(ex·ploring)

1. Investigating in a systematic way: examining. 2. Searching into or ranging over for the purpose of discovery.

Microsoft®

PowerPoint 2016

Comprehensive

Series Editor Mary Anne Poatsy

Krebs | Lawson

Series Created by Dr. Robert T. Grauer

PEARSON

Boston   Columbus   Indianapolis   New York   San Francisco   Hoboken
Amsterdam   Cape Town   Dubai   London   Madrid   Milan   Munich   Paris   Montréal   Toronto ·
Delhi   Mexico City   São Paulo   Sydney   Hong Kong   Seoul   Singapore   Taipei   Tokyo

Vice President of Career Skills: Andrew Gilfillan
Senior Editor: Samantha Lewis
Team Lead, Project Management: Laura Burgess
Project Manager: Laura Karahalis
Program Manager: Emily Biberger
Development Editor: Cheryl Slavik
Editorial Assistant: Michael Campbell
Director of Product Marketing: Maggie Waples
Director of Field Marketing: Leigh Ann Sims
Product Marketing Manager: Kaylee Carlson
Field Marketing Managers: Molly Schmidt & Joanna Sabella
Marketing Coordinator: Susan Osterlitz
Senior Operations Specialist: Diane Peirano
Senior Art Director: Diane Ernsberger
Interior and Cover Design: Diane Ernsberger
Cover Photo: Courtesy of Shutterstock® Images
Associate Director of Design: Blair Brown
Senior Product Strategy Manager: Eric Hakanson
Product Manager, MyITLab: Zachary Alexander
Media Producer, MyITLab: Jaimie Noy
Digital Project Manager, MyITLab: Becca Lowe
Media Project Manager, Production: John Cassar
Full-Service Project Management: Jenna Vittorioso, Lumina Datamatics, Inc.
Composition: Lumina Datamatics, Inc.
Efficacy Curriculum Manager: Jessica Sieminski

Library of Congress Control Number: 2015956948

1 2 3 4 5 6 7 8 9 10 V003 20 19 18 17 16

ISBN 10:   0-13-447948-3
ISBN 13: 978-0-13-447948-4

Dedications

For my husband, Ted, who unselfishly continues to take on more than his share to support me throughout the process; and for my children, Laura, Carolyn, and Teddy, whose encouragement and love have been inspiring.

Mary Anne Poatsy

For my children for all of believing in me, encouraging me, and supporting me. Thank you Marshall Krebs, Jaron Krebs, Jenalee Krebs Behle, and Michelle Krebs. To my writing mentor, Dr. Keith Mulbery, for the same reasons.

Cynthia Krebs

This book is dedicated to my children and to my students to inspire them to never give up and to always keep reaching for their dreams.

Rebecca Lawson

To my husband Dan, whose encouragement, patience, and love helped make this endeavor possible. Thank you for taking on the many additional tasks at home so that I could focus on writing.

Amy Rutledge

About the Authors

Mary Anne Poatsy, Series Editor, Windows 10 Author

Mary Anne is a senior faculty member at Montgomery County Community College, teaching various computer application and concepts courses in face-to-face and online environments. She holds a B.A. in Psychology and Education from Mount Holyoke College and an M.B.A. in Finance from Northwestern University's Kellogg Graduate School of Management.

Mary Anne has more than 12 years of educational experience. She is currently adjunct faculty at Gwynedd-Mercy College and Montgomery County Community College. She has also taught at Bucks County Community College and Muhlenberg College, as well as conducted personal training. Before teaching, she was Vice President at Shearson Lehman in the Municipal Bond Investment Banking Department.

Cynthia Krebs, PowerPoint Author

Cynthia Krebs is the Program Director of Business and Marketing Education at Utah Valley University. She is a tenured professor in the Information Systems and Technology Department at UVU where she teaches the Methods of Teaching Business, Marketing, and Digital Technology course to future teachers, as well as classes in basic computer applications and business proficiency applications. She holds a B.S. and M.S. in Business Education with an emphasis in Economic Education. Cynthia has received numerous awards, and has presented extensively at the local, regional, and national levels as well as consulting with government organizations and businesses.

Cynthia lives by a peaceful creek in Springville, Utah. When she isn't teaching or writing, she enjoys spending time with her children and spoiling her grandchildren Ava, Bode, Solee, Morgan, and Preslee. She loves traveling and reading.

Rebecca Lawson, PowerPoint Author

Rebecca Lawson is a professor in the Computer Information Technologies program at Lansing Community College. She coordinates the curriculum, develops the instructional materials, and teaches for the E-Business curriculum. She also serves as the Online Faculty Coordinator at the Center for Teaching Excellence at LCC. In that role, she develops and facilitates online workshops for faculty learning to teach online. Her major areas of interest include online curriculum quality assurance, the review and development of printed and online instructional materials, the assessment of computer and Internet literacy skill levels to facilitate student retention, and the use of social networking tools to support learning in blended and online learning environments.

Amy Rutledge, Common Features Author

Amy Rutledge is a Special Instructor of Management Information Systems at Oakland University in Rochester, Michigan. She coordinates academic programs in Microsoft Office applications and introductory management information systems courses for the School of Business Administration. Before joining Oakland University as an instructor, Amy spent several years working for a music distribution company and automotive manufacturer in various corporate roles including IT project management. She holds a B.S. in Business Administration specializing in Management Information Systems, and a B.A. in French Modern Language and Literature. She holds an M.B.A from Oakland University. She resides in Michigan with her husband, Dan, and daughters Emma and Jane.

Dr. Robert T. Grauer, Creator of the Exploring Series

Bob Grauer is an Associate Professor in the Department of Computer Information Systems at the University of Miami, where he is a multiple winner of the Outstanding Teaching Award in the School of Business, most recently in 2009. He has written numerous COBOL texts and is the vision behind the Exploring Office series, with more than three million books in print. His work has been translated into three foreign languages and is used in all aspects of higher education at both national and international levels. Bob Grauer has consulted for several major corporations including IBM and American Express. He received his Ph.D. in Operations Research in 1972 from the Polytechnic Institute of Brooklyn.

Brief Contents

Contents

Acknowledgments

The Exploring team would like to acknowledge and thank all the reviewers who helped us throughout the years by providing us with their invaluable comments, suggestions, and constructive criticism.

Adriana Lumpkin
Midland College

Alan S. Abrahams
Virginia Tech

Alexandre C. Probst
Colorado Christian University

Ali Berrached
University of Houston–Downtown

Allen Alexander
Delaware Technical & Community College

Andrea Marchese
Maritime College, State University of New York

Andrew Blitz
Broward College; Edison State College

Angel Norman
University of Tennessee, Knoxville

Angela Clark
University of South Alabama

Ann Rovetto
Horry-Georgetown Technical College

Astrid Todd
Guilford Technical Community College

Audrey Gillant
Maritime College, State University of New York

Barbara Stover
Marion Technical College

Barbara Tollinger
Sinclair Community College

Ben Brahim Taha
Auburn University

Beverly Amer
Northern Arizona University

Beverly Fite
Amarillo College

Biswadip Ghosh
Metropolitan State University of Denver

Bonita Volker
Tidewater Community College

Bonnie Homan
San Francisco State University

Brad West
Sinclair Community College

Brian Powell
West Virginia University

Carol Buser
Owens Community College

Carol Roberts
University of Maine

Carolyn Barren
Macomb Community College

Carolyn Borne
Louisiana State University

Cathy Poyner
Truman State University

Charles Hodgson
Delgado Community College

Chen Zhang
Bryant University

Cheri Higgins
Illinois State University

Cheryl Brown
Delgado Community College

Cheryl Hinds
Norfolk State University

Cheryl Sypniewski
Macomb Community College

Chris Robinson
Northwest State Community College

Cindy Herbert
Metropolitan Community College–Longview

Craig J. Peterson
American InterContinental University

Dana Hooper
University of Alabama

Dana Johnson
North Dakota State University

Daniela Marghitu
Auburn University

David Noel
University of Central Oklahoma

David Pulis
Maritime College, State University of New York

David Thornton
Jacksonville State University

Dawn Medlin
Appalachian State University

Debby Keen
University of Kentucky

Debra Chapman
University of South Alabama

Debra Hoffman
Southeast Missouri State University

Derrick Huang
Florida Atlantic University

Diana Baran
Henry Ford Community College

Diane Cassidy
The University of North Carolina at Charlotte

Diane L. Smith
Henry Ford Community College

Dick Hewer
Ferris State College

Don Danner
San Francisco State University

Don Hoggan
Solano College

Don Riggs
SUNY Schenectady County Community College

Doncho Petkov
Eastern Connecticut State University

Donna Ehrhart
State University of New York at Brockport

Elaine Crable
Xavier University

Elizabeth Duett
Delgado Community College

Erhan Uskup
Houston Community College–Northwest

Eric Martin
University of Tennessee

Erika Nadas
Wilbur Wright College

Floyd Winters
Manatee Community College

Frank Lucente
Westmoreland County Community College

G. Jan Wilms
Union University

Gail Cope
Sinclair Community College

Gary DeLorenzo
California University of Pennsylvania

Gary Garrison
Belmont University

Gary McFall
Purdue University

George Cassidy
Sussex County Community College

Gerald Braun
Xavier University

Gerald Burgess
Western New Mexico University

Gladys Swindler
Fort Hays State University

Hector Frausto
California State University
Los Angeles

Heith Hennel
Valencia Community College

Henry Rudzinski
Central Connecticut State University

Irene Joos
La Roche College

Iwona Rusin
Baker College; Davenport University

J. Roberto Guzman
San Diego Mesa College

Jacqueline D. Lawson
Henry Ford Community College

Jakie Brown Jr.
Stevenson University

James Brown
Central Washington University

James Powers
University of Southern Indiana

Jane Stam
Onondaga Community College

Janet Bringhurst
Utah State University

Jean Welsh
Lansing Community College

Jeanette Dix
Ivy Tech Community College

Jennifer Day
Sinclair Community College

Jill Canine
Ivy Tech Community College

Jill Young
Southeast Missouri State University

Jim Chaffee
The University of Iowa Tippie College of
Business

Joanne Lazirko
University of Wisconsin–Milwaukee

Jodi Milliner
Kansas State University

John Hollenbeck
Blue Ridge Community College

John Seydel
Arkansas State University

Judith A. Scheeren
Westmoreland County Community College

Judith Brown
The University of Memphis

Juliana Cypert
Tarrant County College

Kamaljeet Sanghera
George Mason University

Karen Priestly
Northern Virginia Community College

Karen Ravan
Spartanburg Community College

Karen Tracey
Central Connecticut State University

Kathleen Brenan
Ashland University

Ken Busbee
Houston Community College

Kent Foster
Winthrop University

Kevin Anderson
Solano Community College

Kim Wright
The University of Alabama

Kristen Hockman
University of Missouri–Columbia

Kristi Smith
Allegany College of Maryland

Laura Marcoulides
Fullerton College

Laura McManamon
University of Dayton

Laurence Boxer
Niagara University

Leanne Chun
Leeward Community College

Lee McClain
Western Washington University

Linda D. Collins
Mesa Community College

Linda Johnsonius
Murray State University

Linda Lau
Longwood University

Linda Theus
Jackson State Community College

Linda Williams
Marion Technical College

Lisa Miller
University of Central Oklahoma

Lister Horn
Pensacola Junior College

Lixin Tao
Pace University

Loraine Miller
Cayuga Community College

Lori Kielty
Central Florida Community College

Lorna Wells
Salt Lake Community College

Lorraine Sauchin
Duquesne University

Lucy Parakhovnik
California State University, Northridge

Lynn Keane
University of South Carolina

Lynn Mancini
Delaware Technical Community College

Mackinzee Escamilla
South Plains College

Marcia Welch
Highline Community College

Margaret McManus
Northwest Florida State College

Margaret Warrick
Allan Hancock College

Marilyn Hibbert
Salt Lake Community College

Mark Choman
Luzerne County Community College

Maryann Clark
University of New Hampshire

Mary Beth Tarver
Northwestern State University

Mary Duncan
University of Missouri–St. Louis

Melissa Nemeth
Indiana University-Purdue University
Indianapolis

Melody Alexander
Ball State University

Michael Douglas
University of Arkansas at Little Rock

Michael Dunklebarger
Alamance Community College

Michael G. Skaff
College of the Sequoias

Michele Budnovitch
Pennsylvania College of Technology

Mike Jochen
East Stroudsburg University

Mike Michaelson
Palomar College

Mike Scroggins
Missouri State University

Mimi Spain
Southern Maine Community College

Muhammed Badamas
Morgan State University

NaLisa Brown
University of the Ozarks

Nancy Grant
Community College of Allegheny County–
South Campus

Nanette Lareau
University of Arkansas Community
College–Morrilton

Nikia Robinson
Indian River State University

Pam Brune
Chattanooga State Community College

Pam Uhlenkamp
Iowa Central Community College

Patrick Smith
Marshall Community and Technical College

Paul Addison
Ivy Tech Community College

Paula Ruby
Arkansas State University

Peggy Burrus
Red Rocks Community College

Peter Ross
SUNY Albany

Philip H. Nielson
Salt Lake Community College

Philip Valvalides
Guilford Technical Community College

Ralph Hooper
University of Alabama

Ranette Halverson
Midwestern State University

Richard Blamer
John Carroll University

Richard Cacace
Pensacola Junior College

Richard Hewer
Ferris State University

Richard Sellers
Hill College

Rob Murray
Ivy Tech Community College

Robert Banta
Macomb Community College

Robert Dušek
Northern Virginia Community College

Robert G. Phipps Jr.
West Virginia University

Robert Sindt
Johnson County Community College

Robert Warren
Delgado Community College

Rocky Belcher
Sinclair Community College

Roger Pick
University of Missouri at Kansas City

Ronnie Creel
Troy University

Rosalie Westerberg
Clover Park Technical College

Ruth Neal
Navarro College

Sandra Thomas
Troy University

Sheila Gionfriddo
Luzerne County Community College

Sherrie Geitgey
Northwest State Community College

Sherry Lenhart
Terra Community College

Sophia Wilberscheid
Indian River State College

Sophie Lee
California State University,
Long Beach

Stacy Johnson
Iowa Central Community College

Stephanie Kramer
Northwest State Community College

Stephen Z. Jourdan
Auburn University at Montgomery

Steven Schwarz
Raritan Valley Community College

Sue A. McCrory
Missouri State University

Sumathy Chandrashekar
Salisbury University

Susan Fuschetto
Cerritos College

Susan Medlin
UNC Charlotte

Susan N. Dozier
Tidewater Community College

Suzan Spitzberg
Oakton Community College

Suzanne M. Jeska
County College of Morris

Sven Aelterman
Troy University

Sy Hirsch
Sacred Heart University

Sylvia Brown
Midland College

Tanya Patrick
Clackamas Community College

Terri Holly
Indian River State College

Terry Ray Rigsby
Hill College

Thomas Rienzo
Western Michigan University

Tina Johnson
Midwestern State University

Tommy Lu
Delaware Technical Community College

Troy S. Cash
Northwest Arkansas Community College

Vicki Robertson
Southwest Tennessee Community

Vickie Pickett
Midland College

Weifeng Chen
California University of Pennsylvania

Wes Anthony
Houston Community College

William Ayen
University of Colorado at Colorado Springs

Wilma Andrews
Virginia Commonwealth University

Yvonne Galusha
University of Iowa

Special thanks to our content development and technical team:

Cheryl Slavik

Lynn Bowen

Lisa Bucki

Lori Damanti

Sallie Dodson

Patti Hammerle

Elizabeth Lockley

Joyce Nielsen

Barbara Stover

Preface

The Exploring Series and You

Exploring is Pearson's Office Application series that requires students like you to think "beyond the point and click." In this edition, we have worked to restructure the Exploring experience around the way you, today's modern student, actually use your resources.

The goal of Exploring is, as it has always been, to go farther than teaching just the steps to accomplish a task—the series provides the theoretical foundation for you to understand when and why to apply a skill. As a result, you achieve a deeper understanding of each application and can apply this critical thinking beyond Office and the classroom.

The How & Why of This Revision

Outcomes matter. Whether it's getting a good grade in this course, learning how to use Excel so students can be successful in other courses, or learning a specific skill that will make learners successful in a future job, everyone has an outcome in mind. And outcomes matter. That is why we revised our chapter opener to focus on the outcomes students will achieve by working through each Exploring chapter. These are coupled with objectives and skills, providing a map students can follow to get everything they need from each chapter.

Critical Thinking and Collaboration are essential 21st century skills. Students want and need to be successful in their future careers—so we used motivating case studies to show relevance of these skills to future careers and incorporated Soft Skills, Collaboration, and Analysis Cases with Critical Thinking steps in this edition to set students up for success in the future.

Students today read, prepare, and study differently than students used to. Students use textbooks like a tool—they want to easily identify what they need to know and learn it efficiently. We have added key features such as Tasks Lists (in purple), Step Icons, Hands-On Exercise Videos, and tracked everything via page numbers that allow efficient navigation, creating a map students can easily follow.

Students are exposed to technology. The new edition of Exploring moves beyond the basics of the software at a faster pace, without sacrificing coverage of the fundamental skills that students need to know.

Students are diverse. Students can be any age, any gender, any race, with any level of ability or learning style. With this in mind, we broadened our definition of "student resources" to include physical Student Reference cards, Hands-On Exercise videos to provide a secondary lecture-like option of review; and MyITLab, the most powerful and most ADA-compliant online homework and assessment tool around with a direct 1:1 content match with the Exploring Series. Exploring will be accessible to all students, regardless of learning style.

Providing You with a Map to Success to Move Beyond the Point and Click

All of these changes and additions will provide students an easy and efficient path to follow to be successful in this course, regardless of where they start at the beginning of this course. Our goal is to keep students engaged in both the hands-on and conceptual sides, helping achieve a higher level of understanding that will guarantee success in this course and in a future career.

In addition to the vision and experience of the series creator, Robert T. Grauer, we have assembled a tremendously talented team of Office Applications authors who have devoted themselves to teaching the ins and outs of Microsoft Word, Excel, Access, and PowerPoint. Led in this edition by series editor Mary Anne Poatsy, the whole team is dedicated to the Exploring mission of moving students **beyond the point and click**.

Key Features

The **How/Why Approach** helps students move beyond the point and click to a true understanding of how to apply Microsoft Office skills.

- **White Pages/Yellow Pages** clearly distinguish the theory (white pages) from the skills covered in the Hands-On Exercises (yellow pages) so students always know what they are supposed to be doing and why.

- **Case Study** presents a scenario for the chapter, creating a story that ties the Hands-On Exercises together.

- **Hands-On Exercise Videos** are tied to each Hands-On Exercise and walk students through the steps of the exercise while weaving in conceptual information related to the Case Study and the objectives as a whole.

The **Outcomes focus** allows students and instructors to know the higher-level learning goals and how those are achieved through discreet objectives and skills.

- **Outcomes** presented at the beginning of each chapter identify the learning goals for students and instructors.

- **Enhanced Objective Mapping** enables students to follow a directed path through each chapter, from the objectives list at the chapter opener through the exercises at the end of the chapter.
  - **Objectives List:** This provides a simple list of key objectives covered in the chapter. This includes page numbers so students can skip between objectives where they feel they need the most help.
  - **Step Icons:** These icons appear in the white pages and reference the step numbers in the Hands-On Exercises, providing a correlation between the two so students can easily find conceptual help when they are working hands-on and need a refresher.
  - **Quick Concepts Check:** A series of questions that appear briefly at the end of each white page section. These questions cover the most essential concepts in the white pages required for students to be successful in working the Hands-On Exercises. Page numbers are included for easy reference to help students locate the answers.
  - **Chapter Objectives Review:** Appears toward the end of the chapter and reviews all important concepts throughout the chapter. Newly designed in an easy-to-read bulleted format.

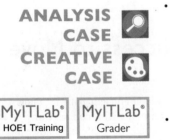

- **MOS Certification Guide** for instructors and students to direct anyone interested in prepping for the MOS exam to the specific locations to find all content required for the test.

End-of-Chapter Exercises offer instructors several options for assessment. Each chapter has approximately 11–12 exercises ranging from multiple choice questions to open-ended projects.

- **Multiple Choice, Key Terms Matching, Practice Exercises, Mid-Level Exercises, Beyond the Classroom Exercises, and Capstone Exercises** appear at the end of all chapters.
  - **Enhanced Mid-Level Exercises** include a **Creative Case** (for PowerPoint and Word), which allows students some flexibility and creativity, not being bound by a definitive solution, and an **Analysis Case** (for Excel and Access), which requires students to interpret the data they are using to answer an analytic question, as well as **Discover Steps**, which encourage students to use Help or to problem-solve to accomplish a task.

- **Application Capstone** exercises are included in the book to allow instructors to test students on the entire contents of a single application.

Resources

Instructor Resources

The Instructor's Resource Center, available at **www.pearsonhighered.com**, includes the following:

- **Instructor Manual** provides one-stop-shop for instructors, including an overview of all available resources, teaching tips, as well as student data and solution files for every exercise.

- **Solution Files with Scorecards** assist with grading the Hands-On Exercises and end-of-chapter exercises.

- **Prepared Exams** allow instructors to assess all skills covered in a chapter with a single project.

- **Rubrics** for Mid-Level Creative Cases and Beyond the Classroom Cases in Microsoft Word format enable instructors to customize the assignments for their classes.

- **PowerPoint Presentations** with notes for each chapter are included for out-of-class study or review.

- **Multiple Choice, Key Term Matching, and Quick Concepts Check Answer Keys**

- **Test Bank** provides objective-based questions for every chapter.

- **Scripted Lectures** offer an in-class lecture guide for instructors to mirror the Hands-On Exercises.

- **Syllabus Templates**
  - Outcomes, Objectives, and Skills List
  - Assignment Sheet
  - File Guide

Student Resources

Student Data Files

Access your student data files needed to complete the exercises in this textbook at **www.pearsonhighered.com/exploring.**

Available in MyITLab

- **Hands-On Exercise Videos** allow students to review and study the concepts taught in the Hands-On Exercises.
- **Audio PowerPoints** provide a lecture review of the chapter content, and include narration.
- **Multiple Choice quizzes** enable you to test concepts you have learned by answering auto-graded questions.
- **Book-specific 1:1 Simulations** allow students to practice in the simulated Microsoft Office 2016 environment using hi-fidelity, HTML5 simulations that directly match the content in the Hands-On Exercises.
- **eText** available in some MyITLab courses and includes links to videos, student data files, and other learning aids.
- **Book-specific 1:1 Grader Projects** allow students to complete end of chapter Capstone Exercises live in Microsoft Office 2016 and receive immediate feedback on their performance through various reports.

(ex·ploring)

SERIES

1. Investigating in a systematic way: examining. 2. Searching into or ranging over for the purpose of discovery.

Microsoft®

PowerPoint 2016

COMPREHENSIVE

Office 2016 Common Features

LEARNING OUTCOME You will apply skills common across the Microsoft Office suite to create and format documents and edit content in Office 2016 applications.

OBJECTIVES & SKILLS: After you read this chapter, you will be able to:

CASE STUDY | Spotted Begonia Art Gallery

You are an administrative assistant for Spotted Begonia, a local art gallery. The gallery does a lot of community outreach and tries to help local artists develop a network of clients and supporters. Local schools are invited to bring students to the gallery for enrichment programs.

As the administrative assistant for Spotted Begonia, you are responsible for overseeing the production of documents, spreadsheets, newspaper articles, and presentations that will be used to increase public awareness of the gallery. Other clerical assistants who are familiar with Microsoft Office will prepare the promotional materials, and you will proofread, make necessary corrections, adjust page layouts, save and print documents, and identify appropriate templates to simplify tasks. Your experience with Microsoft Office 2016 is limited, but you know that certain fundamental tasks that are common to Word, Excel, and PowerPoint will help you accomplish your oversight task. You are excited to get started with your work!

Taking the First Step

The Spotted Begonia Art Gallery

10/06/18

Ms. Jane Hernandez
Executive Director
ABC Arts Foundation
432 Main Street
Detroit, MI 48201

RE: DISCOVER THE ARTIST IN YOU! PROGRAM

Dear Ms. Hernandez,

We are pleased to invite you and your colleagues to our *Discover the Artist in You!* Kickoff party on November 8th at 2pm in the Picasso Wing of the gallery. Light refreshments will be served. Please see the enclosed flyer.

The Spotted Begonia Art Gallery is pleased that the ABC Arts Foundation has accepted our funding proposal for the *Discover the Artist in You!* Program. The *Discover the Artist in You!* Program will introduce elementary students to local artists and will give those students a chance to create their own art projects under the guidance of those artists. We look forward to partnering with you to provide this program to more than 500 local elementary students!

Please RSVP by November 1st to ejhazelton@sbag.org with the number attending. Please let me know if you have any questions.

Thank you,

Emma J. Hazelton

Arts Education Outreach Coordinator
Spotted Begonia Art Gallery
387 Pine Hill Road
Pontiac, MI 48340

Spotted Begonia Art gallery   www.sbag.org   Pontiac, MI

Spotted Begonia Art Gallery

MAY 31, 2018
DISCOVER THE ARTIST IN YOU!

A Special Children's Event
[To replace any tip text with your own, just click it and start typing. To replace the photo or logo with your own, right-click it and then click Change Picture. To try out different looks for this flyer, on the Design tab, check out the Themes, Colors, and Fonts galleries.]

replace with
LOGO

[Add Key Event Info Here!]

[Don't Be Shy—Tell Them Why They Can't Miss It!]

[One More Point Here!]

[Add More Great Info Here!]

[You Have Room for Another One Here!]

[COMPANY NAME]
[Street Address]
[City, ST ZIP Code]
[Telephone]

[Web Address]

[Dates and Times]
[Dates and Times]

FIGURE 1.1 Spotted Begonia Art Gallery Memo and Flyer

CASE STUDY | Spotted Begonia Art Gallery

Starting Files	Files to be Submitted
f01h1Letter	f01h2Flyer_LastFirst
f01h2Flyer	f01h3Letter_LastFirst
Blank document	

Getting Started with Office Applications

Organizations around the world rely heavily on Microsoft Office software to produce documents, spreadsheets, presentations, and databases. **Microsoft Office** is a productivity software suite including a set of software applications, each one specializing in a particular type of output. You can use **Word** to produce all sorts of documents, including memos, newsletters, forms, tables, and brochures. **Excel** makes it easy to organize records, financial transactions, and business information in the form of worksheets. With **PowerPoint**, you can create dynamic presentations to inform and persuade audiences. **Access** is a relational database software application that enables you to record and link data, query databases, and create forms and reports.

You will sometimes find that you need to use two or more Office applications to produce your intended output. You might, for example, find that an annual report document you are preparing in Word for an art gallery should also include a chart of recent sales stored in Excel. You can use Excel to prepare the summary and then incorporate the worksheet in the Word document. Similarly, you can integrate Word tables and Excel charts into a PowerPoint presentation. The choice of which software applications to use really depends on what type of output you are producing. Table 1.1 describes the major tasks of the four primary applications in Microsoft Office.

TABLE 1.1 Microsoft Office Software	
Office 2016 Product	**Application Characteristics**
Word	Word processing software used with text to create, edit, and format documents such as letters, memos, reports, brochures, resumes, and flyers.
Excel	Spreadsheet software used to store quantitative data and to perform accurate and rapid calculations with results ranging from simple budgets to financial and statistical analyses.
PowerPoint	Presentation graphics software used to create slide shows for presentation by a speaker, to be published as part of a website, or to run as a stand-alone application on a computer kiosk.
Access	Relational database software used to store data and convert it into information. Database software is used primarily for decision making by businesses that compile data from multiple records stored in tables to produce informative reports.

As you become familiar with Microsoft Office, you will find that although each software application produces a specific type of output, all applications share common features. Such commonality gives a similar feel to each software application so that learning and working with Office software products is easy.

In this section, you will learn how to open an application, log in with your Microsoft account, and open and save a file. You will also learn to identify features common to Office software applications, including interface components such as the Ribbon, Backstage view, and the Quick Access Toolbar. You will experience Live Preview. You will learn how to get help with an application. You will also learn how to search for and install Office add-ins.

Starting an Office Application

 Microsoft Office applications are launched from the Start menu. Click the Start button, and then click the app tile for the application in which you want to work. If the application tile is not on the Start menu, you can open the program from All apps, or alternatively, you can click in the search box on the task bar, type the name of the program, and press Enter. The program will open automatically.

Change Your Microsoft Account

Although you can log in to Windows as a local network user, you can also log in using a Microsoft account. When you have a Microsoft account, you can sign in to any Windows computer and you will be able to access the saved settings associated with your Microsoft account. That means the computer will have the same familiar look that you are used to seeing on other computers and devices. Your Microsoft account will automatically sign in to all of the apps and services that use a Microsoft account as the authentication. You can also save your sign-in credentials for other websites that you frequently visit. If you share your computer with another user, each user can have access to his own Microsoft account; you can easily switch between accounts so you can access your own files.

To switch between accounts in an application such as Word, complete the following steps:

1. Click the profile name at the top-right of the application.
2. Select Switch account. Select an account from the list, if the account has already been added to the computer, or add a new account.

Logging in with your Microsoft account also provides additional benefits such as being connected to all of Microsoft's resources on the Internet. These resources include a free Outlook email account and access to OneDrive cloud storage. *Cloud storage* is a technology used to store files and to work with programs that are stored in a central location on the Internet. *OneDrive* is an app used to store, access, and share files and folders. It is accessible using an installed desktop app or as cloud storage using a Web address. For Office applications, OneDrive is the default location for saving files. Documents saved in OneDrive are accessible from any computer that has an Internet connection. As long as the document has been saved in OneDrive, the most recent version of the document will be accessible when you log in from any computer connected to the Internet. Moreover, files and folders stored on the computer's hard drive or saved on a portable storage device can be synced with those on the OneDrive account.

OneDrive enables you to collaborate with others. You can easily share your documents with others or edit a document on which you are collaborating. You can even work with others simultaneously on the same document.

Working with Files

When working with an Office application, you can begin by opening an existing file that has already been saved to a storage medium, or you can begin work on a new file. When you open an application within Office, you can select a template to use as you begin working on a new file.

Create a New File

After opening an Office application, such as Word, Excel, or PowerPoint, you will be presented with template choices. Click Blank document (workbook, presentation, etc.) to start a new blank file. Perhaps you are already working with a document in an Office application but want to create a new file.

To create a new Office file, complete the following steps:

1. Click the File tab and click New.
2. Click Blank.

Open a File

STEP 2 »» You will often work with a file, save it, and then continue the project at a later time. To open an existing file, you can click a location such as This PC or OneDrive and navigate to the folder or drive where your document is stored. Once you make your way to the file to be opened, double-click the file name to open the file (see Figure 1.2).

To open a file, complete the following steps:

1. Open the application.
2. Click Open Other Documents (Workbooks, etc.).
3. Click the location for your file (such as This PC or OneDrive).
4. Navigate to the folder or drive and double-click the file to open it.

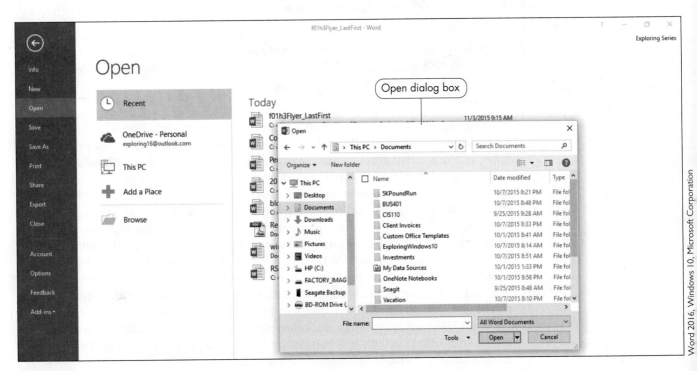

FIGURE I.2 The Open Dialog Box

Office simplifies the task of reopening the file by providing a Recent documents list with links to your most recently opened files. Previously saved files, such as the data files for this book, are available in the Recent documents list, shown in Figure 1.3. If you just opened the application, the recent list displays at the left. If you do not see your file listed, you can click the link to Open Other Documents (or Workbooks, Presentations, etc.)

To access the Recent documents list, complete the following steps:

1. Open the application.
2. Click any file listed in the Recent documents list to open that document.

The list constantly changes to reflect only the most recently opened files, so if it has been quite some time since you worked with a particular file, you might have to browse for your file instead of using the Recent documents list to open the file.

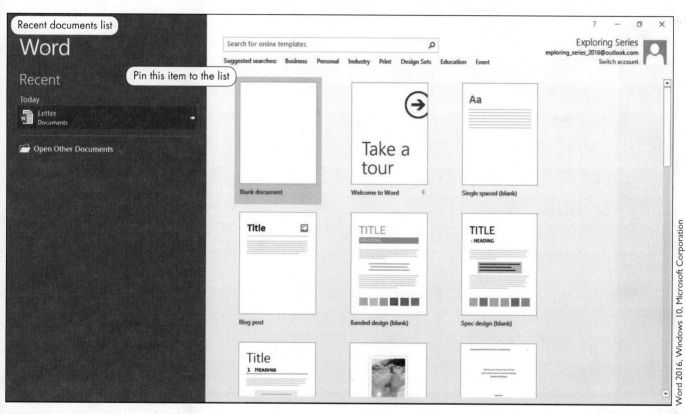

FIGURE 1.3 Recent Documents List

Save a File

STEP 3 ≫ Saving a file enables you to later open it for additional updates or reference. Files are saved to a storage medium such as a hard drive, CD, flash drive, or to the cloud on OneDrive.

The first time that you save a file, you should indicate where the file will be saved and assign a file name. Of course, you will want to save the file in an appropriately named folder so that you can find it easily later. Thereafter, you can quickly save the file with the same settings, or you can change one or more of those settings, perhaps saving the file to a different storage device as a backup copy. Figure 1.4 shows a typical Save As pane for Office that enables you to select a location before saving the file.

It is easy to save a previously saved file with its current name and file location; click the Save icon on Quick Access Toolbar. There are instances where you may want to rename the file or save it to a different location. For example, you might reuse an event flyer for another event and simply update some of the details for the new event.

To save a file with a different name and/or file location, complete the following steps:

1. Click the File tab.
2. Click Save As.
3. Select a location or click Browse to navigate to the desired file storage location.
4. Type the file name.
5. Click Save.

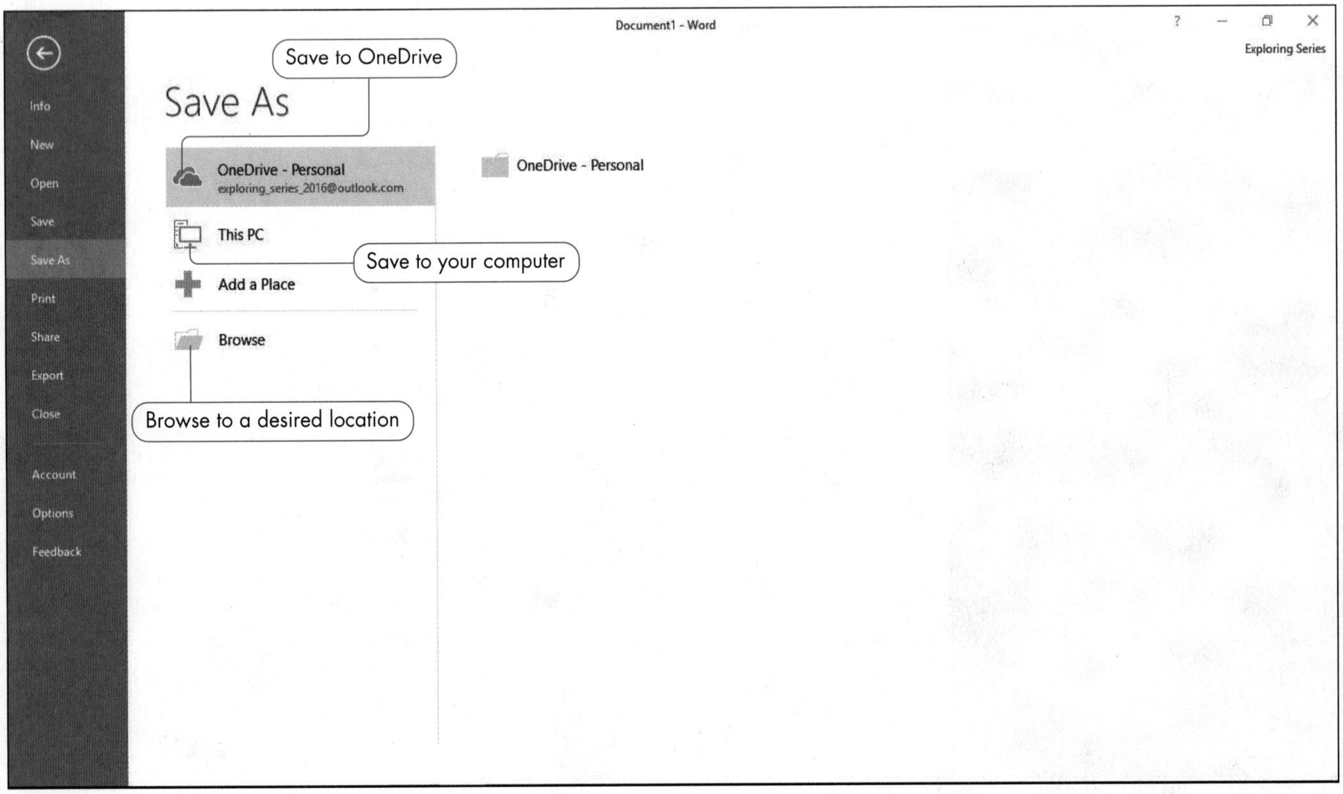

Word 2016, Windows 10, Microsoft Corporation

FIGURE 1.4 Save As in Backstage View

As previously mentioned, signing in to your Microsoft account enables you to save files to OneDrive and access them from virtually anywhere. To save a file to your OneDrive account follow the same steps as saving a file to your hard drive but select OneDrive and then the desired storage location on your OneDrive. You must be connected to the Internet in order to complete this action.

Using Common Interface Components

When you open any Office application you will first notice the title bar and Ribbon. The ***title bar*** identifies the current file name and the application in which you are working. It also includes Ribbon display options and control buttons that enable you to minimize, restore down, or close the application window (see Figure 1.5). The Quick Access Toolbar, on the left side of the title bar, enables you to save the file, and undo or redo editing. Located just below the title bar is the Ribbon. The ***Ribbon*** is the command center of Office applications. It is the long bar located just beneath the title bar, containing tabs, groups, and commands.

Title bar

Ribbon Display Options

Quick Access Toolbar

Home tab

Minimize, Restore Down, Close

FIGURE 1.5 The Title Bar and Quick Access Toolbar

Word 2016, Windows 10, Microsoft Corporation

Use the Ribbon

The Ribbon is composed of tabs. Each *tab* is designed to appear much like a tab on a file folder, with the active tab highlighted. The File tab is located at the far left of the Ribbon. The File tab provides access to Backstage view which contains Save and Print, as well as additional functions. Other tabs on the Ribbon enable you to modify a file. The active tab in Figure 1.6 is the Home tab.

Dialog Box Launcher

Tell me what you want to do box

More

Home tab is active

Collapse the Ribbon

FIGURE 1.6 The Ribbon

Word 2016, Windows 10, Microsoft Corporation

Office applications enable you to work with objects such as images, shapes, charts, and tables. When you include such objects in a project, they are considered separate components that you can manage independently. To work with an object, you must select it. When you select an object, the Ribbon is modified to include one or more *contextual tabs* that contain groups of commands related to the selected object. Figure 1.7 shows a contextual tab related to a selected picture in a Word document. When you click away from the selected object, the contextual tab disappears.

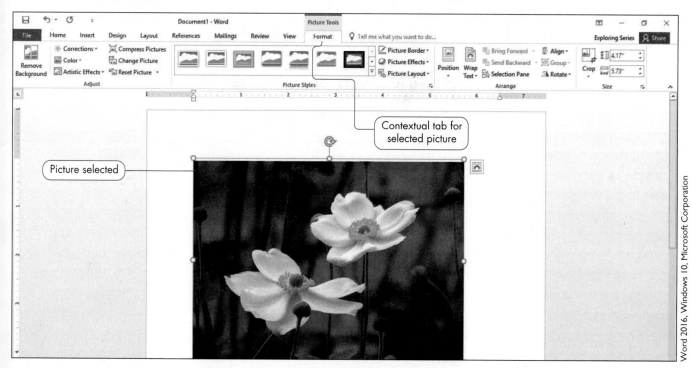

Contextual tab for selected picture

Picture selected

Word 2016, Windows 10, Microsoft Corporation

FIGURE 1.7 A Contextual Tab

On each tab, the Ribbon displays several task-oriented groups, with each group containing related commands. A *group* is a subset of a tab that organizes similar tasks together. A *command* is a button or area within a group that you click to perform tasks. Office is designed to provide the most functionality possible with the fewest clicks. For that reason, the Home tab, displayed when you first open a document in an Office software application, contains groups and commands that are most commonly used. For example, because you often want to change the way text is displayed, the Home tab in each Office application includes a Font group with commands related to modifying text. Similarly, other tabs contain groups of related actions, or commands, many of which are unique to the particular Office application.

Word, PowerPoint, Excel, and Access all share a similar Ribbon structure. Although the specific tabs, groups, and commands vary among the Office programs, the way in which you use the Ribbon and the descriptive nature of tab titles is the same regardless of which program you are using. For example, if you want to insert a chart in Excel, a header in Word, or a shape in PowerPoint, you will click the Insert tab in any of those programs. The first thing that you should do as you begin to work with an Office application is to study the Ribbon. Take a look at all tabs and their contents. That way, you will have a good idea of where to find specific commands and how the Ribbon with which you are currently working differs from one that you might have used in another application.

If you are working with a large project, you can maximize your workspace by temporarily hiding the Ribbon.

To hide the Ribbon, complete one of the following steps:

- Double-click the active tab to hide the Ribbon.
- Click Collapse the Ribbon (refer to Figure 1.6), located at the right side of the Ribbon.

To unhide the Ribbon, double-click any tab to redisplay the Ribbon.

Some actions do not display on the Ribbon because they are not as commonly used, but are related to commands displayed on the Ribbon. For example, you might want to change the background of a PowerPoint slide to include a picture. In that case, you will work with a *dialog box* that provides access to more precise, but less frequently used, commands. Figure 1.8 shows the Font dialog box in Word. Some commands display a dialog box when they are clicked. Other Ribbon groups include a *Dialog Box Launcher* that, when clicked, opens a corresponding dialog box (see Figure 1.8).

TIP: GETTING HELP WITH DIALOG BOXES

Getting help while you are working with a dialog box is easy. Click the Help button that displays as a question mark in the top-right corner of the dialog box. The subsequent Help window will offer suggestions relevant to your task.

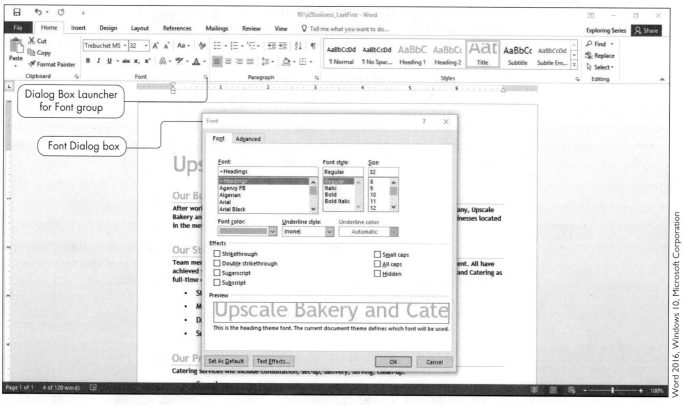

FIGURE 1.8 The Font Dialog Box

The Ribbon contains many selections and commands, but some selections are too numerous to include in the Ribbon's limited space. For example, Word provides far more text styles than it can easily display at once, so additional styles are available in a *gallery*. A gallery also provides a choice of Excel chart styles and PowerPoint transitions. Figure 1.9 shows an example of a PowerPoint Themes gallery. Most often, you can display a gallery of additional choices by clicking the More button ⊡ (refer to Figure 1.6) that is found in some Ribbon selections.

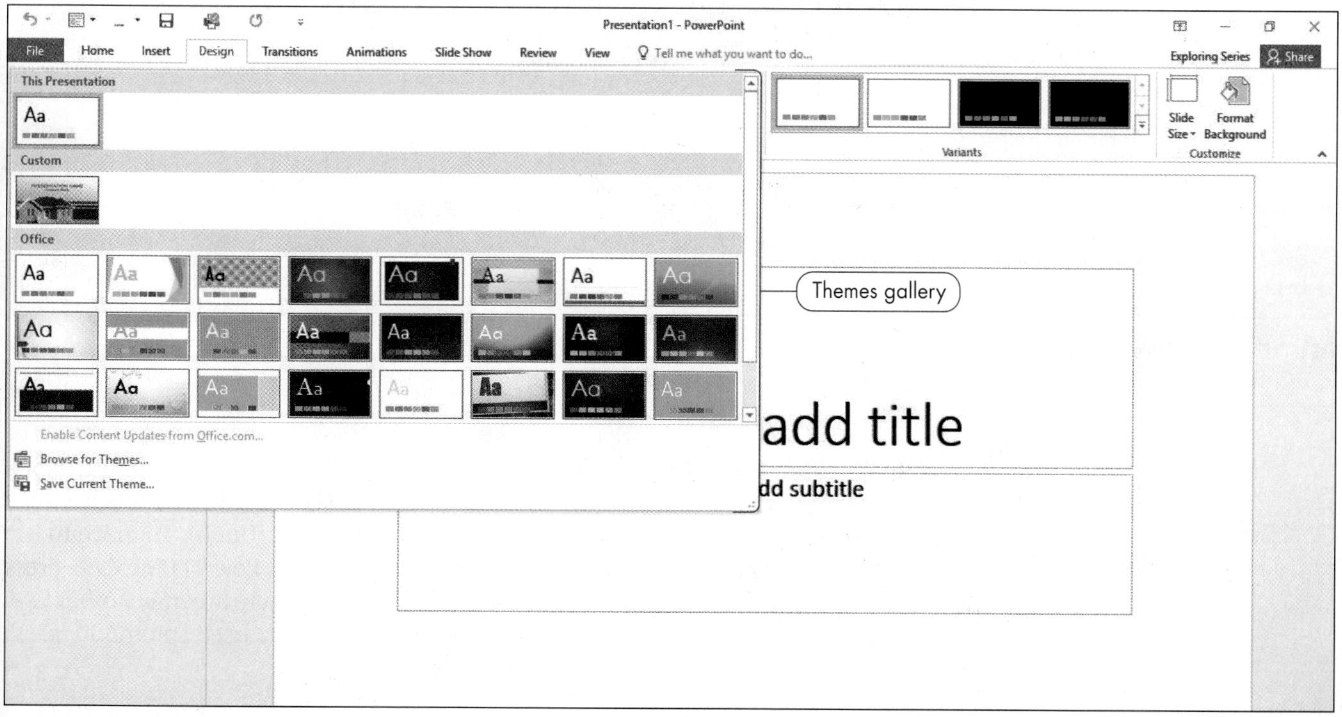

FIGURE 1.9 The Themes Gallery in PowerPoint

When editing a document, worksheet, or presentation, it is helpful to see the results of formatting changes before you make final selections. The feature that displays a preview of the results of a selection is called **Live Preview**. You might, for example, be considering modifying the color of an image in a document or worksheet. As you place the pointer over a color selection in a Ribbon gallery or group, the selected image will temporarily display the color to which you are pointing. Similarly, you can get a preview of how color designs would display on PowerPoint slides by pointing to specific themes in the PowerPoint Themes group and noting the effect on a displayed slide. When you click the item, such as the font color, the selection is applied. Live Preview is available in various Ribbon selections among the Office applications.

Use a Shortcut Menu

STEP 4 ›› In Office, you can usually accomplish the same task in several ways. Although the Ribbon provides ample access to formatting and Clipboard commands (such as Cut, Copy, and Paste), you might find it convenient to access the same commands on a shortcut menu. A **shortcut menu** provides choices related to the object, selection, or area of the document at which you right-click, such as the one shown in Figure 1.10. A shortcut menu is also called a *context menu* because the contents of the menu vary depending on the location at which you right-clicked.

FIGURE 1.10 A Shortcut Menu in PowerPoint

Use Keyboard Shortcuts

You might find that you prefer to use keyboard shortcuts, which are keyboard equivalents for software commands, when they are available. Universal keyboard shortcuts in Office include Ctrl+C (Copy), Ctrl+X (Cut), Ctrl+V (Paste), and Ctrl+Z (Undo). To move to the beginning of a Word document, to cell A1 in Excel, or to the first PowerPoint slide, press Ctrl+Home. To move to the end of those items, press Ctrl+End. There are many other keyboard shortcuts. To discover a keyboard shortcut for a commonly used command, press

Alt to display Key Tips for commands available on the Ribbon and Quick Access Toolbar. You can press the letter or number corresponding to Ribbon commands to invoke the action from the keyboard. Press Alt again to remove the Key Tips.

TIP: USING RIBBON COMMANDS WITH ARROWS

Some commands, such as Paste in the Clipboard group, contain two parts: the main command and an arrow. The arrow may be below or to the right of the command, depending on the command, window size, or screen resolution. Instructions in the *Exploring* series use the command name to instruct you to click the main command to perform the default action (e.g., Click Paste). Instructions include the word *arrow* when you need to select the arrow to access an additional option (e.g., Click the Paste arrow).

Customize the Ribbon

The Ribbon provides access to commands to develop, edit, save, share, and print documents. Office applications enable users to personalize the Ribbon, giving them easier access to a frequently used set of commands that are unique to them or their business. You can create and name custom tabs on the Ribbon, add groups of commands to custom or existing tabs, and alter the positioning of tabs on the Ribbon (see Figure 1.11). By default, the command list displays popular commands associated with other tabs (e.g. Paste, Delete, Save As), but all available commands can be displayed in the list's respective menu. The custom tabs are unique to the Office program in which they are created. You can add and remove Ribbon tabs, as well as rename them.

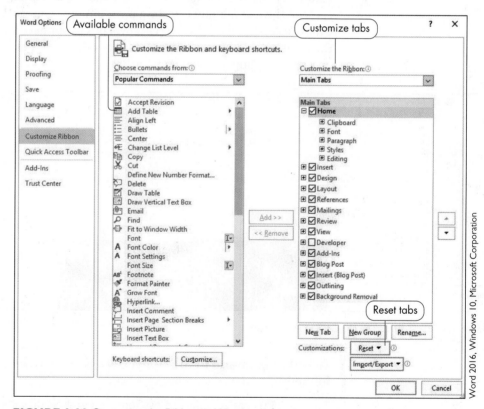

FIGURE 1.11 Customize the Ribbon in Word

To customize the Ribbon, complete the following steps:

1. Click the File tab and click Options.
2. Click Customize Ribbon. By deselecting a tab name, you can remove it from the Ribbon. Later, you can select it again to redisplay it.
3. Click a tab name and click Rename to change the name of the tab.
4. Type a new name and press Enter.

To return to showing all of the original tabs, click Reset and click Reset all customizations (refer to Figure 1.11).

Use the Quick Access Toolbar

The **Quick Access Toolbar**, located at the top-left corner of any Office application window (refer to Figure 1.5), provides one-click access to commonly executed tasks such as saving a file or undoing recent actions. By default, the Quick Access Toolbar includes buttons for saving a file and for undoing or redoing recent actions. You can recover from a mistake by clicking Undo on the Quick Access Toolbar. If you click the arrow beside Undo—known as the Undo arrow—you can select from a list of previous actions in order of occurrence. The Undo list is not maintained when you close a file or exit the application, so you can only erase an action that took place during the current Office session. Similar to Undo, you can also Redo (or Replace) an action that you have just undone. You can also customize the Quick Access Toolbar to include buttons you frequently use for commands such as printing or opening files. Because the Quick Access Toolbar is onscreen at all times, the most commonly accessed tasks are just a click away.

Customize the Quick Access Toolbar

There are certain actions in an Office application that you use often, and for more convenient access, you can add a button for each action to the Quick Access Toolbar (see Figure 1.12). One such action you may want to add is a Quick Print button. Rather than clicking the File tab and selecting print options, you can add a Quick Print icon to the Quick Access Toolbar, and one click will print your document with the default settings of the Print area. Other buttons can also be added such as Spelling & Grammar to quickly check the spelling of the document.

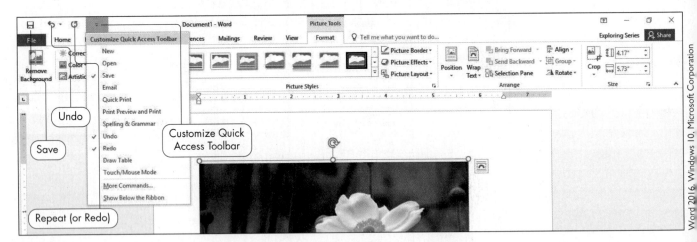

FIGURE 1.12 Customize the Quick Access Toolbar

To add a command to the Quick Access Toolbar, complete one of the following steps:

- Click Customize Quick Access Toolbar and then click More Commands near the bottom of the menu options. Then, select commands from a list and click Add.
- Right-click the command on the Ribbon and click Add to Quick Access Toolbar.

Similarly, remove a command from the Quick Access Toolbar by right-clicking the icon on the Quick Access Toolbar and clicking *Remove from Quick Access Toolbar*. If you want to display the Quick Access Toolbar beneath the Ribbon, click *Customize Quick Access Toolbar* and click *Show Below the Ribbon*.

Getting Help

One of the most frustrating things about learning new software is determining how to complete a task. Microsoft includes comprehensive help with Office so that you are less likely to feel such frustration. As you work with any Office application, you can access help online as well as within the current software installation.

Use the *Tell me what you want to do* Box

STEP 5 ❯❯ New to Office 2016 is the *Tell me what you want to do* box. The **Tell me what you want to do box**, located to the right of the last tab (see Figure 1.13), not only enables you to search for help and information about a command or task you want to perform, but it will also present you with a shortcut directly to that command and in some instances (like Bold) it will complete the action for you. Perhaps you want to find an instance of a word in your document and replace it with another word but cannot locate the command on the Ribbon. You can type *find and replace* in the *Tell me what you want to do* box and a list of commands related to the skill will display. For example, in Figure 1.13, you see that Replace displays as an option in the list. If you click this option, the Find and Replace dialog box opens without you having to locate the button to do so.

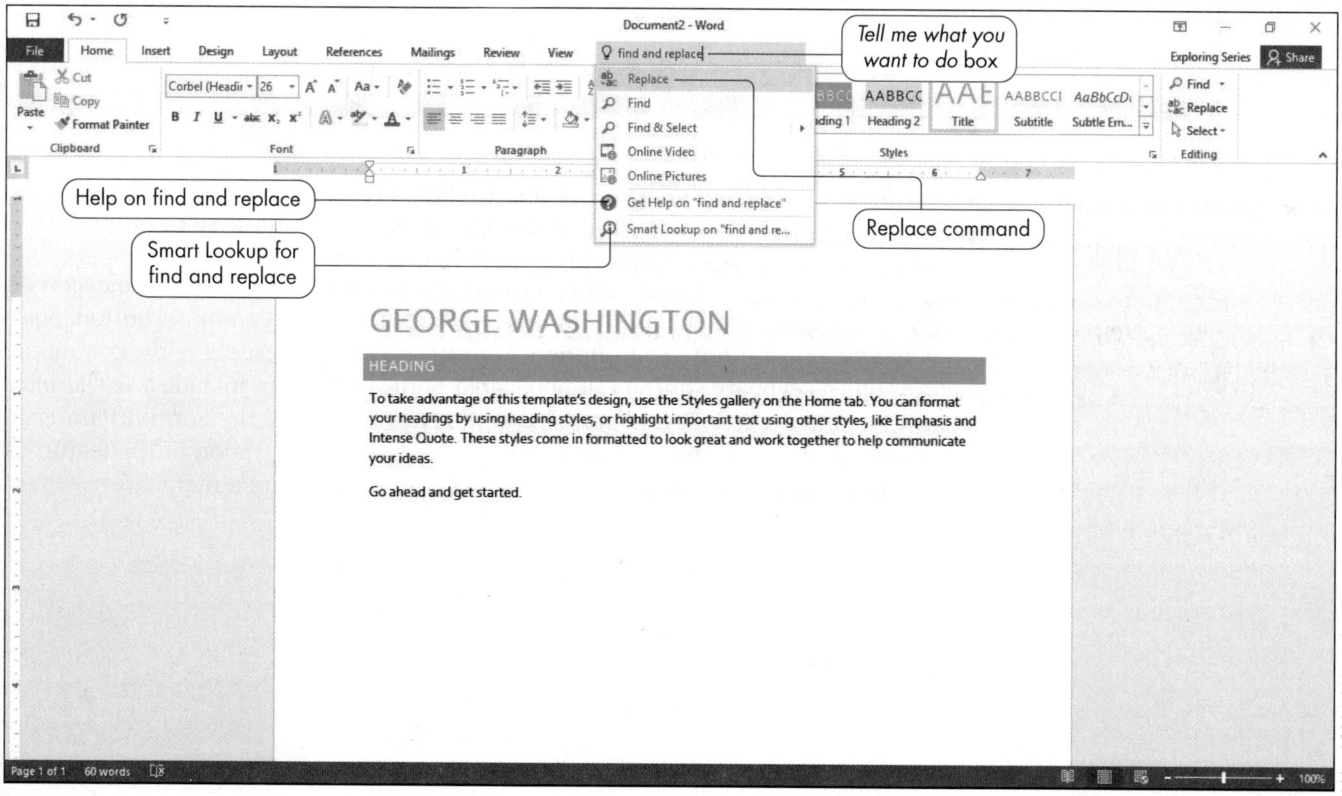

FIGURE 1.13 The *Tell me what you want to do* Box

Should you want to read about the feature instead of apply it, you can click *Get Help on "find and replace"* option, which will open Office Help for the feature. Another new feature is Smart Lookup. This feature opens the Insights pane that shows results from a Bing search on the task description typed in the box (see Figure 1.14). **Smart Lookup** provides information about tasks or commands in Office, and can also be used to search for general information on a topic such as *President George Washington*. Smart Lookup is also available on the shortcut menu when you right-click text.

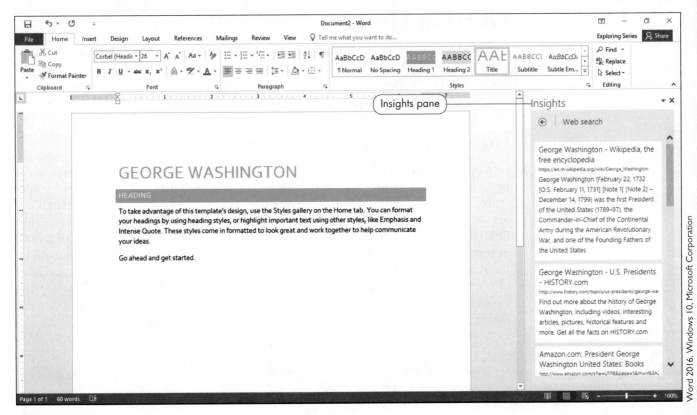

FIGURE 1.14 Smart Lookup

Use Enhanced ScreenTips

As you work on your projects you may wonder about the purpose of a specific icon on the Ribbon. For quick summary information on the purpose of a command button, place the pointer over the button. An ***Enhanced ScreenTip*** displays, describing the command, and providing a keyboard shortcut, if applicable. Some ScreenTips include a *Tell me more* option for additional help. The Enhanced ScreenTip, shown for the Format Painter in Figure 1.15, provides context-sensitive assistance. A short description of the feature is shown in addition to the steps that discuss how to use the Format Painter feature.

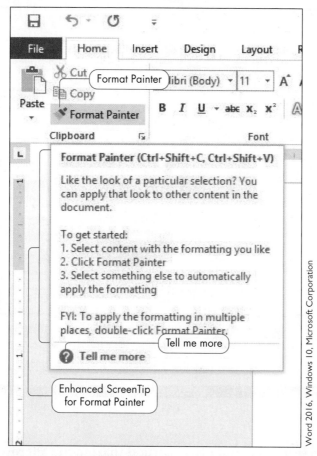

Word 2016, Windows 10, Microsoft Corporation

FIGURE 1.15 Enhanced ScreenTip

Installing Add-ins

Sometimes it is helpful to extend the functionality of Office programs by adding a Microsoft or third-party add-in to the program. An ***add-in*** is a custom program or additional command that extends the functionality of a Microsoft Office program (see Figure 1.16). Some add-ins are available for free while others may have a cost associated with them. For example, in PowerPoint you could add a Poll Everywhere poll that enables you to interact with your audience by having them respond to a question you have asked. The audience's electronic responses will appear on a slide as a real-time graph or word cloud. In Excel, add-ins provide additional functionality that can help with statistics and data mining.

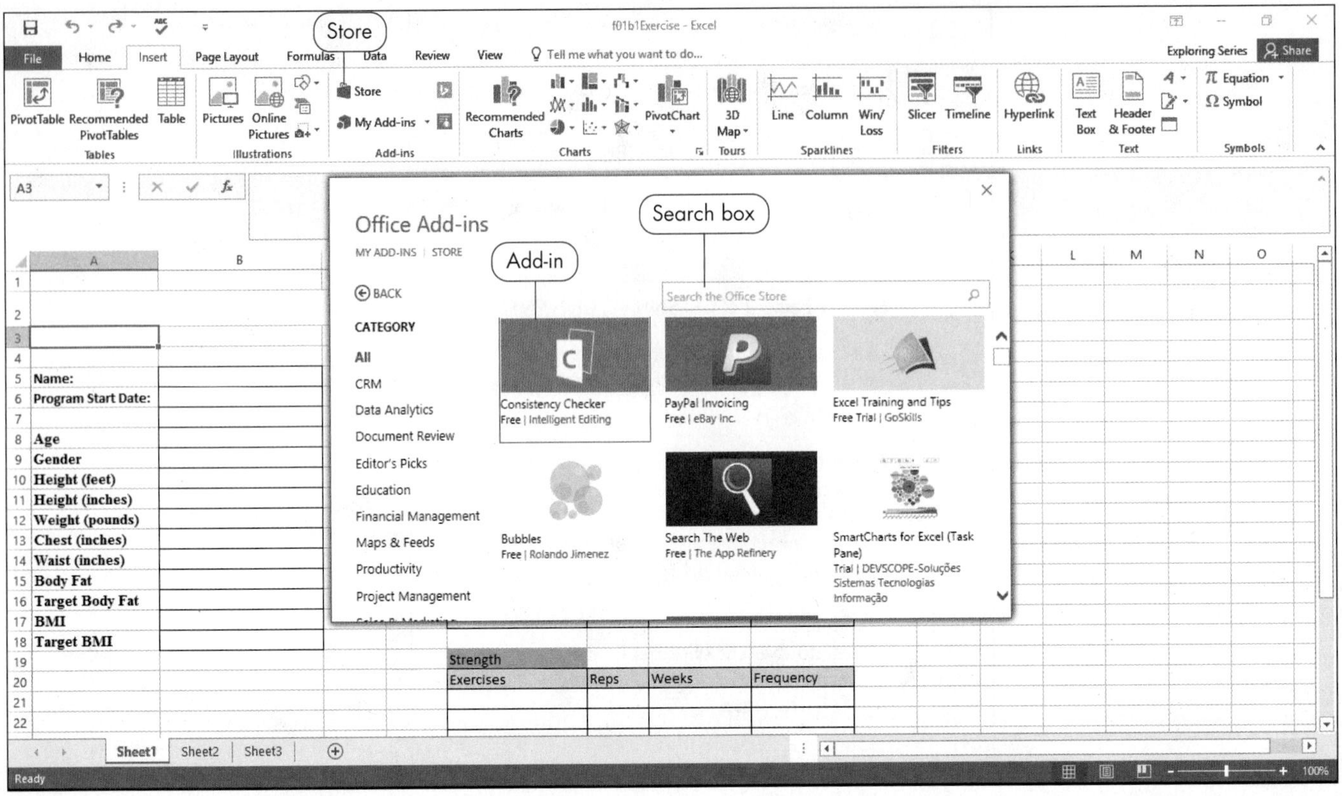

FIGURE 1.16 Add-Ins for Excel

To search for and install an add-in from the Microsoft Store, complete the following steps:

1. Click the Insert tab.
2. Click Store (refer to Figure 1.16). Browse the list of add-ins or use the search box.
3. Click the add-in. A box will display with information about the add-in such as its purpose, the cost (if any), and information it may access.
4. Click Trust It to add the add-in to your application. The newly added add-in will be available for future use in the My Add-ins list located on the Insert tab.

Quick Concepts ✓

1. What are the benefits of logging in with your Microsoft account? **p. 5**
2. What is the purpose of the Quick Access Toolbar? **p. 14**
3. You are having trouble completing a task in Microsoft Word. What are some of the Office application features you could use to assist you in getting help with that task? **pp. 15–16**

Hands-On Exercises

Skills covered: Open a Microsoft Office Application • Open a File • Save a File • Use a Shortcut Menu • Use the *Tell me what you want to do* Box

1 Getting Started with Office Applications

The Spotted Begonia Art Gallery just hired several new clerical assistants to help you develop materials for the various activities coming up throughout the year. A coworker sent you a letter and asked for your assistance in making a few minor formatting changes. The letter is to thank the ABC Arts Foundation for its generous donation to the *Discover the Artist in You!* program and to invite them to the program's kickoff party. To begin, you will open Word and then open an existing document. You will use the Shortcut menu to make simple changes to the document. Finally, you will use the *Tell me what you want to do* box to apply a style to the first line of text.

STEP 1 ›› OPEN A MICROSOFT OFFICE APPLICATION

You start Microsoft Word from the Windows Start menu. Refer to Figure 1.17 as you complete Step 1.

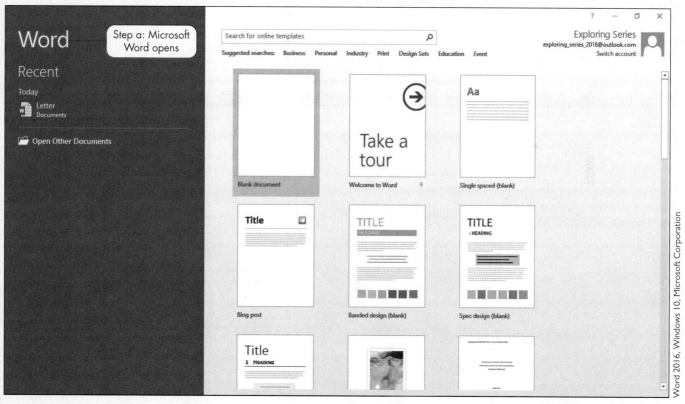

FIGURE 1.17 Open Word

Word 2016, Windows 10, Microsoft Corporation

    a. Start your computer and log into your Microsoft account. On the Start menu, click **All apps** and click **Word 2016**.

    Microsoft Word displays.

You open a thank-you letter that you will later modify. Refer to Figure 1.18 as you complete Step 2.

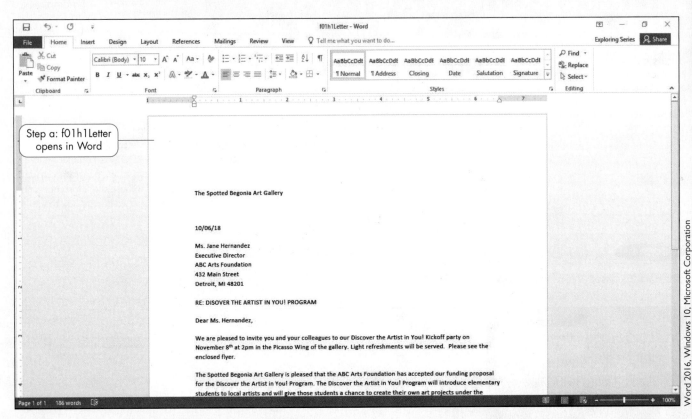

FIGURE 1.18 Open the Letter

a. Click **Open Other Documents** and click **Browse**. Navigate to the location of your student files. Double-click *f01h1Letter* to open the file shown in Figure 1.18. Click Enable Content.

The thank-you letter opens.

TROUBLESHOOTING: When you open an file from the student files associated with this book, you will need to enable the content. You may be confident of the trustworthiness of the files for this book.

You save the document with a different name, to preserve the original file. Refer to Figure 1.19 as you complete Step 3.

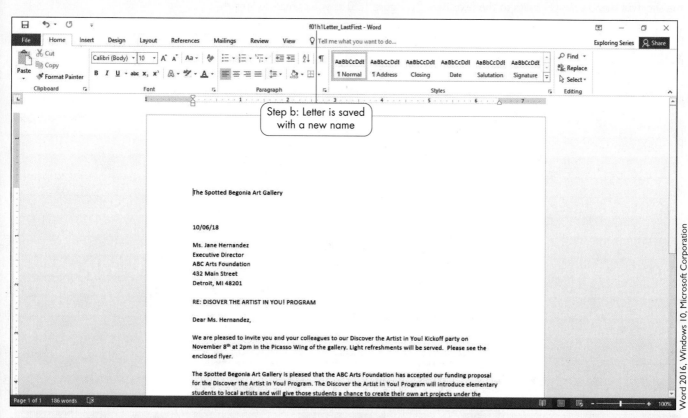

FIGURE 1.19 Save the Letter with a New Name

a. Click the **File tab**, click **Save As**, and then click **Browse** to display the Save As dialog box. Click **This PC** or click the location where you are saving your files.

b. Click in the **File name box** and type **f01h1Letter_LastFirst**.

When you save files, use your last and first names. For example, as the Common Features author, I would name my document "f01h1Letter_RutledgeAmy".

> **TROUBLESHOOTING:** If you make any major mistakes in this exercise, you can close the file, open *f01h1Letter* again, and then start this exercise over.

c. Click **Save**.

The file is now saved as f01h1Letter_LastFirst. You can check the title bar of the workbook to confirm that the file has been saved with the correct name.

You would like to apply italics to the *Discover the Artist in You!* text in the first sentence of the letter. You will select the text and use the shortcut menu to apply italics to the text. Refer to Figure 1.20 as you complete Step 4.

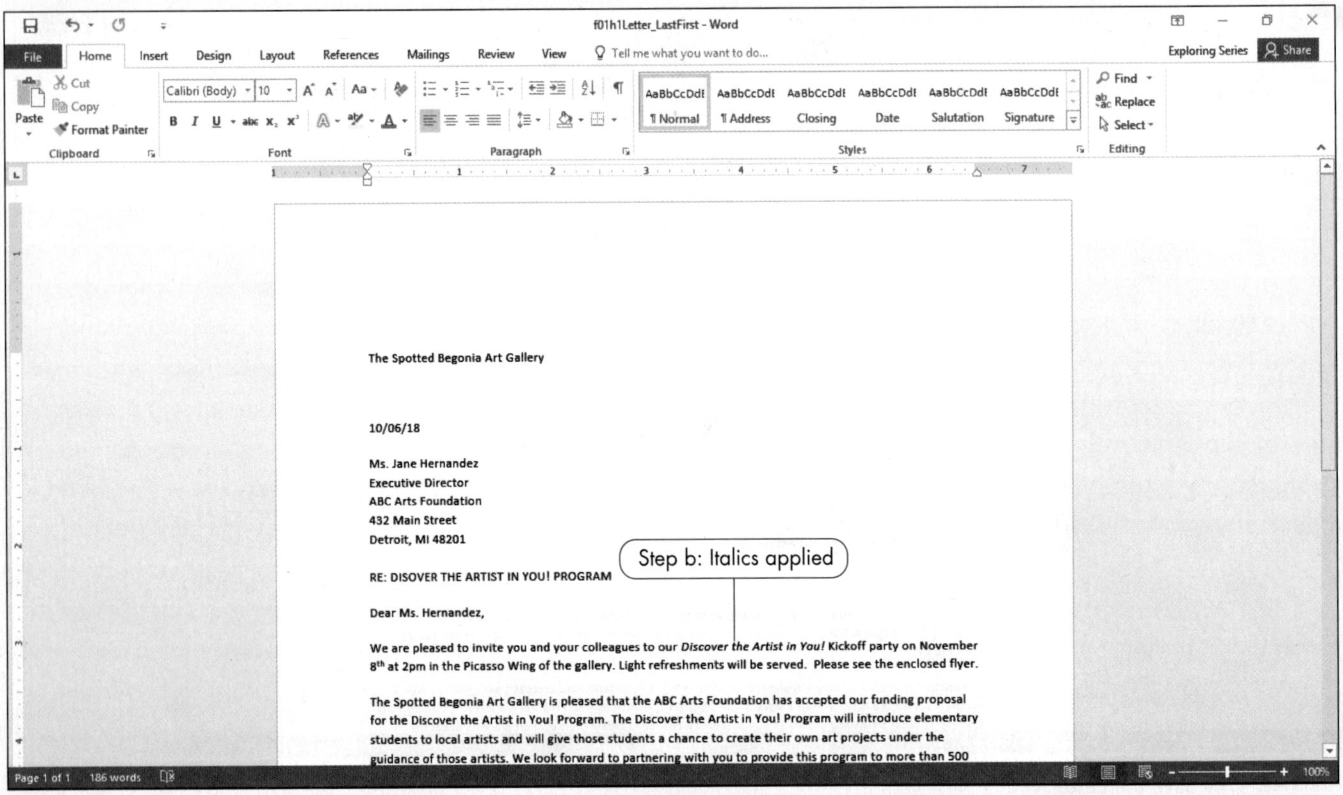

FIGURE 1.20 Apply Italics Using the Shortcut Menu

a. Select the text **Discover the Artist in You!** in the first sentence of the letter that starts with *We are pleased*.

The text is selected.

b. Right-click the selected text. Click **Font** on the Shortcut menu. Click **Italic** under Font style, and click **OK**.

Italics is applied to the text.

c. Click **Save** on the Quick Access Toolbar.

STEP 5 » USE THE *TELL ME WHAT YOU WANT TO DO* BOX

You would like to apply a style to the first line in the letter. Since you do not know how to complete the task, you use the *Tell me what you want to do* box to search for and apply the change. Refer to Figure 1.21 as you complete Step 5.

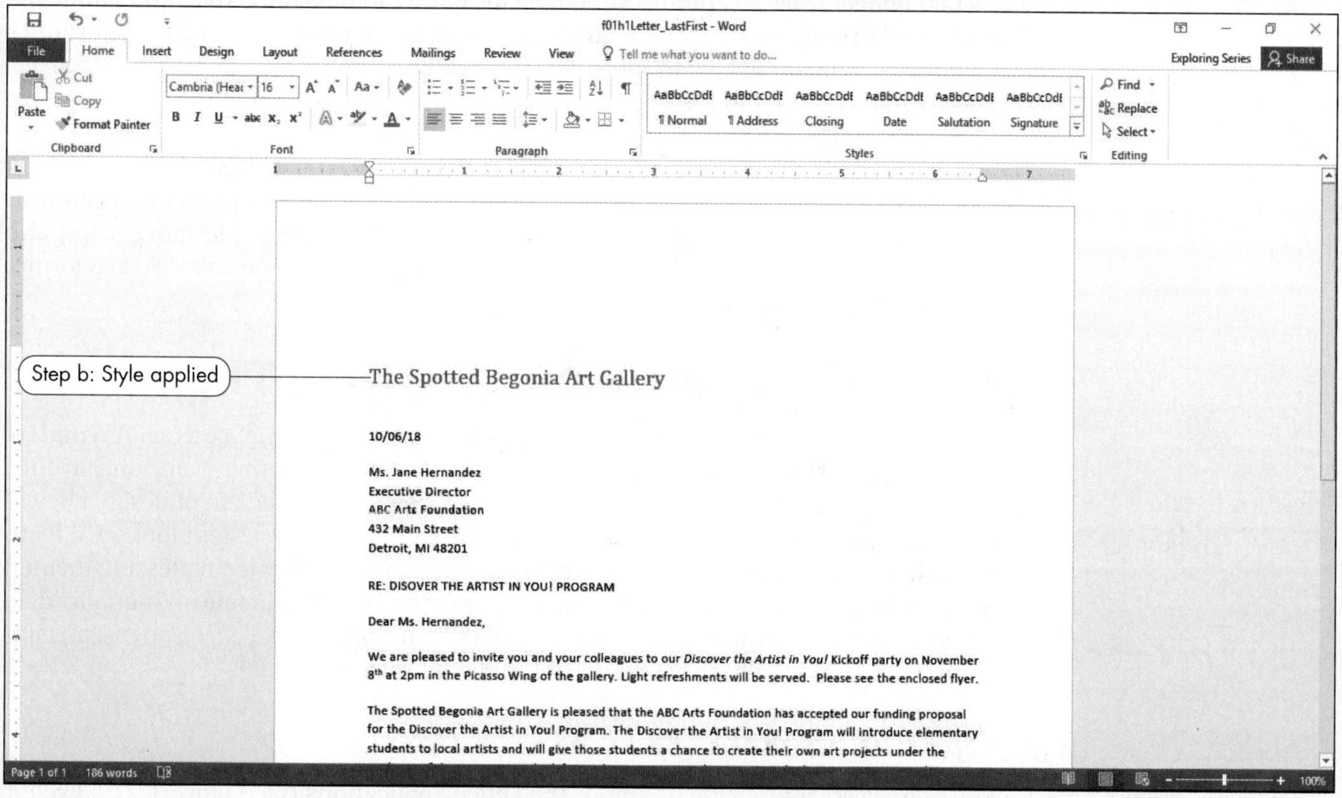

Word 2016, Windows 10, Microsoft Corporation

FIGURE 1.21 Change the Text Style Using the *Tell me what you want to do* Box

a. Triple-click the entire first line of the letter that starts with *The Spotted Begonia Art Gallery* to select it. Click the ***Tell me what you want to do* box**, and type **heading 1**.

A list of options appears below the box.

b. Click **Promote to Heading1** to apply the style to the selected text.

The Heading 1 style is applied to the text.

c. Save the document. Keep the document open if you plan to continue with the next Hands-On Exercise. If not, save and close the workbook, and exit Word.

Format Document Content

After creating a document, worksheet, or presentation, you will probably want to make some formatting changes. You might prefer to center a title, or maybe you think that certain budget worksheet totals should be formatted as currency. You can change the font so that typed characters are larger or in a different style. You might even want to bold text to add emphasis. In all Office applications, the Home tab provides tools for selecting and editing text. You can also use the Mini toolbar for making quick changes to selected text.

In this section you will explore themes and templates. You will learn to use the Mini toolbar to quickly make formatting changes. You will learn how to select and edit text, as well as check your grammar and spelling. You will learn how to move, copy, and paste text, as well as insert pictures. And, finally, you will learn how to resize and format pictures and graphics.

Using Templates and Applying Themes

You can enhance your documents by using a template or applying a theme. A ***template*** is a predesigned file that incorporates formatting elements, such as a theme and layouts, and may include content that can be modified. A ***theme*** is a collection of design choices that includes colors, fonts, and special effects used to give a consistent look to a document, workbook, or presentation. Microsoft provides high quality templates and themes, designed by professional designers to make it faster and easier to create high-quality documents. Even if you use a theme to apply colors, fonts, and special effects, they can later be changed individually or to a completely different theme.

Open a Template

STEP 1 ⟫ You can access a template in any of the Office applications (see Figure 1.22). Even if you know only a little bit about the software, you could then make a few changes so that the file would accurately represent your specific needs. The document also would be prepared much more quickly than if you designed it yourself from a blank file. For example, you might want to prepare a home budget using an Excel template, such as the Family monthly budget planner template, that is available by typing *Budget* in the *Suggested searches* template list.

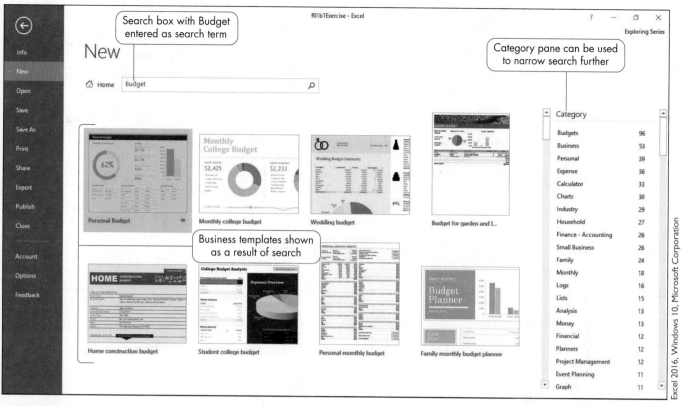

FIGURE 1.22 Templates in Excel

The Templates list is comprised of template groups available within each Office application. The search box enables you to locate other templates that are available online. When you click one of the Suggested searches, additional choices are displayed. Once you select a template, you can view more information about the template including author information, a general overview about the template, and additional views (if applicable).

> **To search for and use a template, complete the following steps:**
>
> 1. Open the Microsoft application with which you will be working.
> 2. Type a search term in the *Search for online templates box*, or click one of the Suggested search terms.
> 3. Scroll through the template options or use the pane at the right to narrow your search further.
> 4. Select a template, and review its information in the window that opens.
> 5. Click Create to open the template in the application.

A Help window may display along with the worksheet template. Read it for more information about the template, or close it to continue working.

Apply a Theme

Applying a theme enables you to visually coordinate various page elements. Themes are a bit different for each of the Office applications. In Word, a theme is a set of coordinating fonts, colors, and special effects, such as shadowing or glows that are combined into a package to provide a stylish appearance (see Figure 1.23). In PowerPoint, a theme is a file that includes the formatting elements like a background, a color scheme, and slide layouts that position content placeholders. Themes in Excel are similar to those in Word in that they are a set of coordinating fonts, colors, and special effects. Themes in Excel will not only change the color of the fill in a cell, but will also affect any SmartArt or charts in the workbook. Access also has a set of themes that coordinate the appearance of fonts and colors for objects such as Forms and Reports. In Word and PowerPoint, themes can be accessed from the Design tab. In Excel they can be accessed from the Page Layout tab. In Access, themes can be applied to forms and reports. To apply a theme, click the Themes arrow, and select a theme from the Themes gallery.

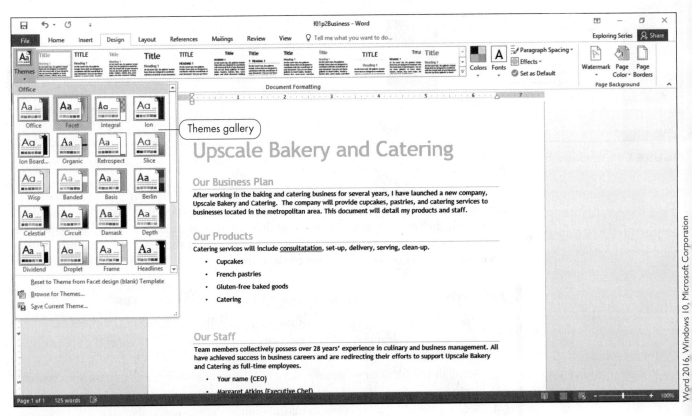

FIGURE 1.23 Themes in Word

Modifying Text

Formatting and modifying text in documents, worksheets, or presentations is an essential function when using Office applications. Centering a title, formatting cells, or changing the font color or size are tasks that occur frequently. In all Office applications, the Home tab provides tools for editing selected text. You can also use the Mini toolbar for making quick changes to selected text.

Select Text

STEP 2 ❱❱ Before making any changes to existing text or numbers, you must first select the characters. A general rule that you should commit to memory is "Select, then do." A foolproof way to select text or numbers is to place the pointer before the first character of the text you want to select, and then drag to highlight the intended selection. Before you drag, be sure that the pointer takes on the shape of the letter *I*, called the *I-beam* ⊤I. Although other methods for selecting exist, if you remember only one way, it should be the click-and-drag method. If your attempted selection falls short of highlighting the intended area, or perhaps highlights too much, click outside the selection and try again.

Sometimes it can be difficult to precisely select a small amount of text, such as a single word or sentence. Other times, the task can be overwhelming large, such as when selecting an entire 550-page document. In either case there are shortcuts to selecting text. The shortcuts shown in Table 1.2 are primarily applicable to text in Word and PowerPoint. When working with Excel, you will more often need to select multiple cells. To select multiple cells, drag the intended selection when the pointer displays as a large white plus sign ⊕.

TABLE 1.2 Shortcut Selection in Word and PowerPoint	
Item Selected	**Action**
One word	Double-click the word.
One line of text	Place the pointer at the left of the line, in the margin area. When the pointer changes to a right-pointing arrow, click to select the line.
One sentence	Press and hold Ctrl, and click in the sentence to select it.
One paragraph	Triple-click in the paragraph.
One character to the left of the insertion point	Press and hold Shift, and press the left arrow on the keyboard.
One character to the right of the insertion point	Press and hold Shift, and press the right arrow on the keyboard.
Entire document	Press and hold Ctrl, and press A on the keyboard.

Pearson Education, Inc.

Once you have selected the desired text, besides applying formatting, you can delete or simply type over to replace the text.

Edit Text

At times, you will want to make the font size larger or smaller, change the font color, or apply other font attributes. For example, if you are creating a handout for a gallery show opening, you may want to apply a different font to emphasize key information such as dates and times. Because such changes are commonplace, Office places those formatting commands in many convenient places within each Office application.

You can find the most common formatting commands in the Font group on the Home tab. As noted earlier, Word, Excel, and PowerPoint all share very similar Font groups that provide access to tasks related to changing the character font. Remember that you can place the pointer over any command icon to view a summary of the icon's purpose, so although the icons might at first appear cryptic, you can use the pointer to quickly determine the purpose and applicability to your desired text change.

The way characters display onscreen or print in documents, including qualities such as size, spacing, and shape, is determined by the font. Office applications have a default font, Calibri, which is the font that will be in effect unless you change it. Other font attributes include bold, italic, and font color, all of which can be applied to selected text. Some formatting commands, such as Bold and Italic, are called **toggle commands**. They act somewhat like light switches that you can turn on and off. Once you have applied bold formatting to text, the Bold command is highlighted on the Ribbon when that text is selected again. To undo bold formatting, click Bold again.

If you want to apply a different font to a section of your project for added emphasis or interest, you can make the change by selecting a font from within the Font group on the Home tab. You can also change the font by selecting from the Mini toolbar.

If the font change that you plan to make is not included as a choice on either the Home tab or the Mini toolbar, you can find what you are looking for in the Font dialog box. Click the Dialog Box Launcher in the bottom-right corner of the Font group. Figure 1.24 shows a sample Font dialog box. Because the Font dialog box provides many formatting choices in one window, you can make several changes at once. Depending on the application, the contents of the Font dialog box vary slightly, but the purpose is consistent—providing access to choices related to modifying characters.

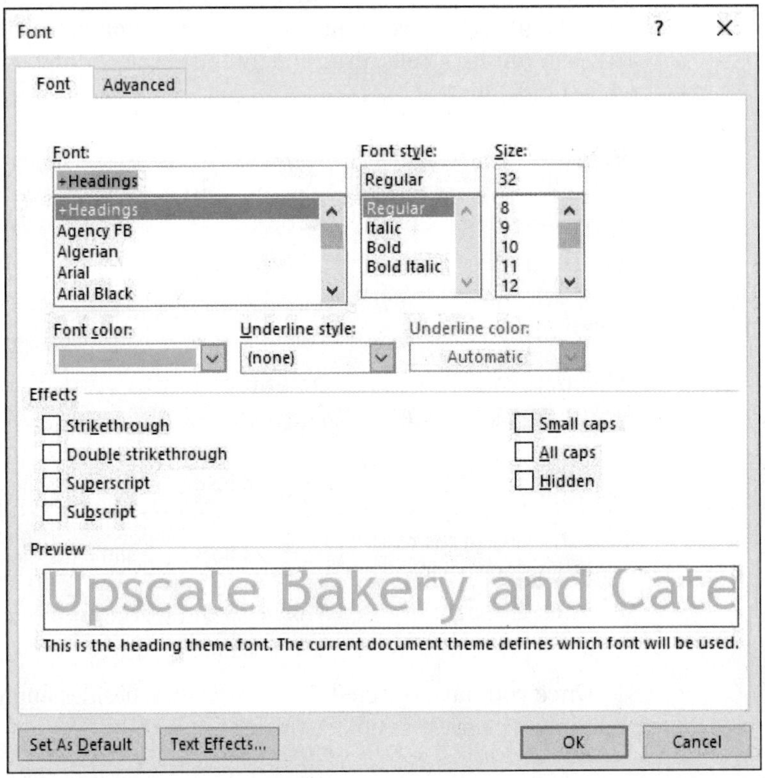

Word 2016, Windows 10, Microsoft Corporation

FIGURE 1.24 The Font Dialog Box

Use the Mini Toolbar

You have learned that you can always use commands on the Home tab of the Ribbon to change selected text within a document, worksheet, or presentation. Although using the Ribbon to select commands is simple enough, the ***Mini toolbar*** provides an even faster way to accomplish some of the same formatting changes. When you select any amount of text within a worksheet, document, or presentation, move the pointer slightly within the selection to display the Mini toolbar (see Figure 1.25). The Mini toolbar provides access to the most common formatting selections, such as bold or italic, or font type or color. Unlike the Quick Access Toolbar, the Mini toolbar is not customizable, which means that you cannot add or remove options from the toolbar.

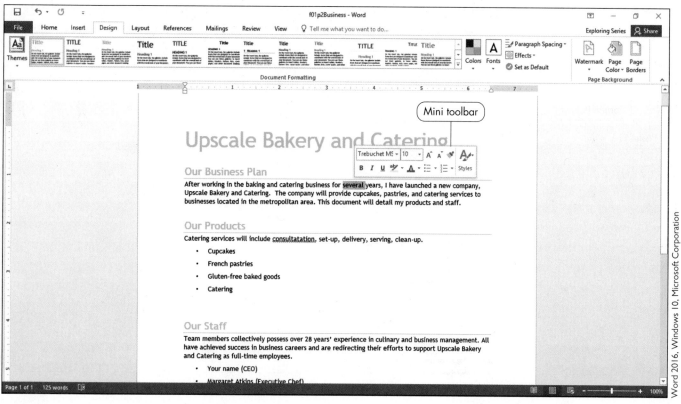

FIGURE 1.25 The Mini Toolbar

The Mini toolbar is displayed only when text is selected. The closer the pointer is to the Mini toolbar, the darker the toolbar becomes. As you move the pointer away from the selected text, the Mini toolbar eventually fades away. If the Mini toolbar is no longer displayed, you can right-click the selection to make the Mini toolbar appear again. To make selections from the Mini toolbar, click a command on the toolbar. To temporarily remove the Mini toolbar from view, press Esc.

> **To permanently disable the Mini toolbar so that it does not display in any open file when text is selected, complete the following steps:**
>
> 1. Click the File tab and click Options.
> 2. Click General.
> 3. Click the *Show Mini toolbar on selection* check box to deselect it.
> 4. Click OK.

Copy Formats with Format Painter

STEP 3 ▶▶ Using ***Format Painter***, you can copy all formatting from one area to another in Word, PowerPoint, and Excel (see Figure 1.26). If, for example, a heading in Word includes multiple formatting features, you will save time by copying the entire set of formatting options to the other headings. In so doing, you will ensure the consistency of formatting for all headings because they will appear exactly alike.

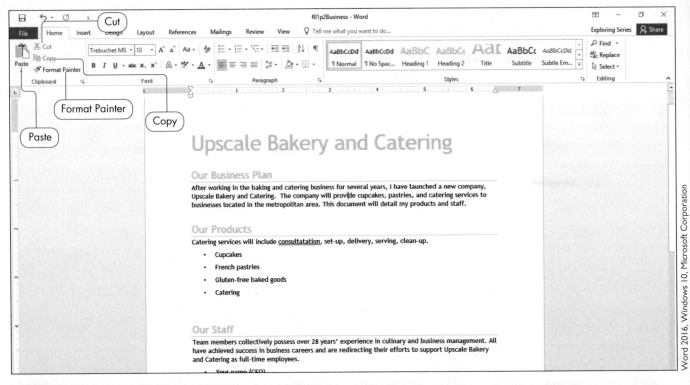

FIGURE 1.26 Format Painter

To copy a format, complete the following steps:

1. Select the text containing the desired format.
2. Single-click Format Painter if you want to copy the format to only one other selection. If, however, you plan to copy the same format to multiple areas, double-click Format Painter.
3. Select the area to which the copied format should be applied.

If you single-clicked Format Painter to copy the format to one other selection, Format Painter turns off once the formatting has been applied. If you double-clicked Format Painter to copy the format to multiple locations, continue selecting text in various locations to apply the format. Then, to turn off Format Painter, click Format Painter again or press Esc.

Relocating Text

On occasion, you will want to relocate a section of text from one area to another. Suppose that you have included text on a PowerPoint slide that you believe would be more appropriate on a different slide. Or perhaps an Excel formula should be copied from one cell to another because both cells should be totaled in the same manner. You can move the slide text or copy the Excel formula by using the cut, copy, and paste features found in the Clipboard group on the Home tab. The Office **Clipboard** is an area of memory reserved to temporarily hold selections that have been cut or copied and allows you to paste the selections. When the computer is shut down or loses power, the contents of the Clipboard are erased, so it is important to finalize the paste procedure during the current session.

Cut, Copy, and Paste Text

 》》 To *cut* means to remove a selection from the original location and place it in the Office Clipboard. To *copy* means to duplicate a selection from the original location and place a copy in the Office Clipboard. Although the Clipboard can hold up to 24 items at one time, the usual procedure is to paste the cut or copied selection to its final destination fairly quickly. To *paste* means to place a cut or copied selection into another location. In addition to using the Clipboard group icons, you can also cut, copy, and paste in any of the ways listed in Table 1.3.

TABLE 1.3	Cut, Copy, and Paste Options
Command	**Actions**
Cut	• Click Cut in Clipboard group. • Right-click selection and select Cut. • Press Ctrl+X.
Copy	• Click Copy in Clipboard group. • Right-click selection and select Copy. • Press Ctrl+C.
Paste	• Click in destination location and select Paste in Clipboard group. • Click in destination location and press Ctrl+V. • Click Clipboard Dialog Box Launcher to open Clipboard pane. Click in destination location. With Clipboard pane open, click arrow beside intended selection and select Paste.

Pearson Education, Inc.

To cut or copy text, complete the following steps:

1. Select the text you want to cut or copy.
2. Click the appropriate icon in the Clipboard group either to cut or copy the selection. Remember that cut or copied text is actually placed in the Clipboard, remaining there even after you paste it to another location. It is important to note that you can paste the same item multiple times, because it will remain in the Clipboard until you power down your computer or until the Clipboard exceeds 24 items.
3. Click the location where you want the cut or copied text to be placed. The location can be in the current file or in another open file within any Office application.
4. Click Paste in the Clipboard group on the Home tab.

When you paste text you may not want to paste the text with all of its formatting. In some instances, you may want to paste only the text, unformatted, so that it fits in with the formatting of its new location. When pasting text, there are several options available and those options will depend on the program you are using.

Use the Office Clipboard

When you cut or copy selections, they are placed in the Office Clipboard. Regardless of which Office application you are using, you can view the Clipboard by clicking the Clipboard Dialog Box Launcher, as shown in Figure 1.27.

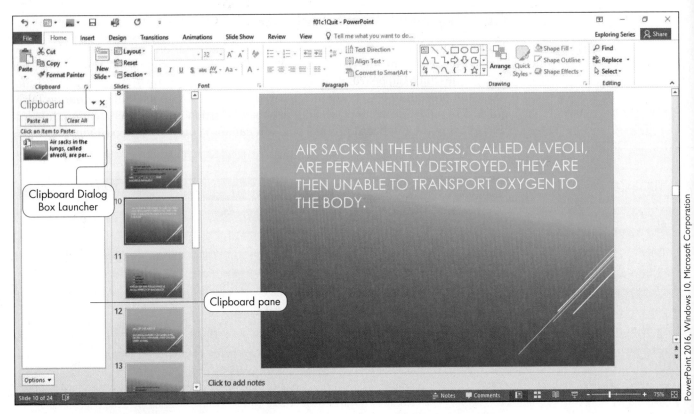

FIGURE 1.27 The Office Clipboard

Unless you specify otherwise when beginning a paste operation, the most recently added Clipboard item is pasted. You can, however, select an item from the Clipboard pane to paste. Click the item in the list to add it to the document. You can also delete items from the Clipboard by clicking the arrow next to the selection in the Clipboard pane and then clicking Delete. You can remove all items from the Clipboard by clicking Clear All. The Options button in the Clipboard pane enables you to control when and where the Clipboard is displayed. Close the Clipboard pane by clicking the Close ☒ button in the top-right corner of the pane or by clicking the arrow in the title bar of the Clipboard pane and selecting Close.

Checking Spelling and Grammar

STEP 5 ≫ As you create or edit a file you will want to make sure no spelling or grammatical errors exist. You will also be concerned with wording, being sure to select words or phrases that best represent the purpose of the document, worksheet, or presentation. On occasion, you might even find yourself at a loss for an appropriate word. Word, Excel, and PowerPoint all provide standard tools for proofreading, including a spelling and grammar checker and thesaurus.

Word and PowerPoint check your spelling and grammar as you type. If a word is unrecognized, it is flagged as misspelled or grammatically incorrect. Even though Excel does not check your spelling as you type, it is important to run the spelling checker in Excel. Excel's spelling checker will review charts, pivot tables, and other reports that all need to be spelled correctly. Misspellings are identified with a red wavy underline, grammatical problems are underlined in green, and word usage errors (such as using bear instead of bare) have a blue underline.

To check the spelling for an entire file, complete the following steps:

1. Click the Review tab.
2. Click Spelling and Grammar.

Beginning at the top of the document, each identified error is highlighted in a pane similar to Figure 1.28. You can then choose how to address the problem by making a selection from the options in the pane.

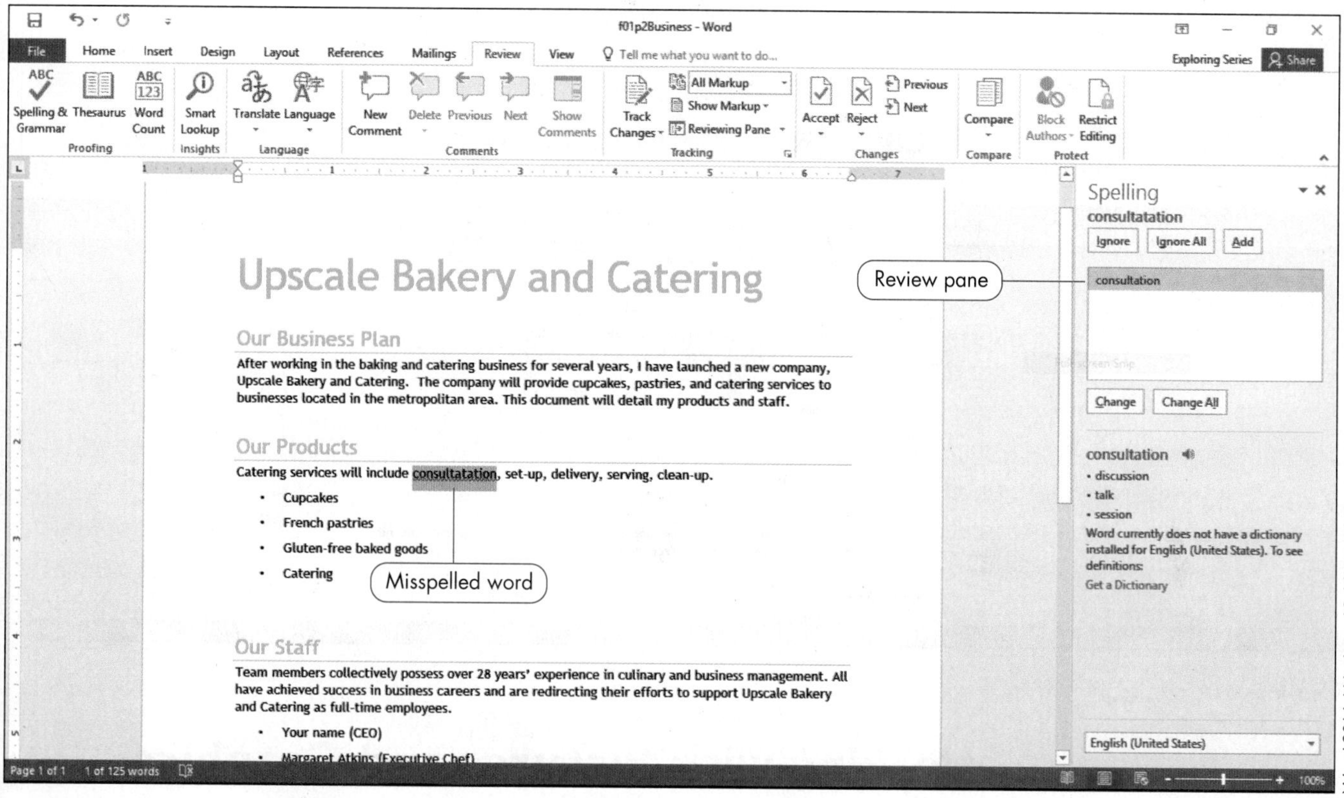

FIGURE 1.28 Checking for Spelling and Grammatical Errors

If the word or phrase is truly in error—that is, it is not a person's name or an unusual term that is not in the application's dictionary—you can correct it manually, or you can let the software correct it for you. If you right-click a word or phrase that is identified as a mistake, you will see a shortcut menu similar to that shown in Figure 1.29. If the Office dictionary makes a suggestion with the correct spelling, you can click to accept the suggestion and make the change. If a grammatical rule is violated, you will have an opportunity to select a correction. However, if the text is actually correct, you can click Ignore or Ignore All (to bypass all occurrences of the flagged error in the current document). Click *Add to Dictionary* if you want the word to be considered correct whenever it appears in any document. Similar selections on a shortcut menu enable you to ignore grammatical mistakes if they are not errors.

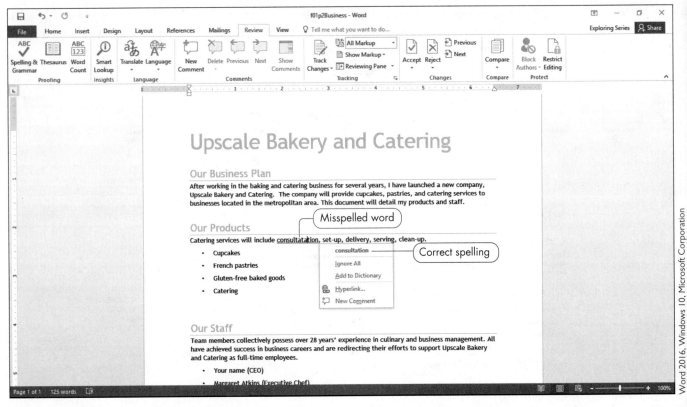

FIGURE 1.29 Correcting Misspelling

Working with Pictures and Graphics

Documents, worksheets, and presentations can include much more than just words and numbers. You can add energy and additional description to a project by including pictures and other graphic elements. Although a ***picture*** is usually just that—a digital photo—it is actually defined as a graphic element.

Insert Pictures and Graphics

You can insert pictures from your own library of digital photos you have saved on your hard drive, OneDrive, or another storage medium, or you can initiate a Bing Image Search for online pictures directly inside the Office program you are using. The Bing search filters are set to use the Creative Commons license system. These are images and drawings that can be used more freely than images from websites. You should read the Creative Commons license for each image you use to avoid copyright infringement. You can also insert a picture from social media sites, such as Facebook, by clicking the Facebook icon at the bottom of the Online Pictures dialog box.

> **To insert an online picture from a Bing Image Search, complete the following steps:**
>
> 1. Click in the file where you want the picture to be placed.
> 2. Click the Insert tab.
> 3. Click Online Pictures in the Illustrations group.
> 4. Type a search term in the Bing Image Search box and press Enter.
> 5. Select your desired image and click Insert (see Figure 1.30).

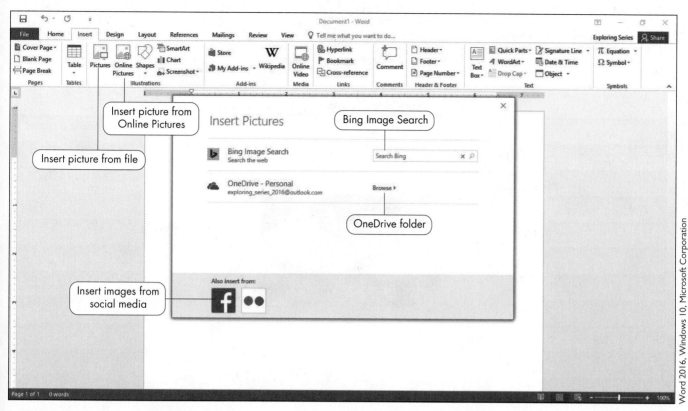

FIGURE 1.30 Inserting Online Pictures

To insert a picture from a file stored on your computer, complete the following steps:

1. Click in the file where you want the picture to be placed.
2. Click the Insert tab.
3. Click Pictures in the Illustrations group to search for a file located on your computer.
4. Locate the file and select it. Click Insert at the bottom of the dialog box to insert the file into your document.

Resize and Format Pictures and Graphics

You have learned how to add a picture to your document, but quite often, a picture is inserted in a size that is too large or too small for your purposes. To resize a picture, you can drag a corner sizing handle. You should never resize a picture by dragging a center sizing handle, as doing so would skew the picture. You can also resize a picture by adjusting settings in the Size group of the Picture Tools Format tab. When a picture is selected, the Picture Tools Format tab includes options for modifying a picture (see Figure 1.31). You can apply a picture style or effect, as well as add a picture border, from selections in the Picture Styles group. Click More (see Figure 1.31) to view a gallery of picture styles. As you point to a style, the style is shown in Live Preview, but the style is not applied until you click it. Options in the Adjust group simplify changing a color scheme, applying creative artistic effects, and even adjusting the brightness, contrast, and sharpness of an image.

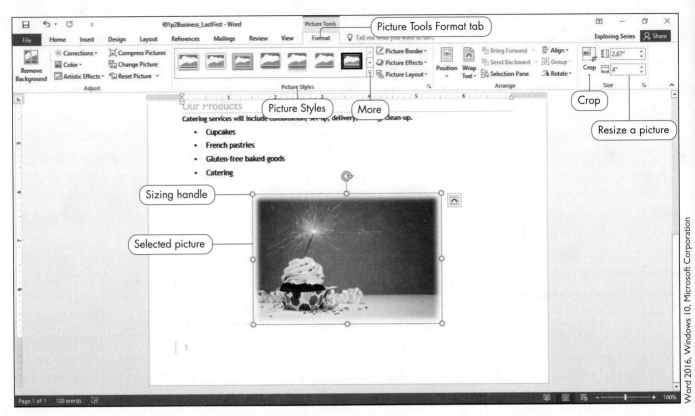

FIGURE 1.31 Formatting a Picture

If a picture contains more detail than is necessary, you can crop it, which is the process of trimming edges that you do not want to display. The Crop tool is located on the Picture Tools Format tab (refer to Figure 1.31). Even though cropping enables you to adjust the amount of a picture that displays, it does not actually delete the portions that are cropped out unless you actually compress the picture. Therefore, you can later recover parts of the picture, if necessary. Cropping a picture does not reduce the file size of the picture or the document in which it displays.

Quick Concepts

4. What is the difference between a theme and a template? *p. 24*

5. Give an example of when Format Painter could be used. *p. 29*

6. When will an Office application identify a word as misspelled that is not actually misspelled? *p. 32*

Hands-On Exercises

Skills covered: Open a
Template • Select Text • Edit Text
• Use the Mini Toolbar • Format
Painter • Cut, Copy, and Paste Text
• Check Spelling and Grammar •
Insert a Picture

2 Format Document Content

As the administrative assistant for the Spotted Begonia Art Gallery, you want to create a flyer to announce
the *Discover the Artist in You!* kickoff event. You decide to use a template to help you get started more
quickly. You will modify the flyer created with the template by adding and editing text and a photo.

STEP 1 》》 OPEN A TEMPLATE

To expedite the process of creating a flyer, you will review the templates that are available in Microsoft Word. You search for flyers
and finally choose one that is appropriate for the gallery, knowing that you will be able to replace the photos with your own. Refer
to Figure 1.32 as you complete Step 1.

[Add Key Event
Info Here!]

[Don't Be Shy—
Tell Them Why

Step b: Flyer template
opened

[One More Point
Here!]

[Add More Great
Info Here!]

[You Have Room
for Another One
Here!]

Word 2016, Windows 10, Microsoft Corporation

[DATE]
[EVENT
TITLE HERE]

FIGURE 1.32 Use a Template

a. Start Word. In the *Search for online templates* box type the search term **event flyer** to
search for event flyer templates Click **Search**.

Your search results in a selection of event flyer templates.

b. Locate the event flyer template in Figure 1.32 and click to select it. The template appears
in a preview. Click **Create** to open the flyer template.

The flyer template that you selected opens in Word.

> **TROUBLESHOOTING:** If you do not find the template in the figure, you may access the
> template from the student data files – *f01h2Flyer*.

c. Click **Save** on the Quick Access Toolbar. Save the document as **f01h2Flyer_LastFirst**. Because this is the first time to save the flyer file, the Save button on the Quick Access Toolbar opens a dialog box in which you must indicate the location of the file and the file name.

You will replace the template text to create the flyer, adding information such as a title, date, and description. After adding the text to the document, you will modify the organization name in the flyer so it is more like the logo text. Refer to Figure 1.33 as you complete Step 2.

FIGURE 1.33 Select and Edit Text

a. Click the [Date] **placeholder** in the main body of the text and type **May 31, 2018** in the placeholder. Click the [Event Title Here] **placeholder** and type **Discover the Artist in You!** in the placeholder. Press **Enter** and continue typing **Spotted Begonia Art Gallery**. Click the [Event Description Heading] **placeholder** and type **A Special Childrens Event**. (Ignore the misspelling at this time.)

You modify the placeholders to customize the flyer for your purposes.

b. Point to the text **Discover the Artist in You!** until the pointer becomes an I-beam. Click and drag to select the text. Click the **Font arrow** on the Mini toolbar. Select **Eras Bold ITC**.

The font is changed.

c. Select the text, **May 31, 2018**. Click the **Font Size arrow** on the Mini toolbar. Select **26** on the Font Size menu.

The font size is changed to 26 pt.

d. Click Save on the Quick Access Toolbar to save the document.

STEP 3 ❯❯ USE FORMAT PAINTER

You want the gallery name font to match that of the event description heading in the flyer. You recently learned about using the Format Painter tool to quickly apply font attributes to text. Refer to Figure 1.34 as you complete Step 3.

FIGURE 1.34 Use Format Painter

a. Click the **Home tab**. Select the text **A Special Childrens Event**, and click **Format Painter** in the Clipboard group. Drag to select the text **Spotted Begonia Art Gallery**.

The text is now modified to match the font and size of the event description heading.

b. Save the document.

STEP 4 ❯❯ CUT, COPY, AND PASTE TEXT

You decide that one of the paragraphs in the flyer would be best near the end of the document. You cut the paragraph and paste it in the new location. Refer to Figure 1.35 as you complete Step 4.

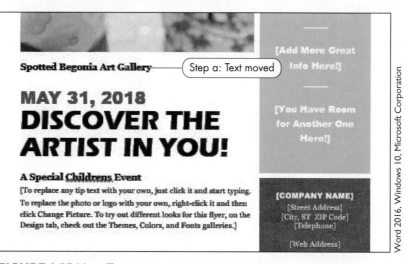

FIGURE 1.35 Move Text

a. Point to the text **Spotted Begonia Art Gallery** until the pointer becomes an I-beam. Click and drag to select the text. Press **Ctrl+X**.

The paragraph text is cut from the document and placed in the Office Clipboard.

b. Click before the word *May*. Press **Ctrl+V** to paste the previously cut text.

The text is now moved above the event date.

c. Save the document.

Because this flyer will be seen by the public, it is important to check the spelling and grammar for your document. Refer to Figure 1.36 as you complete Step 5.

FIGURE 1.36 Check Spelling and Grammar

a. Press **Ctrl+Home**. Click the **Review tab**, and click **Spelling & Grammar**. in the Proofing group Click **Change** to accept the suggested change to *Children's* in the Spelling pane. Click **OK** to close the dialog box.

The spelling and grammar check is complete.

b. Save the document.

You want to add an image saved on your computer that was taken at a previous children's event held at the gallery. Refer to Figure 1.37 as you complete Step 6.

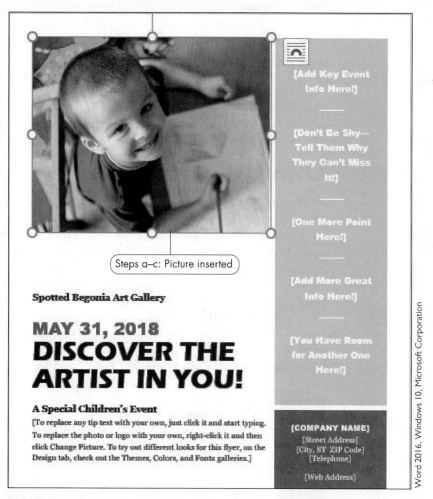

FIGURE 1.37 Insert Picture

a. Click the **image** to select it. Click the **Insert tab** and then click **Pictures**. Browse to your student data files and locate the *f01h2Art* picture file. Click **Insert**.

   The child's image is inserted into the flyer and replaces the template image of the children with ice cream.

b. Save and close the document. You will submit this file to your instructor at the end of the last Hands-On Exercise.

Modify Document Layout and Properties

When working with a document, at some point you must get it ready for distribution and/or printing. Before you send a document or print it, you will want to view the final product to make sure that your margins and page layout are as they should be.

In this section you will learn about Backstage view and explore how to view and edit document properties. You will learn about views and how to change a document view to suit your needs. Additionally, you will learn how to modify the page layout including page orientation and margins as well as how to add headers and footers. Finally, you will explore Print Preview and the various printing options available to you.

Using Backstage View

Backstage view is a component of Office that provides a concise collection of commands related to a file. Using Backstage view, you can view or specify settings related to protection, permissions, versions, and properties. A file's properties include the author, file size, permissions, and date modified. Backstage view also includes options for customizing program settings, signing in to your Office account, and exiting the application. You can create a new document, as well as open, save, print, share, export, and close files using Backstage view. Backstage view also enables you to exit the application.

Click the File tab to see Backstage view (see Figure 1.38). Backstage view will occupy the entire application window, hiding the file with which you are working. You can return to the application in a couple of ways. Either click the Back arrow in the top-left corner or press Esc on the keyboard.

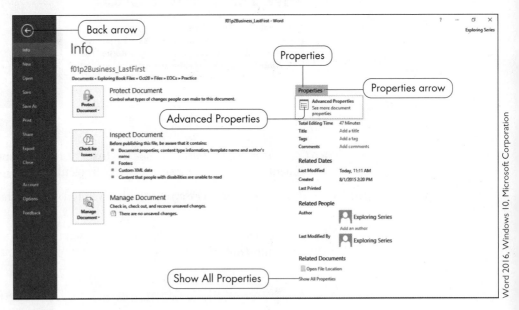

FIGURE 1.38 Backstage View and Document Properties

Customize Application Options

General settings in the Office application in which you are working can also be customized (see Figure 1.39). For example, you can change the AutoRecover settings, a feature that enables Word to recover a previous version of a document, such as the location and save frequency. You can alter how formatting, spelling, and grammar are checked by the application such as ignoring words in all uppercase letters. You can also modify the AutoCorrect feature. Additionally, you can change the language in which the application is displayed or the language for spelling and grammar checking, which may be helpful for a language course.

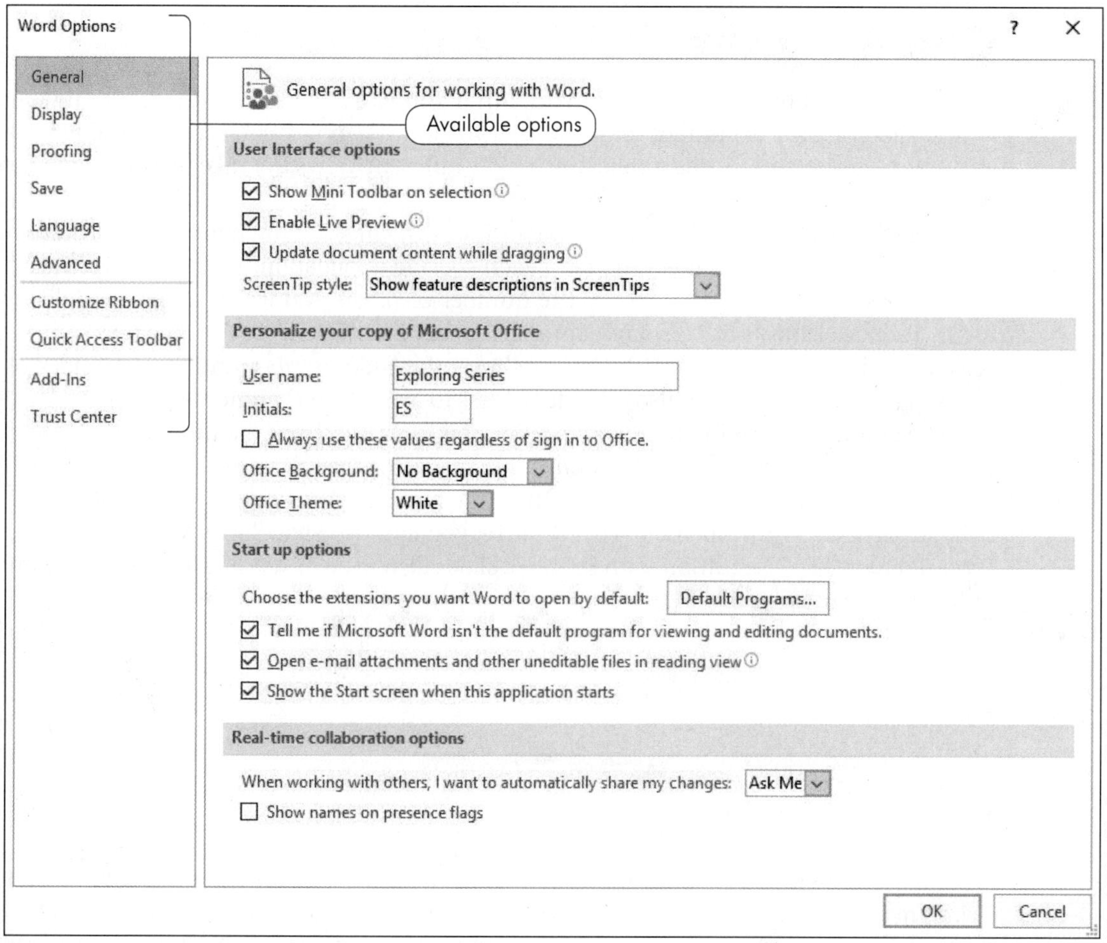

Word 2016, Windows 10, Microsoft Corporation

FIGURE 1.39 Application Options in Word

To customize an Office application, complete the following steps:

1. Click the File tab.
2. Click Options and select the option of your choice.
3. Click OK.

View and Edit Document Properties

STEP 1 It is good to include information that identifies a document, such as the author, document purpose, intended audience, or general comments. Those data elements, or metadata, are saved with the document, but do not appear in the document as it displays onscreen or is printed. You can use the Document Properties, located in Backstage view, to display descriptive information. You can even search for a file based on metadata you assign a document. For example, suppose you apply a tag of *Picasso* to all documents you create that are associated with that particular artist. Later, you can use that keyword as a search term, locating all associated documents. Statistical information related to the current document such as file size, number of pages, and total words are located on the Info page of Backstage view. You can modify some document information, such as adding a title or comments, but for more possibilities, display the Advanced Properties (refer to Figure 1.38).

> **To display the Advanced Properties, complete the following steps:**
>
> 1. Click the File tab.
> 2. Click the Properties arrow on the Info page.

Changing the Document View

STEP 2 >> As you prepare a document, you may find that you want to change the way you view it. A section of your document may be easier to view when you can see it magnified, for example. Alternatively, some applications have different views to make working on your project easier.

The **status bar**, located at the bottom of the program window, contains information relative to the open file and is unique to each specific application. When you work with Word, the status bar informs you of the number of pages and words in an open document. The Excel status bar displays summary information, such as average and sum, of selected cells. The PowerPoint status bar shows the slide number and total number of slides in the presentation. It also provides access to Notes and Comments.

The status bar also includes commonly used tools for changing the **view**—the way a file appears onscreen—and for changing the zoom size of onscreen file contents. The view buttons (see Figure 1.40) on the status bar of each application enable you to change the view of the open file. For instance, you can use Slide Sorter view to look at a PowerPoint slide presentation with multiple slides displayed or use Normal view to show only one slide in large size.

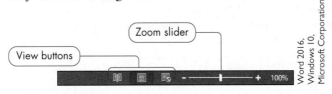

FIGURE 1.40 The Status Bar

Additional views for all Office applications are available on the View tab. Word's Print Layout view is useful when you want to see both the document text and such features as margins and page breaks. Web Layout view is useful to see what the page would look like on the Internet. Read Mode view provides a clean look that displays just the content without the Ribbon or margins. It is ideal for use on a tablet where the screen may be smaller than on a laptop or computer. PowerPoint, Excel, and Access also provide other unique view options. As you learn more about Office applications, you will become aware of the views that are specific to each application.

The **Zoom slider** is a horizontal bar on the bottom-right side of the status bar that enables you to increase or decrease the size of the document onscreen. You can drag the tab along the slider in either direction to increase or decrease the magnification of the file (refer to Figure 1.40). Be aware, however, that changing the size of text onscreen does not change the font size when the file is printed or saved.

Changing the Page Layout

When you prepare a document or worksheet, you are concerned with the way the project appears onscreen and possibly in print. The Layout tab in Word and the Page Layout tab in Excel provide access to a full range of options such as margin settings and page orientation. PowerPoint does not have a Page Layout tab, since its primary purpose is displaying contents onscreen rather than in print.

Because a document or workbook is most often designed to be printed, you may need to adjust margins and change the page orientation for the best display. In addition, perhaps the document or spreadsheet should be centered on the page vertically or the text should be aligned in columns. You will find these and other common page settings in the Page Setup group on the Layout (or Page Layout) tab. For less common settings, such as determining whether headers should print on odd or even pages, you use the Page Setup dialog box.

Change Margins

STEP 3 » A **margin** is the area of blank space that displays to the left, right, top, and bottom of a document or worksheet. Margins display when you are in Print Layout or Page Layout view, or in Backstage view previewing a document to print. As shown in Figure 1.41, you can change the margins by clicking Margins in the Page Setup group. You can also change margins in the Print area on Backstage view.

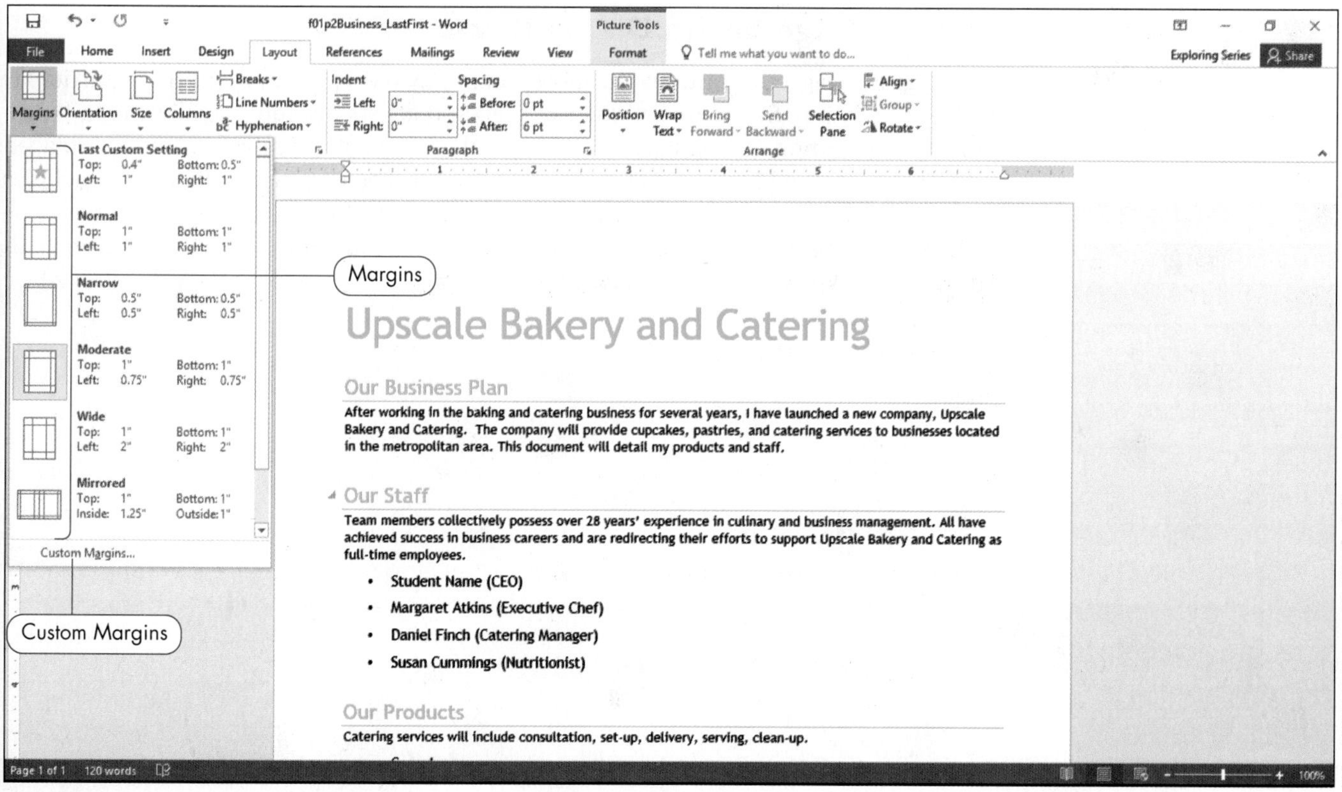

FIGURE 1.41 Page Margins in Word

To change margins in Word and Excel, complete the following steps:

1. Click the Layout (or Page Layout) tab.
2. Click Margins in the Page Setup group.
3. Select a preset margin option or click Custom Margins (refer to Figure 1.41) to display the Page Setup dialog box where you can apply custom margin settings.
4. Click OK to accept the settings and close the dialog box.

Change Page Orientation

Documents and worksheets can be displayed in different page orientations. A page displayed or printed in *portrait orientation* is taller than it is wide. A page in *landscape orientation* is wider than it is tall. Word documents are usually more attractive displayed in portrait orientation, whereas Excel worksheets are often more suited to landscape orientation.

To change the page orientation, complete the following steps:

1. Click the Layout (or Page Layout) tab.
2. Click Orientation in the Page Setup group.
3. Select Portrait or Landscape.

Orientation is also an option in the Print area of Backstage view.

Use the Page Setup Dialog Box

The Page Setup group contains the most commonly used page options in the particular Office application. Some are unique to Excel, and others are more applicable to Word. Other less common settings are available in the Page Setup dialog box only, displayed when you click the Page Setup Dialog Box Launcher. The Page Setup dialog box includes options for customizing margins, selecting page orientation, centering horizontally or vertically, printing gridlines, and creating headers and footers. Figure 1.42 shows both the Excel and Word Page Setup dialog boxes.

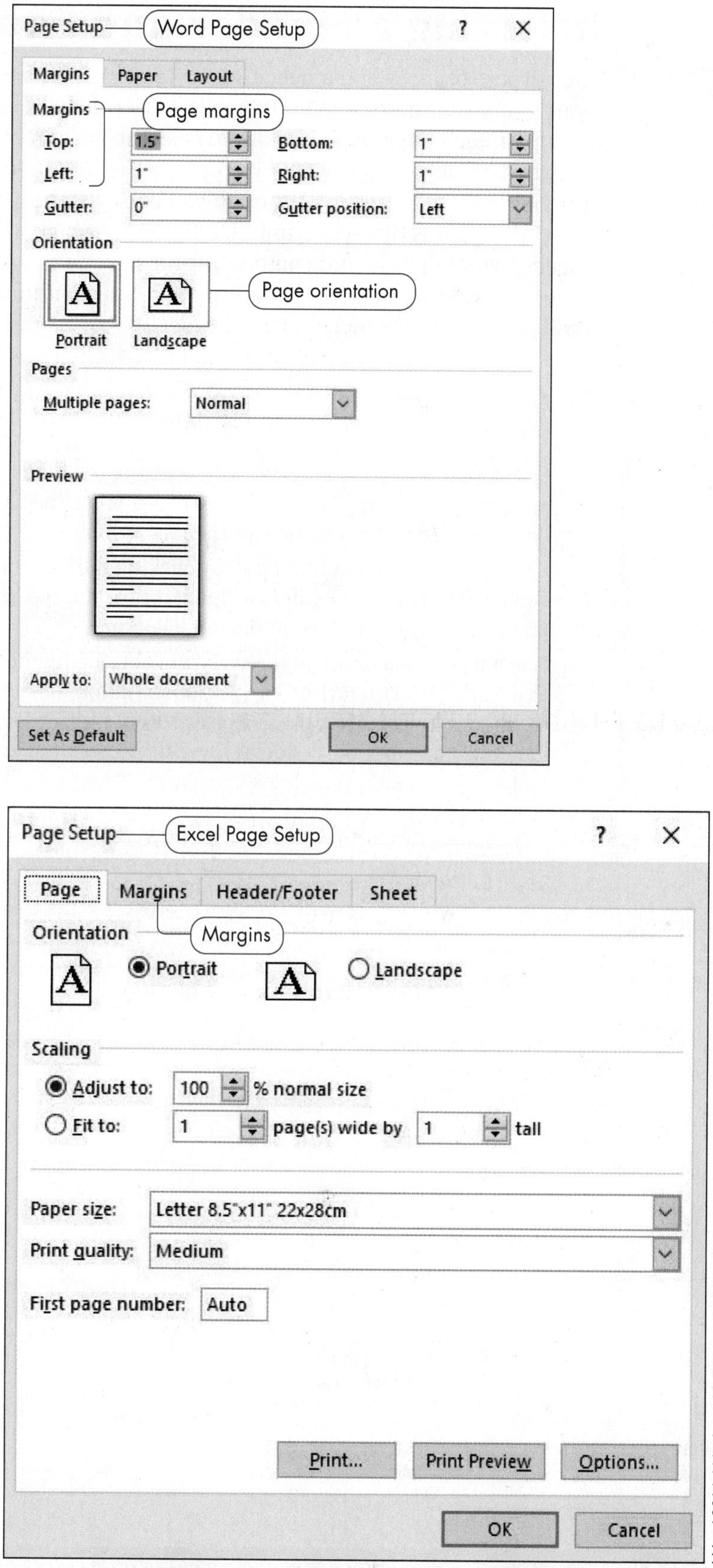

Word 2016, Windows 10, Microsoft Corporation

FIGURE 1.42 Page Setup Dialog Boxes in Word and Excel

Inserting a Header and Footer

STEP 4 »» The purpose of including a header or footer in a document is to better identify the document and give it a professional appearance. A **header** consists of one or more lines at the top of each page. A **footer** displays at the bottom of each page. One advantage of using headers and footers is that you specify the content only once, after which it displays automatically on all pages. Although you can type the text yourself at the top or bottom of every page, it is time-consuming, and the possibility of making a mistake is great. As a header, you might include an organization name or a class number so that each page identifies the document's origin or purpose. A page number is a typical footer, although it could just as easily be included in a header.

To apply a header or footer, complete one of the following steps (based on the application):

- Select a header or footer in Word by clicking the Insert tab and then clicking Header or Footer (see Figure 1.43). Choose from a predefined list, or click Edit Header (or Edit Footer) to create an unformatted header or footer.

- Select a header or footer in Excel by clicking the Insert tab and clicking Header and Footer. Select the left, center, or right section and type your own footer or use a predefined field code such as date or file name.

- Select a header or footer for PowerPoint by clicking the Insert tab, clicking Header and Footer, and then checking the footer option for slides. In PowerPoint, a footer's location will depend on the theme applied to the presentation. For some themes, the footer will appear on the side of the slide rather than at the bottom. Headers and footers are available for Notes and Handouts as well.

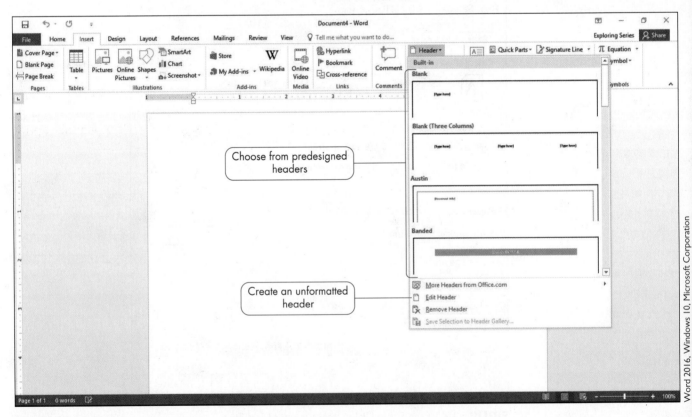

FIGURE 1.43 Insert Header in Word

After typing a header or footer, it can be formatted like any other text. It can be formatted in any font or font size. In Word or Excel, when you want to leave the header and footer area and return to the document, click Close Header and Footer (see Figure 1.44).

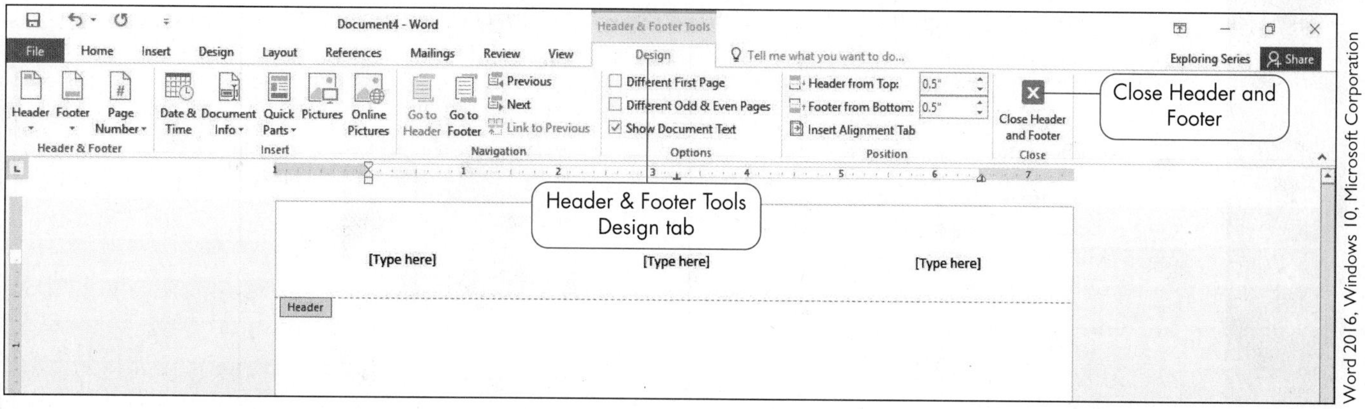

FIGURE 1.44 Close Header and Footer

Previewing and Printing a File

STEP 5 ▶▶ When you want to print an Office file, you can select from various print options, including the number of copies and the specific pages to print. It is a good idea to take a look at how your document or worksheet will appear before you print it. The Print Preview feature of Office enables you to do just that. In the Print Preview pane, you will see all items, including any headers, footers, graphics, and special formatting.

To view a file before printing, complete the following steps:

1. Click the File tab.
2. Click Print.

The subsequent Backstage view shows the file preview on the right, with print settings located in the center of the Backstage screen. Figure 1.45 shows a typical Backstage Print view. If you know that the page setup is correct and that there are no unique print settings to select, you can simply print without adjusting any print settings.

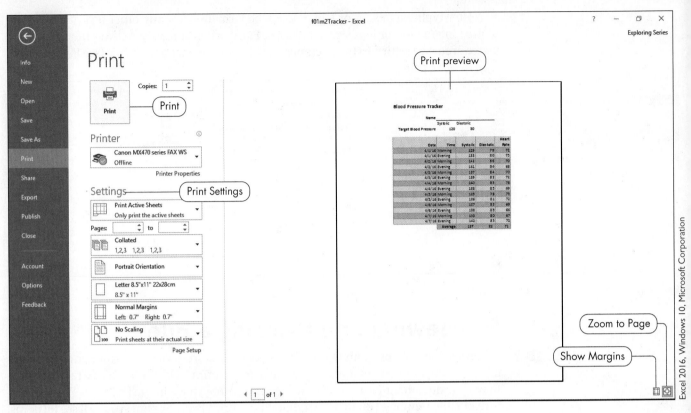

FIGURE 1.45 Backstage Print View in Excel

Options to show the margins (*Show Margins*) and to increase the size of the print preview (*Zoom to Page*) are found on the bottom-right corner of the preview (refer to Figure 1.45). Remember that increasing the font size by adjusting the zoom applies to the current display only; it does not actually increase the font size when the file is printed or saved. To return the preview to its original view, click *Zoom to Page* once more.

Other options in the Backstage Print view vary depending on the application in which you are working. For example, PowerPoint's Backstage Print view includes options for printing slides and handouts in various configurations and colors, whereas Excel's focuses on worksheet selections and Word's includes document options. Regardless of the Office application, you will be able to access Settings options from Backstage view, including page orientation (landscape or portrait), margins, and paper size. To print a file, click the Print button (refer to Figure 1.45).

Quick Concepts

7. What functions and features are included in Backstage view? *p. 42*

8. Why would you need to change the view of a document? *p. 44*

9. What is the purpose of a header or footer? *p. 48*

Hands-On Exercises

Watch the Video for this Hands-On Exercise!

MyITLab® HOE3 Training

Skills covered: Enter Document Properties • Change the Document View • Change Margins • Insert a Footer • Preview a File • Change Page Orientation

3 Modify Document Layout and Properties

You continue to work on the thank-you letter you previously started. As the administrative assistant for the Spotted Begonia Art Gallery, you must be able to search for and find documents previously created. You know that by adding tags to your letter you will more easily be able to find it at a later time. You will review and add document properties, and prepare the document to print and distribute by changing the page setup. Additionally, you will add a footer with Spotted Begonia's information. Finally, you will explore printing options, and save the letter.

STEP 1 ›› ENTER DOCUMENT PROPERTIES

You will add document properties, which will help you locate the file when performing a search of your hard drive. Refer to Figure 1.46 as you complete Step 1.

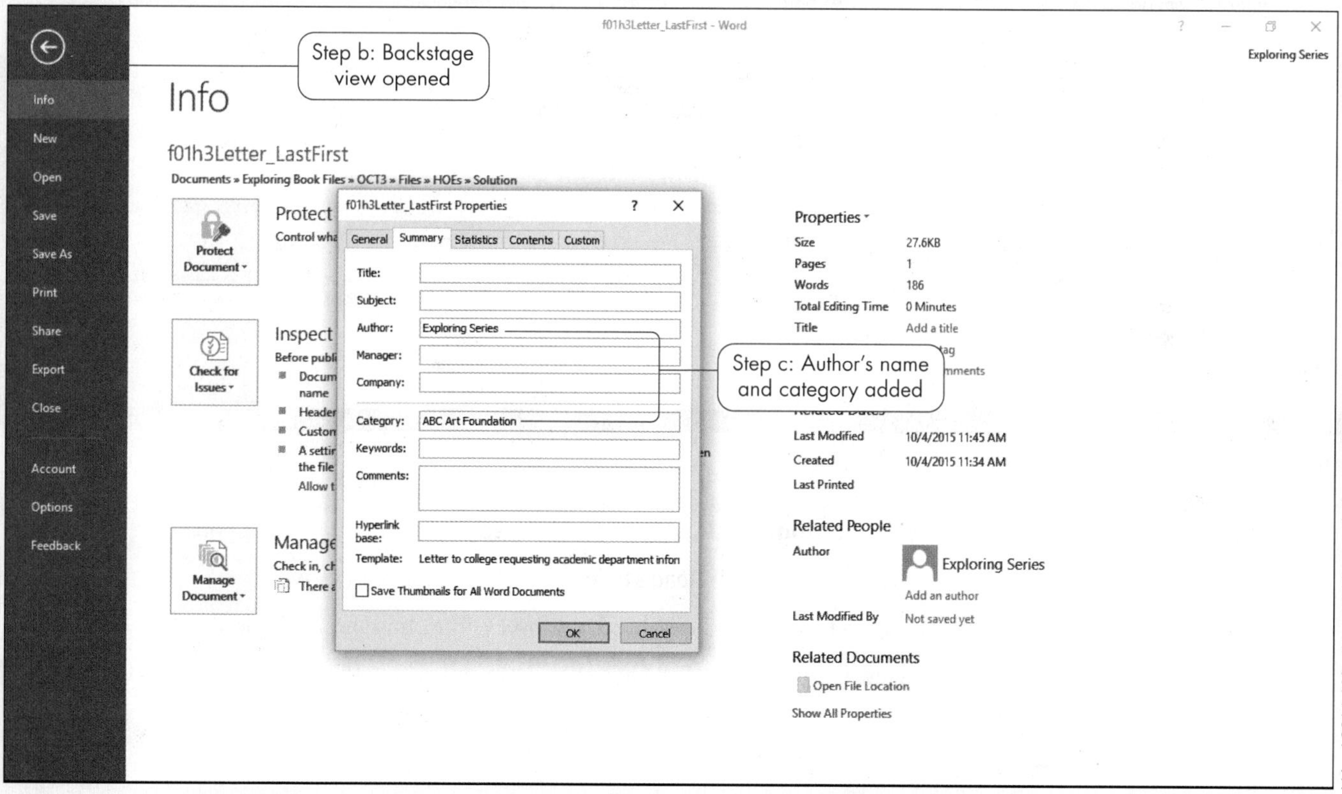

Word 2016, Windows 10, Microsoft Corporation

FIGURE 1.46 Backstage View

a. Open *f01h1Letter_LastFirst* if you closed it at the end of Hands-On Exercise 1, and save it as **f01h3Letter_LastFirst**, changing h1 to h3.

The letter is now open in Word.

b. Click the **File tab** and click **Properties** at the top-right of Backstage view. Click **Advanced Properties**.

The Properties dialog box opens so you can make changes.

c. Select the **Author box** and type your first and last name. Select the **Category box** and type **ABC Art Foundation**. Click **OK**.

You added the Author and Category properties to your document.

d. Save the document.

STEP 2 » CHANGE THE DOCUMENT VIEW

To get a better perspective on your letter, you want to explore the various document views available in Word. Refer to Figure 1.47 as you complete Step 2.

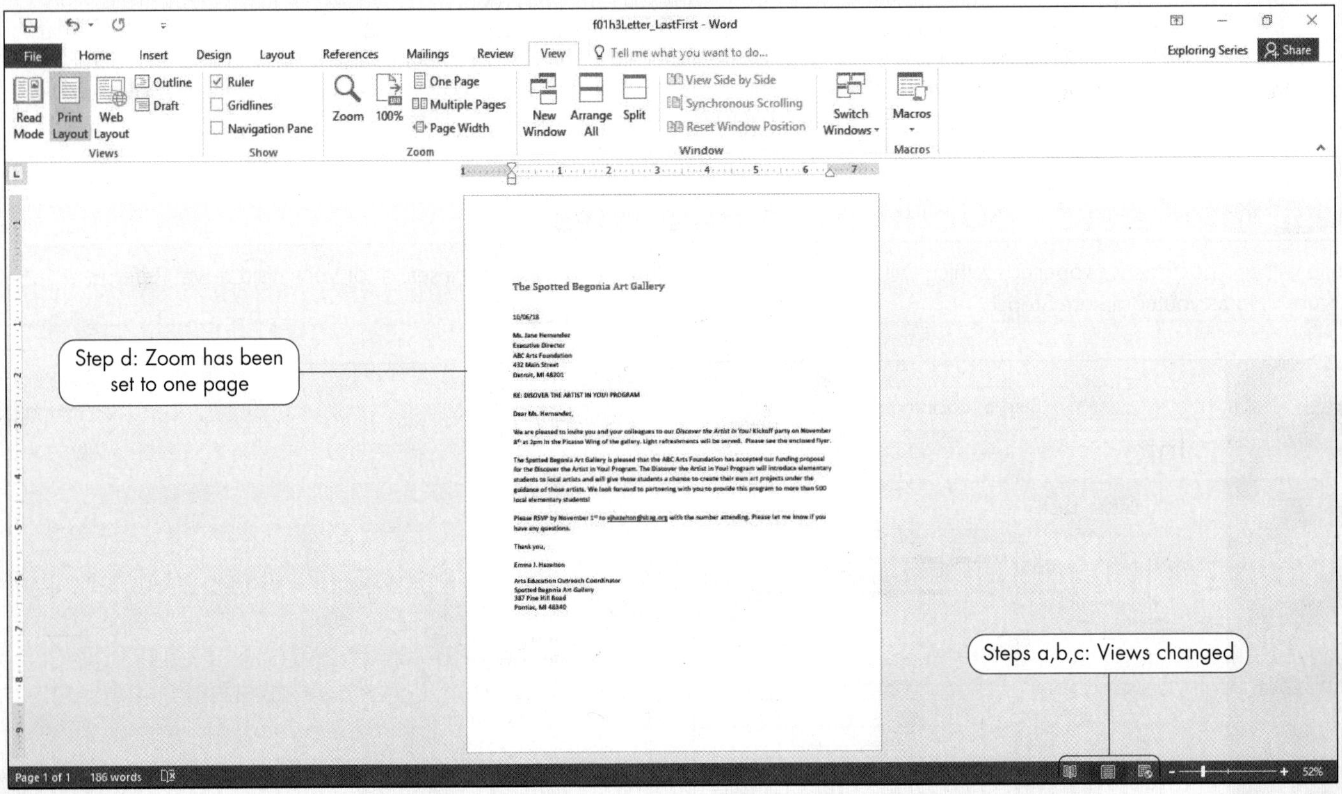

Word 2016, Windows 10, Microsoft Corporation

FIGURE 1.47 Change the Document View

a. Click **Read Mode** on the status bar. Observe the changes to the Ribbon.

The view is changed to Read Mode, which is a full-screen view.

b. Click **Web Layout** on the status bar. Observe the changes to the view.

The view is changed to Web Layout and simulates how the document would appear on the Web.

c. Click **Print Layout** on the status bar. Observe the changes to the view.

The document has returned to Print Layout view.

d. Click the **View tab** and click **Zoom** in the Zoom group. Click the **One Page option**. Click **OK**.

The entire letter is displayed.

STEP 3 »» CHANGE PAGE LAYOUT

While the letter was displayed in One Page zoom, you observed that the margins were too large. You will change the margins so they are narrower. Refer to Figure 1.48 as you complete Step 3.

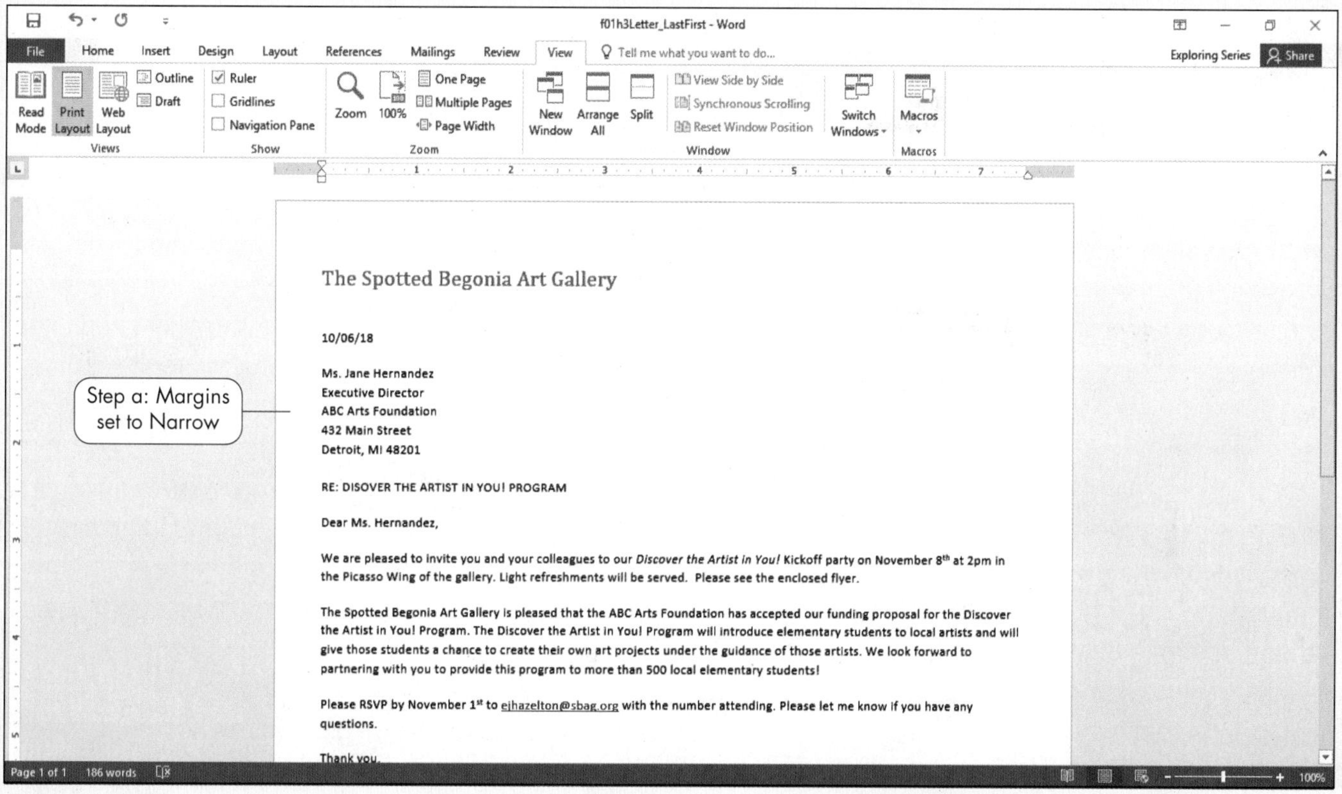

Word 2016, Windows 10, Microsoft Corporation

FIGURE 1.48 Change Margins

a. Click the **Layout tab** and click **Margins** in the Page Setup group. Select **Narrow**. Observe the changes.

The document margins were changed to Narrow.

b. Click the **View tab** and click **100%** in the Zoom group.

The document returns to its previous view.

c. Save the document.

STEP 4 » INSERT A FOOTER

Additional information such as a phone number and website need to be added to the letter. You decide to add these to the letter as a footer. Refer to Figure 1.49 as you complete Step 4.

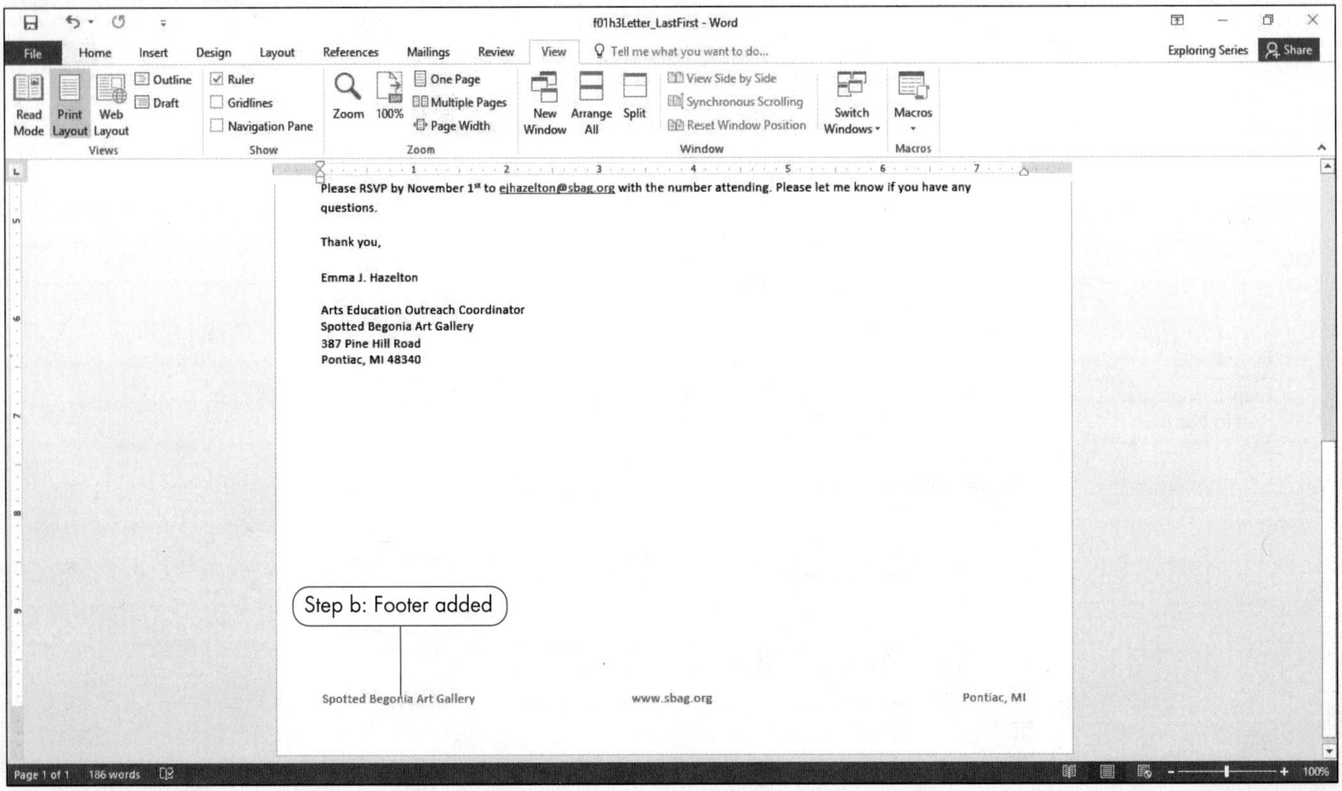

FIGURE 1.49 Footer

a. Click the **Insert tab** and click **Footer** in the Header & Footer group. Click the **Blank (three columns)** footer.

   The document opens in Header and Footer view. You select a footer with little formatting.

b. Click **[Type here]** on the far left of the footer. Type **Spotted Begonia Art Gallery** in that placeholder. Click **[Type here]** in the center of the footer. Type **www.sbag.org** in that placeholder. Click **[Type here]** on the far right of the footer. Type **Pontiac, MI** in that placeholder. On the Header & Footer Tools Design tab, click **Close Header and Footer** in the Close group.

   The footer information is entered.

c. Save the document.

You have reviewed and finalized the letter, so you will print the document so it can be sent to its recipient. You will first preview the document as it will appear when printed. Refer to Figure 1.50 as you complete Step 5.

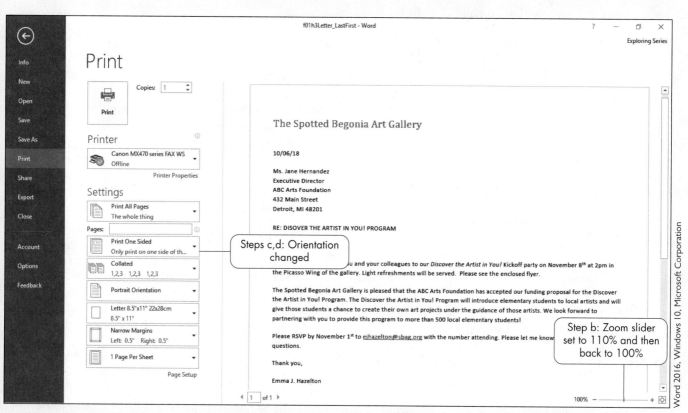

FIGURE 1.50 Backstage Print View

a. Click the **File tab** and click **Print**.

It is always a good idea to check the way a file will look when printed before actually printing it.

b. Drag the **Zoom slider on the status bar** to increase the document view to 110%. Click **Zoom to Page** (located at the far right of the status bar).

Your print preview returns to the original size.

c. Click **Portrait Orientation** in the Settings area. Click **Landscape Orientation**.

The letter appears in a wider and shorter view.

d. Return to Portrait Orientation to see the original view.

You decide that the flyer is more attractive in portrait orientation, so you return to that setting.

e. Save and close the file. Based on your instructor's directions, submit the following:

f01h2Flyer_LastFirst

f01h3Letter_LastFirst

Chapter Objectives Review

After reading this chapter, you have accomplished the following objectives:

1. Start an Office application.

- Your Microsoft account connects you to all of Microsoft's Internet-based resources.
- Change a Microsoft account: If you share your computer with another user, each user can have access to his own Microsoft account; you can easily switch between accounts so you can access your own files.

2. Work with files.

- Create a new file: You can create a document as a blank document or with a template.
- Open a file: You can open an existing file using the Open dialog box. Previously saved files can be accessed using the Recent documents list.
- Save a file: Saving a file enables you to open it later for additional updates or reference. Files are saved to a storage medium such as a hard drive, CD, flash drive, or to the cloud on OneDrive.

3. Use common interface components.

- Use the Ribbon: The Ribbon, the long bar located just beneath the title bar containing tabs, groups, and commands, is the command center of Office applications.
- Use a shortcut menu: A shortcut menu provides choices related to the object, selection, or area of the document on which you right-click.
- Use keyboard shortcuts: Keyboard shortcuts are keyboard equivalents for software commands. Universal keyboard shortcuts in Office include Ctrl+C (Copy), Ctrl+X (Cut), Ctrl+V (Paste), and Ctrl+Z (Undo).
- Customize the Ribbon: You can personalize the Ribbon in your Office applications, giving you easier access to a frequently used set of commands that are unique to you or your business.
- Use the Quick Access Toolbar: The Quick Access Toolbar, located at the top-left corner of any Office application window, provides one-click access to commonly executed tasks such as saving a file or undoing recent actions.
- Customize the Quick Access Toolbar: You use certain actions in an Office application often, and for more convenient access, you can add a button for each action to the Quick Access Toolbar.

4. Get help.

- Use the *Tell me what you want to do* box: The *Tell me what you want to do* box not only links to online resources and technical support but also provides quick access to functions.
- Use Enhanced ScreenTips: An Enhanced ScreenTip describes a command and provides a keyboard shortcut, if applicable.

5. Install add-ins.

- Add-ins are custom programs or additional commands that extend the functionality of a Microsoft Office program.

6. Use templates and apply themes.

- Open a template: Templates are a convenient way to save time when designing a document.
- Apply a theme: Themes are a collection of design choices that include colors, fonts, and special effects used to give a consistent look to a document, workbook, or presentation.

7. Modify text.

- Select text: To select text or numbers, place the pointer before the first character or digit you want to select, and then drag to highlight the intended selection. Before you drag, be sure that the pointer takes on the shape of the letter *I*, called the I-beam.
- Edit text: You can edit the font, font color, size, and many other attributes.
- Use the Mini toolbar: The Mini toolbar provides instant access to common formatting commands after text is selected.
- Copy formats with the Format Painter: Easily apply formatting from one selection to another by using Format Painter.

8. Relocate text.

- Cut, copy, and paste text: To cut means to remove a selection from the original location and place it in the Office Clipboard. To copy means to duplicate a selection from the original location and place a copy in the Office Clipboard. To paste means to place a cut or copied selection into another location.
- Use the Office Clipboard: When you cut or copy selections, they are placed in the Office Clipboard. You can paste the same item multiple times; it will remain in the Clipboard until you power down your computer or until the Clipboard exceeds 24 items.

9. Check spelling and grammar.

- Office applications check and mark spelling and grammar errors as you type for later correction. The Thesaurus enables you to search for synonyms.

10. Work with pictures and Graphics.

- Insert pictures and graphics: You can insert pictures from your own library of digital photos you have saved on your hard drive, OneDrive, or another storage medium, or you can initiate a Bing search for online pictures directly inside the Office program you are using.
- Resize and format pictures and graphics: To resize a picture, drag a corner sizing handle; never resize a picture by dragging a center sizing handle. You can apply

a picture style or effect, as well as add a picture border, from selections in the Picture Styles group.

11. Use Backstage view.

- Customize application options: You can customize general settings in the Office application in which you are working, such as AutoRecover settings and location and save frequency.
- View and edit document properties: Information that identifies a document, such as the author, document purpose, intended audience, or general comments can be added to the document's properties. Those data elements are saved with the document, but do not appear in the document as it displays onscreen or is printed.

12. Change the document view.

- The status bar provides information relative to the open file and quick access to View and Zoom level options. Each application has a set of views specific to the application.

13. Change the page layout.

- Change margins: A margin is the area of blank space that displays to the left, right, top, and bottom of a document or worksheet.

- Change page orientation: Documents and worksheets can be displayed in different page orientations. Portrait orientation is taller than it is wide; landscape orientation is wider than it is tall.
- Use the Page Setup dialog box: The Page Setup dialog box includes options for customizing margins, selecting page orientation, centering horizontally or vertically, printing gridlines, and creating headers and footers.

14. Insert a header and footer.

- A footer displays at the bottom of each page.
- A header consists of one or more lines at the top of each page.

15. Preview and print a file.

- It is important to review your file before printing.
- Print options can be set in Backstage view and include page orientation, the number of copies, and the specific pages to print.

Key Terms Matching

Match the key terms with their definitions. Write the key term letter by the appropriate numbered definition.

a. Access
b. Add-in
c. Clipboard
d. Backstage view
e. Cloud storage
f. Format Painter
g. Footer
h. Group
i. Header
j. Margin

k. Microsoft Office
l. Mini toolbar
m. OneDrive
n. Quick Access Toolbar
o. Ribbon
p. Status bar
q. Tab
r. *Tell me what you want to do* box
s. Template
t. Theme

1. _____ A tool that copies all formatting from one area to another. **p. 29**

2. _____ Stores up to 24 cut or copied selections for use later on in your computing session. **p. 30**

3. _____ A task-oriented section of the Ribbon that contains related commands. **p. 10**

4. _____ An online app used to store, access, and share files and folders. **p. 5**

5. _____ Custom programs or additional commands that extend the functionality of a Microsoft Office program. **p. 17**

6. _____ A component of Office that provides a concise collection of commands related to an open file and includes save and print options. **p. 42**

7. _____ A tool that displays near selected text that contains formatting commands. **p. 28**

8. _____ Relational database software used to store data and convert it into information. **p. 4**

9. _____ Consists of one or more lines at the bottom of each page. **p. 48**

10. _____ A predesigned file that incorporates formatting elements, such as a theme and layouts, and may include content that can be modified. **p. 24**

11. _____ A collection of design choices that includes colors, fonts, and special effects used to give a consistent look to a document, workbook, or presentation. **p. 24**

12. _____ A component of the Ribbon that is designed to appear much like a tab on a file folder. **p. 9**

13. _____ Provides handy access to commonly executed tasks such as saving a file and undoing recent actions. **p. 14**

14. _____ The long bar at the bottom of the screen that houses the Zoom slider and various View buttons. **p. 44**

15. _____ A productivity software suite including a set of software applications, each one specializing in a particular type of output. **p. 4**

16. _____ Allows you to search for help and information about a command or task you want to perform, and will also present you with a shortcut directly to that command. **p. 15**

17. _____ The long bar located just beneath the title bar containing tabs, groups, and commands. **p. 8**

18. _____ The area of blank space that displays to the left, right, top, and bottom of a document or worksheet **p. 45**

19. _____ A technology used to store files and to work with programs that are stored in a central location on the Internet. **p. 5**

20. _____ Consists of one or more lines at the top of each page. **p. 48**

Multiple Choice

1. The Recent documents list shows documents that have been previously:
   - (a) Printed.
   - (b) Opened.
   - (c) Saved in an earlier software version.
   - (d) Deleted.

2. In Word or PowerPoint a quick way to select an entire paragraph is to:
   - (a) Place the pointer at the left of the line, in the margin area, and click.
   - (b) Triple-click inside the paragraph.
   - (c) Double-click at the beginning of the paragraph.
   - (d) Press Ctrl+C inside the paragraph.

3. When you want to copy the format of a selection but not the content, you should:
   - (a) Double-click Copy in the Clipboard group.
   - (b) Right-click the selection and click Copy.
   - (c) Click Copy Format in the Clipboard group.
   - (d) Click Format Painter in the Clipboard group.

4. Which of the following is *not* a benefit of using OneDrive?
   - (a) Save your folders and files to the cloud.
   - (b) Share your files and folders with others.
   - (c) Hold video conferences with others.
   - (d) Simultaneously work on the same document with others.

5. What does a red wavy underline in a document, spreadsheet, or presentation mean?
   - (a) A word is misspelled or not recognized by the Office dictionary.
   - (b) A grammatical mistake exists.
   - (c) An apparent word usage mistake exists.
   - (d) A word has been replaced with a synonym.

6. Which of the following is *true* about headers and footers?
   - (a) They can be inserted from the Design tab.
   - (b) Headers and footers only appear on the last page of a document.
   - (c) Headers appear at the top of a document.
   - (d) Only page numbers can be included in a header or footer.

7. Live Preview:
   - (a) Opens a predesigned document or spreadsheet that is relevant to your task.
   - (b) Provides a preview of the results of a choice you are considering before you make a final selection.
   - (c) Provides a preview of an upcoming Office version.
   - (d) Enlarges the font onscreen.

8. You can get help when working with an Office application in which one of the following areas?
   - (a) The *Tell me what you want to do* box
   - (b) Status bar
   - (c) Backstage view
   - (d) Quick Access Toolbar

9. In PowerPoint, a file that includes formatting elements such as a background, a color scheme, and slide layout is a:
   - (a) Theme.
   - (b) Template.
   - (c) Scheme.
   - (d) Variant.

10. A document or worksheet printed in landscape orientation is:
    - (a) Taller than it is wide.
    - (b) Wider than it is tall.
    - (c) A document with 2" left and right margins.
    - (d) A document with 2" top and bottom margins.

Practice Exercises

1 Designing Webpages

You have been asked to make a presentation to the local business association. With the mayor's renewed emphasis on growing the local economy, many businesses are interested in establishing a Web presence. The business owners would like to know a little bit more about how webpages are designed. In preparation for the presentation, you will proofread and edit your PowerPoint file. You decide to insert an image to enhance your presentation. Refer to Figure 1.51 as you complete this exercise.

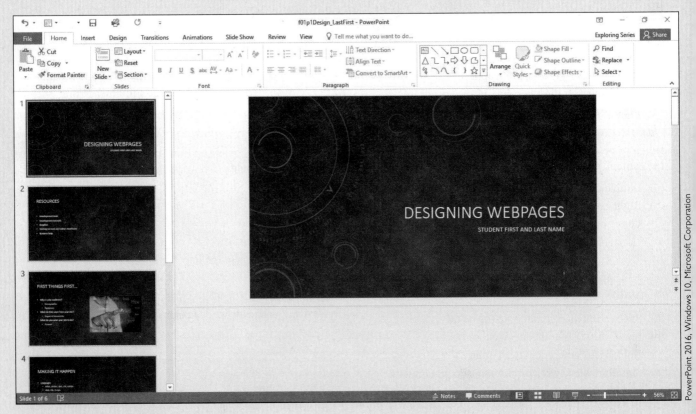

FIGURE 1.51 Designing Webpages Presentation

a. Open *f01p1Design*. Click the **File tab**, click **Save As**, and save the file as **f01p1Design_LastFirst**.

b. Ensure that Slide 1 is visible, select the text *Firstname Lastname*, and type your own first and last names. Click an empty area of the slide to cancel the selection.

c. Click the **Design tab**, then click the **Celestial theme** in the Themes group to apply it to all slides.

d. Click the **Review tab** and click **Spelling** in the Proofing group. In the Spelling pane, click **Change** or **Ignore** to make changes as needed. Most identified misspellings should be changed. The words *KompoZer* and *Nvu* are not misspelled, so you should ignore them when they are flagged. Click **OK** when you have finished checking spelling.

e. Click the **Slide Show tab**. Click **From Beginning** in the Start Slide Show group. Click each slide to view the show and press **Esc** when you reach the last slide, slide 6.

f. Click **Slide 2** in the Slides pane on the left. Triple-click to select the **Other tools** text on the slide and press **Backspace** on the keyboard to delete the text.

g. Click **Slide 4** in the Slides pane. Triple-click to select the **FrontPage,Nvu** text and press **Backspace** to delete the text.

h. Click the **Insert tab**. Click **Header & Footer** in the Text group. Click the **Slide number check box** to select it and click **Apply to All**.

i. Press **Ctrl+End** to place the insertion point at the end of *Templates* on Slide 4 and press **Enter**. Type **Database Connectivity** to create a new bulleted item.

j. Click **Slide 3** in the Slides pane. Click the **Insert tab** and click **Pictures** in the Images group. Browse to the student data files, locate and select *f01p1website*, and then click **Insert**.

k. Click the **Shape height box** in the Size group on the Picture Tools Format tab. Type **4** and then press Enter.

l. Click **Slide 6** in the Slides pane. Click the **Insert tab**, and then click **Store** in the Add-ins group. In the search box, type **multiple response poll**. Press **Enter**. The add-in will resize if the window or resolution is small.

m. Click the **Multiple Response Poll** and then click **Trust It** to insert it into the slide.

n. Click the **Insert question here text box** in the poll window, and type **Do you have a website?**

o. Click the first **Insert option here text box** and type **Yes**. Click the second **Insert option here text box** and type **No**. Click **Preview** in the poll window.

p. Click the **File tab** and click **Print**. Click the **Full Page Slides arrow** and click **6 Slides Horizontal** to see a preview of all of the slides as a handout. Click the **Back arrow**.

q. Click **Slide 1** in the Slides pane to move to the beginning of the presentation.

r. Drag the **Zoom slider** on the status bar to the right to **130%** to magnify the text. Use the **Zoom slider** to move to **60%**.

s. Save and close the file. Based on your instructor's directions, submit f01p1Design_LastFirst.

2 Upscale Bakery

You have always been interested in baking and have worked in the field for several years. You now have an opportunity to devote yourself full time to your career as the CEO of a company dedicated to baking cupcakes and pastries, and to catering. One of the first steps in getting the business off the ground is developing a business plan so that you can request financial support. You will use Word to develop your business plan. Refer to Figure 1.52 as you complete this exercise.

a. Open *f01p2Business*. Click the **File tab**, click **Save As**, and save the file as **f01p2Business_LastFirst**.

b. Click the **Review tab** and click **Spelling & Grammar** in the Proofing group. Click **Change** for all suggestions and then click OK.

c. Select the paragraphs beginning with *Our Staff* and ending with *(Nutritionist)*. Click the **Home tab** and click **Cut** in the Clipboard group. Click to the left of *Our Products* and click **Paste**.

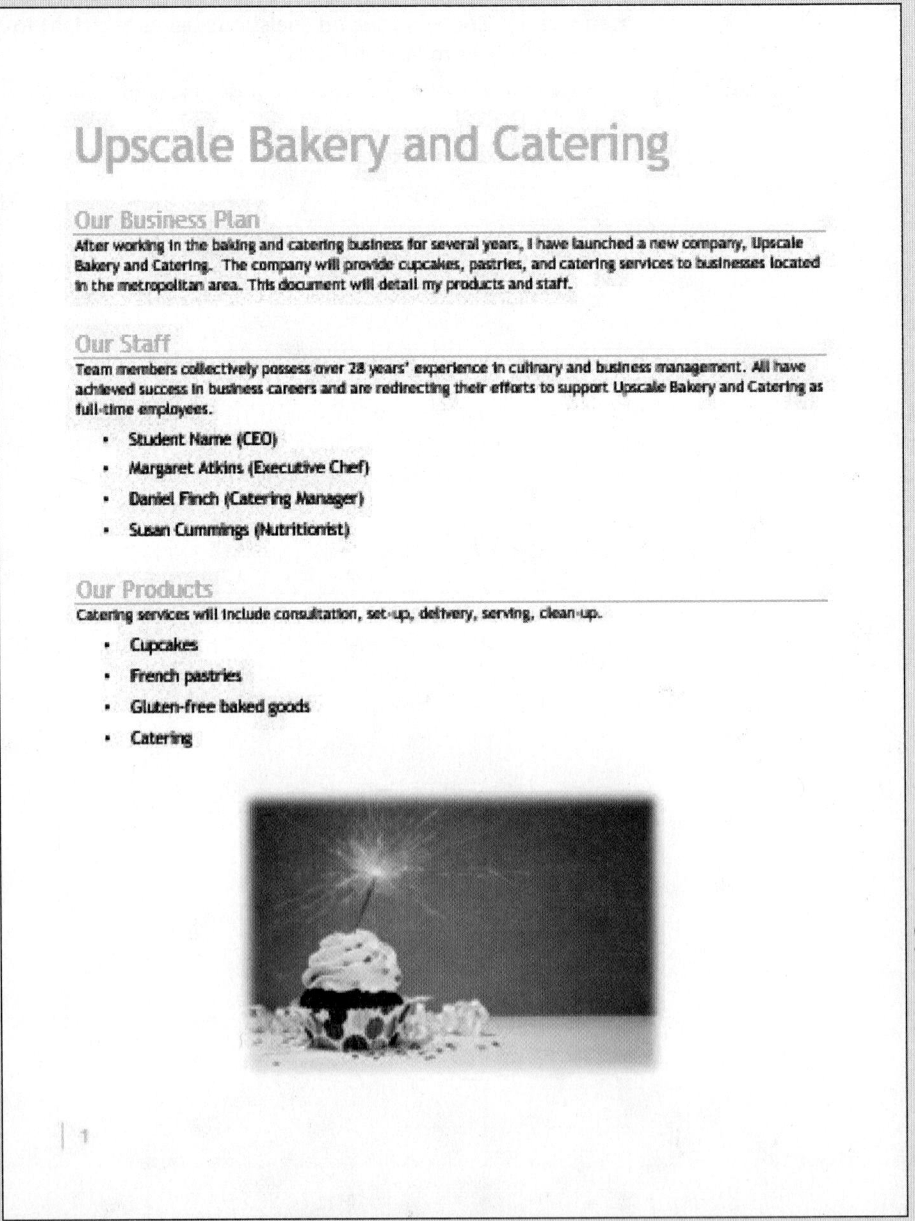

Upscale Bakery and Catering

Our Business Plan
After working in the baking and catering business for several years, I have launched a new company, Upscale Bakery and Catering. The company will provide cupcakes, pastries, and catering services to businesses located in the metropolitan area. This document will detail my products and staff.

Our Staff
Team members collectively possess over 28 years' experience in culinary and business management. All have achieved success in business careers and are redirecting their efforts to support Upscale Bakery and Catering as full-time employees.

- Student Name (CEO)
- Margaret Atkins (Executive Chef)
- Daniel Finch (Catering Manager)
- Susan Cummings (Nutritionist)

Our Products
Catering services will include consultation, set-up, delivery, serving, clean-up.

- Cupcakes
- French pastries
- Gluten-free baked goods
- Catering

1

FIGURE 1.52 Upscale Bakery Business Plan

d. Select the text **Your name** in the first bullet in the *Our Staff* section and replace it with your first and last names. Select the entire bullet list, click the **Font Size arrow** and then click **11**.

e. Double-click **Format Painter** in the Clipboard group on the Home tab. Drag the Format Painter pointer to change the other *Our Staff* bullets' font size to **11 pt**. Drag across all four *Our Products* bullets. Click Format Painter to deselect it.

f. Click the ***Tell me what you want to do* box**, and type **Footer**. Click **Add a Footer** scroll to locate the **Sideline footer**, click to add it to the page. Click **Close Header and Footer** on the Header & Footer Tools Design tab.

g. Select the last line in the document, which says *Insert and position picture here*, and press **Delete**. Click the **Insert tab** and click **Online Pictures** in the Illustrations group.
   - Click in the **Bing Image Search box**, type **Cupcakes**, and then press **Enter**.
   - Select any cupcake image and click **Insert**. Do not deselect the image.

TROUBLESHOOTING: If you are unable to find a cupcake image in the Bing Image Search then you can use f01p2Cupcake from the student data files.

   - Ensure the **Picture Tools Format tab** is active, and in the Picture Styles group, click the **Soft Edge Rectangle**.
   - Click the **Shape width box** in the Size group and change the width to **4**.
   - Click outside the picture.

h. Click the **File tab**. In the Properties section, add the tag **Business Plan**. Add your first and last name to the Author property.

i. Click **Print** in Backstage view. Change Normal Margins to **Moderate Margins**. Click the **Back arrow**.

j. Click the **picture** and click **Center** in the Paragraph group on the Home tab.

k. Save and close the file. Based on your instructor's directions, submit f01p2Business_LastFirst.

Mid-Level Exercises

1 Reference Letter

You are an instructor at a local community college. A student asked you to provide her with a letter of reference for a job application. You have used Word to prepare the letter, but now you want to make a few changes before it is finalized.

a. Open *f01m1RefLetter* and save it as **f01m1RefLetter_LastFirst**.

b. Select the date and point to several font sizes on the Mini toolbar. Use Live Preview to compare them. Click **11**.

c. Change the rest of the letter (below the date) to font size 11.

d. Apply bold to the student's name, *Stacy VanPatten*, in the first sentence.

e. Customize the Quick Access Toolbar so that a Spelling and Grammar button is added.

f. Use the button you just added to correct all errors using Spelling & Grammar. Stacy's last name is spelled correctly.

g. Select the word *intelligent* in the second paragraph, and use the Thesaurus to find a synonym. Replace *intelligent* with **gifted**. Change the word *an* to **a** just before the new word. Close the Thesaurus.

h. Add the tag **reference letter** to the Properties for the file in Backstage view.

i. Move the last paragraph—beginning with *In my opinion*—to position it before the second paragraph—beginning with *Stacy is a gifted*.

j. Move the insertion point to the beginning of the document.

k. Change the margins to **Narrow**.

l. Preview the document as it will appear when printed.

m. Save and close the file. Based on your instructor's directions, submit f01m1RefLetter_LastFirst.

2 Medical Monitoring

You are enrolled in a Health Informatics program of study in which you learn to manage databases related to health fields. For a class project, your instructor requires that you monitor your blood pressure, recording your findings in an Excel worksheet. You have recorded the week's data and will now make a few changes before printing the worksheet for submission.

a. Open *f01m2Tracker* and save it as **f01m2Tracker_LastFirst**.

b. Preview the worksheet as it will appear when printed. Change the orientation of the worksheet to **Landscape**. Close the Preview.

c. Click in the cell to the right of *Name* and type your first and last names. Press **Enter**.

d. Change the font of the text in **cell C1** to **Verdana**. Use Live Preview to try some font sizes. Change the font size to **20**.

e. Add the Spelling and Grammar feature to the Quick Access Toolbar, and then check the spelling for the worksheet to ensure that there are no errors.

DISCOVER f. Get help on showing decimal places. You want to increase the decimal places for the values in **cells E22**, **F22**, and **G22** so that each value shows one place to the right of the decimal. Select the cells and then use the *Tell me what you want to do* box to immediately apply the changes. You might use **Increase Decimals** as a search term. When you find the answer, increase the decimal places to **1**.

DISCOVER g. Click **cell A1** and insert an Online Picture of your choice related to blood pressure. Resize and position the picture so that it displays in an attractive manner. Apply the **Soft Edges** picture effect to the image and set to **5 pt**.

h. Change the page margins to **Wide**.

i. Insert a footer with the page number in the center of the spreadsheet footer area. Click on any cell in the worksheet.

j. Change the View to **Normal**.

k. Open Backstage view and adjust print settings to print two copies. You will not actually print two copies unless directed by your instructor.

l. Save and close the file. Based on your instructor's directions, submit f01m2Tracker_LastFirst.

3 | Today's Musical Artists

CREATIVE
CASE
COLLABORATION
CASE

With a few of your classmates, you will use PowerPoint to create a single presentation on your favorite musical artists. Each student must create at least one slide and then all of the slides will be added to the presentation. Because everyone's schedule is varied, you will use your OneDrive to pass the presentation file among the group.

a. Designate one student to create a new presentation and save it as **f01m3Music_GroupName**.

b. Add your group member names to the Author Properties in Backstage view.

c. Add a theme to the presentation.

d. Add one slide that contains the name of an artist, the genre, and two or three interesting facts about the artist.

e. Insert a picture of the artist or clip art that represents the artist.

f. Put your name on the slide that you created. Save the presentation.

g. Pass the presentation to the next student so that he or she can perform the same tasks in Steps d–f and save the presentation before passing it on to the next student. Continue until all group members have created a slide in the presentation.

h. Save and close the file. Based on your instructor's directions, submit f01m3Music_GroupName.

Beyond the Classroom

Fitness Planner

GENERAL CASE ✓

You will use Microsoft Excel to develop a fitness planner. Open *f01b1Exercise* and save it as **f01b1Exercise_LastFirst**. Because the fitness planner is a template, the exercise categories are listed, but without actual data. You will personalize the planner. Change the orientation to **Landscape**. Move the contents of **cell A2** (*Exercise Planner*) to **cell A1**. Click **cell A8** and use Format Painter to copy the format of that selection to **cells A5** and **A6**. Increase the font size of **cell A1** to **18**. Use the *Tell me what you want to do* box to learn how to insert a header and put your name in the header. Begin the fitness planner, entering at least one activity in each category (warm-up, aerobics, strength, and cooldown). Insert a picture from a Bing Image Search that is appropriate for the planner. You may want to use **exercise** as your search term. Check the spelling in the workbook. Add the tag **Exercise Planner** to the Properties in Backstage view. Review the document in Print Preview. Ensure that the tracker fits on a single sheet of paper when printed. Resize the image if necessary to fit on the page. Save and close the file. Based on your instructor's directions, submit f01b1Exercise_LastFirst.

Household Records

DISASTER RECOVERY ✚

FROM SCRATCH

Use Microsoft Excel to create a detailed (fictional) record of valuables in your household. In case of burglary or disaster, an insurance claim is expedited if you are able to itemize what was lost along with identifying information such as serial numbers. You will then make a copy of the record on another storage device for safekeeping outside your home (in case your home is destroyed by a fire or weather-related catastrophe). Design a worksheet listing at least five fictional appliances and pieces of electronic equipment along with the serial number of each. Change the orientation to **Landscape**. Use the *Tell me what you want to do* box to learn how to insert a header and put your name in the header. Return to Normal view. Insert a picture from a Bing Image Search that is appropriate for the record. You may want to use **appliances** as your search term. Review the document in Print Preview. Ensure that the records fit on a single sheet of paper when printed. Move and resize the image as necessary so that it fits on the page when printed. Check the spelling in the workbook. Add the tag **Disaster Recovery** to the Properties in Backstage view. Save the workbook as **f01b2Household_LastFirst**. Save and close the file. Based on your instructor's directions, submit f01b2Household_LastFirst.

Capstone Exercise

You are a member of the Student Government Association (SGA) at your college. As a community project, the SGA is sponsoring a Stop Smoking drive designed to provide information on the health risks posed by smoking cigarettes and to offer solutions to those who want to quit. The SGA has partnered with the local branch of the American Cancer Society as well as the outreach program of the local hospital to sponsor free educational awareness seminars. As the secretary for the SGA, you will help prepare a PowerPoint presentation that will be displayed on screens around campus and used in student seminars. The PowerPoint presentation has come back from the reviewers with only one comment: A reviewer suggested that you spell out Centers for Disease Control and Prevention, instead of abbreviating it. You will use Microsoft Office to help with those tasks.

Open and Save Files

You will open, review, and save a PowerPoint presentation.

a. Open *f01c1Quit* and save it as **f01c1Quit_LastFirst**.

Select Text, Move Text, and Format Text

A reviewer commented that you should modify the text on slide 12. The last sentence in the paragraph should be first since it is the answer to the question on the previous slide. You also add emphasis to the sentence.

a. Click **Slide 12**, and select the text **Just one cigarette – for some people**.

b. Cut the selected text and then paste it at the beginning of the paragraph.

c. Use the Mini toolbar to apply **Italics** to the text *Just one cigarette – for some people*.

Apply a Theme and Change the View

There is a blank theme for the slides, so you apply a different theme to the presentation.

a. Apply the **Metropolitan** theme to the presentation.

b. Change the View to Slide Sorter. Click **Slide 2** and drag to move Slide 2 to the end of the presentation. It will become the last slide (Slide 22).

c. Return to Normal view.

Insert and Modify a Picture

You will add a picture to the first slide and then resize it and position it.

a. Click **Slide 1**, and insert an online picture appropriate for the topic of **smoking**.

b. Resize the picture and reposition it.

c. Click outside the picture to deselect it.

Use the *Tell me what you want to do* Box

A reviewer suggested that you spell out Centers for Disease Control and Prevention, instead of abbreviating it. You know that there is a find and replace option to do this but you cannot remember where it is. You use the *Tell me what you want to do* box to help you with this function. You then replace the text.

a. Use the *Tell me what you want to do* box to search **replace**.

b. Use the results from your search to find a function that will find and then replace the single occurrence of *CDC* with **Centers for Disease Control and Prevention**.

Customize the Quick Access Toolbar

You often preview and print your presentations and find it would be easier to have a button on the Quick Access Toolbar to do so. You customize the toolbar by adding this shortcut.

a. Add the Print Preview button to the Quick Access Toolbar.

b. Add the Print button to the Quick Access Toolbar.

Use Print Preview, Change Print Layout, and Print

To get an idea of how the presentation will look when printed, you will preview the presentation. You decide to print the slides so that two slides will appear on one page.

a. Preview the document as it will appear when printed.

b. Change the Print Layout to **2 Slides** (under the Handouts section).

c. Preview the document as it will appear when printed.

d. Adjust the print settings to print two copies. You will not actually print two copies unless directed by your instructor.

Check Spelling and Change View

Before you call the presentation complete, you will correct any spelling errors and view the presentation as a slide show.

a. Check the spelling. The word *hairlike* is not misspelled, so it should not be corrected.

b. View the slide show. Click after reviewing the last slide to return to the presentation.

c. Save and close the file. Based on your instructor's directions, submit f01c1Quit_LastFirst.

Introduction to PowerPoint

LEARNING OUTCOME You will plan, create, navigate, and print a basic presentation.

OBJECTIVES & SKILLS: After you read this chapter, you will be able to:

CASE STUDY | Be a Trainer

You teach employee training courses for the Training and Development department of your State Department of Human Resources. You begin each course by presenting your objectives for the course using a Microsoft Office PowerPoint 2016 presentation. You create a slide show to help you organize your content and to help your audience retain the information.

Because of the exceptional quality of your presentations, the director of the State Department of Human Resources has asked you to prepare a new course on presentation skills. In the Hands-On Exercises for this chapter, you will work with two presentations for this course. One presentation will focus on the benefits of using PowerPoint, and the other will focus on the preparation for a slide show, including planning, organizing, and delivering.

Wavebreakmedia/ Shutterstock

Creating a Basic Presentation

CHAPTER 1

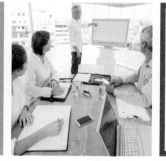

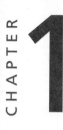

The Essence of PowerPoint
You
Focus on content and enter your information
Add additional elements to create interest
Motivate your audience while presenting
PowerPoint
Helps you organize your thoughts
Provides tools to make slide show creation easy
Allows flexibility in delivery and presentation

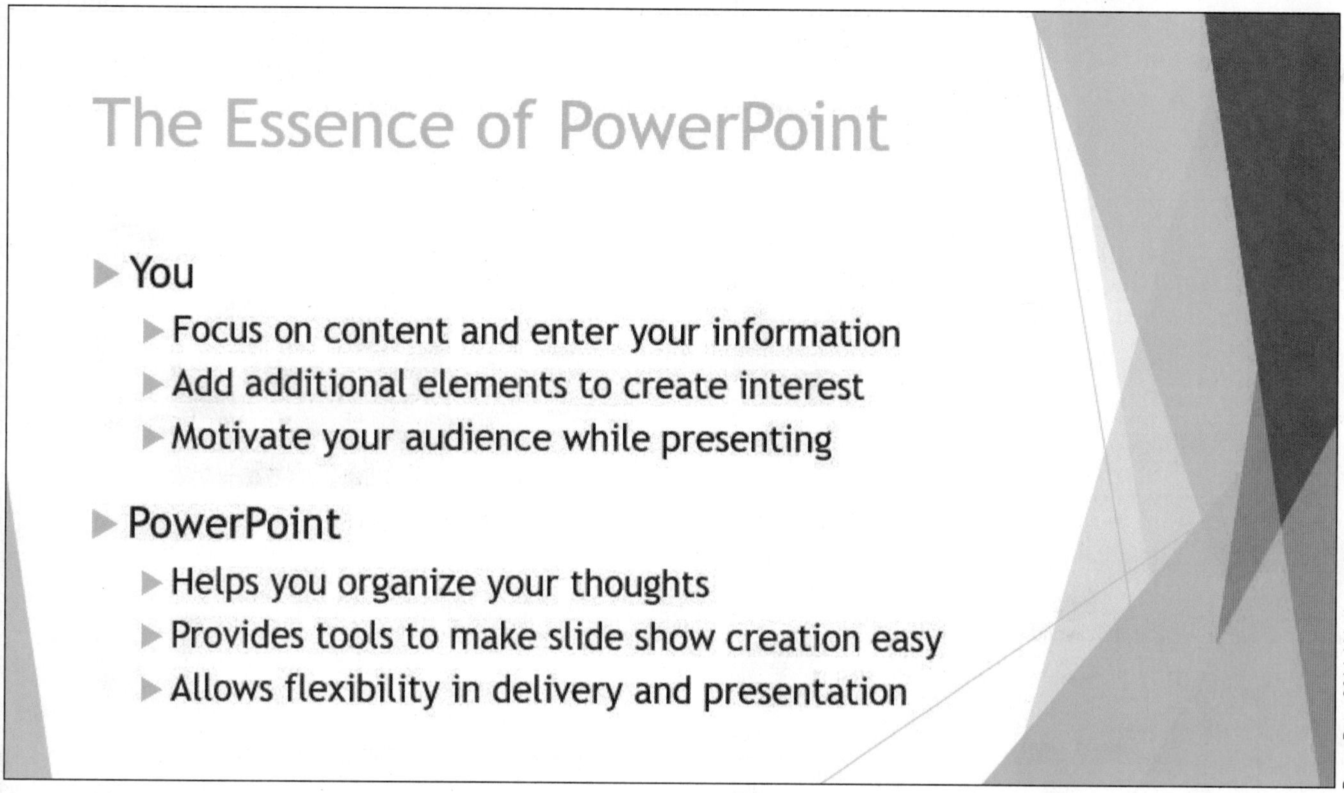

PowerPoint 2016, Windows 10, Microsoft Corporation

FIGURE 1.1 Be a Trainer Slide

CASE STUDY | Be A Trainer

Starting File	Files to be Submitted
p01h1Intro	p01h1Intro_LastFirst p01h1Intro_LastFirst.ppsx p01h4Content_LastFirst

Work with PowerPoint

You can use Microsoft Office PowerPoint 2016 to create an electronic slide show or other materials for use in a professional presentation. A *slide* is the most basic element of PowerPoint (similar to a page being the most basic element of Microsoft Word). A collection of slides is referred to as a *deck* of slides. The slides may be easily arranged just as cards can be easily shuffled in a deck of cards. The arranged slides displayed onscreen for an audience is a *slide show*, often referred to as a presentation. A *PowerPoint presentation* is an electronic slide show that can be edited or delivered in a variety of ways: you can project the slide show on a screen as part of a presentation, run it automatically at a kiosk or from a DVD, display it on the World Wide Web, email it, or create printed handouts.

Figure 1.2 shows the first four slides of a PowerPoint presentation. The slides contain different types of content, such as text, an online picture, and a table. The presentation has a consistent color scheme. It is easy to create presentations with consistent and attractive designs using PowerPoint.

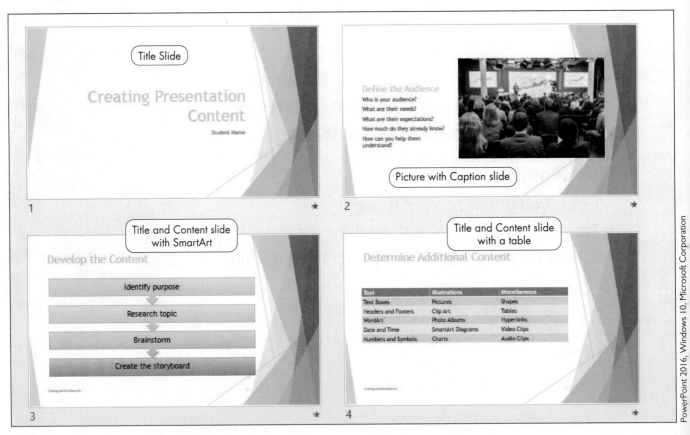

FIGURE 1.2 Various PowerPoint Slide Layouts

In this section, you will start your exploration of PowerPoint by opening and viewing a previously completed presentation. You will modify the presentation by adding identifying information, examining different PowerPoint views to discover the advantages of each, and saving the presentation.

Opening and Viewing a PowerPoint Presentation

 STEP 1 >> When you open a new presentation or a previously created presentation, you see the default PowerPoint workspace, *Normal view*. Figure 1.3 shows Normal view, which displays the Ribbon and other common interface components as well as two panes that

provide maximum flexibility in working with the presentation. The pane on the left side of the screen, the ***Slides pane***, shows the slide deck with ***thumbnails*** (slide miniatures) representing the location of the slides. The slides are numbered to help you select the slide you want to edit. The large pane on the right side of the screen, the ***Slide pane***, is the main workspace and displays the currently selected slide.

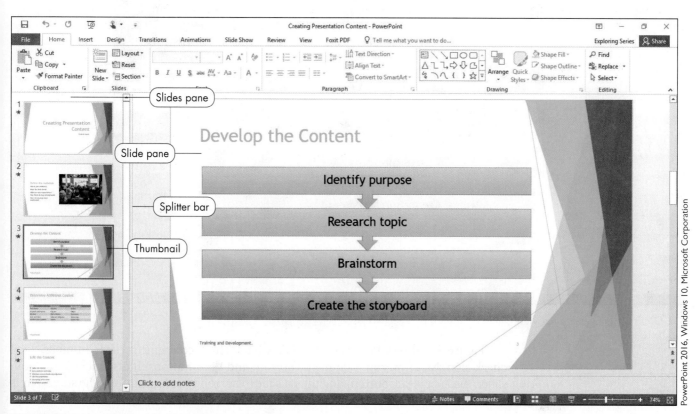

FIGURE 1.3 Normal View (Default PowerPoint View)

TIP: ADD-INS TAB

You may see an Add-Ins tab on the Ribbon. This tab indicates that additional functionality, such as an updated Office feature or an Office-compatible program, has been added to your system. Add-Ins are designed to increase your productivity.

While in Normal view, you can hide the left pane that displays the thumbnails. Doing so will expand the workspace so you can see more detail while editing slide content. To hide the pane with the thumbnails, drag the border that separates the panes one from another to the left until you see the word Thumbnails appear on the left side. Figure 1.4 shows an individual slide in Normal view with the Slides pane closed. You can quickly restore the view by clicking the arrow above Thumbnails or you can click the View tab and click Normal in the Presentation Views group. You can also widen the Slides pane to show more detail by dragging the splitter bar to the right.

FIGURE 1.4 Individual Slide View

Figure 1.5 shows PowerPoint's **status bar**, which contains the slide number, Spell check icon, Notes button, Comments button, and View buttons. It also includes a Zoom slider, the Zoom level button, and the Fit slide to current window button. The status bar is located at the bottom of your screen and can be customized.

To customize the status bar, complete the following steps:

1. Right-click the status bar.
2. Select the options to display from the Customize Status Bar list.
3. Click off the Customize Status Bar list to return to editing.

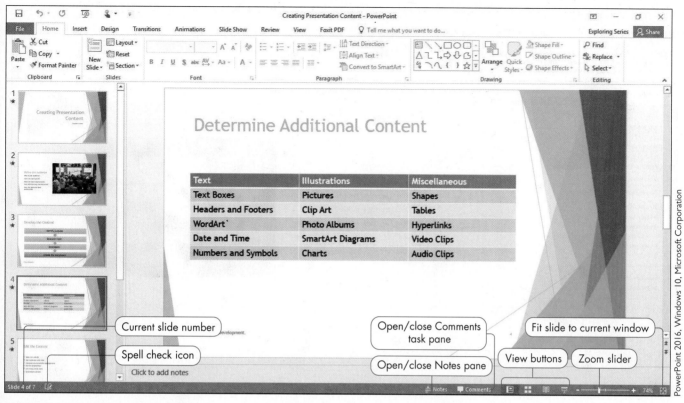

FIGURE 1.5 PowerPoint Status Bar

Use PowerPoint Views Effectively

In addition to Normal view, PowerPoint offers specialty views to enable you to work effectively and efficiently with your slides. The Presentation Views group on the View tab enables you to access these views:

- Normal
- Outline View
- Slide Sorter
- Notes Page
- Reading View

Use *Outline View* when you would like to enter text into your presentation using an outline. In other words, rather than having to enter the text into each placeholder on each slide separately, you can type the text directly into an outline. Figure 1.6 shows an example of Outline View.

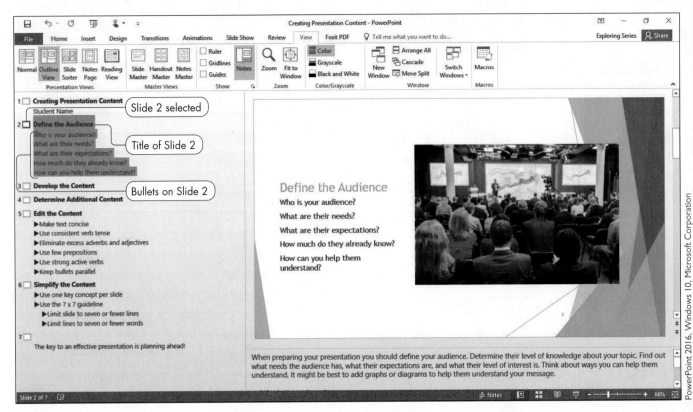

FIGURE 1.6 Outline View

Slide Sorter view displays thumbnails of your presentation slides, which enables you to view multiple slides simultaneously (see Figure 1.7). This view is helpful when you want to change the order of the slides, or to delete one or more slides. You can set transition effects (the way the slides transition from one to another) for multiple slides in Slide Sorter view. If you are in Slide Sorter view and double-click a slide thumbnail, PowerPoint displays the selected slide in Normal view.

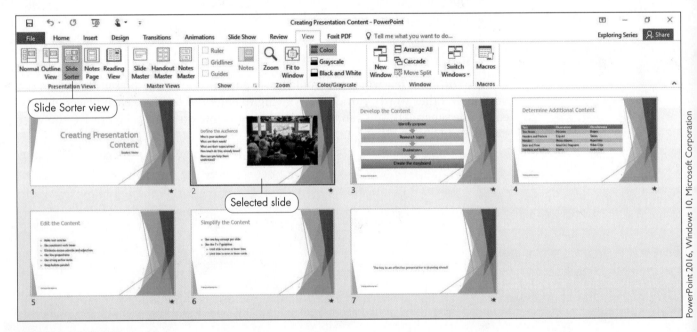

FIGURE 1.7 Slide Sorter View

To rearrange slides in Slide Sorter view, complete the following steps:

1. Move the pointer over the slide thumbnail of the slide you want to move.
2. Drag the slide to the new location.

Use ***Notes Page view*** when you need to enter and edit large amounts of text that you can refer to when presenting. Slides should contain just key points and you should elaborate on the key points verbally as you deliver the presentation. Consequently, speaker notes can be a most useful tool when giving a presentation. Notes do not display when the presentation is shown (except when Presenter view is used), but are intended to help the speaker remember the key points or additional information about each slide. Figure 1.8 shows an example of Notes Page view.

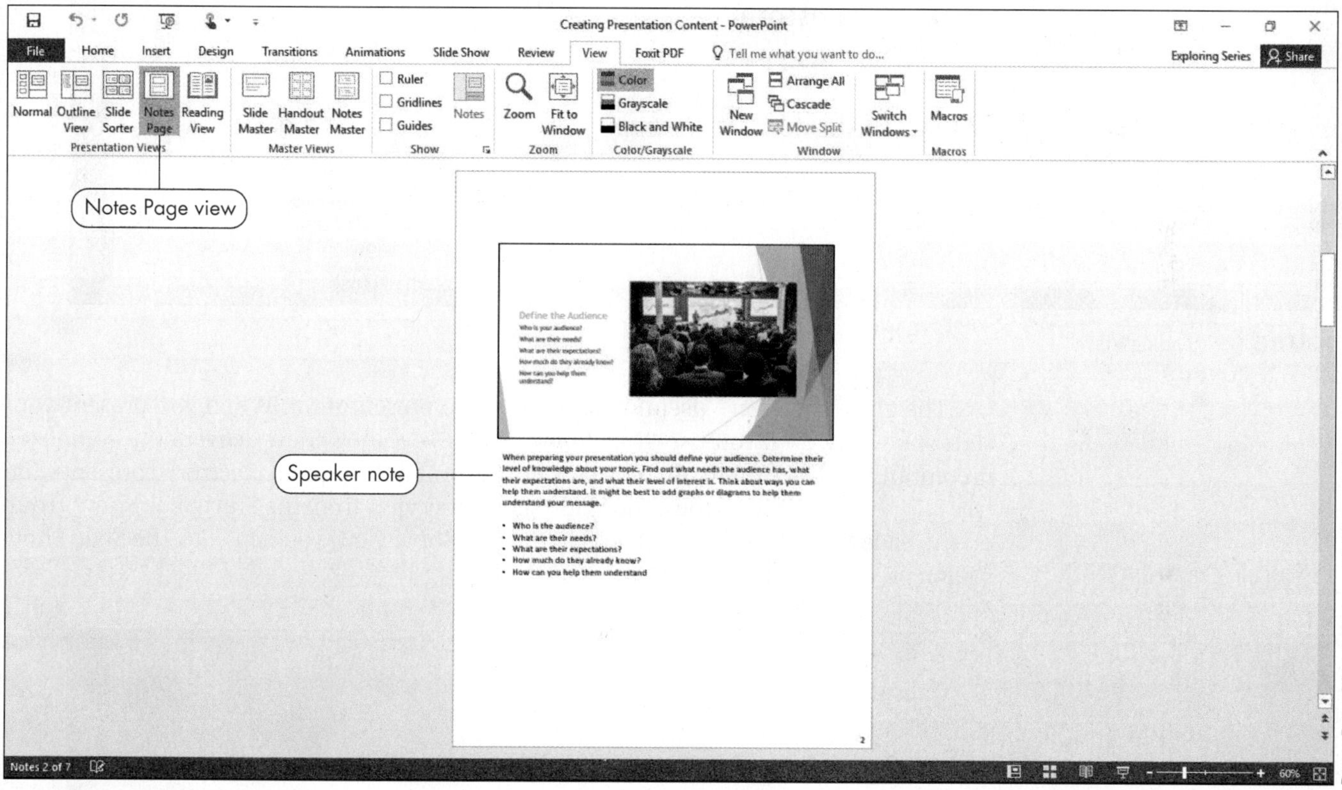

PowerPoint 2016, Windows 10, Microsoft Corporation

FIGURE 1.8 Notes Page View

Use ***Reading View*** to view the slide show full screen, one slide at a time. Animations and transitions are active in Reading View. A title bar, including the Minimize, Maximize/Restore Down (which changes its name and appearance depending on whether the window is maximized or at a smaller size), and Close buttons, is visible, as well as a modified status bar (see Figure 1.9). In addition to View buttons, the status bar includes navigation buttons for moving to the next or previous slide, as well as a menu for accomplishing common tasks such as printing. Press Esc to return quickly to the previous view.

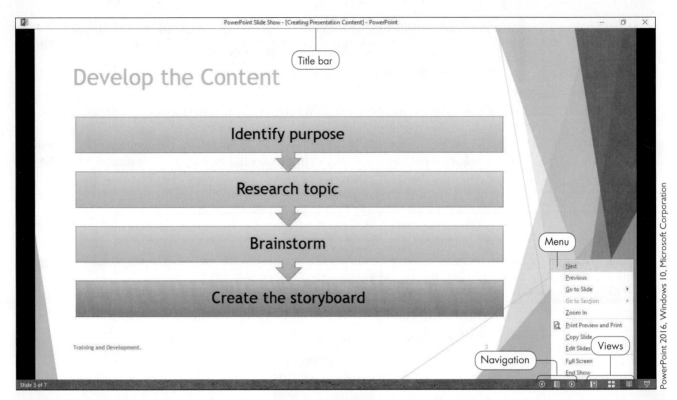

FIGURE 1.9 Reading View

The above views are useful when creating a presentation. When you present your slide show, however, you use ***Slide Show view***. Slide Show view delivers the completed presentation full screen to an audience, one slide at a time, as an electronic presentation (see Figure 1.10). Access the options for Slide Show view from the Start Slide Show group on the Slide Show tab. For quick access to Slide Show view, you can click the Slide Show button on the status bar.

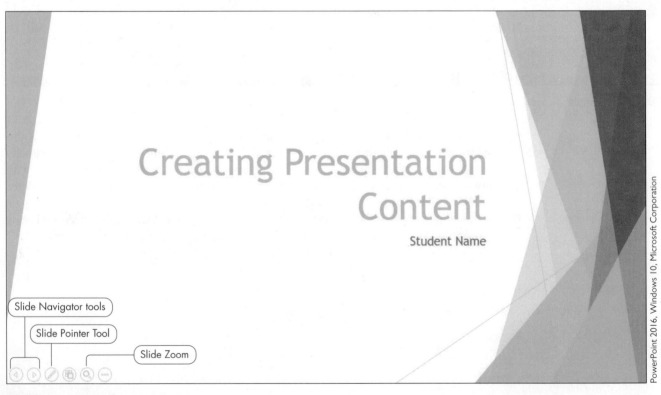

FIGURE 1.10 Slide Show View

The slide show can be presented manually, where you click the mouse to move from one slide to the next, or automatically, where each slide stays on the screen for a predetermined amount of time, after which the next slide appears. A slide show can contain a combination of both methods. To end the slide show, press Esc. This view also includes pointer tools, Slide Navigator that enables you to move between slides as needed without leaving Slide Show view, and Slide Zoom that you can use to focus your audience on your ideas.

Presenter view, accessed from the Monitors group on the Slide Show tab, is an especially valuable view that lets you deliver a presentation using two monitors simultaneously. Typically, one monitor is a projector that delivers the full-screen presentation to the audience; the other monitor is a laptop or computer that displays the presentation in Presenter view. Presenter view includes a slide, a thumbnail image of the next slide, and any speaker notes you have created. The view options are displayed on the second monitor so the presenter can control them. This view includes a timer that displays the time elapsed since the presentation began so you can keep track of the presentation length. Figure 1.11 shows the audience view on the right side of the figure and the Presenter view on the left side.

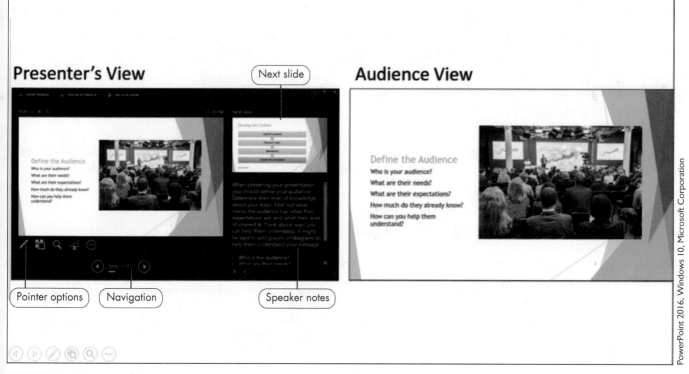

FIGURE 1.11 Presenter View

Typing a Speaker Note

STEP 2 ❯❯ Rather than change your view to Notes Page view to type speaker notes, you can change Normal view from a two-paned view to a three-paned view as shown in Figure 1.12. To display the Notes pane, click Notes on the status bar. The Notes pane will display below the Slide Pane, the main working area.

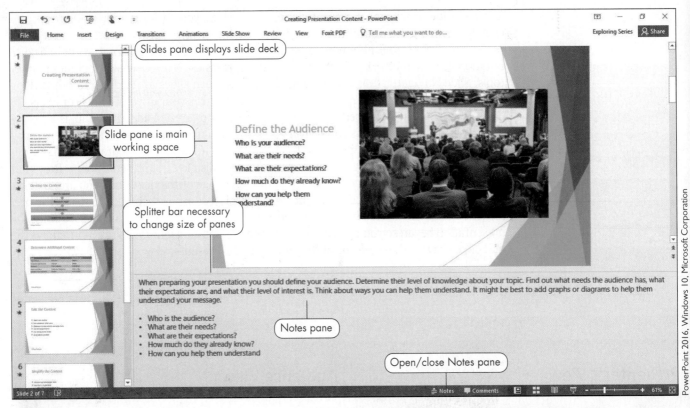

FIGURE 1.12 Tri-pane Normal View

To create a note for the speaker in the Notes pane, complete the following steps:

1. Click Notes on the status bar if the Notes pane is not visible.
2. Drag the splitter bar between the Slide pane and the Notes pane up to expand the Notes pane.
3. Click in the Notes pane and begin typing.

TIP: FORMAT A SPEAKER NOTE

Notes can be formatted much like a Word document using the formatting tools in the Font and Paragraph groups on the Home tab. You can create bulleted lists and italicize or bold key words you want to feature, among other things, to help you stay organized and on track with your presentation. Not all text modifications will be visible in Normal view or in Presenter view. To see modifications such as font and font size, images, and charts, switch to Notes Page view.

Saving as a PowerPoint Show

STEP 3 ▶▶ When you save a *PowerPoint presentation*, by default it is saved with a .pptx file extension. Then, when you open the file, it opens to Normal view, or edit mode, so that you can make changes to the presentation. If you use Save As and save the presentation as a *PowerPoint show* with a .ppsx extension, the presentation opens in Slide Show view. You will not see the PowerPoint interface; the presentation is in play mode. This is valuable when you are ready to present and do not want your audience to see the PowerPoint interface. You double-click the PowerPoint show file with a .ppsx extension in File Explorer to open the presentation in Slide Show view. PowerPoint presentations are often saved as .ppsx files for distributing to others, too. Although a .ppsx file cannot be changed while viewing, you can open the file in PowerPoint and edit it.

Quick Concepts

1. Describe the main advantage for using each of the following views: Normal view, Notes Page view, Slide Sorter view, and Slide Show view. **pp. 73–77**

2. Discuss the purpose of a speaker note. **p. 75**

3. Explain the difference between a PowerPoint presentation (.pptx) and a PowerPoint show (.ppsx). **p. 78**

Hands-On Exercises

Watch the Video
for this Hands-On
Exercise!

MyITLab®
HOE1 Training

Skills covered: View a
Presentation in Normal View
• Use the Notes Pane • Save a
Presentation in PowerPoint Show
Mode

1 Work with PowerPoint

You have been asked to create a presentation on the benefits of PowerPoint for the Training and
Development department. You decide to view an existing presentation to determine if it contains material
you can adapt for your presentation. You view the presentation, add a speaker note, and then save the
presentation as a PowerPoint presentation and as a PowerPoint show.

STEP 1 »» **OPEN AND VIEW A POWERPOINT PRESENTATION**

You open a presentation created by your colleague. You experiment with various methods of advancing to the next slide and then
return to Normal view. As you use the various methods of advancing to the next slide, you find the one that is most comfortable to
you and then use that method as you view slide shows in the future. An audio clip of audience applause will play when you view Slide
4: The Essence of PowerPoint. You will want to wear a headset if you are in a classroom lab so that you do not disturb classmates.
Refer to Figure 1.13 as you complete Step 1.

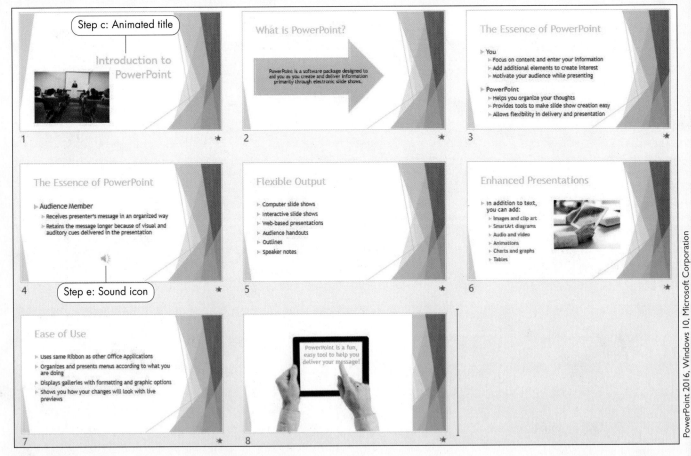

PowerPoint 2016, Windows 10, Microsoft Corporation

FIGURE 1.13 Introduction to PowerPoint Presentation

   a. Start PowerPoint and open the *p01h1Intro* file. Save the file as **p01h1Intro_LastFirst**.
   When you save files, use your last and first names. For example, as the PowerPoint
   author, I would name my presentation "p01h1Intro_KrebsCynthia".

> **TROUBLESHOOTING:** If you make any major mistakes in this exercise, you can close the file,
> open *p01h1Intro* again, and then start this exercise over.

b. Click **Slide Show** on the status bar.

The presentation begins with the title slide, the first slide in all slide shows. The title has an animation assigned, so it displays automatically.

c. Press **Spacebar** to advance to the second slide and read the slide.

The title animation on the second slide automatically wipes down, and the arrow wipes to the right.

d. Position the pointer in the lower-left corner side of the slide, and click the **right arrow** in the Navigation bar to advance to the next slide. Click to read the animated slide content.

The text on the third slide, and all following slides, has the same animation applied to create consistency in the presentation.

e. Press the **left mouse button** to advance to the fourth slide, which has a sound icon displayed on the slide.

The sound icon on the slide indicates sound has been added. The sound has been set to start automatically so you do not need to click anything for the sound to play.

TROUBLESHOOTING: If you do not hear the sound, your computer may not have a sound card or your sound may be muted.

---

f. Continue to navigate through the slides until you come to the end of the presentation (a black screen).

g. Press **Esc** to return to Normal view.

STEP 2 〉〉 **TYPE A SPEAKER NOTE**

You add a speaker note to a slide to help you remember to mention some of the many objects that can be added to a slide. You also view the note in Notes view to see how it will print. Refer to Figure 1.14 as you complete Step 2.

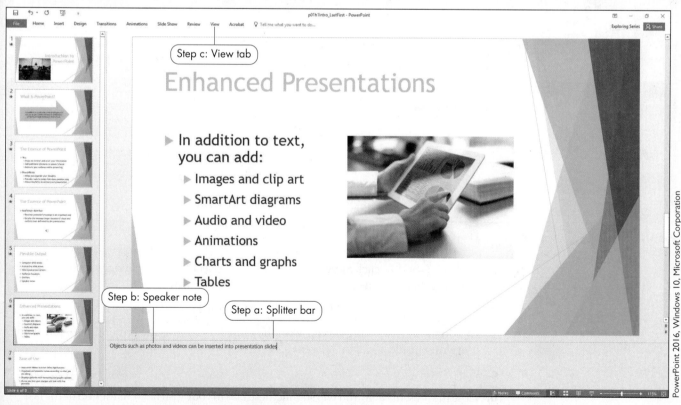

FIGURE 1.14 Speaker Note in Notes Pane of Normal View

a. Click the **Slide 6 thumbnail** and then drag the border between the Slide pane and the Notes pane up to expand the Notes pane.

Slide 6 is selected, and the slide displays in the Slide pane.

> **TROUBLESHOOTING:** If the Notes pane is not visible, click Notes on the status bar.

b. Type **Objects such as pictures and videos can be inserted into presentation slides.** in the Notes pane.

c. Click the **View tab** and click **Notes Page** in the Presentation Views group.

The slide is shown at a reduced size and the speaker note is shown below the slide.

d. Click **Normal** in the Presentation Views group.

This displays the presentation in Normal view.

e. Save the presentation.

STEP 3 ›› **SAVE AS A POWERPOINT SHOW**

You want to save the slide show as a PowerPoint show so that it opens automatically in Slide Show view rather than Normal view. Refer to Figure 1.15 as you complete Step 3.

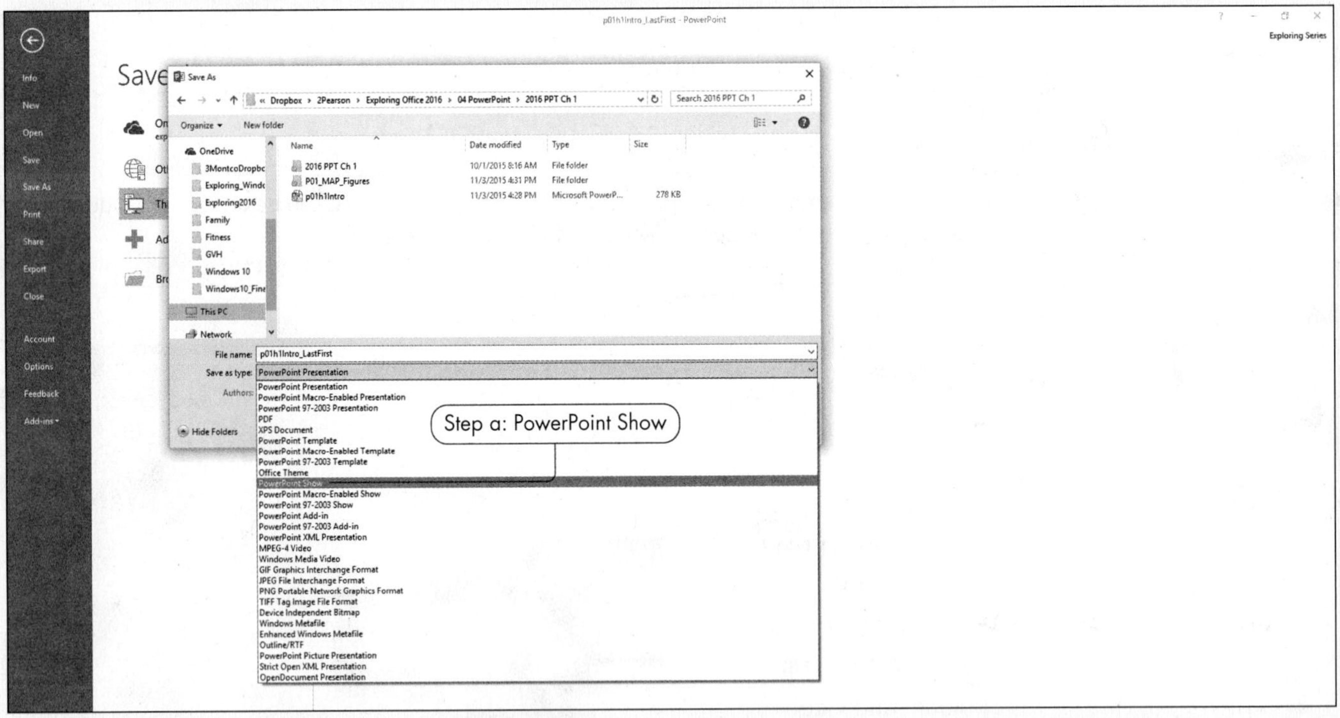

FIGURE 1.15 Saving a Presentation as a PowerPoint Show

a. Click the **File tab**, click **Save As**, click **Browse**, select the file location where the file is to be saved, click **Save as type**, and then select **PowerPoint Show**.

b. Leave the file name **p01h1Intro_LastFirst** for the PowerPoint show.

Although you are saving this file with the same file name as the presentation, it will not overwrite the file, as it is a different file type.

c. Click **Save**.

d. Close the presentation. You will submit these files to your instructor at the end of the last Hands-On Exercise.

Presentation Creation

You are ready to create your own presentation by choosing a theme, adding content, and applying formatting. You create the presentation by adding the content first and then applying formatting so that you can concentrate on your message and its structure without getting distracted by the formatting of the presentation.

In this section, you will create a visual plan called a storyboard. You will also learn to polish your presentation by using layouts, applying design themes, and reviewing your presentation for errors.

Planning and Preparing a Presentation

Creating an effective presentation requires advance planning. First, determine the purpose of your presentation. An informative presentation could notify the audience about a change in policy or procedure. An educational presentation could teach an audience about a subject or a skill. Sales presentations are often persuasive calls to action to encourage the purchase of a product, but they can also be used to sell an idea or process. A goodwill presentation could be used to recognize an employee or acknowledge an organization. You could even create a certificate of appreciation using PowerPoint.

Next, research your audience—determine their level of knowledge about your topic. Find out what needs the audience has, what their expectations are, and what their level of interest is.

After determining your purpose and researching your audience, brainstorm how to deliver your message. Before using your computer, you may want to sketch out your thoughts on paper to help you organize them. After organizing your key points, add them as content to the slide show, and then format the presentation.

Use a Storyboard

A **storyboard** is a visual plan for your presentation that helps you map out the direction of your presentation. It can be a very rough draft that you sketch out while brainstorming, or it can be an elaborate plan that includes the text and objects drawn as they would appear on a slide.

A simple PowerPoint storyboard is divided into sections representing individual slides. The first block in the storyboard is used for the title slide. Subsequent blocks are used to introduce the topics, develop the topics, and then summarize the information. Figure 1.16 shows a working copy of a storyboard for planning presentation content. The storyboard is in rough-draft form and shows changes made during the review process. A blank copy of the document in Figure 1.16 has been included with your student files should you want to use this for presentation planning. The PowerPoint presentation shown in Figure 1.17 incorporates the changes to the storyboard made during the review process.

Purpose: [ ] Informative [X] Educational [ ] Persuasive [ ] Goodwill [ ] Other

Audience: IAAP Membership
Location: Marriott Hotel
Date and Time: September 16, 2019

Content	Layout	Visual Element(s)
Title slide		
Title Slide Planning ~~Before Creating~~ Presentation Content	Title Slide	O Shapes O Chart O Table O WordArt O Picture O Video O Clip Art O Sound O SmartArt O _____ *Description:*
Introduction		
Introduction (Key Pont, Quote, Image, Other) A good plan is like a road map: It shows the final destination and usually the best ways to get there. M. Stanley Judd	Section Header	O Shapes O Chart O Table O WordArt ⊘ Picture O Video O Clip Art O Sound O SmartArt O _____ *Description:*
Key topics with main points		
Key Point #1 Identify the Purpose ~~Selling (e-commercial)~~, Persuading Informing Good Will, ~~Entertaining~~ Educating, Motivating tional vational	Title + ~~Two~~ Content	O Shapes O Chart O Table O WordArt O Picture O Video O Clip Art O Sound O SmartArt ⊘ Text *Description:*
Key Point #2 Define the Audience Who is ~~going to be~~ in the audience What are the ~~audiences~~ needs? What are the expectations? How much do they already know?	Title + ~~Two~~ Content	O Shapes O Chart O Table O WordArt ⊘ Picture O Video O Clip Art O Sound O SmartArt O _____ *Description:*
Key Point #3 Develop the Content • Identify purpose • Research topic • Brainstorm • Create the storyboard	Title and Content + SmartArt	O Shapes O Chart O Table O WordArt O Picture O Video O Clip Art O Sound ⊗ SmartArt O _____ *Description:*
Key Point #4 Simplify the Content Make text concise, Use consistent verb tense, Eliminate excess adverbs and adjectives, Use few prepositions, Use strong active verbs, Keep bullets parallel	Title and Content	O Shapes O Chart O Table O WordArt O Picture O Video O Clip Art O Sound O SmartArt O _____ *Description:*
Summary (Restatement of Key Points, Quote, Other) Quote: The key to an effective presentation is planning ahead!	Section Header	O Shapes O Chart O Table O WordArt ⊘ Picture O Video O Clip Art O Sound O SmartArt O _____ *Description:*

FIGURE 1.16 Rough-Draft Storyboard

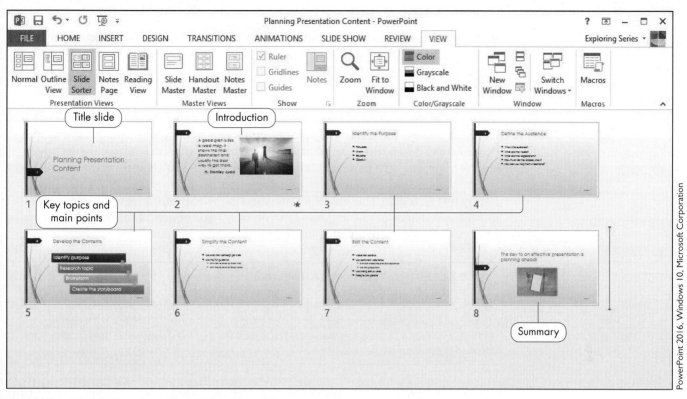

FIGURE 1.17 Slide Show Based on Storyboard

After you create the storyboard, review what you wrote.

Use Short Phrases

Shorten complete sentences to phrases that you can use as bulleted points by eliminating excess adverbs and adjectives and using only a few prepositions. Think like a newspaper editor writing a headline and distill the content into the most important words. For example, "Good computer skills are required of each student attending the CIS 150 course" could be shortened to "CIS 150 course requires good computer skills."

Use Active Voice

Edit the phrases so they begin with active voice when possible to involve the viewer. When using active voice, the subject of the phrase performs the action expressed in the verb. In phrases using passive voice, the subject is acted upon. Passive voice needs more words to communicate your ideas and can make your presentation seem flat. The following is an example of the same thought written in active voice and passive voice:

- Active Voice: Students need good computer skills.
- Passive Voice: Good computer skills are needed by students.

Use Parallel Construction

Use parallel construction so that your bullets are in the same grammatical form to help your audience see the connection between your phrases. If you start your first bullet with a noun, start each successive bullet with a noun; if you start your first bullet with a verb, continue starting your bullets with verbs. Parallel construction also gives each bullet an equal level of importance and promotes balance in your message. In the following example, the fourth bullet is not parallel to the first three bullets because it does not begin with a verb. The fifth bullet shows the bullet in parallel construction.

- Find a good place to study.
- Organize your study time.

- Study for tests with a partner.
- Terminology is important so learn how to use it properly. (Incorrect)
- Learn and use terminology properly. (Correct)

Follow the 7 × 7 Guideline

With all the photographs and graphics available, and features such as Chart and SmartArt, use as little text as possible. Let imagery support your message as you speak to the audience. When text is necessary, keep the information on your slides concise so it is easy for your audience to remember. You can explain and elaborate on the slide content to your audience when delivering your presentation. Follow the 7 × 7 guideline when putting text on a slide. This guideline suggests that you use no more than seven words per line and seven lines per slide. Although you may need to exceed this guideline on occasion when presenting to an audience, follow it as often as possible.

TIP: EXCEEDING THE 7 × 7 GUIDELINE
You may see slides with a great deal of text, multiple charts and graphs, or a combination of multiple objects. This is typically done when the person who created the presentation intends for the slide deck to be printed and distributed rather than viewed by an audience, or to be viewed on a monitor by an individual in control of advancing the slides. These methods give the viewer ample time to absorb any detailed information on the slide.

After you complete the planning and review process, you are ready to select the "look" of your presentation.

Choose a Theme

 When you first open PowerPoint you are provided the opportunity to choose from various design themes. A **theme** is a designer-quality look that includes coordinating colors, matching fonts, and effects such as shadows. The Blank Presentation uses the Office theme.

To create a new presentation, complete the following steps:

1. Click File, and then click New.
2. Click the design theme you want to use.
3. Click Create and a new file will open with the design theme you selected.

You can always change the theme from the one that you initially choose. You can even select a variant for the theme. A **variant** is a variation of the theme design you have chosen. Each variant uses different color palettes and font families. Figure 1.18 shows the Ion theme with four variant options for this theme.

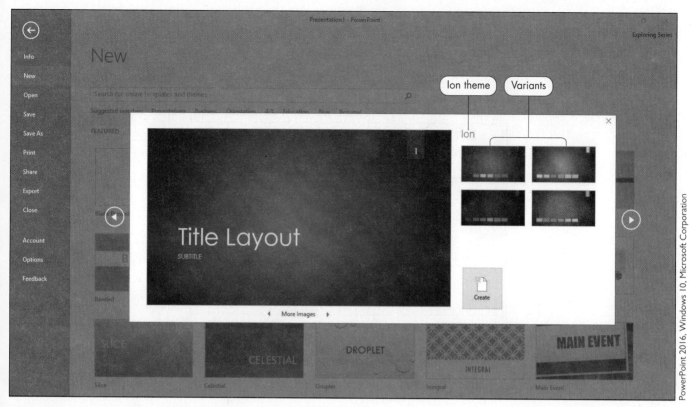

FIGURE 1.18 Ion Theme with Variant Options

> **To change a theme or apply a theme variant, complete the following steps:**
>
> 1. Click the Design tab to display thumbnail previews in the Themes and Variants groups.
> 2. Click More to see all of the available themes.
> 3. Point to different themes to see a Live Preview of the theme applied to your presentation.
> 4. Click a theme to apply it to your presentation.
> 5. Click a variant in the Variants group to apply it to your presentation.

Adding Presentation Content

After you complete the planning and review process, you are ready to prepare the slide deck you will use during your presentation. To prepare the slide deck, you need to understand PowerPoint's use of slide layouts.

Use Slide Layouts

PowerPoint provides a set of predefined slide *layouts* that determine the position of placeholders in various locations. *Placeholders* are objects that hold specific content, such as titles, subtitles, or images. Placeholders determine the position of the objects on the slide. Some layouts also include a small palette of icons that you can use to insert a variety of objects.

When you click the New Slide arrow on the Home tab, a gallery from which you can choose a layout displays. Figure 1.19 shows the Layout Gallery available for you to use when you have selected Blank presentation with the Office theme. Table 1.1 describes some of the most common slide layouts.

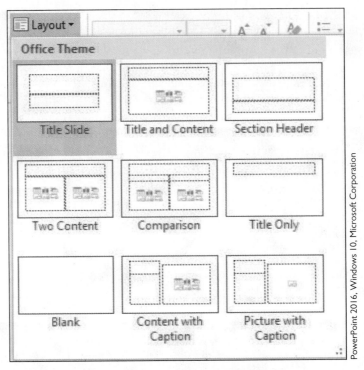

FIGURE 1.19 Layout Gallery for Office Theme

PowerPoint 2016, Windows 10, Microsoft Corporation

TABLE 1.1	Common Layout Options
Slide Layout	**Description**
Title Slide	A new, blank presentation opens to a title slide layout. This slide includes a placeholder for a title and a placeholder for a subtitle.
Title and Content	In addition to a placeholder for the title, this layout includes a content placeholder. Click and type in the content placeholder and you create a bulleted list. Or, click one of the icons on the palette in the center of the placeholder to insert objects such as a table, chart, SmartArt graphic, picture, online picture, or video.
Section Header	The Section Header layout enables you to separate different sections or main topics similar to how a tabbed page separates sections in a notebook.
Two Content	This layout includes two content placeholders which you can use to create two columns on the slide. Often this layout is used to put text on one side of the slide and graphic content on the other side. A title placeholder is also included.
Comparison	Use this layout to make a comparison between two points by listing supporting detail in columns. In addition to having two content placeholders, this layout also includes a heading placeholder over each content placeholder and a title placeholder.
Title Only	Only a title placeholder is included on the slide which gives you a lot of empty area you can use to insert any type of object such as shapes, WordArt, pictures, charts, etc.
Blank	The blank layout contains no placeholders making it ideal for content that will cover the entire slide, such as a picture.
Content with Caption	The left side of this layout includes a placeholder for a title and a placeholder for text. The right side includes a placeholder for content such as a chart or picture.
Picture with Caption	The top of the slide includes a large placeholder for a picture. Beneath the picture placeholder is a placeholder for a caption and a placeholder for descriptive text.

Pearson Education, Inc.

After you select a layout, click a placeholder. The border of the placeholder becomes a dashed line and you are able to enter content. If you click the dashed line placeholder border, the placeholder and all of its content are selected. The border changes to a solid line. Once selected, you can drag the placeholder to a new position, resize it, format the contents of the placeholder, or delete the placeholder. To format the contents of the placeholder, click the placeholder border and use the controls on the Home tab to format the text. If you only want to change a portion of the text, select the text and then use the controls on the Home tab to format the text.

TIP: UNUSED PLACEHOLDERS

It is not necessary to delete unused placeholders on a slide. Unused placeholders in a slide layout do not show when you display a slide show.

Create a Title Slide and an Introduction

STEP 2 ▶▶ The title placeholder should be used for a short title that indicates the purpose of the presentation. Try to capture the title in two to five words. The subtitle placeholder should be used for information such as the speaker's name and title, the speaker's organization, the organization's logo, and the date of the presentation. To add this information to the placeholders, click in the placeholder and begin typing.

After the title slide, you should include an introduction slide that will get the audience's attention. The introduction could be a list of topics covered in the presentation, a thought-provoking quotation or question, or an image that relates to the topic. Introduction slides can also be used to distinguish between topics or sections of the presentation.

Create Key Point Slides

After you create the title slide and introduction, you should create a slide for each of the key points you outlined in your storyboard.

To add a slide, complete the following steps:

1. Click the New Slide arrow on the Home tab.
2. Click the layout that you want for your new slide in the gallery of layouts.

The New Slide button has two parts, the New Slide button and the New Slide arrow. Click the New Slide arrow when you want to choose a layout from the gallery. Click New Slide, which appears above the New Slide arrow, to quickly insert a new slide. If you click New Slide when the title slide is selected, the new slide uses the Title and Content layout. If the current slide uses any layout other than Title Slide, the subsequent new slide uses the same layout.

Each key point should be on a separate slide with the details needed to support it. The Title and Content layout is a very common layout used for presenting a key point and its supporting details. List the key point in the title placeholder, and then create a bulleted list in the content placeholder. To increase or decrease levels, or indents, for bulleted items, click Increase List Level or Decrease List Level in the Paragraph group on the Home tab. You can press Tab as a shortcut to increase a level, or Shift+Tab as a shortcut to decrease a level.

End with a Summary or Conclusion Slide

To give closure to your presentation, end with a summary slide that reiterates your presentation's key points. Or, create a conclusion slide that restates the purpose of the presentation or invokes a call to action. You may also want to repeat your contact information at the end of the presentation so the audience knows how to follow-up with any questions or needs.

Reviewing the Presentation

After you create the presentation, check for spelling errors, incorrect word usage, and inconsistent capitalization. Nothing is more embarrassing or can make you appear more unprofessional than a misspelled word enlarged on a big screen. Also view the slide show to ensure that the content is presented in the proper order, that the layouts provide the content in an effective manner, and that all transitions and animations work.

Check Spelling

 Use a five-step method for checking spelling in PowerPoint. Although proofreading five times may seem excessive, it will help ensure your presentation is professional.

To check spelling, complete the following steps:

1. Read the slide content as you type it looking for wavy red underlines that indicate a potential typographical error or a repeated word. Read each slide after typing its information.
2. Use the Spelling feature located on the Review tab to check the entire presentation.
3. Ask a friend or colleague to review the presentation.
4. Display the presentation in ReadingView and read each word out loud.
5. Correct all spelling or word usage errors found.

> **TIP: PROOFING OPTIONS**
> The Spelling feature, by default, does not catch contextual errors like *to*, *too*, and *two*, but you can set the proofing options to help you find and fix this type of error. To modify the proofing options, click File and click Options. Click Proofing in the PowerPoint Options window and click Check Grammar with Spelling. With this option selected, the spelling checker will flag contextual mistakes with a red wavy underline. To correct the error, right-click the flagged word and select the proper word choice.

Use the Thesaurus

As you create and edit your presentation, you may notice that you are using one word too often, especially at the beginning of bullets. Use the Thesaurus to help you make varied word choices. Access the Thesaurus from the Proofing group on the Review tab.

Check Slide Show Elements

 After checking the wording on the individual slides, it is helpful to view the presentation in Slide Show view to see if the elements you have incorporated are effective. Check the order of the information to make sure the content is presented in a logical order and that the layout showcases the information effectively. Make sure that the transitions and animations are working. Examine any media to make sure it supports the message.

To check the slide show elements, complete the following steps:

1. Click the Slide Show tab.
2. Click From Beginning in the Start Slide Show group.
3. Advance through each slide checking layouts, transitions, and animations.
4. End the slide show and return to Normal view.
5. Change any layouts, placeholder locations, transitions, and animations as needed.

Reorder Slides

 STEP 5 As you review your presentation, you may realize that you need to reorder your slides. This can easily be done using Slide Sorter view.

To reorder slides, complete the following steps:

1. Click the View tab.
2. Click Slide Sorter in the Presentation Views group.
3. Select the slide you want to move and drag the slide to the new location.
4. Double-click any slide to return to Normal view.

Quick Concepts

4. Identify the three advanced planning steps you should follow before adding content to a slide show. *p. 83*

5. Define storyboard and describe how a storyboard aids you in creating a slide show. *p. 83*

6. Describe two guidelines you should follow when assessing your slide content. *pp. 85–86*

7. Explain the purpose of using a presentation theme. *p. 86*

Hands-On Exercises

Watch the Video
for this Hands-On
Exercise!

MyITLab®
HOE2 Training

Skills covered: Choose a Theme
• Add Presentation Content •
Check Spelling • Use the Thesaurus
• Check Slide Show Elements •
Reorder Slides

2 Presentation Creation

To help state employees learn the process for presentation creation, you decide to give them guidelines for determining content, structuring a slide show, and assessing content. You have previously created a storyboard, and now you create the slide show to deliver these guidelines.

STEP 1 ›› PLAN AND PREPARE A PRESENTATION

You are creating a Training and Development presentation for the employees from a previously created storyboard. You begin by selecting a theme, and as you progress through the steps you will add and edit several slides. You begin by choosing the Retrospect theme with a specific variation color and creating the Title Slide content. Figure 1.20 displays the storyboard used to plan the presentation.

Step a: Purpose

Storyboard

Purpose: [X] Informative [ ] Educational [ ] Persuasive [ ] Goodwill [ ] Other

Audience: Training and Development
Location: CS 601a
Date and Time: July 1, 2019

Content	Layout	Visual Element(s)
Title Slide Creating Presentation Content Step a: Introduction slide	Title Slide	○ Shapes ○ Chart ○ Table ○ WordArt ○ Picture ○ Video ○ Clip Art ○ Sound ○ SmartArt ○ ___ Description:
Key Point #1 Define the Audience Who is the audience? What are their needs? What are their expectations? How much do they already know? How can you help them understand?	Two Content	○ Shapes ○ Chart ○ Table ○ WordArt ✗ Picture ○ Video ○ Clip Art ○ Sound ○ SmartArt ○ ___ Description: People at presentation
Key Point #2 Develop the Content • Identify purpose • Research topic • Brainstorm • Create the storyboard	Title and Content	○ Shapes ○ Chart ○ Table ○ WordArt ○ Picture ○ Video ○ Clip Art ○ Sound ○ SmartArt ○ ___ Description:
Key Point #3 Determine Additional Content List types of text, illustrations, and other content	Title and Content	○ Shapes ○ Chart ✗ Table ○ WordArt ○ Picture ○ Video ○ Clip Art ○ Sound ○ SmartArt ○ ___ Description:
Key Point #4 Edit the Content Make text concise. Use consistent verb tense. Eliminate excess adverbs and adjectives. Use few prepositions. Use strong active verbs. Keep bullets parallel.	Title and Content	○ Shapes ○ Chart ○ Table ○ WordArt ○ Picture ○ Video ○ Clip Art ○ Sound ○ SmartArt ○ ___ Description:
Key Point #5 Simplify the Content Make text concise. Use consistent verb tense. Eliminate excess adverbs and adjectives. Use few prepositions. Use strong active verbs. Keep bullets parallel.	Title and Content	○ Shapes ○ Chart ○ Table ○ WordArt ○ Picture ○ Video ○ Clip Art ○ Sound ○ SmartArt ○ ___ Description:
Summary (Restatement of Key Points, Quote, Other) Quote: The key to an effective presentation is planning ahead!	Section Header	○ Shapes ○ Chart ○ Table ○ WordArt ○ Picture ○ Video ○ Clip Art ○ Sound ○ SmartArt ○ ___ Description:

Step a: Summary slide

Step a: Key point slides

PowerPoint 2016, Windows 10, Microsoft Corporation

FIGURE 1.20 Storyboard for Creating Presentation Content Slide Show

a. Review the storyboard displayed in Figure 1.20. Note the purpose, introduction, key points, and summary.

b. Open PowerPoint. Select the **Retrospect theme**. Select the first theme variant, the **Orange variant**, and click **Create**.

c. Save the presentation as **p01h2Content_LastFirst**.

d. Click in the **title placeholder** on the Title Slide and type **Creating Presentation Content**.

e. Type your name in the **subtitle placeholder**.

f. Click **Notes** on the status bar. Type **Training and Development** in the Notes pane.

g. Save the presentation.

STEP 2 ›› ADD PRESENTATION CONTENT

You continue creating your presentation by adding a second slide with the Title and Content layout. After adding a title to the slide, you create a bulleted list to develop your topic. After adding the presentation content, you proofread the presentation to ensure no errors exist. Refer to Figure 1.21 as you complete Step 2.

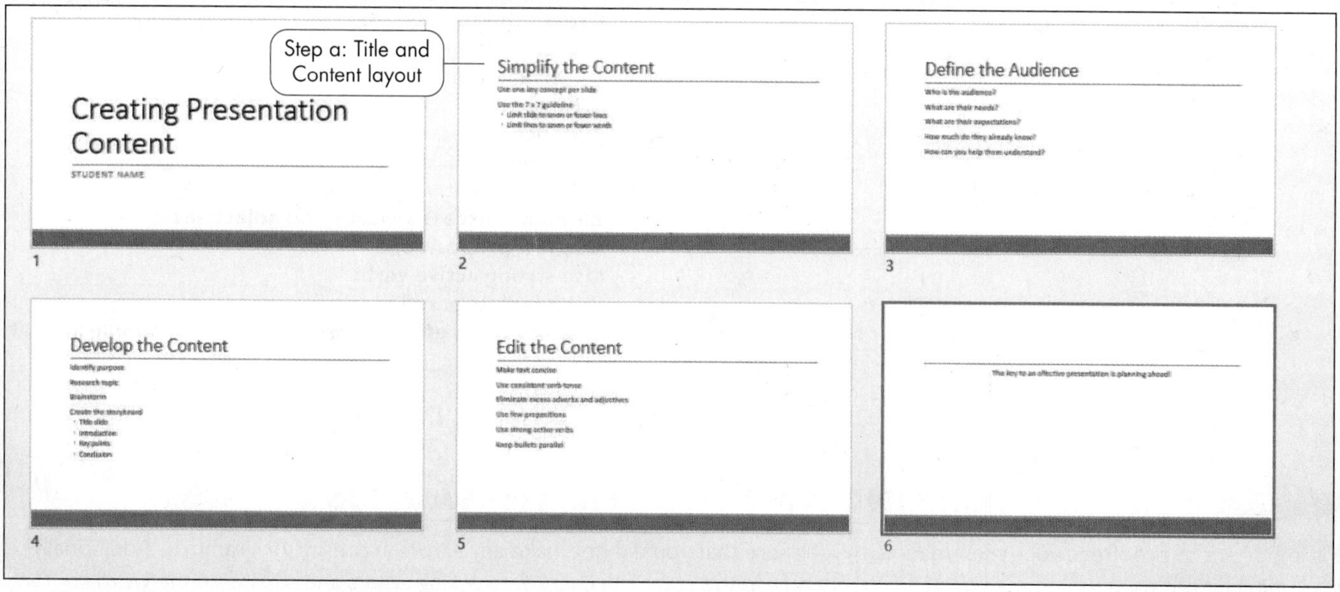

PowerPoint 2016, Windows 10, Microsoft Corporation

FIGURE 1.21 New Slides with Content in Slide Sorter View

a. Click **New Slide** in the Slides group on the Home tab.

Because you clicked the top half of New Slide, the new slide uses the Title and Content layout which is the default slide layout after a Title Slide layout. The new Slide 2 contains two placeholders: one for the title and one for body content.

b. Type **Simplify the Content** in the title placeholder.

c. Click in the **content placeholder** below the title placeholder, type **Use one main concept per slide**, and then press **Enter**.

By default, the list level is the same as the previous level. Note that the Retrospect theme does not automatically place bullets into the body of the presentation.

d. Type **Use the 7 × 7 guideline** and press **Enter**.

e. Click **Increase List Level** in the Paragraph group.

The list level indents and the font size is reduced indicating this is a subset of the main level.

f. Type **Limit slide to seven or fewer lines** and press **Enter**.

g. Type **Limit lines to seven or fewer words**. (Do not include the period.)

By default, the list level is the same as the previous level.

h. Click **New Slide** in the Slides group four times to create four more slides with the Title and Content layout.

To move between slides in the slide deck, click the thumbnail of the slide you want to edit in the Slide pane.

i. Type the following text in the appropriate slide. Use Increase List Level 🔲 and Decrease List Level 🔲 in the Paragraph group to change levels.

Slide	Slide Title	Content Data
3	Define the Audience	Who is the audience?
		What are their needs?
		What are their expectations?
		How much do they already know?
		How can you help them understand?
4	Develop the Content	Identify purpose
		Research topic
		Brainstorm
		Create the storyboard
		Title slide
		Introduction
		Key points
		Conclusion
5	Edit the Content	Make text concise
		Use consistent verb tense
		Eliminate excess adverbs and adjectives
		Use few prepositions
		Use strong active verbs
		Keep bullets parallel
6	No title	The key to an effective presentation is planning ahead!

j. Save the presentation.

STEP 3 ❱❱ **CHECK SPELLING AND USE THE THESAURUS**

It is important to proofread your presentation, making sure that you did not make any errors in spelling or grammar. Additionally, it is important not to use the same words too frequently. In this step, you check for spelling errors and substitute the word *key* for the word *main*.

a. Click **Spelling** in the Proofing group on the Review tab and correct any errors. Carefully proofread each slide.

The result of the spelling check depends on how accurately you entered the text of the presentation.

b. Click **Slide 2**, use the Thesaurus to change *main* in the first bulleted point to **key** and click **Close (X)** on the Thesaurus.

c. Save the presentation.

You view the slide show and decide that the concluding statement emphasizing the importance of planning can be improved by modifying the layout of the slide. Refer to Figure 1.22 as you complete Step 4.

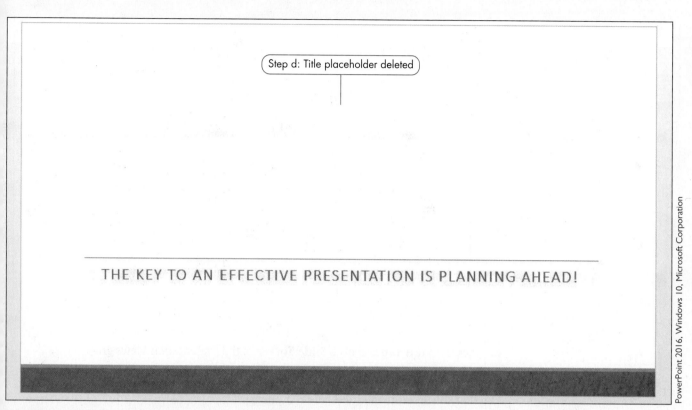

FIGURE 2.22 Slide with Modified Layout

a. View the presentation in Slide Show view and then return to Normal view.

b. Click the **Slide 6 thumbnail** in the Slides pane. Click the **Home tab** and click **Layout** in the Slides group.

c. Click **Section Header** from the Layout gallery.

The layout for Slide 6 changes to the Section Header layout. The Section Header layout adds emphasis to the statement on Slide 6.

d. Click the border of the title placeholder and press **Delete**.

The dotted line border becomes a solid line, which indicates the placeholder is selected. Pressing Delete removes the placeholder and the content of that placeholder. It is not necessary to delete the placeholder because empty placeholders do not display in Slide Show view, but deleting the placeholder gives you a cleaner look in Normal view.

e. Click the **subtitle placeholder** and click **Center** in the Paragraph group on the Home tab.

The layout of Slide 6 has now been modified.

f. Save the presentation.

STEP 5 » REORDER SLIDES

You notice that the slides do not follow a logical order. You change the slide positions in Slide Sorter view. Refer to Figure 1.23 as you complete Step 5.

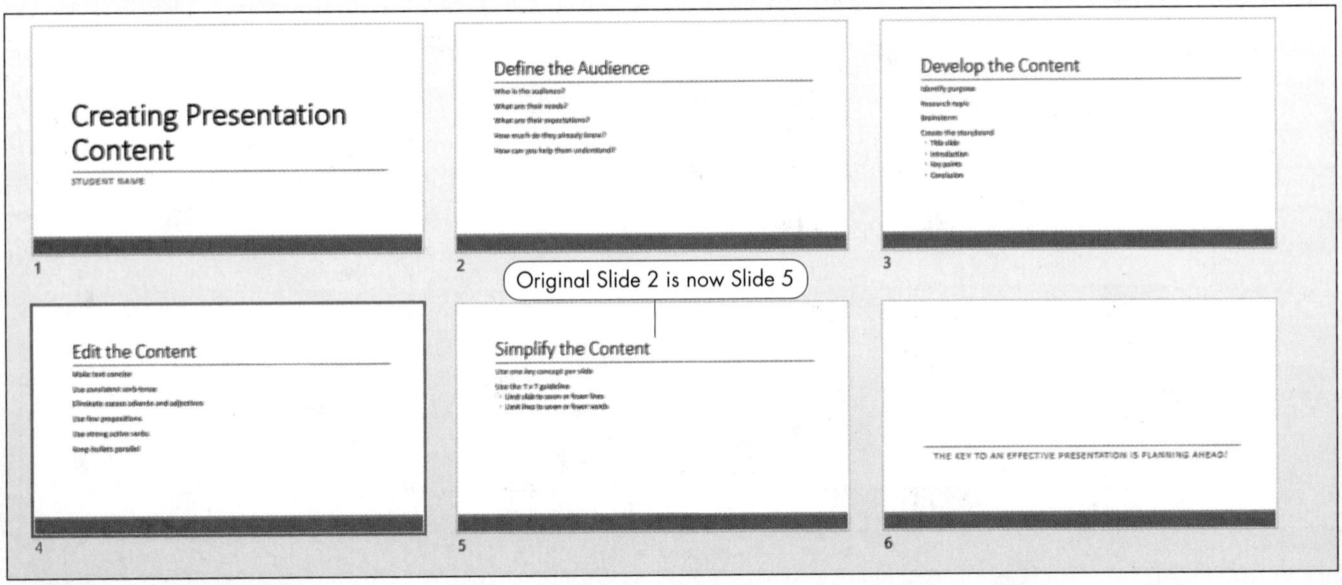

FIGURE 1.23 Reordered Slide Deck

a. Click the **View tab** and click **Slide Sorter** in the Presentation Views group.

b. Select **Slide 2** and drag it before the conclusion (last) slide so that it becomes Slide 5.

After you drop the slide, all slides renumber.

c. Double-click **Slide 6**.

Your presentation returns to Normal view.

d. Save the presentation. Keep the presentation open if you plan to continue with the next Hands-On Exercise. If not, close the presentation and exit PowerPoint.

Presentation Enhancement

You can strengthen your slide show by adding objects that support the message. PowerPoint enables you to include a variety of visual objects to add impact to your presentation. You can add tables, charts, and SmartArt diagrams created in PowerPoint, or you can insert objects that were created in other applications, such as a chart from Microsoft Excel or a table from Microsoft Word. You can add images, WordArt (stylized letters), sound, animated clips, and video clips to increase your presentation's impact. You can add animations and transitions to catch the audience's attention. You can also add identifying information to slides or audience handouts by adding headers and footers.

In this section, you will add a table to a slide to organize data in columns and rows. You will insert an online picture that relates to your topic and then you will move and resize the picture. You will apply transitions to control how one slide changes to another and add animations to text and pictures to add visual interest. You will finish by adding identifying information in a header and footer.

Adding a Table

STEP 1 »» A ***table*** organizes information in columns and rows. Tables can be simple and include just a few words or images, or they can be more complex and include structured numerical data.

To create a table on a new slide, complete the following steps:

1. Create a new slide using any layout.
2. Click the Insert tab, and then click Table in the Tables group.
3. Drag over the grid to highlight the number of rows and columns that you need, and then click.
4. Type your information into the table cells.

You can also click the Insert Table icon on any slide layout that includes the icon. Figure 1.24 shows a table added to a slide. Once a table is created, you can resize a column or a row by positioning the pointer over the border you wish to resize and then dragging the border to the desired position.

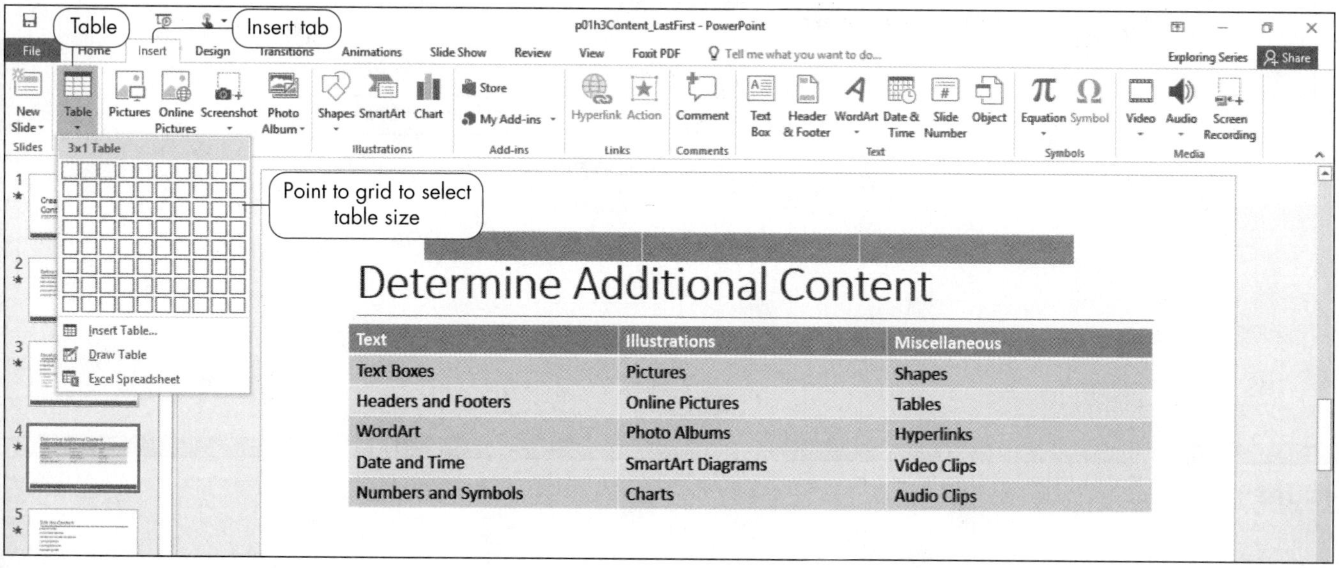

PowerPoint 2016, Windows 10, Microsoft Corporation

FIGURE 1.24 Slide with Table

> **TIP: MOVEMENT WITHIN A TABLE**
> The insertion point will show you where the text you type will appear in the table. Use the arrow keys or click anywhere in the table to move the insertion point to a new cell. You can also use the Tab key to move the insertion point. Press Tab to move to the next cell or press Shift+Tab to move to the previous cell. Pressing Ctrl+Tab inserts an indent within the cell. Pressing Tab in the last cell of a table creates a new blank row at the end of the table.

Inserting Media Objects

 Adding media objects such as pictures, online pictures, audio, and/or video is especially important in PowerPoint, as PowerPoint is a visual medium. Use the Insert tab to insert media objects in any layout. The following layouts include a palette of icons you can use to quickly insert objects:

- Title and Content
- Two Content
- Comparison
- Content with Caption
- Picture with Caption

Clicking the Pictures icon in the content placeholder (or Pictures on the Insert tab) opens a dialog box you can use to browse for picture files on any computer or device to which you are connected. Clicking Online Pictures opens the Insert Pictures dialog box that enables you to search Bing images or your OneDrive account. Figure 1.25 displays the icons for inserting objects on the slide.

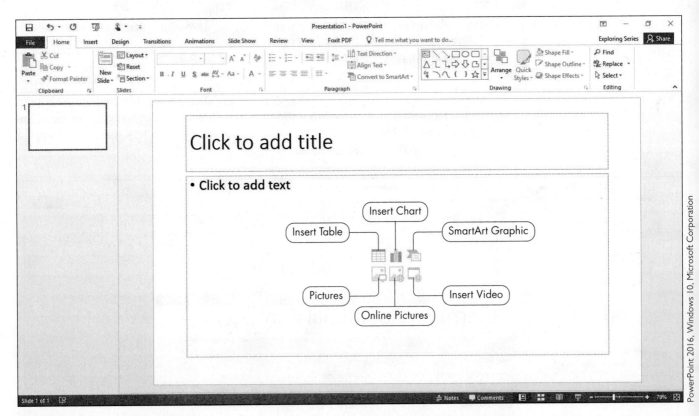

FIGURE 1.25 Layout Palette Icons

Applying Transitions and Animations

A *transition* is a visual effect that takes place when one slide is replaced by another slide while the presentation is displayed in Slide Show view or Reading View. An *animation* is motion that you can apply to text and objects. Animating text and objects can help focus attention on an important point, control the flow of information on a slide, and help you keep the audience's attention.

Apply Transitions

STEP 3 ›› A transition is a specific type of animation that is used to provide visual interest as a slide is replaced by another slide. You can select from the basic transitions displayed on the Ribbon, or from the Transition gallery available in the Transition to This Slide group on the Transitions tab. You can control whether the transition applies to all the slides or just the current slide. Figure 1.26 displays the Transition gallery.

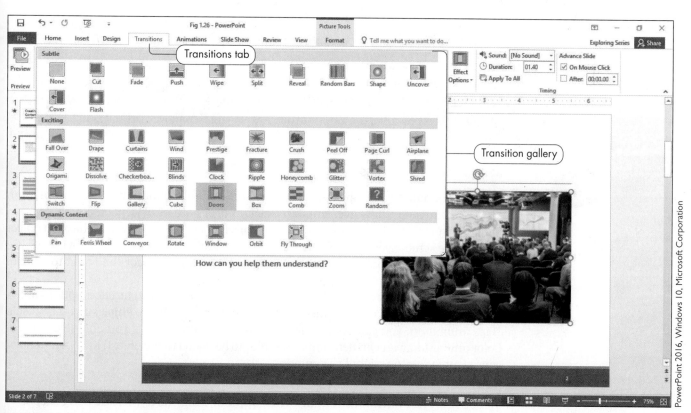

FIGURE 1.26 Transition Gallery

To apply a transition to a slide, complete the following steps:

1. Select the slide to which you want to add a transition.
2. Click the Transitions tab.
3. Click the More button in the Transition to This Slide group.
4. Select a transition from one of the following groups: Subtle, Exciting, and Dynamic Content.
5. Click Preview to see the transition applied to the slide.

After you choose a transition effect, you can select a sound to play when the transition occurs. You can choose the duration of the transition in seconds, which controls how quickly the transition takes place. The sound can be added by choosing an option in the Sound menu found in the Timing group on the Transitions tab.

Another determination you must make is how you want to start the transition process. Use the Advance Slide options in the Timing group to determine whether you want to manually click or press a key to advance to the next slide, or you want the slide to automatically advance after a specified number of seconds. You can set the number of seconds for the slide to display in the same area.

To delete a transition, complete the following steps:

1. Select the slide with the transition you want to delete.
2. Click the Transitions tab.
3. Click None in the Transition to This Slide group.
4. Click Apply to All in the Timing group if you want to remove all transitions.

Animate Objects

 You can animate text or objects using an assortment of animations. Using animation, you can control the entrance, emphasis, exit, and/or path of objects on a slide. In addition, you can add multiple animations to an object. For example, you could have an object fly onto the screen from the left, change color, and then exit the screen by flying off the screen to the right. You can even create your own motion path for the object to control the pattern it follows on the screen.

An animation can be modified by changing its effect options. The effect options available for animations are determined by the animation type. For example, if you choose a Wipe animation, you can determine the direction of the wipe. If you choose an Object Color animation, you can determine the color to be added to the object. Keep animations consistent for a professional presentation.

To apply an animation to text or other objects, complete the following steps:

1. Select the object you want to animate.
2. Click the Animations tab.
3. Click More in the Animation group to display the Animation gallery.
4. Select the animation type.
5. Click Effect Options to display any available options related to the selected animation type.

The slide in Figure 1.27 shows an animation effect added to a quote and an attribution. A tag with the number 1 is attached to the quote to show that it will run first. The attribution has a number 2 to show that it will play after the first animation. The Fly In animation in the gallery is shaded pink to show that it is the selected animation. Click Preview in the Preview group to see all animations on the slide play. You can also see the animations play in Reading View and in Slide Show view. Slides that include an animation display a star icon beneath the slide when viewed in Slide Sorter view or the Slides tab in Normal view.

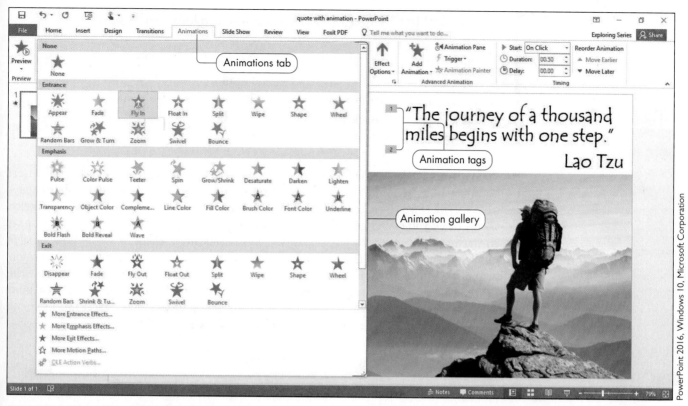

FIGURE 1.27 Animation Gallery

PowerPoint's Animation Painter feature enables you to copy an animation from one object to another. Animation Painter picks up the animation from the first object and applies it to the second on the same slide or a different slide.

> **To apply an animation to text or other objects, complete the following steps:**
>
> 1. Select the object that has the animation effect you want to copy to another object.
> 2. Click Animation Painter in the advanced Animation group on the Animations tab.
> 3. Click the text or object to which you want to apply the animation.

> **TIP: EFFECTIVELY ADDING TRANSITIONS, ANIMATIONS, AND SOUND**
> When you select transitions, sounds, and animations, remember that too many sounds, transitions, and animations can be distracting. The audience will be wondering what is coming next rather than paying attention to your message. The speed of the transition is important, too—very slow transitions will lose the interest of your audience. Too many sound clips can be annoying. Consider whether you need to have the sound of applause with the transition of every slide. Is a typewriter sound necessary to keep your audience's attention, or will it grate on their nerves if it is used on every word? Ask someone to review your presentation and let you know of any annoying or jarring elements.

Inserting a Header or Footer

STEP 5 ❯❯ The date of the presentation, the presentation audience, a logo, a company name, and other identifying information are very valuable, and you may want such information to appear on every slide, handout, or notes page. Use the Header and Footer feature to do this. The header generally appears at the top of pages in a handout or on a notes page, while a footer generally appears at the bottom of slides in a presentation or at the bottom of pages in a handout or on a notes page. Because the theme controls the placement of the header/footer elements, you may find headers and footers in various locations on the slide.

To insert text in a header or footer, complete the following steps:

1. Click the Insert tab.
2. Click Header & Footer in the Text group.
3. Click the Slide tab or the Notes and Handouts tab.
4. Click desired options and enter desired text.
5. Click Apply to All to add the information to all slides or pages, or if you are adding the header or footer to a single slide, click Apply.

With the Header and Footer dialog box open, click the Date and time check box to insert the current date and time signature. Click Update automatically if you want the date always to be current. Once you select Update automatically, you can select the date format you prefer. Alternatively, you can choose the option to enter a fixed date to preserve the original date, which can help you keep track of versions. Click the Slide number check box to show the slide number on the slide. Click the Footer check box and then click in the Footer box to enter information. The Preview window enables you to see the position of these fields. Always note the position of the fields, as PowerPoint layouts vary considerably in header and footer field positions. If you do not want the header or footer to appear on the title slide, select *Don't show on title slide*. Figure 1.28 shows the Slide tab of the Header and Footer dialog box.

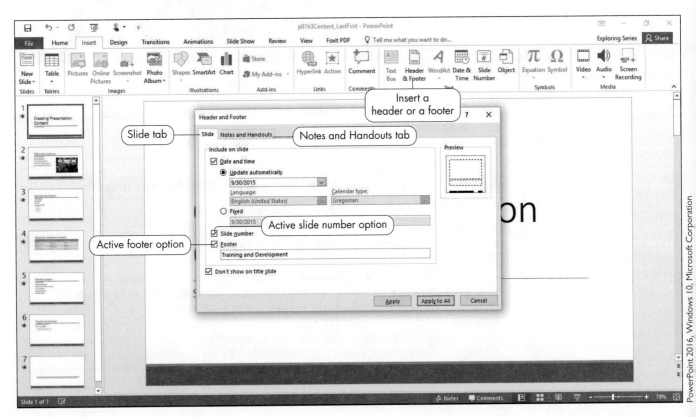

FIGURE 1.28 Header and Footer Dialog Box

The Notes and Handouts tab contains the same date/time options as the Slide tab, but it also gives you an option for a header. As you activate the fields, the Preview window shows the location of the fields. The header field is located in the upper-left corner of the printout. The date and time are located on the upper-right. The footer field is on the lower-left and the page number is located on the lower-right.

Quick Concepts

8. Explain why adding media objects to a PowerPoint slide show is important. *p. 98*

9. How does a table organize information? *p. 97*

10. Describe three benefits that can occur when objects are animated in a slide show. *p. 100*

11. Give an example of when you would use the Update automatically option in the Header and Footer feature. When would you use the Fixed date option? *p. 102*

Hands-On Exercises

Skills covered: Add a Table • Insert Media Objects • Apply Transitions • Animate Objects • Insert a Footer

3 Presentation Enhancement

You decide to strengthen the slide show by adding a table and an online picture that will help state employees stay interested in the presentation and retain the information longer. You insert a table, add a picture, apply a transition, and animate the picture you have included. Finally, you create a slide footer and a Notes and Handouts header and footer.

STEP 1 ›› ADD A TABLE

To organize the list of objects that can be added to a PowerPoint slide, you create a table on a new slide. Listing these objects as bullets would take far more space than a table takes. Refer to Figure 1.29 as you complete Step 1.

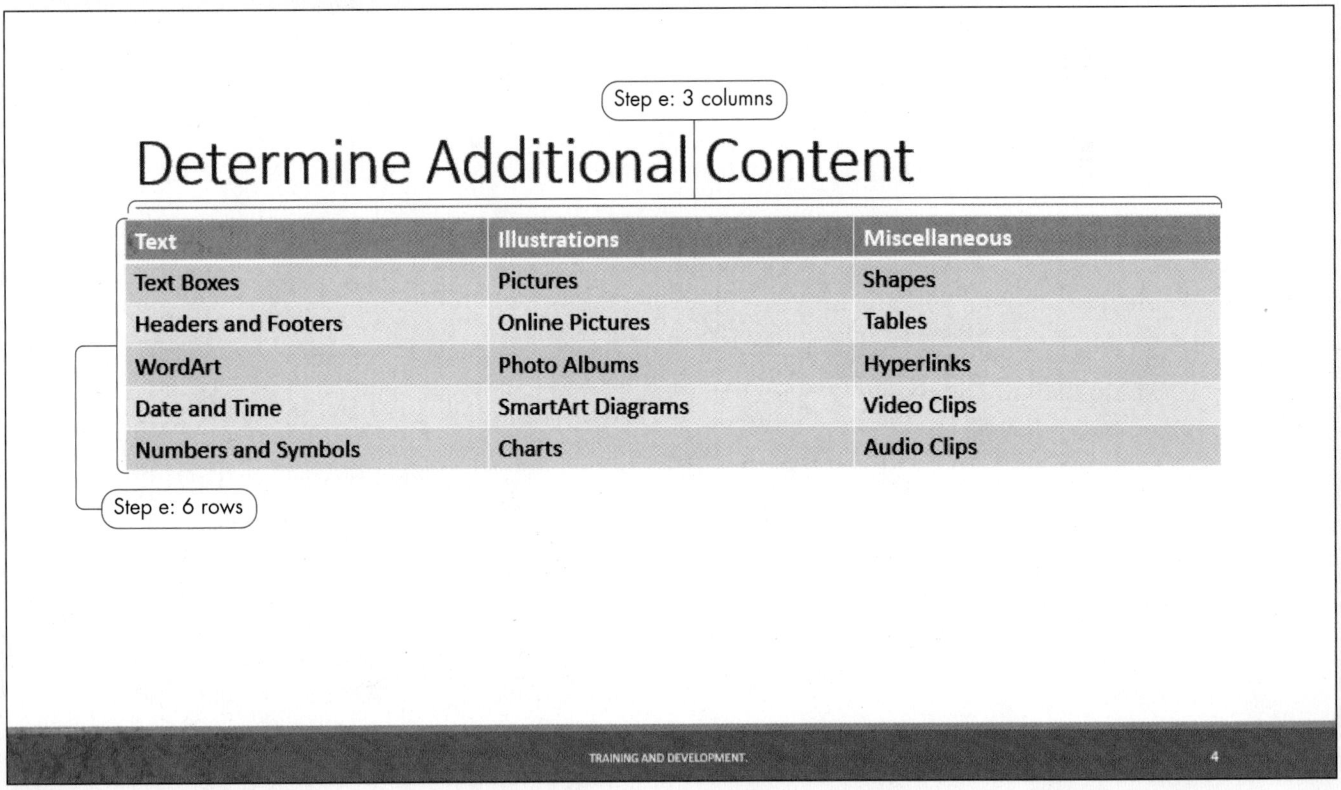

Step e: 3 columns

Determine Additional Content

Text	Illustrations	Miscellaneous
Text Boxes	Pictures	Shapes
Headers and Footers	Online Pictures	Tables
WordArt	Photo Albums	Hyperlinks
Date and Time	SmartArt Diagrams	Video Clips
Numbers and Symbols	Charts	Audio Clips

Step e: 6 rows

TRAINING AND DEVELOPMENT.   4

PowerPoint 2016, Windows 10, Microsoft Corporation

FIGURE 1.29 PowerPoint Table

a. Open *p01h2Content_LastFirst* if you closed it after the last Hands-On Exercise and save it as **p01h3Content_LastFirst**, changing h2 to h3.

b. Click **Slide 5** and click **New Slide** in the Slides group.

A new slide with the Title and Content layout is inserted after Slide 5.

c. Click the **title placeholder** and type **Determine Additional Content**.

d. Click **Insert Table** in the content placeholder in the center of the slide.

The Insert Table dialog box opens.

e. Set the number of columns to **3** and the number of rows to **6** and click **OK**.

PowerPoint creates the table and positions it on the slide. The first row is formatted differently from the other rows so that it can be used for column headings.

f. Type **Text** in the upper-left cell of the table. Press **Tab** to move to the next cell and type **Illustrations**. Press **Tab**, type **Miscellaneous**, and then press **Tab** to move to the next row.

g. Type the following text in the remaining table cells, pressing **Tab** after each entry.

Text Boxes	**Pictures**	**Shapes**
Headers and Footers	**Online Pictures**	**Tables**
WordArt	**Photo Albums**	**Hyperlinks**
Date and Time	**SmartArt Diagrams**	**Video Clips**
Numbers and Symbols	**Charts**	**Audio Clips**

h. Save the presentation.

STEP 2)) INSERT MEDIA OBJECTS

In this step, you insert a picture and then resize it to better fit the slide. The picture you insert relates to the topic and adds visual interest. Refer to Figure 1.30 as you complete Step 2.

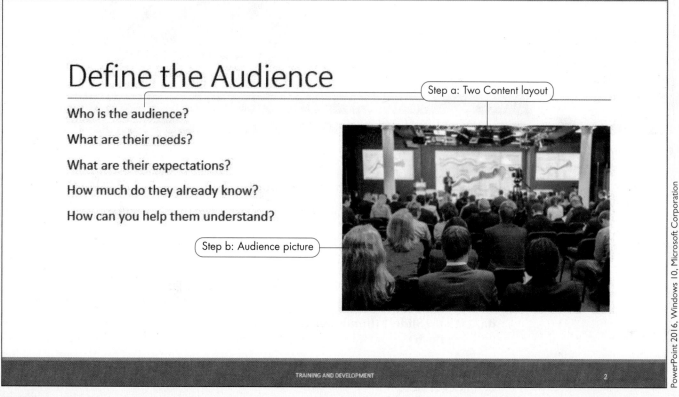

FIGURE 1.30 Online Picture Inserted

a. Display **Slide 2**, click **Layout** in the Slides group on the Home tab, and then click the **Two Content layout**.

Changing the layout for this slide will better accommodate the photo you will add in the next step.

b. Click the **Pictures icon** in the right content placeholder, navigate to the folder containing your student data files, and then select *p01h3Audience*. Refer to Figure 1.30 for a sample image. Click **Insert**.

c. Save the presentation.

To add motion when one slide changes into another, you apply a transition to all slides in the presentation. You select a transition that is not distracting but that adds emphasis to the slide show. You will also include a sound as the transition occurs. Refer to Figure 1.31 as you complete Step 3.

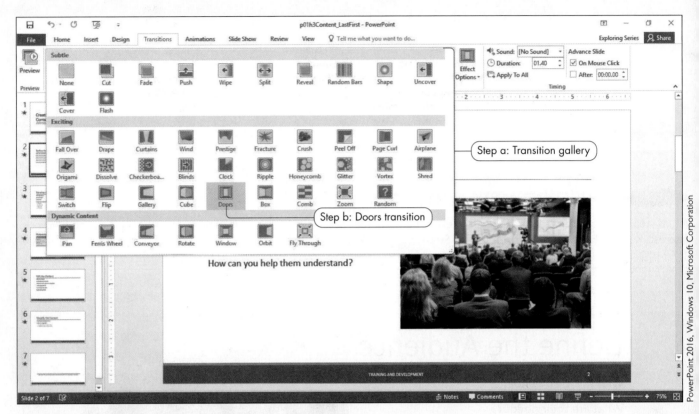

FIGURE 1.31 Transition Gallery

a. Click the **Transitions tab** and click **More** in the Transition to This Slide group.

The Transition gallery displays.

b. Click **Doors** under Exciting.

c. Click **Apply to All** in the Timing group.

The transition effect will apply to all of the slides in the presentation. Notice that a star has been added next to the thumbnail of each slide where a transition has been applied.

d. Select the **Slide 1 thumbnail**, click the **Sound arrow** in the Timing group, and then select **Push**.

The Push sound will play as Slide 1 enters when in Slide Show view.

e. Click **Preview**.

The Transition effect will play along with the sound for the first slide.

> **TROUBLESHOOTING:** If you are completing this activity in a classroom lab, you may need to plug in headphones or turn on speakers to hear the sound.

f. Save the presentation.

STEP 4 » ANIMATE AN OBJECT

You add animation to your slide show by controlling how individual objects such as lines of text or images enter or exit the slides. Refer to Figure 1.32 as you complete Step 4.

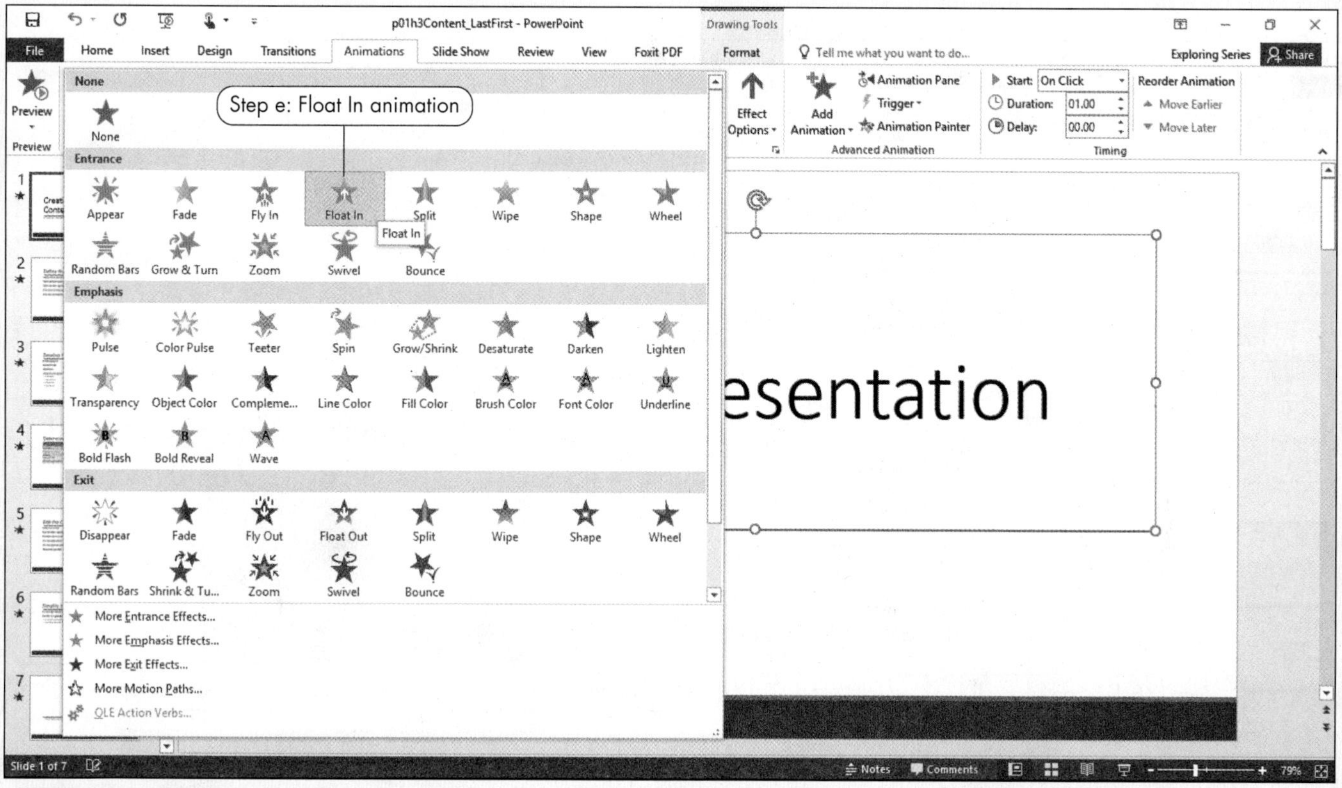

FIGURE 1.32 Title Placeholder with Animation

a. Select the **title placeholder** on Slide 1.

b. Click the **Animations tab** and click **More** in the Animation group.

c. Click **Float In** (under Entrance).

The Float In animation is applied to the title placeholder.

d. Select the **picture** on Slide 2.

You decide to apply and modify the Zoom animation and change the animation speed.

e. Click **More** in the Animation group and click **Zoom** (under Entrance).

f. Click **Effect Options** in the Animation group and select **Slide Center**.

The picture now grows and zooms from the center of the slide.

g. Save the presentation.

STEP 5 » CREATE A HANDOUT FOOTER

Because you are creating this presentation for the Training and Development department, you include this identifying information in a slide footer. You also decide to include your personal information in a Notes and Handouts header and footer. Refer to Figure 1.33 as you complete Step 5.

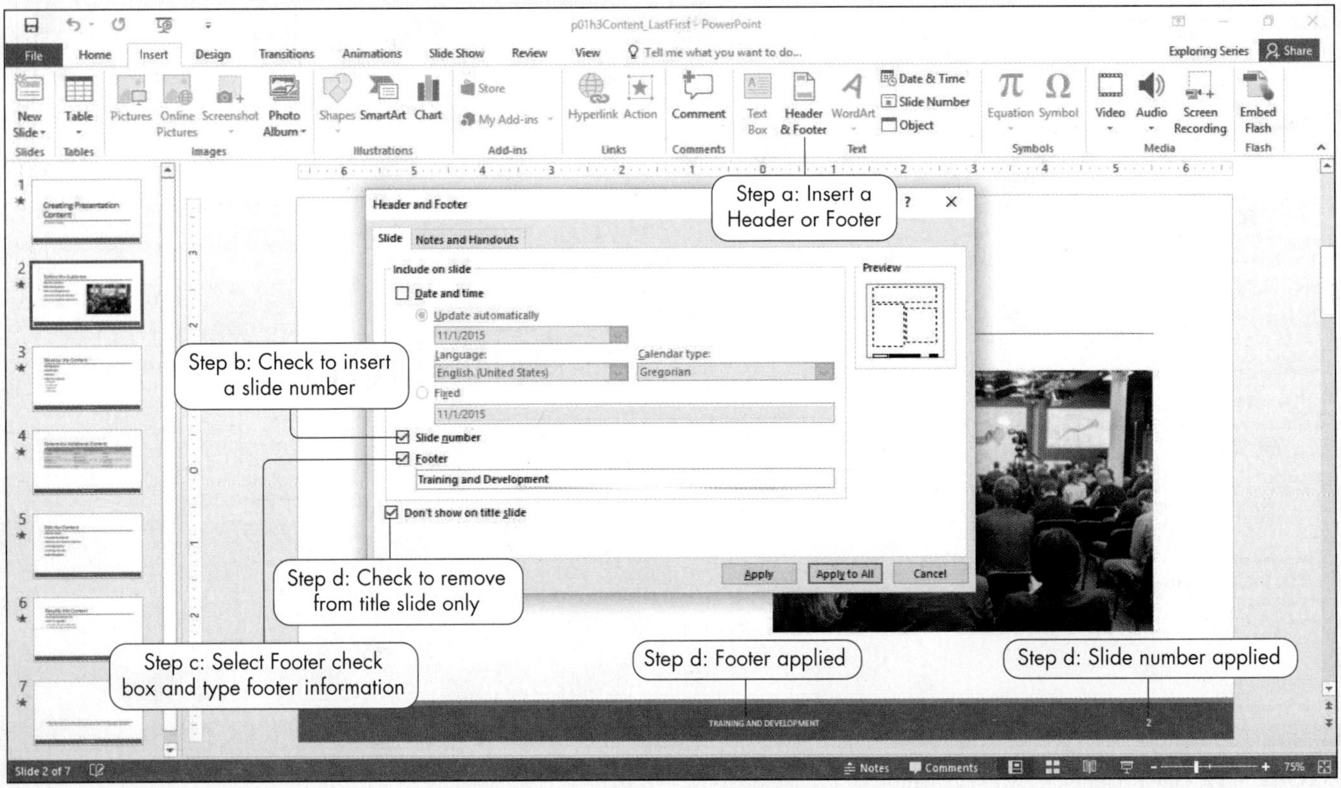

FIGURE 1.33 Slide Footer

a. Click the **Insert tab** and click **Header & Footer** in the Text group.

The Header and Footer dialog box opens, with the Slide tab active.

b. Click **Slide number check box** to select it.

The slide number will now appear on each slide. Note the position of the slide number in the Preview window: lower-right corner of the slide. The theme determined the position of the slide number.

c. Click the **Footer check box** to select it and type **Training and Development**.

Training and Development will appear on each slide. Note the position of the footer in the Preview window: bottom center of the slide.

d. Click the **Don't show on title slide** check box to select it and click **Apply to All**.

The slide footer and page number appear on all slides except the title slide.

e. Save the presentation. Keep the presentation open if you plan to continue with the next Hands-On Exercise. If not, close the presentation and exit PowerPoint.

Navigation and Printing

In the beginning of this chapter, you opened a slide show and advanced one by one through the slides by clicking the mouse. Audiences may ask questions that can be answered by going to another slide in the presentation. As you respond to the questions, you may find yourself jumping back to a previous slide or moving forward to a future slide. You may even find that during your presentation you wish to direct your audience's attention to a single area of a slide. PowerPoint's navigation options enable you to maneuver through a presentation easily.

To help your audience follow your presentation, you can choose to provide them with a handout. Various options are available for audience handouts. Be aware of the options, and choose the one that best suits your audience's needs. You may distribute handouts at the beginning of your presentation for note taking or provide your audience with the notes afterward.

In this section, you will run a slide show and navigate within the show. You will practice a variety of methods for advancing to new slides or returning to previously viewed slides. You will annotate a slide during a presentation and will change from screen view to black-screen view. Finally, you will print handouts of the slide show.

Navigating a Slide Show

STEP 1 ▶▶ PowerPoint provides multiple methods to advance through the slide show. You can also go back to a previous slide or jump to a specific slide, if needed. Use Table 1.2 to identify navigation options, and then experiment with each navigation method. Find the method that you are most comfortable using and stay with that method.

TABLE 1.2 Navigation Options

Navigation Option	Mouse	Keyboard	On-Screen
Advance to next slide or animation	Left-click	Press spacebar Press Page Down Press N Press down or right arrow Press Enter	Click right arrow
Return to previous slide or animation	Right-click, choose Previous	Press Backspace Press Page Up Press P Press up or left arrow	Click left arrow
End slide show	Right-click, choose End Show	Press Esc Press Ctrl+Break	Click … , choose End Show
Go to specific slide	Right-click, click See All Slides, click slide	Type slide number, press Enter	Click <art> select slide.
Zoom in	Right-click, click Zoom In, move pointer to highlight area, click	+ or Ctrl ++	Click Magnifying glass icon, move pointer to highlight area, click
Zoom out	Right-click	Press Esc	

The See All Slides command displays all of your slides so you can easily identify and select the slide to which you want to go. You can access the See All Slides command in the navigation controls on the lower-left corner of the screen. Once you see all of the slides, you can click the slide of your choice.

To move to a specific slide on the screen using the See All Slides command, complete the following steps:

1. Right-click a slide while in Slide Show view.
2. Click See All Slides.
3. Click the slide you want to display.

If an audience member asks you a question that is best explained by a chart or diagram you have on a slide in your presentation, you can zoom in on a single section of the slide to answer the question. Figure 1.34 displays a slide in Slide Show view with an area highlighted for zooming on the left and a slide with the zoomed area on the right.

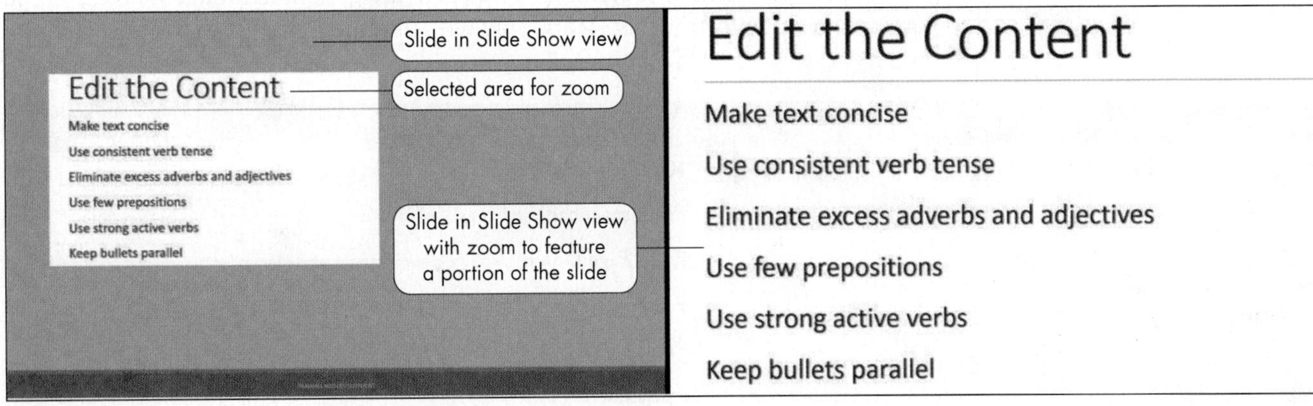

Slide in Slide Show view	
Edit the Content — Selected area for zoom	# Edit the Content
Make text concise	Make text concise
Use consistent verb tense	Use consistent verb tense
Eliminate excess adverbs and adjectives	Eliminate excess adverbs and adjectives
Use few prepositions — Slide in Slide Show view with zoom to feature a portion of the slide	Use few prepositions
Use strong active verbs	Use strong active verbs
Keep bullets parallel	Keep bullets parallel

PowerPoint 2016, Windows 10, Microsoft Corporation

FIGURE 1.34 Zoom to Emphasize Part of a Slide

To enlarge a section of a slide on the screen, complete the following steps:

1. Navigate to the slide.
2. Point to the lower-left side of the screen to display the navigation controls.
3. Click the magnifying glass icon in the navigation controls on the lower-left corner. This will display a highlighted rectangular area on your slide.
4. Move the rectangular box over the area of the slide you want to emphasize. (Figure 1.34 shows the rectangular box.)
5. Click Esc to return to Normal view.

After the last slide in your slide show displays, the audience sees a black slide. This slide has two purposes: It enables you to end your show without having your audience see the PowerPoint design screen, and it cues the audience to expect the room lights to brighten. If you need to blacken the screen at any time during your presentation, you can press B. (If you blacken the screen in a darkened room, you must be prepared to quickly brighten some lights.) When you are ready to start your slide show again, simply press B again.

If you prefer bringing up a white screen, press W. White is much harsher on your audience's eyes, however. Only use white if you are in an extremely bright room. Whether using black or white, you are enabling the audience to concentrate on you, the speaker, without the slide show interfering.

Annotate the Slide Show

STEP 2 ▶▶ You may find it helpful to add *annotations* (notes or drawings) to your slides during a presentation. You can draw directly on your slide using the Pen tool. You can underline or circle words to call attention to them, draw an arrow to an object, or draw a simple illustration.

To add annotations, complete the following steps:

1. Point to the lower-left side of the slide to display the slide show controls.
2. Click the Pen tool to display the options for annotating a slide, or right-click a slide in Slide Show view.
3. Point to Pointer Options.
4. Click Pen or Highlighter.
5. Press and hold the left mouse button and write or draw on the screen.

To change the ink color for the Pen or Highlighter, complete the following steps:

1. Right-click on a slide to display the shortcut menu.
2. Point to Pointer Options.
3. Click Ink Color.
4. Click the color of your choice.

To erase what you have drawn, press E. With each slide, you must again activate the drawing pointer, in order to avoid accidentally drawing on your slides. The annotations you create are not permanent unless you save the annotations when exiting the slide show and then save the changes upon exiting the file. You may want to save the annotated file with a different file name from the original presentation so that you have both versions of the presentation.

Rather than annotate a slide, you may simply want to point to a specific section of the screen. The laser pointer feature enables you to do this.

To use the laser pointer, complete the following steps:

1. Right-click a slide in Slide Show view.
2. Point to Pointer Options.
3. Click Laser Pointer.
4. Move the pointer to the desired position.
5. Press Esc to end the laser pointer.

TIP: ANNOTATING SHORTCUTS

Press Ctrl+P to change the pointer to a drawing pointer while presenting, and click and draw on the slide, much the same way your favorite football announcer diagrams a play. Use Page Down and Page Up to move forward and backward in the presentation while the annotation is in effect. Press Ctrl+A to return the pointer to an arrow.

Printing in PowerPoint

A printed copy of a PowerPoint slide show can be used to display speaker notes for reference during the presentation, for audience handouts or a study guide, or as a means to deliver the presentation if there were an equipment failure. A printout of a single slide with text on it can be used as a poster or banner. Figure 1.35 shows the print options. Depending on your printer and printer settings, the names may vary.

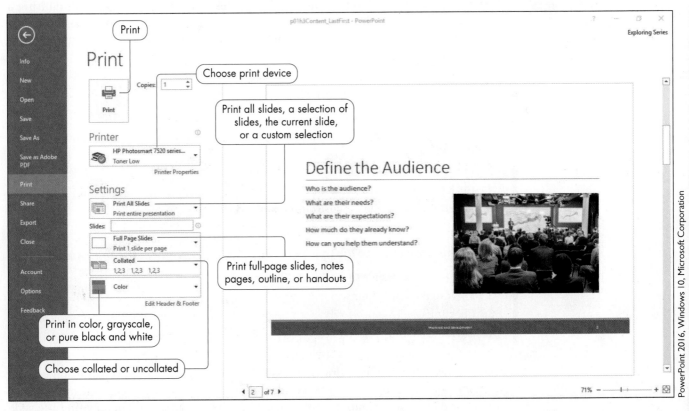

FIGURE 1.35 Print Options

To print a copy of the slide show using the default PowerPoint settings, complete the following steps:

1. Click the File tab and click Print.
2. Click the currently displayed printer to choose the print device you want to use.
3. Click Print All Slides and then select one of the options for the print area or for a custom range.
4. Click Full Page Slides to select the layout of the printout.
5. Click to select Collated or Uncollated.
6. Click Color to select Color, Grayscale, or Pure Black and White.
7. Click Print.

Print Full Page Slides

Use the Full Page Slides option to print the slides for use as a backup or when the slides contain a great deal of detail the audience needs to examine. You will be grateful for the backup if your projector bulb blows out or if your computer quits working during a presentation.

If you are printing the slides on paper smaller than the standard size, be sure to change the slide size and orientation before you print. By default, PowerPoint sets the slides for landscape orientation for printing so that the width is greater than the height (11" × 8 1/2"). If you are going to print a flyer or overhead transparency, however, you need to set PowerPoint to portrait orientation, to print so that the height is greater than the width (8 1/2" × 11").

To change your slide orientation, complete the following steps:

1. Click the Design tab.
2. Click Slide Size in the Customize group.
3. Click Customize Slide Size.
4. Click Portrait or Landscape in the Slides sized for section. You can also change the size of the slide as well as the orientation in this dialog box. If you want to create a custom size of paper to print, enter the height and width.

When you click Full Page Slides, several print options become available:

- Frame Slides: puts a black border around the slides in the printout, giving the printout a more polished appearance.

- Scale to Fit Paper: ensures that each slide prints on one page even if you have selected a custom size for your slide show, or if you have set up the slide show so that it is larger than the paper on which you are printing.

- High Quality: ensures that the shadows print if you have applied shadows to text or objects.

- Print Comments and Ink Markup: prints any comments or annotations; this option is active only if you have used added annotations to the slides.

After you click the File tab and click Print, you can determine the color option with which to print.

- Color: prints your presentation in color if you have a color printer or grayscale if you are printing on a black-and-white printer.

- Grayscale: prints in shades of gray, but be aware that backgrounds do not print when using the Grayscale option. By not printing the background, you make the text in the printout easier to read and you save ink or toner.

- Pure Black and White: prints in black and white only, with no gray color.

Print Handouts

STEP 3 ⟩⟩ The principal purpose for printing handouts is to give your audience something they can use to follow and take notes on during the presentation. With your handout and their notes, the audience has an excellent resource for the future. Handouts can be printed with one, two, three, four, six, or nine slides per page. Printing three slides per page is a popular option because it places thumbnails of the slides on the left side of the printout and lines on which the audience can write on the right side of the printout. Figure 1.36 shows the option set to Handouts and the Slides per page option set to 6.

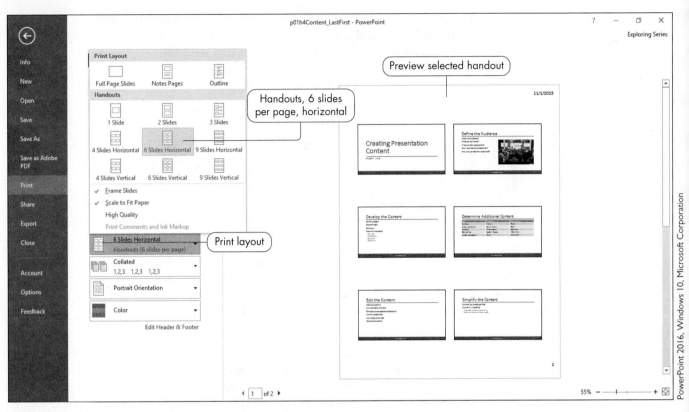

FIGURE 1.36 Setting Print Options

Print Notes Pages

If you include charts, technical information, or references in a speaker note, print a Notes Page if you want the audience to have a copy. To print a specific notes page, change the print layout to Notes Pages and click the Print All Slides arrow. Click Custom Range and enter the specific slide numbers to print.

Print Outlines

You may print your presentation as an outline made up of the slide titles and main text from each of your slides if you only want to deal with a few pages while presenting. The outline generally gives you enough detail to keep you on track with your presentation, but does not display speaker notes.

Remember, you, the speaker, are the most important part of any presentation. Do not rely on slides or handouts to get your message to the audience. These are supplemental materials for your presentation. The audience is there to hear YOU! Poor delivery will ruin even the best presentation. Speak slowly and clearly, maintain eye contact with your audience, and only use the information on the slides to guide you. Refer to the delivery tips in Table 1.3 before presenting.

TABLE 1.3 Practice the following delivery tips to gain confidence and polish your delivery

Before the presentation:

- Practice or rehearse your PowerPoint presentation until you are comfortable with the material and its corresponding slides.
- Know your material thoroughly. Glance at your notes infrequently.
- Arrive early to set up so you do not keep the audience waiting while you manage equipment.
- Have a backup in case the equipment does not work: Handouts work well.
- If appropriate, prepare handouts for your audience so they can relax and participate in your presentation rather than scramble taking notes.
- Make sure your notes pages acknowledge quotes, notes, data, and sources.

During the presentation:

- Speak naturally. Do not read from a prepared script or your PowerPoint Notes.
- Never post a screen full of small text and then torture your audience by saying, "I know you can't read this, so I will …"
- Speak to the person farthest away from you to be sure the people in the last row can hear you. Speak slowly and clearly.
- Vary your delivery. Show emotion or enthusiasm for your topic. If you do not care about your topic, why should the audience?
- Pause to emphasize key points when speaking.
- Look at the audience, not at the screen, as you speak to open communication and gain credibility.
- Use the three-second guide: Look into the eyes of a member of the audience for three seconds and then scan the entire audience. Continue doing this throughout your presentation. Use your eye contact to keep members of the audience involved.
- Blank the screen by pressing B or W at any time during your presentation when you want to solicit questions, comments, or discussion.
- Be judicious. Do not overwhelm your audience with your PowerPoint animations, sounds, and special effects. These features should enhance your message.

After the presentation:

- Thank the audience for their attention and participation. Leave on a positive note.

Quick Concepts

12. How do you go to a specific slide when displaying a slide show? *p. 109*

13. Describe at least three uses for a printed copy of a PowerPoint slide show. *p. 113*

14. Discuss three things you should do while delivering a presentation and why you think doing these things strengthens your presentation. *p. 115*

Hands-On Exercises

4 Navigation and Printing

To prepare for your presentation to Training and Development department employees, you practice displaying
the slide show and navigating to specific slides. You also annotate a slide and print audience handouts.

STEP I ›› NAVIGATE A SLIDE SHOW

In this step, you practice various slide navigation techniques to become comfortable with their use. You also review the Slide Show
Help feature to become familiar with navigation shortcuts. Refer to Figure 1.37 as you complete Step 1.

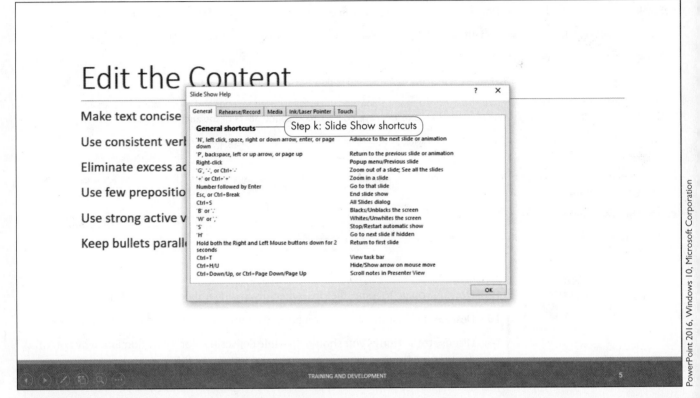

FIGURE I.37 Slide Show Help

a. Open *p01h3Content_LastFirst* if you closed it at the end of Hands-On Exercise 3 and save
   it as **p01h4Content_LastFirst**, changing h3 to h4.

b. Click the **Slide Show tab** and click **From Beginning** in the Start Slide Show group.

   Note the transition effect and sound you applied in Hands-On Exercise 3.

c. Press **Spacebar** to display the animated title.

d. Press the **left mouse button** to advance to Slide 2.

e. Press **Spacebar** to play the animation.

   Note that the picture animation plays on click.

f. Click the **Magnifying glass icon** and zoom in only on the text for Slide 2.

g. Press **Enter** to advance to Slide 3.

h. Press **N** to advance to Slide 4.

i. Press **Backspace** to return to Slide 3.

j. Press the number **5** and press **Enter**.

Slide 5 displays.

k. Press **F1** and read the Slide Show Help window showing the shortcut tips that are available during the display of a slide show.

TROUBLESHOOTING: If you are using a laptop, press FN+F1.

---

l. Close the Help window. Practice moving between slides using the shortcuts shown in Help.

STEP 2 ⟫ **ANNOTATE A SLIDE**

You practice annotating a slide using a pen, and then you remove the annotations. You practice darkening the screen and returning to the presentation from the dark screen. Refer to Figure 1.38 as you complete Step 2.

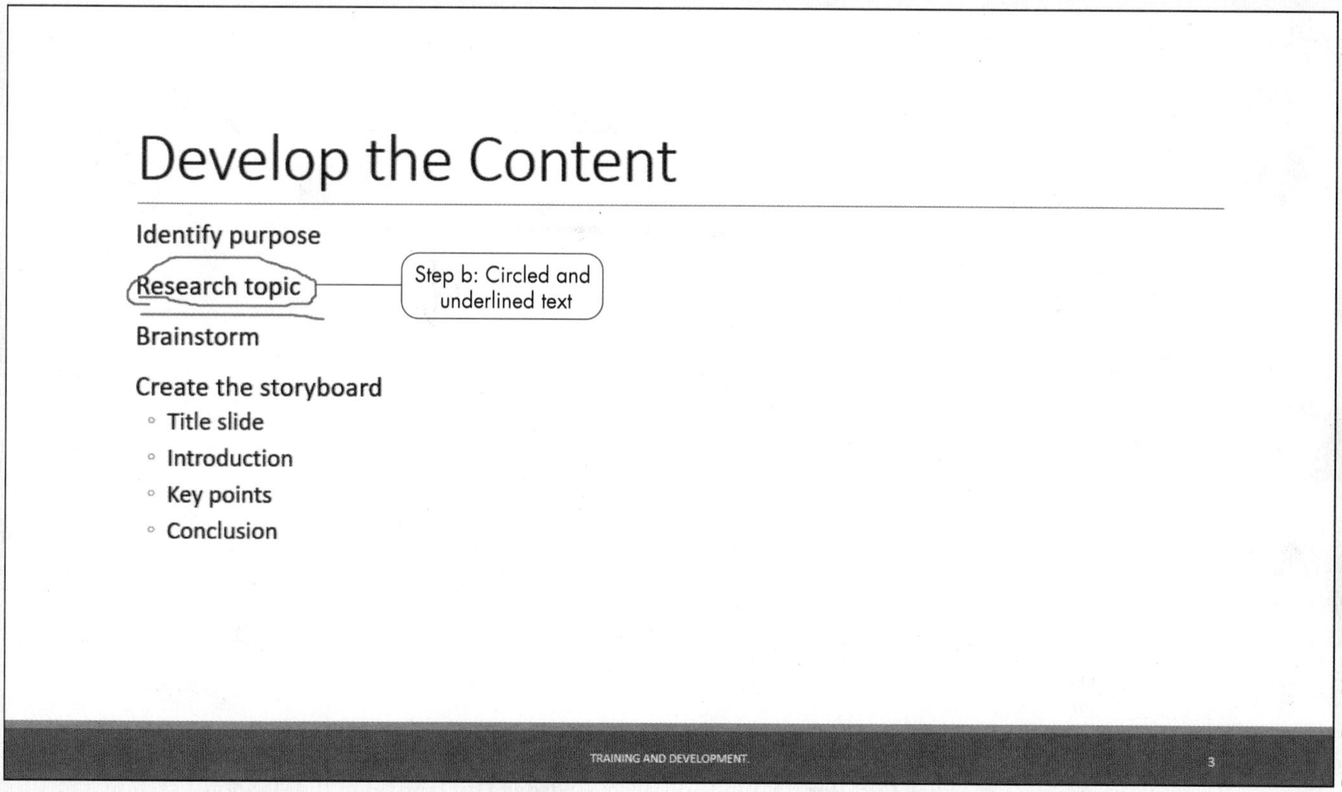

Develop the Content

Identify purpose

(Research topic) ——— Step b: Circled and underlined text

Brainstorm

Create the storyboard
- ° Title slide
- ° Introduction
- ° Key points
- ° Conclusion

TRAINING AND DEVELOPMENT.

3

PowerPoint 2016, Windows 10, Microsoft Corporation

FIGURE 1.38 Annotated Slide

a. Go to Slide 3 and then press **Ctrl+P**.

The pointer becomes a pen.

b. Circle and underline the words *Research topic* on the slide.

c. Press **E**.

The annotations erase.

d. Draw a box around *storyboard*.

e. Press **B**.

The screen blackens.

f. Press **B** again.

The slide show displays again.

g. Press **Esc** to end annotations.

h. Press **Esc** to end the slide show.

i. Save the presentation.

STEP 3 ›› PRINT HANDOUTS

To enable your audience to follow along during your presentation, you print handouts of your presentation. You know that audience members may want to keep your handouts for future reference. Refer to Figure 1.39 as you complete Step 3.

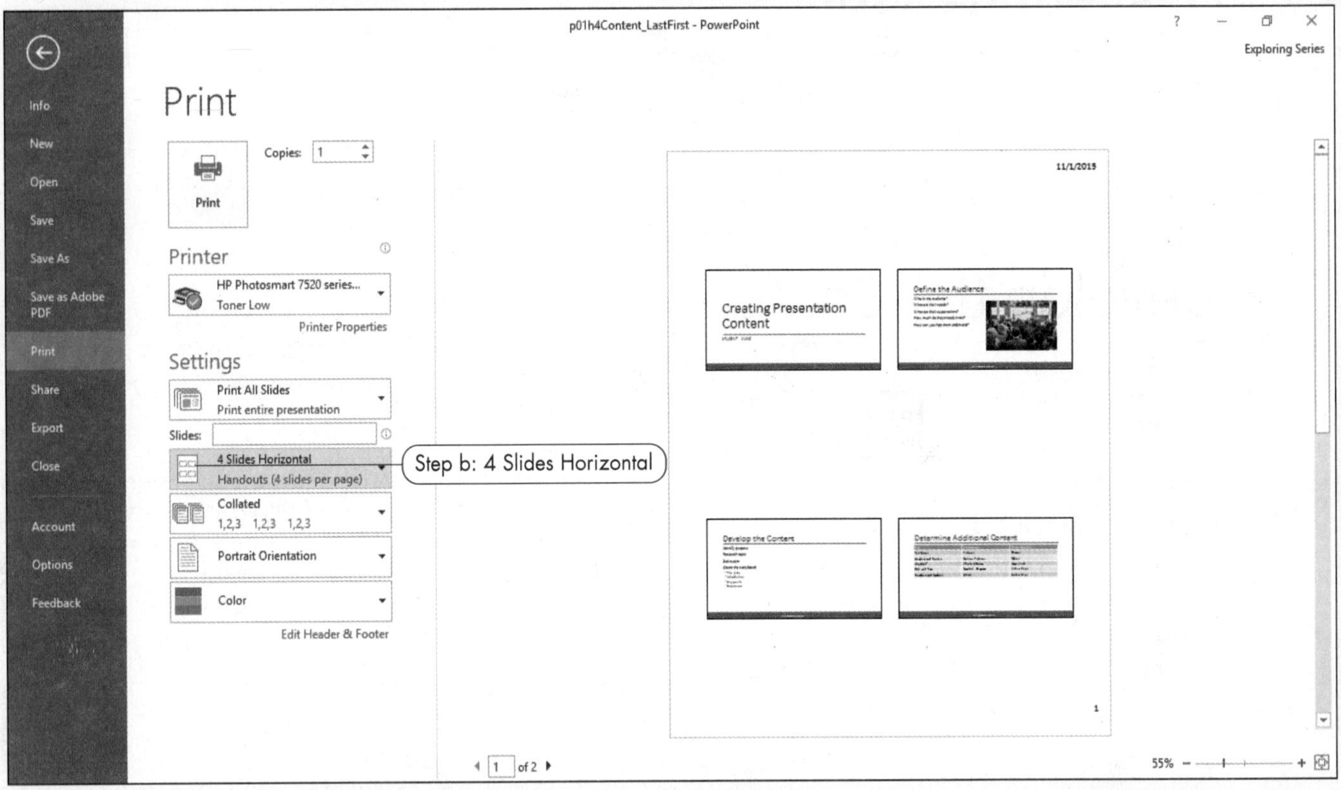

PowerPoint 2016, Windows 10, Microsoft Corporation

FIGURE 1.39 Audience Handout

a. Click **File** and then click **Print**.

b. Click **Full Page Slides** and select **4 Slides Horizontal** in the Handouts section.

> **TROUBLESHOOTING:** If you have previously selected a different print layout, Full Page Slides will be changed to that layout. Click the arrow next to the displayed layout option to select a different layout..

c. Click **Print** to print the presentation if requested by your instructor.

d. Save and close the file. Based on your instructor's directions, submit the following:

p01h1Intro_LastFirst

p01h1Intro_LastFirst.ppsx

p01h4Content_LastFirst

Chapter Objectives Review

After reading this chapter, you have accomplished the following objectives:

1. Open and view a PowerPoint presentation.

- Slide shows are electronic presentations that enable you to advance through slides containing content that will help your audience understand your message.
- Normal view, PowerPoint's default view, displays the slide deck in the Slides pane and the workspace in the Slide pane. A third pane, the Notes pane, may be displayed.
- Use PowerPoint views effectively: The Presentation Views group on the View tab enables you to access specialty views designed to help you work effectively and efficiently.
- Slide Sorter view displays thumbnails of slides to enable you to organize your presentation.
- Outline View enables you to easily create a presentation from an outline or view the outline of a presentation you have created.
- Notes Page view displays a thumbnail of the slide and any speaker notes that have been created.
- Slide Show view displays the slide show in full-screen view for an audience.
- Presenter view gives the presenter additional options while presenting, whereas the audience views the full-screen presentation.

2. Type a speaker note.

- Slides should contain only a minimum amount of information, and the speaker should deliver the majority of the information throughout the presentation.
- Speaker notes can be added to the PowerPoint presentation to provide the speaker with additional notes, data, or other comments to refer to during the presentation.

3. Save as a PowerPoint Show.

- By default, when you save a presentation it is saved with the file extension .pptx and, when opened, the presentation opens in Normal view for editing.
- You can save a presentation as a slide show, so that if you open it from a File Explorer winder, the file opens in Slide Show mode. Slide shows are saved with the file extension .ppsx.

4. Plan and prepare a presentation.

- Use a storyboard: Organize your ideas on a storyboard, and then create your presentation in PowerPoint.
- Review the storyboard to ensure that you use active voice, parallel construction, and follow the 7×7 guideline.
- Choose a theme: A theme applies coordinating colors, matching fonts, and effects to provide your presentation with a designer-quality look.

5. Add presentation content.

- Use slide layouts: When you add a slide, you can choose from a set of predefined slide layouts that determine the position of the objects or content on a slide.
- Placeholders hold content and determine the position of the objects on the slide.
- Create a title slide and introduction: The title slide should have a short title that indicates the purpose. An introduction slide will get the audience's attention.
- Create key point slides: The content of your presentation follows the title slide and the introduction. Create a slide for each of the key points in the storyboard.
- End with a summary or conclusion slide: The final slide of your presentation reviews the main points, restates the purpose, or invokes a call to action.

6. Review the presentation.

- Check spelling: Read each slide after typing its information, use the spelling feature, ask others to proofread the presentation, and display the presentation in Reading View then read each word out loud. Correct all spelling or word usage errors found for a professional presentation.
- Use the Thesaurus: The Thesaurus helps you make varied word choices.
- Check slide show elements: View the presentation in Slide Show view and check slide layouts, transitions, and animations to ensure that slides present information in a clear and orderly manner. Make changes as needed.
- Reorder slides: Change the order of the slides by dragging them to a new location in Slide Sorter view.

7. Add a table.

- Tables organize information in rows and columns to present structured data.

8. Insert media objects.

- Media objects such as online pictures, images, movies, and sound can be added to enhance the message of your slides and to add visual interest.

9. Apply animations and transitions.

- Apply transitions: Use transitions to control the movement of slides as one slide changes to another.
- Animate objects: Apply animation to objects to control the movement of an object on one slide.

10. Insert a header or footer.

- Headers and footers are used for identifying information on the slide or on handouts and notes pages. Header and footer locations vary depending on the theme applied.

11. Navigate a slide show.

- Various navigation methods advance the slide show, return to previously viewed slides, or go to specific slides.
- Annotate the slide show: Annotations are useful for adding comments to slides.

12. Print in PowerPoint.

- Print full page slides: Print full page slides for use as a backup or when the slides contain a great deal of detail the audience needs to examine.
- Print handouts: Handouts print miniatures of the slides using 1, 2, 3, 4, 6, or 9 slide thumbnails per page. Handouts are useful to an audience.
- Print notes pages: The Notes Page method prints a single thumbnail of a slide with its associated notes per page.
- Print outlines: Outline View prints the titles and main points of the presentation in outline format.

Key Terms Matching

Match the key terms with their definitions. Write the key term letter by the appropriate numbered definition.

a. Animation

b. Annotation

c. Layout

d. Normal view

e. Notes Page view

f. Placeholder

g. PowerPoint presentation

h. PowerPoint show

i. Presenter view

j. Reading View

k. Slide

l. Slide show

m. Slide Show view

n. Slide Sorter view

o. Status bar

p. Storyboard

q. Theme

r. Thumbnail

s. Transition

t. Variant

1. _____ Defines containers, positioning, and formatting for all of the content that appears on a slide. **p. 87**

2. _____ The default PowerPoint view, containing two panes that provide maximum flexibility in working with the presentation. **p. 70**

3. _____ A container that holds content. **p. 87**

4. _____ The movement applied to an object or objects on a slide. **p. 99**

5. _____ The most basic element of PowerPoint, analogous to a page in a Word document. **p. 70**

6. _____ A note or drawing added to a slide during a presentation. **p. 111**

7. _____ Located at the bottom of the screen in Normal view, this contains the slide number, spelling check, Notes, and Comments buttons, and options that control the view of your presentation. **p. 72**

8. _____ Used to view a slide show full screen, one slide at a time, for performing a thorough review of the slides without the full interface onscreen. **p. 75**

9. _____ A presentation saved with a .pptx extension. **p. 78**

10. _____ An electronic method to deliver your message using multiple slides. **p. 70**

11. _____ Used if the speaker needs to enter and edit large amounts of text for reference in the presentation. **p. 77**

12. _____ Uses a .ppsx extension. **p. 78**

13. _____ A specialty view that delivers a presentation on two monitors simultaneously. **p. 77**

14. _____ A variation of the theme you have chosen, using different color palettes and font families. **p. 86**

15. _____ The view used to deliver a completed presentation full screen to an audience, one slide at a time. **p. 76**

16. _____ A slide miniature. **p. 71**

17. _____ A specific animation that is applied when a previous slide is replaced by a new slide. **p. 99**

18. _____ Displays thumbnails of your presentation slides, allowing you to view multiple slides simultaneously. **p. 74**

19. _____ A visual design that helps you plan the direction of your presentation slides. **p. 83**

20. _____ A collection of formatting choices that includes colors, fonts, and special effects. **p. 86**

Multiple Choice

1. Which of the following features enable you to change the color of objects in your slide show without changing text?

    (a) Themes
    (b) Insert
    (c) Format Variants
    (d) Slide Color

2. Which of the following statements is *not* accurate about placeholders?

    (a) Placeholders may be resized.
    (b) All of the content contained in a placeholder is selected when the border of the placeholder is double-clicked.
    (c) Placeholder positions are determined by the slide layout and may not be changed.
    (d) Placeholders can contain text, pictures, tables, and more.

3. What is the term for theme alternatives using different color palettes and font families?

    (a) Palettes
    (b) Designs
    (c) Variants
    (d) Layouts

4. Which print method provides lined space for note taking by the audience?

    (a) Handout, 6 Slides Horizontal
    (b) Outline
    (c) Notes Pages
    (d) Handout, 3 Slides

5. Which of the following components are contained in Normal view?

    (a) Slide Sorter pane, Slides tab, and Reading pane
    (b) Slides pane and Slide pane
    (c) Slides tab, Slide pane, and Reading pane
    (d) Slide pane, Notes pane, and Slide Sorter pane

6. What view is the best choice if you want to reorder the slides in a presentation?

    (a) Slide Sorter view
    (b) Presenter view
    (c) Reading View
    (d) Slide Show view

7. Which of the following layouts is most commonly used when introducing the topic of the presentation and the speaker?

    (a) Blank
    (b) Title Slide
    (c) Comparison
    (d) 3 column

8. In reference to content development, which of the following points is *not* in active voice and is not parallel to the others?

    (a) Identify the purpose of the presentation.
    (b) Sketch out your thoughts on a storyboard.
    (c) Brainstorm your thoughts.
    (d) Your topic should be researched thoroughly.

9. Which feature will enable you to apply motion as one slide exits and another enters?

    (a) Transition
    (b) Timing
    (c) Animation
    (d) Advance

10. During a slideshow, which of the following would *not* focus audience attention on a specific object?

    (a) Put nothing on the slide but the object.
    (b) Apply an animation to the object.
    (c) Use the Pen tool to circle the object.
    (d) Apply a transition to the object.

Practice Exercises

1 Managing Your Stress

FROM SCRATCH The slide show you create in this practice exercise covers concepts and skills that will help you manage your stress as a college student. You create a title slide, an introduction, four slides containing main points of the presentation, and a conclusion slide. Then, you review the presentation and edit a slide so that the text of the bulleted items is parallel. Finally, you print a title page to use as a cover and notes pages to staple together as a reference. Refer to Figure 1.40 as you complete the exercise.

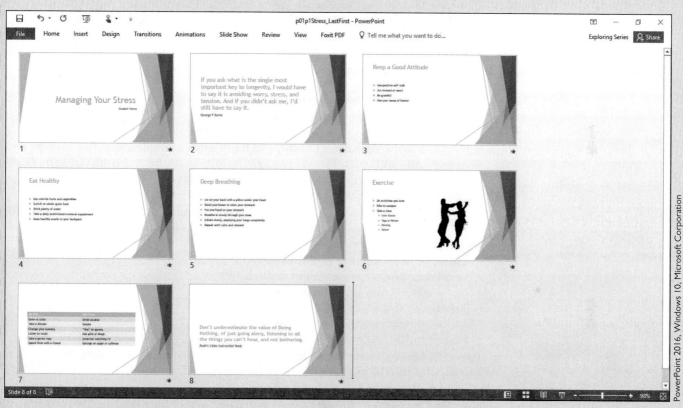

FIGURE 1.40 Managing Your Stress

a. Click **File** and click **New**.

b. Click the **Facet theme**. Click the variant with the blue color (upper-right corner) and click **Create**.

c. Save the presentation as **p01p1Stress_LastFirst**.

d. Click the **Insert tab**, click **Header & Footer** in the Text group, and then click the **Notes and Handouts tab** in the Header and Footer dialog box. Make the following changes:

   • Select the **Date and time check box** and ensure that *Update automatically* is selected.

   • Click to select the **Header check box** and type your name in the **Header box**.

   • Click the **Footer check box** and type your instructor's name and your class name in the **Footer box**. Click **Apply to All**.

e. Click in the **title placeholder** and type **Managing Your Stress**. Click in the **subtitle placeholder** and type your name.

f. Click the **New Slide arrow** in the Slides group on the Home tab to create a new slide (Slide 2) using the **Section Header layout** for the introduction of the slide show. You use a quote for the introduction. Type **Don't underestimate the value of Doing Nothing, of just going along, listening to all the things you can't hear, and not bothering.** in the title placeholder. Type **Pooh's Little Instruction Book** in the subtitle placeholder.

g. Click the **New Slide arrow** in the Slides group on the Home tab to create a new slide (Slide 3) using the **Title and Content layout** for the first main point of the slide show. Type **Keep a Good Attitude** in the title placeholder and type the following bulleted text in the content placeholder:

- **Use positive self-talk**
- **Instead of reacting, act**
- **Be thankful**
- **Use your sense of humor**

h. Click **New Slide** in the Slides group on the Home tab to create a new slide (Slide 4) for the second main point of the slide show. Type **Eat Healthy** in the title placeholder and type the following bulleted text in the content placeholder:

- **Eat colorful fruits and vegetables**
- **Switch to whole-grain food**
- **Drink plenty of water**
- **Take a daily multivitamin/mineral supplement**
- **Keep healthy snacks in your backpack**

i. Click **Notes** on the status bar. Drag the Splitter bar up to provide more room for note text. Type the following in the Notes pane: **Eat colorful fruits and vegetables. Eat blue, purple, and deep red fruits and vegetables every day to help keep the heart healthy and the brain functioning. Eat green vegetables to help prevent cancer. Eat yellow and green vegetables to help prevent age-related macular degeneration.**

j. Click **New Slide** in the Slides group on the Home tab to create a new slide (Slide 5) for the third main point of the slide show. Type **Deep Breathing** in the title placeholder and enter the following bulleted text in the content placeholder:

- **Lie on your back with a pillow under your head**
- **Bend your knees to relax your stomach**
- **Put one hand on your stomach**
- **Breathe in slowly through your nose**
- **Exhale slowly, emptying your lungs completely**
- **Repeat until calm and relaxed**

k. Type the following in the Notes pane for Slide 5: **Practice deep breathing daily until it becomes natural to you when you want to relax.**

l. Click the **New Slide arrow** in the Slides group on the Home tab to create a new slide (Slide 6) using the **Two Content layout** for the fourth main point of the slide show. Type **Exercise** in the title placeholder and enter the following text in the content placeholder on the left side of the slide following the title:

- **Do activities you love**
- **Bike to campus**
- **Take a class**
  - **Latin Dance**
  - **Yoga or Pilates**
  - **Fencing**
  - **Soccer**

m. Click the **Online Pictures icon** in the content placeholder on the right side of the slide. Type **Latin dancing** in the search box for Bing images. Press **Enter**. Click an image of dancers and then click **Insert** to insert the image.

> **TROUBLESHOOTING:** If you cannot locate an image of dancers that you like, use one of the other suggested classes from Step l as your search string.

n. Type the following in the Notes pane: **Learning more about an activity you are interested in gets you moving and is a good stress reliever.**

o. Click the **New Slide arrow** in the Slides group on the Home tab. Click **Title and Content** to create a new slide (Slide 7) for the last main point of the slide show. Select the **title place-holder** and press **Delete**.

p. Click the **Insert Table icon** in the content placeholder. Set Number of columns to **2** and Number of rows to **7**. Click **OK**. Type the following text in the columns, pressing **Tab** after each entry except the last:

Do this!	Not this!
Draw or color	Drink alcohol
Take a shower	Smoke
Change your scenery	"Veg" on games
Listen to music	Use pills or drugs
Take a power nap	Zone out watching TV
Spend time with a friend	Splurge on sugar or caffeine

q. Type the following in the Notes pane for Slide 7: **Use healthy activities to relieve your stress. Many activities students use to relieve stress actually cause them a great deal more stress.**

r. Click the **New Slide arrow** in the Slides group on the Home tab and add a new slide (Slide 8) using the **Section Header layout**. You use a quote for the conclusion slide of the slide show. Type **If you ask what is the single most important key to longevity, I would have to say it is avoiding worry, stress, and tension. And if you didn't ask me, I'd still have to say it.** in the title placeholder and then type **George F Burns** in the subtitle placeholder.

s. Click Slide 3. Note that the slide bullets are not in parallel construction. The second bulleted point needs to be changed to active voice. Select *Instead of reacting, act* and type **Act instead of react**.

t. Click **thankful** in the third bullet. Click the **Review tab** and click **Thesaurus**. Click **grateful** in the Thesaurus. Click the **arrow** and then click **Insert**.

u. Click the **Transitions tab** and click **More** in the Transition to This Slide group. Click **Push** in the Transition gallery. Click **Apply to All** in the Timing Group.

v. Click the **View tab**, and click **Slide Sorter** in the Presentation Views group. Drag **Slide 8**, the George Burns quote, so that it becomes **Slide 2**. Drag the new **Slide 3**, the Pooh quote, so that it becomes **Slide 8**.

w. Click the **File tab**, click **Print**, and then click **Full Page Slides**. Click **Full Page Slides** and select **Notes Pages**, click **Frame Slides**, and click **Print**, if your instructor asks you to submit printed slides.

x. Click the **Review tab** and click **Spelling**. Correct any errors.

y. Click the **File tab** and click **Save** to save the presentation as a normal PowerPoint presentation type.

z. Click the **File tab** and click **Save As**. In the Save As dialog box, change the Save as type to **PowerPoint Show** and click **Save**. Close the file. Based on your instructor's directions, submit the following:

p01p1Stress_LastFirst.pptx

p01p1Stress_LastFirst.ppsx

2 Tips for a Successful Presentation

FROM SCRATCH Your employer is a successful business person who has been asked by the local Chamber of Commerce to give tips for presenting successfully using a PowerPoint presentation. She created a storyboard of her presentation and has asked you to create the presentation from the storyboard. Refer to Figure 1.41 as you complete this exercise.

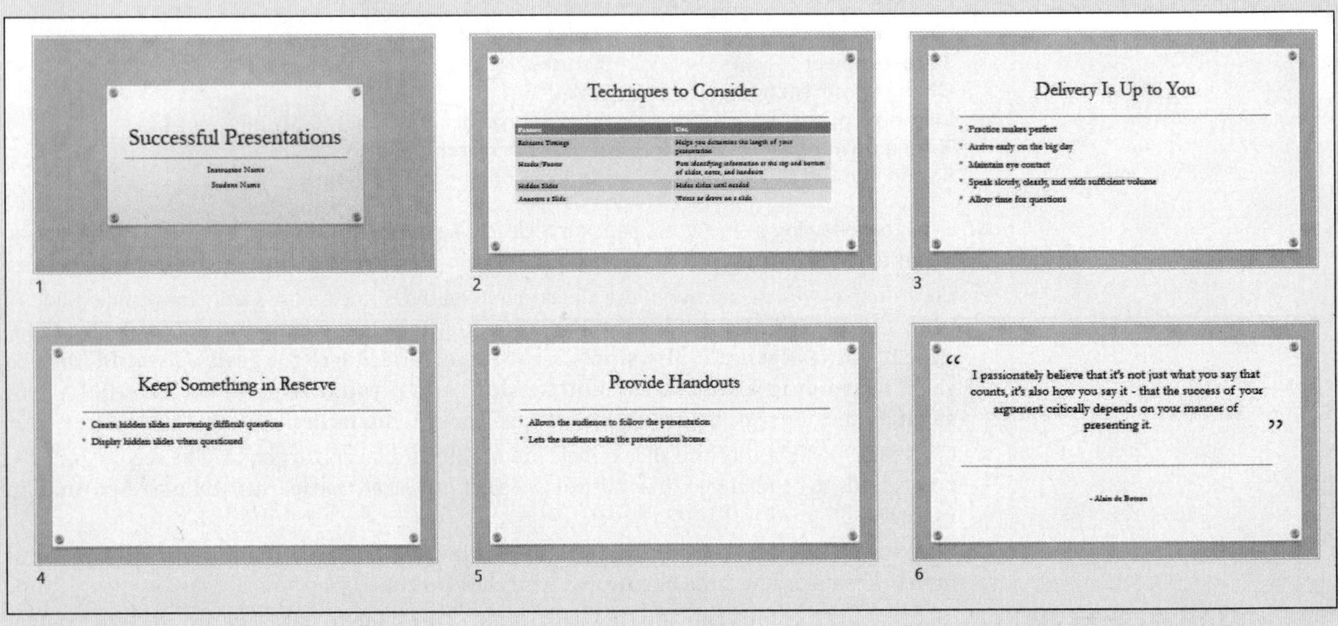

FIGURE 1.41 Successful Presentations

a. Click **File** and then click **New**.

b. Select **Organic**, select the variant in the lower-right corner, and then click **Create**.

c. Save the presentation as **p01p2Presenting_LastFirst**.

d. Click the **Insert tab**, click **Header & Footer**, and then click the **Notes and Handouts tab** in the Header and Footer dialog box.
   - Click to select the **Date and time check box** and click **Update automatically**.
   - Click to select the **Header check box** and type your name in the **Header box**.
   - Click to select the **Footer check box** and type your instructor's name and your class name. Click **Apply to All**.

e. Click in the **title placeholder** on Slide 1, and type **Successful Presentations**. Click in the **subtitle placeholder** and type your instructor's name. Press **Enter**. On the new line, type your name.

f. Click the **Home tab** and click **New Slide** in the Slides group.

g. Click in the **title placeholder** and type **Techniques to Consider**.

h. Click the **Insert Table icon** in the content placeholder and enter **2** columns and **5** rows.

i. Type the following information in the table cells, pressing **Tab** after each item except the last:

Feature	Use
Rehearse Timings	Helps you determine the length of your presentation
Header/Footer	Puts identifying information on the top and bottom of slides, notes, and handouts
Hidden Slides	Hides slides until needed
Annotate a Slide	Writes or draws on a slide

j. Click the **Home tab** and click **New Slide** in the Slides group. Type **Delivery Is Up to You** in the title placeholder.

PowerPoint 2016, Windows 10, Microsoft Corporation

k. Click in the **content placeholder** and type the following bulleted text:
- **Practice makes perfect**
- **Arrive early on the big day**
- **Maintain eye contact**
- **Speak slowly, clearly, and with sufficient volume**
- **Allow time for questions**

l. Click **New Slide** and type **Keep Something in Reserve** in the title placeholder.

m. Click in the **content placeholder** and type the following bulleted text:
- **Create hidden slides answering difficult questions**
- **Display hidden slides when questioned**

n. Click **New Slide** and type **Provide Handouts** in the title placeholder.

o. Click in the **content placeholder** and type the following bulleted text:
- **Allows the audience to follow the presentation**
- **Lets the audience take the presentation home**

p. Click the **New Slide arrow** and click **Quote with Caption**.

q. Type **I passionately believe that it's not just what you say that counts, it's also how you say it — that the success of your argument critically depends on your manner of presenting it.** in the title placeholder.

r. Click the **center placeholder** and press **Delete**.

s. Type **- Alain de Botton** in the bottom placeholder.

t. Select the **bottom placeholder** and then click the **Animations tab**. Click **Fly In** in the Animations group.

u. Click the **Review tab** and click **Spelling** in the Proofing group. Accept *Lets* in Slide 5. Review the presentation in Slide Show view to fix any spelling errors.

v. Click the **Slide Show tab** and click **From Beginning** in the Start Slide Show group. Press **Page Down** to advance through the slides. When you reach the last slide of the slide show, press the number **3** and press **Enter** to return to Slide 3.

w. Right-click, point to **Pointer Options**, and then click **Highlighter**. Highlight **Speak slowly, clearly, and with sufficient volume**.

x. Press **Page Down** to advance through the remainder of the presentation. Press **Esc** when you reach the black slide at the end of the slide show and click **Keep** to keep your slide annotations.

y. Click the **File tab**, click **Print**, and then click **Full Page Slides**. Click **Outline** and click **Print**, if your instructor asks you to submit printed slides.

z. Save and close the file. Based on your instructor's directions, submit p01p2Presenting_LastFirst.

Mid-Level Exercises

1 Planning Presentation Content

CREATIVE CASE

FROM SCRATCH

You received a high-definition mini action cam for Christmas and you have been using it to video your snowboarding, paddle boarding, and fishing trips. A friend who has seen your videos asked you to present a workshop on characteristics of HD mini action cams and why they are becoming commonly used, popular models, as well as tips for use. You create a slide show for your audience to view as you present.

a. Create a new presentation, applying the design theme of your choice to the presentation. Save the presentation as **p01m1Cam_LastFirst**.

b. Create a title slide that includes **Using a Mini Action Cam** as the title and your name and class in the subtitle placeholder.

c. Create a Title and Content slide using **Popular Models** as the title. Create the following two-column table in the content placeholder.

GoPros	Muvis
Garmins	Rolleis
Ghosts	iVues
Sonys	Panasonics
iONs	HTCs

d. Create a slide using the Content with Caption layout. Type **Characteristics** as the title, and list the following in the content placeholder on the left side of the slide: **Small, Lightweight, Tough, Attachable, POV video, Fish-eye perspective**. Insert an online picture of a mini action camera in the content placeholder on the right side of the slide.

e. Create a slide using the Two Content layout. Type **Popular Features** as the title. List the following in the content placeholder on the left side of the slide: **Slow motion, GPS tracking, Wrist remote, Waterproof casing**. List the following in the content placeholder on the right side of the slide: **Box cam style, Bullet cam style, Sunglasses mount, WiFi connectivity**.

f. Create a slide using the Title and Content layout. Type **Tips** as the title, and then type this list in the content placeholder:
   - **Know your mount**
   - **Practice running the camera by touch**
   - **Get the light right**
   - **Avoid water spots on the lens**

g. Create a slide using the Title and Content layout. Type **Sample Video** as the title. Use the Insert Video button on the palette of content options to insert the video *p01m1Video* located in your student files.

h. Change the view to Slide Sorter view, and then move Slide 3 (Characteristics) so that it becomes Slide 2. While in Slide Sorter view, assign the transition of your choice to all slides in the slide show. Note the star that appears under each slide that indicates the slide has a transition attached.

i. Double-click **Slide 2** to return to Normal view. Select the content placeholder that contains the list of characteristics. Apply the Wipe animation.

j. Change the view to Notes Page view. Add the notes for the speaker's reference as follows:

Slide	Note
2	Action cameras are small, lightweight cameras that are designed to attach to objects like helmets, surf or paddle boards, cars, sticks, and other objects to create point of view (POV) video.
4	When purchasing a mini action camera, determine how you are most likely to use the camera, then look at cameras that will provide those features.

5
- **Check to see where the mount is steadiest so you don't get a choppy video while getting the shot you want.**
- **Practice until you can operate the camera by touch, as different mounts make it impossible to see the buttons.**
- **Use camera settings for different lighting conditions.**
- **Apply an anti-beading solution to the lens to prevent water spots from forming.**

k. Add a slide number in the footer to all of the slides except the title slide. (Note: The slide number position on the slide will depend on the theme you selected.)

l. Review the slide show in Slide Show view to check spelling and word usage. Adjust layouts and placeholder location until all elements fit attractively and professionally on the slide.

m. Print notes pages.

n. Save and close the file. Based on your instructor's directions, submit p01m1Cam_LastFirst.

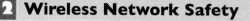

2 Wireless Network Safety

MyITLab®
Grader

FROM SCRATCH

You volunteer at the local community center. You have been asked to present to a group of young teens about staying safe when using wireless computer networks. You have researched the topic and using your notes you are ready to prepare your presentation.

a. Start a new presentation. Apply the Banded theme. Apply the black, blue, and green variant. Save the presentation as **p01m2Wifi_LastFirst**.

b. Add **Wi-Fi Safety** as a footer on all slides except the title slide. Also include an automatically updated date and time and a slide number.

c. Create a Notes and Handouts header with your name and a footer with your instructor's name and your class name. Apply to all.

d. Add the title **WiFi Safety** in the title placeholder. Type **Keeping Your Personal Information Safe** in the subtitle placeholder.

e. Insert a new slide using the Two Content layout. Type **Wireless Fidelity (WiFi)** as the title.

f. Type the following into the left content placeholder:
- **Uses radio waves to exchange data wirelessly via a computer network**
- **Commonly found at coffee shops and other public places**
- **Also called hotspots**

g. Add an online picture to the right content placeholder: Search for **WiFi photo** in the search box. Insert the photo of your choosing.

h. Insert a new slide using the **Title and Content layout** as the third slide in the presentation. Type **WiFi Hotspot Security** as the title.

i. Type the following into the content placeholder:
- **Avoid unsecured networks if possible**
- **Don't access confidential information**
- **Set network locations to "Public"**
- **Keep firewall and antivirus software up-to-date**

j. Click **Notes** on the status bar. Add the following text to the Notes pane:

Although a number of threats exist when using public WiFi hotspots, there are several ways you can protect yourself and your computer.

k. Insert a new slide using the Blank layout as the fourth slide in the presentation.

l. Click the **Insert tab**, click **Table**, and then insert a table with four rows and two columns. Type the following text in the table:

Threat	Explanation
Identity Theft	Criminal act involving the use of your personal information for financial gain.
Hacking	Unauthorized access to a computer or network.
Malware	Software programs that are designed to be harmful. A virus is a type of malware.

m. Position the table at the approximate center of the slide.

n. Apply the **Fade transition** from the Subtle category to all slides in the slide show.

DISCOVER 🔍

o. Add the **Bounce animation** from the Entrance category to the content placeholder and then to the image on Slide 2. Start the animation for the image with the previous animation so they start at the same time.

p. Move Slide 4 so that it becomes Slide 3.

q. Review the presentation and correct any errors you find.

r. Print the handouts, three per page, framed.

s. Save and close the file. Based on your instructor's directions, submit p01m2Wifi_LastFirst.

3 Creating a Free Website and Blog for Your PowerPoint Experiences

COLLABORATION CASE ⌬

FROM SCRATCH ☕

Web 2.0 technologies make it easy for people to interact using the Internet. Web applications often combine functions to help us create our online identity, share information, collaborate on projects, and socialize. In this exercise, you will create an online identity for your use in your PowerPoint class, share information about your PowerPoint experience with others, and get to know a few of your classmates. You will create a website for use during your PowerPoint class, add information to the pages in your website, and then share the address of your site with others. You will also visit the websites of others in your class.

a. Open a Web browser and search for a site that enables you to create a free website or blog. For example: Google Sites, Web.com, Weebly, or any other free site.

b. Register for the site and then begin creating your site.

c. Enter a title for your website as follows: use your first name and last name followed by PPT to indicate this is your PowerPoint site.

d. Use whatever free design elements the site provides to create the look of your site.

e. Add a blog to your site. Add an entry to your blog that explains your previous experience with PowerPoint and why you have registered for this class. Search YouTube for a video about PowerPoint or presentation skills. Create a second blog entry about what you learned and include the link for others to view if interested.

f. Publish your website.

g. Exchange website addresses with at least three other students in your class. Visit your classmates' websites and leave a comment to indicate you have visited. Then, revisit your website to see what comments your classmates entered.

h. Email your instructor your website address so your instructor can visit your site.

Beyond the Classroom

Using Creative Commons

Research copyright law as it applies in education, and then research the nonprofit organization Creative Commons (CC). Prepare a slide show to present to others that explains what Creative Commons is and how it enables you to legally use online media in your slide show. Create a storyboard on paper outlining your slide show. Then, create a PowerPoint presentation named **p01b1CC_LastFirst** based on your storyboard. Include a title slide and at least four slides related to this topic. Choose a theme, transitions, and animations. Insert at least one appropriate online picture with an attribution to its creator. Include speaker notes on most slides as necessary. Create a handout header with your name and the current date. Include a handout footer with your instructor's name and your class name. Review the presentation to ensure there are no errors and that your transition and animations work by viewing each slide in Slide Show view. Print as full page slides, or as directed by your instructor. Save and close the file. Based on your instructor's directions, submit p01b1CC_LastFirst.

Polishing a Business Presentation

DISASTER RECOVERY

A neighbor has created a slide show to present to a local business explaining his company's services. He has asked you to refine the slide show so it has a more professional appearance. Open *p01b2Green* and save the file as **p01b2Green_LastFirst**. View the slide show. Note that the text is difficult to read because of a lack of contrast with the background, there are capitalization errors and spelling errors, the bulleted points are not parallel, and images are positioned and sized poorly. Select and apply a design theme and a variant. Modify text following the guidelines presented throughout this chapter. Reposition placeholders as needed. Size and position the images in the presentation or replace them with your choice of images. Text may be included in speaker notes to emphasize visuals, if desired. Apply a transition to all slides. Add a minimum of two animations. Make other changes you choose. Create a handout header with your name and the current date. Include a handout footer with your instructor's name and your class name. Review the presentation to ensure there are no errors by viewing each slide in Slide Show view. Save your file and then save it again as a PowerPoint show. Close the file. Print notes pages if directed by your instructor. Based on your instructor's directions, submit the following:

p01b2Green_LastFirst
p01b2Green_LastFirst.ppsx

Want'n Waffles is a small, successful mobile food business. The company was started by two culinary arts students and their families as a way to finance the students' college education. A year later they own three food trucks that sell breakfast waffles, waffle sandwiches, and dessert waffles. Street-food lovers line up around the block when the food trucks park in their neighborhood. The truck locations are advertised via Twitter and on Facebook so waffle lovers can follow the trucks from place to place. The business has increased its revenue and profits and the owners are looking to expand their operation by offering franchises in other college cities. They need to prepare a presentation for an important meeting with financiers.

Create a Title Slide

You add your name to the title slide, apply a theme, and create a slide for the Want'n Waffles mission statement.

a. Open *p01c1Waffles* and save it as **p01c1Waffles_LastFirst**.

b. Create a Notes and Handouts header with your name and a footer with your instructor's name and your class name. Include the date and time, updated automatically. Apply to all.

c. Replace YOUR NAME in the **subtitle placeholder** on Slide 1 with your name.

d. Apply the **Retrospect theme**.

Add Content

You add the information about your business as content slides.

a. Create a new slide after Slide 1 using the **Section Header layout**. Type the following in the title placeholder: **Want'n Waffles provides gourmet quality food prepared on the spot in a clean mobile truck.**

b. Double-click the border of the title placeholder, then change the font size to **60 pt** and apply **Italic**.

c. Add the following speaker note to Slide 3: **We can sell inexpensive breakfasts, lunches, and desserts because our overhead is low. We don't have to pay for a "brick and mortar" restaurant with all of the expenses of a building. Because we don't have to pay for servers, prices stay down while sales increase. Our trucks are a favorite with employees because they get quick service, excellent food, and the convenience of a location close to them. We are mobile so we can change location as needed to increase sales. Best of all, our food is FUN!**

Create Tables

You create a table to show the increase in sales from last year to this year and a table showing a few of your waffle specialties.

a. Create a table of four columns and seven rows in the content placeholder on Slide 4. Type the data from the table below in your table.

TABLE 1

Category	Last Year	This Year	Increase
Breakfast waffles	$125,915	$255,856	$129,941
Breakfast crepes	45,404	97,038	51,634
Waffle-wiches	61,510	138,555	77,045
Waffle cookies	22,100	43,200	21,100
Dessert waffles	151,012	246,065	95,053
Totals	$405,941	$780,714	$374,773

b. Apply the **Medium Style 2 – Accent 2** Table Style to the table.

c. Format the table text font to **18 pt**. Center align the column headings and right align all numbers.

d. Add a new slide after Slide 4 that uses the **Comparison layout**. Type **Want'n Waffle Specialties** as the title of the slide, use **Luncheon Waffles** as the heading for the left column, and type **Dessert Waffles** as the heading for the right column. Type the data from Table 2 below in your table and apply the same formatting to this table that you applied in Step c.

TABLE 2

Chicken and Waffle Grilled Cheese	Waffle Confetti Cake
PB&J Waffle Panini	Waffled Banana Bread
Zucchini-Parmesan Waffle	Chocolate Chip Waffle Cookies
Maple Bacon Waffle	Waffled Carrot Cake
Margherita Waffle Pizza	Waffle Sundae

e. View the slide show in Slide Sorter view.

f. Move Slide 5 (A Natural Franchise) so that it becomes Slide 3.

g. Note that Slide 2 includes the mission statement as the introduction slide, Slides 3 through 7 cover the key points of the presentation and include supporting data, and Slide 8 uses a plan for the future as the conclusion (summary) slide.

Add an Online Picture and Animate Content

You want to include a picture of a waffle creation to inspire interest in the franchise. To emphasize the profits the business has realized, you add animations. To help the audience absorb the next steps on the summary slide, you animate the text.

a. Display Slide 3. Use the content placeholder on the right side to open Online Pictures. Use **waffles** as your search keyword in the search box. Locate an image of a waffle and insert it in the placeholder.

b. Use the same online picture of a waffle on the last slide of your slide show. Position the image in the lower-right portion of your slide, and size it appropriately.

c. Select the **Our first year was profitable box** on Slide 5 and apply the **Fly In entrance animation**.

d. Select the **Our second year was significantly better box** and apply the **Fly In entrance animation**. Change the Start option to **After Previous**.

e. Apply the **Fly In entrance animation** to the text content placeholder on Slide 8.

f. Check the spelling in the slide show, and review the presentation for any other errors. Fix anything you think is necessary.

Navigate and Print

You proofread the presentation in Slide Show view and check the animations. You notice an error on a slide and correct it. When all errors have been corrected, you print a handout with four slides per page.

a. Start the slide show and navigate through the presentation, experimenting with various navigation methods.

b. Note the parallel construction error on Slide 4. The third bulleted point, *Profits are increasing*, does not start with an active verb as the other bulleted points do.

c. Annotate the conclusion slide, *The Next Steps*, by underlining **detailed financial proposal** and circling **two** and **ten** with a red pen.

d. Exit the presentation and keep the annotations.

e. Use the Slides pane in Normal view to navigate to Slide 4. Modify the third bulleted point as follows: **Increase profits.**

f. Print a handout with four slides, horizontal per page if directed to print by your instructor.

g. Save the file as a presentation and as a show. Close the file. Based on your instructor's directions, submit the following:

p01c1Waffles_LastFirst
p01c1Waffles_LastFirst.ppsx

PowerPoint

Presentation Development

LEARNING OUTCOME   You will apply tools to create and modify a presentation.

OBJECTIVES & SKILLS: After you read this chapter, you will be able to:

CASE STUDY | The Wellness Education Center

The Wellness Education Center at your school promotes overall good health to students and employees. The director of the Center asked you to create two slide shows that she can use to deliver presentations to the campus community.

You create a presentation to inform campus groups about the Center by downloading a template with a wellness theme from Microsoft Office Online. You modify several of the layouts the template provides to customize the template to your needs. To concentrate on the content of the slides, you use Outline view to enter slide text and edit the presentation outline.

You create a second presentation for the Center using an outline the director created in Microsoft Word. You import the outline, supplement it with slides you reuse from another presentation, and divide the presentation into sections. Using standard slide show design guidelines, polish the presentation by editing the content and the theme.

PowerPoint 2016, Windows 10, Microsoft Corporation

FIGURE 2.1 Wellness Education Center Slide

CASE STUDY | The Wellness Education Center

Starting Files	Files to be Submitted
Blank presentation p02h3MedOutline p02h3Wellness p02h4Logo	p02h2Center_LastFirst p02h4Mission_LastFirst

Templates

One of the hardest things about creating a presentation is getting started. You may have a general idea of what you want to say but not how to organize your thoughts. Or you may know what you want to say but need help designing the look for the slides. PowerPoint's templates enable you to create professional-looking presentations and may even include content to help you decide what to say.

In this section, you will learn how to create a presentation using a template that you modify to fit your needs.

Creating a Presentation Using a Template

STEP 1 ▶▶ Templates and themes are not the same thing. A theme is a collection of design choices that includes colors, fonts, and special theme effects. A *template* is a file that includes the formatting elements like a background, a theme with a color scheme and font selections for titles and text boxes, and slide layouts that position content placeholders. Some templates include suggestions for how to modify the template, whereas others include ideas about what you could say to inform your audience about your topic. These suggestions can help you learn to use many of the features in PowerPoint.

PowerPoint offers templates online for you to use. You can quickly and easily download additional professional templates in a variety of categories. These templates were created by Microsoft, a Microsoft partner, or a member of the Microsoft community. You can select a suggested search term or type your own search term in the Search box. Then you can filter by category to narrow your search further. For example, you can download a template for a renewable energy presentation created by a Microsoft partner, an active listening presentation created by a Microsoft community member, or a business financial report created by Microsoft. Figure 2.2 shows four PowerPoint templates.

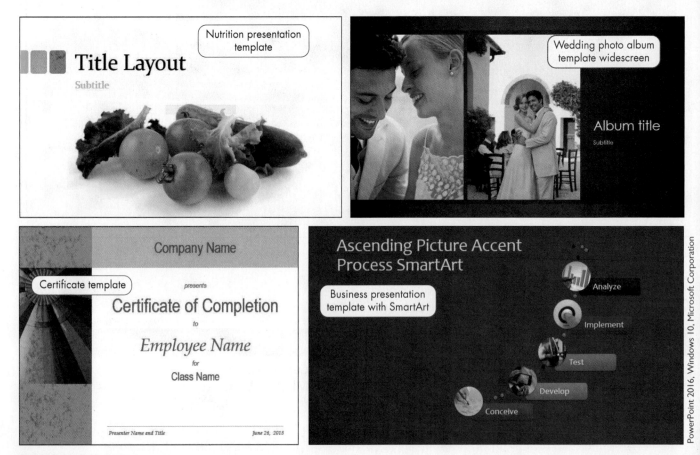

FIGURE 2.2 Templates

When you open PowerPoint you are presented with a variety of design themes from which to choose. If you want to use a template with suggested content or additional design themes, you need to search online.

To begin a presentation using a template, complete the following steps:

1. Start PowerPoint.
2. Click one of the suggested search terms, or click in the search box and type the text for which you would like to search. Press Enter. For example, you may want to search for Marketing templates, and thus you would type Marketing as your search term.
3. Click a template or theme to preview it in a new window.
4. Click Create to download the template. A new presentation file is created based on the template.

Figure 2.3 displays some of the templates available and where to search for templates and themes described in Step 2 above. Your view may show different template options, as Microsoft frequently updates the available templates.

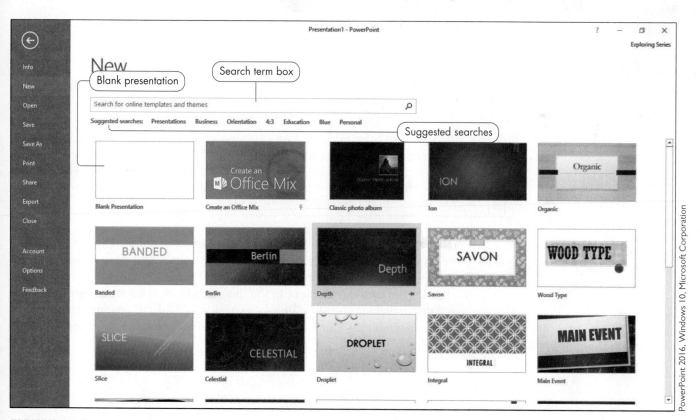

FIGURE 2.3 Templates and Themes

You can filter your results further by using one of the categories on the right side of the screen. For example, Figure 2.4 shows the search results for a search for Photo Albums. The column on the right shows several of the categories. Depending on your search criteria, you may also see non-PowerPoint templates in your search results.

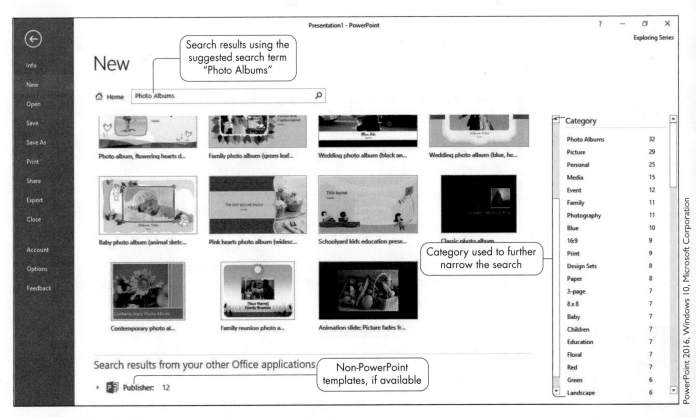

FIGURE 2.4 Template Categories

> **TIP: SEARCHING BY TEMPLATE DIMENSIONS**
> In the category list, you can search using 4:3 for templates with the typical screen dimensions or 16:9 for widescreen templates. Because most screens and televisions have moved to the widescreen format, you may want to choose the 16:9 dimension size.

If you know you want to work with a particular template, double-click its thumbnail to open the presentation. If you would like to preview it first, click once on the template to open a preview window. In Figure 2.5, the Classic Photo Album template is selected. The title slide for the template displays in the new screen. You can view the other slides in the template by clicking the More Images arrows. Click the left or right white arrows to preview other templates. Click Create to download the template and create a new presentation file.

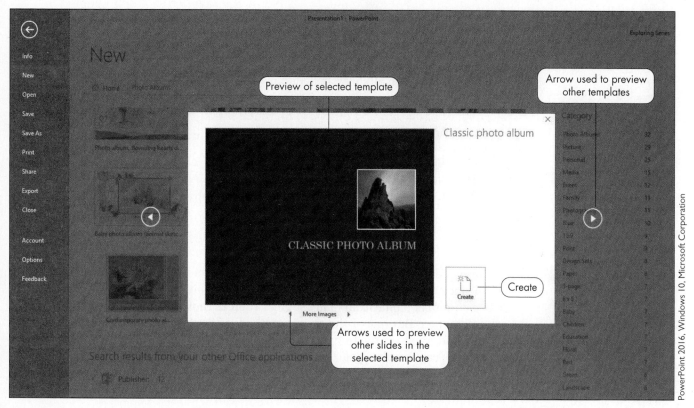

FIGURE 2.5 Template Preview

Modifying a Presentation Based on a Template

STEP 2 ⟫ The templates you download may have custom slide layouts unique to that particular template. After you download a template, you can modify it, perhaps by changing a font style or size, moving or deleting a placeholder, or moving an object on the slide. After you modify the presentation, you can save it and use it repeatedly. The ability to save these changes as a new template can save you a tremendous amount of time, because you will not have to redo your modifications the next time you use the presentation.

Modify a Placeholder and Layout

STEP 3 ⟫ A template may be customized in several ways. Slide layouts, also called layouts, are an obvious point at which to customize a template. You can change the layout by clicking the Layout arrow in the Slides group and selecting a new layout from those listed there. You can also change the layout by moving title, subtitle, or picture placeholders to a new position on individual slides. The placeholders can be resized or deleted.

To modify a layout by moving or resizing a placeholder, complete the following steps:

1. Advance to the slide that you would like to modify.
2. Click the placeholder's border.
3. Drag the placeholder to a different part of the slide to change the position, or drag the border to resize the placeholder.

The colors and background fill for placeholders can be changed to visually carry out a theme. For example, the recruiters at your school may have a presentation developed that is used to explain to prospective students the types of support and academic services that are available at your school. The presentation's theme displays your school's colors in its placeholders on all slides. In addition, although the placeholders for a template may be assigned a default font type, size, or color, these characteristics are easily modified.

To modify the text within a placeholder, complete the following steps:

1. Click the placeholder text.
2. Type the text and then select it.
3. Apply any of the features available in the Font group on the Home tab.

Add Pictures and Captions

Pictures add visual interest to a presentation and can be used to effectively convey meaning. Some templates include slide layouts with placeholders for both pictures and text. The pictures can come from many sources such as those you have taken and stored on your computer. But one of the easiest methods to get pictures for your presentation is to search for them on the Internet and then add them to your slide in the picture placeholder. The caption placeholder can be used for additional information to explain or support the picture or idea. Note that some pictures located on the Internet may not be used without permission or license from the creator.

To locate pictures from the Internet to add to your template, complete the following steps:

1. Advance to a slide where you want to add a picture.
2. Select the picture placeholder.
3. Click Online Pictures in the Insert tab.
4. Type your search term into the Bing Image Search box.

Quick Concepts

1. Are a template and a theme the same thing? Why or why not? ***p. 136***

2. Why might someone use a template rather than start from a blank presentation? ***p. 136***

3. What are some of the Suggested searches templates available in PowerPoint? What are some of the categories used to filter one of the Suggested searches? ***p. 138***

Hands-On Exercises

Skills covered: Create a New Presentation Based on a Template • Modify a Placeholder • Modify a Layout • Add Pictures and Modify a Caption

1 Templates

To promote the Wellness Education Center at your school, you decide to create a presentation that can be shown to campus groups and other organizations to inform them about the Center and its mission.

STEP 1 >> CREATE A NEW PRESENTATION BASED ON A TEMPLATE

You begin the Wellness Education Center presentation by looking for a template that is upbeat and that represents the idea that being healthy makes you feel good. You locate the perfect template (a photo album with warm sunflowers on the cover) from the Photo Albums Suggested search that you conduct. You open a new presentation based on the template and save the presentation. Refer to Figure 2.6 as you complete Step 1.

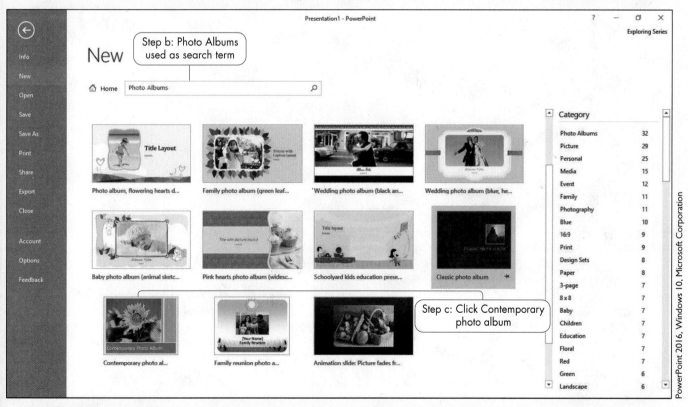

FIGURE 2.6 New Presentation Dialog Box

a. Start PowerPoint.

b. Type **Photo Albums** in the Search box and press **Enter**.

   Thumbnails of sample Photo Album templates will display. The exact results may vary.

c. Scroll to locate, and then click **Contemporary photo album**. Click **Create** in the Preview window.

d. View the slide show and read each of the instructions included in the template.

   Templates may include instructions for their use or tips on the content that may be added to create a specific presentation. For example, Slide 2 includes instructions to follow for adding your own pages to the album.

e. Click the **Insert tab** and click **Header & Footer** in the Text group. Click the **Notes and Handouts tab** in the Header and Footer dialog box. Create a handout header with your name and a handout footer with your instructor's name and your class. Include the current date. The page number feature can remain active. Click **Apply to All**.

f. Save the presentation as **p02h1Center_LastFirst**.

STEP 2)) **MODIFY A PLACEHOLDER**

The template you selected and downloaded consists of a Title Slide layout you like, but the text in the placeholders needs to be changed to the Wellness Education Center information. You edit the title slide to include the Center's name and slogan. You also modify the title placeholder to make the Center's name stand out. Refer to Figure 2.7 as you complete Step 2.

FIGURE 2.7 Edited Title Slide

a. Click **Slide 1**, select the text **Contemporary Photo Album** in the title placeholder, and type **Wellness Education Center**.

> **TROUBLESHOOTING:** If you make any major mistakes in this exercise, you can close the file, open *p02h1Center_LastFirst* again and then start this exercise over.

b. Select the title text, and click **Italic** and **Text Shadow** in the Font group on the Home tab.

You modify the template's title placeholder to make the title text stand out.

c. Click the **subtitle text,** *Click to add date or details,* and type **Dedicated to Promoting Healthy Lifestyles!**

d. Save the presentation.

The Contemporary Photo Album template includes many layouts designed to create an interesting photo album. Although the layout you selected conveys the warm feeling you desire, the layouts will be modified to fit your needs. You modify a section layout and add a new slide with the layout of your choice. You also delete unnecessary slides. Refer to Figure 2.8 as you complete Step 3.

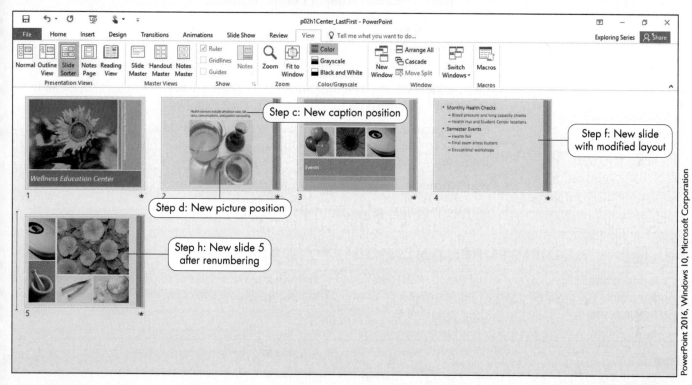

FIGURE 2.8 Title and Content Layout

a. Click **Slide 2,** replace the sample text with **Health services include physician care, lab tests, immunizations, and patient counseling.**

b. Click **Layout** in the Slides group and click the **Square with Caption layout.**

Note that the Contemporary photo album template has many more layouts than the default Office Theme template. The number of layouts provided with a template varies, so always check to see your options.

c. Select the caption, and drag it to the top of the picture (not above it).

As you drag, you will notice red line guides appear to help you as you move the object. You can press and hold Shift to constrain the movement of the caption as you drag for additional control.

d. Select the picture and drag the picture below the caption.

The location of the placeholder is modified to show the caption above the picture.

e. Click **Slide 3,** select the placeholder text **Choose a layout,** and type **Events.** Delete the subtitle text.

When you delete existing text in a new template placeholder, it is replaced with instructional text such as *Click to add subtitle.* It is not necessary to delete this text, as it will not display when the slide show is viewed.

f. Click the **New Slide arrow** and click the **Title and Content layout**.

> **TROUBLESHOOTING:** Clicking the New Slide arrow opens the Layout gallery for you to select a layout. Clicking New Slide directly above the New Slide arrow creates a new slide using the layout of the current slide.

g. Delete the title placeholder and drag the content placeholder to the top of the slide. Type the following information:

- **Monthly Health Checks**
  - **Blood pressure and lung capacity checks**
  - **Health Hut and Student Center locations**
- **Semester Events**
  - **Health fair**
  - **Final exam stress busters**
  - **Educational workshops**

h. Click the **View tab** and click **Slide Sorter** in the Presentation Views group. Click the **Slide 5 thumbnail**, and then press and hold **Ctrl** to also select the **Slide 6 thumbnail**. Press **Delete**.

The presentation now contains five slides. After you make the deletions, the remaining slides are renumbered, and the slide that becomes Slide 5 is a collage of images from the template.

i. Click **Normal** in the Presentation Views group.

j. Save the presentation.

STEP 4 ⟫ ADD PICTURES AND MODIFY A CAPTION

You decide to add a slide using one of the template's layouts to add pictures that are reminders of the importance of controlling blood pressure. You modify the layout by deleting a caption placeholder and changing the size of another. Refer to Figure 2.9 as you complete Step 4.

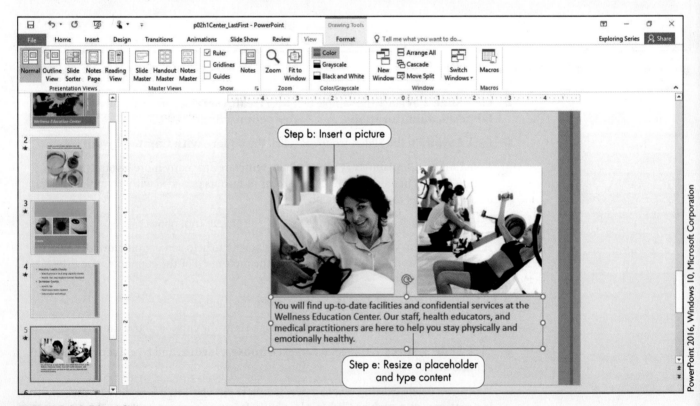

FIGURE 2.9 Edited Slide

a. Ensure that Slide 4 is the active slide, click the **New Slide arrow** on the Home tab, and then click **2-Up Landscape with Captions**.

A new slide is created. The layout includes two picture placeholders and two caption placeholders.

b. Select the **left picture placeholder** and click **Online Pictures** on the Insert tab. In the Bing Image Search box, type **blood pressure check**, press **Enter**, and then insert a picture of your choice.

The image is added to the placeholder.

> **TROUBLESHOOTING:** Clicking the icon in the center of the picture placeholder will open the Insert Picture dialog box. If this happens, click Cancel. Click somewhere in the white space around the icon to select the placeholder. Once the placeholder is selected, you will be able to continue with the instructions for adding an Online Picture.

c. Select the **right picture placeholder** and click **Online Pictures** on the Insert tab. In the Bing Image Search box, type **gym**, press **Enter**, and then insert a picture of your choice.

d. Delete the right caption placeholder and select the remaining caption placeholder. Click the **Format tab**. In the Size group, change the Width to **9"**. The caption placeholder is now the width of both pictures.

e. Type the following in the caption placeholder: **You will find up-to-date facilities and confidential services at the Wellness Education Center. Our staff, health educators, and medical practitioners are here to help you stay physically and emotionally healthy.**

f. Left align the text and then run the spelling checker. Save the presentation. Keep the presentation open if you plan to continue with the next Hands-On Exercise. If not, close the presentation, and exit PowerPoint.

Outlines

An *outline* organizes text using a *hierarchy* with main points and subpoints to indicate the levels of importance of the text. When you use a storyboard to determine your content, you create a basic outline. An outline is the fastest way to enter or edit text for a presentation. Think of an outline as the road map you use to create your presentation. Rather than having to enter the text in each placeholder on each slide separately, you can type the text directly into an outline, and it will populate into the slides automatically.

In this section, you will learn how to add content to a presentation using Outline view. After creating the presentation, you will modify the outline structure. Finally, you will print the outline.

Creating a Presentation in Outline View

To create an outline for your presentation you must be in Outline view. *Outline view* shows the presentation in an outline format displayed in levels according to the points and subpoints on each slide. There are two panes in Outline view, the outline and an image of the active slide. Instead of the slide thumbnails displayed in Normal view, the presentation is displayed as a hierarchy of the titles and text for each individual slide. Each slide is denoted by a slide number and a slide icon, followed by the slide title if the slide contains a title placeholder. The slide title is formatted as bold. Slide text is indented under the slide title. A slide with only an image (no text) will not have a title in the outline and will display only the slide number and icon.

Use Outline View

> **To change to Outline view, complete the following steps:**
>
> 1. Click the View tab.
> 2. Click Outline View in the Presentation Views group.

 One benefit of working in Outline view is that you get a good overview of your presentation without the distraction of design elements, and you can move easily from one slide to the next. You can copy text or bullets from one slide to another and rearrange the order of the slides or bullets. Outline view makes it easy to see relationships between points and to determine where information belongs. Figure 2.10 shows a portion of a presentation in Outline view.

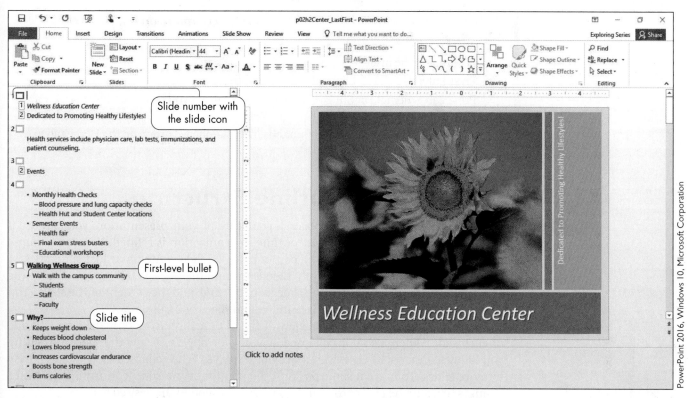

FIGURE 2.10 Outline View

Edit in Outline View

STEP 2 ❯❯ PowerPoint accommodates nine levels of indentation, although you will likely only use two or three per slide as a design best practice. Levels make it possible to show hierarchy or relationships between the information on your slides. The main points appear on Level 1; subsidiary items are indented below the main point to which they apply, and their font size is decreased.

You can promote any item to a higher level or demote it to a lower level, either before or after the text is entered, by clicking Increase List Level or Decrease List Level in the Paragraph group on the Home tab. When designing your slides, consider the number of subsidiary or lower-level items you add to a main point; too many levels within a single slide make the slide difficult to read or understand because the text size becomes smaller with each additional level.

TIP: CHANGING LIST LEVELS IN AN OUTLINE
As a quick alternative to using Increase and Decrease List Level commands on the Home tab, press Tab to demote an item or press Shift+Tab to promote an item.

Outline view can be an efficient way to create and edit text in a presentation.

> **To use Outline view to create a presentation, complete one or more of the following steps:**
>
> - Ensure that the insertion point is in the Outline pane located on the left.
> - Press Enter to create a new slide or bullet at the same level.
> - Press Tab to demote or Shift+Tab to promote items as you type to create a hierarchy of information on each slide.
> - Use the Cut, Copy, and Paste commands in the Clipboard group on the Home tab to move and copy selected text.

Modifying an Outline Structure

STEP 3 ⟩⟩ Because Outline view shows the overall structure of your presentation, you can use it to move bullets or slides until your outline's organization is refined. You can collapse or expand your view of the outline contents to see slide contents or just slide titles. A *collapsed outline* view displays only slide icons and the titles of the slides, whereas the *expanded outline* view displays the slide icon, the title, and the content of the slides. You can collapse or expand the content in individual slides or in all slides.

Figure 2.11 shows a collapsed view of the outline displaying only the icon and title of each slide. When a slide is collapsed, a wavy line appears below the slide title, letting you know additional levels exist but are not displayed. The collapsed view makes it easy to move slides. To move a slide, position the pointer over a slide icon until the pointer changes to a four-headed arrow, and then drag the icon to the desired position.

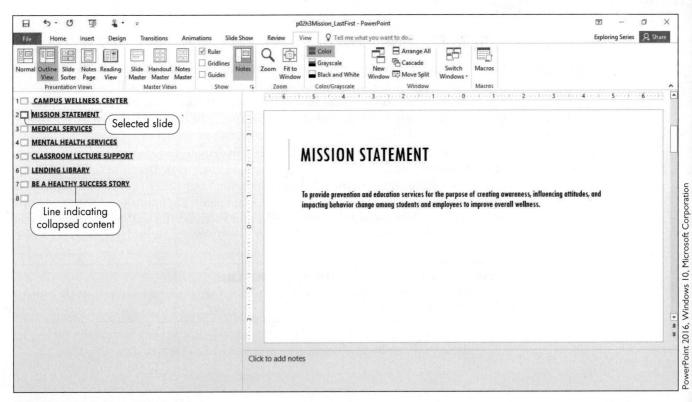

FIGURE 2.11 Collapsed Outline View

To collapse or expand a slide, complete the following steps:

1. Double-click the slide icon in the Outline pane. Doing this action collapses or expands the slide contents in the pane.
2. Right-click the text following an icon to display Expand or Collapse. Pointing to either will display the shortcut menu with options for collapsing or expanding the selected slides or all slides (see Figure 2.12).

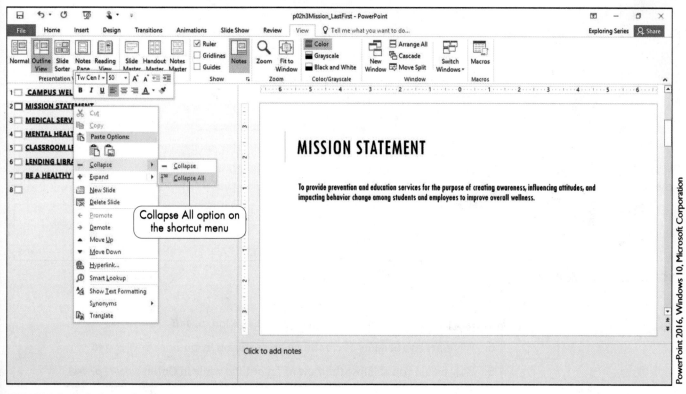

FIGURE 2.12 Collapse Outline Process

Printing an Outline

You can print an outline in either expanded or collapsed view. Figure 2.13 displays a preview of an expanded view of the outline ready to print. The slide icon and slide number will print with the outline.

To print the outline, complete the following steps:

1. Click the File tab and click Print.
2. Click Full Page Slides, Notes Pages, or Outline (whichever displays) to open a gallery of printing choices.
3. Click Outline.
4. Click Print.

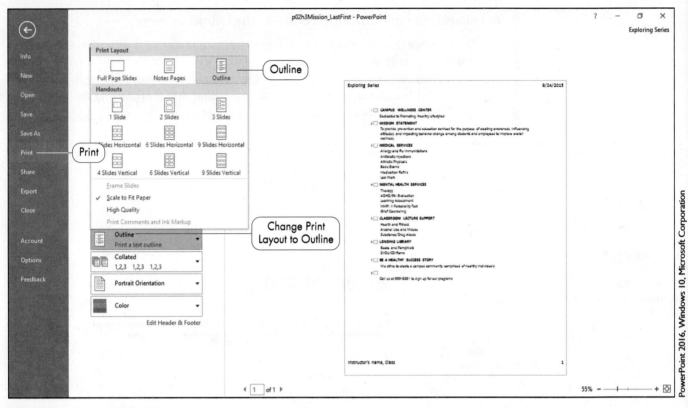

FIGURE 2.13 Outline Printing

Quick Concepts

4. Describe how an outline organizes a presentation. *p. 146*

5. What are two benefits of creating a presentation in Outline view? *p. 146*

6. Why would you collapse the view of an outline while in Outline view? *p. 148*

Hands-On Exercises

Watch the Video for this Hands-On Exercise!

MyITLab®
HOE2 Training

Skills covered: Use Outline View • Edit in Outline View • Modify the Outline Structure and Print

2 Outlines

The Wellness Education Center sponsors a Walking Wellness group to help campus members increase their physical activity and cardiovascular fitness. The director of the Wellness Education Center believes that joining a group increases a member's level of commitment and provides an incentive for the member to stay active. She asks you to edit the slide show you created in Hands-On Exercise 1 to include information about the walking group.

STEP 1 ►► USE OUTLINE VIEW

Because you want to concentrate on the information in the presentation rather than the design elements, you use Outline view. You add the information about the walking group as requested by the director. Refer to Figure 2.14 as you complete Step 1.

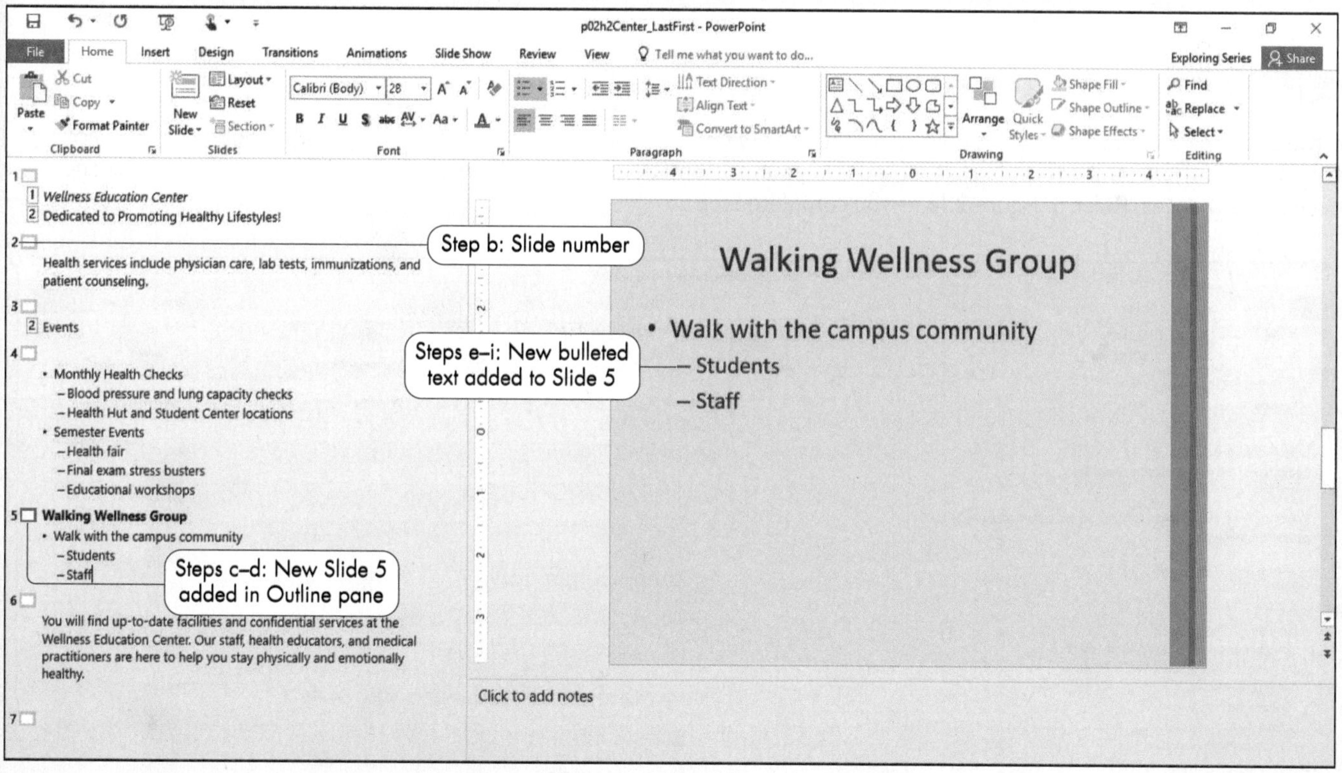

FIGURE 2.14 Revised Outline

a. Open *p02h1Center_LastFirst* if you closed it at the end of Hands-On Exercise 1, and save it as **p02h2Center_LastFirst**, changing h1 to h2.

b. Click the **View tab** and click **Outline View** in the Presentation Views group.

Note that each slide in the presentation is numbered and has a slide icon. Slides 1 through 5 include text on the slides. Slide 6 contains images only, so no text is displayed in the outline. None of the slides has a title. The text in the Outline pane on the left is also displayed on the slide in the Slide pane on the right.

c. Click at the end of the last bullet for Slide 4 in the Outline pane and press **Enter**.

The insertion point is now positioned to enter text at the same level as the previous bullet point. To create a new slide at a higher level, you must decrease the indent level.

d. Click **Decrease List Level** in the Paragraph group on the Home tab twice.

A new Slide 5 is created, the previous Slide 5 is renumbered as Slide 6, and Slide 6 is renumbered as Slide 7.

e. Type **Walking Wellness Group** and press **Enter**.

Pressing Enter moves the insertion point to the next line and creates a new slide, Slide 6. The title is bold in the Outline.

f. Press **Tab** to demote the text in the outline.

The insertion point is now positioned to enter bulleted text on Slide 5.

g. Type **Walk with the campus community** and press **Enter**.

h. Press **Tab** to demote the bullet and type **Students**.

Students becomes Level 3 text.

i. Press **Enter** and type **Staff**.

j. Save the presentation.

While proofreading your outline, you discover that you did not identify one of the campus community groups. You also notice that you left out one of the most important slides in your presentation: why someone should walk. You edit the outline and make these changes. Refer to Figure 2.15 as you complete Step 2.

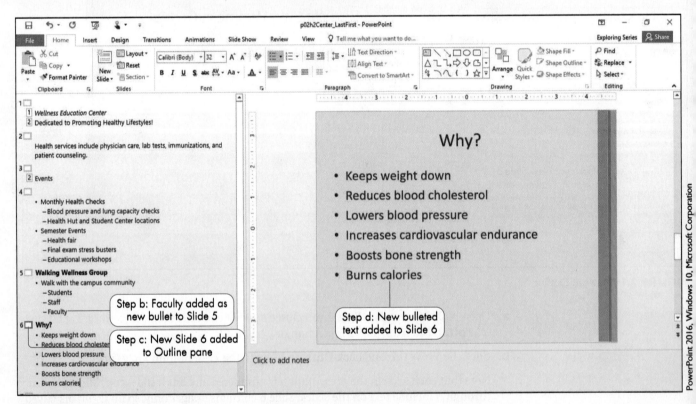

FIGURE 2.15 Edited Outline

a. Ensure that the word *Staff* on Slide 5 is selected in the outline.

b. Press **Enter** and type **Faculty**.

> **TROUBLESHOOTING:** If your text does not appear in the correct position, check to see if the insertion point was in the wrong location. To enter a blank line for a new bullet, the insertion point must be at the end of an existing bullet point, not at the beginning.

c. Press **Enter** and press **Shift+Tab** twice.

Pressing Shift+Tab promotes the text to create a new Slide 6.

d. Use the Outline pane to type the information for Slide 6 as shown below:

Why?

- **Keeps weight down**
- **Reduces blood cholesterol**
- **Lowers blood pressure**
- **Increases cardiovascular endurance**
- **Boosts bone strength**
- **Burns calories**

e. Save the presentation.

STEP 3 ❭❭ **MODIFY THE OUTLINE STRUCTURE AND PRINT**

The director of the Wellness Education Center has reviewed the slide show and made several suggestions about its structure. She feels that keeping weight down belongs at the bottom of the list of reasons for walking and asks you to reposition it. Refer to Figure 2.16 as you complete Step 3.

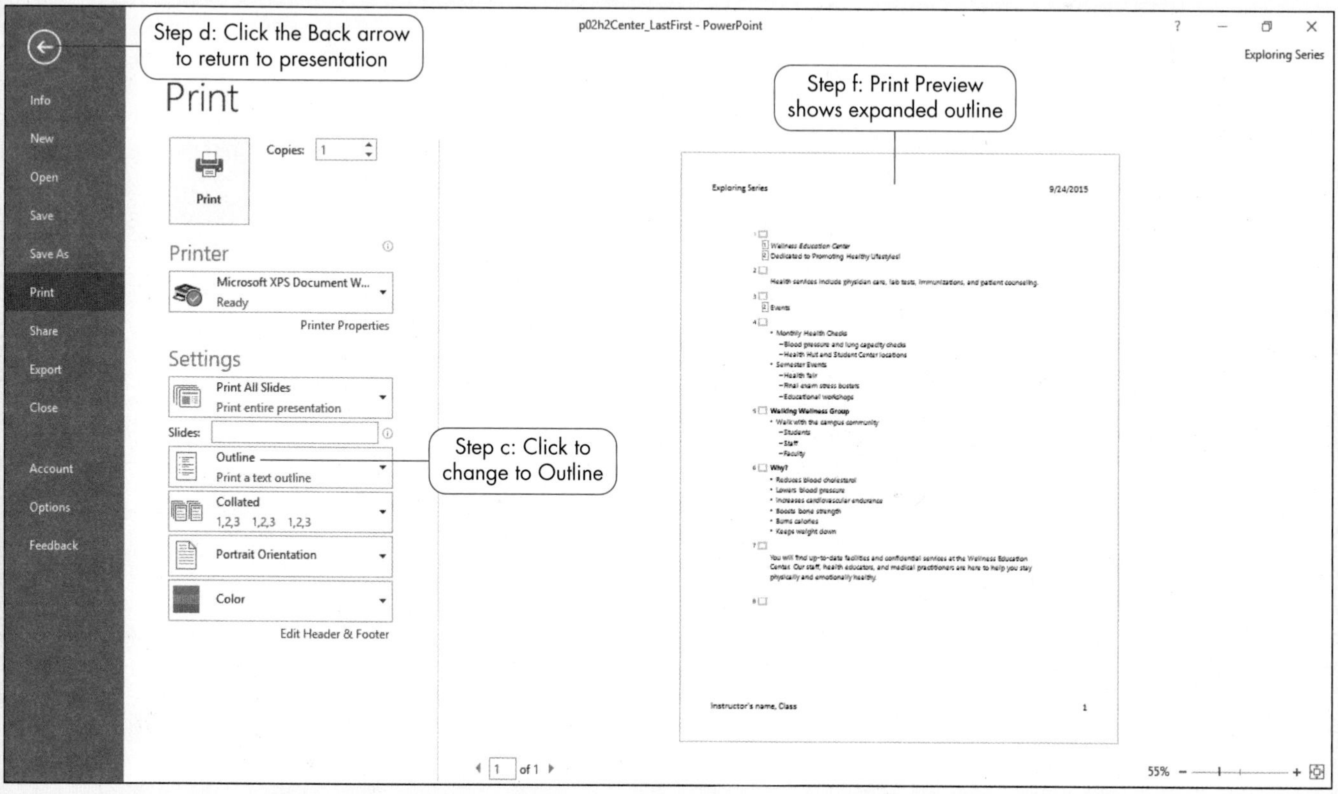

FIGURE 2.16 Expanded Outline in Print Preview

a. Position the pointer over the first bullet, *Keeps weight down*, on Slide 6 in the outline. When the pointer looks like a four-headed arrow, click and drag the text until it becomes the last bullet on the slide.

b. Right-click anywhere in the Slide 6 text, point to **Collapse**, and then click **Collapse All**.

Only the slide titles will be shown in the Outline.

c. Click the **File tab**, click **Print**, and then click the **Full Page Slides arrow**. Click **Outline**.

A preview of the collapsed outline shows in the Preview pane. Because so few slides contain titles, the collapsed outline is not helpful.

d. Click the **Back arrow** to return to the presentation.

The Outline pane is once again visible.

e. Right-click any text visible in the Outline pane, point to **Expand**, and then select **Expand All**.

f. Click the **File tab** and click **Print**.

The Outline Print Layout is retained from Step c and the expanded outline shows in the Preview pane.

g. Click the **Back arrow** to return to the presentation.

h. Check spelling in the presentation. Save and close the presentation. You will submit this file to your instructor at the end of the last Hands-On Exercise.

Data Imports

You can add slides to a presentation in several ways if the content exists in other formats, such as an outline in Word or slides from other presentations. PowerPoint can create slides based on Microsoft Word outlines (.docx or .doc formats) or outlines saved in another word-processing format that PowerPoint recognizes (.rtf format). You can import data into a slide show to add existing slides from a previously created presentation. This is a very efficient way to add content to a slide show.

In this section, you will learn how to import an outline into a PowerPoint presentation and how to add slides from another presentation into the current presentation.

Importing an Outline

STEP 1 ⟫ Outlines created using Outline view in Microsoft Word can be imported to quickly create a PowerPoint presentation. To create an outline in Word, you must click the View tab, click Outline, and then type your text.

PowerPoint also recognizes outlines created in Word and saved in ***Rich Text Format (.rtf)***, a file format you can use to transfer formatted text documents between applications such as word-processing programs and PowerPoint. You can even transfer documents between different platforms such as Mac and Windows. The structure and most of the text formatting are retained when you import the outline into PowerPoint.

> **To create a new presentation from an outline, complete the following steps:**
>
> 1. Click the New Slide arrow on the Home tab.
> 2. Click Slides from Outline.
> 3. Locate and select the file and click Insert.

Solve Problems While Importing Word Outlines

You may encounter problems when trying to import an outline. For example, a list using the numbered list or bullet feature in the Paragraph group on the Home tab in Word (that was not created in Outline view) will not import easily to PowerPoint.

If you import a Word document that appears to be an outline and after importing, each line of the Word document becomes a title for a new slide, the Word document is actually a bulleted list rather than an outline. These two features are separate and distinct in Word and do not import into PowerPoint in the same manner. Open the bulleted list in Word, apply outline heading styles, save the file, and then re-import it to PowerPoint.

PowerPoint also recognizes outlines created and saved in a ***plain text format*** (which uses the file extension ***.txt***), a file format that retains text without any formatting. But because .txt outlines have no saved hierarchical structure, each line of the outline becomes a slide. Avoid saving outlines you create in this format. If you receive an outline in a .txt format, you can create a hierarchy in PowerPoint without having to retype the text by simply moving the text around to create the structure.

Reusing Slides from an Existing Presentation

STEP 2 ⟫ You can reuse slides from an existing PowerPoint presentation when creating a new presentation without having to open the other file. The imported slides display in a pane on the right so that you can select the slides you want to import into your existing presentation. This feature can save you considerable time.

To import existing slides without having to open the other file, complete the following steps:

1. Click the New Slide arrow in the Slides group on the Home tab.
2. Click Reuse Slides.
3. Click Browse, click Browse File, and then navigate to the folder containing the presentation that has the slides you want to use.
4. Click Open.
5. Select each slide individually to add it to the presentation. Or right-click any slide and click Insert All Slides to add all of the slides to the presentation.
6. Close the Reuse Slides pane.

By default, when you insert a slide into the presentation, it takes on the formatting of the open presentation. If the new slides do not take on the formatting of the open presentation, select the imported text in Outline view and click Clear all Formatting in the Font group of the Home tab. It will format the slides using the active theme. If you wish to retain the formatting of the original presentation, click the Keep source formatting check box at the bottom of the Reuse Slides pane, shown in Figure 2.17.

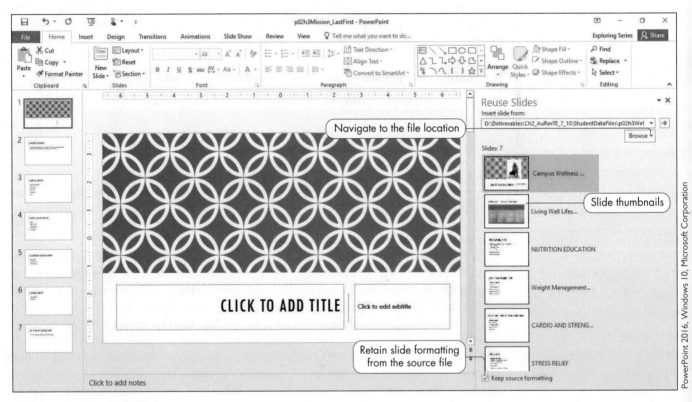

FIGURE 2.17 Reuse Slides Pane

Quick Concepts ✓

7. Describe two problems and their solutions that you may encounter when importing an outline into PowerPoint. *p. 155*

8. Describe how you would use slides from another presentation in your current presentation. *p. 156*

9. When you insert a slide into a presentation, what formatting does it use? How would you change this default setting? *p. 156*

Hands-On Exercises

Watch the Video
for this Hands-On
Exercise!

MyITLab®
HOE3 Training

Skills covered: Import a Rich
Text Format Outline • Reuse Slides
from Another Presentation

3 Data Imports

The director of the Wellness Education Center is impressed with the center's overview presentation
you created. She gives you an electronic copy of an outline she created in a word-processing software
package and asks if you can convert it into a slide show. You create a slide show from the outline and then
supplement it with content from another slide show.

STEP 1 >> IMPORT A RICH TEXT FORMAT OUTLINE

The director of the Wellness Education Center saves an outline for a presentation in Rich Text Format. You import the outline
into PowerPoint to use as the basis for a presentation about the center, its mission, and the services it provides to students, staff,
and faculty. Refer to Figure 2.18 as you complete Step 1.

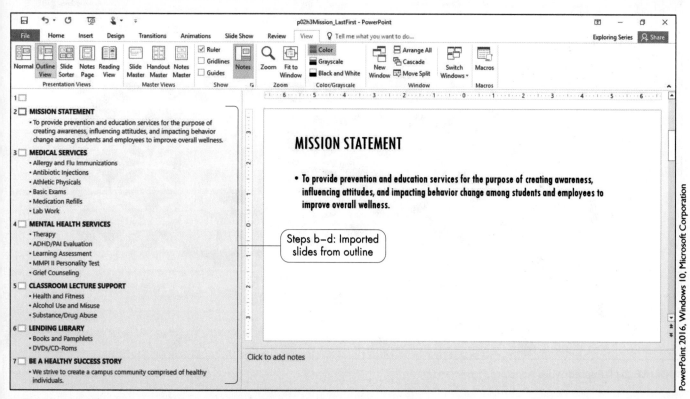

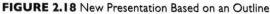

FIGURE 2.18 New Presentation Based on an Outline

a. Click the **File tab**, click **New**, and then double-click **Blank Presentation**. Save the
presentation as **p02h3Mission_LastFirst**.

A new blank presentation opens and is saved.

b. Click the **New Slide arrow** on the Insert tab, click **Slides from Outline**, and then
navigate to the location of your student data files.

c. Browse and insert file *p02h3MedOutline*.

The outline is opened and new slides are added to the presentation.

d. Click the **View tab** and click **Outline View** in the Presentation Views group.

Because the file was created in Word with heading styles applied and saved in Rich Text Format, the outline retains its hierarchy. Each slide has a title and bulleted text.

e. Create a handout header with your name and a handout footer with your instructor's name and your class. Include the current date.

f. Apply the **Integral theme** to all slides.

The Integral theme adds a subtle blue line next to the title.

g. Save the presentation.

While reviewing the Wellness Education Center presentation, you realize you do not have a title slide or a final slide inviting students to contact the Center. You reuse slides from another presentation created for the Center containing slides that would fit well in this presentation. Refer to Figure 2.19 as you complete Step 2.

FIGURE 2.19 Reused Slides Added to Presentation

a. Switch to **Normal view**. Click **Slide 1**, click the **New Slide arrow** in the Slides group on the Home tab, and then click **Reuse Slides** at the bottom of the New Slides gallery.

b. Click **Browse**, click **Browse File**, and then locate your student data files. Select *p02h3Wellness*, and then click **Open**.

> **TROUBLESHOOTING:** If you do not see the *p02h3Wellness* file, click Files of type and select All PowerPoint Presentations.

c. Click to select the **Keep source formatting check box** at the bottom of the Reuse Slides pane.

With *Keep source formatting* selected, the images and design of the slides you reuse will transfer with the slide.

d. Click the **first slide**, *Campus Wellness*, in the Reuse Slides pane.

The slide is added to your presentation after the current slide, Slide 1.

e. Delete the blank title slide that is currently Slide 1.

The newly reused slide will be in the Slide 1 position to serve as the title slide of your presentation.

f. Select the **Slide 7 icon**, *BE A HEALTHY SUCCESS STORY*, in the Slides pane of the original presentation.

g. Click **Slide 7** in the Reuse Slides pane and close the Reuse Slides pane.

h. Save the presentation. Keep the presentation open if you plan to continue with the next Hands-On Exercise. If not, close the presentation, and exit PowerPoint.

Design

After you are satisfied with the content, then you can consider the visual aspects of the presentation. You should evaluate many aspects when considering the visual design of your presentation. Those aspects include layout, background, typography, color, and animation, as well as dividing the content into sections. Sections can help you effectively organize and manage the parts of the presentation.

In this section, you will work with tools that allow you to create well-designed presentations. Using these features, you can create a slide show using a professional template and themes and then modify it to reflect your own preferences. Before doing so, however, you need to consider some basic visual design principles for PowerPoint. Finally, you will customize the slide master and slide layouts controlled by the slide master.

Using Sections

STEP 1 ≫ Content divided into **sections** can help you group slides meaningfully. This is similar to how tabs help to organize a binder. These sections provide organization to a presentation by giving a point at which to collapse or expand the slide hierarchy.

When you create a section, it is given the name Untitled Section. You will want to change this to a meaningful name, which enables you to jump to a section quickly. For example, you may be creating a slide show for a presentation on geothermal energy. You could create sections for Earth, plate boundaries, plate tectonics, and thermal features.

> **TIP: USING A SECTION HEADER**
> It is easy to confuse term *section* with *section header*. If you need to create a visual break in the presentation, such as stopping to pose questions for the audience, then you will want to use a section header slide instead of a section. Section header slides can be added through Slide Master view.

Use either Normal view or Slide Sorter view to create sections. Figure 2.20 shows a section added to a presentation in Normal view. Slide sections can be collapsed or expanded. The collapsed view makes it easier to move groups of slides around to reorganize a presentation.

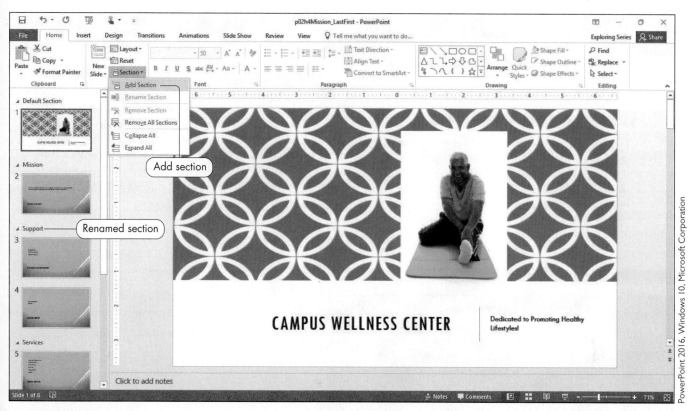

FIGURE 2.20 Using Sections

> **To create a section, complete the following steps:**
>
> 1. Select the first slide of the new section.
> 2. Click Section in the Slides group on the Home tab.
> 3. Click Add Section.
> 4. Right-click Untitled Section and select Rename Section.
> 5. Type a new name for the section.

Examining Slide Show Design Principles

STEP 2 ▶▶ When applied to a project, universally accepted design principles can increase its appeal and professionalism. Some design aspects may be applied in specific ways to the various types of modern communications: communicating through print media such as flyers or brochures, through audio media such as narrations or music, or through a visual medium such as a slide show. Table 2.1 focuses on principles that apply to slide shows and examines examples of slides that illustrate these principles.

TABLE 2.1 Slide Show Design Principles

Example	Design Tip

FIGURE 2.21 Examples of Templates Appropriate for Different Audiences

PowerPoint 2016, Windows 10, Microsoft Corporation

FIGURE 2.22 Example of a Clean Design

PowerPoint 2016, Windows 10, Microsoft Corporation

- **Choose design elements appropriate for the audience.**
Consider the audience. A presentation to elementary students might use bright, primary colors and cartoon-like images. For an adult audience, use photographs rather than cartoon-like images to give the slide show a more professional appearance. Figure 2.21 shows design examples suitable for grade school and business audiences, respectively.

- **Keep the design neat and clean.**
Avoid using multiple fonts and font colors on a slide. Avoid using multiple images. Use white space (empty space) to open up your design. Figure 2.22 shows an example of a clean design.

TABLE 2.1   Continued

Example	Design Tip
 FIGURE 2.23 Example of an Effective Focal Point FIGURE 2.24 Example of Unified Design Elements	• **Create a focal point that leads the viewer's eyes to the critical information on the slide.** The focal point should be the main area of interest. Pictures should always lead the viewer's eyes to the focal point, not away from it. Images should not be so large that they detract from the focal point, unless your goal is to make the image the focal point. Figure 2.23 illustrates examples of an effective focal point. • **Use unified design elements for a professional look.** Visual unity creates a harmony between the elements of the slide and between the slides in the slide show. Unity gives the viewer a sense of order and peace. Create unity by repeating colors and shapes. Use images in only one style such as all photographs or all line art throughout the presentation. Figure 2.24 shows a disjointed and a unified design.
 FIGURE 2.25 Sans Serif (left) and Serif (right) Fonts	• **Choose fonts appropriate for the output of your presentation.** If a presentation is to be delivered through a projection device, consider using sans serif fonts with short text blocks. If your presentation will be delivered as a printout, consider using serif fonts. Figure 2.25 displays an example of sans serif and serif fonts.

PowerPoint 2016, Windows 10, Microsoft Corporation

TABLE 2.1   Continued

Example	Design Tip

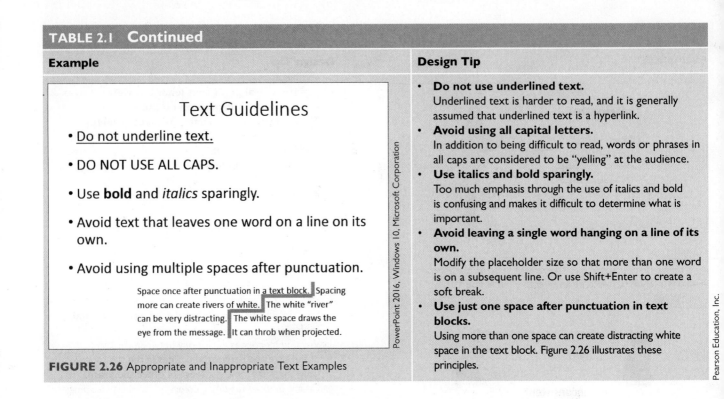	• **Do not use underlined text.**
	  Underlined text is harder to read, and it is generally assumed that underlined text is a hyperlink.
	• **Avoid using all capital letters.**
	  In addition to being difficult to read, words or phrases in all caps are considered to be "yelling" at the audience.
	• **Use italics and bold sparingly.**
	  Too much emphasis through the use of italics and bold is confusing and makes it difficult to determine what is important.
	• **Avoid leaving a single word hanging on a line of its own.**
	  Modify the placeholder size so that more than one word is on a subsequent line. Or use Shift+Enter to create a soft break.
	• **Use just one space after punctuation in text blocks.**
	  Using more than one space can create distracting white space in the text block. Figure 2.26 illustrates these principles.

FIGURE 2.26 Appropriate and Inappropriate Text Examples

PowerPoint 2016, Windows 10, Microsoft Corporation

Pearson Education, Inc.

Remember that these design principles are guidelines. For example, the use of all capital letters is found for headings and titles in certain themes. You may choose to avoid applying one or more of the principles, but you should be aware of the principles and carefully consider why you are not following them. If you are in doubt about your design, ask a classmate or colleague to review the design and make suggestions. Fresh eyes can see things you might miss.

Modifying a Theme

 Themes can be modified once they have been applied. You can change the variants, colors, fonts, and effects used in the theme. You can even change the background styles. Each of these options is on the Design tab, and each has its own gallery. Figure 2.27 shows the locations for accessing the galleries.

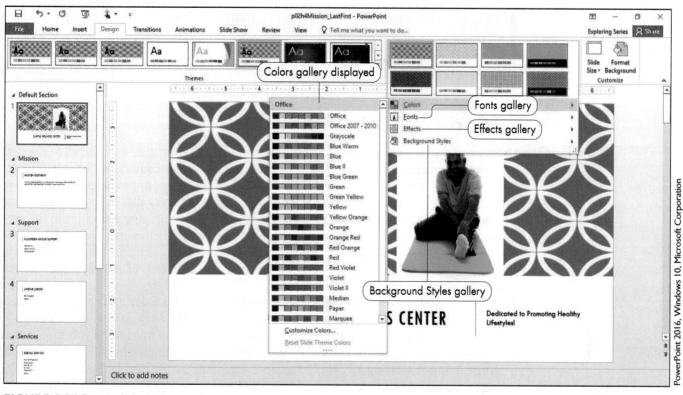

FIGURE 2.27 Design Galleries

Each PowerPoint theme includes a ***Colors gallery***, a gallery that provides a set of colors with each color assigned to a different element in the theme design. Once the theme is selected, you can change the colors by displaying the Colors gallery. Use Live Preview as you move the pointer along the various color sets to see how each color theme applies to your slides. You can even customize one or more of the colors in each color set.

Selecting a font for the title and another for the bullets or body text of your presentation can be difficult. Without a background in typography, determining which fonts go together well is difficult. The ***Fonts gallery*** is a gallery that pairs a title font and a body font. Click any of the samples in the Fonts gallery, and the font pair is applied to your theme.

The ***Effects gallery*** displays a full range of special effects that can be applied to all shapes in the presentation. Using effects aids you in maintaining a consistency to the appearance of your presentation. The gallery uses effects such as a soft glow, soft edges, shadows, or three-dimensional (3-D) look.

You can change the background style of the theme by accessing the ***Background Styles gallery***, a gallery containing backgrounds consistent with the selected theme colors. Simply changing your background style can liven up a presentation and give it your individual style.

Some of the themes include background shapes to create the design. If the background designs interfere with other objects on the slide, such as tables, images, or charts, you can select Format Background in the Customize group of the Design tab, and then click Hide Background Graphics by clicking so that the background shapes will not display for that slide.

> **To access these galleries, complete the following steps:**
>
> 1. Click the Design tab.
> 2. Click More in the Variants group and choose the gallery you want to change (Colors, Fonts, Effects, or Background Styles).

Modifying the Slide Master

STEP 4 ▶▶ You can further modify and customize your presentation through the slide master. *Masters* control the layouts, background designs, and color combinations for handouts, notes pages, and slides, giving the presentation a consistent appearance. By changing the masters, you make universal style changes that affect every slide in your presentation and the supporting materials. This is more efficient than changing each slide in the presentation. When you want two or more different styles or themes in a presentation, you can add a different slide master for each theme. The design elements you already know about, such as themes and layouts, can be applied to each type of master. Slide masters can be reused in other presentations.

Each of the layouts available to you when you choose a design theme has consistent elements that are set by a *slide master* containing design information. The slide master is the top slide in a hierarchy of slides based on the master. As you modify the slide master, elements in the slide layouts related to it are also modified to maintain consistency. A slide master includes associated slide layouts such as a title slide layout, various content slide layouts, and a blank slide layout. The associated slide layouts designate the location of placeholders and other objects on slides as well as formatting information.

> **To modify a slide master or slide layout based on a slide master, complete the following steps:**
>
> 1. Click the View tab.
> 2. Click Slide Master in the Master Views group.
> 3. Click the slide master at the top of the list or click one of the associated layouts.
> 4. Make modifications.
> 5. Click Close Master View in the Close group.

In Slide Master view, the slide master is the larger, top slide thumbnail shown in the left pane that coordinates with the Title and Content Layout. The Title Slide Layout is the second slide in the pane. The number of slides following it varies depending upon the template. Figure 2.28 shows the Integral Theme Slide Master and its related slide layouts. The ScreenTip for the slide master indicates it is used by one slide because the slide show is a new slide show composed of a single title slide.

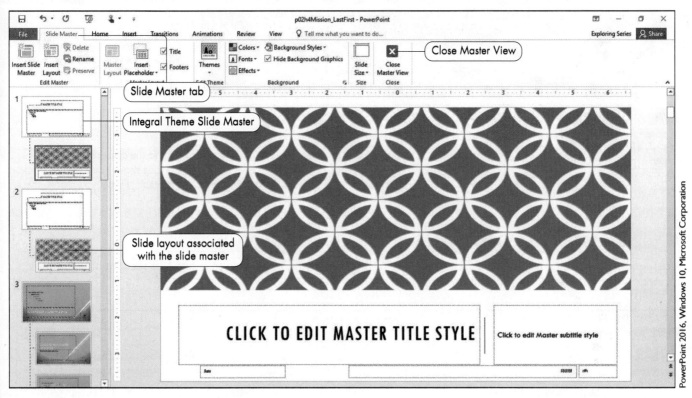

FIGURE 2.28 Slide Master View

The slide master is the most efficient way of setting the fonts, color scheme, and effects for the entire slide show. For example, you may wish to add a small company logo to the right corner of all slides. To set this choice, click the slide master thumbnail in the slide pane to display the slide master. The main pane shows the placeholders for title style, text styles, a date field, a footer field, and a page number field. Double-click the text in the Master title style or any level of text in the Master text styles placeholder and insert the logo.

You can move and size the placeholders on the slide master. The modifications in position and size will be reflected on the associated slide layouts. This may conflict with some of the slide layout placeholders, however. The placeholders can be moved on the individual slide layouts as needed.

Quick Concepts ✓

10. How are sections in a presentation similar to tabs in a binder? *p. 160*

11. Why is it important to have unified design elements in a presentation? *p. 163*

12. Which elements of a theme can be modified? Where do you access these elements to make the change? *p. 164*

13. In what ways can a slide master give a consistent appearance to presentations? *p. 166*

Hands-On Exercises

Watch the Video
for this Hands-On
Exercise!

MyITLab®
HOE4 Training

Skills covered: Create
Sections • Apply Design Principles
• Modify a Theme • Modify a Slide
Master

4 Design

The director of the Wellness Education Center plans to add more content to the center's mission presentation. To help her organize the content, you create sections in the slide show. You apply your knowledge of design principles to make the text more professional and readable. Finally, you change the theme and make modifications to the presentation through the slide master.

STEP 1 ›› CREATE SECTIONS

After reviewing the Campus Wellness Education Center mission slide show, you decide to create four sections organizing the content. Refer to Figure 2.29 as you complete Step 1.

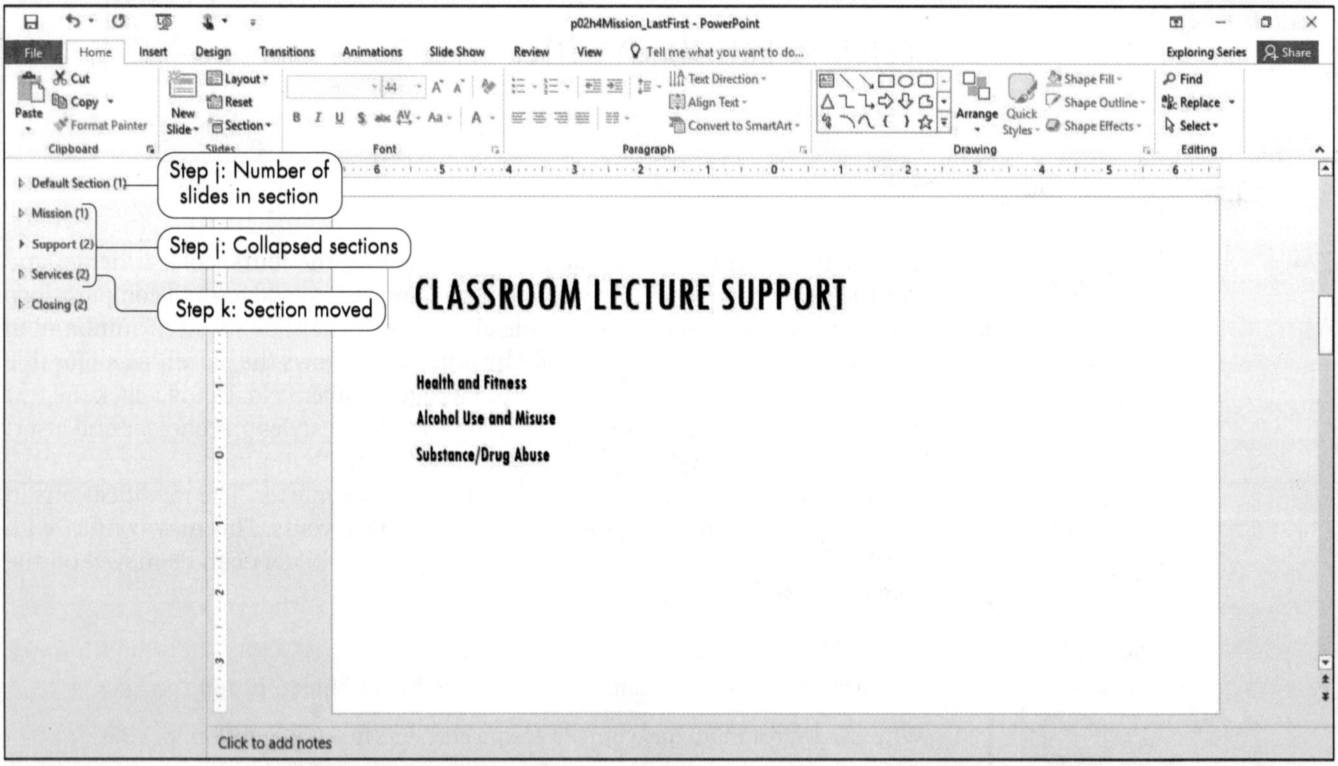

FIGURE 2.29 Content Divided into Sections

a. Open *p02h3Mission_LastFirst* if you closed it at the end of Hands-On Exercise 3, and save it as **p02h4Mission_LastFirst**, changing h3 to h4.

b. Click the **View tab**, click **Normal**, and then click the **Slide 2 thumbnail**.

c. Click **Section** in the Slides group on the Home tab and select **Add Section**.

A section divider is positioned between Slide 1 and Slide 2 in the Slides tab. It is labeled *Untitled Section*.

d. Right-click the **Untitled Section divider** and select **Rename Section**.

The Rename Section dialog box opens.

e. Type **Mission** in the Section name box and click **Rename**.

The section divider name changes and displays in the Slides tab.

f. Create a new section between Slides 2 and 3.

g. Right-click **Untitled Section**, click **Rename Section**, and then name the section **Services**.

h. Right-click between Slide 4 and Slide 5, click **Add Section**, and then rename the section **Support**.

i. Right-click between Slide 6 and Slide 7 and create a section named **Closing**.

The slide show content is divided into logical sections.

j. Right-click any section divider and select **Collapse All**.

The Slides tab shows the four sections you created: Mission, Services, Support, and Closing, as well as the Default section. Each section divider displays the section name and the number of slides in the section.

k. Right-click the **Support section** and click **Move Section Up**.

The Support section and all its associated slides are moved above the Services section.

l. Right-click any section divider and click **Expand All**.

m. Click the **View tab** and click **Slide Sorter** in the Presentation Views group.

Slide Sorter view displays the slides in each section.

n. Click **Normal** in the Presentation Views group. Save the presentation.

STEP 2 ›› APPLY DESIGN PRINCIPLES

You note that several of the slides in the presentation do not use slide show text design principles. You edit these slides so they are more readable. Refer to Figure 2.30 as you complete Step 2.

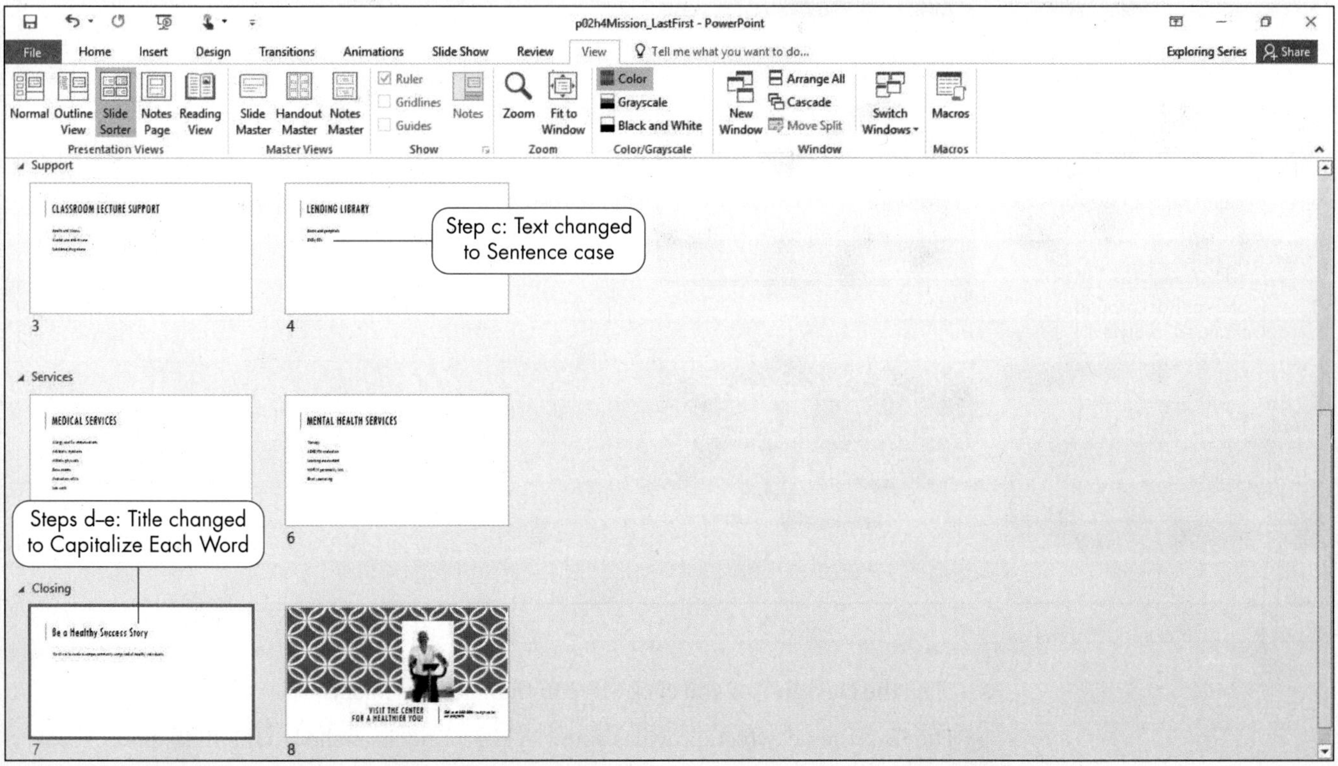

FIGURE 2.30 Portion of Slide Show in Slide Sorter View

a. Click **Slide 3**, select the text below the title placeholder, click the **Change Case arrow** in the Font group on the Home tab, and then select **Sentence case**.

The text now meets the guideline and is more readable.

b. Change the text below the titles in Slides 4, 5, and 6 to **Sentence case**.

c. Click **Slide 4**, change the second line to **DVDs/CDs**.

Always proofread to ensure that the case feature accurately reflects proper capitalization.

d. Click **Slide 7**, select the **title text**, click **Change Case** in the Font group, and then click **Capitalize Each Word**.

Each word in the title begins with a capital letter.

e. Change the uppercase *A* in the title to a lowercase *a*.

Title case capitalization guidelines state that only significant parts of speech of four or more letters should be capitalized. Minor parts of speech including articles and words shorter than four letters should not be capitalized.

f. Click the **View tab** and click **Slide Sorter** in the Presentation Views group.

Note the sentence case in the Services section.

g. Save the presentation.

STEP 3 ›› **MODIFY A THEME**

Although you are satisfied with the opening and closing slides, you think the main body of slides should be enhanced. You decide to change the theme and then modify the new theme to customize it. Refer to Figure 2.31 as you complete Step 3.

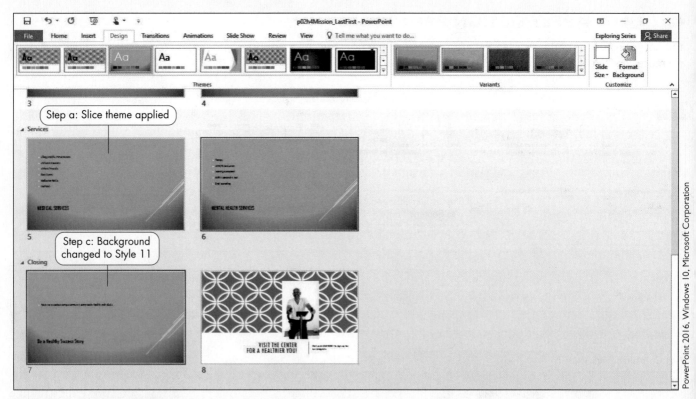

FIGURE 2.31 Modified Theme

a. Click the **Design tab** and click **Slice** in the Themes gallery.

The Slice theme, which provides a new background, is applied to the slide show except for the title and conclusion slides.

b. Click the **Design tab** and click **More** in the Variants group.

The Variants Gallery opens.

c. Select **Background Styles** and click **Style 11**.

d. Save the presentation.

STEP 4 ›› MODIFY A SLIDE MASTER

You want to add the Wellness Education Center's logo to slides 2 through 7 using the slide master. Refer to Figure 2.32 as you complete Step 4.

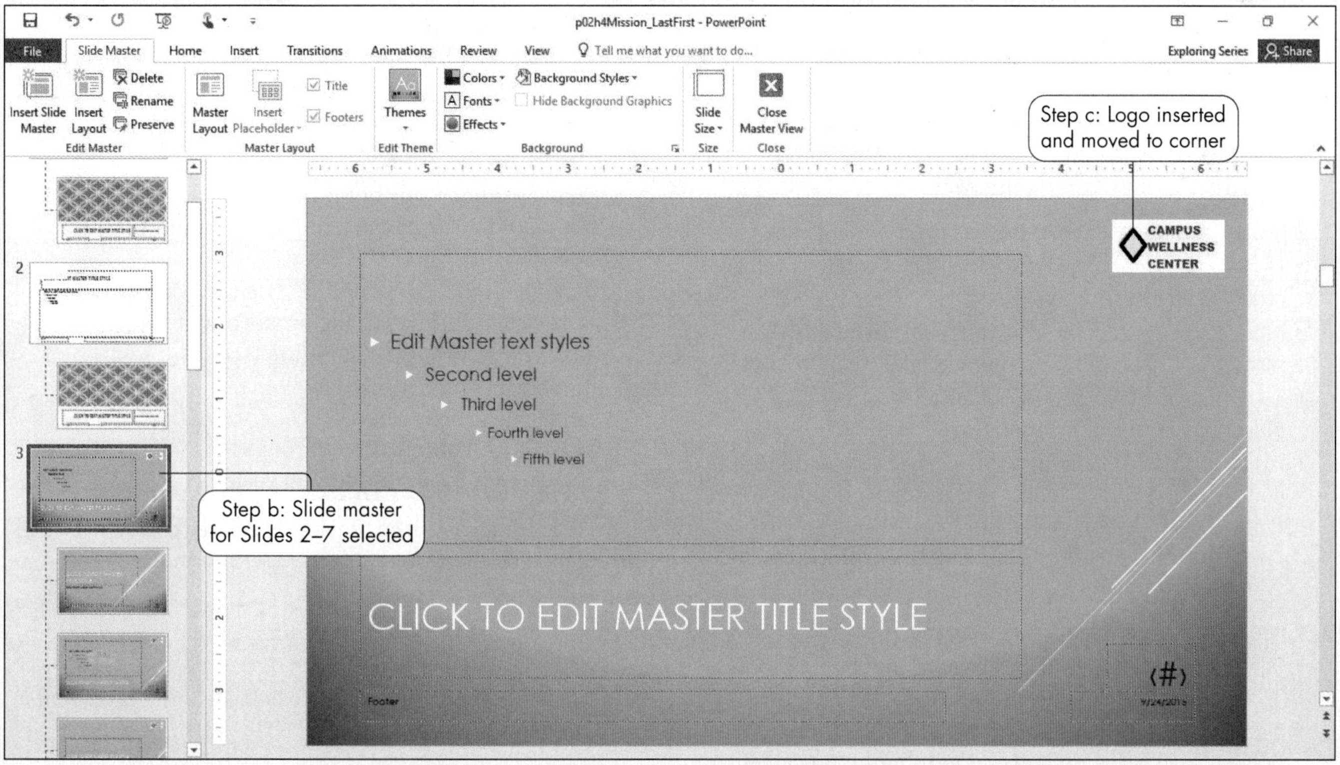

FIGURE 2.32 Modified Slide Master

a. Click the **View tab** and click **Slide Master** in the Master Views group. Scroll to the top of the slide pane.

Note the masters labeled 1 and 2. These masters control the first and last slides of the presentation.

b. Click the **slide master thumbnail** next to the number 3.

The third slide master controls slides 2 through 7.

c. Click the **Insert tab** and click **Pictures**. Locate the *p02h4Logo* picture file in the student files folder and click **Insert**.

The logo is inserted. The logo will display in the slide pane thumbnails and slide show, but not on the full slide in Normal view.

d. Move the logo to the top right corner of the slide master.

e. Click the **Slide Master tab**. Click **Close Master View** in the Close group.

Observe that the logo has been inserted on Slides 2 through 7 in the presentation.

f. Check spelling in the presentation. Save and close the file. Based on your instructor's directions, submit the following:

p02h2Center_LastFirst

p02h4Mission_LastFirst.

Chapter Objectives Review

After reading this chapter, you have accomplished the following objectives:

1. Create a presentation using a template.
- Templates incorporate a background, theme, a layout, and in some instances, content that you can modify.
- You can search for and download templates from Microsoft or elsewhere on the Web.

2. Modify a presentation based on a template.
- Using a template saves time and enables you to create a customized presentation.
- Modify a placeholder and layout: You can modify the structure of a template by changing the layout of a slide.
- To change the layout, resize placeholders or drag placeholders to new locations on a slide.
- Add pictures and captions: You can add visual interest to your presentation by adding pictures that you have taken and stored on your computer or by searching for them on the Internet and then saving and inserting them into your presentation.

3. Create a presentation in Outline view.
- When you use a storyboard to determine your content, you create a basic outline.
- Working in Outline view enables you to edit the presentation easily, and saves time because you can enter information efficiently without moving from placeholder to placeholder on slides.
- Use Outline view: Entering your presentation in Outline view enables you to organize the content of the presentation in a hierarchy of main points and subpoints.
- Edit in Outline view: Levels of indention makes it easy to show the relationships between information on the slide. You can promote or demote either before or after the information is entered on the slide.

4. Modify an outline structure.
- Because Outline view helps you see the structure of the presentation, you are able to see where content needs to be strengthened or where the flow of information needs to be revised.
- If you decide a slide contains content that would be presented better in another location in the slide show, use the Collapse and Expand features to easily move it.
- After collapsing the slide content, you can drag the slide to a new location and then expand it.
- To move individual bullet points, cut and paste the bullet points, or drag and drop them.

5. Print an outline.
- An outline can be printed in either collapsed or expanded form to be used during a presentation.

6. Import an outline.
- You can import any outline that has been saved in a format PowerPoint can read, such as a Word outline (.doc or .docx).
- In addition to a Word outline, you can use a common generic format such as Rich Text Format (.rtf).
- Solve problems while importing Word outlines: Importing outlines saved in plain text (.txt) can be problematic because each line of the outline becomes a slide instead of retaining the hierarchy.

7. Reuse slides from an existing presentation.
- Slides that have been previously created can be reused in new slide shows for efficiency and continuity.

8. Use sections.
- Sections help organize slides into meaningful groups of slides that can be collapsed or organized.
- Each section can be named to help identify the contents of the sections.

9. Examine slide show design principles.
- Using basic slide show principles and applying the guidelines make presentations more polished and professional.

10. Modify a theme.
- A template includes themes that define its font attributes, colors, and backgrounds.
- Using galleries, you can change a template's theme colors, fonts, effects and backgrounds.

11. Modify the slide master.
- A slide master controls the layouts, background designs, and color combinations associated with the handouts, notes pages, and slides in a presentation.
- By changing the slide master, you make changes that affect every slide in a presentation.

Key Terms Matching

Match the key terms with their definitions. Write the key term letter by the appropriate numbered definition.

a. Background Styles gallery
b. Collapsed outline
c. Colors gallery
d. Effects gallery
e. Expanded outline
f. Fonts gallery
g. Hierarchy
h. Master

i. Outline
j. Outline view
k. Plain text format (.txt)
l. Rich text format (.rtf)
m. Section
n. Slide master
o. Template

1. _____ A file that incorporates a theme, a layout, and content that can be modified. **p. 136**

2. _____ A method of organizing text in a hierarchy to depict relationships. **p. 146**

3. _____ A method used to organize text into levels of importance in a structure. **p. 146**

4. _____ A view showing the presentation in an outline format displayed in levels according to the points and any subpoints on each slide. **p. 146**

5. _____ An Outline view that displays only the slide number, icon, and title of each slide in Outline view. **p. 148**

6. _____ An Outline view that displays the slide number, icon, title, and content of each slide in the Outline view. **p. 148**

7. _____ A Word outline saved in this format can be used when transferring documents between platforms. **p. 155**

8. _____ A file format that retains only text but no formatting when transferring documents between applications or platforms. **p. 155**

9. _____ A set of colors available for every theme. **p. 165**

10. _____ A gallery that pairs a title font with a body font. **p. 165**

11. _____ A range of special effects for shapes used in the presentation. **p. 165**

12. _____ A gallery providing both solid color and background styles for application to a theme. **p. 165**

13. _____ The top slide in a hierarchy of slides based on the master. **p. 166**

14. _____ A slide view where the control of the layouts, background designs, and color combinations for handouts, notes pages, and slides can be set giving a presentation a consistent appearance. **p. 166**

15. _____ A division to presentation content that groups slides meaningfully. **p. 160**

Multiple Choice

1. A widescreen template that can be used for display on most screens and televisions is found in the category:
   - (a) 4:3.
   - (b) 11:17.
   - (c) 16:9.
   - (d) 20:20.

2. To add pictures to a presentation, you can:
   - (a) Use your own photos.
   - (b) Search for and insert pictures from Bing Image Search.
   - (c) Use the default images that came with the template.
   - (d) Use any of the above options.

3. What is the advantage to collapsing the outline so only the slide titles are visible?
   - (a) Transitions and animations can be added.
   - (b) Graphical objects become visible.
   - (c) More slide titles are displayed at one time, making it easier to rearrange the slides in the presentation.
   - (d) All of the above.

4. Which of the following is *true*?
   - (a) The slide layout can be changed after the template has been chosen.
   - (b) Themes applied to a template will not be saved with the slide show.
   - (c) Placeholders downloaded with a template cannot be modified.
   - (d) Slides cannot be added to a presentation after a template has been chosen.

5. In Outline view, levels of indentation showing the hierarchy of information *cannot* be created by:
   - (a) Pressing TAB to demote a bullet point from the first level to the second level.
   - (b) Pressing SHIFT+TAB to promote a bullet point from the second level to the first level.
   - (c) Pressing ALT+TAB to demote a bullet point from the first level to the second level.
   - (d) Pressing Decrease List Level to demote a bullet point from the first level to the second level.

6. Which of the following is the easiest method for adding existing content to a presentation?
   - (a) Import an outline using heading styles created in Word.
   - (b) Import a numbered list created in Word.
   - (c) Import a bulleted list created in Word.
   - (d) Import a document saved in plain text format.

7. How is formatting affected when reusing slides from an existing presentation?
   - (a) The slide being reused takes on the formatting of the open presentation.
   - (b) You can click Clear All Formatting to format slides using the active theme.
   - (c) The original presentation's formatting can be retained by clicking Keep Source Formatting.
   - (d) Any of the above may happen.

8. Which of the following is *not* true of sections?
   - (a) Sections can be renamed.
   - (b) Sections can be created in Normal view or Slide Sorter view.
   - (c) Sections can be collapsed.
   - (d) A slide show can be divided into only six logical sections.

9. Which of the following formats *cannot* be imported to use as an outline for a presentation?
   - (a) .jpg
   - (b) .docx
   - (c) .txt
   - (d) .rtf

10. You own a small business and decide to institute an Employee of the Month award program. Which of the following would be the fastest way to create the award certificate with a professional look?
    - (a) Enter the text in the title placeholder of a slide, change the font for each line, and then drag several images of awards onto the slide.
    - (b) Select a theme, modify the placeholders, and then enter the award text information.
    - (c) Create a table, enter the award text in the table, and then add images.
    - (d) Search for online templates and themes and download an Award certificate template.

Practice Exercises

1 Classic Photo Album

FROM SCRATCH You enjoy using your digital camera to record nature shots during trips you take on weekends. You decide to store these pictures in an electronic slide show that you can display for your family. You use the Classic Photo Album template. Refer to Figure 2.33 as you complete this exercise.

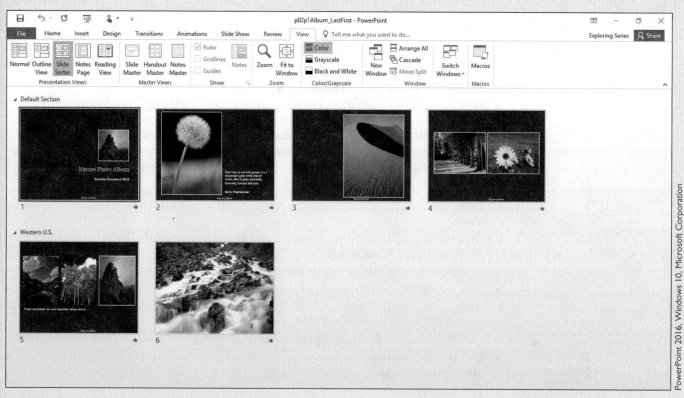

FIGURE 2.33 Classic Photo Album in Slide Sorter View

a. Start PowerPoint.

b. Type **Photo Albums** in the Search box and press **Enter**.
   Thumbnails of sample templates will display.

c. Click **Classic photo album** and click **Create**.

d. Save the presentation file as **p02p1Album_LastFirst**.

e. Create a Notes and Handouts header with your name and a footer with your instructor's name and your class. Include the current date set to update automatically. The page number feature can remain active. Click **Apply to All**.

f. Select the word **CLASSIC** in the title placeholder of the first slide and type **Nature**.

g. Change the case of the title to **Capitalize Each Word**.

h. Replace the text in the **subtitle placeholder**, *Click to add date and other details*, with **Favorite Pictures in 2018**.

i. Click the **New Slide arrow** to display the Layout gallery.

j. Click the **Portrait with Caption layout** to add a new Slide 2.

k. Click the **Picture icon**, locate the image *p02p1Nature* from your student data files, and then click **Insert**.

l. Click in the **caption placeholder** and type **Our way is not soft grass, it's a mountain path with lots of rocks. But it goes upwards, forward, toward the sun.** Press **Enter** twice and type **Ruth Westheimer**.

m. Click **Slide 3**, read the text in the placeholder, and click anywhere in the text.

n. Click the border of the caption placeholder and press **Delete** to remove the content. Select the placeholder again and press **Delete** to remove the placeholder. Modify the layout of the slide by dragging the picture placeholder to the right side of the slide.

o. Select the **Slide 4 thumbnail**, click **Layout** in the Slides group, and then click the **2-Up Landscape with Captions layout** to apply it to the slide.

p. Select the extra photograph (the smaller one) and press **Delete**. Select a border surrounding one of the caption placeholders and press **Delete**. Repeat selecting and deleting until all caption placeholders have been deleted. Delete the CHOOSE A LAYOUT placeholder.

q. Select the **Slide 5 thumbnail**, press and hold **Ctrl**, and select the **Slide 7 thumbnail** in the Slides tab, and then press **Delete** to delete Slides 5 and 7 entirely.

r. Ensure that Normal view is selected, and then click **Slide 5**.

s. Replace the text in the subtitle placeholder with **Clear mountain air and beautiful skies above.**

t. Click **Section** in the Slides group and click **Add Section**. Right-click the **Untitled Section** divider and select **Rename Section**.

u. Type **Western U.S.** and click **Rename**.

v. Click the **Slide Show tab** and click **From Beginning** in the Start Slide Show group to view the presentation. Note the variety of layouts. Proofread to ensure all text is in serif font and that Slides 2 and 5 use sentence case. Press **Esc** when you are finished viewing the presentation.

w. Click the **View tab**, and then click **Slide Master**.

x. Click the **slide master thumbnail** labeled 1. Add your first and last name as a footer. Click **Close Master View**.

y. Save and close the file. Based on your instructor's directions, submit p02p1Album_LastFirst.

2 A Guide to Successful Presentations

FROM SCRATCH Your community's Small Business Development Center (SBDC) asks you to provide training to local small business owners on preparing and delivering presentations. You create an outline and then supplement it by reusing slides from another presentation and by adding slides from an outline. Because the slides come from different sources, they have different fonts, and you change the fonts to match one of the design principles discussed in the chapter. You create sections to organize the presentation and then polish the presentation by adding and modifying a theme. Refer to Figure 2.34 as you complete this exercise.

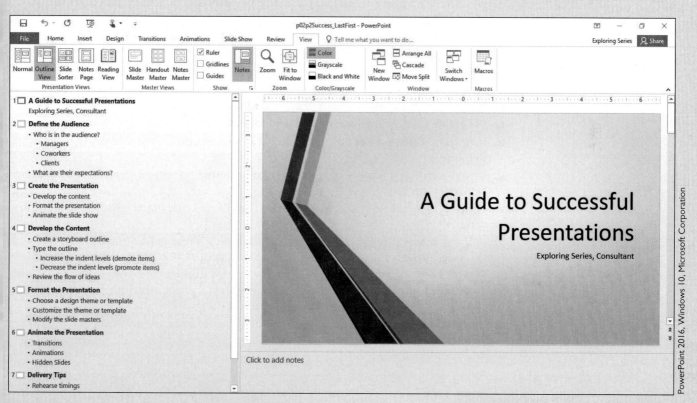

FIGURE 2.34 Presentation Created from an Outline and Reused Slides

a. Create a new, blank presentation. Click the **View tab** and click **Outline View**. Click next to the Slide 1 icon and type **A Guide to Winning Presentations**. Press **Enter** and press **Tab**. Type your name and add the title **Consultant**.

b. Save the new presentation as **p02p2Success_LastFirst**.

c. Create a Notes and Handouts header with your name and a footer with your instructor's name and your class. Include the current date set to update automatically. The page number feature can remain active.

d. Click the **New Slide arrow** in the Slides group on the Home tab, click **Slides from Outline**, locate *p02p2TipsOutline* in your student data files, and then click **Insert**.

e. Select the word **Winning** on Slide 1 while in Outline view, and type **Successful**.

f. Click at the end of the last bulleted text on Slide 3, press **Enter**, and then press **Shift+Tab** to create a new Slide 4. Type **Develop the Content** and press **Enter**.

g. Press **Tab**, type **Create a storyboard outline**, and then press **Enter**.

h. Type **Type the outline** and press **Enter**.

i. Press **Tab** to create a subpoint and type **Increase the indent levels (demote items)**. Press **Enter**.

j. Type **Decrease the indent levels (promote items)** and press **Enter**.

k. Press **Shift+Tab** to return to the previous level and type **Review the flow of ideas**.

l. Click at the end of the last bulleted text on Slide 4 and click the **New Slide arrow** in the Slides group.

m. Click **Reuse Slides** at the bottom of the gallery to open the Reuse Slides pane. Click **Browse**, click **Browse File**, select *p02p2Reuse*, and then click **Open**.

n. Double-click each of the slides in the Reuse Slides pane to insert the slides into the slide show. Close the Reuse Slides pane.

o. Press **Ctrl+A** to select all text in the outline, change the font to **Calibri (Body)**, and then deselect the text.

p. Right-click any bullet point to collapse, point to **Collapse**, and then select **Collapse All**.

q. Drag the Slide 5 icon below the Slide 7 icon.

r. Right-click one of the slide titles, point to **Expand**, and then select **Expand All**.

s. Click the **View tab**, click **Normal**, and then click the **Design tab**. Click **More** in the Themes group and click **Parallax**. Choose the Green variant (the third variant from the left).

t. Click **Slide 2**, click the **Home tab**, click **Section**, and then select **Add Section**.

u. Right-click **Untitled Section** and select **Rename Section**. Type **Create**, and then click **Rename**.

v. Repeat Steps t and u to create a section named **Refine** before Slide 5 and a section named **Deliver** before Slide 7.

w. Click the **View tab** and click **Slide Master**. Click the top slide (numbered Slide 1) in the slide pane.

x. Click the **Insert tab** and click **Pictures**. Locate *p02p2PresenterLogo* and click **Insert**. Move the image to the bottom-right corner of the slide. Click the **Slide Master tab** and click **Close Master View**.

y. Click the **File tab**, click **Print**, click **Full Page Slides**, and select **Outline**. View the outline in the Preview pane and then press **Back** to return to the presentation.

z. Check spelling in the presentation. Save and close the file. Based on your instructor's directions, submit p02p2Success_LastFirst.

Mid-Level Exercises

1 Nutrition Guide

FROM SCRATCH

You have been asked to help create a presentation for a local Girl Scout troop that is featuring good nutrition as its theme for the month. You locate a template online for nutrition that has some fun colors that you think the young girls will enjoy. Since you have given similar presentations, you decide to reuse basic slide content you have previously created on standard nutritional guidelines supported by the U.S. Department of Agriculture. Lastly, you modify the presentation using the slide master so all the changes are easily implemented to all slides.

a. Start PowerPoint, and in the *Search for online templates and themes* box, type **Nutrition**.

b. Select **Fresh food presentation** and click **Create**.

c. Save the presentation as **p02m1Food_LastFirst**.

d. Create a Notes and Handouts header with your name and a footer with your instructor's name and your class. Include the current date.

e. View the slides in Slide Show view.

f. Review the presentation, noting the several types of slide layouts.

g. Click **Slide 1**, replace the Title layout text with **Nutritional Guide**. Replace the subtitle with **June 2018**.

h. Click **Slide 6** and replace the title text with **Food!** Type **Make Good Choices** as the subtitle text.

i. Make the following changes to Slide 2:
   • Replace Title of the Presentation with **Great Nutritional Choices**.
   • Add three bullets: **Colorful fruits and vegetables, Fresh food over processed foods, Reasonable portions.**

j. Delete Slides 3 through 5 and then delete all remaining blank slides.

k. Click the **New Slide arrow** in the Slides group of the Home tab and select **Reuse Slides**.

l. Browse to locate and select the *p02m1Diet* presentation from the student data files in the Reuse Slides pane.

m. Select all seven slides in the Reuse Slides pane. Close the Reuse Slides pane.

n. Move Slide 3 so it becomes the last slide of the presentation.

o. Click the **View tab** and click **Slide Master** from the Master Views group.

DISCOVER

p. Click the third slide in the left pane and make the following changes to the Title and Content Layout slide master:
   • Select the five levels of text in the content placeholder, click the **Font Color arrow** in the Mini toolbar, select the **Eyedropper**, and then click the orange rectangle in the upper-left corner to select one of the colors found in the graphics.
   • Select the text in the title **Click to edit Master title style**, click the **Font Color arrow** in the Mini toolbar, and then select **Dark Green, Accent 6** (theme color, last column).
   • Increase the font size of the slide title to **40**.
   • Close the Slide Master.

q. View Slides 2 through 9 to ensure the changes in the slide master are reflected in the slides.

r. Select Slide 10 and make the following changes:
   • Replace *Food!* with **Food is fun for everyone!**

s. Run the spelling checker and proofread the presentation. Save and close the file. Based on your instructor's directions, submit p02m1Food_LastFirst.

2 Go Digital

CREATIVE CASE

FROM SCRATCH

The local senior citizens' center asked you to speak on photography. The center has many clients interested in learning about digital photography. You decide to create a presentation with sections on learning the advantages of a digital camera, choosing a camera, taking pictures with a digital camera, and printing and sharing photos. In this exercise, you begin the presentation by importing data from an outline and then complete it by reusing some slides from another presentation.

a. Create a new blank PowerPoint presentation and create slides from the *p02m2Outline* outline. Save the slide show as **p02m2Digital_LastFirst**.

b. Apply the **Wisp theme** to the slides.

c. Delete the blank Slide 1 and change the layout of the new Slide 1 to **Title Slide**. Add your name in the subtitle.

d. Review the presentation in PowerPoint's Outline view and add the following information as the last bullets on Slide 2:
    • **Instant feedback**
    • **Sharing**

e. Promote the text **Free Experimentation** on Slide 4 so that it creates a new slide.

> **TROUBLESHOOTING:** If you cannot select a bullet, place your insertion point at the end of the bullet and click to select the bulleted line.

f. Select all text in Outline view and click **Clear All Formatting** in the Font group on the Home tab.

g. Open the Reuse Slides pane and browse to locate and open the *p02m2Slides* presentation. Click the last slide in the original presentation in the Outline pane. Right-click any slide in the Reuse Slides pane and click **Insert All Slides**. The new slides should be inserted as Slides 6 and 7. Close the Reuse Slides pane.

h. Select **More** in the Variants Gallery on the Design tab and change the presentation font to **Corbel**. Using the Colors gallery, change the presentation colors to **Red**. Apply **Background Style 10**.

i. Return to Normal view.

j. Create a section between Slides 1 and 2 named **Advantages**.

k. Create a section after Slide 7 named **Choosing a Digital Camera**.

DISCOVER

l. Use the Web to research things to consider when purchasing a digital camera. Be sure to include the major types of cameras available.

m. Insert a new Slide 8 in the **Choosing a Digital Camera** section to explain your findings.

n. Create a Notes and Handouts header with your name and a footer with your instructor's name and your class. Include the current date.

o. Save and close the file. Based on your instructor's directions, submit p02m2Digital_LastFirst.

3 Using Social Technologies for Ideas and Resources

COLLABORATION CASE

FROM SCRATCH

Social networking enables us to connect with others who share common interests via the Internet. Social networking also helps businesses connect with their customers. In this exercise, you will give an overview of some of the popular social media technologies such as Facebook, Twitter, LinkedIn, etc. and discuss how businesses can utilize them to engage their customers. Choose a business that interests you and discuss which social media technologies it uses and how they are used to connect with its customers. You will visit Microsoft's Office.com website, download a template from the Design Gallery, modify the template with your information, and then post the PowerPoint presentation you create to a location where others can view and comment on it.

a. Access the Internet and go to **http://templates.office.com**. Click **PowerPoint**. Click to see all available PowerPoint 2016 templates.

b. Click several of the thumbnails to see further details about the presentation.

c. Select one of the templates and download the slides to the location you use to store your files for this class. Save the file as **p02m3Resources_GroupName**. Open the saved slide show and modify the slides so they reflect your information and ideas. Be sure to follow the design principles discussed in the chapter. Your presentation should be approximately six to nine slides in length, including the title and credit slides. Delete any unnecessary slides found in the template. Make sure you create a final slide that credits the source for the template design. Provide the URL for the location from where you downloaded the template.

d. Load your edited presentation to an online location for others to review. Upload your presentation to your Microsoft OneDrive account or use another method for sharing your presentation with your instructor and classmates. (If you do not already have a OneDrive account, you can create a free account at https://onedrive.live.com.)

e. Invite three classmates to view the presentation you saved at the site, and then add a comment about your presentation. If using OneDrive to add comments, click the **Comment button** in PowerPoint Online. If you saved to another online storage location, share the location with three classmates and ask them to download the presentation. After viewing the presentation, ask them to email you with their comments.

f. Visit three of your classmates' presentations from their storage locations. Leave a comment about their presentations or email your classmates, sharing a comment about their presentations.

g. Review the comments of your classmates.

h. Save and close the file. Based on your instructor's directions, submit p02m3Resources_GroupName.

Beyond the Classroom

Social Media Marketing

You have a bright, creative, and energetic personality, and you are using these talents in college as a senior majoring in marketing. You hope to work in social media marketing. The Marketing 405 course you are taking this semester requires every student to create a social media marketing plan for a fictional company and to present an overview of the company to the class. This presentation should include the company purpose, the company's history, and past and present projects—all of which you are to "creatively invent."

Search http://templates.office.com for an appropriate template to use in creating your presentation. Save your presentation as **p02b1Marketing_LastFirst**. Research what a social media marketing campaign entails, and use what you learn to add your own content to comply with the case requirements. Add images, transitions, and animations as desired. Organize using sections. Create a handout header with your name and a handout footer with your instructor's name and your class. Include the current date and page number. Save and close the file. Based on your instructor's directions, submit p02b1Marketing_LastFirst.

Michigan, My State

DISASTER RECOVERY ✚

Your sister spent a lot of time researching and creating a presentation on the state of Michigan for a youth organization leader and team members. She does not like the presentation's design and has asked for your help. You show her how to download the state history report presentation template from Office.com, Presentations category, Education subcategory. Save the new presentation as **p02b2State_LastFirst**. Reuse her slides, which are saved as *p02b2Michigan*. Cut and paste the images she gathered into the correct placeholders and move bulleted text to the correct slide. Resize placeholders as needed. You tell your sister that mixing cartoons and drawings with photos is contributing to the cluttered look. Choose one format based on your preference. Create new slides with appropriate layouts as needed. You remind her that although federal government organizations allow use of their images in an educational setting, your sister should give proper credit if she is going to use their data. Give credit to the State of Michigan's website for the information obtained from Michigan.gov (http://michigan.gov/kids). Give credit to the U.S. Census Bureau (http://www.census.gov) for the Quick Facts. Finalize the presentation by deleting unneeded slides, adding appropriate sections, modifying themes, checking spelling, proofreading, and applying transitions. Create a handout header with your name and a handout footer with your instructor's name and your class. Include the current date. Print the outline as directed by your instructor. Save and close the file. Based on your instructor's directions, submit p02b2State_LastFirst.

Capstone Exercise

You are developing a report for your sociology class about the roles of women in the science, technology, engineering, and mathematics (STEM) fields. After doing some research, you begin to see that throughout history, women have had very few opportunities in these areas for historical and societal reasons. You want to demonstrate to your classmates the key and increasingly important role women have played in STEM advances. You will use your PowerPoint presentation to inform them of some key contributors in the STEM areas. In this capstone project, you concentrate on developing the content of the presentation.

Design Template

You download a template from http://templates.office.com to create the basic design and structure for your presentation, save the presentation, and create the title slide.

a. Create a new presentation using one of the available templates. Search for the template using the search term **Technology** and locate and download the **Technology at work design slides template**.

b. Save the presentation as **p02c1Women_LastFirst**.

c. Type **Women in STEM** as the title on the title slide.

d. Type the subtitle **Science, Technology, Engineering, and Mathematics** and change the font size to 20.

e. Insert 6 blank new slides.

f. Create a handout header with your name and a handout footer with your instructor's name and your class. Include the current date. Apply to all slides.

Outline and Modifications

Based on the storyboard you created after researching women in STEM on the Internet, you type the outline of your presentation. As you create the outline, you also modify the outline structure.

a. Open Outline view.

b. Type **Name 3 women in STEM** as the title for Slide 2.

c. Type each of the following as Level 1 bullets for Slide 2: **My biology teacher**, **My computer applications teacher**, **My math teacher**.

d. Type **Think on a bigger scale** as the title for Slide 3. Enter each of the following as Level 1 bullets for Slide 3: **National names?**, and **International names?**

e. Add this speaker note to Slide 3: **These may be hard questions to answer quickly because there are relatively few women in these fields**.

f. Type **Here are some names to get you started** as the title for Slide 4.

g. Type each of the following as Level 1 bullets for Slide 4: **Sally Ride**, **Christa McAuliffe**.

h. Add this speaker note to Slide 4: **For different reasons, both of these women were important in the development of the aerospace industry.**

Imported Outline

You have an outline on women in STEM that was created in Microsoft Word and also a slide show on that topic. You reuse this content to build your slide show.

a. Position the insertion point at the end of the outline after Slide 4.

b. Use the **Slides from Outline option** to insert the *p02c1Stem* outline.

c. Delete Slide 5 and any blank slides.

d. Demote the last two bullets on the new Slide 5.

e. Click the first bullet on Slide 6. Cut and paste the text after the name and date from the bullet point to the Notes pane. Replace *She* with **Hypatia**. Repeat for the remaining two bullets.

f. Delete all text after *physics* for the first bullet of Slide 7. Replace the comma with a period.

g. Position the insertion point at the end of the outline.

h. Reuse Slides 2 and 3, using the same order, from *p02c1Work* to add two slides to the end of the presentation.

i. Modify the outline structure by reversing slides 8 and 9.

Design

The content of some of the imported slides does not fit well and the font colors are not uniform across all of the slides. You want to adjust the layout and font color to create a well-designed presentation. Then you decide to view a slide show to verify your changes.

a. Switch to Normal view. Change the layout of Slide 9 to Blank.

b. Check Slides 5–7 to ensure the title placeholder font is Arial Black (Heading) with the color set to Black, Text 2. Check the subtitle font to Arial Body with the color set to Grey 80%, Text 1.

c. Use the spelling checker and proofread the presentation.

d. View a slide show from the beginning.

e. Move Slide 5 to just before Slide 8.

Sections

To facilitate organization of the presentation and moving between the slides, you create sections.

a. Add a section before Slide 2 and rename it **Quiz**.

b. Add a section before Slide 5 and rename it **History**.

c. Add a section before Slide 7 and rename it **Reasoning**.

d. Print the outline as directed by your instructor.

e. Save and close the file. Based on your instructor's directions, submit p02c1Women_LastFirst.

Presentation Design

LEARNING OUTCOME You will use shapes, diagrams, and objects to enhance a presentation.

OBJECTIVES & SKILLS: After you read this chapter, you will be able to:

Shapes

OBJECTIVE 1: CREATE SHAPES 188
Create Shapes, Draw Lines and Connectors, Create and Modify Freeform Shapes

OBJECTIVE 2: APPLY QUICK STYLES AND CUSTOMIZE SHAPES 194
Apply Quick Styles and Customize Shapes, Change Shape Fills, Change Shape Outlines, Change Shape Effects

HANDS-ON EXERCISE 1:
Shapes 205

SmartArt and WordArt

OBJECTIVE 3: CREATE SMARTART 210
Create SmartArt

OBJECTIVE 4: MODIFY SMARTART 214
Modify Smart Art, Change SmartArt Theme Colors, Use Quick Styles with SmartArt, Change the SmartArt Layout, Change SmartArt Type, Convert Text to a SmartArt Diagram

OBJECTIVE 5: CREATE WORDART AND MODIFY WORDART 217
Create WordArt, Modify WordArt

HANDS-ON EXERCISE 2:
SmartArt and WordArt 220

Object Manipulation

OBJECTIVE 6: MODIFY OBJECTS 225
Resize Objects, Flip and Rotate Objects, Merge Shapes, Group and Ungroup Objects, Recolor Objects

OBJECTIVE 7: ARRANGE OBJECTS 233
Order Objects

HANDS-ON EXERCISE 3:
Object Manipulation 239

CASE STUDY | Illustrations and Infographics Workshop

This summer, you are working with several IT interns. You want to introduce the interns to drawing using computer-based drawing tools, creating infographics, and working with online pictures. You decide to teach the concepts in a PowerPoint workshop because you want to introduce the participants to an application they all have access to and because PowerPoint has many tools for creating and modifying illustrations.

You begin training by teaching the participants how to create and modify lines and shapes, how to use shapes to create flow charts, how to use SmartArt diagrams, and how to modify online pictures to meet their needs. You also demonstrate WordArt manipulation as a creative way to enhance text used in illustrations and infographics. You conclude the workshop by showing the interns how to modify and arrange objects to better meet their needs.

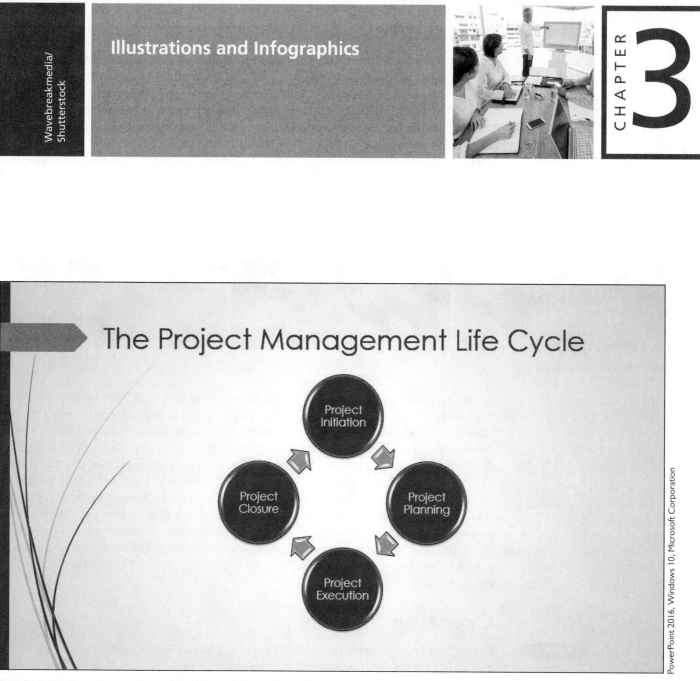

FIGURE 3.1 Illustrations and Infographics Workshop Slide

PowerPoint 2016, Windows 10, Microsoft Corporation

CASE STUDY | Illustrations and Infographics Workshop

Starting Files	Files to be Submitted
p03h1Project p03h2ProjectManagement	p03h1Project_LastFirst p03h3ProjectManagement_LastFirst

Shapes

Text can be very effective when giving a presentation, but sometimes an illustration or diagram can add additional clarity to the idea that is being presented. One type of visual element is a **shape**, a geometric or non-geometric object used to create an illustration or to highlight information. For example, you can create a quote inside a shape to call attention to it. You can also combine shapes to create complex images. Figure 3.2 shows three PowerPoint themes using shapes. The Berlin theme uses a rectangular shape to draw attention to the information in the title placeholder. The Vapor Trail theme uses curved shapes to create an interesting design. SmartArt in the Quotable theme uses rounded rectangles to emphasize each concept.

PowerPoint 2016, Windows 10, Microsoft Corporation

FIGURE 3.2 Using Shapes

Infographics, a shortened term for information graphics, are visual representations of data or knowledge. Infographics typically use shapes to present complex data or knowledge in an easily understood visual representation. PowerPoint includes powerful drawing tools you can use to create lines and shapes, which are the basis for infographics. Because drawn images are created with shapes, you should learn to modify the shapes used for drawn images to meet your needs. In addition to using the drawing tools, you can enhance shapes by adding effects such as 3-D, shadow, glow, warp, bevel, and others. These effects are accessible through style galleries. Using these visual effects makes it easy for you to create professional-looking infographics to enhance your presentation.

In this section, you will create and modify various shapes and lines. You will also customize shapes and apply special effects to objects. Finally, you will learn how to apply and change outline effects.

Creating Shapes

 PowerPoint provides tools for creating shapes. You can insert a multitude of standard geometric shapes such as circles, squares, hearts, or stars. You can insert equation shapes, such as + and ÷, and a variety of banners. After you create a shape, you can modify it and apply fills and special effects. Text may also be added to a shape by clicking inside of the shape and typing, or by pasting text into the shape. Text in a shape may be formatted using the standard formatting tools.

To create a shape, complete the following steps:

1. Click the Insert tab.
2. Click Shapes in the Illustrations group.
3. Click the shape you want from the Shapes gallery.
4. Click the desired position in which to place the shape, or drag the cross-hair pointer to control the approximate size of the shape.

To resize the shape, drag any of the sizing handles that surround the shape after it is created. Figure 3.3 shows the Shapes gallery and the many shapes from which you can choose. Notice that the most recently used shapes are at the top of the list so you can conveniently reuse them.

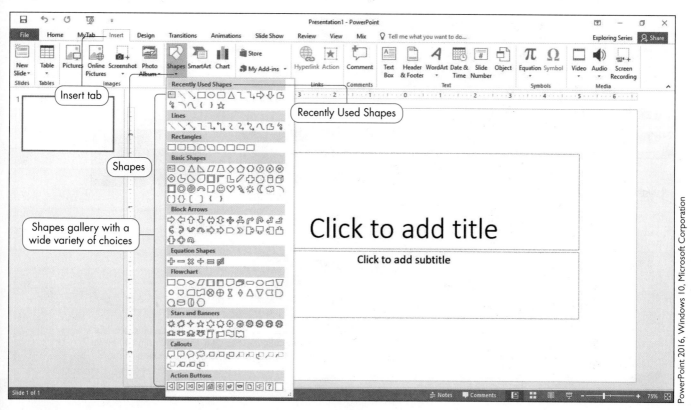

FIGURE 3.3 Shapes Gallery

TIP: USING THE DRAWING GROUP

You can also access the Shapes gallery from the Drawing group on the Home tab. The Drawing group enables you to choose a shape, arrange its order and position, apply a Quick Style, and then change properties of the shape. If you have a widescreen monitor or if your monitor is set for a higher resolution, the Drawing group displays individual shapes instead of one Shapes command. If you only see one shape, click the More button to open the Shapes gallery.

The Shapes command deactivates the selected shape after you draw it once, forcing you to reselect the shape each time you want to use it. By activating the **Lock Drawing Mode** feature, you can add several shapes of the same type on your slide without selecting the shape each time.

To activate Lock Drawing Mode, complete the following steps:

1. Right-click the shape you want to use in the Shapes gallery and select Lock Drawing Mode.
2. Click anywhere on the slide or drag to create the first shape.
3. Click or drag repeatedly to create additional shapes of the same type.
4. Press Esc to release Lock Drawing Mode.

Figure 3.4 shows a series of rectangles created with Lock Drawing Mode activated, a basic oval, and smiley face all of that are located in the Basic Shapes category in the Shapes gallery. In addition, a **callout** is shown that was created using the Cloud Callout located in the Callouts category. A callout is a shape that can be used to add text, often used in cartooning. Notice that the smiley face shape is selected on the slide. The sizing handles display around the shape. A yellow circle is located on the mouth of the shape. This is an **adjustment handle** that you can drag to change the shape. If you drag the adjustment handle upward, the smile becomes a frown. Some shapes have an adjustment handle, and some do not.

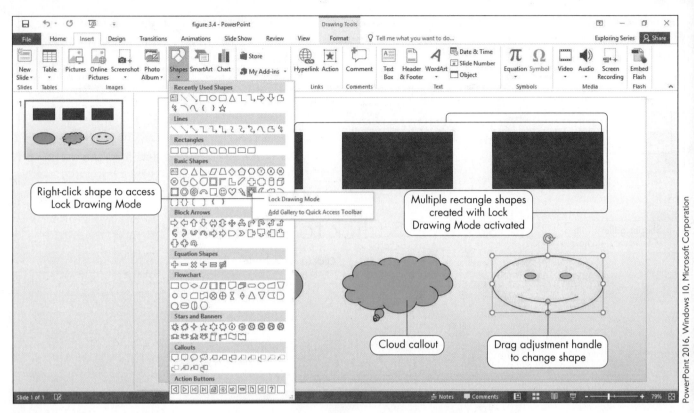

FIGURE 3.4 Basic Shapes

TIP: CONSTRAIN A SHAPE
A rectangle can be constrained or forced to form a perfect square, and an oval or ellipse can be constrained to form a perfect circle. To constrain a shape, press and hold Shift as you drag to create the shape. Or, if you click on the screen instead of dragging when you initially create the shape, you get a perfect 1-inch square or a perfect 1-inch diameter circle.

Draw Lines and Connectors

STEP 2 ▶▶ Lines are shapes that can be used to point to information, to connect shapes on a slide, or to divide a slide into sections. Lines also are often used in slide design.

To draw a straight line, complete the following steps:

1. Select Line in the Lines category of the Shapes gallery.
2. Position the pointer on the slide where you want the line to begin.
3. Drag to create the line. Hold Shift as you drag to constrain to a perfectly horizontal, vertical, or any multiple of a 45-degree angle line.

You can also create curved lines. These may take a little practice to get the curve you want.

To create a curved line, complete the following steps:

1. Click Curve in the Lines category of the Shapes gallery.
2. Click the slide at the location where you want to start the curve.
3. Click again where the peaks or valleys of the curve occur and continue to click and move the pointer to shape the curve in the desired pattern.
4. Double-click to end the curve.

As you click while creating the curve, you set a point for the curve to bend around. To draw a shape that looks like it was drawn with a pen, select the Scribble shape.

In addition to drawing simple lines to create dividing lines and waves, you may need *connectors*, or lines with connection points at each end. Connectors stay connected to the shapes or placeholders to which you attach them. Connector lines move with shapes when the shapes are moved. The three types of connectors are: line (to create straight lines), elbow (to create angled lines), and curved. Not all line shapes are connectors. To determine which line shapes are connectors, point to the line in the gallery and a ScreenTip will appear with the shape name, such as Curved Arrow Connector.

The first step in working with connectors is to create the shapes you want to connect with lines. Once the shapes are created, you can use connectors to join them.

To connect shapes, complete the following steps:

1. Create the shapes you wish to connect.
2. Select a connector line from the Lines category of the Shape gallery.
3. Move the pointer over a shape; circles appear around the shape. These are the locations where you can attach the connector.
4. Click one of the circles to connect the line and drag to the next shape, releasing the mouse button when you see the circle on the shape to which you want to connect. You can also drag to control the direction and size of the connector line.

If you move a shape that is joined to another shape using a connector line, the line moves with it, extending or shortening as necessary to maintain the connection. Sometimes when you rearrange the shapes, the connectors may no longer extend to the shape that was not moved, or the connectors may cross shapes and be confusing. If that happens, you can use the yellow adjustment handle located on the connector line to reshape the connectors. Select the connector lines and drag the handles to obtain a clearer path.

A *flow chart* is an illustration that shows a sequence to be followed or a plan containing steps. For example, you could use a flow chart to illustrate the sequence to follow when implementing a new product. Connector lines join the shapes in a flow chart.

The typical flow chart sequence includes start and end points shown in oval shapes, steps shown in rectangular shapes, and decisions to be made shown in diamond shapes. Colored shapes are optional, but be sure to be consistent when you apply color. Connectors with arrows demonstrate the order in which the sequence should be followed to accomplish the goal. Each shape in a flow chart has a label to which you can add text.

When you select a shape and type text in it or when you paste text into a shape, the text becomes part of the shape. Sometimes, however, it is necessary to add a text to a slide and you do not have a placeholder or shape in which to place the text. You can add a *text box*, an object that provides space for text. A text box can be more flexible than content placeholders and can be added to slides in which the chosen layout does not include a content placeholder, but text is still necessary. For example, use a text box to add a quote to a slide that is separate from the slide content placeholder. Text inside a text box can be formatted just as text in placeholders is formatted. You can even add a border, fill, shadow, or 3-D effect to the text in a text box. Figure 3.5 shows a basic flow chart created with shapes, connectors, and text boxes.

Lines and Connectors

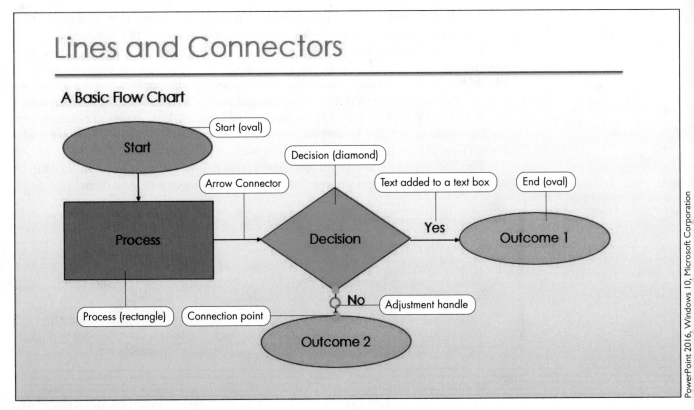

FIGURE 3.5 Basic Flow Chart

Create and Modify Freeform Shapes

A *freeform shape* is a shape that can be used to create customized shapes using both curved and straight-line segments. It enables you to draw whatever you want, like you would draw with a pencil on a sheet of paper. A freeform shape can be comprised of straight-line segments and curved segments. One use for the freeform tool is to trace a picture.

To create a freeform shape, complete the following steps:

1. Select the Freeform shape in the Lines category of the Shapes gallery and click the slide to set the starting point for the shape.
2. Click to draw straight lines and drag to create curves.
3. Double-click to end the freeform shape.

> **TIP: CREATE A CLOSED SHAPE**
> If you use the Curve, Freeform, or Scribble line tool to create a shape and end the shape at its starting point, the starting point and ending points join to create a closed shape. The advantage of joining the ends of the line and creating a closed shape is that you can include a fill, or interior content.

Sometimes, the freeform shape you have drawn is not exactly as you desired. You can modify the freeform shape to achieve the desired shape. This can be achieved through the help of a vertex. A *vertex*, also known as an anchor point, is a black square that controls a curved line segment and indicates where two line segments meet or end. You can control the shape by using these anchor points. Click a point to move and drag it to a new position or to modify the shape's line segment curve. A vertex can be deleted if you right-click the point and select Delete Point. Either moving a vertex or deleting it will redefine the object's shape. Figure 3.6 shows a freeform shape with its vertexes displayed. Figure 3.7 shows a selected vertex dragged to a new position. When you release the left mouse button, the freeform will take the new shape.

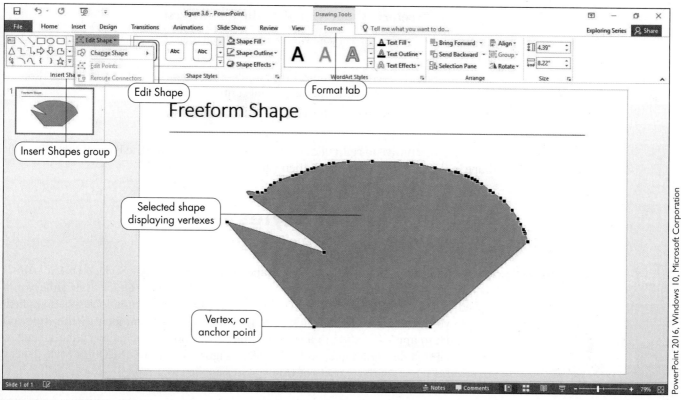

FIGURE 3.6 Modifying a Freeform Shape

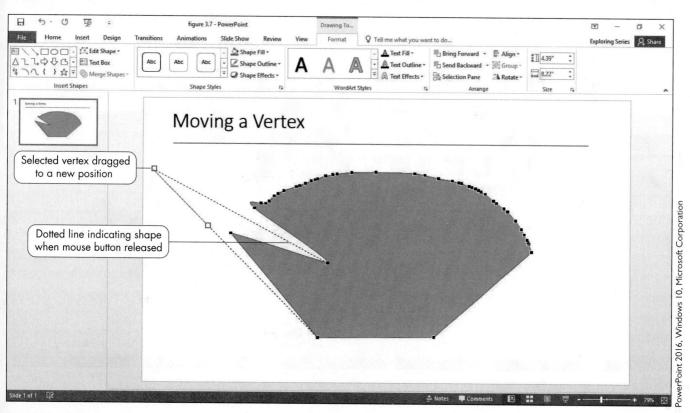

FIGURE 3.7 Moving a Vertex

> **To modify a freeform shape, complete the following steps:**
>
> 1. Select the freeform object you want to change, and then right-click.
> 2. Click Edit Points.
> 3. Drag one of the vertexes or one of the handles that extend from the vertex point. You can also right-click a vertex for additional control options.
> 4. Click off the shape or press Esc to finish editing points.

As an alternative to right clicking the shape, you can click the Format tab, click Edit Shape in the Insert Shapes group, then click Edit Points.

Applying Quick Styles and Customizing Shapes

 You can add a professional look to your shapes by applying a Quick Style. A ***Quick Style*** is a combination of different formats that can be selected from the Quick Style gallery and applied to a shape or other objects. To see how a Quick Style would look when applied, position your pointer over the Quick Style thumbnail. When you identify the style you want, click to apply the style to a selected object. Options in the gallery include edges, shadows, line styles, gradients, and 3-D effects. Figure 3.8 shows the Quick Style gallery and several shapes with a variety of Quick Styles applied to them.

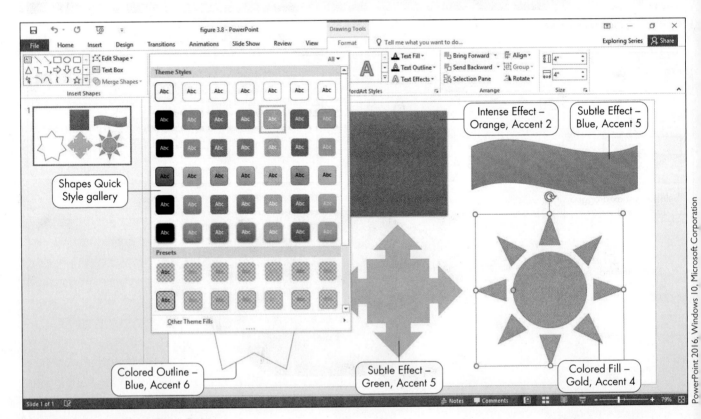

FIGURE 3.8 Using Shape Quick Styles

To apply a Quick Style to a shape, complete the following steps:

1. Select the shape and click the Format tab.
2. Click the More button in the Shape Styles group. This enables you to apply a Quick Style or to select the fill and outline of the shape manually and apply special effects.
3. Preview the styles in the Quick Styles gallery by moving the pointer over the various styles.
4. Click the Quick Style you wish to apply.

As an alternative to using the Format tab, you can click the Home tab and click Quick Styles in the Drawing group.

To apply a Quick Style to multiple objects, use a ***selection net*** or ***marquee***. A selection net or marquee is a selection of multiple objects and is created by dragging a rectangle around all of the objects you want to select and ending the selection by releasing the mouse button. All objects contained entirely within the net will be selected. With the objects selected, you can apply a Quick Style to all the objects at the same time.

TIP: SELECTING MULTIPLE OBJECTS

If objects are difficult to select with a selection net because of their placement or because they are nonadjacent, press and hold Ctrl or Shift as you click each object. While the Ctrl or Shift keys are pressed, as you click each object it is added to the selection. When you have selected all objects, choose the style or effect you want, and it will apply only to the selected objects. If you click an object you do not want to include, simply click it a second time and it will be removed from the selection.

Change Shape Fills

One way to customize a shape is by changing the shape fill, or the interior format of the shape. You can choose a solid color fill, no fill, a picture fill, a gradient fill, or a texture fill. These options are available from the Shape Fill gallery in the Shape Styles group on the Format tab. The Shape Fill gallery provides color choices that match the theme colors or color choices based on standard colors. Figure 3.9 shows the Shape Fill options and a shape filled with the Theme color Gold, Accent 4.

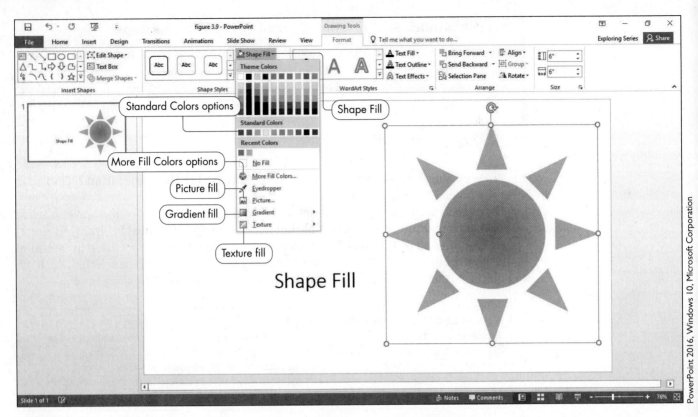

FIGURE 3.9 Shape Fill Options

> **To change the fill of a selected object, complete the following steps:**
>
> 1. Select the shape and click the Format tab.
> 2. Click the Shape Fill arrow in the Shape Styles group.
> 3. Select the fill option you want.

You may want to recreate an exact color in another part of your presentation by using the ***Eyedropper***. The Eyedropper enables you to match colors used in other slides to create a unified look to your presentation. For example, you want to re-create the yellow in a sunset used in the introduction slide of your presentation. Figure 3.10 shows a color picked up by the Eyedropper and applied to another object.

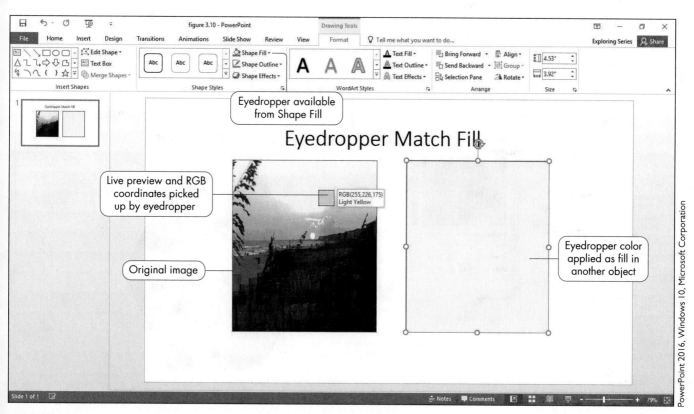

FIGURE 3.10 Using the Eyedropper

To use the Eyedropper to match colors, complete the following steps:

1. Click the shape you want to fill, click the Shape Fill arrow in the Shape Styles group on the Format tab, and then select Eyedropper.
2. Point to the color you want to recreate. While pointing to different colors, you will see a Live Preview of the color aiding you in your decision of which color to select.
3. Click and the shape will fill with the color in the Eyedropper. If you decide you do not want to use the Eyedropper, press Esc.

Alternatively, you may also select More Fill Colors to open the Colors dialog box where you can mix colors based on an RGB color model (Red Green Blue) or an HSL color model (Hue Saturation Luminosity). The default RGB color model gives each of the colors red, green, and blue a numeric value that ranges from 0 to 255. The combination of these values creates the fill color assigned to the shape. When all three RGB values are 0, you get black. When all three RGB values are 255, you get white. By using different combinations of numbers between 0 and 255, you can create more than 16 million shades of color.

The Colors dialog box also enables you to determine the amount of *transparency*, or visibility of the fill. At 0% transparency, the fill is *opaque* (or solid), while at 100% transparency, the fill is clear. The Colors dialog box enables you to drag a slider to specify the percentage of transparency. Figure 3.11 shows the Colors dialog box with the RGB color model selected, Red assigned a value of 236, Green assigned a value of 32, Blue assigned a value of 148, and a transparency set at 0%.

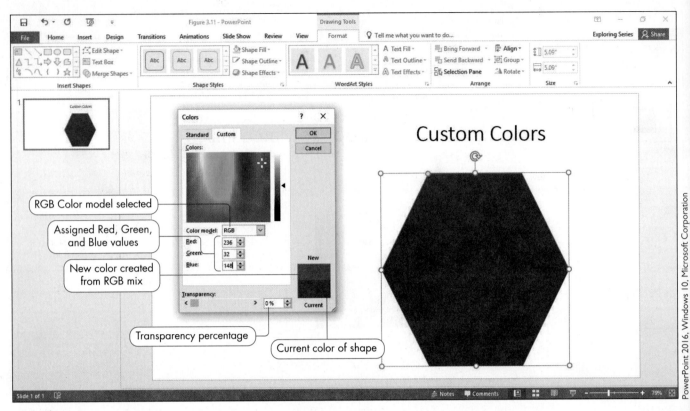

FIGURE 3.11 Colors Dialog Box

You can fill shapes with images using the ***picture fill*** option. This option enables you to create unusual frames for your pictures and can be a fun way to vary the images in your presentation.

To insert a picture as a fill, complete the following steps:

1. Click the shape you want to fill, click the Shape Fill arrow in the Shape Styles group on the Format tab, and then click Picture.
2. Click Browse to locate a picture from a file that you want to add and double-click the picture to insert it. To insert an online picture, click Search Bing to search the Web for a Bing image.

Figure 3.12 shows the 7-Point Star shape filled with a picture that was saved on the computer hard drive. The image is of a wildflower growing through snow that the presenter selected to enhance a presentation about perseverance.

FIGURE 3.12 Shape Filled with a Picture

You can fill shapes with a *gradient fill*, a blend of two or more colors. When you select Gradient from the Shape Fill gallery, another gallery of options opens, enabling you to select Light and Dark Variations that blend the current color with white or black in linear or radial gradients. Figure 3.13 shows the gradient options for a selected object.

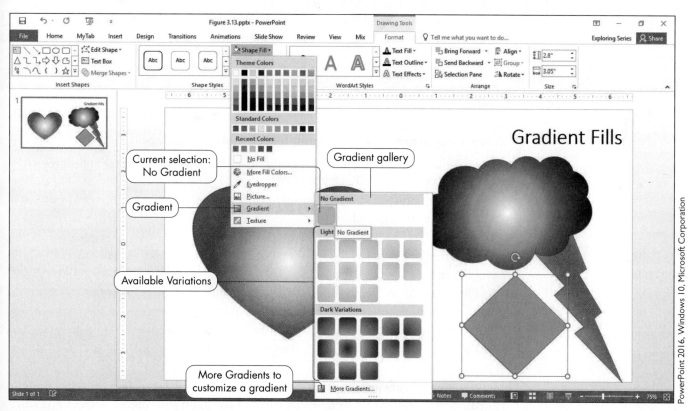

FIGURE 3.13 Light and Dark Gradient Variations

When you select More Gradients at the bottom of the Gradients gallery, the Format Shape pane opens. The Gradient fill option in the Fill section provides access to the Preset gradients gallery. This gallery gives you a variety of gradients using a multitude of colors based on the theme for the presentation.

You can create a custom gradient in the Format Shape pane. Select the colors to blend for the gradient, the direction and angle of the gradient, the brightness of the colors, and the amount of transparency to apply. Figure 3.14 shows a custom gradient created in the Format Shape pane.

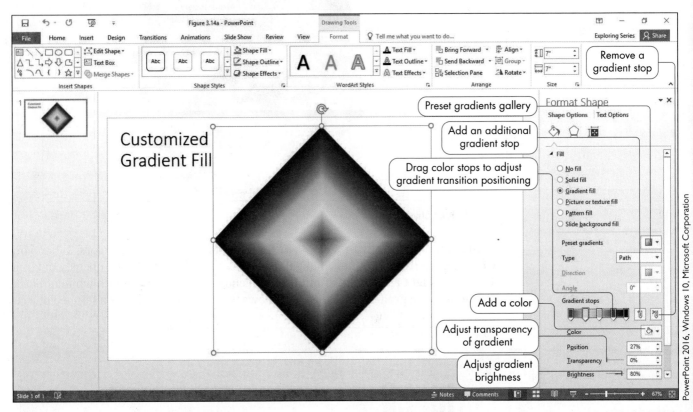

FIGURE 3.14 Creating a Custom Gradient

To create a custom gradient, complete the following steps:

1. Click the shape you want to fill, click the Shape Fill arrow in the Shape Styles group on the Format tab, and then click Gradient.
2. Click More Gradients to open the Format Shape pane.
3. Click Fill and click Gradient Fill.
4. Click the first Gradient stop.
5. Click the Color arrow and select the color from one of the color categories.
6. Click the last Gradient stop.
7. Click the Color arrow and select the color from one of the color categories.
8. Click *Add gradient stop* to add an additional color if desired.
9. Drag the new gradient stop until you create the desired blend.
10. Click a gradient stop and click *Remove gradient stop* to remove a color.

Selecting *Picture or texture fill* gives you access to common ***texture fills***, such as canvas, denim, marble, or cork, which you can use to fill your object. Selecting Texture opens the Texture gallery, with options for setting a transparency level and tiling. Tiled textures have seamless edges so that you cannot tell where one tile ends and another begins. Figure 3.15 shows the Texture gallery and a Plaque shape with an Oak texture applied. The first plaque is scaled at 100% while the second plaque Scale X was scaled to 75% and and Scale Y was scaled to 50%.

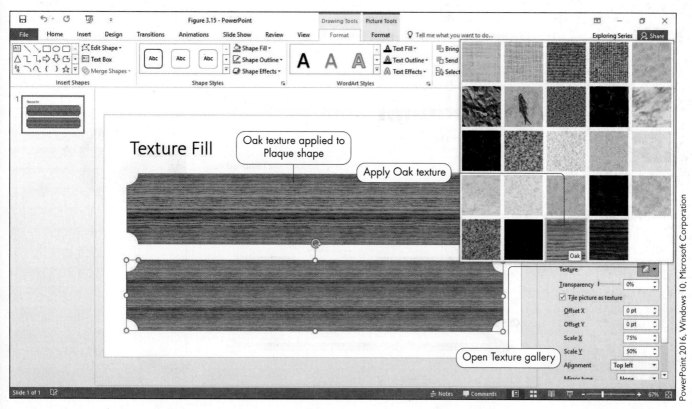

FIGURE 3.15 Texture Fills

To apply a texture fill, complete the following steps:

1. Click the shape you want to fill, click the Shape Fill arrow Shape Styles group on the Format tab, and then click Texture.
2. Select More Textures to open the Format Shape pane.
3. Click Picture or texture fill and then click the Texture arrow.
4. Click the texture you want to apply to your shape.
5. Select scaling, if desired.

Change Shape Outlines

By default, outlines form a border around a shape. You can modify a shape's outline by changing its color, style, or **_line weight_** (thickness). Figure 3.16 shows examples of each of these modifications. You can modify outlines by using the Shape Styles feature accessible in the Shape Styles group on the Format tab, or by clicking the Shape Styles Dialog Box Launcher to open the Format Shape pane. Click the Fill & Line icon and then click Line.

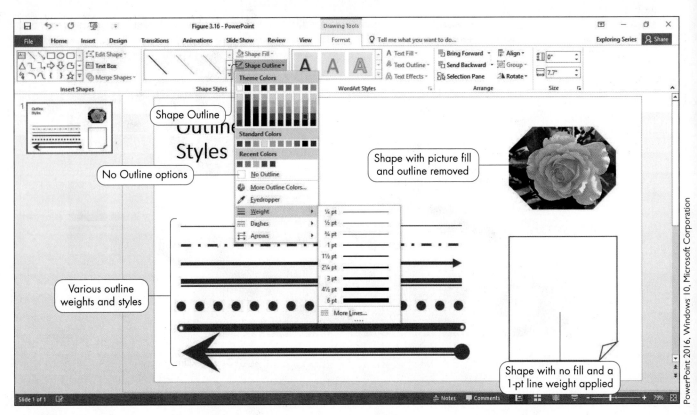

FIGURE 3.16 Outline Colors, Styles, and Weights

You can customize outlines using the Shape Outline gallery options available in the Shape Styles group or the Line options in the Format Shape pane.

To change an outline color, complete the following steps:

1. Click the shape you want to change the outline color of and then click the Shape Outline arrow in the Shape Styles group on the Format tab.
2. Select a theme color, a standard color, or a color from the More Outline Colors option.

The width or thickness of a line is measured in **points** (pt), the smallest unit of measurement in typography. One vertical inch contains 72 pt. If you do not want an outline around a shape, click No Outline in the Shape Outline gallery. See Figure 3.16 to see an example of a shape with a picture fill that has the outline removed so it does not detract from the image.

To set the line width, complete the following steps:

1. Select a line or an object with an outline and click the Format tab.
2. Click the Shape Outline arrow in the Shape Styles group, and point to Weight to display line weight choices from 1/4 pt to 6 pt.
3. Click one of the weight options or click More Lines.

Selecting More Lines opens the Format Shape pane with the Line options displayed. The Format Shape pane enables you to change the line weight using the spin arrows in the Width box or by typing the weight directly into the Width box. You can also use the Format Shape pane to create Compound type outlines, which combine thick and thin lines.

For variety, you can change a solid line to a dashed line. Dashed lines make interesting boxes or borders for shapes and placeholders by using round dots, square dots, and combinations of short dashes, long dashes, and dots.

To make a line or object outline dashed, complete the following steps:

1. Select a line or an object with an outline.
2. Click the Shape Outline arrow in the Shape Styles group on the Format tab, and point to Dashes to display dash options.
3. Click the desired dash style.

You can add an arrowhead to the beginning or end of a line to create an arrow that points to critical information on the slide. The Shape Outline feature enables you to create many different styles of arrows using points, circles, and diamonds.

To add an arrowhead, complete the following steps:

1. Select a line.
2. Click the Shape Outline arrow in the Shape Styles group on the Format tab, and point to Arrows to display start and end arrow options.
3. Click the desired arrow style.

Change Shape Effects

STEP 4 ⟫ PowerPoint enables you to apply many stunning effects to shapes: preset three-dimensional effects, shadow effects, reflections, glows, soft edge effects, bevels, and 3-D rotations. Shape effects will change if you choose a new theme. Figure 3.17 shows an example of some of the shape effects available.

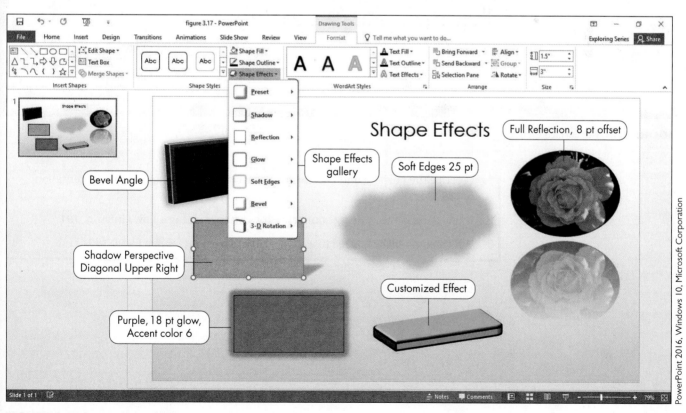

FIGURE 3.17 Sample Shape Effects

To apply effects to a selected shape, complete the following steps:

1. Click the shape to which you want to add effects, and then click the Shape Effects arrow in the Shape Styles group on the Format tab.
2. Point to Preset and select a built-in combination, or select one of the options listed below Preset to set individual effects.

To customize an effect, click 3-D Options at the bottom of the Preset gallery to open the Format Shape pane, where you can define the bevel, depth, contour, and surface of the effect. Figure 3.18 displays the Format Shape options and the Material options for the surface of a shape.

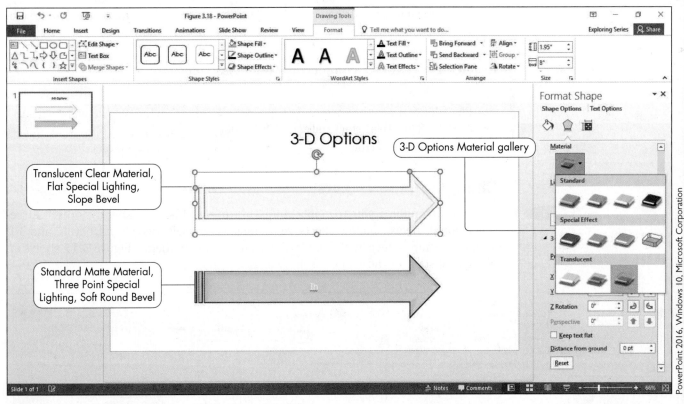

FIGURE 3.18 3-D Surface Options

Quick Concepts

1. Describe the purpose and effectiveness of incorporating shapes into a presentation. *p. 188*
2. What is the value of using connector lines when creating a flow chart? *p. 191*
3. Why might a fill be applied to a shape? Give two examples of a fill. *p. 195*

Hands-On Exercises

Watch the Video
for this Hands-On
Exercise!

MyITLab®
HOE1 Training

1 Shapes

You begin the illustrations and infographics workshop by having the interns work with a project status report. They will create basic shapes using PowerPoint's drawing tools. You also ask the group to customize the shapes by adding styles and effects.

STEP 1 » CREATE SHAPES

Knowing how to use a flow chart to diagram the processes or steps needed to complete a project or task is a valuable skill. To teach participants how to create multiple shapes using Lock Drawing Mode, you have them create several ovals as part of a project flow chart. Refer to Figure 3.19 as you complete Step 1.

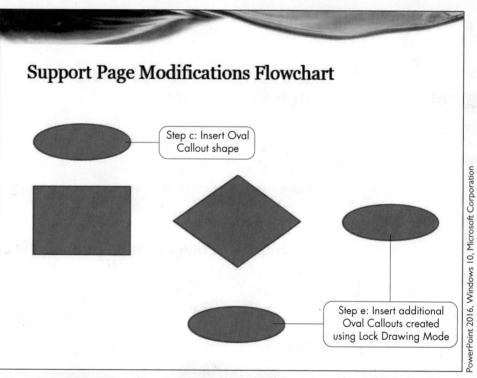

FIGURE 3.19 Basic Shapes

a. Open *p03h1Project*, and save it as **p03h1Project_LastFirst**.

> **TROUBLESHOOTING:** If you make any major mistakes in this exercise, you can close the file, open *p03h1Project* again and then start this exercise over.

b. Replace *First Name Last Name* on Slide 1 with your name. Create a handout header with your name and a handout footer with your instructor's name and your class. Include the current date. Apply to all.

c. Move to Slide 6, and click **Oval** in the Basic Shapes in the Drawing group on the Home tab. Position the pointer on the top-left side of the slide above the square shape and below the title and drag to create the shape.

> **TROUBLESHOOTING:** If you do not see the Oval shape, click More for the Basic Shapes or click the Insert tab and click Shapes in the Illustrations group.

Do not worry about the exact placement or size of the shapes you create at this time. You will learn how to precisely place and size shapes in the steps to follow.

d. Click the **Insert tab** and click **Shapes** in the Illustrations group. Right-click **Oval** in the Basic Shapes category and select **Lock Drawing Mode**.

You activate Lock Drawing Mode so that you can create multiple shapes of the same kind.

e. Position the pointer to the right of the diamond and drag to create an oval. Repeat this process below the diamond to mimic Figure 3.19.

f. Press **Esc** to turn off Lock Drawing Mode.

You created two additional Oval shapes.

g. Save the presentation.

STEP 2 ›› DRAW LINES AND CONNECTORS

To continue building the flow chart, the workshop interns practice creating connecting lines between shapes. You also teach the group how to add a text box to a slide so they can add text, because the Title Only layout is being used. Refer to Figure 3.20 as you complete Step 2.

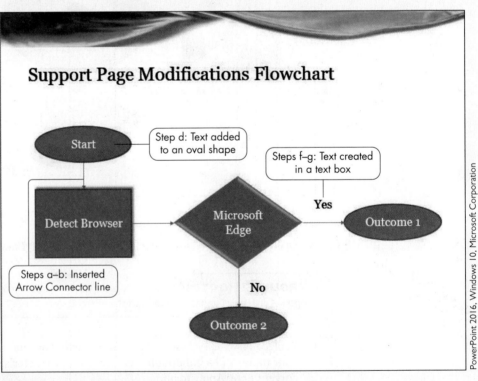

FIGURE 3.20 Basic Flow Chart

a. Click **Shapes** in the Illustrations group from the Insert tab, click **Arrow** in the Lines category, move the cross-hair pointer over the oval on the left side of the slide, and then position the pointer on the bottom-center handle.

The shape's connector handles appear when a connector line is selected and the cross-hair pointer is moved onto the shape.

b. Drag a connecting line that attaches the bottom-center connecting handle of the oval to the top-center connecting handle of the rectangle below it.

A connector arrow is placed between the oval and the rectangle. The default line weight is thin at 3/4 pt.

c. Click **Shapes** in the Illustrations group on the Insert tab, right-click the **Arrow**, and then select **Lock Drawing Mode**. Create connecting arrows using the technique just practiced that will attach the rectangle to the diamond and the diamond to the two remaining ovals, as shown in Figure 3.20. Press **Esc**.

d. Right-click the oval on the top-left of the slide, select **Edit Text**, and then type **Start**.

The text you typed becomes part of the oval shape.

e. Select the **square shape** and type **Detect Browser**. Use either of these methods to select each of the remaining shapes and type the text shown in Figure 3.20.

f. Click the **Insert tab** and click **Text Box** in the Text group.

Clicking Text Box enables you to create text anywhere on a slide.

g. Position the pointer above the connector between the Decision diamond and the Outcome 1 oval, click once, and then type **Yes**.

> **TROUBLESHOOTING:** If the text box is not positioned above the connector line between the Decision diamond and the Outcome 1 oval, click the border (not the sizing handle) of the text box and drag it into position.

h. Click **Text Box** in the Insert Shapes group on the Format tab, position the pointer to the right side of the connector between the Decision diamond and the Outcome 2 oval, click once, and then type **No**. Reposition the text box if necessary.

i. Save the presentation.

You encourage participants of the workshop to experiment with Quick Styles and to modify shape fills, but you ask them to set the shapes to styles of your choice in this slide show to demonstrate that they can meet specifications when asked. Refer to Figure 3.21 as you complete Step 3.

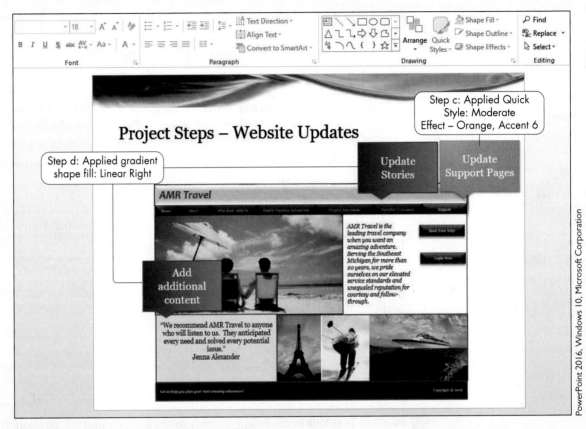

FIGURE 3.21 Quick Styles and Customized Fills

a. Click **Slide 5** and then select the far-right callout shape, **Update Support Pages**.

b. Click the **Format tab** and click **More** in the Shape Styles group.

The Quick Style gallery opens.

c. Move the pointer over the Quick Styles and note the changes in fill, outline, and effects to the shape as you do so. After you are through experimenting, click **Moderate Effect - Orange, Accent 6** (fifth row, seventh column). Click in an empty area to deselect the callout.

Live Preview shows the effects on the object as you move the pointer over the Quick Style options.

d. Press and hold **Ctrl** and click the remaining two callout shapes to select them. Click the **Format tab**, click **Shape Fill arrow** in the Shape Styles group, and then click **Blue, Accent 1** (first row, fifth column). Click **Shape Fill arrow** again, point to **Gradient**, and then click **Linear Right** under Dark Variations. Click **Text Fill arrow** in the WordArt Styles group and click **White, Background 1** to change the text to white.

You apply a gradient fill to more than one shape at a time.

e. Save the presentation.

PowerPoint provides many shape effects that you can use for emphasis. You ask the participants to apply effects to the flow chart shapes so they become familiar with the options available. Refer to Figure 3.22 as you complete Step 4.

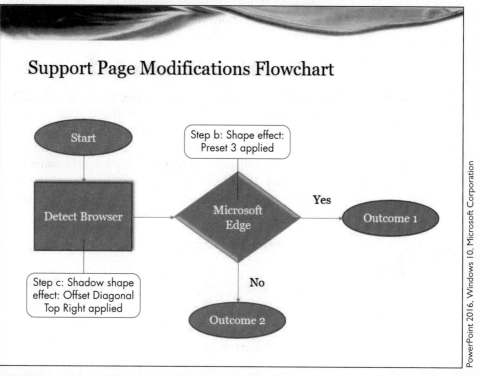

FIGURE 3.22 Shape Effects

a. Click **Slide 6** and click the **diamond shape**.

b. Click the **Format tab**, click the **Shape Effects arrow** in the Shape Styles group, point to **Preset**, and then click **Preset 3**.

Preset 3 combines a bevel type, a depth, contours, and a surface effect.

c. Select the **rectangle shape**, click the **Shape Effects arrow** in the Shape Styles group, point to **Shadow**, and then click **Offset Diagonal Top Right** (Outer category).

The Offset Diagonal option applies a soft shadow to the top-right of the rectangle.

d. Spell check and review the presentation.

e. Save and close the presentation. You will submit this file to your instructor at the end of the last Hands-On Exercise.

SmartArt and WordArt

Diagrams are infographics used to illustrate concepts and processes. PowerPoint includes a feature to create eye-catching diagrams: SmartArt. Another eye-catching PowerPoint feature, WordArt, draws attention to an infographic using text.

In this section, you will create and modify SmartArt diagrams and WordArt text.

Creating SmartArt

STEP 1 ▶▶ The *SmartArt* feature enables you to create a visual representation of information. You can type the text of your message in one of many existing layouts. The resulting illustration is professional looking and is complemented by the selected theme. You can also convert existing text to a SmartArt diagram. Figure 3.23 compares a text-based slide in the common bullet format to a slide showing the same information converted to a SmartArt diagram. The arrows and colors in the SmartArt diagram make it easy for the viewer to understand the message and remember the concept of a cycle. It is especially effective when you add animation to each step.

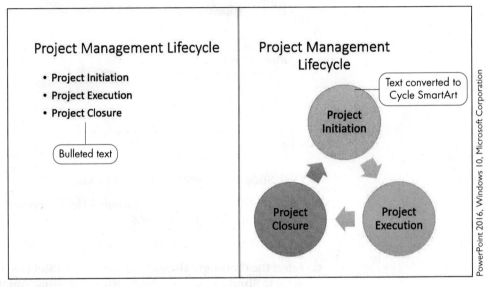

FIGURE 3.23

Choose a SmartArt Diagram Type

To create a SmartArt diagram, first choose a diagram type that fits your message. The SmartArt gallery has nine different categories of diagrams: List, Process, Cycle, Hierarchy, Relationship, Matrix, Pyramid, Picture, and Office.com. At the top of the list of categories is All, which you can click to display the choices from all categories. Each category includes a description of the type of information appropriate for the layouts in that category. The following Table 3.1 shows the SmartArt categories and their purposes.

TABLE 3.1	SmartArt Types and Purposes	
Type	**Purpose**	**Sample SmartArt**
List	Show nonsequential information. For example, a list of items to be checked on a roof each year.	
Process	Display steps in a process or a timeline. For example, the steps involved in washing a car.	
Cycle	Show a continual process. For example, the recurring business cycle.	
Hierarchy	Display a decision tree, organization chart, or pedigree. For example, a pedigree chart showing the parents of an individual.	
Relationship	Illustrate connections. For example, the connections among outdoor activities.	
Matrix	Display how parts relate to a whole. For example, the Keirsey Temperament Theory of four groups describing human behavior.	
Pyramid	Show proportional relationships with the largest component on the top or bottom. For example, an ecology chart.	

(Continued)

TABLE 3.1	Continued		
Type	**Purpose**	**Sample SmartArt**	
Picture	Display nonsequential or grouped blocks of information. Maximizes both horizontal and vertical display space for shapes.	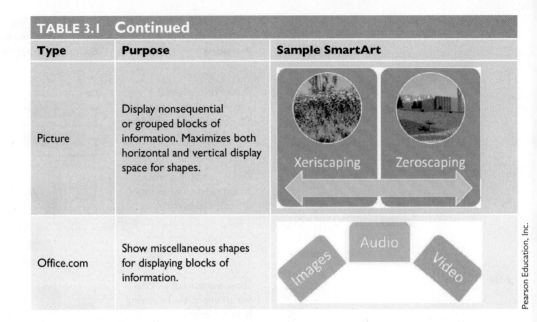	
Office.com	Show miscellaneous shapes for displaying blocks of information.		

Pearson Education, Inc.

A SmartArt diagram creates a layout for information, provides a pane for quickly typing text, automatically sizes shapes and text, and enables you to switch between layouts, making it easy to choose the most effective layout. Some layouts can be used for any type of information and are designed to be visually attractive, while other layouts are created specifically for a certain type of information, such as a process or hierarchy. SmartArt types include options for presenting lists of information in ordered (steps to complete a task) or unordered (features of a product) formats.

Figure 3.24 shows the Choose a SmartArt Graphic dialog box. The pane on the left side shows the types of SmartArt diagrams available. Each type of diagram includes subtypes that are displayed in the center pane. Clicking one of the subtypes enlarges the selected graphic and displays it in the preview pane on the right side. The preview pane describes purposes for which the SmartArt subtype can be used effectively. Some of the descriptions include tips for the type of text to enter.

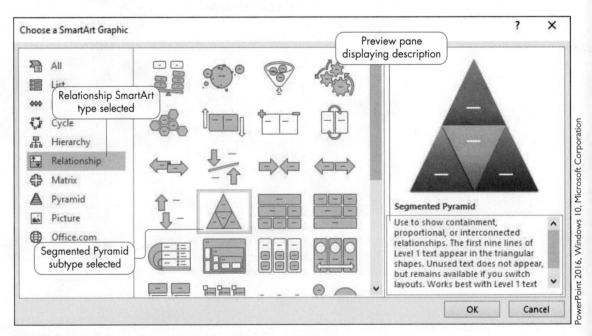

PowerPoint 2016, Windows 10, Microsoft Corporation

FIGURE 3.24 Choose a SmartArt Graphic Gallery

> **To create a SmartArt diagram, click the SmartArt icon on the icon palette of a layout, or complete the following steps:**
>
> 1. Click the Insert tab.
> 2. Click SmartArt in the Illustrations group.
> 3. Click the type of SmartArt diagram you want in the left pane.
> 4. Click the SmartArt subtype you want in the center pane.
> 5. Preview the selected SmartArt and subtype in the right pane.
> 6. Click OK.

Use the SmartArt Text Pane

Once you select the SmartArt diagram type and the subtype, a ***Text pane*** opens in which you type text. If the Text pane does not open, click Text Pane in the Create Graphic group on the SmartArt Tools Design tab. The Text pane works like an outline—type a line of text, press Enter, and then press Tab or Shift+Tab to increase or decrease the indent level. The font size will adjust to fit text inside the shape, or the shape may resize to fit the text, depending on the size and number of shapes in your SmartArt diagram.

The layout accommodates additional shapes as you add text unless the type of shape is designed for a specific number of shapes, such as the Relationship Counterbalance Arrows layout, which is designed to show two opposing ideas. If you choose a diagram with more shapes than you need, you can delete the extra shapes; PowerPoint will automatically rearrange the remaining shapes to eliminate any blank space.

Some layouts are limited in the space available for text. Some layouts allow for points and subpoints. Read the description of the layout in the gallery for information relating to these limitations and special features. Figure 3.25 shows text typed into the Text pane for a Basic Cycle SmartArt diagram. Because four lines of text were typed, four shapes were created. The description for the Basic Cycle SmartArt diagram states that the diagram works best with Level 1 text only.

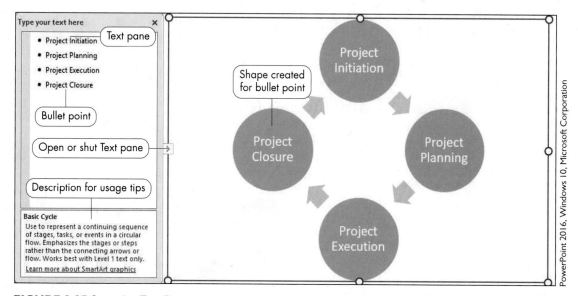

FIGURE 3.25 SmartArt Text Pane

TIP: TEXT IN SMARTART

Some SmartArt layouts allow only one level of text, while others are set up for one or two levels of text. So, if there are main and subpoints that need to be displayed, a SmartArt graphic that allows two levels of text is necessary. Be sure to keep the text short and limit it to key points to create a visually appealing diagram.

Modifying SmartArt

You can modify SmartArt diagrams with the same tools used for other shapes and text boxes. You can reposition or resize a SmartArt diagram by dragging its borders. You can modify SmartArt text in the Text pane just as if it were in a placeholder, or you can modify the text in the shape itself. If you need an additional shape, click to position the insertion point in the Text pane at the beginning or end of the text where you want to add a shape, press Enter, and then type the text. An alternative method for adding shapes is to use the Add Shape command.

To add a shape to the SmartArt, complete the following steps:

1. Click an existing shape in the SmartArt diagram.
2. Click the SmartArt Tools Design tab.
3. Click the Add Shape arrow in the Create Graphic group.
4. Select an available option

SmartArt diagrams have two galleries used to enhance the appearance of the diagram, both of which are located in the SmartArt Tools Design tab in the SmartArt Styles group. One gallery changes colors, and the other gallery applies a combination of special effects.

Change SmartArt Theme Colors

 STEP 2 To change the color scheme of a SmartArt diagram, click Change Colors to display the Colors gallery (see Figure 3.26). The gallery contains Primary Theme Colors, Colorful, and Accent color schemes. Click a color variation to apply it to the SmartArt diagram.

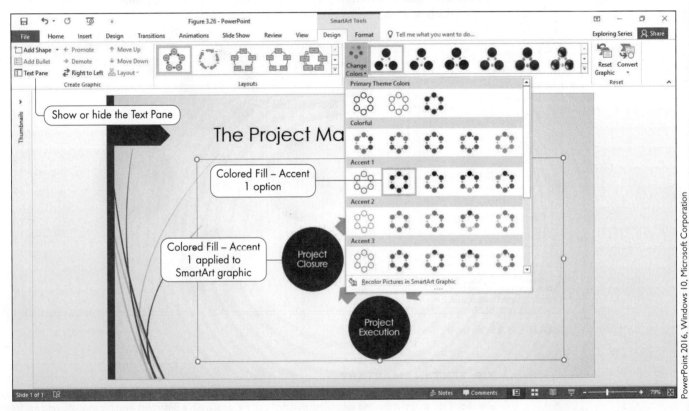

FIGURE 3.26 SmartArt Theme Color Options

Use Quick Styles with SmartArt

After creating the diagram, use SmartArt Quick Styles in the SmartArt Styles group to adjust the style of the SmartArt to match other styles you have used in your presentation. The style you select, however, should make the diagram easier to understand. The SmartArt Quick Styles gallery displays combinations of special effects, such as shadows, gradients, and 3-D effects that combine perspectives and surface styles. Figure 3.27 displays the SmartArt Quick Styles gallery.

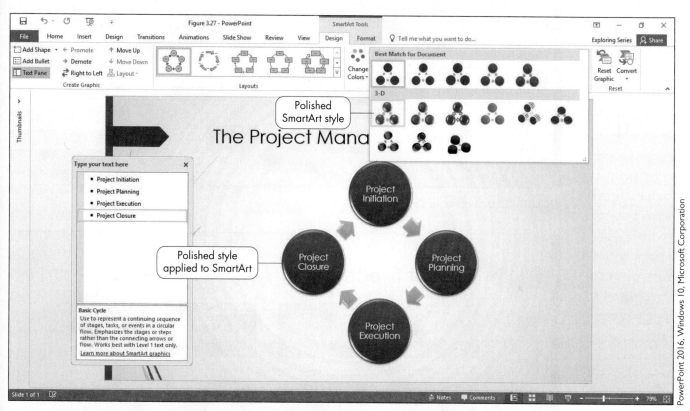

FIGURE 3.27 SmartArt Quick Style Gallery

Change the SmartArt Layout

 After creating a SmartArt diagram, you may find that the layout needs adjusting. For example, as you type text, PowerPoint reduces the size of the font. If you type too much text, the font size becomes too small. Figure 3.28 shows a Process diagram displaying the sequential steps to execute a project. To allow the text to fit in the shapes of the diagram, PowerPoint reduced the font size to 12 pt making it difficult to read. By adjusting the layout, you can make the diagram easier to read. Figure 3.29 shows the same process from Figure 3.28, modified to utilize the Basic Bending Process layout.

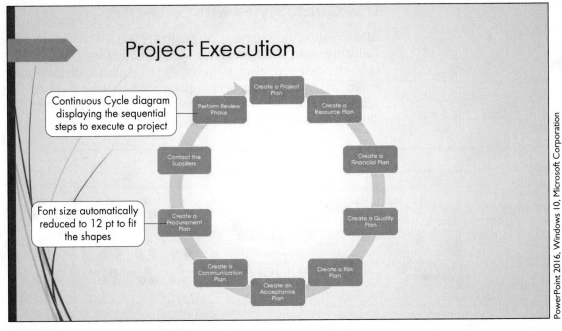

FIGURE 3.28 Continuous Cycle SmartArt

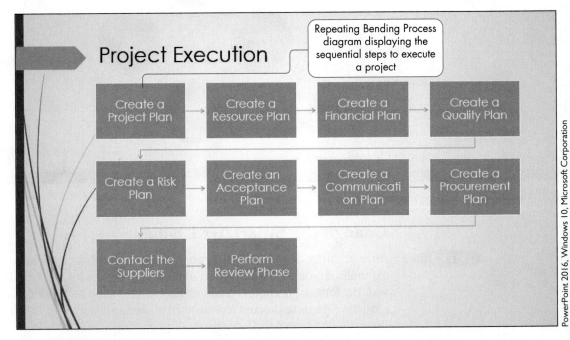

FIGURE 3.29 Modified SmartArt Layout

To change the layout of a SmartArt diagram, complete the following steps:

1. Select the SmartArt diagram and click the SmartArt Tools Design tab.
2. Click More in the Layouts group to display the Layouts gallery.
3. Use Live Preview to determine which layout subtype presents your information in the best way.
4. Select the layout you want to use.

Change SmartArt Type

You can change the SmartArt diagram type if you decide a completely different type of diagram would be better. The process is similar to changing the SmartArt layout subtypes. Changing the diagram type may affect the audience's perception of your diagram.

For example, if you have created a list of unordered items, switching to a cycle diagram implies that a specific order to the items exists. Also, if you have customized the shapes, keep in mind that changes to colors, line styles, and fills will transfer from the old diagram to a new one. However, some effects, such as rotation, do not transfer.

To change the SmartArt diagram type, complete the following steps:

1. Select the SmartArt diagram.
2. Click More in the Layouts group on the Design tab and click More Layouts. The Choose a SmartArt Graphic gallery opens, displaying all the layouts grouped by category.
3. Click the type and layout you want.

Convert Text to a SmartArt Diagram

You can also convert existing text to a SmartArt diagram by selecting the placeholder containing the text and clicking Convert to SmartArt Graphic in the Paragraph group on the Home tab. You can also select the text, right-click the placeholder, and then select Convert to SmartArt. When the gallery opens, click the desired layout for the SmartArt diagram. See Figure 3.30.

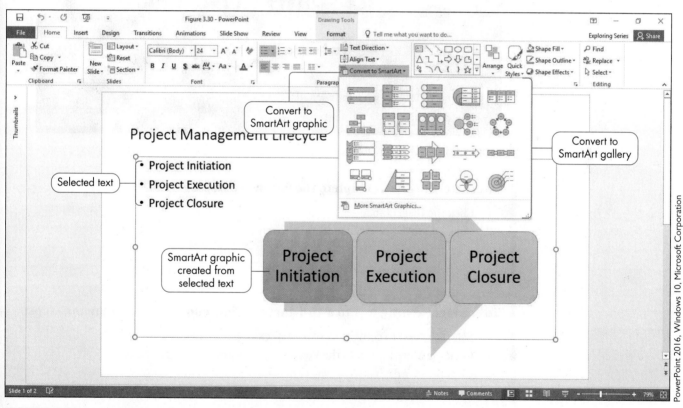

FIGURE 3.30 Convert to SmartArt

Creating WordArt and Modifying WordArt

 You may want to call attention to text on a slide by using WordArt. **WordArt** uses special effects based on text rather than a shape. In WordArt, special effects apply to the text itself, not to the shape surrounding the text. For example, in a WordArt graphic the text may have a 3-D reflection rather than the box surrounding the text. By applying special

effects, such as curves or waves, directly to the text, you can create text that emphasizes the information for your audience.

Create WordArt

When you create WordArt, PowerPoint provides a gallery of WordArt styles that has a variety of text styles to choose from, as well as the option to change individual settings or elements to modify the style. You can convert existing text to WordArt text, or you can create a WordArt object and then type text. The colors depend upon the theme you have selected. Figure 3.31 shows a slide with a WordArt effect enhancing text on the slide.

FIGURE 3.31 WordArt Used on a Slide

To create WordArt, complete the following steps:

1. Click the Insert tab.
2. Click WordArt in the Text group to open the WordArt gallery.
3. Click the WordArt style of your choice.
4. Type text in the WordArt placeholder.

To convert existing text to a WordArt graphic, complete the following steps:

1. Select the text to convert to WordArt text.
2. Click the More button in the WordArt Styles group on the Format tab.
3. Click the WordArt style of your choice.

Modify WordArt

You can change the style of a WordArt object by clicking a Quick Style located in the WordArt Styles group on the Format tab. Alternatively, you can modify the individual elements of the WordArt by clicking Text Fill, Text Outline, or Text Effects in the WordArt Styles group. WordArt Text Effects includes a unique Transform option. Transform can rotate the WordArt text around a path or add a warp to stretch, angle, or bloat letters. Figure 3.32 shows the warp options available in the WordArt Transform category.

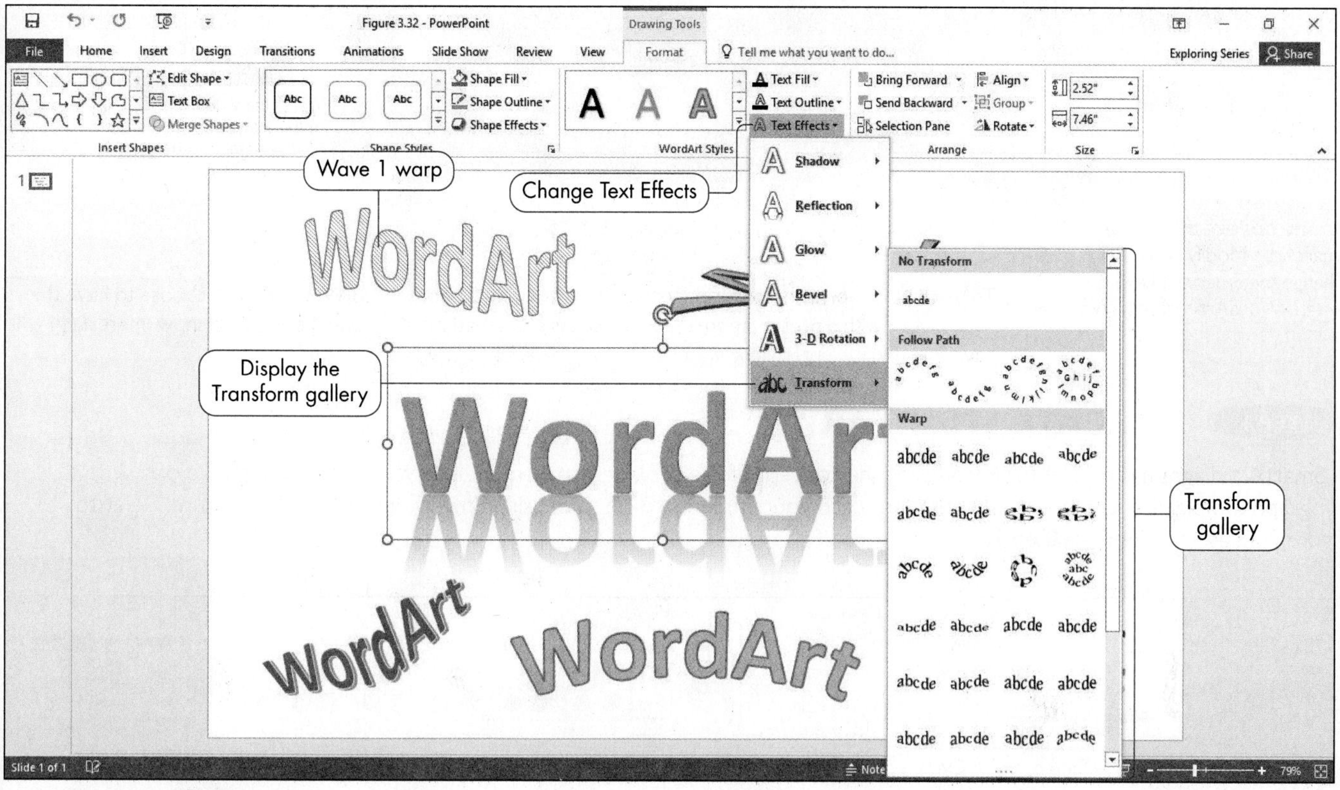

FIGURE 3.32 Warp Options

Quick Concepts ✓

4. Which SmartArt diagram type would be most effective to show an organization chart or pedigree? *p. 211*

5. How does typing text in a SmartArt text pane work like an outline? *p. 213*

6. Why would you convert existing text to a SmartArt diagram? *p. 210*

7. Why would you use WordArt on a slide? *p. 217*

Hands-On Exercises

Watch the Video for this Hands-On Exercise!

Skills covered: Create SmartArt • Modify SmartArt • Change the SmartArt Layout • Create WordArt • Modify WordArt

2 SmartArt and WordArt

To teach your workshop participants how to work with SmartArt and WordArt, you choose to have the group work with a presentation about a process—the water cycle. To make the slide show interesting, you have included fun, interesting water facts.

STEP 1 ⟩⟩ CREATE SMARTART

A SmartArt diagram is perfect for introducing the concept of the project management life cycle and is an example of a simple infographic explaining a complex concept. You teach your students to diagram using PowerPoint's SmartArt feature. Refer to Figure 3.33 as you complete Step 1.

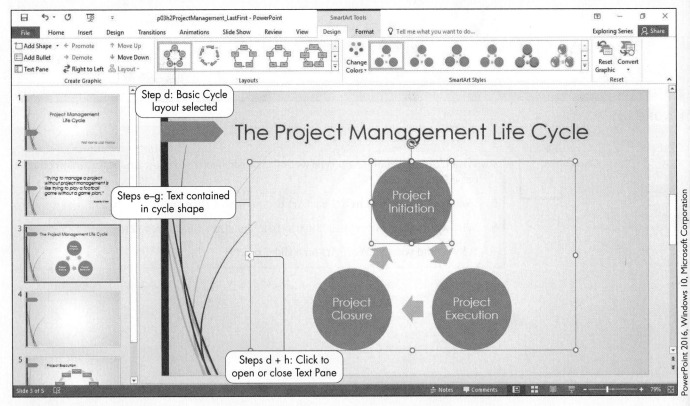

FIGURE 3.33 Basic Cycle SmartArt

a. Open the *p03h2ProjectManagement* presentation and save it as **p03h2ProjectManagement_LastFirst**.

b. Replace *First Name Last Name* with your name on Slide 1. Create a handout header with your name and a handout footer with your instructor's name and your class. Include the current date. Apply to all.

c. Click **Slide 3**. Click the **Insert tab** and click **SmartArt** in the Illustrations group.

The *Choose a SmartArt Graphic* dialog box opens.

d. Click **Cycle**, click the subtype **Basic Cycle**, read the description of the SmartArt diagram, and then click **OK**.

The Text pane opens with the insertion point in the first bullet location so that you can type the text for the first cycle shape.

> **TROUBLESHOOTING:** If the Text pane is not displayed, click Text Pane in the Create Graphic group or click the arrow on the center-left side of the SmartArt boundary.

e. Type **Project Initiation**.

As you type, the font size for the text gets smaller so the text fits in the shape.

f. Press ⬇ to move to the second bullet and type **Project Execution**. Repeat this technique to add a third bullet and type **Project Closure**.

g. Press ⬇ to move to the blank bullet point and press **Backspace**. Repeat to remove the remaining blank bullet point.

The extra shapes in the Basic Cycle SmartArt are removed.

h. Click **Open/Close Text pane** or **Close (X)** on the top-right of the Text pane to close it.

i. Drag the SmartArt object down so that it does not overlap the title.

j. Ensure that the SmartArt object is still selected. Click the **resizing handle** on the top-right corner of the SmartArt diagram, drag a corner of the object inward approximately an inch, and then reposition it so the object is approximately centered under the title (Refer to Figure 3.33).

k. Save the presentation.

STEP 2 ❯❯ MODIFY SMARTART

You need to modify the structure of the SmartArt diagram because a step in the cycle was omitted. The diagram could also be enhanced with a color style change. You teach your participants these skills. Refer to Figure 3.34 as you complete Step 2.

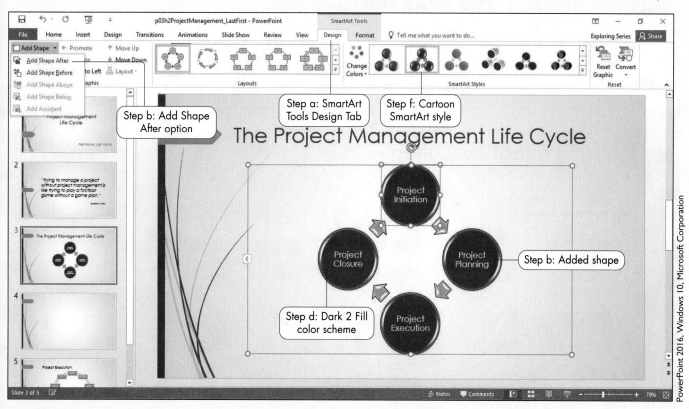

FIGURE 3.34 Modified SmartArt

a. Click the **Project Initiation shape** and ensure that the SmartArt Tools Design tab is selected.

b. Click the **Add Shape arrow** in the Create Graphic group and select **Add Shape After**.

You have added a new shape after *Project Initiation* and before *Project Execution*.

> **TROUBLESHOOTING:** If you had clicked Add Shape, you would have automatically added a shape after the selected shape. Using the Add Shape arrow gives you a choice of adding before or after.

c. Type **Project Planning** in the new shape.

d. Click the **SmartArt border** to select all the shapes in the SmartArt diagram, click **Change Colors** in the SmartArt Styles group, and then click **Dark 2 Fill** in the Primary Theme Colors category.

e. Click **More** in the SmartArt Styles group and move the pointer over the styles.

Live Preview shows the impact each style has on the shapes and text in the SmartArt diagram.

f. Click **Cartoon** in the 3-D category (first row, third column).

This choice makes the text readable and enhances the appearance of the SmartArt diagram.

g. Save the presentation.

STEP 3 ›› **CHANGE THE SMARTART LAYOUT**

Many different layouts are available for SmartArt diagrams, and you teach the workshop participants that for an infographic to be effective, it must be understood quickly. You ask the group to note the reduced font size on the process SmartArt showing the Project Execution. You teach them to change the layout of the SmartArt to make it more effective. Refer to Figure 3.35 as you complete Step 3.

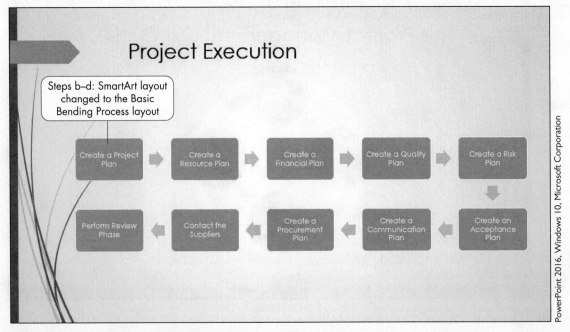

FIGURE 3.35 Basic Bending Process SmartArt

a. Click **Slide 6**. Select the **SmartArt Continuous Cycle shape** by clicking any shape.

b. Click the **SmartArt Tools Design tab**, click **More** in the Layouts group, select **More Layouts** at the bottom of the Layouts gallery, and then click **Process** in the left pane of the *Choose a SmartArt Graphic* dialog box. Click **Basic Bending Process** in the center pane and click **OK**.

c. Ensure that the SmartArt border is selected. Click the **Format tab**, type **4.03** in the **Shape Height box** in the Size group, and then press **Enter**.

d. Open the Size Dialog Box Launcher. Click **Position** and **type 1.6** in the **Horizontal Position box** and **2.44** in the **Vertical Position box**. Close the Format Shape pane. Deselect the SmartArt diagram by clicking outside of the SmartArt.

e. Save the presentation.

STEP 4 ▶▶ CREATE AND MODIFY WORDART

You teach the participants how to use WordArt to call attention to text and how to modify Text Effects applied to WordArt. You also have them insert text in a text box so they can compare the options available with each method for adding text to a slide. Refer to Figure 3.36 as you complete Step 4.

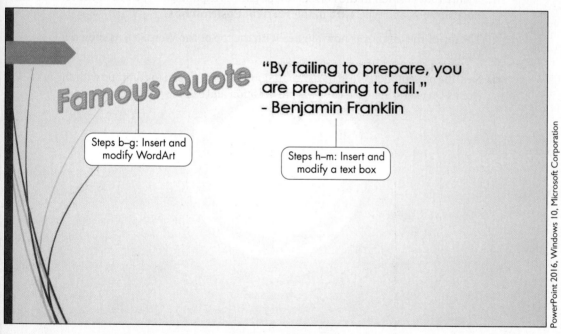

FIGURE 3.36 Modified WordArt

a. Click **Slide 4**. Click the **Insert tab** and click **WordArt** in the Text group.

b. Click **Pattern Fill - Orange, Accent 1, 50%, Hard Shadow - Accent 1 (**fourth row, third column).

A WordArt placeholder is centered on the slide.

c. Type **Famous Quote** in the **WordArt placeholder**.

d. Click **Text Effects** on the **Format tab** in the WordArt Styles group, and then point to **3-D Rotation**.

The 3-D Rotation gallery opens, showing No Rotation, Parallel, Perspective, and Oblique categories.

e. Click **Off Axis 1 Right** (under Parallel category, second row, second column).

f. Type **1.5** in the **Shape Height box** in the Size group and press **Enter**.

The height of the WordArt shape adjusts to 1.5.

g. Open the Size Dialog Box Launcher and ensure that Position is expanded so the options are available. Type **0.87** in the **Horizontal Position box** and **1.33** in the **Vertical Position box**. Close the Format Shape pane and deselect the shape.

h. Click the **Insert tab** and click **Text Box** in the Text group.

i. Click to the bottom-right of the WordArt shape and type **"By failing to prepare, you are preparing to fail." – Benjamin Franklin**.

The text box expands to fit the text, with the result that the text is contained in one long line that flows off the slide.

j. Click the **Format tab**, type **5.2** in the **Shape Width box** in the Size group, and then press **Enter**.

k. Click the **Size Dialog Box Launcher**, scroll down to see the Text Box options, click to expand and view the options, and then click the **Wrap text in shape check box**.

l. Click the **border** of the text box to select all the text. Click the **Home tab** and change the font size of the text to **28 pt**.

m. Ensure that Position in the Format Shape pane is expanded. Type **6.2** in the **Horizontal Position box** and type **1.08** in the **Vertical Position box**.

The top of the text box is now aligned with the top of the WordArt, as shown in Figure 3.36.

n. Save the presentation. Keep the presentation open if you plan to continue with the next Hands-On Exercise. If not, close the presentation and exit PowerPoint.

Object Manipulation

As you add objects to your slides, you may want to manipulate them by arranging them differently on the slide or recoloring them. Perhaps you have several shapes created, and you want to align them at their left edges or arrange them by their center points and then determine the order of the shapes. You may have inserted a drawn image, and then find that the colors used in the image do not match the colors of the theme of your presentation. You may have added a drawn image that includes something you do not want.

In this section, you will learn to modify objects. You will isolate objects, flip and rotate objects, group and ungroup objects, and recolor an image. You will also learn to determine the order of objects and align objects to one another and to the slide.

Modifying Objects

Many images are made from a series of combined shapes. You can modify existing drawings by breaking them into individual shapes and removing pieces you do not need, changing or recoloring shapes, rotating shapes, and combining shapes from several objects to create a new object. Figure 3.37 shows a picnic illustration available from Microsoft Office Online. In the bottom-right corner of the figure, the illustration was broken apart; the fireworks, flag, fries, and tablecloth removed; the hamburger, hotdogs, and milkshake flipped and resized; and the hamburger and chocolate milkshake recolored.

FIGURE 3.37 Modified Objects

Resize Objects

 Resizing objects is the most common modification procedure, and it is important for you to know a precise resizing method for times when you need exact measurements. For example, you use PowerPoint to create an advertisement for an automobile trader magazine, and the magazine specifies that the ad must fit in a 2" by 2" space. You can specify the exact height and width measurement of an object or adjust to a specific proportion of its original size.

The controls to resize an object to an exact measurement are found in the Size group on the Format tab or the Format pane. The Size group contains controls to change the height and width of an object. The Format pane also contains boxes for typing exact measurements for shape height and width, but additionally allows you to use a precise rotation angle and to scale an object based on its original size (note that not all Online Pictures are added at full size). To keep the original height and width proportions of an image, make sure the *Lock aspect ratio* check box is selected. ***Aspect ratio*** is the ratio of an object's width to its height. Figure 3.38 shows the sizing options available on the Format Picture pane.

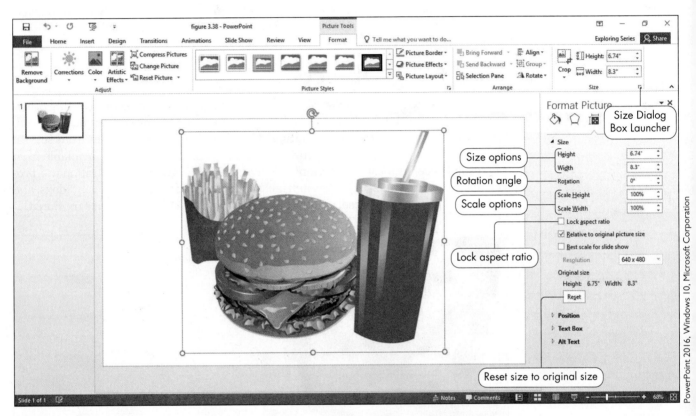

FIGURE 3.38 Sizing Options

Flip and Rotate Objects

STEP 2 ⟩⟩ Sometimes you will find that an object is facing the wrong way and you need to reverse the direction it faces, or ***flip*** it. You can flip an object vertically or horizontally to get a mirror image of the object. You may find that you need to ***rotate*** an object, or move the object around its axis. Perhaps you took a photograph with your digital camera sideways to get a full-length view, but when you download the image, it displays sideways. You can quickly rotate an object left or right 90°, flip it horizontally or vertically, or freely rotate it any number of degrees.

You rotate a selected object by dragging the rotation handle located at the top of the object in the direction you want it to rotate. To constrain the rotation to 15° angles, press and hold Shift while dragging. To rotate exactly 90° to the left or the right, click Rotate in the Arrange group on the Format tab. If you want a mirror image, click Rotate and select Flip Vertical or Flip Horizontal. You can also drag one of the side sizing handles over the opposite side to flip it. However, this method will cause distortion if you do not drag far enough to keep the height and width measurements proportional. Figure 3.39 shows the original and its flipped counterpart along with the rotate options.

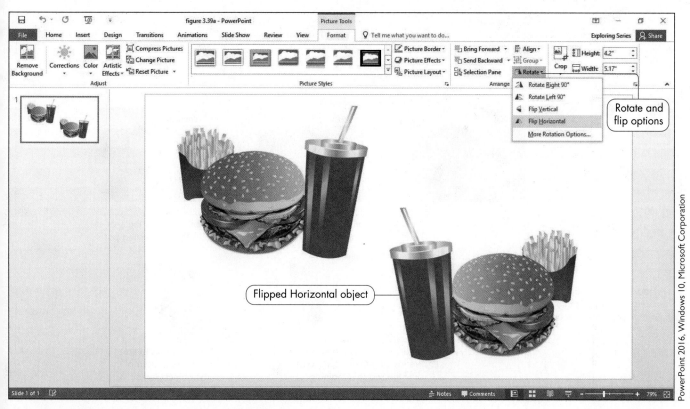

FIGURE 3.39 Rotating and Flipping Options

Merge Shapes

The Merge Shapes feature enables you to take individual shapes that you have inserted and merge them together to create one image. There are five different merging options: Union, Combine, Fragment, Intersect, and Subtract. Figure 3.40 shows the five different merging option results of a square and a circle created using Shapes in the Insert Shapes group on the Format tab. The five merged objects are blue because in every case, the blue square was selected first.

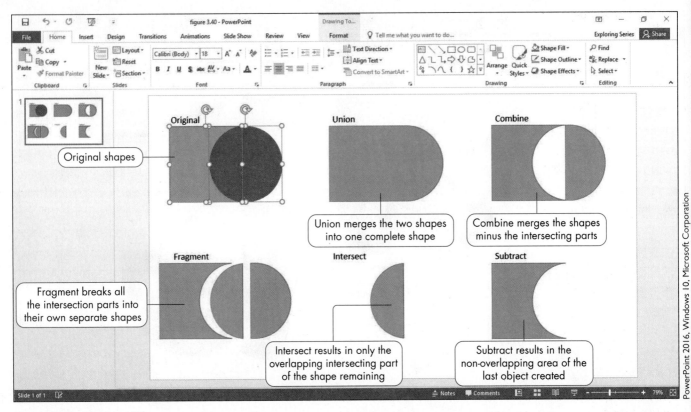

FIGURE 3.40 Merging Shapes

To merge shapes, complete the following steps:

1. Arrange the shapes so they overlap as desired.
2. Select the overlapping shapes.
3. Click the Format tab.
4. Click Merge Shapes in the Insert Shapes group.
5. Click the merge option of your choice.

> **TIP: USING SUBTRACT SHAPES**
> When applying the Subtract Shapes merging option, you will have a different result depending on the shape you select first. In Figure 3.40, the square was selected first, and the circle second.

Group and Ungroup Objects

STEP 3 ⟫ A drawn object is usually created in pieces, layered, and then grouped to create the final image. These images can be *ungrouped*, or broken apart, so you can modify or delete the individual pieces. *Grouping* enables multiple objects to act or move as though they were a single object, whereas ungrouping separates an object into individual shapes. Grouping is different from merging a shape. Grouping simply makes it easier to move the newly grouped object or apply formatting, whereas merging may create a new object altogether.

Some images are typically created and saved as *vector graphics*, which are math-based. Drawing programs such as Adobe Illustrator and CorelDRAW are used to create vector graphic images. The advantage of vector files is that they retain perfect clarity when edited or resized due to the fact that the computer simply recalculates the math. Vector files also use a smaller amount of storage space compared to their pixel-based counterparts such as photographs. Many company logos are vector graphics, which leads to another advantage of vector images.

To convert a vector graphic into a drawing object of grouped shapes, complete the following steps:

1. Right-click the image on the slide and select Edit Picture if the option is available. If the option is not available, the graphic cannot be converted into a drawing object.

2. Click Yes if after you select Edit Picture, a message opens asking if you want to convert the picture into a drawing object.

If a vector image is inserted, it is automatically a grouped image, and thus, the option to ungroup is available. This ability to ungroup (or group) the image enables you to separate the parts of the image and edit or adjust the image to tailor it to your needs. Some vector graphics that have been grouped have to be converted into drawing objects by ungrouping them.

TIP: AN IMAGE THAT WILL NOT UNGROUP

If your selected image will not ungroup for editing, it is not in a vector format. Often pictures from the Web are in .bmp, .jpg, .gif, and .png formats, which are not vector-based images and cannot be ungrouped.

To ungroup a drawing object, complete the following steps:

1. Right-click the drawing object on the slide.
2. Point to Group.
3. Select Ungroup to view the individual shapes.

Alternatively, you can ungroup an object using Group in the Arrange group on the Format tab. Select Ungroup to see each individual shape surrounded by adjustment handles. Click outside of the image borders to deselect the shapes.

Some images may have more than one grouping. The artist may create an image from individual shapes, group it, layer it on other images, and then group it again. If this occurs, the ungroup option will be available to repeat again. Figure 3.41 is an example of an image that has been ungrouped with some of the pieces selected.

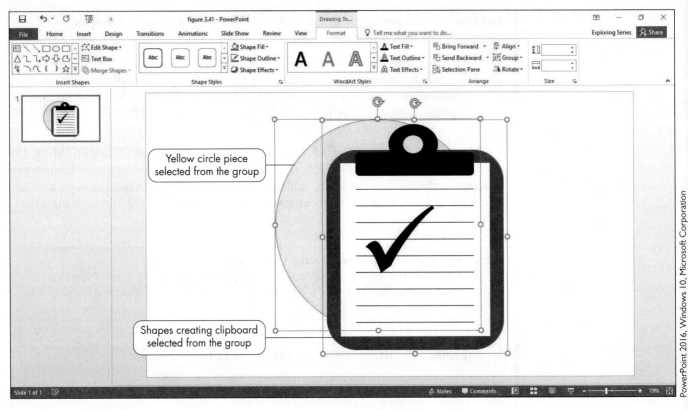

FIGURE 3.41 Modified Objects

If necessary, to continue ungrouping, select the image, right-click, click Group, and then click Ungroup as many times as necessary to break the image down to all shapes. Figure 3.42 shows a graphic that has been ungrouped to its lowest level. All of the individual parts are selected.

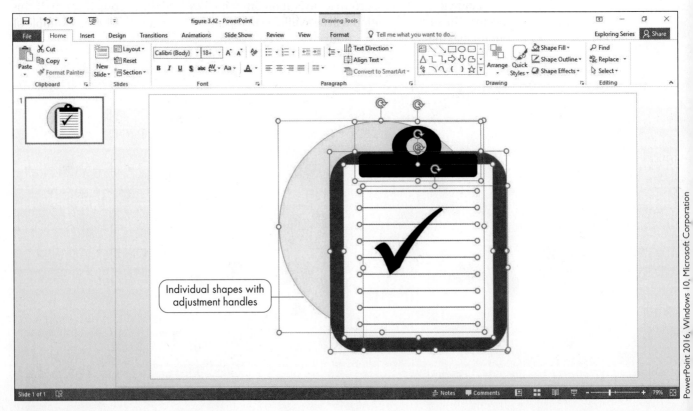

FIGURE 3.42 Ungrouped Complex Image

When working with the individual shapes of an image, it is helpful to zoom in on the image. Zooming helps you make sure you have the correct shape before you make modifications. Figure 3.43 shows a selected shapes (lines) that have their fill changed to a theme color. Once you have made all of your needed changes, drag a selection net around all the shapes of the image and group or regroup the image. If you do not group the image, you risk moving the individual pieces inadvertently.

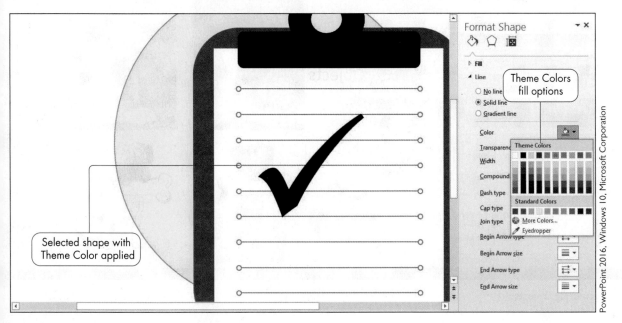

FIGURE 3.43 Modifying Ungrouped Shapes

Recolor Objects

 You can quickly change the colors in an image using the Recolor Picture option regardless of image file type, which enables you to match your image to the color scheme of your presentation without ungrouping the image and changing the color of each shape. You can select either a dark or a light variation of your color scheme.

You also can change the color mode of your picture to Grayscale, Sepia, Washout, or Black and White. Grayscale changes your picture up to 256 shades of gray. Sepia gives you that golden tone often used for an old-fashioned photo look. Washout is used to create watermarks, whereas Black and White is a way to reduce image color to black and white. Figure 3.44 shows two different file types of a dog with variations of color.

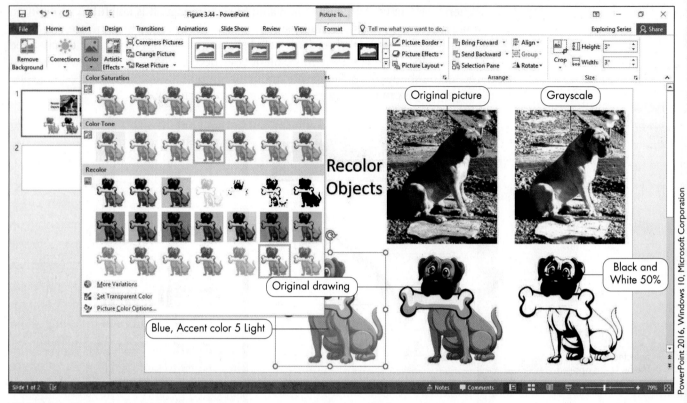

FIGURE 3.44 Recoloring Objects

To change the colors of an image, complete the following steps:

1. Select the image you want to change.
2. Click the Format tab.
3. Click Color in the Adjust group.
4. Click the color variation of your choice, or select More Variations to open the Theme Colors options and select a theme color.

You may want an image without a background, or decide that a portion of the image needs to be transparent. The Recolor gallery includes a Set Transparent Color option that is valuable for creating a transparent area in many pictures. In Figure 3.45 the black is set to transparent so the purple background shows.

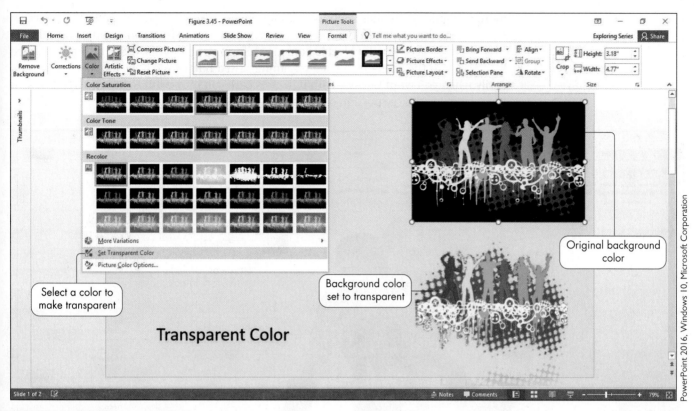

FIGURE 3.45 Set Transparent Color

> **To set a transparent color in your image, complete the following steps:**
> 1. Select the image in which you want to set a transparent color.
> 2. Click the Format tab.
> 3. Click Color in the Adjust group.
> 4. Click Set Transparent Color and point to the color you want to make transparent.
> 5. Click to make the color transparent.

Arranging Objects

When you have multiple objects such as shapes, online pictures, SmartArt, and WordArt on the slide, it can become challenging and time consuming to arrange them. While Smart Guides are good for simple alignment, they do not work for all situations. For more complex situations, PowerPoint has several features to control the order and position of the objects, how the objects align to one another, and how they align to the slide. Before using any of these features, you must select the object(s).

Sometimes there are so many objects placed so closely together that it is difficult to select the individual object you need on the slide. You can select the object(s) by using the *Selection Pane*. The Selection Pane, found in the Arrange group on the Format tab, lists all objects on the slide and enables you to select, multiselect, show, hide, or change the order of objects on the slide. The Selection Pane is incredibly helpful when you are working with complex images comprised of overlapping objects. Every object displays on the pane and you can click through the objects to identify them.

The object you selected is highlighted in the Selection Pane. If an object is not selected, click the Home tab, click Select in the Editing group, and then select Selection Pane. Because the Selection Pane is so valuable, you may want to memorize the keyboard shortcut for opening it—Alt+F10—or add it to the Quick Access Toolbar.

If you have many objects of the same shape type listed in the Selection Pane, it might be difficult to identify which to select. In a case like this, you can rename objects with more recognizable names such as Red Ball. Just double-click the name in the Selection Pane to select it, and then type a new name. Figure 3.46 shows an example of multiple overlapping objects. Each object is named Freeform with a number. The red ball is named Freeform 6 in the Selection Pane. Renaming it Red Ball would help you identify it more easily when you want to work with it. In this case you may want to hide the red ball so it is not blocking a large portion of the image.

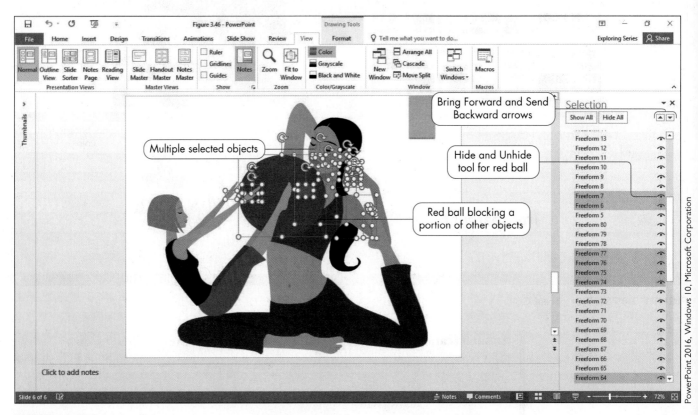

FIGURE 3.46 Selection Pane

If you are having a difficult time identifying objects, you can use Hide and Unhide (the eye) on the Selection Pane to identify objects: select an object on the list, and then click to hide it and click again to unhide it. An even more valuable use of Hide and Unhide, however, is to make objects invisible so you can work on the areas you need without objects getting in the way.

Order Objects

STEP 5 ❯❯ You can layer shapes by placing them under or on top of one another. The order of the layers is called the ***stacking order***. PowerPoint adds shapes or other objects in a stacking order as you add them to the slide. The last shape you place on the slide is on top and is the highest in the stacking order. Drawn images are comprised of shapes that have been stacked. Once you ungroup an image and modify it, you may need to change the stacking order. You can open the Selection Pane to see the order in which objects are placed. The topmost object on the list is at the top of the stacking order. You can use the Bring Forward and Send Backward arrows in the Selection Pane to change the order of the selected object. Figure 3.46 shows the location of the Bring Forward and Send Backward arrows in the Selection Pane.

The Arrange group on the Format tab also includes the Bring Forward and Send Backward arrows. Use the Bring Forward arrow to bring an object forward one layer or to bring it all the way to the front to become the top layer of a stack. Use the Send Backward arrow to move an object back one layer, or move it all the way to the back behind all layers. Figure 3.47 shows the results of reordering a circle at the back of a stack of objects to the top of the stacking order.

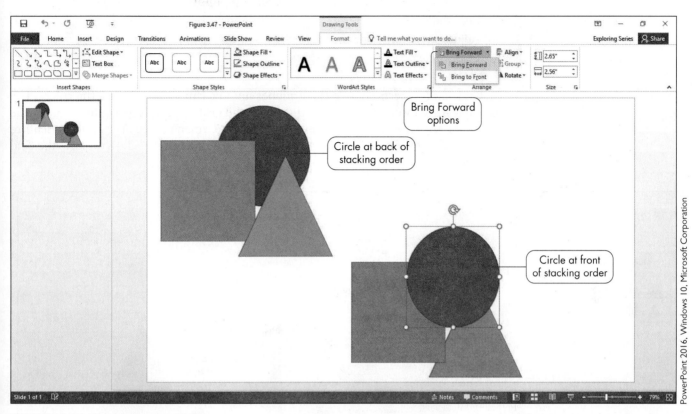

FIGURE 3.47 Changing Stacking Order

TIP: ORDERING SHORTCUTS

You can right-click a shape and select *Bring to Front* or *Send to Back*. Using this method, you can still choose whether to move one layer or all layers.

Align Objects

Dragging an object to position it on the slide is an easy way to position objects when you use Smart Guides. ***Smart Guides*** display when you drag an object on your slide to help you quickly align objects in relation to other objects. For example, you might want to align a series of rectangles at their tops or adjust the amount of space between the rectangles so that they are evenly spaced. PowerPoint has rulers, a grid, and drawing guides that enable you to complete the aligning process quickly.

Rulers provide you with visual cues that help you keep your objects aligned. They enable you to see the size of an object or the distance between shapes. PowerPoint provides both a horizontal ruler and a vertical ruler.

To view and then hide the ruler, complete the following steps:

1. Click the View tab.
2. Click the check box for Ruler in the Show group.
3. Click the check box for Ruler again to turn off the Ruler.

Each slide can also display a ***grid*** containing intersecting lines, which, by default, are hidden. You can display the grid to align your objects and to keep them evenly spaced. When you activate the grid, you will not see it in Slide Show view, and it will not print.

To view the grid and change the grid settings:

1. Click the View tab.
2. Click the check box for Gridlines in the Show group.
3. Click the Show Dialog Box Launcher in the Show group.
4. Adjust the settings for Snap to and Spacing.
5. Click *Display grid on screen* and click OK.

By default, objects snap to the gridlines and measurement lines on the rulers. The *Snap to* feature forces an object to align with the grid by either the center point or the edge of the object, whichever is closer to the gridline. You can turn off the *Snap to* feature or change the setting so that objects snap to other objects. Figure 3.48 displays the Grid and Guides dialog box options.

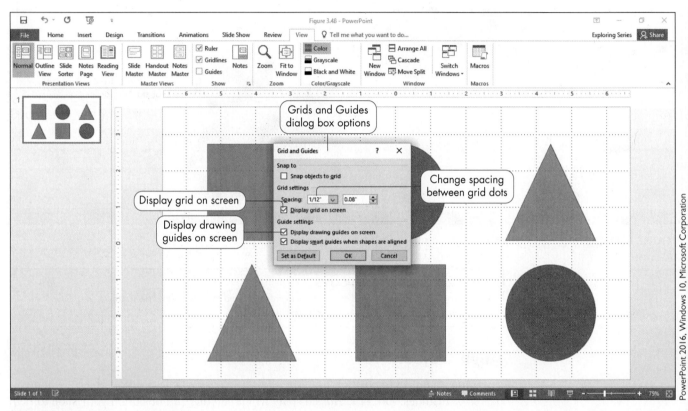

FIGURE 3.48 Grid and Guides Setting

Guides are nonprinting, temporary vertical or horizontal lines that you can place on a slide to help you align objects or determine regions of the slide.

To activate guides, complete the following steps:

1. Click the View tab.
2. Click the check box next to Guides.

When you first display the guides, you see two guides that intersect at the center of the slide (the zero setting on both the horizontal and vertical rulers). To move a guide, point to it and drag. A directional arrow will appear as well as a measurement telling you how far from the center point you are moving the guide. To create additional guides, press Ctrl+Shift while dragging. To remove guides, drag them off the slide. Figure 3.49 displays the default horizontal and vertical guides as well as two additional guides that were created to the left and the right of the zero point on the horizontal ruler.

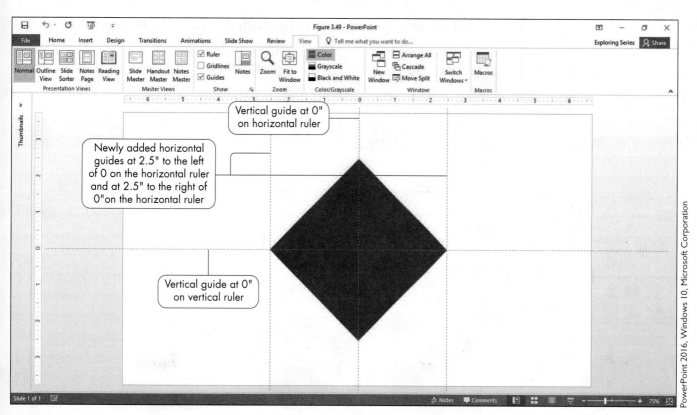

FIGURE 3.49 Creating a Guide

> **TIP: RULE OF THIRDS**
>
> Grids and guides can help you utilize the rule of thirds, a photography strategy that breaks a composition up into horizontal and vertical thirds to draw attention to part of the shot. Change the settings for your grid and guides to divide the screen into horizontal and vertical thirds and then place your objects accordingly. Generally it is easy to center the object on one of the guide intersections.

The **Align** feature makes it simple to line up shapes and objects in several ways. You can align with other objects by lining up the sides, middles, or top/bottom edges of objects. Or, if you have only one object or group selected, you can align in relation to the slide—for example, the top or left side of the slide.

> **To align objects, complete the following steps:**
>
> 1. Select the objects you want to align.
> 2. Click Align in the Arrange group on the Format tab.
> 3. Select Align to Slide or Align Selected Objects depending on if you want to align the objects to the slide or align the objects to one another.
> 4. Click Align in the Arrange group on the Format tab. This step is not necessary if the option you want is already selected in Step 3.
> 5. Click one of the following: Align Left, Align Center, Align Right, Align Top, Align Middle, or Align Bottom.

The Align feature also includes options to **distribute** selected shapes evenly over a given area. Perhaps you have shapes on the page but they are unequally spaced and you want to have an equal amount of space between all the shapes. Use the distribute options to assign an equal amount of space between the shapes.

To distribute objects, complete the following steps:

1. Select the objects you want to distribute.
2. Click Align in the Arrange group on the Format tab.
3. Select Distribute Horizontally or Distribute Vertically.

Figure 3.50 shows three shapes on two rows that are aligned at their middles, aligned to the middle of the slide, and distributed horizontally so that the space between them is equidistant.

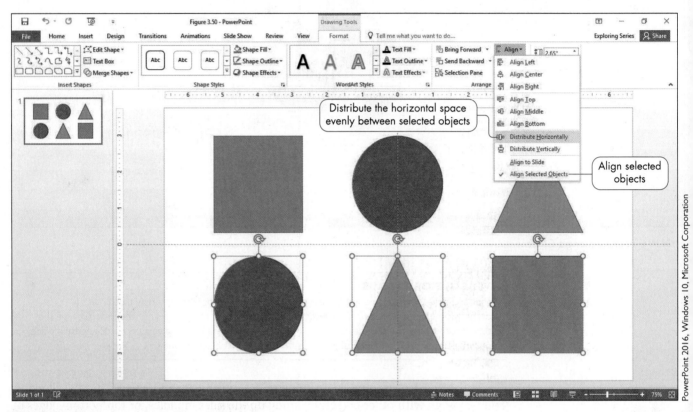

FIGURE 3.50 Alignment Options

Quick Concepts ✓

8. Why would you ungroup a picture? ***p. 228***

9. Why is the Selection Pane useful? ***p. 233***

10. Why would you use the Recolor Picture tool? ***p. 231***

11. How are rulers, a grid, and drawing guides used when aligning objects? ***p. 235***

Hands-On Exercises

Skills covered: Resize Objects • Flip Objects • Group and Ungroup Objects • Recolor Objects • Order Objects

3 Object Manipulation

You teach the workshop participants how to size, position, align, ungroup, and use other object manipulation techniques to images. The ability to manipulate pictures by grouping and ungrouping, recoloring, combining, and using other techniques offers unlimited possibilities for creativity. You want your group members to have these skills.

STEP 1 ›› RESIZE OBJECTS

You teach your workshop participants to use the Size Dialog Box Launcher. You want them to be able to precisely size and position objects on the slide. Refer to Figure 3.51 as you complete Step 1.

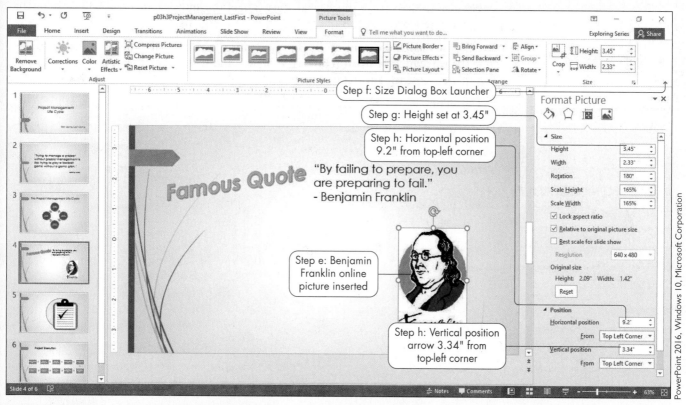

FIGURE 3.51 Size and Position Alignment Options

a. Open *p03h2ProjectManagement_LastFirst* if you closed it at the end of Hands-On Exercise 2, and save it as *p03h3ProjectManagement_LastFirst*, changing h2 to h3.

b. Click **Slide 4**. Click the **Insert tab** and click **Online Pictures** in the Images group.

   The Insert Pictures dialog box opens.

c. Type **Benjamin Franklin** in the **Bing Image Search box** and press **Enter**.

   The search results of Benjamin Franklin are images licensed under Creative Commons.

d. Click **Close** to close the Creative Commons Information Box.

TROUBLESHOOTING: If you selected *Show all web results* instead of closing the Creative Commons information box, there will be thousands more pictures. This makes trying to find a specific picture time consuming, and the image you select may be subject to copyright. Click BACK TO SITES to return to the Insert Pictures dialog box and then repeat Steps c and d.

e. Insert the image of Benjamin Franklin as shown in Figure 3.51.

   You have inserted the image in the center of Slide 4.

TROUBLESHOOTING: If you cannot locate the image in Figure 3.51, select another image of Benjamin Franklin.

f. Click the **Size Dialog Box Launcher** in the Size group on the Format tab.

   The Format Picture pane opens with the Size option expanded.

g. Type **3.45** in the **Height box** and click in the **Width box**.

   Because *Lock aspect ratio* is selected, the width of the image changes to 2.33, keeping the image in proportion.

h. Click the **Position arrow** in the Format Picture pane to expand the options. Type **9.2** in the **Horizontal position box**, type **3.34** in the **Vertical position box**, press **Enter**, and then close the Format Picture pane.

   The picture is moved to a new position.

i. Save the presentation.

Rotating and flipping are both ways to angle an object on the slide. You can rotate using precise measurements or, for an imprecise method of rotation, you can rotate the object using the Rotation handle. You ask your participants to use these methods so that they are familiar with the benefits of each. Refer to Figure 3.52 as you complete Step 2.

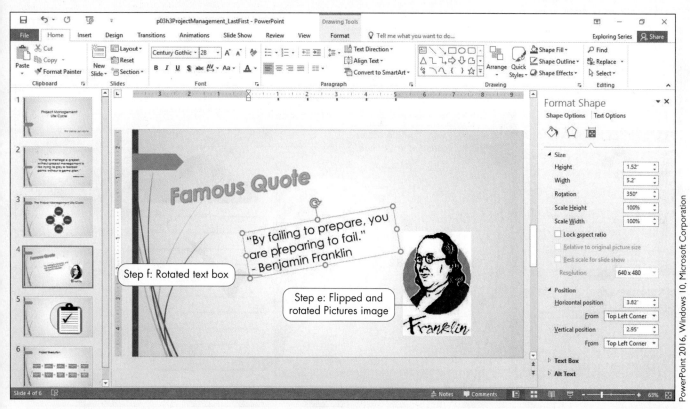

FIGURE 3.52 Flipping and Rotating

a. Click the **Benjamin Franklin image** and click **Rotate** in the Arrange group on the Format tab.

The rotate and flip options appear.

b. Click **Flip Horizontal**.

Benjamin Franklin now faces to the right side of the slide.

c. Click **Rotate** in the Arrange group and select **More Rotation Options**.

d. Type **180** in the Rotation box and press **Enter**.

The picture is rotated upside down.

e. Click **Rotate** in the Arrange group and select **Flip Vertical**. Close the Format Shape pane.

The Online Pictures picture appears to be in its original position, but the rotation angle is still set at 180°.

f. Select the text box in the top-right of the slide and drag it down and to the left to the approximate center of the slide using the Smart Guides to help you position the text box. Position the insertion point over the rotation handle and drag the rotation handle to the left until the text box is rotated to approximately match the slant in the *Famous Quote* WordArt.

> **TROUBLESHOOTING:** As you change the angle of rotation for the text box, you may need to reposition the text box on the slide so that it does not overlap the picture. An easy way to make small position adjustments is to press the arrow keys on the keyboard.

g. Save the presentation.

Being able to change colors, remove shapes, add shapes, and group, ungroup, and regroup images are important skills you want your participants to master. You ask the participants to ungroup an image, change the color of a portion of an image, and regroup the image. Refer to Figure 3.53 as you complete Step 3.

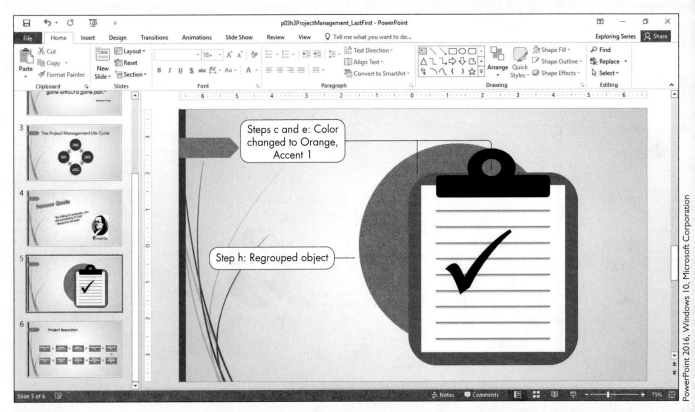

FIGURE 3.53 Grouping, Ungrouping, Regrouping

a. Right-click the **clipboard picture** on Slide 5, click **Group**, click **Ungroup**.

The picture breaks into two groups: a circle and a clipboard comprised of multiple shapes.

> **TROUBLESHOOTING:** If Group does not appear as an option when you right-click the picture, right-click another area of the picture.

b. Click the **Format tab**, click **Group** in the Arrange group, select **Ungroup**, and then click outside the picture border.

When you ungroup this time, objects are selected and surrounded with adjustment handles but there are still grouped shapes forming the clipboard. Clicking outside the border deselects the shapes so that you can select just the one you wish to modify.

c. Select the **large yellow circle**, click **Shape Fill** in the Shape Styles group, and then click **Orange, Accent 1** (first row, fifth column).

You change the harsh yellow fill to one of the theme colors of the presentation. You note, however, that the small circle on the clipboard handle is still yellow.

d. Select the **handle** of the clipboard, click **Group** in the Arrange group, and then select **Ungroup**. Click outside of the image again.

All of the shapes making up the clipboard handle have now been ungrouped.

e. Select the **small yellow circle**, and then click the **Shape Fill button** (not the arrow) to change the fill color to **Orange, Accent 1**. Click outside of the image.

The Shape Fill button will default to the last color selected.

f. Right-click the **clipboard picture**, click **Group**, and then click **Regroup**.

g. Drag diagonally from the lower-left and create a selection net around all the shapes used to make the clipboard picture and the background circle.

All the shapes are selected.

h. Click the **Format tab**, click **Group** in the Arrange group, and then select **Regroup**.

i. Save the presentation.

STEP 4 ▶▶ RECOLOR OBJECTS

You teach your workshop participants to recolor a picture so that it matches the color scheme of the presentation. Refer to Figure 3.54 as you complete Step 4.

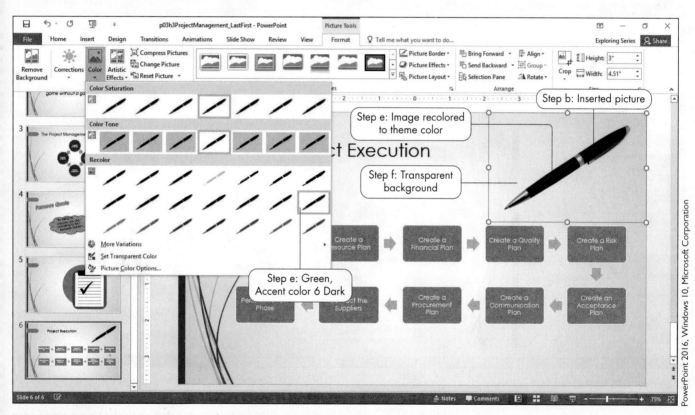

FIGURE 3.54 Recolored picture

a. Click **Slide 6**. Click the **Insert tab** and click **Pictures** in the Images group.

b. Locate *p03h3Pen* in your data files and click **Insert**.

c. Ensure the image is selected, and click the **Format tab**. In the Size group, change the height to **3**.

The width will change automatically.

d. Click **Align** in the Arrange group and select **Align Top** to move the object to the top of the slide. Once the picture is aligned to the top, click **Align** again and select **Align Right**.

The picture is now aligned to the top-right of the slide.

e. Click **Color** in the Adjust group and click **Green, Accent color 6 Dark** under the Recolor category (second row, seventh column).

The color of the image now matches the colors in the theme.

f. Click **Color** and click **Set Transparent Color**. Click anywhere in the background around the pen.

The distracting background becomes transparent leaving the pen.

g. Save the presentation.

STEP 5 »» **ORDER OBJECTS**

Being able to create and reorder shapes allows you to be creative, enabling you to create backgrounds, borders, and corners. Refer to Figure 3.55 as you complete Step 5.

FIGURE 3.55 Reordered Shapes

a. Click **Slide 4**. Click the **View tab** and click the **Ruler check box** in the Show group to view the ruler if it is not currently displayed.

The horizontal and vertical rulers display.

b. Click the **Insert tab**, click **Shapes** in the Illustrations group, and then click the **Cloud Callout** in the Callouts category.

c. Position the cross-hair pointer on the slide so that the indicator on the ruler is at the **3.5" mark** to the left of the zero point on the horizontal ruler and the **0.5" mark** above the zero point on the vertical ruler.

This is the beginning point for the cloud callout.

d. Drag to the **2.5" mark** to the right of the zero point on the horizontal ruler and the **2" mark** below the zero point on the vertical ruler and release.

A large cloud callout shape in the theme color is created on top of the text box on the slide. You will use the cloud callout as a callout for the Online Pictures image. Currently, it is hiding the quote and must be reordered.

TROUBLESHOOTING: Drag the top-left handle of the selected shape to adjust the starting point. Drag the bottom-right handle of the selected shape to adjust the ending point.

e. Drag the adjustment handle (yellow circle) at the bottom of the callout shape to the **3" mark** to the right of the zero point on the horizontal ruler and the **1" mark** below 0 on the vertical ruler until it looks similar to the position shown in Figure 3.55.

f. Click the **Format tab**, click the **Shape Fill arrow** in the Shape Styles group, and then click **Orange, Accent 1, Lighter 40%** (fourth row, fifth column). Click the **Send Backward arrow** in the Arrange group of the Format tab and select **Send to Back**.

g. Select the **Benjamin Franklin picture**. Click the **Send Backward arrow** in the Arrange group and select **Send to Back**. If necessary, move the text box into position as seen in Figure 3.55.

TROUBLESHOOTING: Adjust position and the size of the text box to fit within the cloud callout if the text does not fit within the shape.

h. Save and close the file. Based on your instructor's directions, submit the following:

p03h1Project_LastFirst

p03h3ProjectManagement_LastFirst.

Chapter Objectives Review

After reading this chapter, you have accomplished the following objectives:

1. Create shapes

- You can use shapes to highlight information, as a design element, as the basis for creating illustrations, or to contain information in infographics.
- Draw lines and connectors: Lines are shapes that can be used to point to information, or to divide a slide into sections. Connectors are lines that attach to the shapes you create and move with shapes when the shapes are moved.
- Create and modify freeform shapes: PowerPoint provides tools for creating, sizing, and positioning shapes. You can modify a freeform shape to achieve the desired shape through the help of vertexes.

2. Apply Quick Styles and customize shapes

- A Quick Style is a format that can be applied to a shape or object to add a professional look.
- Applying a Quick Style enables you to apply preset options.
- Change shape fills: A shape can be customized by changing its default fill to another color, to a picture, to a gradient, to a texture, or to no fill.
- Change shape outlines: The shape outline color, weight, or dash style can be modified.
- Change shape effects: Special effects such as shadows, reflections, and glows may be added.

3. Create SmartArt

- SmartArt graphics are diagrams that present information visually to effectively communicate a message.
- Type text in an existing SmartArt layout or convert existing text into a SmartArt diagram.
- Choose a SmartArt diagram type: Select a diagram type from one of the nine categories of diagrams in the SmartArt gallery. Refer to the description of the layout to ensure that it is appropriate to the information type.
- Use the SmartArt Text pane: SmartArt diagrams include a Text pane which enables you to type text in the pane like you would type an outline.

4. Modify SmartArt

- Change SmartArt theme colors: SmartArt diagrams can be modified to fit nearly any color scheme.
- SmartArt can be modified to include additional shapes, to delete shapes, to apply a SmartArt style, to revise the color scheme, or to add special effects.
- The direction, size, and positioning of a SmartArt diagram can be changed.
- Use Quick Styles with SmartArt: After creating the diagram, you can use Quick Styles to adjust the style to match other styles you have used in your presentation or to make the diagram easier to understand.
- Change the SmartArt layout: Once a SmartArt diagram type has been chosen, it can easily be converted to another layout.
- Change SmartArt type: You can change the SmartArt diagram type if you decide a different type would be better.
- Convert text to a SmartArt diagram: Bullets and other text can be converted directly to a SmartArt diagram.

5. Create WordArt and Modify WordArt

- WordArt is text with decorative effects applied to draw attention to the text.
- Create WordArt: Select a WordArt style and type the text you desire.
- Modify WordArt: WordArt can be modified by transforming the shape of the text and by applying special effects and colors. Special effects available include 3-D presets and rotations.
- Text created as WordArt can be edited.

6. Modify objects

- Resize objects: To precisely resize objects, specify the exact height and width measurement in the Size group on the Format tab or in the Format pane.
- Flip and rotate objects: An object may be flipped horizontally or vertically, or rotated by dragging its green rotation handle.
- Merge shapes: The Merge Shapes feature enables you to take shapes that you have inserted and merge them together. There are five different merging options: Union, Combine, Fragment, Intersect, and Subtract.
- Group and ungroup objects: Vector images can be ungrouped so basic shapes can be customized, and objects can be regrouped so they can be moved as one object.
- Recolor objects: Pictures can be recolored by changing their color mode or by applying dark or light variations of a theme color or custom color.

7. Arrange objects

- Objects are stacked in layers.
- The object at the top of the layer is the one that fully displays, while other objects in the stack may have some portions blocked.
- Order objects: The stacking order of shapes can be reordered so that objects can be seen as desired.
- Align objects: Features such as rulers, grids, guides, align, and distribute can be used to arrange objects on a slide and arrange objects in relation to one another.

Key Terms Matching

Match the key terms with their definitions. Write the key term letter by the appropriate numbered definition.

a. Adjustment handle

b. Aspect ratio

c. Callout

d. Connector

e. Distribute

f. Eyedropper

g. Freeform shape

h. Gradient fill

i. Group

j. Guide

k. Infographic

l. Line weight

m. Lock Drawing Mode

n. Picture fill

o. Selection net

p. SmartArt

q. Stacking order

r. Texture fill

s. Vector graphic

t. Vertex

1. _____ Inserts an image from a file into a shape. **p. 198**

2. _____ A blend of two or more colors or shades. **p. 199**

3. _____ A marquee that selects all objects in an area you define by dragging. **p. 195**

4. _____ A yellow circle that enables you to modify a shape. **p. 189**

5. _____ Enables the creation of multiple shapes of the same type. **p. 189**

6. _____ A tool used to recreate an exact color. **p. 196**

7. _____ A visual representation of data or knowledge. **p. 188**

8. _____ A line shape that is attached to and moves with other shapes. **p. 191**

9. _____ Diagram that presents information visually to effectively communicate a message. **p. 210**

10. _____ A feature which keeps an object's proportion the same with respect to width and height. **p. 226**

11. _____ Combines two or more objects. **p. 228**

12. _____ Point where a curve ends or the point where two line segments meet in a freeform shape. **p. 192**

13. _____ To divide or evenly spread shapes over a given area. **p. 187**

14. _____ Inserts a fill such as marble into a shape. **p. 200**

15. _____ A shape that combines both curved and straight lines. **p. 192**

16. _____ An object that provides space for text anywhere on a slide. **p. 189**

17. _____ The order of objects placed on top of one another. **p. 234**

18. _____ An object-oriented graphic based on geometric formulas. **p. 228**

19. _____ A straight horizontal or vertical line used to align objects. **p. 236**

20. _____ The width or thickness of a line. **p. 201**

Multiple Choice

1. Which of the following presents information as a diagram?

   (a) Text box
   (b) WordArt
   (c) Text pane
   (d) SmartArt

2. An object that provides space for text anywhere on a slide:

   (a) Text box
   (b) WordArt
   (c) Text pane
   (d) SmartArt

3. Which of the following is a reason for ungrouping a drawn object?

   (a) To resize the group as one piece
   (b) To move the objects as one
   (c) To add text on top of the group
   (d) To be able to individually change shapes used to create the composite image

4. Which of the following breaks all intersecting parts of selected shapes into their own separate shapes?

   (a) Fragment
   (b) Intersect
   (c) Subtract
   (d) Union

5. You have inserted a picture of a field with a dog on the right side. If you flip the picture vertically, what would the resulting image look like?

   (a) The image would show right side up, but the dog would be on the left side.
   (b) The image would be upside down with the dog's head pointing down.
   (c) The image would be rotated 270°, and the dog would be at the top.
   (d) The image would be rotated 90°, and the dog would be on the bottom.

6. You have items needed for a camping trip in a bullet placeholder. Which of the following SmartArt diagrams would you use to display the data as an infographic?

   (a) Hierarchy
   (b) Cycle
   (c) List
   (d) Relationship

7. Which of the following is *not* a layout available from the SmartArt gallery?

   (a) Information table
   (b) Horizontal bullet list
   (c) Process graphic
   (d) Cycle matrix

8. Which of the following might be a reason for changing the stacking order of shapes?

   (a) To show a relationship by placing shapes in front of or behind each other
   (b) To hide something on a shape
   (c) To uncover something hidden by another shape
   (d) All of the above

9. Which of the following SmartArt diagram layouts is used to illustrate connections?

   (a) Relationship
   (b) Matrix
   (c) Cycle
   (d) Pyramid

10. Which of the following may be used to precisely align objects?

    (a) Gridlines
    (b) Smart Guides
    (c) Ruler
    (d) All of the above

Practice Exercises

1 Hiring Flow Chart

FROM SCRATCH To help explain the hiring process at your company, you create a Hiring Flow Chart. You want the flow chart to show the four stages of the hiring. Refer to Figure 3.56 as you complete this exercise.

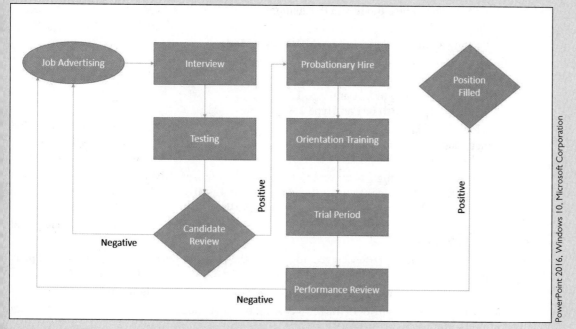

FIGURE 3.56 Hiring Flow Chart

a. Open a blank presentation file and save it as **p03p1Hiring_LastFirst**. Create a Notes and Handouts header with your name and a footer with your instructor's name and your class. Include the current date.

b. Click the **Home tab** and click **Layout** in the Slides group. Select the **Blank layout**.

c. Click the **Insert tab** and click **Shape** in the Illustrations group. Click **Oval** in the Basic Shapes category. Drag to create an oval on the slide.

d. Change the size of the oval shape by doing the following:
   - Click the **Format tab** and click the **Size Dialog Box Launcher** to open the Format Shape pane.
   - Click in the **Height box** and type **1**.
   - Click in the **Width box** and type **2.5**.
   - Click the **Position arrow** and type **.3** in the **Horizontal position box** and **0.89** in the **Vertical position box**.
   - Type **Job Advertising** in the oval.

e. Click the **Insert tab** and click **Shapes** in the Illustrations group. Click **Diamond** in the Basic Shapes category. Drag to create a diamond on the slide.

f. Change the size of the diamond shape in the Format Shape pane by doing the following:
   - Click in the **Height box** and type **2**.
   - Click in the **Width box** and type **2.5**.
   - Click the **Position arrow** and type **10.03** in the **Horizontal position box** and **0.89** in the **Vertical position box**.
   - Type **Position Filled** in the diamond.

g. Create another diamond shape in the Format Shape pane with the following formatting:
- Click in the **Height box** and type **2**.
- Click in the **Width box** and type **2.5**.
- Click the **Position arrow** and type **3.54** in the **Horizontal position box** and **4.46** in the **Vertical position box**.
- Type **Candidate Review** in the diamond.

h. Click the **Insert tab** and click **Shapes** in the Illustrations group. Right-click **Rectangle** in the Rectangle category and select **Lock Drawing Mode**.

i. Draw six rectangles on the screen in the approximate locations shown in Figure 3.56. Select all six rectangles and:
- Click in the **Height box** and type **1**.
- Click in the **Width box** and type **2.5**.

j. Select the oval, the diamond, and the two top rectangles. Click **Format tab**, click **Align**, and then click **Align Top**. Type **Interview** in the rectangle on the left and type **Probationary Hire** in the rectangle on the right.

k. Drag another rectangle between the *Interview* rectangle and the *Candidate Review* diamond using the Smart Guides to align the objects. Type **Testing** in the rectangle. Select all three shapes, click **Format**, click **Align**, and then click **Distribute Vertically**.

l. Type the following in the remaining rectangles: **Orientation Training**, **Trial Period**, and **Performance Review**.

m. Select the Performance Review rectangle. Click the **Position arrow** in the Format Shape pane and type **6.78** in the **Horizontal position box** and **6.25** in the **Vertical position box**.

n. Use the Smart Guides to position the remaining two rectangles as shown in Figure 3.56.

o. Select the four rectangles in the third column of shapes and then click **Align** and **Distribute Vertically**.

p. Click the **Insert tab**, click **Shapes**, and then right-click **Elbow Arrow Connector** in the Lines category.

q. Position the pointer over the oval labeled *Job Advertising* to view the connecting points. Drag from the connecting point on the right side of the oval to the connection point on the left side of the *Interview* rectangle. Continue to connect shapes as shown in Figure 3.56. PowerPoint will automatically determine where to bend the arrow as you are dragging the line.

r. Click the **Insert tab** and then click **Text Box** in the Text group. Position the pointer below the connector line to the left of *Candidate Review*. Type **Negative**. Create the three remaining text boxes to complete the flow chart.

s. Save and close the file. Based on your instructor's directions, submit p03p1Hiring_LastFirst.

2 | Principles of Pilates

You have created a slide show about Pilates for your Pilates instructor to show prospective students. You use infographics, shapes, and online pictures to share the message. Refer to Figure 3.57 as you complete this exercise.

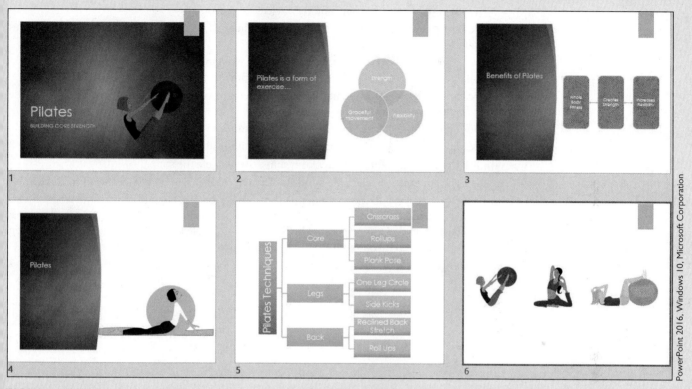

FIGURE 3.57 Pilates Presentation

a. Open *p03p2Pilates* and save it as **p03p2Pilates_LastFirst**.

b. Create a Notes and Handouts header with your name and a footer with your instructor's name and your class. Include the current date.

c. Click **Slide 2**. Click the placeholder containing the bullet points and click the **Home tab**.

d. Click **Convert to SmartArt** in the Paragraph group and click **Basic Venn**.

e. Click **Change Colors** in the **Design tab** in the SmartArt Styles group. Click **Transparent Gradient Range - Accent 1** in the Accent 1 section.

f. Click **Slide 3**. Click the **Insert tab**, click **Shapes** in the Illustrations group, and then select **Double Arrow** in the Lines section. Drag an arrow from the right-center connecting point on the Whole Body Fitness shape to the left-center connecting point on the Creates Strength shape. Repeat this step to create a connector between the Creates Strength shape and the Increases Flexibility shape.

g. Click **Slide 5**. Select the **Hierarchy SmartArt** and click the **SmartArt Tools Design tab**.

h. Select the **Core shape** and click the **Add Shape arrow** in the Create Graphic group. Select **Add Shape Below** and type **Plank Pose**.

i. Click **More** in the Layouts group on the Design tab and select **More Layouts**. Click **Horizontal Multi-Level Hierarchy** in the Hierarchy category.

j. Click **Intense Effect** in the SmartArt Styles group.

k. Click **Slide 1**. Select the image, click the **Format tab**, and then click **Color** in the Adjust group. Click **Sepia** in the Recolor variations category (first row, third column).

l. Click **Slide 4**. Right-click the image and select **Edit Picture**. Click **Yes** to convert the picture into a drawing object. Select the image again.

m. Click the **Format tab** and click **Group** in the Arrange group. Select **Ungroup**.

n. Click the **View tab** and click **Zoom** in the Zoom group. Select **200%** and click **OK**. Deselect the shapes and select the circle.

o. Click the **Format tab** and click **Shape Fill**. Select **Lime, Accent** 1 (top row, fifth column).

p. Click **Fit to Window** in the Zoom group.

q. Drag a selection net around all the shapes comprising the image, click the **Format tab**, click **Group** in the Arrange group, and then select **Regroup**.

r. Click the **Insert tab** and click **Shapes** in the Illustrations group. Click **Freeform** in the Lines section.

s. Click approximately **0.5"** from the foot of the woman to create the first point of a freeform shape you create to resemble a mat (see Figure 3.57).

t. Click approximately **0.5"** from the right hand of the woman to create the second point of the freeform shape.

u. Click approximately **1/4"** vertically and horizontally from the bottom-right of the slide.

v. Click approximately **1/4"** vertically and horizontally from the bottom-left of the slide.

w. Click the starting point of the freeform shape to complete the shape.

x. Click the **Format tab**, click the **Send Backward arrow**, and then select **Send to Back**.

y. Click **Slide 6**. Line up the three figures in a horizontal line beginning with the woman with the red ball and ending with the woman with the purple ball. Drag a selection net around all the images and click the **Format tab**. Click **Align**, then click **Align Middle**. Click **Align**, then click **Distribute Horizontally** to evenly distribute the images.

z. Save and close the file. Based on your instructor's directions, submit p03p2Pilates_LastFirst.

Mid-Level Exercises

1   SmartArt and Online Pictures Ideas

To help you become familiar with the SmartArt Graphic gallery and the types of information appropriate for each type of diagram, you create a slide show of SmartArt ideas. You also manipulate an image. In this activity, you work extensively with sizing, placement, and fills.

a. Open *p03m1Ideas* and save it as **p03m1Ideas_LastFirst**. On Slide 1, replace *First Name Last Name* with your name.

b. Create a Notes and Handouts header with your name and a footer with your instructor's name and your class. Include the current date.

c. Display the gridlines.

d. Click **Slide 2**. Insert a **Vertical Box List SmartArt diagram** (second row, second column in the List category) and make the following modifications:

- Apply the **Subtle Effect** from SmartArt Styles.
- Apply **Colored Outline – Accent 3** Color style.
- Type the following list items into the **Text Pane**:
  - **List**
  - **Process**
  - **Cycle**
  - **Hierarchy**
  - **Relationship**
  - **Matrix**
  - **Pyramid**
  - **Picture**
- Change the text font size to **20 pt**.
- Size the SmartArt diagram to **7"** wide and drag it so that it is at the horizontal center of the slide using the grid to help you determine placement.
- Align the bottom border of the SmartArt diagram with the last line of the gridline.

e. Click **Slide 3**. Convert the text to an **Upward Arrow Process SmartArt diagram** and make the following modifications:

- Apply the **Simple Fill SmartArt Style**.
- Change the height of the SmartArt diagram to **6.17"** and the width to **10"**.
- **Align Center** the diagram. Then **Align Middle** the diagram.

f. Click **Slide 4**. Insert a **Diverging Radial SmartArt diagram** and make the following modifications:

- Apply the **3-D Polished SmartArt Style**.
- Change the SmartArt colors to **Colorful - Accent Colors** (first row, first column in the Color section).
- Type **Residential College** as the center hub and type **Build Community**, **Promote Personal Growth**, and **Support Academic Success** as the spokes around the hub. Remove the extra shape.
- Set the height of the SmartArt to **5.5"** and the width to **6.67"**.

g. Click **Slide 5**. Insert a **Horizontal Hierarchy SmartArt diagram** (third row, fourth column in the Hierarchy category) and make the following modifications:

- Apply the **Flat Scene SmartArt Style**.
- Type **School of Business** as the first-level bullet in the **Text Pane**. Type **M&M** and **DIS** as the second-level bullets. Type **Marketing**, and **Management** as third-level bullets under M&M, Type **MIS**, and **POM** as third-level bullets under DIS.
- Click **Right to Left** in Create Graphic group on the SmartArt Tools Design tab to change the orientation of the diagram.
- Drag the borders of the SmartArt graphic until it fits the page and the text is large enough to read.

DISCOVER    **h.** Click **Slide 6**. Insert a **Basic Venn SmartArt diagram** (tenth row, fourth column in the Relationship category) and make the following modifications:

- Type the following as three bullets in the **Text Pane**: **Anesthesiology**, **Nurses**, and **Surgeon**.
- Insert a picture fill in the *Anesthesiology* shape using an Online Picture with **Doctor** as the key term.
- Insert a picture fill in the *Nurses* shape using an Online Picture with **Nurse** as the key term.
- Insert a picture fill in the *Surgeon* shape using an Online Picture with **Surgeon** as the key term.
- Recolor all images using the **Grayscale variation**.
- Format the SmartArt text with the **Fill - White, Outline - Accent 2, Hard Shadow - Accent 2 Style**.
- Set the height of the SmartArt to **4.5"** and the width to **5.5"**.
- Use the grid to center the Venn diagram in the available space.

i. Click **Slide 7**. Insert a **Basic Matrix SmartArt diagram** (first row, first column in the Matrix category) and make the following modifications:
- Apply the **Subtle Effect SmartArt Style**.
- Change the colors to **Colorful - Accent Colors**.
- Type the following text in the Text Pane:
  - **Urgent & Important**
  - **Not Urgent & Important**
  - **Urgent & Not Important**
  - **Not Urgent & Not Important**

j. Click **Slide 8**. Insert a **Basic Pyramid SmartArt diagram** (first row, first column in the Pyramid category) and make the following modifications:
- Apply the **Subtle Effect SmartArt Style**.
- Press **Spacebar** to create a blank space at the top pyramid level and add the following text to the remaining levels. You will add the text for the top pyramid level in a text box in a later step so that the font in the SmartArt is not reduced to a difficult-to-read font size.
  - **Esteem**
  - **Belonging and Love**
  - **Safety**
  - **Biological Needs**
- Drag the border of the SmartArt diagram until it fills the available white space on the slide. Deselect the pyramid.
- Create a text box on the top left of the slide and type **Self-Actualization** in the text box. Change the font size to **39 pt**. Drag the text box so it is centered over the top of the empty pyramid.
- Apply the **Fill – Dark Red, Accent 1, Shadow WordArt Style** to the text box *Maslow's Hierarchy of Needs*.
- Apply the **Deflate Transform Text Effect** to the WordArt text.

k. Click **Slide 9**. Ungroup the complex image until all grouping is undone. Make the following changes:
- Change the color of the bird so it is red.
- Regroup the pieces of the image.

l. View the slide show. Save and close the file. Based on your instructor's directions, submit p03m1Ideas_LastFirst.

2 The Arts

CREATIVE CASE

A presentation created for a local children's arts center can be improved by adding a theme, using shapes and SmartArt, and adding online pictures. You will update the presentation using the theme of your choice and the SmartArt style and colors of your choice.

a. Open *p03m2Perform* and save it as **p03m2Perform_LastFirst**. Create a Notes and Handouts header with your name and a footer with your instructor's name and your class. Include the current date.

b. Apply the theme of your choice to the presentation.

c. Click **Slide 3**. Select the bulleted text and convert it to a **Continuous Block Process SmartArt diagram** available in the Process SmartArt category. Apply the SmartArt colors and style of your choice.

d. Click **Slide 4**. Select the existing SmartArt diagram and change the layout to a **Segmented Pyramid** in the Pyramid SmartArt category. Change the height of the SmartArt to **6"** and the width to **10"**. Set its position at **0"** from the Top Left Corner both horizontally and vertically. Apply the SmartArt colors and style of your choice.

e. Click **Slide 5**. Insert a minimum of two online pictures of items that could be donated to the center. For example, you could add tables, musical instruments, easels, clay, chalk, etc. Adjust colors as desired.

f. Click **Slide 6.** Ungroup the images and change the fill color of several shapes to theme colors. Resize and position the image as appropriate. Regroup the image.

g. Save and close the file. Based on your instructor's directions, submit p03m2Perform_LastFirst.

---

3 Learning from an Expert

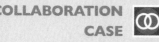

COLLABORATION CASE

Video-sharing sites such as YouTube.com make it possible to learn from PowerPoint industry experts as well as everyday PowerPoint users. You can learn through step-by-step instructions or by inspiration after seeing others use PowerPoint. The video source may also refer you to a professional website that will provide you with a wealth of tips and ideas for creating slide shows that move your work from ordinary to extraordinary. In this exercise, you will view a YouTube video featuring the work of Nancy Duarte, a well-known PowerPoint industry expert. After viewing the video and related website, you will use shapes and animation to recreate one of the effects in Duarte's presentation. Finally, you will present your slides online to other classmates, and then use WordOnline to discuss the experience with your classmates.

a. Access the Internet and go to www.youtube.com. Search for the video *Duarte Design's Five Rules for Presentations by Nancy Duarte.* View the video, click the supporting link beneath the video (http://blog.duarte.com/), and note the additional resources available to viewers of the video.

b. Advance to 2:29 in the video clip on YouTube and rewatch Duarte's Rule 4—Practice Design Not Decoration.

c. Open *p03m3Duarte*, which contains the slide Duarte's Rule 4. Apply animations to the shapes and text contained in the file to reproduce the effect of Duarte's slide. Add a shape to the slide that applies Duarte's Rule 4. Save the file as **p03m3Duarte_LastFirst**.

d. Click the File tab, then click Share. Click Present Online and present your slide to another classmate. Have that classmate also present their slide to you.

e. Go to Office.live.com, and open a Word Online Blank document. Write a brief description of Duarte's rules, noting how you can apply Rule 4 to future presentations. Ask the classmate with whom you shared your Online Presentation to add his or her own thoughts about Duarte's rules to the Word Online document. Save the file as p03m3DuarteNotes_LastFirst_LastFirst (adding the Last and First name of you and your classmate).

f. Based on your instructor's directions, submit p03m3Duarte_LastFirst_LastFirst. Using the Share feature in Word Online, invite your instructor to view your document.

Beyond the Classroom

Human Rights

GENERAL CASE ✓

FROM SCRATCH

Plan a presentation about one or more human rights leaders you admire, such as Helen Keller, Martin Luther King, Jr., Thurgood Marshall, Nelson Mandela, Cesar Chavez, or Michelle Bachelet. Research the person or persons of your choice and sketch out a storyboard of at least four slides sharing information about the person or persons. Create the presentation and name it **p03b1Rights_LastFirst**. Include an appropriate title slide, key topic slides, and conclusion slide. Add text boxes and shapes to add emphasis to information, and a slide with SmartArt that shows a timeline or list of accomplishments. Include a slide with a quote enclosed by a shape and include the name of the person you are quoting. Type a speaker note for the introduction slide that summarizes why you admire this person or these people. Apply a design theme and modify it and other elements as desired to make your presentation interesting and informative. Apply a transition to all slides. In addition to the SmartArt, include several pictures in appropriate locations. Add transitions and animations to enhance the show. Include a Notes and Handouts header with your name and a handout footer with your instructor's name and your class. Save and close the file. Based on your instructor's directions, submit p03b1Rights_LastFirst.

Predators

DISASTER RECOVERY ✚

Your friend who teaches in a middle school asked you to fix the presentation she created about sharks to make it more interesting for her students. Open *p03b2Predators* and save the new presentation as **p03b2Predators_LastFirst**. View the presentation and note visually jarring WordArt that was applied as well as images that are positioned poorly. Convert the bulleted text on Slide 2 into a pyramid demonstrating the food chain using a SmartArt diagram. Use the following levels from top level to bottom level: **Predators**, **Secondary Consumers**, **Primary Consumers**, and **Primary Producers**. The food chain is shown as a pyramid to show that meat-eating predators at the top of the food chain are rarer than plant-eating primary consumers, which are rarer than primary producers such as plants. Type a speaker note for the food chain slide that summarizes how the levels of the food chain work. After Slide 2, review the slides and edit layouts, fonts, and other style elements to make the slides readable and effective. Add at least three shapes, and add shape effects to them to present information located in the speaker notes. On the title slide, modify the WordArt so that it is legible. Add a transition and animations to enhance the show. Include a Notes and Handouts header with your name and a handout footer with your instructor's name and your class. Save and close the file. Based on your instructor's directions, submit p03b2Predators_LastFirst.

Capstone Exercise

You are working on a presentation about energy use in the home. You decide to incorporate shapes to demonstrate heat loss in a home and use the SmartArt feature to create infographics relating to energy use and efficiency.

Create a "Heat Loss" Illustration Using Shapes

You decide to create shapes to explain the concept of heat loss and insulation. You stack three oval shapes to create the zones, and you use a combination of text boxes and online pictures to create the landscape.

a. Open *p03c1Energy* and save it as **p03c1Energy_LastFirst**. Create a handout footer with a fixed date and time, a page number, your name and your class. Replace Student Name with your name on Slide 1.

b. Click **Slide 3**. Insert a Right Arrow shape from the Block Arrows category in the approximate center of the blank area to the left of the slide. This will be the shape containing the information about insulation. Apply the following modifications to the arrow shape:

- Change the arrow shape size to a height of **1.75"** and width of **3.4"**.
- Change the arrow shape position to a horizontal position of **0.4"** from the Top Left Corner and a vertical position of of **4"** from the Top Left Corner.
- Change the Shape Fill, under More Fill Colors, to a custom RGB color: **Red:255**, **Green:255**, and **Blue:50**, and a **Transparency** of **10%**.
- Change the Shape Outline to **Blue** in the Standard Colors category.
- Type **Insulation can reduce heat loss by 2/3**. (Do not include the period.)
- Change the text color to **Dark Blue** in the Standard Colors category.

c. Create an Arrow shape from the Lines category. Begin the arrow at the left center connecting point on the top circle and ending at the roof. Use Shift while dragging the arrow to ensure you create a horizontal line with no angle. Apply the following modifications to the arrow shape:

- Change the arrow width of **1.45"**.
- Change the arrow color to the theme color **Gray - 80%, Background 1**.
- Change the arrow weight to **2 ¼ pt**.

d. Ensure that the arrow is still selected and press **Ctrl+D** three times to create three more arrows.

e. Ensure that the bottom (last) arrow is still selected and then activate the Selection Pane. Rename the selected object **Arrow 4**. Select the arrow above Arrow 4 on the slide and rename it **Arrow 3**. Continue this process to rename **Arrow 2** and **Arrow 1**.

f. Position Arrow 4 at **7.37"** horizontal position from the Top Left Corner and vertical position **6.68"** from the Top Left Corner.

g. Use the Selection Pane to select Arrows 1 through 4, and then use the Align feature to distribute the lines vertically. With the four arrows still selected, **Align Left**.

h. Ensure that the four arrows are still selected, and then bring the object to the front so the arrow heads are on top of the house.

i. Select the house and ungroup twice. Select the window on the left and press **Ctrl+D** to duplicate it. Drag the new window down, and using the Smart Guides, align the window on the left with the window above it and the top with the top of the windows on the door.

j. Regroup the house shapes. Select the house and the new window and then group them.

k. Move to **Slide 5** and insert a text box in the blank space at the bottom of the slide. Type **Change your lifestyle** inside the text box. Make the following modifications:

- Change the font size to **44 pt**.
- Align the text box to the center of the slide.

Convert Text to SmartArt

To add visual interest to slides, you review the slide show and convert some of the bulleted lists to SmartArt graphics.

a. Click **Slide 2**. Convert the bulleted text to a **Basic Venn SmartArt graphic**. Change the colors of the diagram to **Colorful Range – Accent Colors 3 – 4**.

b. Click **Slide 4**. Select the **Insulation Can Help bulleted text** and convert it to a **Target List SmartArt graphic**. Apply the **Moderate Effect SmartArt Style**. Change the colors of the diagram to **Colorful Range – Accent Colors 3 – 4**.

Create SmartArt

You have a list of three ways that someone could save that you decide would present well as a SmartArt list.

a. Add a new slide after Slide 2 using a **Title and Content layout**.

b. Type **What Can You Do** in the title placeholder.

c. Insert a **Vertical Picture Accent List SmartArt**. Type the following text in the following the Text Pane and then close the Text Pane:

- **Conserve electricity**
- **Change thermostat setting**
- **Insulate**

d. Click the picture icon for the Conserve electricity shape and insert *p03c1Electricity*. Insert *p03c1Thermostat* in the picture shape for Change thermostat setting, Insert *p03c1Insulate* in the picture shape for Insulate.

e. Make the following modifications to the SmartArt diagram:

- Change the color of the SmartArt to **Colored Fill - Accent 3**.
- Recolor the three pictures to **Orange, Accent color 6 Dark**.

Convert Text to WordArt

You want to convert some of the text in the slide show to WordArt for emphasis. After converting text to WordArt, you will apply an animation scheme.

a. Click **Slide 4** and select **Heat Loss**.

b. Apply the **Fill - Blue, Background 2, Inner Shadow WordArt Style** to the text.

c. Apply the **Triangle Up Warp Transform effect**.

d. Click **Slide 6**. Select the placeholder for the **Change your lifestyle** text box and apply the **Fill - White, Outline - Accent 1, Glow - Accent 1 WordArt Style**. Apply the **Square Transform Text Effect**.

Apply the **Fly In animation** to the WordArt.

e. Check the spelling in the slide show and accept or correct all spellings on the slide.

f. View the slide show.

g. Save and close the file. Based on your instructor's directions, submit p03c1Energy_LastFirst.

PowerPoint

Enhancing with Multimedia

LEARNING OUTCOME You will prepare a slide show featuring pictures, photos, video, and audio.

OBJECTIVES & SKILLS: After you read this chapter, you will be able to:

CASE STUDY | Engagement Album

Your sister was recently married. As a gift to the couple, you decide to create two memory slide shows to celebrate the occasion. The first slide show will feature images of the couple in a few engagement photos and on their honeymoon in Europe. The second slide show will display photos taken during a family vacation.

As you prepare the first slide show, you edit the images using PowerPoint's Picture Tools tab. Each slide in the first slide show is created individually, and each image is manipulated individually. You download an image from the Internet representing the couple's honeymoon and insert a video of fireworks recorded by the groom during the honeymoon. You insert a fireworks sound clip and music file to complement the fireworks display. Finally, you create the second slide show, a family vacation, using PowerPoint's Photo Album feature. You utilize the Photo Album options for image manipulation.

PowerPoint Rich Media Tools

AMY AND DAN | September 9th

FIGURE 4.1 Engagement Photo Album

CASE STUDY | Engagement Album

Starting Files	Files to be Submitted
p04h1Memory p04h1Memory_Media folder Blank PowerPoint presentation p04h4Album_Media folder	p04h3Memory_LastFirst p04h4Album_LastFirst

Pictures

Multimedia refers to multiple forms of media, such as graphics, sound, animation, and video, that are used to entertain or inform an audience. You can use any of these types of media in PowerPoint by placing the multimedia object on a slide. Multimedia graphics include images, objects created using drawing programs, diagrams and illustrations, scanned images, digital pictures or photographs, and more.

In this section, you will expand your experience with multimedia by inserting digital pictures and modifying their appearance, properties, or location on a slide.

Inserting a Picture

STEP 1 ›› Pictures are bitmap images that computers can read and interpret to create a photorealistic image. Unlike ***vector graphics*** which are created by mathematical statements, ***bitmap images*** are created by bits or pixels placed on a grid or map. In a bitmap image, each pixel contains information about the color to be displayed. A bitmap image is required to have the realism necessary for a photograph. Think of vector graphics as connect-the-dots and bitmap images as paint-by-number, and you begin to see the difference in the methods of representation.

Each type of image has its own advantages and disadvantages. Vector graphics can be sized easily and still retain their clarity but are not photorealistic. Bitmap images represent a much more complex range of colors and shades but can become pixelated (individual pixels are visible and display square edges for a jagged effect) when they are enlarged. A bitmap image can also be a large file, so ***compression***, a method applied to data to reduce the amount of space required for file storage, may be applied. The compression may be lossy (some data may be lost when decompressed) or lossless (no data is lost when decompressed).

> **TIP: COMPRESSION: LOSSY VERSUS LOSSLESS**
>
> Depending on the image's use, you may want to choose a specific image format so that images do not appear pixelated when enlarged. Certain formats can be either lossy or lossless. Lossy compression reduces a file by permanently eliminating certain data, especially redundant data. This makes the file size smaller. However, when the file is uncompressed, only a part of the original data is still there. Pixelation may not even be noticeable for certain image uses, so it might not be an issue. The JPEG image file, a common format, is an image that has lossy compression.
>
> Alternatively, with lossless compression, data that was originally in the file remains after the file is uncompressed. All of the information is completely restored. The Graphics Interchange File (GIF) image format provides lossless compression.

Figure 4.2 displays a pumpkin created as a vector graphic and one created as a bitmap image. Note the differences in realism. The boxes show a portion of the images enlarged. Note the pixilation, or jaggedness, in the enlarged portion of the bitmap image.

FIGURE 4.2 Types of Graphics

PowerPoint does not have to be all bullets; a good image can be more memorable than a simple list of words. You can accomplish this task by scanning and saving a photograph or piece of artwork, by downloading images from a digital camera or smartphone, by downloading an image from Bing Image Search or the Internet, or by creating an image in a graphics-editing software package like Adobe Photoshop™. Table 4.1 displays in alphabetical order by file extension the types of graphic file formats that you can add to a PowerPoint slide.

TABLE 4.1 Types of Graphic File Formats Supported by PowerPoint

File Format	Extension	Description
Bitmap	.bmp, .dib	**Device Independent Bitmap** A representation consisting of rows and columns of dots. The value of each dot is stored in one or more bits of data. Uncompressed and creates large file size.
Windows Enhanced Metafile	.emf	**Windows Enhanced Metafile** A Windows 32-bit file format.
GIF File	.gif	**Graphics Interchange Format** Limited to 256 colors. Effective for scanned images such as illustrations rather than for color photographs. Good for line drawings and black-and-white images. Supports transparent backgrounds.
JPEG File Interchange Format	.jpg, .jpeg	**Joint Photographic Experts Group** Supports 16 million colors and is optimized for photographs and complex graphics. Format of choice for most photographs on the Web. Uses lossy compression.
PICT File	.pict, .pic, .pct	**Macintosh PICT** Holds both vector and bitmap images. PICT supports 8 colors; PICT2 supports 16 million colors.
PNG File	.png	**Portable Network Graphics** Supports 16 million colors. Approved as a standard by the World Wide Web Consortium (W3C). Intended to replace .gif format. Uses lossy compression.
TIFF File	.tif, .tiff	**Tagged Image File Format** Best file format for storing bitmapped images on personal computers. Can be any resolution. Lossless image storage creates large file sizes. Not widely supported by browsers.
Windows Metafile	.wmf	**Windows Metafile** A Windows 16-bit file format.

There are multiple ways to add a picture that you have saved on your computer to a PowerPoint slide. You can use a placeholder or you can insert the image without a placeholder. Both methods have advantages and disadvantages.

To add a picture to a slide using a placeholder, complete the following steps:

1. Select a layout with a placeholder that includes a Pictures icon.
2. Click the Pictures icon to open the Insert Picture dialog box.
3. Navigate to the location of your picture files and select the picture you want to use.
4. Click Insert.

Figure 4.3 shows two examples of placeholders with Pictures icons. When you insert a picture in this manner, the picture is centered within the placeholder frame and is sometimes cropped to fit within the placeholder. This effect can cause unwanted results, such as the tops of heads cropped off. If this situation occurs, undo the insertion, enlarge the placeholder, and then repeat the steps for inserting an image. Avoid enlarging the placeholders when possible because any changes you make to the slide master or theme may not appear correctly once those changes are applied to the slide where you modified the placeholder.

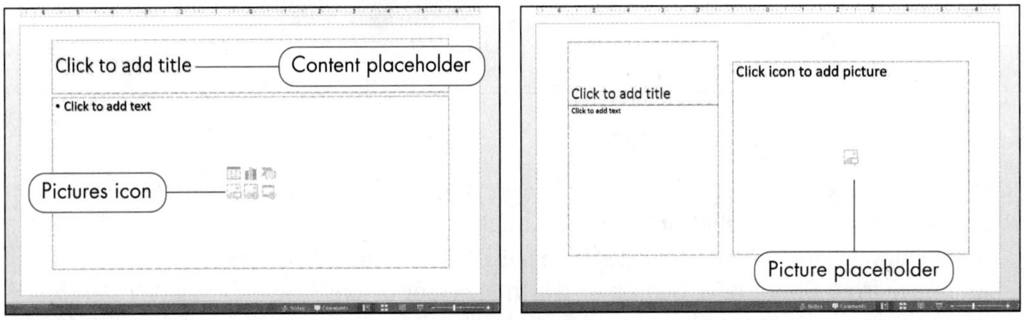

FIGURE 4.3 Insert Picture Using Placeholders

Another way to insert an image is to click Pictures on the Insert tab. The advantage of this method is that your image comes in at full size rather than centered and cropped in a placeholder, and you do not need a picture placeholder. You can then resize the image to fit the desired area. The disadvantage is the time you may spend resizing and positioning the image.

To add a picture using the Insert tab, complete the following steps:

1. Click the Insert tab.
2. Click Pictures in the Images group.
3. Navigate to the location of your picture files and select the picture you want to use.
4. Click Insert.
5. Adjust the size and position of the picture as necessary.

TIP: ADDING IMAGES USING FILE EXPLORER

If you are adding multiple images to a slide show, you can speed up the process by inserting images directly from File Explorer. Open File Explorer and navigate to the folder where the images are located. Position the File Explorer window next to the PowerPoint window and drag the images from the Explorer window onto the slides of your choice.

Transforming a Picture

Once you insert a picture onto a slide, PowerPoint provides tools that you can use to adjust the image. Found on the Picture Tools Format tab (see Figure 4.4), the Picture Tools tab is designed to adjust an image background, correct image problems, manipulate image color, or add artistic or stylized effects. You can also arrange, crop, or resize an image using Picture Tools tab. Additionally, when you right-click on the picture and select Format Picture, you will open the Format Picture task pane, where you can also access these same tools.

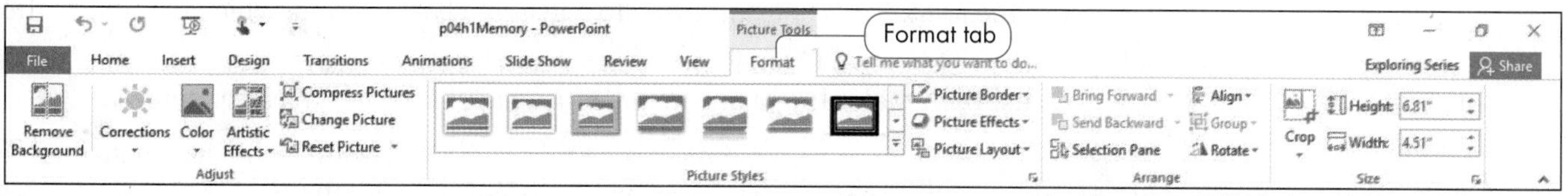

PowerPoint 2016, Windows 10, Microsoft Corporation

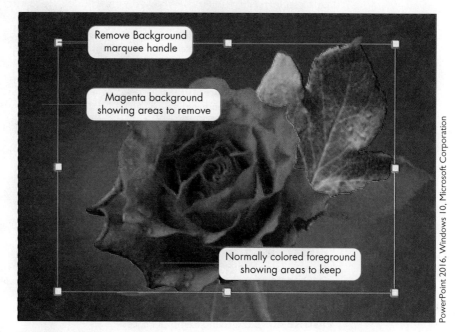

FIGURE 4.4 Picture Tools

Remove a Picture Background

The Remove Background tool in the Adjust group on the Format tab enables you to remove portions of a picture you do not want to keep. Rather than have a rectangle-shaped picture on your slide, you can have an image in the shape of the desired object on the slide. For example, if you remove the background in a picture of a flower, you can have a flower-shaped image on your slide instead. This can create a more interesting and creative look for your slide.

When you select a picture and click the Remove Background tool, PowerPoint creates an automatic marquee selection area in the picture that determines the ***background***, or area to be removed, and the ***foreground***, or area to be kept. PowerPoint identifies the background selection with magenta coloring. You then adjust PowerPoint's automatic selection by marking areas you want to keep, marking areas you want to remove, and deleting any markings you do not want. You can discard all changes you have made or keep your changes. Figure 4.5 shows a picture in which the Remove Background tool has created a marquee identifying the foreground and background.

PowerPoint 2016, Windows 10, Microsoft Corporation

FIGURE 4.5 Remove Background Marquee, Foreground, and Background

Once the background has been identified by the marquee, you can refine the marquee size and shape so that it contains everything you want to keep without extra areas.

To resize the marquee, complete the following steps:

1. Select the picture and drag a marquee handle to indicate the desired foreground.
2. Refine the picture further by using the tools available on the Background Removal tab (see Figure 4.6):

   - Use the *Mark Areas to Keep* tool to add to the foreground, which keeps the area.
   - Use the *Mark Areas to Remove* tool to add to the background, which eliminates the area.
   - To use both tools, drag a line to indicate what should be added or removed.

3. Press Esc or click away from the selection to see what the picture looks like. Note that the thumbnail also shows what the image will look like with the changes applied.

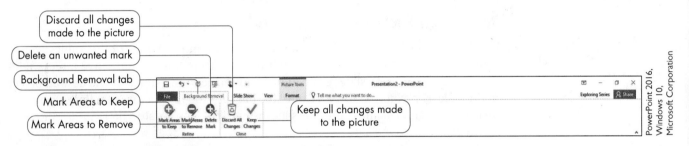

FIGURE 4.6 Background Removal Tools

You can make further changes by returning to Background Removal and continuing to work with your picture. Figure 4.7 shows a resized marquee with enlarged areas marked to show areas to keep and to remove. Figure 4.8 shows the flower picture with the background removed.

FIGURE 4.7 Background Removal Process

PowerPoint 2016, Windows 10, Microsoft Corporation

FIGURE 4.8 Background Removed from Flower

Correct a Picture

STEP 2 ▶▶ PowerPoint includes Corrections, a set of tools in the Adjust group. Corrections enables you to adjust brightness and contrast of an image and also soften or sharpen a picture. You can see what a correction will look like by previewing it in Live Preview.

You can enhance a picture by *sharpening* it—bringing out the detail by making the boundaries of the content more prominent. Or you may enhance the picture by *softening* the content—bluring the edges so the boundaries are less prominent. Sharpening a picture can make it clearer, but oversharpening can make the picture look grainy. Softening is a technique often used for a more romantic image or to make skin appear softer, but applying too much blur can make the picture difficult to see.

To sharpen or soften a picture, complete the following steps:

1. Select the picture.
2. Click the Format tab.
3. Click Corrections in the Adjust group.
4. Point to the thumbnails in the Sharpen/Soften section to view the corrections in Live Preview.
5. Click the thumbnail to apply the degree of correction you want.

You can make fine adjustments to the amount of sharpness and softness you apply to a picture. To make adjustments, follow Steps 1–3 above and click Picture Corrections Options at the bottom of the gallery. The Format Picture pane opens. Drag the Sharpness slider or enter a percentage in the box next to the slider until the desired effect is obtained. Figure 4.9 shows the Corrections gallery, a picture that has been softened, and a picture that has been sharpened.

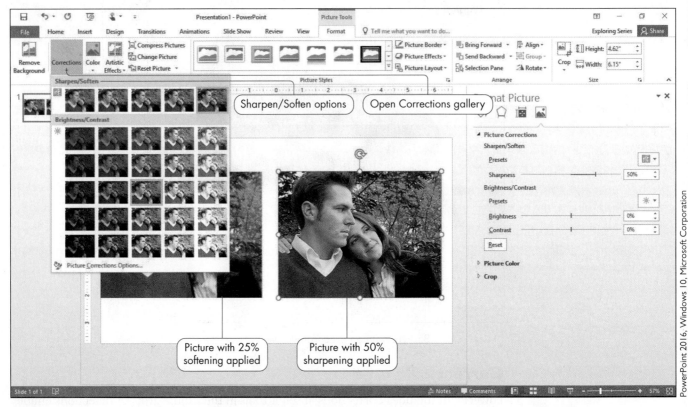

FIGURE 4.9 Corrections Gallery and Softened and Sharpened Pictures

The **brightness** (lightness or darkness) of a picture is often a matter of individual preference. You might want to change the brightness of your picture for reasons other than preference, however. For example, sometimes printing a picture requires a different brightness than is needed when projecting an image. This situation occurs because during printing the ink may spread when placed on the page, making the picture darker. Or, you might want a picture as a background and need to reduce the brightness so that text will show clearly on the background.

Contrast refers to the difference between the darkest area (black level) and lightest area (white level) of an image. If your picture has too little contrast, it can look washed out or muddy; too much contrast, and the light portion of your image will appear to explode off the screen or page. Your setting may vary depending on whether you are going to project the image or print it. Projecting impacts an image because of the amount of light in the room. In a very light room, the image may seem to need a greater contrast than in a darker room, and you may need to adjust the contrast accordingly. Try to set your control for the lighting that will appear when you display the presentation.

To adjust the brightness and contrast of a picture, complete the following steps:

1. Select the picture.
2. Click the Format tab.
3. Click Corrections in the Adjust group.
4. Point to the thumbnails in the Brightness/Contrast section to view the corrections in Live Preview.
5. Click the thumbnail to apply the degree of correction you want.

You can make fine adjustments to the amount of brightness or contrast you apply. To make adjustments, follow Steps 1–3 above and click Picture Corrections Options at the bottom of the gallery. The Format Picture task pane opens. Drag the Brightness and

Contrast sliders or enter percentages in the boxes next to the sliders until you get the result you want. Figure 4.10 shows the Corrections gallery displaying the same picture before and after it has been adjusted for brightness.

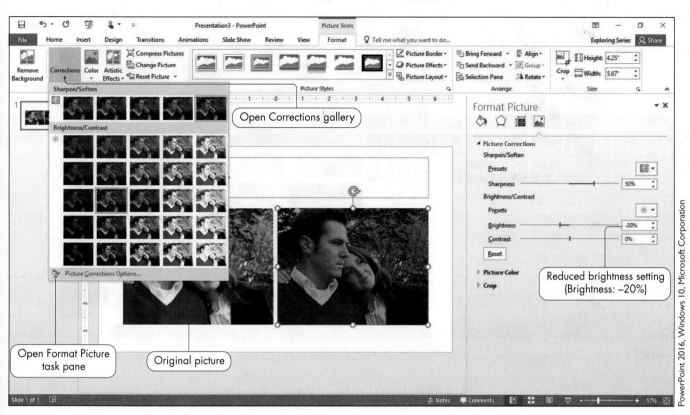

FIGURE 4.10 Format Picture Task Pane and Adjusted Picture

Change Picture Color

You can change the colors in your picture by using PowerPoint's color tools.

To access the color tools, complete the following steps:

1. Select the picture.
2. Click the Format tab.
3. Click Color in the Adjust group.
4. Point to the thumbnails in the gallery to view the corrections in Live Preview.
5. Click the thumbnail to apply the color effect you want.

You can change a picture's *saturation*, or the intensity of the colors in an image. A high saturation level makes the colors more vivid, whereas 0% saturation converts the picture to grayscale. Figure 4.11 shows a picture at its original (100%) intensity and with various levels of intensity.

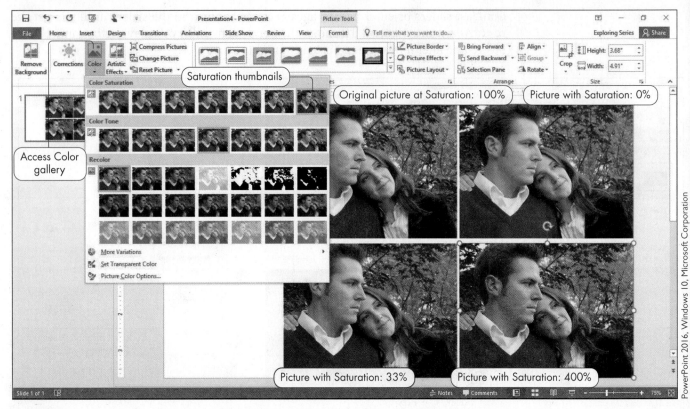

FIGURE 4.11 Picture Saturation

The *tone*, or temperature, of a color is a characteristic of lighting in pictures. It is measured in **kelvin** (K) units of absolute temperature. Lower color temperatures are cool colors and appear blueish white, whereas higher color temperatures are warm colors and appear yellowish to red. PowerPoint enables you to increase or decrease a picture's temperature to enhance its details. Point to a thumbnail to see the amount of temperature in kelvin units that would be applied. Figure 4.12 shows a picture with its original cooler tone and a copy of the picture at a higher temperature with a warmer tone.

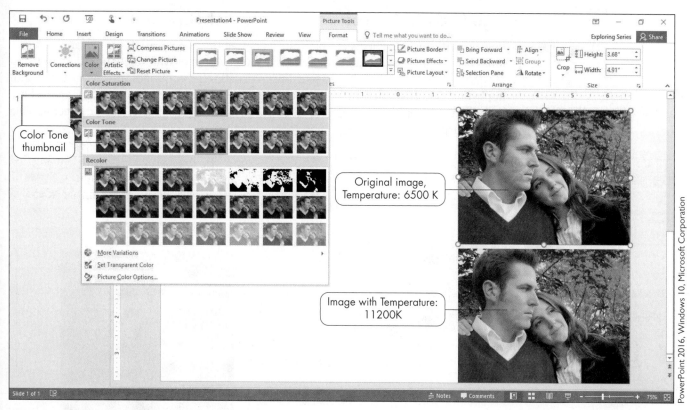

FIGURE 4.12 Picture Color Tone

In an earlier chapter, you *recolored* objects by using the Format tab. You can use the same process to change pictures by adjusting the image's colors. You can click a preset thumbnail from the gallery or click More Variations to pick from additional colors. To return a picture to its original color, click the No Recolor preset thumbnail under the Recolor section. Figure 4.13 shows a picture with the Sepia Recolor preset applied.

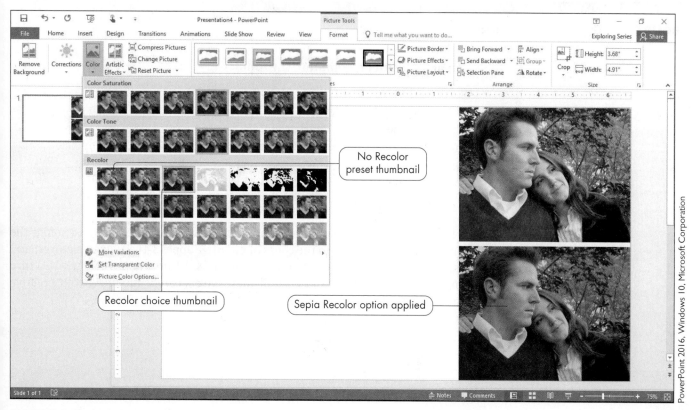

FIGURE 4.13 Sepia Recolor Preset

Use Artistic Effects

STEP 3 ▶▶ PowerPoint's artistic effects enable you to change the appearance of a picture so that it looks like it was created with a marker, as a pencil sketch or watercolor painting, or using other effects. Use Live Preview to see how an artistic effect changes your picture. You can apply only one effect at a time. Any artistic effects that you have previously applied are lost when you apply a new effect. Figure 4.14 shows a Glow Edges artistic effect applied to a picture.

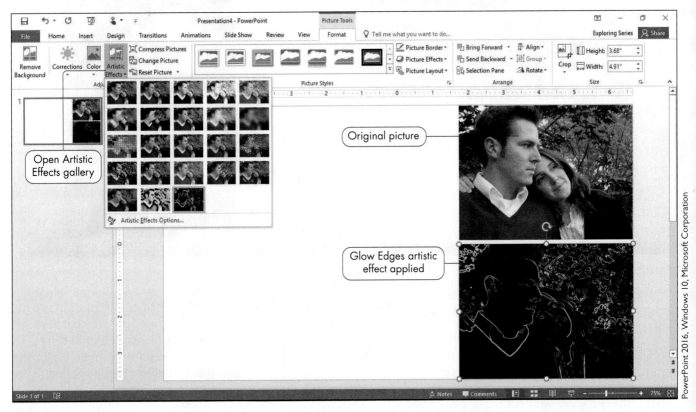

FIGURE 4.14 Glow Edges Artistic Effect

To use an artistic effect, complete the following steps:

1. Select the picture.
2. Click the Format tab.
3. Click Artistic Effects in the Adjust group.
4. Point to the thumbnails in the gallery to view the artistic effects in Live Preview.
5. Click the thumbnail of the artistic effect you want to use.

Apply Picture Styles

With Picture Styles, you can surround your picture with attractive frames, soften the edges of pictures, add shadows to the edges of pictures, apply 3-D effects to pictures, and add glossy reflections below your pictures. Many other effects are possible with Picture Styles, and when you consider that each of these effects can be modified, your creative opportunities are endless! Figure 4.15 shows a few of the possibilities.

Snip Diagonal Corner,
White Picture Style applied

Metal Oval Picture
Style Applied

Bevel Perspective Left,
White Picture Style applied

PowerPoint 2016, Windows 10, Microsoft Corporation

FIGURE 4.15 Picture Style Applications

To apply a picture style, complete the following steps:

1. Select the picture.
2. Click More in the Picture Styles group to open the gallery, then point to a style to see a Live Preview or click the style to apply it to the picture.
3. Apply additional image changes by completing one or more of the following steps:
   - Click Picture Border in the Picture Styles group to select the border color, weight, or dash style.
   - Use the Picture Effects option to select from Preset, Shadow, Reflection, Glow, Soft Edges, Bevel, and 3-D Rotation effects.
   - Select Picture Layout to apply your picture to a SmartArt diagram.

Resize or Crop a Picture

STEP 4 ⟩⟩ You can resize a picture by dragging the sizing handles for the image. You can also use the Format Picture task pane to change the size of the picture to a percent of the original. When *Lock aspect ratio* is checked, the image is resized proportionally.

To resize a picture, complete the following steps:

1. Click the Size Dialog Box Launcher in the Size group on the Picture Tools Format tab to open the Format Picture task pane.
2. Click in the Scale Height or Scale Width box, and then type the new size.

Cropping a picture using the Crop tool lets you eliminate unwanted portions of an image, focusing the viewer's attention on the most important part of the graphic. Remember that if you crop an image and try to enlarge the resulting picture, pixelation may occur that reduces the quality of the image. Figure 4.16 shows a picture with the areas to be cropped from view displayed in gray.

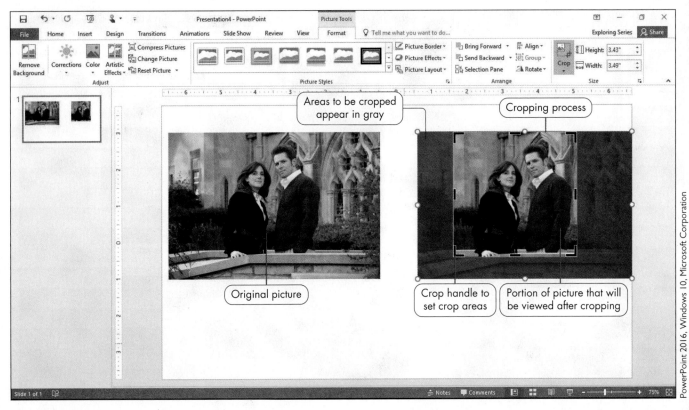

FIGURE 4.16 Use Crop to Focus Attention

To crop a picture, complete the following steps:

1. Select the picture.
2. Click the Format tab.
3. Click Crop in the Size group.
4. Point to a cropping handle and drag inward to eliminate the portion of the image you do not want to view. Use a corner cropping handle to crop in two directions at once.
5. Repeat Step 4 for the remaining sides of the picture.
6. Click Crop again to toggle it off.

When you crop a picture, the cropped portion does not display on the slide, but it is not removed from the presentation file. This is helpful in case you decide later to reset the picture to its original state. When you crop an image, because the unwanted portions of the image are not deleted, the file size is not reduced. Use the Compress Pictures feature to reduce the file size of the image, or all images at once, to reduce the file size of the presentation.

Compress Pictures

The Compress Pictures feature enables you to reduce file sizes by permanently deleting any cropped areas of a selected picture and by changing the resolution of pictures. When you add pictures to your PowerPoint presentation, especially high-resolution pictures downloaded from a digital camera, the presentation file size increases dramatically. It may increase to the point that the presentation becomes slow to load and sluggish to play. Use the Compress Pictures feature to eliminate a large part of this problem. The Compress Pictures feature is in the Adjust group on the Picture Tools Format tab.

By default, you apply compression to only the selected image. If you remove the check in the Compress Pictures dialog box, all pictures in the presentation are compressed. Figure 4.17 shows the Compress Pictures dialog box. You select the amount of compression applied by determining your output. Select 330 pixels per inch (ppi) for use on high-definition displays. Select 220 ppi to ensure that you will obtain excellent quality printouts. Select 150 ppi, however, if you will be displaying the slide show only onscreen or using it for a webpage. Select 96 ppi if you plan to share the slide show by email.

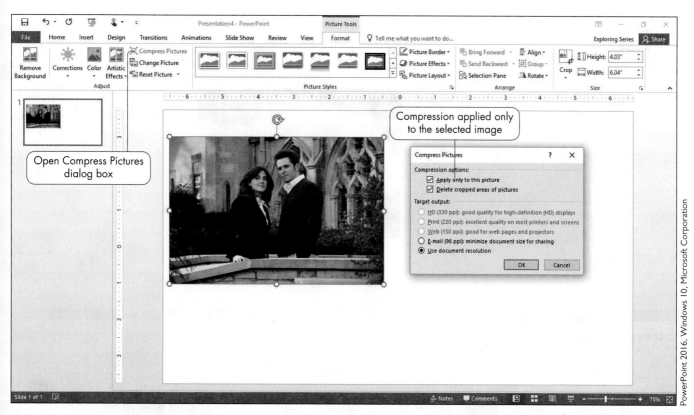

FIGURE 4.17 Picture Compression Options

Create a Background from a Picture

Pictures can make appealing backgrounds if they are transparent enough that text on top of them can be easily read. Picture backgrounds personalize your presentation. To use a photograph as a background, use the Format Background command on the Design tab rather than the Insert Picture feature. Using Insert Picture involves more time because when the picture is inserted it must be resized and the order of the objects on the screen has to be changed to prevent the photograph from hiding placeholders. Figure 4.18 shows an image inserted using Insert Picture that must be resized if it is to be used as a background. It hides the placeholders, so it needs to be positioned at the back and its transparency must be adjusted. Figure 4.19 shows the same picture as Figure 4.18, but in this figure, it was inserted as a background. It is automatically placed behind placeholders and resized to fit the slide, and the transparency is adjusted.

If the background image is too busy or not transparent enough, it can make the presentation difficult to read or distract the audience. Test several images and settings if its color does not contrast enough with the text.

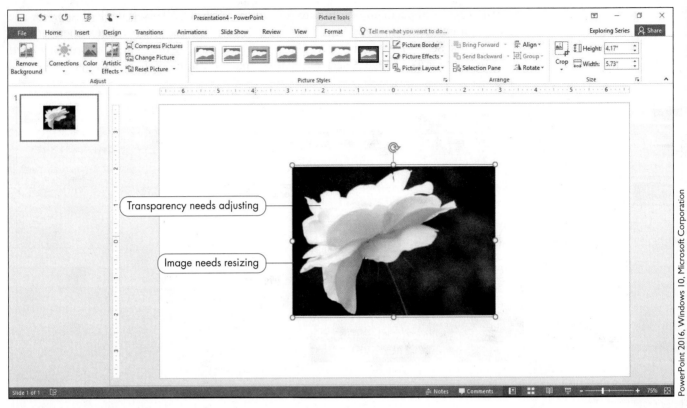

FIGURE 4.18 Background from Insert Picture Option

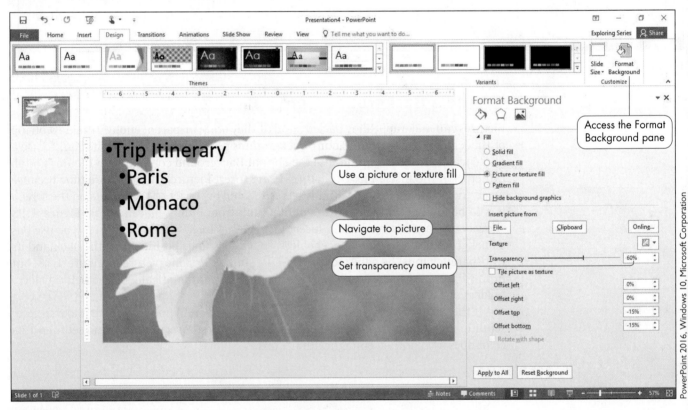

FIGURE 4.19 Background from Format Background Option

To create a background from a picture using the Background command, complete the following steps:

1. Click the Design tab.
2. Click Format Background in the Customize group. The Format Background task pane displays.
3. Click Picture or texture fill.
4. Click File and navigate to the location where your picture is stored.
5. Click the picture file and click Insert.
6. Adjust the transparency for the picture by dragging the Transparency slider.
7. Click Close to apply the picture background to the current slide or click Apply to All to apply it to all slides in the presentation.

The task pane also includes options for moving the picture by offsetting it to the left or right or the top or bottom.

Using the Internet as a Resource

STEP 5 ▶▶ You can use the Internet as a resource for pictures, video, and audio. PowerPoint interacts with the Internet in three important ways:

- You can download pictures, video, and audio from some webpages for inclusion in a PowerPoint presentation. Note, however, that some of these resources may not be used without permission or license from the creator.

- You can insert hyperlinks into a PowerPoint presentation and click those links to display the associated webpage in your browser provided you have an Internet connection during the presentation.

- You can convert any PowerPoint presentation into a webpage.

Regardless of how you choose to use the Internet for resources in your presentations, your first task is to locate the required resource. For example, if you want to use an image of a dolphin in your presentation on oceanography, you can use a search engine and a search term such as *dolphin images* and save the images to be inserted into the presentation. Or you could use Online Pictures in PowerPoint to access the Bing Image Search and insert them directly from the search results. You could also use a search engine to locate videos or audio of dolphins using *dolphin video* or *dolphin audio.* A search results page will display and you can review the list of results to see what you want to include in the presentation.

After you have found an image on the Internet, to save or copy the image, complete one of the following steps:

- Right-click the image to display a shortcut menu and select *Save picture* to save the file on your computer. (This command may vary among Web browsers.) Then, in PowerPoint, click the Insert tab and click Pictures in the Images group. Navigate to the picture and click Insert.

- Right-click the image to display a shortcut menu and select Copy to copy the picture onto the Clipboard. Then, simply, paste it onto the slide.

Saving audio files from the Internet can be accomplished by right-clicking the link of the audio file and then selecting the command *Save Target As* from the shortcut menu. Note that different browsers may call the command differently. Videos are typically very large files, so you may want to link to a video by inserting a hyperlink to the resources website. You can click Insert Hyperlink in the Links group on the Insert tab to add it to your slide. Again, you need to be connected to the Internet during your presentation in order for the video to play. Some websites may provide instructions on how to embed a video into your presentation.

Understand Copyright Protection

A *copyright* provides legal protection to a written or artistic work, including pictures, drawings, poetry, novels, movies, songs, computer software, and architecture. It gives the author of a work the exclusive right to the use and duplication of that work. A copyright does not protect facts, ideas, systems, or methods of operation, although it may protect the way these things are expressed.

The owner of the copyright may sell or give up a portion of his or her rights; for example, an author may give distribution rights to a publisher and/or grant movie rights to a studio. *Infringement of copyright* occurs anytime a right held by the copyright owner is used without permission of the owner. Anything on the Internet should be considered copyrighted unless the site specifically says it is in the *public domain*, in which case the author is giving everyone the right to freely reproduce and distribute the material, thereby making the work owned by the public at large. A work also may enter the public domain when the copyright has expired. Facts themselves are not covered by copyright, so you can use statistical data without fear of infringement. Images are protected unless the owner gives his or her permission for downloading.

TIP: USING MEDIA ELEMENTS

Photographs, fonts, sounds, and videos available from Microsoft and its partners through Office.com are part of Microsoft's Media Elements and are copyright protected by Microsoft. To see what uses of Media Elements are prohibited, go to http://support.microsoft.com and search for *Use of Microsoft Copyrighted Content*.

The answer to what you can use from the Web depends on many things, including the amount of the information you reference, as well as the intended use of that information. It is considered fair use, and thus not an infringement of copyright, to use a portion of a work for educational or nonprofit purposes, or for critical review or commentary. In other words, you can use quotes, facts, or other information from the Web in an educational setting, but you should cite the original work in your footnotes, or list the resource on a bibliography page or slide. Table 4.2 presents guidelines for students and teachers to help determine what multimedia can be used in an educational project based on the Proposal for Fair Use Guidelines for Educational Multimedia created in 1996. These guidelines were created by a group of publishers, authors, and educators who gathered to interpret the Copyright Act of 1976 as it applies to educational and scholarly uses of multimedia. You should note that although these guidelines are part of the Congressional Record, they are not law. They can, however, help you determine when you can use multimedia materials under Fair Use principles in a noncommercial, educational use.

TABLE 4.2 Multimedia Copyright Guidelines for Students and Teachers

The following guidelines are based on Section 107 of the U.S. Copyright Act of 1976 and the Proposal for Fair Use Guidelines for Educational Multimedia (1996), which sets forth fair use factors for multimedia projects. These guidelines cover the use of multimedia based on Time, Portion, and Copying and Distribution Limitations. You can learn more about copyright at http://copyright.gov/.

General Guidelines

- Student projects for specific courses may be displayed and kept in personal portfolios as examples of their academic work.
- Students in specific courses may use multimedia in projects with proper credit and citations. Full bibliographic information must be used when available.
- Students and teachers must display copyright notice if copyright ownership information is shown on the original source. Copyright may be shown in a sources or bibliography section unless the presentation is being used for distance learning. In distance learning situations, copyright must appear on the screen when the image is viewed.
- Teachers may use media for face-to-face curriculum-based instruction, for directed self-study, in demonstrations on how to create multimedia productions, for presentations at conferences, and for distance learning. Teachers may also retain projects in their personal portfolios for personal use such as job interviews or tenure review.
- Teachers may use multimedia projects for educational purposes for up to two years, after which permission of the copyright holder is required.
- Students and teachers do not need to write for permission to use media if it falls under multimedia guidelines unless there is a possibility that the project could be broadly distributed at a later date.

Text Guidelines

- Up to 10 percent of a copyrighted work, or up to 1,000 words, may be used, whichever is less.
- Up to 250 words of a poem may be used, but no more than five poems (or excerpts) from different poets or an anthology; no more than three poems (or excerpts) from a single poet.

Illustrations

- A photograph or illustration may be used in its entirety.
- No more than 15 images may be used from a collection.
- No more than 5 images of an artist's or photographer's work may be used.

Motion Media

- Up to 10 percent of a copyrighted work or 3 minutes may be used, whichever is less.
- The clip cannot be altered in any way.

Music and Sound

- Up to 10 percent of a copyrighted musical composition or sound recording may be used, not to exceed 30 seconds.
- Alterations cannot change the basic melody or fundamental character of the work.

Distribution Limitations

- Multimedia projects should not be posted to unsecured websites.
- No more than two copies of the original may be made, only one of which may be placed on reserve for instructional purposes.
- A copy of a project may be made for backup purposes, but may be used only when the original has been lost, damaged, or stolen.
- If more than one person created a project, each person may keep only one copy.

Quick Concepts ✓

1. What is the difference between bitmap images and vector graphics? Name one advantage and disadvantage of each type of graphic. **p. 262**
2. Why would you compress an image? **p. 262**
3. List five ways to transform an image by using PowerPoint's Picture Tools tab. **p. 265**
4. What is infringement of copyright? What is "fair use"? **p. 278**

Skills covered: Insert Pictures
• Remove a Background • Correct
a Picture • Change Picture Color
• Apply an Artistic Effect • Apply a
Picture Style • Create a Background
from a Picture • Crop a Picture
• Compress a Picture • Insert a
Picture from the Internet

1 Pictures

You decide to create a memories slide show for your sister and her husband, who were recently married. You include their engagement and honeymoon pictures.

STEP 1 ›› INSERT PICTURES AND REMOVE A BACKGROUND

You start the memory album with a picture from the couple's engagement. Because the Title Slide layout does not include a placeholder for content, you add a picture using the Insert Picture from File feature. You then insert images into content placeholders provided in the album layout. Refer to Figure 4.20 as you complete Step 1.

Steps e–f: Resized and positioned

Step g–i: Image inserted and background removed

AMY AND DAN   September 9th

Steps m–n: Images inserted using content placeholders

PowerPoint 2016, Windows 10, Microsoft Corporation

FIGURE 4.20 Inserted Pictures

a. Open *p04h1Memory* and save it as **p04h1Memory_LastFirst**.

> **TROUBLESHOOTING:** If you make any major mistakes in this exercise, you can close the file, open *p04h1Memory* again, and then start this exercise over.

b. Create a handout header with your name and a handout footer with your instructor's name and your class. Apply to all slides. Include the current date.

c. Ensure that you are on Slide 1, click the **Insert tab**, and then click **Pictures** in the Images group.

You add a picture using the Insert Picture command because the Title Slide layout does not include a placeholder for content. The Insert Picture dialog box opens.

d. Locate the *p04h1Mem1* picture in the *p04h1Memory_Media* folder and click **Insert**.

The picture is inserted and centered on the slide.

e. Click the **Size Dialog Box Launcher** in the Size group on the Format tab to open the Format Picture task pane. Click in the **Scale Height box**, select **100**, and then type **96**. Press **Enter**.

Typing 96 in the Scale Height box automatically sets the Scale Width to 96% because the *Lock aspect ratio* check box is selected.

f. Click **Position** in the Format Picture task pane and set the Horizontal Position to **1.00"** from the Top Left Corner. Set the Vertical Position to **0.11"** from the Top Left Corner. Click the **Close** button for the Format Picture task pane.

g. Click the **Insert tab**, click **Pictures** in the Images group, and then locate and insert *p04h1Mem2*.

h. Click **Remove Background** in the Adjust group on the Format tab.

A marquee that includes most of the flower appears around the image. Some petals are cut off and need to be added back in.

i. Drag the left-center, left-bottom, and right-center sizing handles of the marquee as necessary until all petals and the stem are included in the picture (see Figure 4.21).

FIGURE 4.21 Adjusted Marquee

j. Click **Keep Changes** in the Close group on the Background Removal tab.

The background is removed from the flower.

k. Click the **Size Dialog Box Launcher** in the Size group to open the Format Picture task pane and click the **Relative to original picture size check box** to deselect it in the Size section. Click in the **Scale Height box** and type **50**. Press **Enter**.

l. Click **Position** in the Format Picture task pane and set the Horizontal Position to **11.59"** from the Top Left Corner. Set the Vertical Position to **4.79"** from the Top Left Corner. Close the Format Picture task pane.

The flower is now positioned in the lower-right section of the slide. Refer to Figure 4.20.

m. Click **Slide 2**. Click the **Pictures** icon in the large content placeholder on the left side of the slide. Click the *p04h1Mem3* file to select it and click **Insert**.

n. Use the Pictures icons in the two small content placeholders on the right side of the screen to insert *p04h1Mem4* into the top placeholder and *p04h1Mem5* into the bottom placeholder.

Note that the images were centered inside the placeholders.

o. Save the presentation.

You want to include two pictures of the couple in the memory presentation, but the pictures were taken in different lighting conditions. You decide to use PowerPoint's correction tools to enhance the pictures. You also change the color tone of a picture to warm it up to match the warm color of the background graphic color on the slide where it appears. Refer to Figure 4.22 as you complete Step 2.

FIGURE 4.22 Picture Correction and Color Tone Adjustment

a. Click **Slide 3**. Click the **Pictures** in the content placeholders to insert *p04h1Mem6* into the left placeholder and *p04h1Mem7* into the right placeholder.

b. Select the image on the left and click **Corrections** in the Adjust group on the Format tab. Click **Brightness: –20% Contrast: +20%** (fourth row, second column of the Brightness/Contrast section).

The image becomes slightly darker, and the increased contrast brings out the picture detail.

c. Select the image on the right and click **Corrections** in the Adjust group on the Format tab. Click **Brightness: –20% Contrast: 0% (Normal)** (third row, second column of the Brightness/Contrast section).

The brightness is reduced in the image.

d. Click **Slide 4** and select the picture of the woman.

e. Click **Color** in the Adjust group on the Format tab and click **Temperature: 11200 K** in the Color Tone gallery. Next, click **Corrections** in the Adjust group and click **Brightness: +40% Contrast: 0% (Normal)** (third row, fifth column).

The cooler tones in the image are converted to warmer tones, which casts a gold hue over the picture. The picture is also brighter, emphasizing the Colosseum in the background.

f. Click **More** in the Picture Styles group and click **Rotated, White**.

g. Save the presentation.

STEP 3 **» APPLY AN ARTISTIC EFFECT AND A PICTURE STYLE**

The title slide includes a picture of the couple that you want to stand out. The Artistic Effects gallery includes many picture effects, and the Picture Styles gallery includes a variety of Picture Border effects. You decide to experiment with the options available in the galleries to see the impact they have on the title slide picture. You also apply an artistic effect. Refer to Figure 4.23 as you complete Step 3.

FIGURE 4.23 Applied Artistic Effect and Picture Styles

a. Click **Slide 1**, select the picture of the couple, and then click the **Format tab**.

b. Click **Artistic Effects** in the Adjust group on the Format tab.

The Artistic Effects gallery opens. Point to the effects and watch how each effect impacts the image.

> **TROUBLESHOOTING:** Some of the artistic effects involve extensive changes, so expect a slowdown as the preview is created.

c. Click **Texturizer** (fourth row, second column).

A light texture is applied to the picture.

d. Click **More** in the Picture Styles group.

The Picture Styles gallery opens. Point to the styles and watch how each style impacts the image.

e. Click **Center Shadow Rectangle**.

A gray shadow displays evenly around the picture.

f. Click the **Home tab**, click **Format Painter** in the Clipboard group, and then click the **flower picture**.

You copied the picture style, and applied it to the flower.

g. Select the picture of the couple again and click the **Format tab**.

h. Click **Picture Border arrow** in the Picture Styles group and click **Brown, Text 2** (first row, fourth column) in the Theme Colors section.

i. Click **Picture Effects** in the Picture Styles group, point to **Bevel**, and then click **Cool Slant** (first row, fourth column of the Bevel section).

The Bevel effect is applied to the outer edges of the picture.

j. Save the presentation.

The honeymooners stayed in a suite with a gorgeous view of a garden, and you want to include a picture of one of the flowers as the background setting of a picture of the honeymooners. Refer to Figure 4.24 as you complete Step 4.

FIGURE 4.24 Background from a Picture

a. Click the **Design tab**.

b. Click **Slide 5** and click **Format Background** in the Customize group.

The Format Background task pane displays.

c. Select the **Hide background graphics check box** in the Format Background task pane.

d. Click **Picture or texture fill** and click **File** to open the Insert Picture dialog box.

e. Select *p04h1Mem8*, click **Insert**, and then close the Format Background task pane.

f. Examine the picture on the far right of the slide.

g. Click the **View tab** and ensure that the Ruler is selected in the Show group.

Activating the ruler will make it easier for you to determine the area to crop.

h. Select the picture, click the **Format tab**, and then click **Crop** in the Size group.

i. Drag the top-left corner down and to the right until the vertical ruler reaches approximately the +2 1/2" mark and the horizontal ruler reaches approximately the +2" mark.

The resulting size of the image is 5.81" high and 4.25" wide—yours may differ.

j. Click **Crop** in the Size group again to crop the area from view and to turn off the Crop feature.

k. Select the cropped picture and ensure that the Format tab is selected.

l. Click **Compress Pictures** in the Adjust group.

The Compress Pictures dialog box opens.

m. Ensure that Use document resolution is selected in the Target output section.

n. Click the **Apply only to this picture check box** to deselect it.

You need to compress all the pictures you have used in the presentation to reduce the presentation file size, not just the selected picture.

o. Click **OK**.

The portions of the image that were cropped from view are deleted, and all pictures in the slide show are compressed.

p. Save the presentation.

STEP 5 ›› INSERT A PICTURE FROM THE INTERNET

The couple visited Rome, Italy, during their honeymoon, so you want to insert a picture of the Colosseum to end the slide show. You insert an image from Morguefile.com, a website that provides pictures free for personal or commercial use. Refer to Figure 4.25 as you complete Step 5.

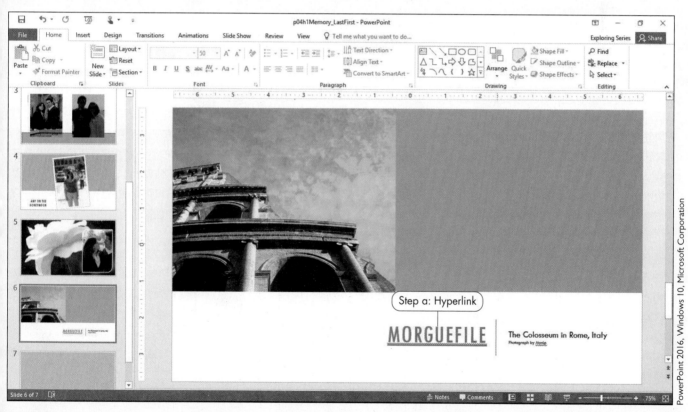

FIGURE 4.25 Hyperlink to Morguefile.com

a. Click **Slide 6**. Click **Slide Show** view.

Note that the text *Morguefile* is a hyperlink. The hyperlink to Morguefile.com will display if you view the presentation in Slide Show view.

b. Click the link to launch the website in your default browser.

> **TROUBLESHOOTING:** If you are not connected to the Internet, the hyperlink will not work. Connect to the Internet and repeat Step b.

The Morguefile website displays a thumbnail of an image of the Colosseum in Rome.

c. Right-click the image, select **Copy picture**, and then close the browser.

The Copy picture command may be named something else depending on the Web browser you are using.

d. Press **Esc** to return to Slide 6 in the presentation. Right-click anywhere on Slide 6 and paste the image using the Picture paste option in the submenu.

e. Adjust the image size so that it covers the left half of the color block on the slide (see Figure 4.25).

Depending on the size of the image you insert, you may or may not need to do this step.

f. Drag the picture to position it on the left side of the slide, leaving the Morguefile text box visible.

The Morguefile website provides royalty-free images, but they ask that credit be given to the photographer. The text box should be visible to give credit to the image source.

g. Save the presentation. Keep the presentation open if you plan to continue with the next Hands-On Exercise. If not, close the presentation and exit PowerPoint.

Video

With video added to your project, you can greatly enhance and reinforce your story, and your audience can retain more of what they see. For example, a video of water tumbling over a waterfall would stir the emotions of a viewer far more than a table listing the number of gallons of water falling within a designated period of time. Anytime you can engage a viewer's emotions, he or she will better remember your message.

In this section, you will learn the types of video file formats that PowerPoint supports and where to search for videos. You will learn about different methods for adding them to your presentation. You will examine the options available when using video and insert a video clip into the memories presentation.

Adding Video

STEP 1 ◗◗ Table 4.3 displays the common types of video file formats you can add to a presentation, listed in alphabetical order by file extension. Different file formats use different types of *codec* (coder/decoder) software, which use algorithms to compress or code videos, and then decompress or decode the videos for playback. Video playback places tremendous demands on your computer system in terms of processing speed and memory. Using a codec reduces those demands. In order for your video file to be viewed correctly, the video player must have the appropriate software installed and the correct version of the software. Even though your video file extension is the same as the one listed in Table 4.3, the video may not play correctly if the correct version of the codec software is not installed.

TABLE 4.3 Types of Video File Formats Supported by PowerPoint

File Format	Extension	Description
Windows Media File	.asf	**Advanced Streaming Format** Stores synchronized multimedia data. Used to stream audio and video content, images, and script commands over a network.
Windows Video File	.avi	**Audio Video Interleave** Stores sound and moving pictures in Microsoft Resource Interchange File Format (RIFF).
MP4 Video	.mp4	**Moving Picture Experts Group 4** File format commonly used with video cameras. Supported by all browsers.
Movie File	.mpg or .mpeg	**Moving Picture Experts Group** Evolving set of standards for video and audio compression developed by the Moving Picture Experts Group.
Adobe Flash Media	.swf	**Flash Video** File format that can be used to deliver video over the Internet. Uses Adobe Flash Player.
Windows Media Video File	.wmv	**Windows Media Video** Compresses audio and video by using Windows Media Video compressed format. Requires minimal amount of storage space on your computer's hard drive.

Pearson Education, Inc.

When you add video to your presentation, you can *embed* the video and store the video within the presentation, or you can *link* to the video, which creates a connection from the presentation to another location such as a storage device or website. The advantage of embedding video is that a copy of the video file is placed in the slide, so moving or deleting the original video will not impact your presentation. The advantage of linking a video file is that your presentation file size is smaller. Another advantage of linking over embedding is that the presentation video is updated automatically if the original video object is changed. One caution for using a linked video from a file—the video is not part of the presentation. You can save the video file and the presentation file in the same folder and then compress the folder to help reduce its overall size. Having the two files in the same folder ensures that the link will still work in case the compressed folder is copied or transferred to a new storage location.

To insert a video in a presentation, complete the following steps:

1. Click the Insert tab.
2. Click Video in the Media group.
3. Click Video on My PC.
4. Browse, locate, and select the video you want to use in the presentation.
5. Click Insert to insert the video in your presentation or click the Insert arrow and select Link to File to link the video to your presentation.

PowerPoint has made it even easier to add online video, such as a video from YouTube, to a presentation. You can search for an online video from within PowerPoint, and the video will be inserted directly into your slide. You can then move the video to a different location on the slide or resize the video just as you would a photograph. Figure 4.26 shows the search box options for Online Video. Video can be inserted from your OneDrive account (if you have video saved there), YouTube, or a website where you have been given the embed code for the video.

Figure 4.27 shows the results of a whales video search. The search term *whales* in the YouTube Search box was used for the search.

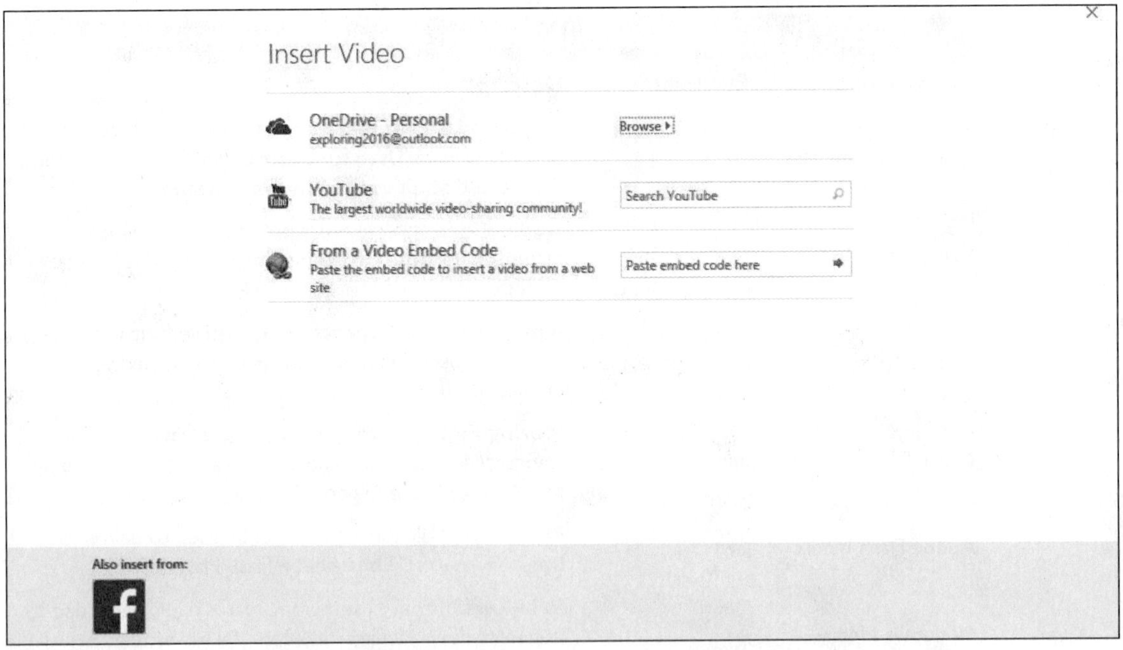

PowerPoint 2016, Windows 10, Microsoft Corporation

FIGURE 4.26 Online Video Search Options

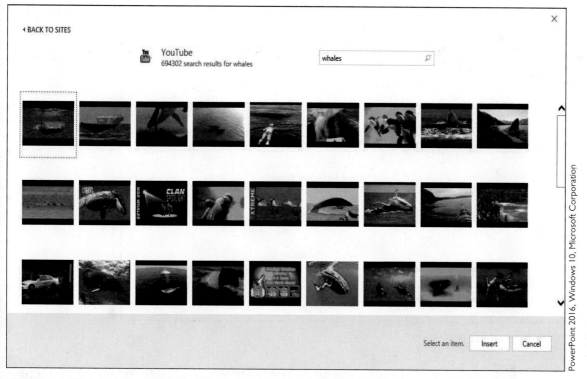

FIGURE 4.27 Search Results for YouTube Search

To search for and insert an online video in a presentation, complete the following steps:

1. Click the Insert tab.
2. Click Video in the Media group.
3. Click Online Video.
4. Browse, locate, and select the video you want to use in the presentation.
5. Click Insert to insert the video in your presentation.

You can also embed video from an online website. When you embed video from the online site, you have to copy and paste the embed code from the site into the *From a Video Embed Code* box (see Figure 4.28). If you have embedded video from an online site, you must be connected to the Internet when you display the presentation.

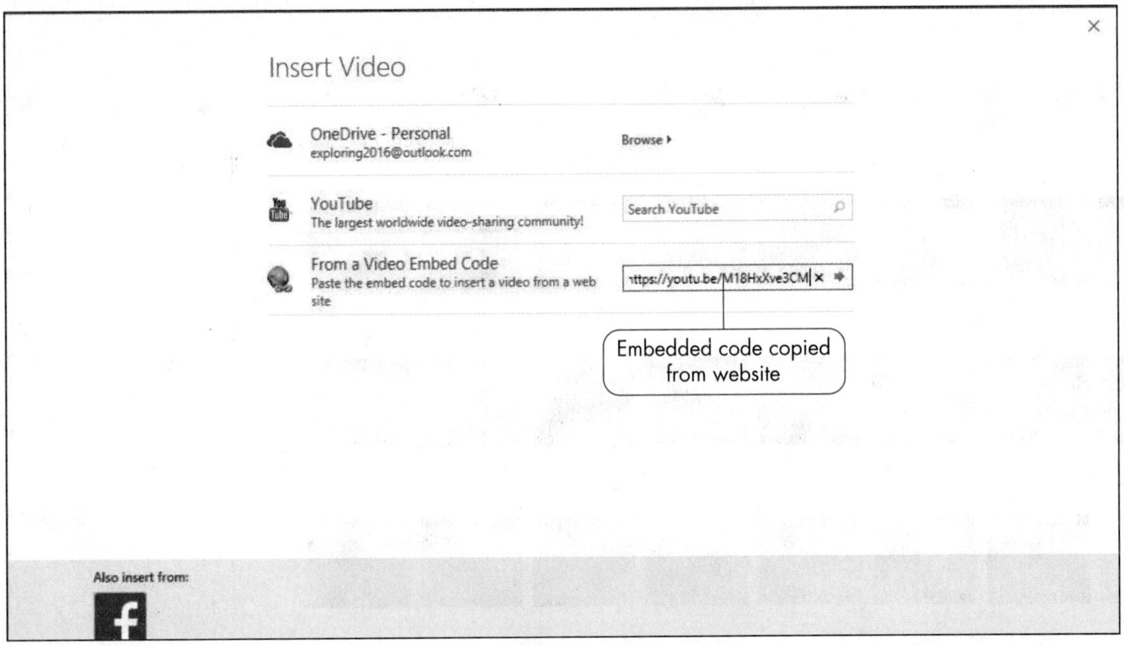

Insert Video

☁ OneDrive - Personal   Browse ▸
  exploring2016@outlook.com

▶ YouTube   Search YouTube   🔍
  The largest worldwide video-sharing community!

⬤ From a Video Embed Code   ╎ttps://youtu.be/M18HxXve3CM╎ × ➡
  Paste the embed code to insert a video from a web
  site

                                          ┌─────────────────────┐
                                          │ Embedded code copied │
                                          │   from website   │
                                          └─────────────────────┘

Also insert from:

[f]

PowerPoint 2016, Windows 10, Microsoft Corporation

FIGURE 4.28 Embed Code from a Website in PowerPoint

To insert embed code from an online video site, complete the following steps:

1. Locate video on an online video site.
2. Copy the embed code.
3. Click the Insert tab in PowerPoint.
4. Click Video in the Media group.
5. Click Online Video.
6. Paste the embed code into the *From a Video Embed Code* box.
7. Click the Insert arrow at the right side of the box.

Whether you have inserted your own video or video from a website, the video will include a Media Controls bar with a Play/Pause button, a Move Back button, a Move Forward button, a time notation, and a Mute/Unmute control slider. The Move Back and Move Forward buttons aid you when editing your own video. However, these controls may auto-hide and become visible only when the pointer is moved. Additionally, videos inserted from websites may use their own control bars instead of the PowerPoint Media Controls bar shown in Figure 4.29.

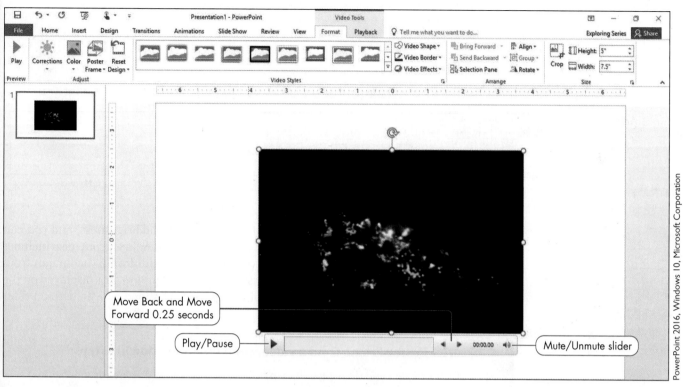

FIGURE 4.29 Media Controls Bar

Using Video Tools

PowerPoint includes tools for working with video. You can format the video's brightness and contrast, color, and style. You can apply most artistic image effects, add or remove bookmarks, trim the video, and set fade in or fade out effects. When you select an inserted video, the Video Tools contextual tab displays with two subtabs: the Format tab and the Playback tab.

Format a Video

STEP 2 >> The Format tab includes options for playing the video for preview purposes, adjusting the video, applying a style to the video, arranging a video on the slide, and cropping and sizing the video. Figure 4.30 displays the Video Tools Format tab. Some of these tools will not work with embedded website videos.

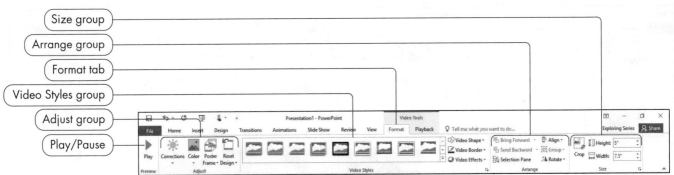

FIGURE 4.30 Video Tools Format Tab

PowerPoint 2016, Windows 10, Microsoft Corporation

Using the Adjust group, you can adjust video contrast and brightness, and you can recolor a video as you did when you worked with images. The Adjust group also includes the ***Poster Frame*** option, which enables you to choose a still frame (or image) from within the video or any image file from your storage device. This image is displayed on the PowerPoint slide when the video is not playing. Figure 4.31 shows a video with a Poster Frame option set to the current frame.

To create a Poster Frame from a video, complete the following steps:

1. Select the video and then click Play in the Preview group to display the video.
2. Pause the video when the frame you want to use as the poster frame appears.
3. Click Poster Frame in the Adjust group.
4. Click Current Frame.

To create a Poster Frame from an image stored in your storage device, complete the following steps:

1. Select the video and click Poster Frame in the Adjust group.
2. Click Image from File.
3. Locate and select desired image.
4. Click Insert.

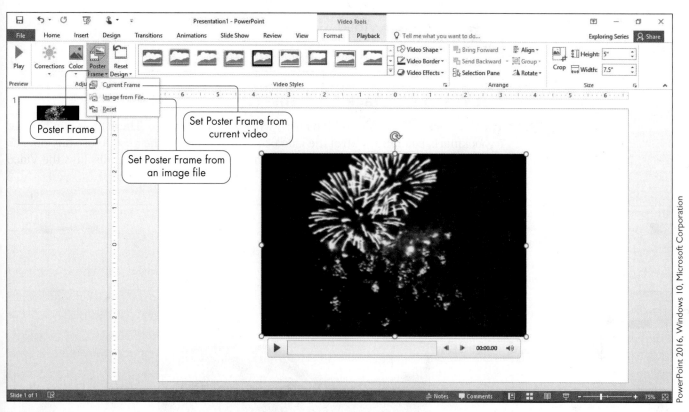

FIGURE 4.31 Poster Frame Option

The Style effects available for images are also available for videos. In addition to the styles in the Video Styles gallery, you can edit the shape of a video, change the border of the video, and add video effects such as Shadow, Reflection, Glow, Soft Edges, Bevel, and 3-D Rotation. Figure 4.32 shows a video formatted to fit a PowerPoint shape, with a gray border and reflection added.

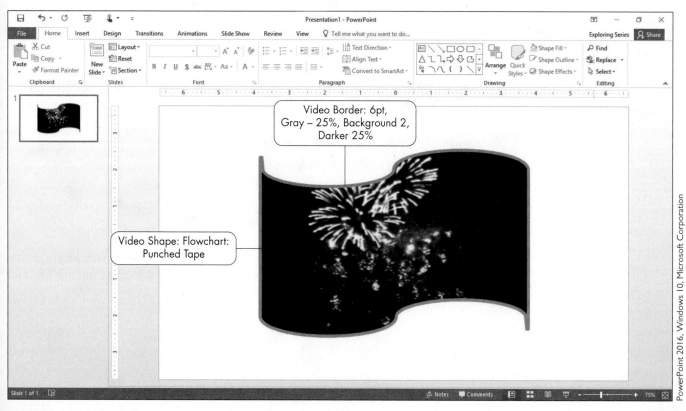

FIGURE 4.32 Video Styles

> **TIP: RESETTING A VIDEO**
> To discard all formatting changes from a selected video, click the Reset Design arrow in the Adjust group on the Format tab and select Reset Design or Reset Design & Size.

Set Video Playback Options

 The Playback tab includes options used when viewing a video. These tools can be used to bookmark, edit, and control the video, and can eliminate the need to use any outside video-editing software for basic video-editing functions. Figure 4.33 displays the Video Tools Playback tab.

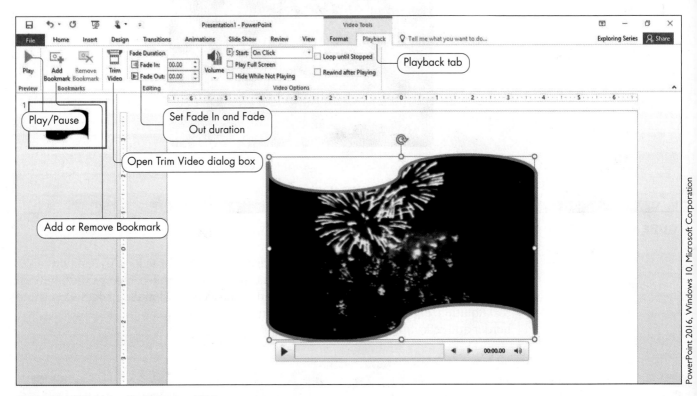

FIGURE 4.33 Video Tools Playback Tab

You can use ***bookmarks*** to mark specific locations in a video, making it possible to quickly advance to the part of the video you want to display or to trigger an event in an animation.

To bookmark a video, complete the following steps:

1. Select the video and click the Playback tab.
2. Click Play on the Media Controls bar. Pause the video at the desired frame.
3. Click Add Bookmark in the Bookmarks group when the video reaches the location you want to be able to move quickly to during your presentation.

A circle displays on the Media Controls bar to indicate the bookmark location (see Figure 4.34). To remove the bookmark, click the circle on the Media Controls bar and click Remove Bookmark in the Bookmarks group.

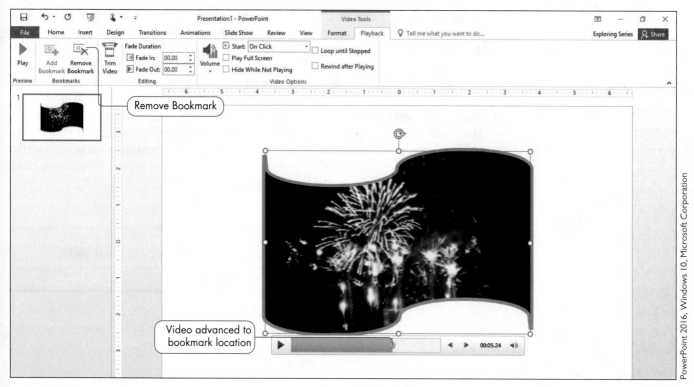

FIGURE 4.34 Bookmarked Video

PowerPoint provides basic video editing by enabling you to determine the starting and ending of a video and set a Fade In and Fade Out duration. In the Trim Video dialog box, which you access in the Editing group on the Playback tab, you can use the Trim option to specify the Start Time and End Time for a video, or you can drag the Start marker and the End marker on the Timing bar to select the time. The advantage to dragging the markers is that as you drag, you can view the video. Any bookmarks you set will also display in the Trim Video dialog box. Figure 4.35 shows the Trim Video dialog box.

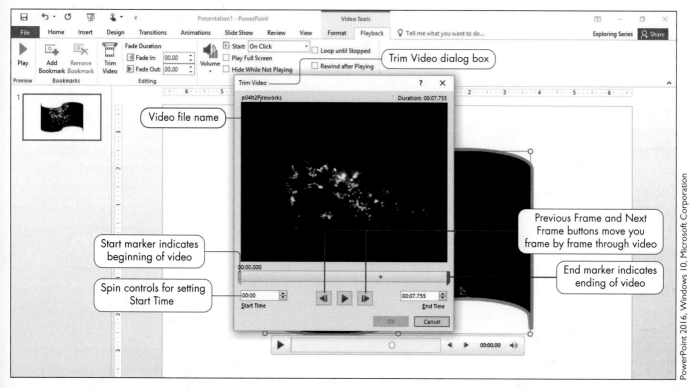

FIGURE 4.35 Trim Video Dialog Box

To set a Fade In or Fade Out duration, click the spin arrows or enter an exact time in the appropriate boxes in the Editing group on the Playback tab. If you have selected a Poster Frame for your video, the Poster Frame will fade into the first frame of your video.

The Video Options group of the Playback tab enables you to control a variety of display options. You can control the volume of the video by clicking the Volume arrow and selecting Low, Medium, or High. You can also mute any sound attached to the video.

The Video Options group also enables you to determine whether the video starts on the click of the pointer (the default setting) or automatically when the slide displays. You can choose to play the video at full screen, hide the video when it is not playing, loop continuously until you stop the playback, and rewind after playing.

Quick Concepts ✔

5. What is a video codec, and why is it usually necessary? *p. 289*

6. Explain the difference between embedding a video and linking a video. *p. 289*

7. Why would you add a bookmark to a video? *p. 296*

Hands-On Exercises

Watch the Video
for this Hands-On
Exercise!

MyITLab®
HOE2 Training

Skills covered: Insert a Video
from a File • Format a Video • Set
Video Playback Options

2 Video

In Europe, the couple recorded some fireworks displayed during a sports event. The groom gave you a copy of the fireworks video because you think it would be an excellent finale to the slide show. You insert the video, add a photo frame, and set the video playback options.

STEP 1 ›› **INSERT A VIDEO FROM A FILE**

You create a copy of the previous presentation and insert the fireworks video. Refer to Figure 4.36 as you complete Step 1.

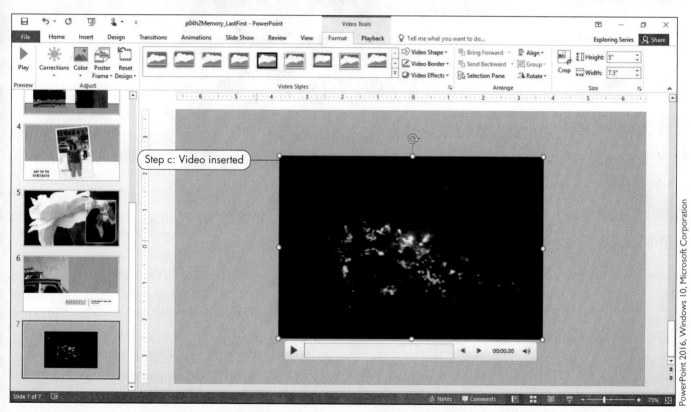

FIGURE 4.36 Inserted Windows Media Video File

a. Open *p04h1Memory_LastFirst* if you closed it at the end of Hands-On Exercise 1, and save it as **p04h2Memory_LastFirst**, changing h1 to h2.

b. Select **Slide 7**. Click the **Insert tab** and click **Video** in the Media group.

c. Click **Video on My PC**, open the *p04h1Memory_Media* folder, select *p04h2Fireworks*, and then click **Insert**.

d. Save the presentation.

The first image of the video shows the fireworks in the beginning stages. You decide to use a Poster Frame of the fireworks while they are fully bursting so the slide has an attractive image on display before the video begins. You also decide that a shape removing the edges of the video would be an improvement. Finally, you add a shadow video effect. Refer to Figure 4.37 as you complete Step 2.

FIGURE 4.37 Formatted Video File

a. Click **Move Forward 0.25 Seconds** on the Media Controls bar located beneath the video to advance the video to the frame at 2.00 seconds.

b. Click the **Poster Frame** in the Adjust group on the Format tab, and then click **Current Frame**.

The frame you selected becomes the poster frame and displays on the slide.

c. Click **Video Shape** in the Video Styles group and click **Hexagon** in the Basic Shapes category.

The video shape changes to a hexagon.

d. Click **Video Effects**, point to **Shadow**, and then click **Perspective Diagonal Lower Left** in the Perspective category.

The shadow displays in a hexagon shape with a perspective view.

e. Click the **Slide Show tab** and click **From Current Slide** in the Start Slide Show group.

Slide 7 opens with the video displayed on the slide. The poster frame shows the fireworks at full cascade with the video shadow. Note that the Controls will display if you move the pointer to the bottom of the video.

f. Move the pointer to the bottom of the video to display the Media Controls bar and click **Play**. Press **Esc** when you are finished.

g. Save the presentation.

The last burst of fireworks does not finish its crescendo, so you decide to trim away this last portion of the video. Because you do not want the viewers of the presentation to have to click to begin the video, you change the start setting to start automatically. You decide to loop the video to play continuously until stopped because it is so short. Refer to Figure 4.38 as you complete Step 3.

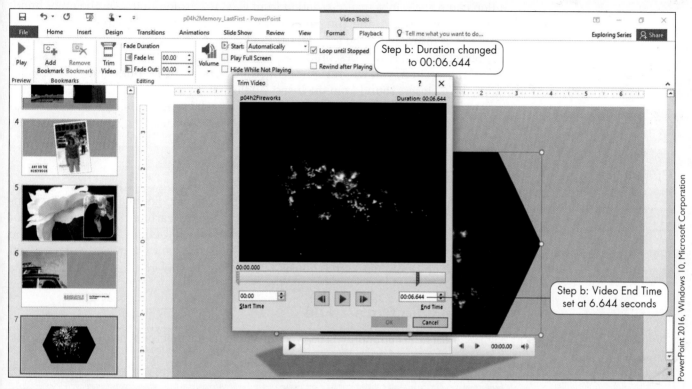

FIGURE 4.38 Video Duration Change

a. Select the video object, click the **Playback tab**, and then click **Trim Video** in the Editing group.

The Trim Video dialog box opens.

b. Drag the red **End Time marker** on the slider until *00:06.644* appears in the End Time box, or type **00:06.644** in the End Time box, and click **OK**.

The duration of the video changes from 7.755 seconds to 6.644 seconds.

c. Click the **Start arrow** in the Video Options group and select **Automatically**.

d. Select the **Loop until Stopped check box** in the Video Options group.

The fireworks video will continue to play until you advance to end the slide show.

e. Click the **Slide Show tab** and click **From Beginning** in the Start Slide Show group.

Advance through the slide show. Note that the video plays in the hexagon shape.

f. Save the presentation. Keep the presentation open if you plan to continue with the next Hands-On Exercise. If not, close the presentation and exit PowerPoint.

Audio

Audio can draw on common elements of any language or culture—screams, laughs, sobs—to add excitement, provide a pleasurable background, set the mood, or serve as a wake-up call for the audience. Harnessing the emotional impact of sound in your presentation can transform your presentation from good to extraordinary. On the other hand, use sound incorrectly, and you can destroy your presentation, leaving your audience confused or distracted. Keep in mind the guideline emphasized throughout this book—any object you add to the presentation should enhance, not detract from, your message.

In this section, you will review the methods for inserting sound and tips for each method. You insert sound from the Insert Audio dialog box or saved audio file and learn how to determine the number of times a sound clip plays, the number of slides through which the sound plays, and the method for launching the sound.

Adding Audio

Your computer needs a sound card and speakers to play audio. In a classroom or computer laboratory, you will need a headset or headphones/earbuds for playback so that you do not disturb other students. You can locate and play sounds and music from the Insert Audio dialog box, or from a hard drive, flash drive, or any other storage device. You can also record your own sounds, music, or narration to play from PowerPoint.

Insert Audio from a File

STEP 1 ⟩⟩ Table 4.4 lists the commonly used types of audio file formats supported by PowerPoint, listed in alphabetical order by extension.

TABLE 4.4	Commonly Used Audio File Formats Supported by PowerPoint	
File Format	**Extension**	**Description**
MIDI File	.mid or .midi	**Musical Instrument Digital Interface** Standard format for interchange of musical information between musical instruments, synthesizers, and computers.
MP3 Audio File	.mp3	**MPEG Audio Layer 3** Sound file that has been compressed by using the MPEG Audio Layer 3 codec (developed by the Fraunhofer Institute).
Windows Audio File	.wav	**Wave Form** Stores sounds as waveforms. Depending on various factors, one minute of sound can occupy as little as 644 kilobytes or as much as 27 megabytes of storage.
Windows Media Audio File	.wma	**Windows Media Audio** Sound format used to distribute recorded music, usually over the Internet. Compressed using the Microsoft Windows Media Audio codec.

Pearson Education, Inc.

To insert audio from a file, complete the following steps:

1. Click the Insert tab.
2. Click Audio in the Media group.
3. Click Audio on My PC.
4. Browse, locate, and select the desired file.
5. Click Insert.

A gray speaker icon representing the file displays in the center of the slide with a Media Controls bar beneath it. The same controls are available when you select audio as when you select video.

Record and Insert Audio

Sometimes you may find it helpful to add recorded audio to a slide show. Although you could record music, **_narration_** (spoken commentary) is more common. One example of a need for recorded narration is when you want to create a self-running presentation, such as a presentation displaying in a kiosk at the mall or online. Rather than adding a narration prior to a presentation, you could create the narration during the presentation. For example, recording the discussion and decisions made during a meeting would create an archive of the meeting.

Before creating the narration, keep in mind the following:

- Your computer will need a sound card, speakers, and a microphone.
- Comments on selected slides may be recorded rather than narrating the entire presentation.
- Voice narration takes precedence over any other sounds during playback, making it possible for a voice to play over inserted audio files.
- PowerPoint records the amount of time it takes you to narrate each slide, and if you save the slide timings, you can use them to create an automatic slide show.
- You can pause and resume recording during the process.

To record narration, complete the following steps:

1. Click the Slide Show tab.
2. Click the Record Slide Show arrow in the Set Up group.

You can choose from Start the Recording from the Beginning or Start Recording from the Current Slide. The Set Up group provides other options to Play Narrations, Use Timings, or Show Media Controls.

Another example when you would want to include audio in your presentations is the creation of an association between words and an image on the screen for a presentation. This could be helpful for a group learning a new language and for helping young children build their vocabulary. These examples differ from narration because the audio is associated with a specific slide.

To record an audio clip, complete the following steps:

1. Click the Insert tab.
2. Click Audio in the Media group.
3. Click Record Audio.
4. Click Record (see Figure 4.39).
5. Record your message.
6. Click Stop.
7. Click Play to check the recording.
8. Type a name for the recording and click OK.

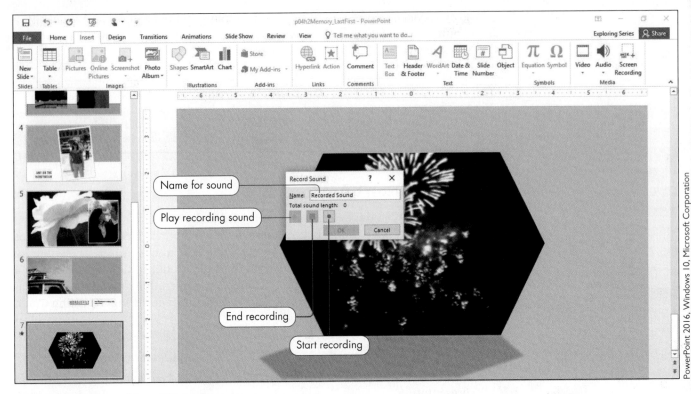

FIGURE 4.39 Record Sound Dialog Box

> **TIP: CREATE NOTES OF YOUR NARRATION**
> A transcript of your narration should be available for those in your audience who are hearing impaired. Providing the transcript lets this audience gain from your presentation, too. Put the transcript in the Notes pane and print the notes pages to provide a transcript.

Changing Audio Settings

When the icon for an inserted audio clip is selected, the Audio Tools contextual tab appears with two subtabs: Format and Playback. The Format tab provides options relating to the inserted sound icon. The Playback tab provides options for playing and pausing the audio clip, adding a bookmark, trimming, fading in and out, adjusting volume, determining starting method, hiding the audio icon while playing, looping, and rewinding after playing. All of these features work similarly to the video features, except that the Trim audio feature provides an audio timeline rather than a video preview window.

Animate an Audio Sequence

STEP 2 ⟫ Although the Playback tab gives you only two options for starting—On Click or Automatically—you have other options available through the Timing group on the Animations tab. You can choose whether the audio plays with a previous event or after a previous event; for example, you can have the audio play as a picture appears or after.

> **To set the audio to play with or after a previous event, complete the following steps:**
> 1. Select the sound icon.
> 2. Click the Animations tab.
> 3. Click the Start arrow in the Timing group.
> 4. Click With Previous or After Previous.

The Timing group on the Animations tab also includes a Delay spin box that you can use to delay the playback of an audio clip (see Figure 4.40).

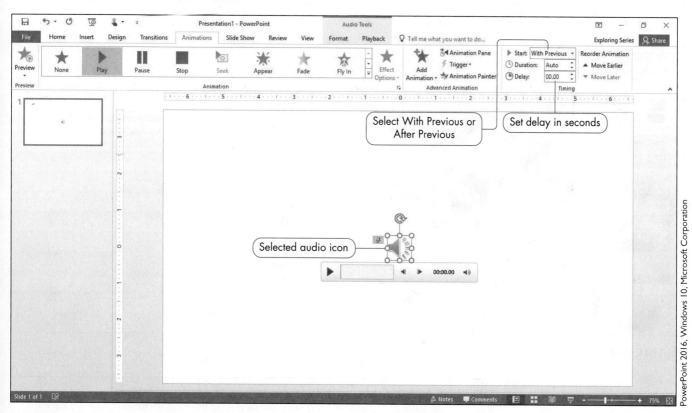

FIGURE 4.40 Audio Sequencing Options

Play a Sound over Multiple Slides

By default, audio plays until it ends or until the next mouse click. If you are playing background music, this means the music ends when you click to advance to the next slide.

To continue audio over multiple slides, complete the following steps:

1. Select the sound icon and click the Animations tab.
2. Click Animation Pane in the Advanced Animation group.
3. Select the sound you want to continue over multiple slides.
4. Click the arrow to the right of the sound.
5. Click Effect Options.
6. Click the After option in the Stop playing section of the Effect tab.
7. Enter the number of slides during which you want the sound to play (see Figure 4.41).

If the background music stops before you get to the last slide, use the Loop Until Stopped feature to keep the sound repeating. Click the Playback tab and click the Loop Until Stopped check box in the Audio Options group.

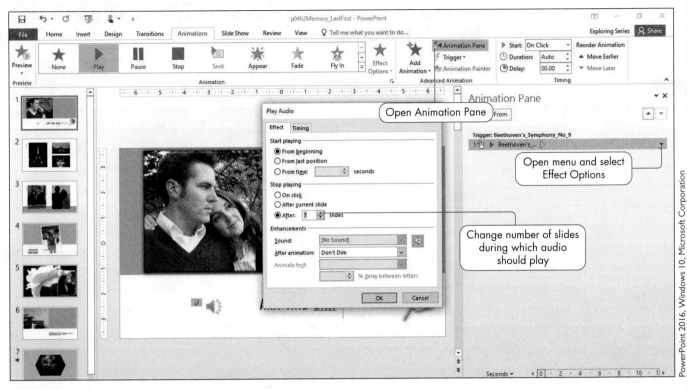

FIGURE 4.41 Audio Effects

TIP: PLAY ACROSS ALL SLIDES
You can set an audio clip to play across slides easily by clicking the Playback tab and selecting the Play Across Slides check box. This option does not let you set the number of slides over which you want the audio to play, however.

Quick Concepts ✓

8. What are two methods for inserting audio into a presentation? *p. 302*

9. Describe a situation where a narrated PowerPoint presentation would be advisable. *p. 303*

10. What audio options are available from the Audio Tools Playback tab? *p. 304*

Hands-On Exercises

Watch the Video for this Hands-On Exercise!

MyITLab®
HOE3 Training

Skills covered: Add Audio from a File • Change Audio Settings

3 Audio

You decide to create a background mood for the memories presentation by inserting a favorite audio clip of the bride—Beethoven's Symphony No. 9.

STEP 1 ❯❯ ADD AUDIO FROM A FILE

The bride is a classically trained musician, so you decide to enhance the slide show with one of her favorite pieces. Refer to Figure 4.42 as you complete Step 1.

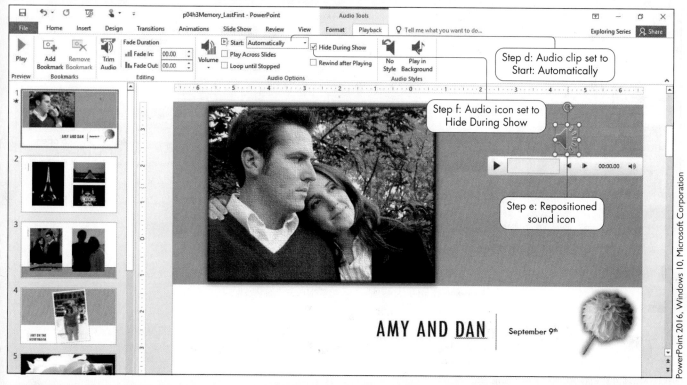

FIGURE 4.42 Slide 1 Audio Settings

a. Open *p04h2Memory_LastFirst* if you closed it at the end of the Hands-On Exercise 2, and save it as **p04h3Memory_LastFirst**, changing h2 to h3.

> **TROUBLESHOOTING:** To complete this exercise, it is best that you have a sound card and speakers. Even if this equipment is not available, however, you can still perform these steps to gain the knowledge.

b. Click **Slide 1**. Click the **Insert tab**, click **Audio** in the Media group, and then select **Audio on My PC**.

The Insert Audio dialog box opens.

c. Locate the *p04h1Memory_Media* folder, select *Beethoven's_Symphony_No_9*, and then click **Insert**.

The sound icon and Media Controls bar are displayed in the center of the slide.

d. Click the **Playback tab**, click the **Start arrow** in the Audio Options group, and then select **Automatically**.

e. Drag the **sound icon** to the top-right corner of the slide.

f. Click the **Hide During Show check box** in the Audio Options group.

g. Click **Play** in the Preview group.

h. Save the presentation.

STEP 2 ›› CHANGE AUDIO SETTINGS

Because PowerPoint's default setting ends a sound file when a slide advances, the Beethoven file is abruptly cut off when you advance to the next slide. You adjust the sound settings so the file plays continuously through all slides in the slide show. Refer to Figure 4.43 as you complete Step 2.

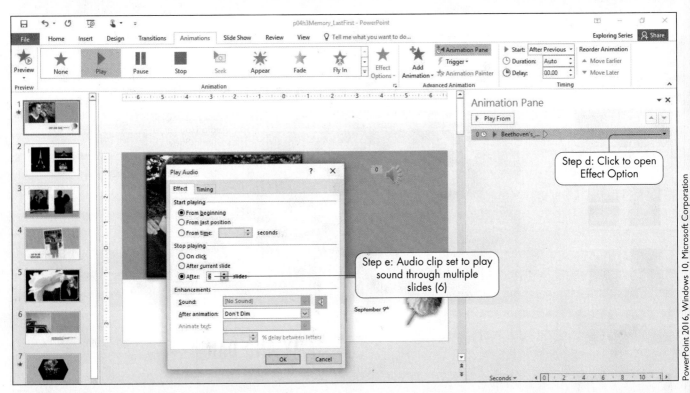

FIGURE 4.43 Play Audio Dialog Box

a. Click the **Slide Show tab** and click **From Beginning** in the Start Slide Show group. Advance through the slides and end the slide show.

Note that the sound clip on Slide 1 discontinues playing as soon as you click to advance to the next slide.

b. Select the **sound icon** on the top-right of Slide 1.

c. Click the **Animations tab** and click **Animation Pane** in the Advanced Animation group.

d. Click the **Beethoven's Symphony sound arrow** in the animation list and select **Effect Options**.

e. Click **After** in the Stop playing section, type **6** in the box, and then click **OK**. Close the Animation Pane.

f. Play the slide show and note the music plays through the sixth slide.

g. Save and close the file. You will submit this file to your instructor at the end of the last Hands-On Exercise.

Photo Albums

PowerPoint has a Photo Album feature designed to speed up the album creation process. This feature takes the images you select and arranges them on album pages based on selections you make.

In this section, you will use the Photo Album feature to create an album. Then you will use the feature settings to customize your album for picture selection, picture order, adjusting contrast and brightness, adding captions, and adjusting the album layout.

Creating a Photo Album

STEP 1 ▶▶ A PowerPoint ***Photo Album*** is a presentation that contains multiple pictures that are imported and formatted through the Photo Album feature. Because each picture does not have to be formatted individually, you save a considerable amount of time. The photo album in Figure 4.44 took less than two minutes to create and assign a theme. Because a four-per-page layout was selected, images were reduced to fit the size of the placeholder. This setting drastically reduced the size of some images.

FIGURE 4.44 PowerPoint Photo Album

PowerPoint 2016, Windows 10, Microsoft Corporation

To create a photo album, complete the following steps:

1. Click the Insert tab.
2. Click Photo Album in the Images group.
3. Click File/Disk.
4. Navigate to your pictures and select the pictures to include in the album.
5. Click Insert.
6. Repeat Steps 3–5 to add additional photos from other folders.
7. Select the Photo Album options you want.
8. Click Create.

If you click the Photo Album arrow, you may choose between creating a new album and editing a previously created album. When you select the pictures you want to include in the album, do not worry about the order of the pictures. You can change the order later. Once an album has been created, you can edit the album settings by clicking the Photo Album arrow in the Images group on the Insert tab and selecting Edit Photo Album.

TIP: CREATING FAMILY ALBUMS

After creating an album, add transitions and you have a beautiful presentation for a family gathering or special event. Loop the presentation to let it run continuously so that people can watch as they desire. Burn the presentation to a DVD/CD or save it on a USB to send it as a memento of the event.

Setting Photo Album Options

Using the photo album features can save you some time formatting and setting various design options. Several tools allow you to do things such as selecting picture order, rotating images, changing contrast and brightness, inserting captions for your photos, and finally selecting an album layout. Figure 4.45 shows the location of these tools. Each is discussed in detail in the following sections.

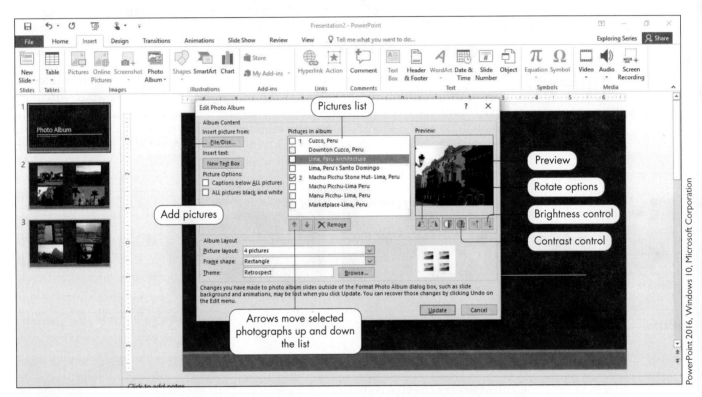

FIGURE 4.45 PowerPoint Photo Album Content Options

Select Pictures and Setting the Picture Order

After pictures are selected, they will display in a list in the Pictures in album section of the Edit Photo Album dialog box. Click the name of a picture to display a preview to help you determine the order of pictures in the album. Click the check box to the left of any picture to select or deselect it within the Pictures in album list.

To set the picture order, complete the following steps:

1. Click the check box next to any image to select it, or use Ctrl or Shift to select more than one image.
2. Use the Move up arrow and the Move down arrow to reposition a selected photograph.
3. Delete any unwanted photographs by selecting them and clicking Remove.

If you have downloaded photographs from a digital camera, you may need to rotate some images. Select the photo you want to rotate and use the rotate left or rotate right button. Rotate buttons are included in the Album Content section under the image preview.

Change Picture Contrast and Brightness

 Contrast and brightness controls enable you to fine-tune your pictures by enhancing details in over- or underexposed photos. Brightening the picture overall may make some details easier to see. Changing the contrast will increase the definition of the borders between light and dark portions of a picture.

To set the contrast or brightness, complete the following steps:

1. Click the check box next to the photo you want to modify.
2. Click the contrast or brightness controls until the photo is modified as desired.

Insert Captions

The New Text Box button allows you to insert a text box with the photo caption in the album. The text placeholder is the same size as the placeholders for pictures. The *Captions below ALL pictures* option will not become available until you choose an album layout, which is discussed next. When this option is active, the file name of the picture displays as a caption below the picture in the album. You can modify the caption text once the album is created.

Set an Album Layout

 The Album Layout section of the Photo Album dialog box gives many options for personalizing the album. First, you can select a Picture layout: a single picture fitted to a full slide; one, two, or four pictures on a slide; or one, two, or four pictures and a title placeholder per slide. When you select a single picture per slide, the image is maximized on the slide.

You can select from a variety of frame shapes in the Album Layout section. Options include rectangles, rounded rectangles, simple black or white frames, a compound black frame, a center shadow rectangle, or a soft edge rectangle.

You can apply a theme for the background of your album while in the Photo Album dialog box. This helps to personalize the album. If you are in a networked lab situation, it may be difficult to navigate to the location where themes are stored. If this is the case, create the album and in the main PowerPoint window, click the Design tab, click the More button in the Themes group, and then select a theme from the gallery.

Quick Concepts

11. What advantages does the Photo Album feature offer? *p. 309*

12. List two image transformation tools available in the Album Content section of the Photo Album dialog box. *p. 311*

13. Describe one way to personalize an album. *p. 311*

Skills covered: Create an Album • Select and Order Pictures • Adjust Contrast and Brightness • Set Album Layout • Select Frame Shape • Edit Album Settings • Apply a Theme

4 Photo Albums

The bride and groom also took a trip to Peru, capturing photos of the gorgeous scenery. You prepare a photo album to help them preserve their memories. You take the time to improve the picture quality by adjusting the brightness and contrast. You also apply an album layout, apply frame shapes, and apply a theme to further personalize the album.

STEP 1 ≫ **CREATE AN ALBUM, AND SELECT AND ORDER PICTURES**

You have a folder in which you have saved the images you want to use for the vacation album. In this step, you add the images to the album and order the images by the date during which the trip was taken. Refer to Figure 4.46 as you complete Step 1.

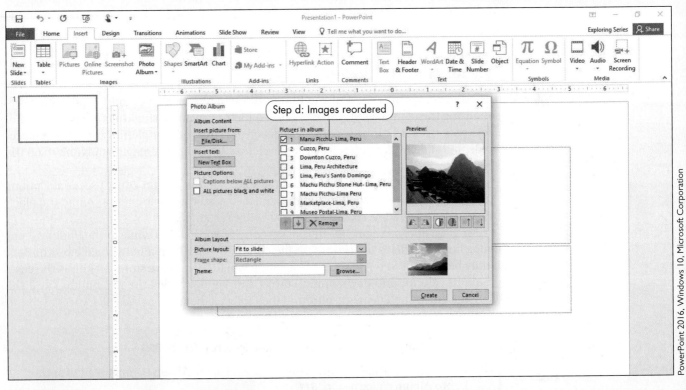

FIGURE 4.46 PowerPoint Photo Album Dialog Box

a. Open a new blank presentation. Click the **Insert tab** and click **Photo Album** in the Images group.

The Photo Album dialog box opens.

b. Click **File/Disk**. Open the *p04h4Album_Media* folder.

c. Click one of the files in the list, press **Ctrl+A** to select all pictures in the folder, and then click **Insert**.

The list of pictures displays in the *Pictures in album* box.

d. Click to select the **7 Manu Picchu - Lima, Peru** picture and click the **Move up arrow** to reposition the picture so that it is the first picture in the list. Refer to Figure 4.46 to ensure that the images are in the correct order and click **Create**.

The Photo Album feature includes buttons that enable you to adjust the contrast and brightness of images without having to access PowerPoint's Picture Tools tab. You use the Photo Album buttons to adjust the contrast in one of the Peruvian pictures. Refer to Figure 4.47 as you complete Step 2.

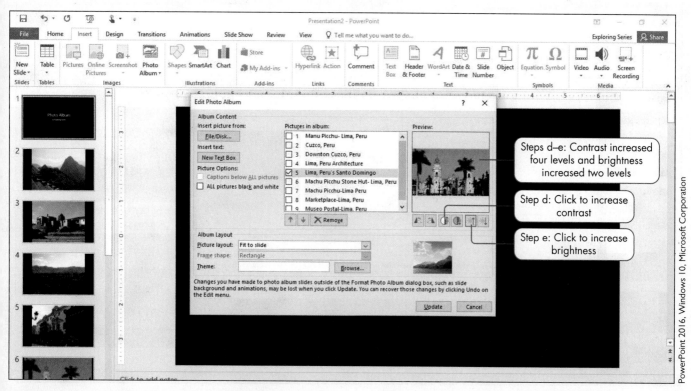

FIGURE 4.47 PowerPoint Photo Album Picture Tools

a. Click the **Photo Album arrow** located in the Images group on the Insert tab.

b. Select **Edit Photo Album**.

> **TROUBLESHOOTING:** If the list of photos does not display, you have selected the Photo Album button and not the Photo Album arrow.

c. Select **5 Lima, Peru's Santo Domingo** in the Pictures in album list.

d. Click **Increase Contrast** (third button from the left) four times.

e. Click **Increase Brightness** (fifth button from the left) twice.

The adjusted image can be viewed in the Preview window. If you had changed brightness only, the image would be washed out.

You change the layout of the album pages to four pictures per page. Then, to help identify the location the image was taken from during the trip, you include captions. Refer to Figure 4.48 as you complete Step 3.

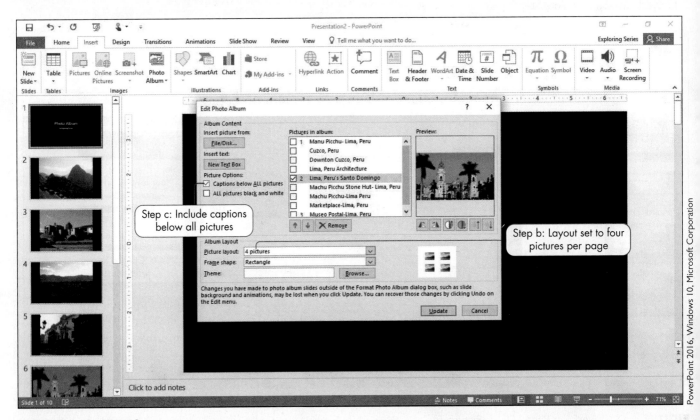

FIGURE 4.48 Album Setup

a. Click the **Picture layout arrow** in the Album Layout section of the Photo Album dialog box.

b. Click one of the layouts and view the layout in the Album Layout Preview window on the right (below the larger Album Content Preview window). Then repeat to select **4 pictures**.

Clicking *4 pictures* will create an album of four pages—a title page and three pages with pictures.

c. Click the **Captions below ALL pictures check box** in the Picture Options section.

Captions below ALL pictures only becomes available after the layout is selected.

You decide to use a simple white frame to enhance the pictures taken during the trips. Refer to Figure 4.49 as you complete Step 4.

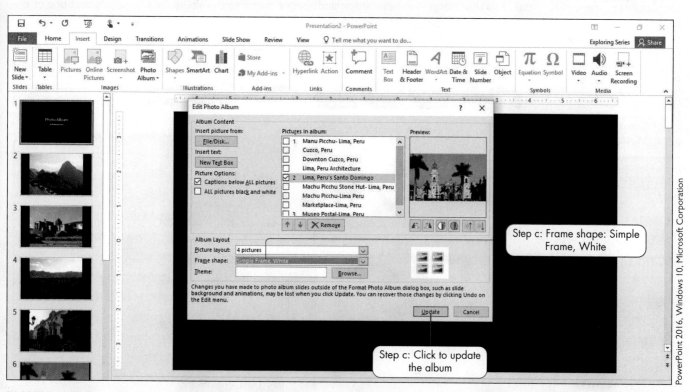

FIGURE 4.49 Frame Shape Selection

a. Click the **Frame shape arrow** in the Album Layout section.

b. Select each of the frames and view the layout in the Preview window on the right.

c. Select **Simple Frame, White** and click **Update**.

d. Create a handout header with your name and a handout footer with your instructor's name and your class. Include the current date.

e. Ensure that your name is in the subtitle placeholder on Slide 1.

f. Save the presentation as **p04h4Album_LastFirst**.

STEP 5 » EDIT ALBUM SETTINGS AND APPLY A THEME

You decide to edit your album settings so that you include only one picture per page rather than four. This allows more space for the pictures to show more detail. You also change the frame shape and apply a theme to the album. Finally, you correct one of the captions for an image. Refer to Figure 4.50 as you complete Step 5.

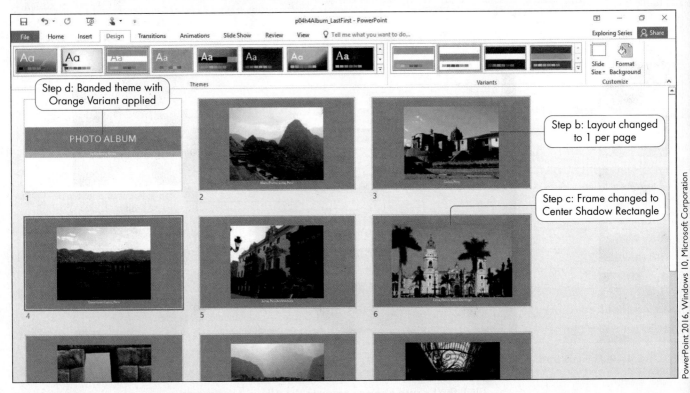

FIGURE 4.50 The Revised Photo Album

a. Click the **Insert tab**, click the **Photo Album arrow** in the Images group, and then select **Edit Photo Album**.

The Edit Photo Album dialog box opens displaying the current settings, which you may now change.

b. Click the **Picture layout arrow** and select **1 picture**.

c. Click the **Frame shape arrow** and select **Center Shadow Rectangle**. Click **Update**. Delete any blank slides from the album.

The pictures now display one per page.

d. Click the **Design tab**, apply **Banded theme** in the Themes group, and then click the **Orange Variant** in the Variants group.

e. Click **Slide 4**. Edit the text box to correct the spelling of *Downtown*.

The text box caption below the image has been corrected, since the picture file name was misspelled.

f. Save and close the file. Based on your instructor's directions, submit the following:

p04h3Memory_LastFirst

p04h4Album_LastFirst

Chapter Objectives Review

After reading this chapter, you have accomplished the following objectives:

1. Insert a picture.
- Bitmap images, represented by pixels placed on a grid, produce photorealistic portrayals.
- Pictures can be inserted using the Insert Picture option, which centers the image on the slide, or by using placeholders that center and crop the image inside the placeholder.

2. Transform a picture.
- Pictures can be transformed in a variety of ways, including removing the background, applying corrections, changing colors, applying artistic effects and picture styles, and cropping.
- Remove a picture background: The Remove Background tool enables you to remove portions of a picture you do not want to keep.
- Correct a picture: You can enhance a picture by sharpening or softening it, or you can increase or decrease a picture's brightness and contrast.
- Change picture color: Use the color tools to adjust the saturation and tone of your pictures.
- Use artistic effects: With artistic effects you can change the appearance of a picture so that it looks like it was created with a marker, as a pencil sketch, and more.
- Apply picture styles: You can surround your pictures with attractive frames, soften the edges of pictures, add shadows to the edges of pictures, apply 3-D effects to pictures, add glossy reflections, and more.
- Resize or crop a picture: You can resize pictures or crop them to remove unwanted portions of the image.
- Compress pictures: Pictures can be compressed to save file storage space.
- Create a background from a picture: Pictures can make appealing backgrounds when you adjust the transparency.

3. Use the Internet as a resource.
- The Internet can be extremely valuable when searching for information for a presentation.
- Understand copyright protection: Although students and teachers have rights under the Fair Use Act, care should be taken to honor all copyrights.
- Before inserting any information or clips into your slide show, research the copyright ownership.
- To be safe, contact the website owner and request permission to use the material.
- Any information used should be credited and include hyperlinks when possible, although attribution does not relieve you of the requirement to honor copyrights.

4. Add video.
- You can insert video located on your hard drive or storage device or YouTube, or embed coding from an online site.

5. Use video tools.
- PowerPoint includes video editing tools.

- Format a video: You can adjust the brightness and contrast, recolor, set a poster frame, select a style, and arrange and size a video.
- Set video playback options: You can also add a bookmark, trim, set a fade in and fade out effect, control the volume, determine how to start the video, set the video to play full screen, hide the video when not playing, loop until stopped, rewind after playing, and show media controls.

6. Add audio.
- Audio catches audience attention and adds excitement to a presentation.
- Take care when adding sound that it enhances your message rather than detracts from it.
- Insert audio from a file: PowerPoint supports many different audio file formats that enable you to include sounds with your presentation.
- Record and insert audio: You may find it helpful to add recorded audio to a slide show by using narration (spoken commentary) or record individual audio clips for individual slides.
- You can hide the speaker icon when not playing, loop until stopped, rewind after playing, and show media controls.

7. Change audio settings.
- Animate an audio sequence: You can add a bookmark, trim, set a fade in and fade out effect, control the volume, and determine how to start audio.
- Play a sound over multiple slides: By default, audio plays during one slide and stops when you advance to a new slide, but it can be set to play over multiple slides.

8. Create a photo album.
- When you have multiple images to be inserted, using the Photo Album feature enables you to quickly insert the images into a slide show.
- After identifying the images you want to use, you can rearrange the order of the pictures in the album.
- You also can choose among layouts for the best appearance.

9. Set Photo Album options.
- Select pictures and set the picture order: PowerPoint enables you to determine the order of pictures in the album.
- Change picture contrast and brightness: Album options for contrast and brightness enable you to make image changes without having to leave the Photo Album dialog box.
- Insert captions: File names can be turned into captions for the pictures.
- Set an album layout: A frame shape can be selected and a theme applied to complete the album appearance.

Key Terms Matching

Match the key terms with their definitions. Write the key term letter by the appropriate numbered definition.

<table>
<tr><td>

a. Background

b. Bitmap image

c. Brightness

d. Compression

e. Contrast

f. Copyright

g. Cropping

h. Embed

i. Foreground

j. Link

</td><td>

k. Multimedia

l. Narration

m. Photo Album

n. Poster frame

o. Public domain

p. Recolor

q. Saturation

r. Sharpening

s. Softening

t. Tone

</td></tr>
</table>

1. _____ An image created by bits or pixels placed on a grid to form a picture. **p. 262**

2. _____ Spoken commentary that is added to a presentation. **p. 303**

3. _____ Process of changing a picture by adjusting the image's colors. **p. 271**

4. _____ A characteristic of lighting that controls the temperature of a color. **p. 270**

5. _____ A characteristic of color that controls its intensity. **p. 269**

6. _____ A technique that enhances the edges of the content in a picture to make the boundaries more prominent. **p. 267**

7. _____ Legal protection afforded to a written or artistic work. **p. 278**

8. _____ A method of storing an object from an external source within a presentation. **p. 289**

9. _____ The difference between the darkest and lightest areas of a picture. **p. 268**

10. _____ The process of eliminating any unwanted portions of an image. **p. 273**

11. _____ The rights to a literary work or property owned by the public at large. **p. 278**

12. _____ Method applied to data to reduce the amount of space required for file storage. **p. 262**

13. _____ The portion of the picture that is kept, which is also the main subject of the picture. **p. 265**

14. _____ Various forms of media used to entertain or inform an audience. **p. 262**

15. _____ Presentation containing multiple pictures organized into album pages. **p. 309**

16. _____ The portion of a picture that can be removed because it is not desired in the picture. **p. 265**

17. _____ A connection from the presentation to another location such as a storage device or website. **p. 289**

18. _____ The image that displays on a slide when a video is not playing. **p. 294**

19. _____ A technique that blurs the edges of the content in a picture to make the boundaries less prominent. **p. 267**

20. _____ A picture correction that controls the lightness or darkness of a picture. **p. 268**

Multiple Choice

1. Which of the following are images that are created by mathematics?

   (a) Photography

   (b) Poster frame

   (c) Vector graphics

   (d) Bitmap images

2. Which of the following is *not* permitted for a student project containing copyrighted material?

   (a) The student markets the project on a personal website.

   (b) Only a portion of copyrighted material is used, and the portion was determined by the type of media used.

   (c) The student receives permission to use copyrighted material to be distributed to classmates in the project.

   (d) The educational project is produced for a specific class and then retained in a personal portfolio for display in a job interview.

3. Which of the following in the Picture Tools tab would help you manage large image files by permanently deleting any cropped areas of a selected picture and by changing the resolution of the pictures?

   (a) Brightness

   (b) Contrast

   (c) Recolor

   (d) Compress Pictures

4. Which type of compression reduces a file by permanently eliminating certain data?

   (a) Linked

   (b) Lost

   (c) Lossy

   (d) Lossless

5. Which of the following stores sound and moving pictures in Microsoft Resource Interchange File Format (RIFF)?

   (a) .gif

   (b) .wmv

   (c) .avi

   (d) .bmp

6. What is used to measure the tone of a color in pictures?

   (a) Saturation percentage

   (b) Kelvin unit

   (c) Contrast level

   (d) Aspect ratio

7. Which of the following is a *false* statement regarding recording a narration?

   (a) Narrations cannot be paused during recording.

   (b) Narrations can be created for presentations displayed in kiosks.

   (c) PowerPoint records the amount of time it takes you to narrate each slide.

   (d) Voice narration takes precedence over any other sounds during playback.

8. Anytime a right held by a copyright owner is used without permission is known as:

   (a) Duplication.

   (b) Infringement.

   (c) Public domain.

   (d) Fair Use.

9. Which of the following reduces the demand on your computer as it plays back a video?

   (a) The contrast

   (b) A bookmark

   (c) Added narration

   (d) A codec

10. Audio Playback tools enable you to do all of the following *except*:

    (a) Add a bookmark.

    (b) Fade the audio in.

    (c) Rewind after playing.

    (d) Change the saturation.

Practice Exercises

1 Geocaching Slide Show

The slide show in Figure 4.51 is designed to be used with a presentation introducing a group to the sport of geocaching. Geocaching became a new sport on May 2, 2000, when 24 satellites around the globe stopped the intentional degradation of GPS signals. On May 3, Dave Ulmer hid a bucket of trinkets in the woods outside Portland, Oregon, and the sport was born! Your geocaching presentation is designed to teach the basic geocaching skills of taking something, leaving something, and signing the logbook. Refer to Figure 4.51 as you complete this exercise.

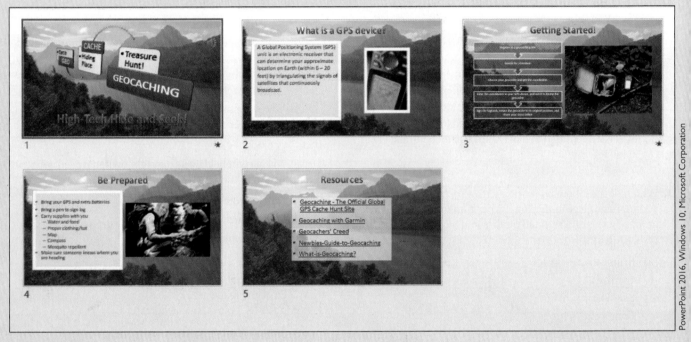

FIGURE 4.51 Geocaching Slide Show

a. Open the *p04p1Cache* slide show and save it as **p04p1Cache_LastFirst**.

b. Create a handout header with your name and a handout footer with your instructor's name and your class. Include the current date.

c. Click the **Design tab** in any slide and click **Format Background** in the Customize group to open the Format Background task pane.

d. Click **Picture or texture fill**, click **Online**, type **mountain lake** in the Bing Image Search box, and press **Enter**. Select the photo shown in the background of Figure 4.51 (or a similar photo) and click **Insert**. Drag the Transparency slider to **30%** or type **30** in the Transparency box. Click **Apply to All** and click **Close** to close the Format Background task pane.

e. Click **Slide 2**. Click the **Pictures button** in the right placeholder. In the *p04p1Cache_Media* folder, click and examine the *p04p1Gps* picture. Click **Insert** and examine the image on Slide 2 and note the resizing of the placeholder to keep the image in proportion.

f. Click **Color** in the Adjust group and change the **Color Saturation** to **0%**.

g. Click the border of the text box on the left side of the slide, click the **Home tab**, click **Format Painter** in the Clipboard group, and then click the **gps picture**.

h. Open your browser and type **morguefile.com/archive** in the address bar and press Enter to open the website. Search for a free photo using the search term *geocaching*. Right-click one of the resulting pictures and select **Save Picture**. Save the image as **p04p1geocache** to your student data folder for this chapter. Close your browser.

TROUBLESHOOTING: If you are using Edge as your browser, you may get prompted to copy the image to a social media site. Click More actions in the upper-right corner of the browser and select Open with Internet Explorer to complete Step h. The Save Background As option is available in Internet Explorer. If you are using Firefox, select the image, and then right-click and save the image.

---

i. Click **Slide 3**. Click the **Pictures button** in the placeholder on the right. Locate the *p04p1geocach* image that you saved and click **Insert**. Crop or resize the picture as needed.

j. Click **Slide 4**. Click the picture of the geocachers and click the **Format tab**. Click **Artistic Effects** in the Adjust group and select **Paint Strokes**.

k. Click **Slide 1**. Complete one of the following steps:
- If you are able to record sound in your computer lab, click the **Insert tab**, click the **Audio arrow** in the Media group, and then select **Record Audio**. Click the red **Record Sound button** and read the Speaker Note at the bottom of Slide 1. When finished reading, click the blue **Stop button** and click **OK**. Proceed to Step m.
- If you are not able to record sound, proceed to Step l.

l. Click **Insert**, if you are not able to record narration in your computer lab. Click the **Audio arrow** in the Media group, and then select **Audio on My PC**. Locate *p04p1Speaker* in the *p04p1Cache_Media* folder and click **Insert**.

m. Click the **Playback tab** and select the **Hide During Show check box** in the Audio Options group. Drag the audio icon to the top right of the slide.

n. Click the **Start arrow** in the Audio Options group and select **Automatically**.

o. Click the **Animations tab** and click **Animation Pane** in the Advanced Animation group. The audio object displays on the Animation Pane. Click the **Re-Order up arrow** until the sound object moves to the top of the list.

p. Click the **Start arrow** in the Timing group and select **With Previous**. Close the Animation Pane.

q. View the slide show.

r. Save and close the file. Based on your instructor's directions, submit p04p1Cache_LastFirst.

2 Geocaching Album

FROM SCRATCH Geocachers are asked to share their geocaching experience in the geocache logbook. *Geocaching — The Official Global GPS Cache Hunt Site* includes some easy steps for logging a geocache find and even enables you to upload a photo with your log entry. Often, geocachers also put their geocaching stories, photos, and videos online in the form of slide shows using a variety of software packages. In this exercise, you create a geocache slide show quickly and easily using the PowerPoint Photo Album feature and add video and text to the slide show. Refer to Figure 4.52 as you complete this exercise.

FIGURE 4.52 Geocaching Album

a. Open a new blank presentation. Click the **Insert tab** and click **Photo Album** in the Images group.

b. Click **File/Disk** in the Insert picture from section, open the *p04p2Geo_Media* folder, click one of the files, and then press **Ctrl+A** to select all pictures in the folder. Click **Insert**.

c. Click the check box for *p04p2Img3* in the Pictures in album section to select it and click **Rotate Right** (second option from the left). Click the check box again to deselect the picture after the rotation. Repeat to rotate *p04p2Img5* and *p04p2Img8* to the right.

d. Click the **Picture layout arrow** in the Album Layout section and select **2 pictures with title**.

e. Click the **Frame shape arrow** in the Album Layout section and select **Center Shadow Rectangle**.

f. Click **Create** and save the album as **p04p2Geo_LastFirst**.

g. Create a handout header with your name and a handout footer with your instructor's name and your class. Include the current date.

h. Ensure Slide 1 is displayed. Change the title to **Geocaching in Provo Canyon**. Ensure that the subtitle includes your name.

i. Click the **Design tab**, click **More** in the Themes group, and then click the **Ion theme**.

j. Enter the following slide titles:

Slide 2 **Marking the Jeep as a waypoint for safe return**
Slide 3 **Using our GPS to find the cache**
Slide 4 **Cache contained a waterproof container with coins and the log**
Slide 5 **Trip completed**

k. Click **Slide 3**. Click the **Home tab**, click the **New Slide arrow**, and then select **Title Only**. Change the title of the slide to **Hitching a ride on a windy day**.

l. Click the **Insert tab**, click the **Video arrow** in the Media group, and then select **Video on My PC**. Click *p04p2Vid1* from the *p04p2Geo_Media* folder and click **Insert**.

m. Click the **Playback tab** and click **Trim Video** in the Editing group. Type **00:17.491** in the **Start Time box** and click **Play**. Type **00:22.337** in the **End Time box** and click **OK**.

n. Type **00.01** in the **Fade Out box** in the Editing group.

o. Click the **Start arrow** in the Video Options group and select **Automatically**.

p. Click the **Format tab** and select the video frame at 4.75 seconds. Click **Poster Frame** in the Adjust group and select **Current Frame**.

q. Insert a new **Title Only** slide, change the title to **Nothing Stops Ava**, and then insert *p04p2Vid2* from the *p04p2Geo_Media* folder.

r. Click the **Playback tab** and click **Move Forward 0.25 Seconds** on the Media Controls bar to advance the video to the frame at 14 seconds. Click **Add Bookmark** in the Bookmarks group.

s. Click the **Format tab**, click **Video Shape** in the Video Styles group, and then click **Heart** in the Basic Shapes gallery.

t. Select one of the images in your album, click the **Format tab**, click **Compress Pictures** in the Adjust group, and then click the **Apply only to this picture check box** to deselect it. Click **OK**.

u. View the slide show. On Slide 5, point to the Media Controls bar, click the **bookmark**, and then click **Play** to begin the video at the bookmark site.

v. Run the spelling checker. Save and close the file. Based on your instructor's directions, submit p04p2Geo_LastFirst.

Mid-Level Exercises

1 Impressionist Paintings

CREATIVE CASE

In this exercise, you will use the Internet to obtain images of paintings by some of the masters of the Impressionist style. The paintings may be viewed at the Web Museum (http://www.ibiblio.org/wm/paint) that is maintained by Nicolas Pioch for academic and educational use.

a. Open the *p04m1Painting* presentation and save it as **p04m1Painting_LastFirst**.

b. Create a handout header with your name and a handout footer with your instructor's name and your class. Include the current date. On Slide 1, change the subtitle *First Name Last Name* to your name.

c. View the slide show and click the hyperlink to *The Web Museum* on Slide 1 to open the Famous Artworks exhibition. Click the Impressionism (1860–1900) link on the Famous Artworks exhibition page.

d. Locate and click the link for each artist listed below. Review the paintings and locate the thumbnail of each title listed below. Click the thumbnail to enlarge it. Then right-click it and save the image to a new folder on your storage device named **Impressionist Paintings**. Ensure that the name of the file includes the last name of the artist and the first word of the title of the painting. Repeat this process until you have saved each of the images of the paintings shown in the table below and close the browser.

Slide #	Artist	Title
Slide 1	Alfred Sisley	*Autumn: Banks of the Seine near Bougival*
Slide 2	Claude Monet	*Impression: soleil levant (pink version)*
Slide 4	Edgar Degas	*Ballet Rehearsal*
Slide 5	Claude Monet	*Waterlilies, Green Reflection, Left Part*
Slide 6	Berthe Morisot	*The Artist's Sister at a Window*
Slide 7	Pierre-Auguste Renoir	*On the Terrace*

e. Return to your slide show. Insert the picture for Slide 1 as a background and insert each of the remaining pictures on the appropriate artist's slide. Resize and position the images as needed. Use picture styles. You do not need to compress the images, as they are already low resolution.

f. Change the font on the Slide 1 Subtitle Placeholder to **White Bold**.

DISCOVER

g. Insert an audio clip of your choice in Slide 1. As an alternative to recording your own audio clip, search for audio using the keywords **copyright free classical music** on the Internet. Save the file and then insert it in Slide 1.

h. Position the audio icon on the slide and hide it during the show. Loop the audio clip and set the song so it plays continuously across slides and does not stop with the next mouse click.

i. Check the spelling in the presentation but ignore any suggestions for the names of the artists. Save and close the file. Based on your instructor's directions, submit p04m1Painting_LastFirst.

2 Red Butte Garden

FROM SCRATCH

You visited Red Butte Garden, a part of the University of Utah, and enjoyed the natural gardens and the botanical garden. You want to create a Photo Album of the pictures you took that day.

a. Create a new Photo Album and insert all of the pictures in the *p04m2Garden_Media* folder.

b. Remove the *p04m2Img1* (Red Butte Garden & Arboretum) picture.

c. Locate *p04m2Img2*, increase the brightness six times, and then increase the contrast twice.

d. Locate *p04m2Img14*, increase the brightness twice, and then increase the contrast six times.

e. Apply a **2 pictures layout** and the **Simple Frame, White frame** shape style.

f. Create the album and save it as **p04m2Garden_LastFirst**.

g. Create a handout header with your name and a handout footer with your instructor's name and your class. Include the current date.

h. Edit the album so only one picture per page displays and click **Update**.

i. Insert *p04m2Img1* as the background for Slide 1 and remove the title and subtitle placeholders.

j. Move Slide 2 to the end of the slide show, select the image, and then apply the **Paint Brush Artistic Effect**.

k. Click **Slide 14**. Select the image and apply a **Sharpen: 50% correction**.

l. Apply the **Reveal transition** on any slide and set the advance to automatically advance after **00:02:00**. Apply to all slides.

m. Save and close the file. Based on your instructor's directions, submit p04m2Garden_LastFirst.

3 Collaborating on a Group Project

CREATIVE CASE

COLLABORATION CASE

In this exercise, you will collaborate with two to three students from your class to create a PowerPoint presentation advertising a product. Your group will determine the product you want to sell. Be inventive! Find an existing product that you can use as a prop to represent your new product (see example in second paragraph). Create a storyboard for that product and use a digital camera or cell phone to capture images for the product. You will upload your version of the pictures to a location all team members can access, such as a OneDrive account. You will then view your team's pictures, download the ones you want to use, and create a presentation based on the storyboard—each group member prepares his or her own storyboard and presentation. Only the images are shared. You will insert the images you want to use in the slides. You will edit the images as needed. You will create a final slide that lists all of the team members in your group. Finally, you will blog about your experience.

For example, after talking using chat technology, a group decides to use green mouthwash as their product. But rather than have it represent mouthwash, they are going to use it as a "brain enhancer." They create a storyboard that lists Slide 1 as a Title and Content slide using the image of the mouthwash and the name of the product—Brain ++. For the second slide, they illustrate the problem by having a picture of a person holding a test paper with the grade F plainly visible. For the third slide, they illustrate the solution by having the same person pretending to drink the Brain ++. The fourth slide demonstrates the result by showing the same person holding a test paper with the grade A plainly visible. The last slide lists all members of the group. Note: This exercise assumes you have done the Collaboration exercise for Chapter 1. If you have not completed that exercise, use OneDrive or another method for sharing your presentation with your instructor and classmates.

a. Create a group with two to three class members and exchange contact information so you will be able to message each other. For example, have each member create a Microsoft account, a Yahoo! account, a Facebook account, or use some type of text or video chat technology.

b. Determine, as a group, the product you will be advertising and its use. Discuss the story line for your product with the group, then each member should create a storyboard.

c. Each member should use a digital camera or cell phone to take pictures of the product.

d. Upload your images to OneDrive, which will enable all group members to access the pictures.

e. View all of the images your group uploaded, determine which ones you want to use in your presentation, and then download those images.

f. Create a PowerPoint presentation and insert the product images into slides following the storyboard you created. Edit the slides and images as needed. Enhance slides as desired. Save the presentation as **p04m3Product_LastFirst**.

g. Create a blog posting about this experience, or write an essay using Microsoft Word, answering the following questions: Was collaborating with others through a chat tool a good experience or was it difficult? What did you like about the experience? How could it have been improved? How easily did your group reach agreement on your product?

h. Save and close the file. Based on your instructor's instructions, submit p04m3Product_LastFirst.

Beyond the Classroom

Zeroscaping Versus Xeriscaping

GENERAL CASE ✓

While on a trip through the Southwest, you took pictures of zeroscaping examples. You plan to use them in an existing slide show on waterwise landscaping. You also want to know more about xeriscaping, however, so you research xeriscaping online.

Open *p04b1Landscape* and save it as **p04b1Landscape_LastFirst**. Add a handout header with your name and a handout footer with your instructor's name and your class. Include the current date. Research zeroscaping and xeriscaping online and include the websites on a Resources slide at the end of the slide show. Please remember that giving credit to your source does not mean you are released from copyright requirements. Create several speaker notes with information you find during your research. Use the zeroscaping images located in the *p04b1Landscape_Media* folder where appropriate, and search the Internet to obtain images for the xeriscaping portion of the slide show. Use a xeriscaping picture for the background of the Title slide. You may change the template and add animations as desired. Add an audio clip and set it to play across all slides. Insert a related video on its own slide. Save and close the file. Based on your instructor's directions, submit p04b1Landscape_LastFirst.

Cascade Springs Ecosystem

DISASTER RECOVERY ✚

You are working with another fifth-grade teacher to create slide shows for your science students. The other teacher visited Cascade Springs, took pictures, and created a PowerPoint Photo Album of the pictures. Open *p04b2Springs* and save the new presentation as **p04b2Springs_LastFirst**. Review the album and read the speaker notes created from National Forest Service signs available to hikers to help them understand the fragile ecosystem. Your role is to review the presentation created by the album and determine which slides and speaker notes to keep. When necessary, rotate images. You may also change the template or slides as desired. If it is possible to record sound clips in your classroom lab, read and record shortened versions of at least three speaker notes and add the audio files to the slides. If you are unable to record the narration, insert the audio files in the *p04b2Springs_Media* folder in appropriate locations. Set the audio files to play when the sound icon is clicked. This allows a teacher to determine if he or she wants to use recordings during the presentation or lecture himself or herself. Finalize the presentation by proofreading, applying transitions and animations, and testing sound icons to ensure that they work properly. Compress all images to Web Target output. Finally, create a handout header with your name and a handout footer with your instructor's name and your class. Include the current date. Save and close the file. Based on your instructor's directions, submit p04b2Springs_LastFirst.

Capstone Exercise

The Science Club at your school wants to raise awareness of the fragility of the world's oceans. You volunteer to create a slide show that can be used at promotional events put on by the club. You use a modified version of Microsoft's Classic Photo Album template. The album has been modified to use the Blue II Color theme. In this activity, you will create the content, insert the photos, modify the photos, add sound, and insert a video clip of the ocean floor. All media for this activity are located in the p04c1Ocean_Media folder.

Insert Pictures

Using template layouts and picture placeholders, you insert photos of the ocean. You modify template placeholders for better fit.

a. Open the file named *p04c1Ocean* and save it as **p04c1Ocean_LastFirst**.

b. Create a handout header with your name and a handout footer with your instructor's name and your class. Include the current date.

c. Ensure that Slide 1 is selected. Click the existing picture and delete it. Locate the *p04c1Ocean_Media* folder and insert *p04c1Ocean1* into the picture placeholder to replace the deleted image.

d. Change the Title placeholder to **Our Fragile Oceans**. Change the subtitle to your first and last name.

e. Click **Slide 2** and replace the existing image by inserting *p04c1Ocean2*. Replace the existing text with **Whales are amazing creatures**.

f. Insert a new **Slide 3** with the **Panorama** layout. Insert *p04c1Ocean3* in the picture placeholder and replace the caption text with **Colorful fish swim together**. Delete Slide 4.

g. Delete **Slide 4** with three picture placeholders.

h. Click the new **Slide 4**. Change the layout to **2-Up Mixed with Captions**.

i. Replace the text in the caption placeholder with **Fish live in coral reefs**. Insert *p04c1Ocean4* in the left picture placeholder and insert *p04c1Ocean5* replacing the existing image that is in the right placeholder.

j. Insert a new **Slide 5** with the Portrait with Caption layout. Replace the text in the caption placeholder with **A close-up of brightly colored coral**. Insert *p04c1Ocean6*. Delete **Slide 6** and **Slide 7**. Then insert *p04c1Ocean7* as a full page picture on the new Slide 6.

k. View and save the presentation.

Apply and Modify a Picture Style, Change Images

After viewing the presentation, you decide to make some modifications. The picture on Slide 1 would stand out better if it had

the background removed. The picture on Slide 6 can be improved with an artistic effect. Some of the captions are too small.

a. Click **Slide 1**. Select the picture and remove the background. Resize the picture so image has a height and width of 3.66".

b. Click **Slide 6**. Apply the Artistic Effect **Plastic Wrap** to the picture (fourth row, last column).

c. Click **Slide 4**. Change the font to **UPPERCASE** and ensure the font size is set to **18**. Apply these same effects to the Slides 2 and 5. **Right-align** the text on Slides 2 and 5.

d. Save the presentation.

Adjust and Compress Images

The picture on Slide 2 needs the brightness, contrast, and color tones adjusted. You use the Picture Tools tab to adjust the pictures, and you apply compression to all of the photographs.

a. Click **Slide 2**, select the picture, and then increase the image sharpness **+25%**.

b. Set the saturation to **200%**, and then set the color tone to **4700 K**.

c. Compress all images using document resolution.

d. Save the presentation.

Insert a Video

You insert a video clip of the ocean and modify the settings. Finally, you add a clip of a whale song that plays on one slide.

a. Click **Slide 5**. Insert a New Slide using the **Blank** layout.

b. Search for and insert a YouTube video showing the ocean.

c. Set the video to play automatically.

d. Change the Video Options to **Hide While Not Playing** and to **Rewind after Playing**.

e. Check spelling in the presentation. Save the presentation.

Create a Photo Album

Your club wants to have something to use as handouts at the upcoming presentations. They ask you for a printed copy of all of the images. You prepare a photo album and print it.

a. Create a New Photo Album using the images in the *p04c1Ocean_Media* folder.

b. Rearrange the pictures so they appear in the following order: Ocean1, Ocean3, Ocean2, and then the remaining pictures in numerical order.

c. Edit the album using two pictures per slide and a **Simple Frame, White frame shape**.

d. Update the album and then save it as **p04c1OceanPix_LastFirst**.

e. Create a handout header with your name and a handout footer with your instructor's name and your class. Include the current date.

f. Change the title on the Title Slide to **Our Fragile Oceans**. Ensure that your name is in the subtitle.

g. Save and close the file. Based on your instructor's directions, submit the following:

p04c1Ocean_LastFirst
p04c1OceanPix_LastFirst

Posters, Tables, and Statistical Charts

LEARNING OUTCOME You will design, create, and modify custom-sized charts, tables, and statistical charts to enhance the presentation of information.

OBJECTIVES & SKILLS: After you read this chapter, you will be able to:

CASE STUDY | Healthy Living: Antioxidants

The county health department is sponsoring a health fair, and you have been invited to present a session on antioxidants. Studies show there is a correlation between eating foods rich in antioxidants, and better overall health, so you want to share this information with others.

You prepare a poster that quickly and efficiently communicates the message that antioxidants promote good health and invites participants to enter the room for more information. After preparing the poster, you work on the PowerPoint slide show you will present. You plan to present information about top foods rich in antioxidants in tables so the information is neatly organized. Finally, you decide to add a chart displaying the antioxidant levels in "superfoods" and format another chart displaying the top 20 common food sources of antioxidants.

Advanced Tables and Basic Charts

CHAPTER 5

FIGURE 5.1 Healthy Living: Antioxidants Room Poster

PowerPoint 2016, Windows 10, Microsoft Corporation

CASE STUDY | Healthy Living: Antioxidants

Starting Files	Files to be Submitted
p05h1Poster	p05h1Poster_LastFirst
p05h1Antioxidants	p05h4Antioxidants_LastFirst
p05h2MediaFolder	
p05h2Orac.xlsx	

Create Custom-sized Charts and Draw Tables

In today's electronic environment, information is readily and quickly available, but is often unorganized. Organizing information into customized charts, tables, and statistical charts makes information easier to understand. Charts and tables primarily arrange and organize information to illustrate relationships among words, numbers, and/or graphics. These charts communicate relationships both verbally and visually.

Examples of three common custom-sized charts are shown in the following figures. Figure 5.2 shows an example of a banner that has been printed locally on vinyl for durability.

Tomasz Zajda/Fotolia

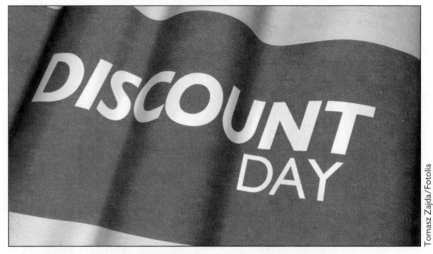

FIGURE 5.2 Custom-sized Chart: A Vinyl Banner

Figure 5.3 shows a table showing the relationship between numbers. This example, a simple multiplication table, is used to teach multiplication to elementary students. The table shows the product derived when a number in the column heading is multiplied by a number in the row heading. The intersection of the first row and the first column shows the multiplication operator.

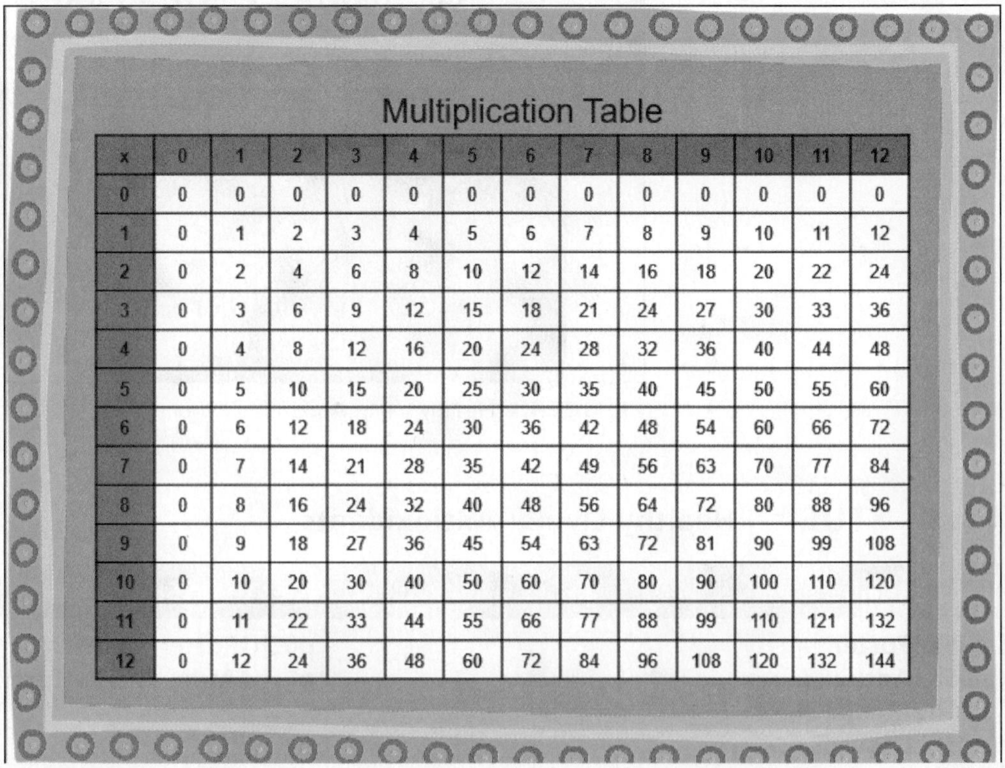

Multiplication Table

x	0	1	2	3	4	5	6	7	8	9	10	11	12
0	0	0	0	0	0	0	0	0	0	0	0	0	0
1	0	1	2	3	4	5	6	7	8	9	10	11	12
2	0	2	4	6	8	10	12	14	16	18	20	22	24
3	0	3	6	9	12	15	18	21	24	27	30	33	36
4	0	4	8	12	16	20	24	28	32	36	40	44	48
5	0	5	10	15	20	25	30	35	40	45	50	55	60
6	0	6	12	18	24	30	36	42	48	54	60	66	72
7	0	7	14	21	28	35	42	49	56	63	70	77	84
8	0	8	16	24	32	40	48	56	64	72	80	88	96
9	0	9	18	27	36	45	54	63	72	81	90	99	108
10	0	10	20	30	40	50	60	70	80	90	100	110	120
11	0	11	22	33	44	55	66	77	88	99	110	121	132
12	0	12	24	36	48	60	72	84	96	108	120	132	144

PowerPoint 2016, Windows 10, Microsoft Corporation

FIGURE 5.3 Multiplication Table Showing Relationship Between Numbers

Figure 5.4 shows a PowerPoint table that includes arrow graphics. This example illustrates a more complex relationship. Text, color, and font size, along with cell shading and arrow graphics, are used to guide the viewer through the process.

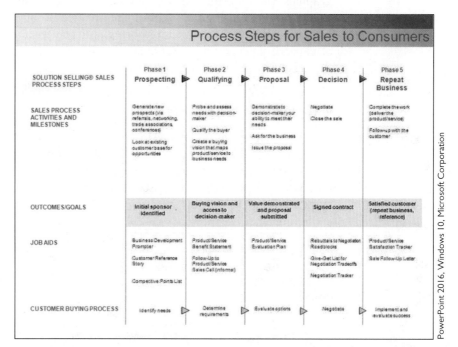

PowerPoint 2016, Windows 10, Microsoft Corporation

FIGURE 5.4 Table Illustrating a Complex Relationship Between Steps in a Process

In this section, you learn how to create custom-sized charts. You create a poster and a banner. You will also learn how to draw a table on a slide. Finally, you will learn how to design a table to effectively communicate and organize your ideas.

Creating a Poster or a Banner

Posters and hanging signs printed on paper, vinyl, or cloth are used for advertising and publicizing. Although graphic professionals use other tools for professional print jobs, you can create posters and banners in PowerPoint by using a custom-sized single slide. Though text can communicate a message by its appearance (typeface, color, size, style, contrast), it can also communicate a message by how it is positioned or arranged. Therefore, when you design a chart on a single slide you need to carefully plan how the information is arranged within the slide and fully utilize formatting tools.

Figure 5.5 displays an attention-grabbing banner announcing a local sporting event.

Chromaco/Fotolia; Christos Georghiou/Fotolia

FIGURE 5.5 Banner Created in PowerPoint

An important part of planning for a poster or banner is considering how you will print the item, because this often determines how you format the single slide. Consider the printer when determining margins. Printers have margins beyond which text and graphics will not print. For commercial printing, it is important to identify all specifications, such as width and height of the finished product, not just margins. Also, when printing wide-format banners or posters, the printer may not support large-sized sheets of paper. If your printer does not support banner- or poster-sized paper, you can submit the file to a local or online printing service.

Customize Slide Size

STEP 1 You can create slides that range in size from wide-format documents such as posters and banners to small banners that appear at the tops of webpages using the Slide Size dialog box. You use the Slide Size dialog box to create a custom size such as 17" x 22", a common size for a poster. The Slide Size, dialog box displaying a custom 17" × 22" setting, is shown in Figure 5.6.

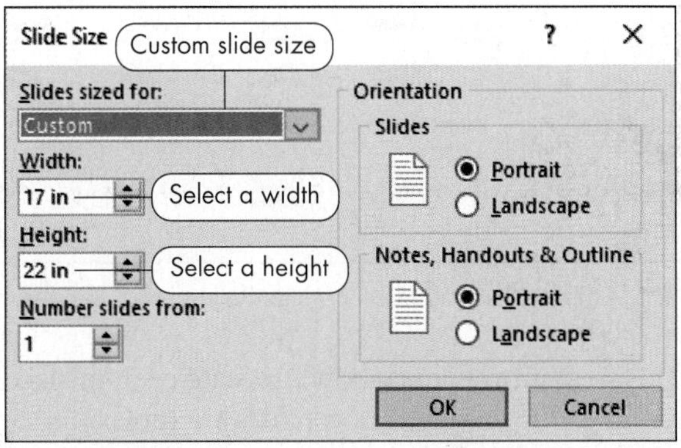

FIGURE 5.6 Custom Setting in Slide Size Dialog Box

To change the slide size, complete the following steps:

1. Click the Design tab.
2. Click Slide Size in the Customize group.
3. Select Custom Slide Size.
4. Click the *Slides sized for* arrow, and click to select the slide size based upon the desired output.
5. Use the Width and Height spin arrows to further adjust the size or, if a desired option is not available in the *Slides sized for* box, to create a custom-sized output.
6. Choose the orientation, found on the right side of the Slide Size dialog box, for Slides and for Notes, Handouts & Outline based upon the desired output.
7. Choose Maximize or Ensure Fit if you chose Custom, and are prompted to adjust content or scale.

TIP: WEBPAGE BANNERS
The Banner option in the *Slides sized for* section is 8" × 1"—an ideal size for a Web banner that displays across the top of a webpage.

Drawing a Table

STEP 2 ›› As you learned in an earlier chapter, tables organize information into a highly structured grid (up to 75 rows and columns in PowerPoint). Because tables are such a common way to present information, they can be created in PowerPoint, Word, Excel, and Access. If you create a table in Word, Excel, or Access, you can then insert it into a PowerPoint slide.

In the earlier chapter, you inserted a table by using the Insert feature to automatically create a table grid. You can also use the Draw Table feature to create tables by manually drawing the grid. This method provides much more flexibility in table design and enables you to create complex tables. With this method you use a pencil pointer that you drag to create horizontal and vertical borders and to create multiple cell heights and widths and diagonal borders. You are also provided with a set of drawing tools to customize the borders you create.

To draw a table, complete the following steps:

1. Click the Insert tab and click the Table arrow in the Tables group.
2. Select Draw Table.
3. Drag the pencil pointer to define the outer table boundary.
4. Click Draw Table in the Draw Borders group on the Table Tools Design tab.
5. Position the pencil along an edge of the table and drag a line to the opposite side.
6. Continue dragging the pencil tool from one border to another to create table cells.
7. Press Esc or click outside of the table to finish drawing your table.

You do not need to be exact when drawing a table because the Layout tab includes buttons that distribute the width of the columns or the height of the rows so that they are uniformly spaced. To distribute columns or rows, select the cells you want to equalize and click Distribute Columns or Distribute Rows in the Cell Size group on the Layout tab.

TIP: ERASE BORDERS

You can erase a border by positioning the Eraser tool, located in the Draw Borders group on the Table Tools Design tab, over the row or column border you wish to eliminate and then clicking the Eraser tool.

Creating a Table Structure

Think carefully about the structure of a table before you create it to maximize the impact of the data it will contain. Tables should convey essential facts that supplement the message in the presentation but should omit distracting details. The table should be easy to understand and consistent with other objects in the presentation.

A table needs a title to communicate its purpose. Keep the title short, but ensure that it gives enough information to accurately identify the table's purpose. Use a subtitle to give further information about the purpose, if necessary, but it should be in a smaller font size. The top row of the table body usually contains **column headers** to identify the contents of the columns. Column headers should be distinguishable from cell contents. Set the headers apart by using color, bold font, italics, or a larger font than you use for the table body cells. Make sure that the font size of the column headers is not larger than the title and subtitle.

TIP: MERGE CELLS TO CREATE A TITLE ROW

To create a title row that stretches across several cells, select the cells to merge, and then click Merge Cells in the Merge group on the Layout tab. You can also use the Eraser tool on the Table Tools Design tab to erase the border between the cells or right-click selected cells and click Merge Cells.

The first column of a table, or the stub column, typically contains the information that identifies the data in each row. The first cell in the stub column should include a heading (stub heading) describing the content of the column. The last row of a table can be used for totals, a note, or source information. Use a smaller font size for the note or source, but make sure it is still large enough to be readable.

You can use table and cell borders to help clarify the information. Typically, horizontal borders are used to set off the title and subtitle from the headings and to set off headings from the table body. Vertical borders help define the columns. Figure 5.7 shows a basic table structure with the table elements identified. Bold is used to emphasize the table title and column headings. One of the columns is shaded in blue and one of the rows is shaded in pale pink to help identify the differences. This is for illustration purposes only—this is not a table style. The intersection of the column and row, or the cell, is shaded in purple. The table is boxed, or surrounded by borders, and borders surround each cell. A heavier border is used to set off the title information from the column headings, the column headings from the body of the table, and the note information from the rest of the table.

Table Title		
Subtitle		
Stub Heading	**Column Heading**	**Column Heading**
Stub (Row Heading)	cell	
Stub (Row Heading)		
Stub (Row Heading)		
Stub (Row Heading)		
Note or Source information		

FIGURE 5.7 Table Elements

PowerPoint 2016, Windows 10, Microsoft Corporation

> **TIP: FORMAT TABLE ELEMENTS**
> The formatting of table elements is no longer as rigid as in years past unless you are preparing a table to adhere to specific guidelines such as American Psychological Association (APA) style. If this is the case, be sure to check a style guide for the style requirements and format the table per the guidelines.

Simplify Table Data

Table data on a slide should be as simple as possible to convey the message. When working with text-based tables, limit the number of entries in tables to keep the font size large enough to read. For example, rather than listing 30 items in a table, list the top 5. Consider providing the audience with a printed Word table if you want them to have a list of all 30 items. Occasionally you may have to left-align or center text in other columns. Generally speaking, however, you want to keep the alignment consistent throughout the table.

When working with numeric-based tables, simplify data by shortening numbers. A good practice is rounding numbers to whole numbers. Another method is to show numbers with a designation stating that the number is in thousands or millions. How you align the numbers in a cell depends on the type of data the cell contains. For example, numbers that do not have a decimal point can be right-aligned, or they can align on the decimal point if one exists.

Change Row Height, Column Width, and Table Size

STEP 3 ⟫ The row height or column width can be changed to accommodate information or to call attention to a cell, row, or column. For example, title rows are often taller than the rows containing body cells. To quickly adjust row height or column width, position the pointer over the target border of a row or column until the pointer changes into a sizing pointer (double-headed arrow) and drag the border to adjust the row or column to the desired height or width. If you require an exact height or width, use the Height and Width spin arrow in the Table Tools Layout tab.

To precisely change the height of a row or the width of the column, complete the following steps:

1. Select the row or the column you want to resize.
2. Click the Table Tools Layout tab.
3. Click the spin arrows in the Height or Width boxes in the Cell Size group, or enter an exact size in the box for the height or width.
4. Press Enter to apply the new size.

Sometime the overall size of a table needs to be modified. You can resize the table manually by dragging a corner or middle sizing handle. Dragging the top- or bottom-middle handles changes the table height, whereas dragging the left- or right-middle handles changes the table width. To keep the ratio of height to width consistent when resizing the table, drag a corner handle while holding down Shift; this sizes the table in both the vertical and horizontal directions simultaneously.

To precisely change the size of the table, complete the following steps:

1. Select the table.
2. Click the Table Tools Layout tab.
3. Click the spin arrows in the Height or Width boxes in the Table Size group, or enter an exact size in the box for the height or width of the table.
4. Check the Lock Aspect Ratio box to keep the table proportions intact when changing the height or width of the table.

Align Text Within Cells, Rows, and Columns

The Alignment group on the Layout tab includes features that not only align the contents of a cell horizontally and vertically but also change the direction of the text by rotating it or changing its orientation. You can also change the margins inside the cell. Once you have selected the text you want to align, click the Table Tools Layout tab. Select Align Left, Center, or Align Right in the Alignment group to align text horizontally. Select Align Top, Center Vertically, or Align Bottom in the Alignment group to align text vertically.

While the Table Tools Layout tab is open, you can also change the direction of text within a cell, row, or column. Click Text Direction in the Alignment group and select Horizontal, Rotate All Text 90°, Rotate All Text 270°, or Stacked in the Alignment group. Rotate All Text 90° positions text vertically facing to the right and Rotate All Text 270° positions text vertically facing to the left. Stacked changes the text orientation from horizontal to vertical for each individual character. Figure 5.8 shows a table with text rotated 270° within a column.

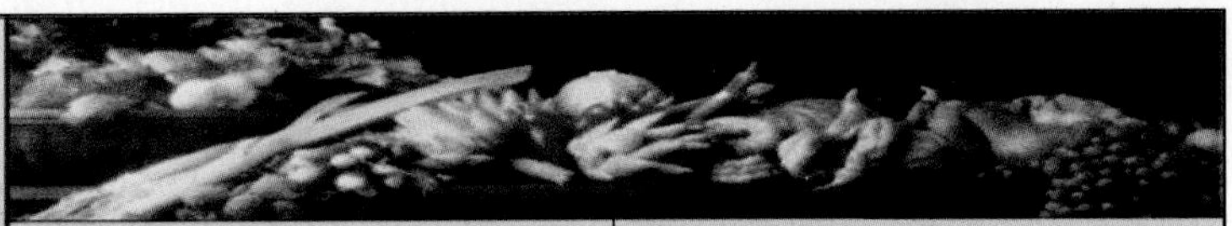

ANTIOXIDANTS		
	Vitamin C	Citrus fruits and juices, berries, dark green vegetables, red and yellow peppers, tomatoes
	Vitamin E	Vegetable oils such as olive, soybean
	Selenium	Brazil nuts, brewer's yeast, oatmeal, brown rice
	Beta Carotene	Variety of dark orange, red, yellow and green vegetables and fruits

PowerPoint 2016, Windows 10, Microsoft Corporation

FIGURE 5.8 Rotated Text Within a Column

You can change the internal margins of a cell from a default of 0.05" for top and bottom margins and 0.1" for left and right margins to no margins, narrow margins, wide margins, or custom margins.

To change the margins of a cell, row, or column, complete the following steps:

1. Select the cells for which you want to change the margins.
2. Click the Table Tools Layout tab.
3. Click Cell Margins in the Alignment group.
4. Select Normal, None, Narrow, Wide, or Custom, which enables you to set each cell margin individually.

Quick Concepts

1. Explain how charts show relationships. *p. 332*
2. When would it be valuable to draw a table instead of using the Insert Table feature? *p. 335*
3. List the purposes of a table title and subtitle. *p. 335*

Skills covered: Design a Poster or Banner • Customize Slide Size • Draw a Table • Change Row Height, Column Width, and Table Size • Align Text Within Cells, Rows, and Columns

1 Create Custom-sized Charts and Draw Tables

You prepare a poster that visitors at the county health fair can see as they walk by the room in which you are presenting. After preparing the poster, your focus turns to the work on the PowerPoint presentation that will be delivered. Information about top foods rich in antioxidants will be presented and neatly organized in tables.

STEP 1 ›› CREATE CUSTOM-SIZED SLIDES

The poster you prepare will be displayed outside your room to communicate the simple message that antioxidants promote good health. You also want the poster to follow the same design as the antioxidant slide show already created, so you use the slide-show title slide as the basis for the poster and resize it to a standard poster size. Finally, you print a scaled-down version of the poster as a record of the presentation. Refer to Figure 5.9 as you complete Step 1.

Step g: Two-line title

Antioxidants = Good Health

Session 6A—Oak Room

Step j: Repositioned slide footer

2018 County Health Fair

PowerPoint 2016, Windows 10, Microsoft Corporation

FIGURE 5.9 Antioxidant Session Poster

a. Open *p05h1Poster* and save it as **p05h1Poster_LastFirst**.

> **TROUBLESHOOTING:** If you make any major mistakes in this exercise, you can close the file, open *p05h1Poster* again, and then start this exercise over.

b. Create a handout header with your name and a handout footer with your instructor's name and your class. Include the current date.

c. Click the **Design tab**, click **Slide Size** in the Customize group, and then select **Custom Slide Size**.

d. Change the width to **17"**.

e. Change the height to **22"**.

The *Slides sized for* box changes to Custom. Orientation changes to portrait for the Slides option and the Notes, Handouts & Outline option because the height of the slide is now greater than its width.

f. Click **OK**. Click **Maximize** and note the change in orientation.

The Maximize option scales the slide to show the entire slide. The Ensure Fit option scales the slide to fit in the window.

g. Select the title placeholder and type **Antioxidants = Good Health**.

h. Change the font size of the title placeholder to **144 pt**.

The session title is split into two lines. It is important to use a font large enough to be viewed easily by health-fair participants.

i. Create a slide footer that reads **2018 County Health Fair**. Click **Apply**.

By default, the slide footer is positioned at the bottom center of the slide, which makes it very difficult to read.

j. Click the footer placeholder to select it. Hold down **Shift** to constrain the movement horizontally and drag the slide footer border straight across to the right side of the poster so that it is positioned under the picture of the artichokes with the right border of the placeholder on the edge of the slide.

This new position increases the readability of the footer.

k. Change the font of the footer to **Arial (Headings)**, **32 pt**, and **Gray- 50%, Background 2, Darker 50%**.

These font changes also increase the readability of the footer.

l. Click the **File tab** and click **Print**.

The Preview display may show only a portion of the poster because the poster size is larger than the typical printer paper size.

m. Click the **Full Page Slides arrow** in the Settings section and ensure that a check appears next to Scale to Fit Paper.

The poster can now be printed to the paper size in the printer.

n. Save and close the file. You will submit this file to your instructor at the end of the last Hands-On Exercise.

STEP 2 ›› DRAW A TABLE

With the poster done, you open the Antioxidants = Healthy Living slide show you want to use during your health-fair presentation. You have sketched out a plan for an antioxidant table that lists a vitamin or mineral and some foods that include this antioxidant type. You realize that because of the varied columns and rows, the most efficient way to create the table is to draw it. Refer to Figure 5.10 to see the table structure that will result when you complete Step 2.

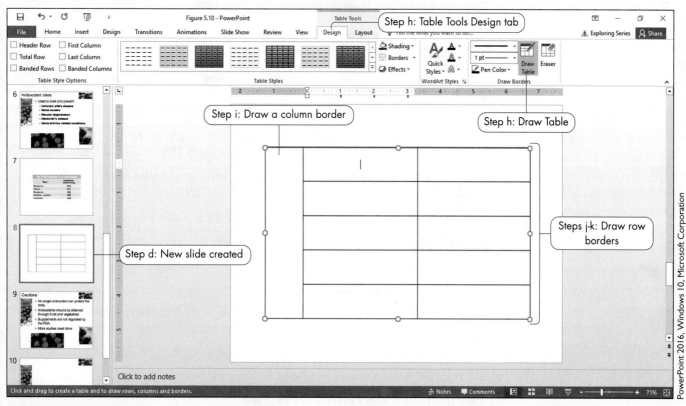

FIGURE 5.10 Table Drawn with Pencil Tool

a. Open *p05h1Antioxidants* and save it as **p05h1Antioxidants_LastFirst**.

b. Create a handout header with your name and a handout footer with your instructor's name and your class. Include the current date.

c. Click the **View tab** and ensure that the Ruler check box is checked to display the ruler. Click **Zoom** in the Zoom group and click **100%**.

   The horizontal and vertical rulers and zoomed view are helpful when drawing a table.

d. Click **Slide 7**. Click the **Home tab**, click the **New Slide arrow**, and then click **Blank**.

   A new slide is created after Slide 7.

e. Click the **Design tab** on the new Slide 8 and click **Format Background** in the Customize group. Click to select the **Hide background graphics check box** in the Format Background pane. Close the Format Background pane.

   The background pictures are removed so they will not distract from the information in the table.

f. Click the **Insert tab**, click **Table** in the Tables group, and then select **Draw Table**.

   The pointer changes to a pencil.

g. Use the ruler as a guide to draw a table starting at 4" to the left of the zero mark on the horizontal ruler and 2.5" above the zero mark on the vertical ruler. End the table at 4" to the right of the zero mark on the horizontal ruler and 2.5" below the zero mark on the vertical ruler.

Hands-On Exercise I   341

The outer border of the table is created.

h. Click **Draw Table** in the Draw Borders group on the **Table Tools Design tab**.

i. Drag the pencil **down** to create a column border, beginning at approximately 1" on the horizontal ruler. Release the mouse button as soon as you see the complete border appear.

Inches are measured from the top-left edge of the table.

> **TROUBLESHOOTING:** If a new table is created in this step, you may have dragged the pencil inside of the table boundaries. Click Undo on the Quick Access Toolbar and select Draw Table in the Draw Borders group on the Table Tools Design Tab. Beginning on the table border, drag the pencil straight down and release it when you see the complete border.

j. Create a row border by dragging **horizontally** beginning from the first column right border to the right boundary of the table approximately 1" from the top boundary.

k. Drag three more row borders without worrying whether the rows are exactly the same height at this time.

Your table now contains five rows to the right of the first column.

l. Split the new rows of the table into two columns by dragging a vertical border.

Your table now contains three columns.

m. Press **Esc** to deactivate the table-drawing mode.

n. Select the center cell and the right cell in the top row, click the **Layout tab**, and then click **Distribute Columns** in the Cell Size group.

The width of the selected cells is distributed equally.

o. Select all five rows that were created by drawing the four borders in Steps j and k.

p. Click **Distribute Rows** in the Cell Size group.

The height of the selected cells is distributed equally.

q. Select the center column and click **Center** in the Alignment group.

Any text typed into the center column is centered horizontally in the cells.

r. Select the center and right columns and click **Center Vertically** in the Alignment group.

Any text typed into the two right column cells is centered vertically.

s. Save the presentation.

You save the table and will add the content in Hands-On Exercise 2.

You review the Antioxidants = Healthy Living slide show and note that the table on Slide 7 does not include a title row or column headings. Without this information, the data in the table are meaningless. You create structure in the table by adding a row for a title and by adding headers to the columns. Refer to Figure 5.11 as you complete Step 3.

Top Five Foods Rich in Antioxidants	
Food *Step i: Column headers added*	Antioxidants mmol/serving
Blackberries	5746
Walnuts *Step b: Table title row added*	3721
Strawberries	3584
Artichokes, prepared	3559
Cranberries	3125

PowerPoint 2016, Windows 10, Microsoft Corporation

FIGURE 5.11 Restructured Table

a. Select the table on Slide 7. Click the **Table Tools Design tab** and click **Draw Table** in the Draw Borders group.

b. Drag the pencil **horizontally** through the blank row at the top of the table.

A new row is created above *Blackberries*. You now have two blank rows available that you can use to create and format the table title and column headings.

> **TROUBLESHOOTING:** If a new table is created in this step instead of a new row, click Undo on the Quick Access Toolbar and drag the pencil through the row without touching the border of the existing table.

c. Press **Esc** to exit Draw Table mode and select both cells in the top row of the table.

d. Click the **Table Tools Layout tab** and click **Merge Cells** in the Merge group.

The selected cells merge into one cell for the table title.

e. Type the title **Top Five Foods Rich in Antioxidants** in the title row.

The wording of the title now clearly defines the table's purpose. The table title is formatted with a white font color for emphasis.

f. Click **Center** in the Alignment group and click **Center Vertically** in the Alignment group.

g. Change the Height value in the Cell Size group to **0.76"**.

The Cell Size group is located in the center of the Ribbon. Be careful to not use the Table Size group on the right end of the Ribbon.

h. Select the title and change the font size to **24 pt**. Click the **Table Tools Design tab**, click the **Text Effects arrow** in the WordArt Styles group, point to **Shadow**, and then click **Offset Diagonal Bottom Right** (the first option under *Outer*) to add a text shadow.

The formatting of the title enhances the title message.

i. Type **Food** in the left cell of the blank row 2 and press **Tab**. Type **Antioxidants mmol/serving** in the right cell of the blank row 2.

j. Select the column headings in row 2 and apply **Bold**.

The column heading for the second column wraps to fit the text on two lines in the cell.

k. Click the **Table Tools Layout tab** and click **Center** in the Alignment group.

l. Click **Center Vertically** in the Alignment group.

m. Save the presentation. Keep the presentation open if you plan to continue with the next Hands-On Exercise. If not, close the presentation and exit PowerPoint.

Table Design

After you create a table, you may find that its appearance or structure must be modified to ensure the tabular information can be quickly read and understood. You may also find that there is an existing table created in other software applications that you could import or paste into PowerPoint and modify.

In this section, you will learn how to set a background fill; change table borders and table effects; insert and delete columns and rows; and adjust text within cells, rows, and columns—all with the goal of making information meaningful to the audience. You will also learn how to share information between applications.

Formatting Table Components

To change the appearance of a table, you can apply formatting to table components, such as the header or total rows, or use the tools in the Table Style Options group on the Table Tools Design tab. You can change table components using a ***table style***, a combination of formatting choices for table components based on the theme of the presentation.

Whether you choose to format and customize the individual style options or apply a full table style, you should understand the different types of formatting available. Table 5.1 shows what is formatted when a table style is applied to a table component.

TABLE 5.1	Table Components and Table Style Formatting Options
Header Row	Formats the row used for the table title or column headers
Total Row	Formats the last row in the table and displays column totals
First Column	Formats the stub (first column) differently than other columns
Last Column	Formats the last column differently than the other columns
Banded Rows	Formats even rows differently than odd rows
Banded Columns	Formats even columns differently than odd columns

Pearson Education, Inc.

To apply a table style from the Table Styles gallery that impacts all of the formatting options based on the theme of the presentation, click More in the Table Styles group. This gallery displays the Best Match for Document at the top of the gallery along with Light, Medium, and Dark styles. Note that at the bottom of the Table Styles gallery there is an option to clear the table of all styles. It does not remove individual attributes such as bold if those attributes were applied separately, however. Figure 5.12 shows the Table Styles gallery and a table style applied to a table. The table style includes the Header Row and Banded Rows table style options.

Table Style Options

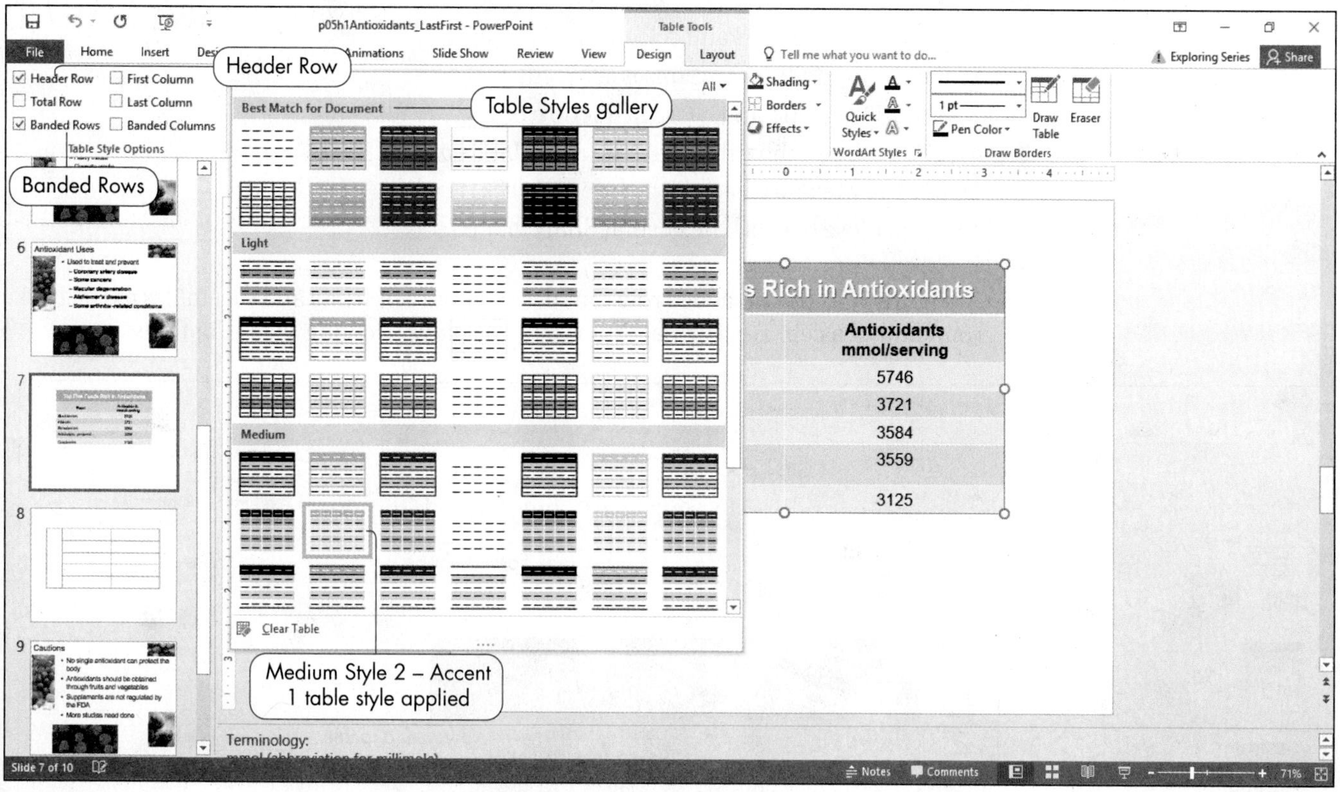

FIGURE 5.12 Table Styles Gallery

Set a Background Fill

STEP 1 You can add pictures or other background fills to individual cells or to a table. This can add an interesting element to the background of the table or selected cells. For example, a table displaying information about specific fruits can include cells with individual pictures of each fruit or the table could include a background image of a bowl of fruits.

> **To change the background fill style, complete the following steps:**
>
> 1. Select the cells in which you want a background change, or select the table.
> 2. Click the Table Tools Design tab.
> 3. Click the Shading arrow in the Table Styles group.
> 4. Select from Theme Colors, Standard Colors, Picture, Gradient, Recent Colors Texture, or Table Background or use the eyedropper tool to pick a color from another object.

As an alternative method of changing the background of a cell, you can right-click and select Format Shape to display the Format Shape pane. Then you can select the desired options from the Format Shape pane. The main advantage of using the right-click method is that the Format Shape pane enables you to choose multiple options including shape and text options, which are not available through the Table Styles group. For example, you could add a text effect to the text in the cell as well as changing the background.

When a picture is placed in a table cell as the background, the cell can still contain text. Choose a light picture if the picture is serving as the background to text so that the text is still legible.

To add a picture background to a table cell using the Format Shape pane, complete the following steps:

1. Right-click the cell and select Format Shape.
2. Ensure that Shape Options is selected.
3. Click Fill & Line and click the Picture or texture fill option.
4. Click File, Clipboard, or Online under *Insert picture from*.
5. Navigate to and locate the picture and click Insert.
6. Click Close to close the Format Shape pane.

Figure 5.13 has an added row that uses a picture of fruits and vegetables as the background fill of a cell. The Format Shape pane displays showing the Fill options.

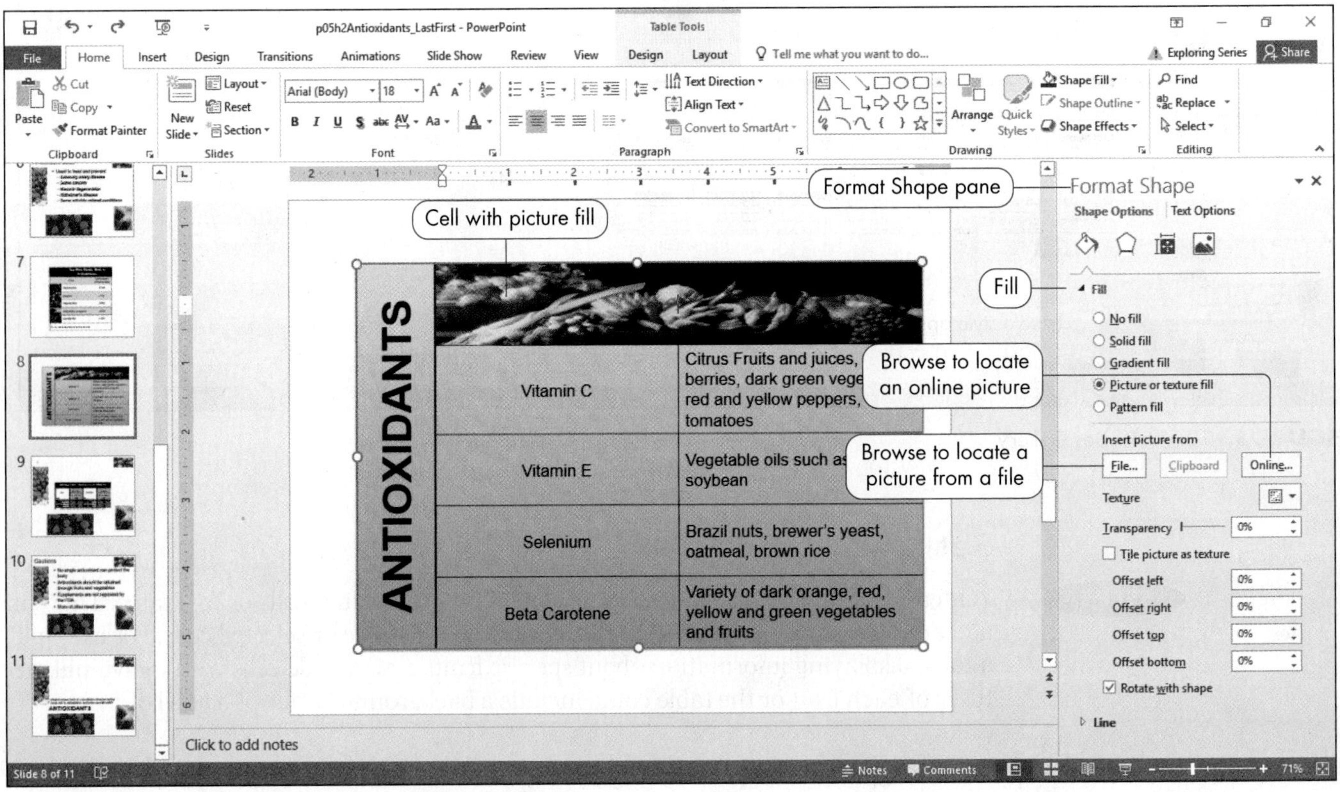

PowerPoint 2016, Windows 10, Microsoft Corporation

FIGURE 5.13 Format Shape Pane

Change Table Borders

Change border style, weight, and color by using the pen options located in the Draw Borders group on the Table Tools Design tab. The Pen Style option changes the style of the line used to draw borders and includes options for dotted and dashed lines. The Pen Weight option changes the width of the border, and the Pen Color option changes the color of the border.

After selecting the style, weight, and color of a border, click the border you want to change with the pencil. You can also drag to create additional borders with the pencil. If you have multiple borders to change, however, it is faster to use Borders in the Table Styles group on the Table Tools Design tab. Select the cell or cells you want to affect, or select the entire table. You can choose to have no border; all cells bordered; only outside borders; only inside borders; just a top, bottom, left, or right border; inside horizontal or vertical borders; or diagonal down or up borders.

Apply a Table Special Effect

Special effects may be added to a cell, selected cells, or a table. Three effects options include Cell Bevel, Shadow, and Reflection and can be found in Effects in the Table Styles group on the Table Tools Design tab. Pointing to one of these options opens that effect's gallery.

As with other galleries, you can preview the effects on the selected cells or the table to view the impact of the effects before committing to a choice. The gallery also includes a No option for each effect that removes any previously applied effects. Figure 5.14 shows four tables: the original table with the default style settings, a table with the Relaxed Inset effect applied to all cells, a table with the Perspective Diagonal Lower Left shadow effect, and a table showing a Full Reflection, touching reflection style.

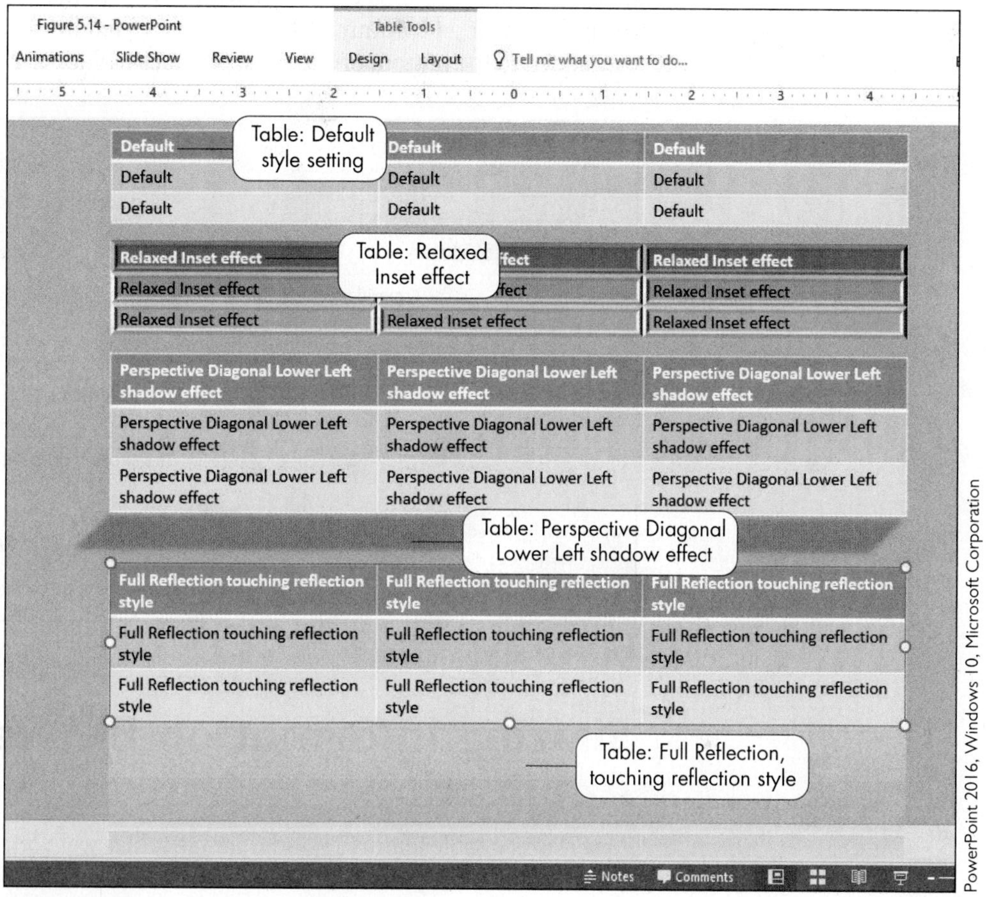

FIGURE 5.14 Table Special Effect Styles

Changing Table Layout

After creating a table, or even while creating it, you can use the tools on the Table Tools Layout tab to change the layout of the table by inserting or deleting columns and rows. View Gridlines is also included on the Layout tab in the Table group, which is a toggle button that enables you to show or hide the table gridlines.

Insert Columns and Rows

STEP 2 ≫ To insert additional information into a table, you can add a row or a column—the process is basically the same for adding rows or columns. To control where the row appears, click in a cell next to where you want to add the new row. If you want the new row to appear at the bottom of a table, click in the last cell of the table and press Tab. After positioning the pointer, click the Table Tools Layout tab, and then click Insert Above or Insert Below in the Rows and Columns group.

The process is similar for inserting a column to the left or right of an existing column: click in a cell next to where you want the new column, and then click Insert Left or Insert Right in the Rows & Columns group on the Layout tab. As an alternative to using the Layout tab, you can right-click in a selected cell, click Split Cells on the context menu that displays, and then use the Number of columns or Number of rows option.

Delete Columns and Rows

To delete selected columns and rows, click Delete in the Rows & Columns group on the Layout tab and click Delete Columns, Delete Rows, or Delete Table. You can also right-click in selected cells, click Delete on the Mini toolbar, and then click Delete Columns, Delete Rows, or Delete Table. Figure 5.15 displays two tables: an original table on the left and the same table after modifications on the right. The table style was changed. The modified table no longer contains a top row with a picture fill, instead featuring a new column to the left of the food column and a picture inserted in each of the resulting cells. Finally, a row added to the bottom of the table provides a place to include source information.

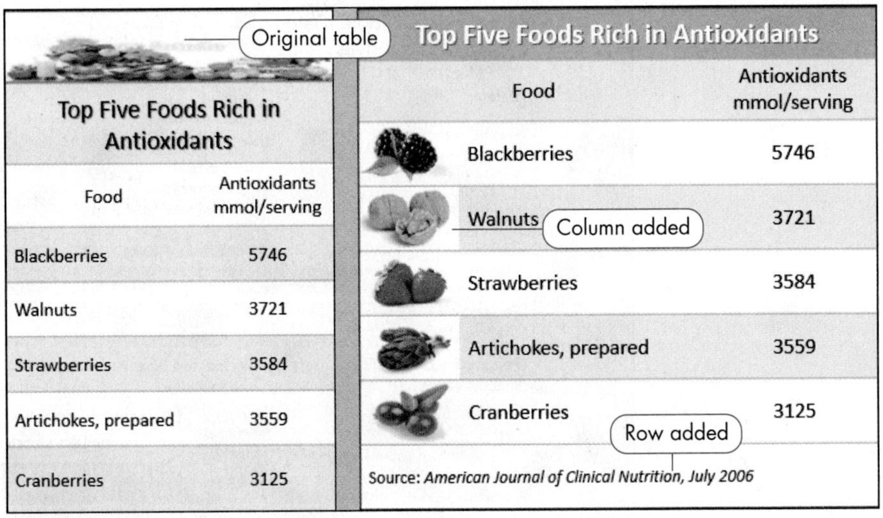

FIGURE 5.15 Table with Modified Layout

Sharing Information Between Applications

PowerPoint's table features handle simple tables well, but if the table contents require calculations, it will be best to create it in Word or Excel. Word tables are good for basic calculations, and Excel tables are best used for complex calculations. After creating the table in Word or Excel, you can insert the table in a presentation slide as an object or link the slide to the Excel worksheet or a Word table. ***Object linking and embedding (OLE)*** lets you insert an object created in one application into a document created in another application.

Link and Embed Objects

STEP 3 ▶▶ Linking an object differs from embedding an object. To understand the differences, you need to understand four key terms used in the object linking and embedding process (see Table 5.2).

TABLE 5.2 Object Linking and Embedding Key Terms

Key Term	Definition
Source application	The application you used to create the original object, such as Word or Excel
Destination application	The application into which the object is being inserted, such as PowerPoint
Source file	The file that contains the original table or data that is used to create a linked or embedded object, such as a Word document or an Excel worksheet
Destination file	The file that contains the inserted object, such as a PowerPoint presentation with an Excel worksheet embedded in it

If you create a table in Excel and paste it into a PowerPoint slide, Excel is the source application and PowerPoint is the destination application. The Excel file containing the table is the source file for the object. Once you insert the table object into PowerPoint, the PowerPoint presentation is the destination file. The simplest way to transfer any object is to copy it within the source application, and paste it into the destination application. This embeds the copied object into the application.

An **embedded object** becomes a part of the destination file. An embedded object does not maintain a connection to the source file or source application in which the object was created. For example, a range of data copied from Excel and pasted into PowerPoint results in a table object displaying the data that can be edited as a table in PowerPoint. Changes to the table data in PowerPoint do not change the source cells within the original Excel file (or vice-versa). The PowerPoint table tool options appear on the Ribbon when the data is selected in PowerPoint, and the table is treated as any other table of data.

In the case of a chart created in Excel, the default option to paste creates a linked object. You would need to choose the option to paste as a picture to embed the chart into PowerPoint without a link to the source file. The PowerPoint Ribbon would display picture tool options. Figure 5.16 shows a PowerPoint slide with an embedded table. It is important to note that if you edit the embedded table, the source document (an Excel document in this example) is *not* changed.

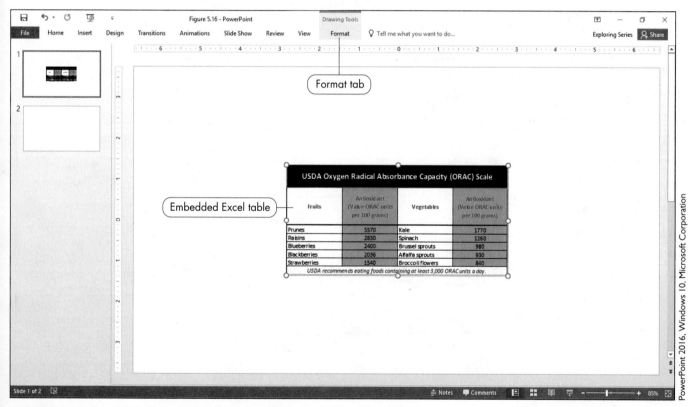

FIGURE 5.16 Excel Table Embedded in PowerPoint Slide

To embed a new object, complete the following steps:

1. Open the source file.
2. Select and copy the object or data.
3. Click to make the destination PowerPoint file active and click at the insertion point.
4. Paste the object into PowerPoint.

With a **linked object**, the information is stored in the source file, and the object in the destination file is updated when you modify it in the source file. When you double-click a linked object, the source application opens, and you are actually editing the source file. The changes you make in the source file display in PowerPoint. The destination file stores only the location of the source file while displaying a picture or representation of the linked data from the source file. The representation in PowerPoint is only a shortcut to the source file so that changes to the source file are reflected and updated in the presentation.

One advantage of linking is the destination file does not increase in size because PowerPoint stores only the link to the data needed to display the information. Another advantage is the data only needs to be changed once in the source file, and any files linked to that source file automatically update the information.

To link to an object, complete the following steps:

1. Open the source file.
2. Select and copy the object or data.
3. Click to make the destination PowerPoint file active and click at the insertion point.
4. Click the Paste arrow and click Paste Special.
5. Click the Paste link option to select it in the Paste Special dialog box, choose the object type in the As box, such as a Microsoft Excel Worksheet Object, and then click OK.

To use an alternative method for linking an object as shown in Figure 5.17, complete the following steps:

1. Click the Insert tab and click Object in the Text group.
2. Click the Create new option, which links to a new file, or click the Create from file option, which enables navigating (Browse) to an existing file.
3. Click the Display as icon option to display an icon in the PowerPoint presentation (double-clicking the icon launches the source file).
4. Click OK.

PowerPoint 2016, Windows 10, Microsoft Corporation

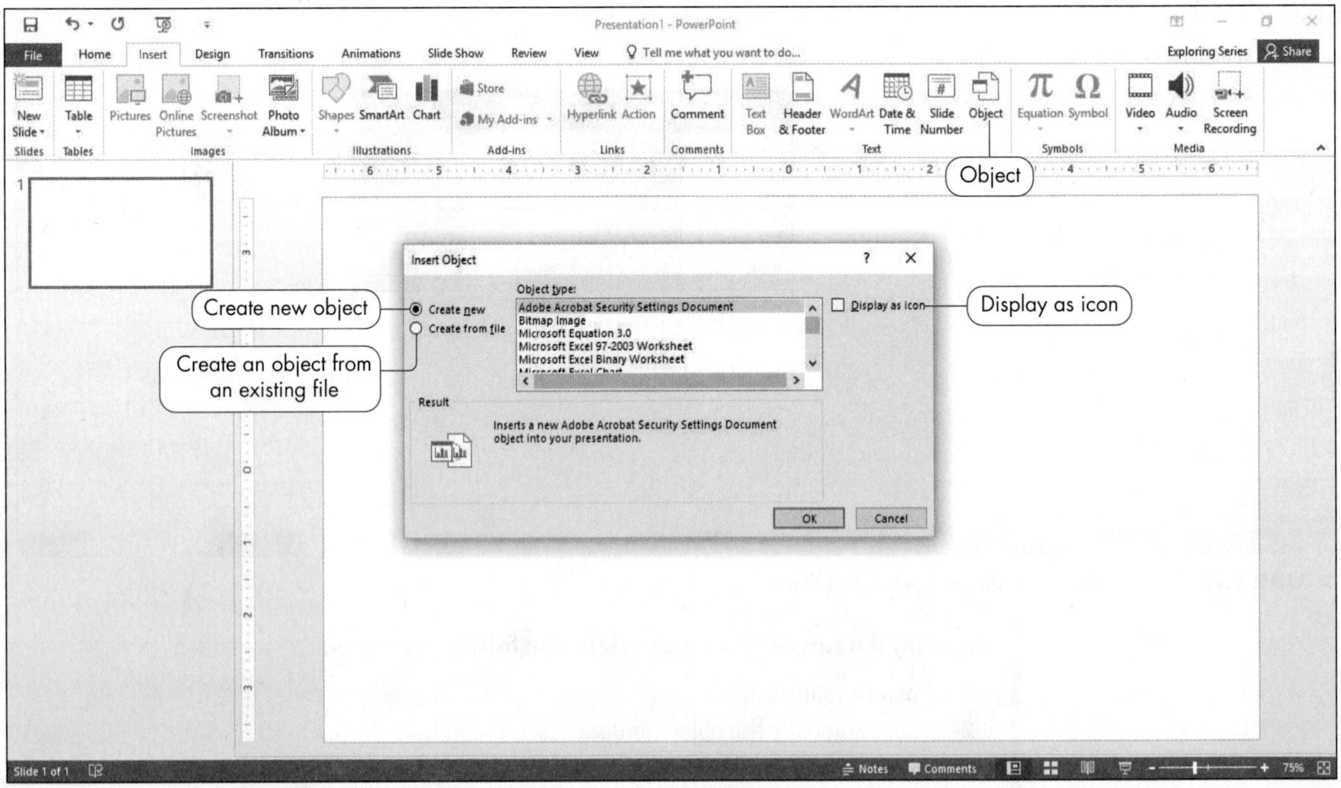

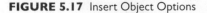

FIGURE 5.17 Insert Object Options

Quick Concepts

4. Why would it be considered a best practice to format a table? ***p. 344***
5. What is the difference between an embedded object and a linked object? ***p. 349***
6. Why would you use an embedded object instead of a linked object in a slide? ***p. 349***

Hands-On Exercises

 Watch the Video for this Hands-On Exercise!

2 Table Design

You continue revising the county health fair antioxidants presentation to make the information in the tables easy to read and to enhance their appearance.

STEP 1 ❯❯ SET A BACKGROUND FILL

You enhance the table on Slide 7 by changing the table style to a clean, clear style. You add a column to the table, and format the cells in the column to include pictures of the food mentioned in the middle column. As a final step, you add a row to the table so that you can acknowledge a source. Refer to Figure 5.18 as you complete Step 1.

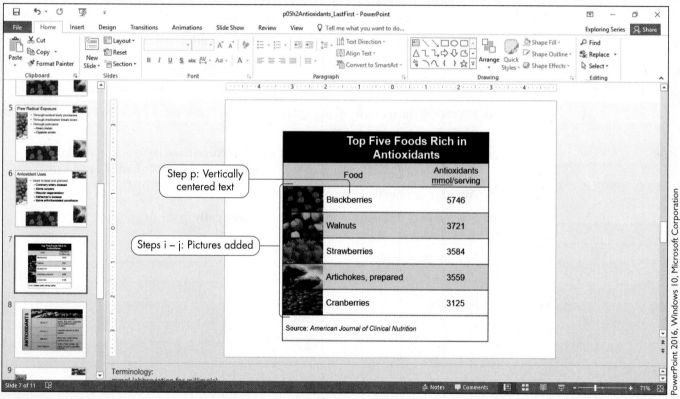

FIGURE 5.18 Formatted and Restructured Table

a. Open *p05h1Antioxidants_LastFirst* if you closed it at the end of the Hands-On Exercise 1, and save it as **p05h2Antioxidants_LastFirst**, changing h1 to h2.

b. Ensure Slide 7 is displayed and select the **table**. Click the **Table Tools Design tab**, click **More** in the Table Styles group, and then select **Medium Style 1 – Accent 4** (first row, fifth column, Medium category).

Medium Style 1 – Accent 4 includes a Header Row style and a Banded Rows style. The black font color can be easily read.

c. Click in any of the cells in the first column, click the **Table Tools Layout tab**, and then click **Insert Left** in the Rows & Columns group.

A new column is inserted to the left of the Food column.

d. Select all of the cells in the top row and click **Merge Cells** in the Merge group.

e. Click in the new left column, click in the **Width box** in the Cell Size group, type **1.2**, and then press **Enter** to apply the change. Change the width of the middle column to **3"** and the width of the right column to **2"**.

f. Select the last five rows of the table (exclude the title and column heading rows), click in the **Height box** in the Cell Size group, and then type **.75**.

g. Click in the cell to the left of *Blackberries* and right-click.

h. Click **Format Shape** to open the Format Shape pane, ensure that Fill & Line (image of bucket) is selected, and then click **Fill** to open the fill options. Click the **Picture or texture fill option**.

A texture appears in your cell.

i. Click **File** to open the Insert Picture dialog box, locate *p05h2Blackberries.jpg* in the p05h2MediaFolder, and then click **Insert** to close the Insert Picture dialog box. Close the Format Shape pane.

j. Repeat Steps h and i to insert *p05h2Walnuts.jpg* in the cell to the left of Walnuts, *p05h2Strawberries.jpg* in the cell to the left of Strawberries, *p05h2Artichokes.jpg* in the cell to the left of Artichokes, and *p05h2Cranberries.jpg* in the cell to the left of Cranberries. Close the Format Shape pane.

k. Position the pointer in the last cell of the table and press **Tab**.

A new row is created with the properties of the row above it.

l. Select the cells in the newly created last row and click **Merge Cells** in the Merge group.

m. Right-click the merged cell to display the Format Shape pane. Click **No Fill** in the Format Shape pane and click **Close**.

n. Type **Source: *American Journal of Clinical Nutrition***. Be sure to apply italic formatting to the text as shown. Select the text and change the font size to **14 pt**.

o. Align the table to the vertical center of the slide.

p. Select rows 3 through 8 and click **Center Vertically** in the Alignment group on the Table Tools Layout tab.

q. Save the presentation.

STEP 2 » INSERT COLUMNS AND ROWS

As you work with the design of the tables in your slide show, you often find that changing the structure of a table requires that you change the formatting of a table and vice versa. Each choice you make entails making further choices as you refine the presentation. In this exercise, you continue refining the tables in your antioxidants presentation. Refer to Figure 5.19 as you complete Step 2.

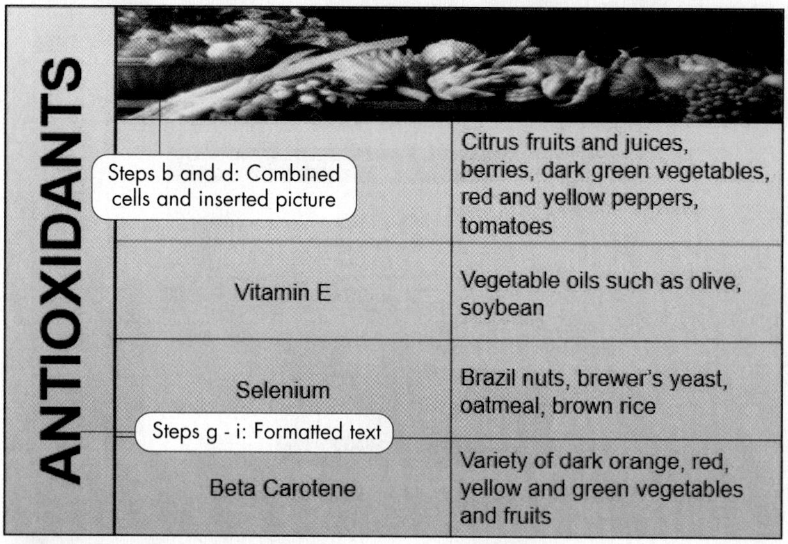

PowerPoint 2016, Windows 10, Microsoft Corporation

FIGURE 5.19 Changed Table Layout

a. Select the table on Slide 8. Click the **Table Tools Design tab**, click **More** in the Table Styles group, and then click **Themed Style 1 - Accent 4** (first row, fifth column, Best Match for Document category).

b. Click **Eraser** in the Draw Borders group and click the vertical border that splits row 1 into two cells. (Do not click the border that divides columns 2 and 3 for the remaining rows.) Press **Esc**.

The border disappears, and the cells merge into one.

c. Click in the top row. Click the **Shading arrow** in the Table Styles group and click **Picture**.

d. Click **Browse** in the Insert Pictures dialog box, locate and select *p05h2Fruits.jpg*, and then click **Insert**.

e. Click the **Layout tab**, change the row height to **1.2"**, and then press **Enter**.

f. Enter the remaining data, as shown in Figure 5.19, without worrying about the text size or position.

g. Click in **column 1**, click **Text Direction** in the Alignment group, and then click **Rotate all text 270°**.

h. Click **Center Vertically** in the Alignment group.

i. Select *Antioxidants* in column 1, change the font size to **44 pt**, and then click **Center** for the alignment. Click the **Table Tools Design tab**. Click **Effects** in the Table Styles group and click **Shadow** and **Offset Bottom** (under *Outer*).

j. Click the **First Column option** in the Table Style Options group.

Activating the First Column table style bolds the text in the first column and creates a bold black border between the first column and the remaining columns.

k. Ensure that the table is selected, click **Align Center**, and then click **Align Middle** to align the table on the slide.

l. Save the presentation.

You have an Excel file that contains data for the USDA Oxygen Radical Absorbance Capacity (ORAC) Scale that you want to include in the presentation. Rather than re-create this information, you insert a linked copy of the table in your presentation. Refer to Figure 5.20 as you complete Step 3.

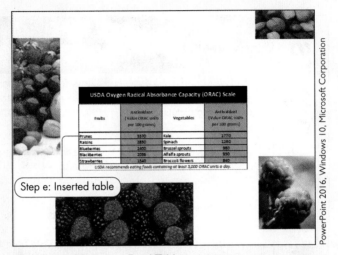

FIGURE 5.20 Linked Excel Table

a. Create a new slide after Slide 8 using the Blank layout.

b. Open *p05h2Orac.xlsx*.

c. Select the **range A1:D8** to select all the table data in the Excel file. Click **Copy** in the Clipboard group on the Home tab.

d. Click the **PowerPoint file** on the Windows taskbar to make the presentation the active file. Click the **Paste arrow** in the Clipboard group on the Home tab and click **Paste Special**.

e. Click the **Paste link option** in the Paste Special dialog box. Click **Microsoft Excel Worksheet Object** in the As box, and then click **OK**.

   A copy of the Excel table is inserted into your presentation. The copy is a shortcut link to the original data file so that changes to the source data file are reflected in your presentation.

f. Close the Excel file. Double-click the **table object** in the presentation.

   The source application, the Microsoft Excel file, opens for editing.

g. Select row 2 in Excel, click the **Font Color arrow**, and then select **Red** under Standard Colors.

   The column headings in the linked table change to reflect the editing you performed in Excel.

h. Observe the color change to the column headings in the presentation. Save the changes in the Excel file. Close Excel. You will not submit the Excel file.

i. Save the presentation. Keep the presentation open if you plan to continue with the next Hands-On Exercise. If not, close the presentation and exit PowerPoint.

Basic Charts

Statistical charts use points, lines, circles, bars, or other shapes to visually communicate numerical relationships, such as changes in time or comparisons. They help you communicate numerical relationships more effectively than using words to describe them. A chart can compare data and show trends or patterns. Summarizing information in a chart helps your audience understand and retain your message.

Whereas the term *chart* can refer to visual displays of information such as tables, maps, lists, SmartArt diagrams, and others, the term *graph* is specific to a chart that displays a relationship between two sets of numbers plotted as data points with coordinates on a grid. These two terms have become synonymous and are used interchangeably now. Microsoft Office applications use the term *chart* to describe the charts and graphs provided for your use, so this chapter will use the term *chart*.

In this section, you will identify chart types and elements. Then you will learn how to create and insert a chart in a slide.

Creating and Inserting Charts

STEP 1 PowerPoint includes tools to create professional-looking charts. You can even save your chart as a template so you can apply the same formatting to new charts of the same type. When you create a chart using PowerPoint, you enter the information in an Excel workbook. The Excel worksheet you use to create the chart is then embedded in your presentation.

Create a chart quickly by clicking the Insert Chart icon in a content placeholder or by clicking the Insert tab, and then clicking Chart in the Illustrations group. The Insert Chart dialog box opens with two panes. The left pane contains the chart types, and the right pane contains chart styles, or subtypes, and a preview of the selected chart type. Figure 5.21 displays the default chart type, a column chart, in the left pane and the default chart style, Clustered Column, in the right pane.

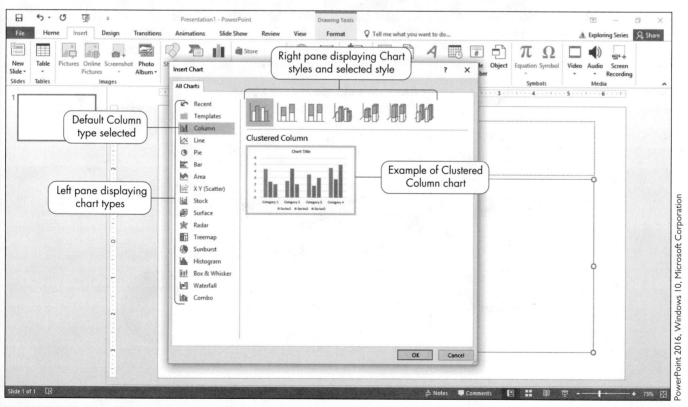

FIGURE 5.21 Basic Elements of a Column Chart

To create a chart, complete the following steps:

1. Click the Insert Chart icon in a content placeholder or click the Insert tab, and then click Chart in the Illustrations group.
2. Select the chart type in the left pane of the Insert Chart dialog box.
3. Select the chart style in the right pane.
4. Click OK.
5. Enter the desired chart data in Excel.
6. Close Excel.

Understand Basic Chart Types

Before beginning to create a chart, think about the information you are presenting and determine what message you want to convey using a chart. Are you representing changes over time? Are you comparing or summarizing data? Are you representing a single series or multiple series? What type of chart will your audience understand quickly?

Each of the basic chart types has appropriate uses. Choose the type that portrays your message most effectively. The chart should be clear and easy to read and should present enough detail to provide the audience with an understanding of your message without overwhelming people with detail. Generally, audiences can easily understand the commonly used charts, such as pie, line, column, and bar charts.

Excel includes a wide variety of charts: column charts, line charts, pie and dough-nut charts, bar charts, area charts, XY (scatter) and bubble charts, stock charts, sur-face charts, radar charts, treemap charts, sunburst charts, histogram charts, and box and whisker charts. The most common purposes of some of these charts are listed in Table 5.3. For greater detail on the available chart types, including chart subtype infor-mation, enter chart types in the *Tell me what you want to do* box for PowerPoint Help and click the hyperlink for *Get Help on "chart types."*

TABLE 5.3	Chart Purposes	
Type	**Purpose**	**Sample Chart**
Column chart	Use to show data changes over a period of time or comparisons among items.	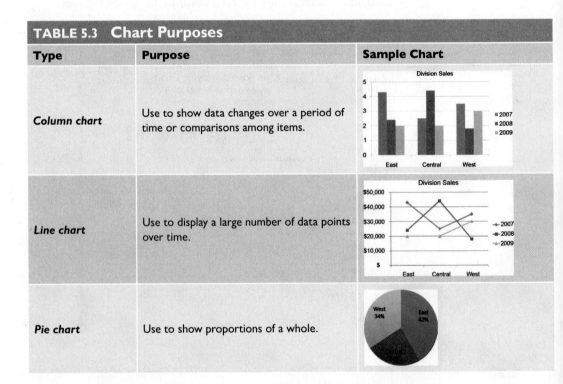
Line chart	Use to display a large number of data points over time.	
Pie chart	Use to show proportions of a whole.	

TABLE 5.3 Chart Purposes (Continued)

Type	Purpose	Sample Chart
Doughnut chart	Use to show the relationship of parts to a whole; like a pie chart but can contain more than one data series.	
Bar chart	Use to show comparisons between items.	
Area chart	Use to emphasize the magnitude of change over time.	
XY (scatter) chart	Use to show the relationships among the numeric values in several data series, or plot two groups of numbers as one series of XY coordinates.	
Bubble chart	Use to show relationships like an XY(scatter) chart but with three values instead of two.	
Stock chart	Use to show fluctuations or the range of change between the high and low values of a subject over time.	
Surface chart	Use to plot a surface using two sets of data.	

Pearson Education, Inc.

Identifying and Modifying Chart Elements

 When you enter the data for your table in an Excel workbook, the cells that contain numeric values are called data points. A ***data series*** contains the data points representing a set of related numbers. The data series can be a ***single-series chart*** (representing only one set of data) or a ***multi-series chart*** (representing two or more sets of data). For example, you would plot the profits for one store in Destin, Florida on a single-series chart, and the profits for several stores in Destin, Fort Walton Beach, and Pensacola, Florida on a multi-series chart.

A pie chart is an example of a single-series chart. With the whole represented as a circle, a pie chart shows the proportional relationship of each segment to the whole. A fill may be applied to each segment, or slice, or applied to the entire pie. A **label** identifies data in a chart—for example, in a pie chart, the label identifies the slices in the pie. The slices can be labeled with the series name, category name, value, or percentage. The labels can be centered, positioned inside a slice, positioned outside of the slice, or positioned according to the Best Fit option, which is based on the amount of text inside the label. **Leaders** are lines used to connect the label to the slice of pie. Though it is preferable to have the labels within a pie slice, often they do not fit. In that case, leaders become necessary to avoid possible confusion. **Exploded pie charts** emphasize data by separating, or exploding, a slice or slices from the pie.

Figure 5.22 shows a pie chart with a single data series representing the categories in a spending plan. The chart includes a title and labels indicating the category names and the percentage each slice of the pie contributes to the total. The Savings slice is exploded for emphasis. The **chart area** (the chart and all of its elements) is bounded by the placeholder borders, whereas the **plot area** (the area representing the data) is defined by a bounding box comprised of single lines. The icons next to the chart are used to finalize the chart. Use the **Chart Elements** icon to show, hide, or format the chart title, data labels, or legend. Use the **Chart Styles** icon to change the style or color of the chart. Use the **Chart Filters** icon to show or hide data in the chart.

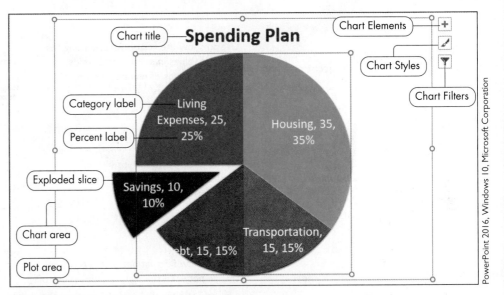

FIGURE 5.22 Basic Elements of a Pie Chart

Other chart types available in Office are plotted on a coordinate system and may be single-series or multi-series charts. The chart is created by plotting data points between two reference lines, or scales, called axes. The **X-axis** is the horizontal axis and usually contains the category information, such as products, companies, or intervals of time. The **Y-axis** is the vertical axis and usually contains the values or amounts. Three-dimensional charts have a third axis, the **Z-axis**, used to plot the depth of a chart. Axes can be given titles to describe what the data represent. Note that some chart types, such as pie charts, do not have axes.

Gridlines, lines that extend from the horizontal or vertical axes, can be displayed to make the chart data easier to read and understand. Tick marks are short lines on the axes that mark the category and value divisions. Data points plotted on the chart may be indicated by data markers, or graphical representations such as bars, dots, or slices that can be enhanced with lines, filled areas, or pictures. To help identify the data series, a *legend* assigns a format or color to each data series and displays that information with the data series name. Legends are only necessary for multi-series charts. Figure 5.23 shows the basic elements of a column chart.

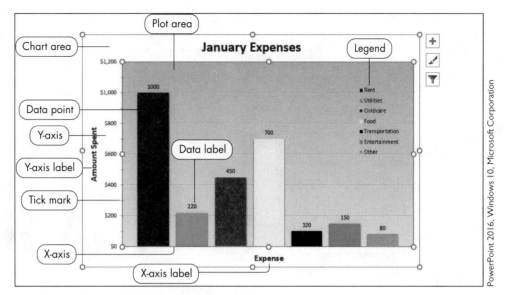

FIGURE 5.23 Basic Elements of a Column Chart

Modifying a Chart within Excel

After selecting the chart type and style, Microsoft Excel opens with a worksheet containing sample data with the title of the Excel workbook as *Chart in Microsoft PowerPoint*. The PowerPoint presentation contains a chart based on the sample data. Replace the sample data in the Excel worksheet with your own data, and the PowerPoint chart updates to reflect the updated information.

The Excel worksheet contains a grid of rows and columns. When you type in a cell, you replace the sample data, and your data point is created in your chart. When you enter the data, you might need to change the row heights or column widths to fit the data. If pound signs display (#####) in a cell, there is not enough room in the cell to display the data. To increase the width of the column, position the pointer on the line to the right of the column heading, and double-click to adjust the column width automatically. To resize the chart data range, drag the bottom-right corner of the range. When you finish entering the data, click Close in Excel and view the chart embedded in PowerPoint.

> **TIP: DELETE THE SAMPLE CHART DATA**
> To quickly delete the sample data in a chart, click Select All (the intersection between the column designations and the row designations), which is located in the top left of the worksheet. This selects all of the cells in the worksheet. Once they are selected, press Delete on the keyboard.

If you close Excel and then need to edit the data the chart is based upon, click the chart, click the Chart Tools Design tab, and then click Edit Data in the Data group. The Excel worksheet reopens so you can edit your data. When you are done editing, click Close on the Excel worksheet to return to PowerPoint. Figure 5.24 shows the sample Excel worksheet, and the associated sample chart created in PowerPoint.

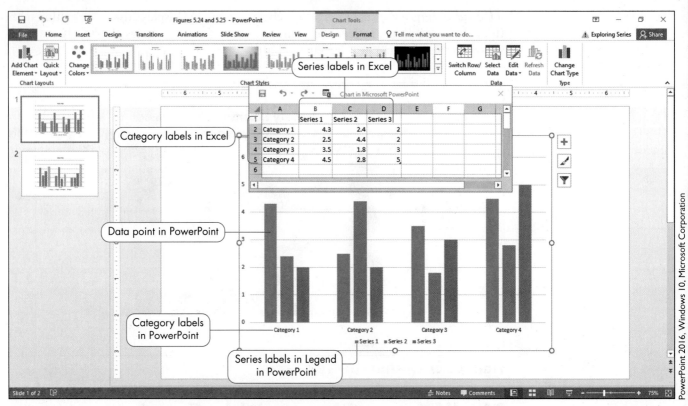

FIGURE 5.24 Excel Worksheet and Associated Chart in PowerPoint

Switch Row and Column Data

STEP 3 ⟩⟩ By default, a chart is plotted based on the series data displayed in the columns of the worksheet and the column headings displayed in the legend. You can switch the emphasis if you want to emphasize the changes by category. Figure 5.25 shows the same data as in Figure 5.24, but the rows and columns have been switched.

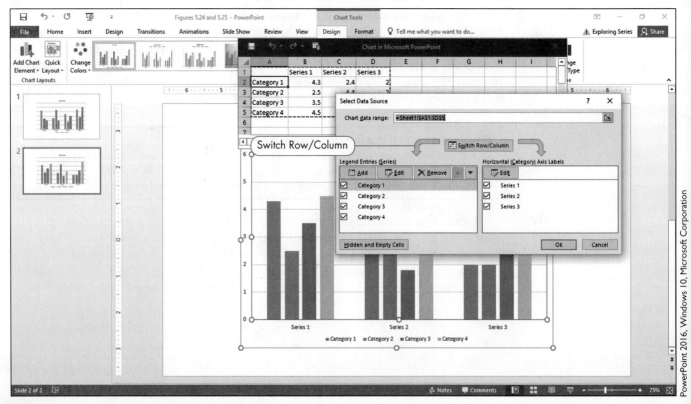

FIGURE 5.25 Chart Emphasizing Changes by Series

To switch rows and columns, complete the following steps:

1. Select the existing chart.
2. Click Select Data or Edit Data in the Data group on the Chart Tools Design tab.
3. Click Switch Row/Column in the Data group.

The chart shown in Figure 5.25 is at its most basic level. Charts should be modified and formatted to ensure that the chart conveys the intended message. For example, without a descriptive title or labels, it is impossible to tell the purpose of the chart or what the amounts represent.

Quick Concepts

7. Charts and graphs are used to communicate what type of data? *p. 355*

8. List the type of data relationships represented by a column chart. *p. 356*

9. A pie chart is used to represent what type of data? *p. 356*

Hands-On Exercises

Watch the Video for this Hands-On Exercise!

MyITLab®
HOE 3 Training

Skills covered: Understand Basic Chart Types • Format Chart Elements • Switch Row and Column Data

3 Basic Charts

Although antioxidants are available in common foods, some fruits are referred to as superfruits because of the high level of antioxidants per serving. You want to show the audience at the county health fair a comparison of the antioxidant levels in a top "common" food and some of the superfruits. You create a chart to illustrate this comparison and also create a chart to show the ideal percentage of each food group in an average diet.

STEP 1 »» CREATE AND INSERT CHARTS

You create a clustered column chart to compare the antioxidant levels in fruits. While proofreading the chart, you notice an incorrect amount and a missing fruit, so you edit the chart. Refer to Figure 5.26 as you complete Step 1.

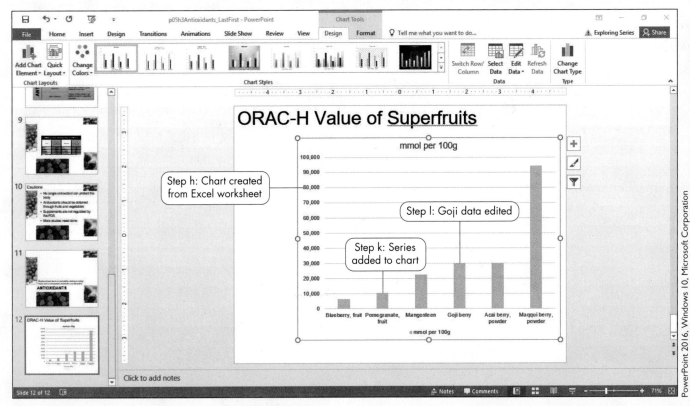

FIGURE 5.26 PowerPoint Chart Based on an Excel Worksheet

a. Open *p05h2Antioxidants_LastFirst* if you closed it at the end of the Hands-On Exercise 2, and save it as **p05h3Antioxidants_LastFirst**, changing h2 to h3.

b. Insert a new slide after Slide 11 using the **Title and Content** layout.

c. Type **ORAC-H Value of Superfruits** on the new Slide 12 in the title placeholder. Click outside the title placeholder.

d. Click the **Design tab**, click **Format Background** in the Customize group, and then click the **Hide background graphics option** in the Format Background pane. Close the Format Background pane.

e. Click the **Insert Chart icon** on the slide. Note the default setting of Column chart, Clustered Column subtype, in the Insert Chart dialog box. Click **OK**.

Excel opens with sample data.

f. Replace the worksheet data with the following data:

	mmol per 100g
Blueberry, fruit	6,500
Mangosteen	22,500
Goji berry	10,000
Acai berry, powder	30,000
Maqui berry, powder	94,500

g. Drag the bottom-right corner of the chart data range to resize the range to fit the data you just entered and exclude any remaining sample data.

Series 2 and Series 3 of the sample data are not needed, and the data do not display on the PowerPoint chart once you resize the range to fit the data. If you want to clean up the source data file, the unwanted sample Series 2 and Series 3 data can be deleted.

h. Close the Excel worksheet and return to PowerPoint.

i. Click the **Chart Tools Design tab**, and click the **Edit Data arrow** in the Data group. Click **Edit Data in Excel**. Maximize the Excel window.

Excel opens, displaying the chart data again.

j. Click the **row 3 indicator** (Mangosteen row) to select it, right-click, and then click **Insert**.

A new row 3 is inserted above the original row 3.

k. Type **Pomegranate, fruit** above Mangosteen in the empty **cell A3**, press **Tab**, and then type **10,500** in **cell B3**.

l. Click in **cell B5**, type **30,000**, and then press **Enter**.

m. Close the Excel worksheet and return to PowerPoint.

n. Save the presentation.

Because antioxidants are available from so many different food sources, you decide that, as part of the summary, you will discuss the ideal percentage of each food group in an average diet. As you discuss each food group, you will suggest foods in that group that contain antioxidants. You create a basic pie chart displaying the food groups as an aid for this discussion. You use chart elements to make the chart easier to read. Refer to Figure 5.27 as you complete Step 3.

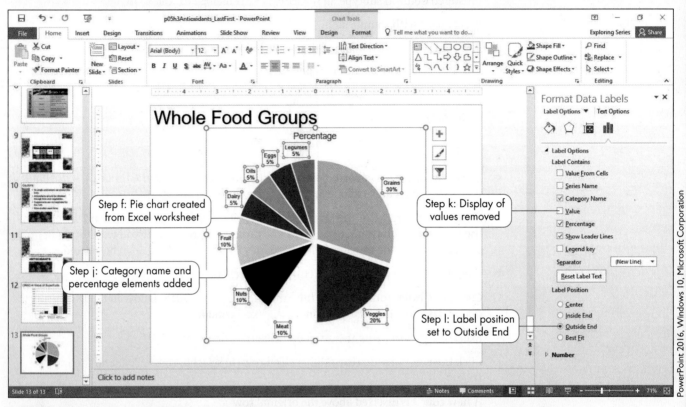

FIGURE 5.27 Pie Chart with Labels

a. Create a new slide after Slide 12 using the **Title Only layout**.

b. Type **Whole Food Groups** in the title placeholder. Click outside of the title placeholder.

c. Click the **Design tab**, click **Format Background** in the Customize group, and then click the **Hide background graphics** option in the Format Background pane. Close the Format Background pane.

d. Click the **Insert tab** and click **Chart** in the Illustrations group.

   The Insert Chart dialog box opens.

e. Click **Pie** in the left pane and click **OK**.

   The default pie chart type is automatically selected, and Excel opens with sample pie chart data.

f. Enter the following data for your pie chart in Excel.

	Percentage
Grains	30
Veggies	20
Meat	10
Nuts	10
Fruit	10
Dairy	5
Oils	5
Eggs	5
Legumes	5

Because a pie chart is a single-series chart, only one data series (Percentage) is entered.

g. Ensure that the chart data range fits the data you just entered by dragging the bottom-right corner of the chart to resize the range if it does not fit.

TROUBLESHOOTING: If you close Excel before resizing the range, not all the categories will display. Click Edit Data in the Data group on the Chart Tools Design tab to reopen Excel and resize the range to fit all categories.

---

h. Close the Excel worksheet.

A basic pie chart is displayed in PowerPoint. The chart needs to be modified because duplicate colors exist, and the white slice disappears into the background. You will make these modifications in Hands-On Exercise 4.

i. Click **Chart Elements** to the right of the chart, click the **Data Labels arrow**, and then click **More Options**.

j. Click **Category Name** and **Percentage** in Label Options in the Format Data Labels pane.

k. Uncheck **Value** in Label Options.

l. Click **Outside End** in Label Position and close the Format Data Labels pane.

m. Click the **Format tab**, and click the **Size and Position dialog box launcher** in the Size group.

n. Click the **chart area** to select it and deselect the labels, click **Lock aspect ratio** in the Size options, and then change the Scale Height to **140%**.

o. Align the chart to the center and middle of the slide.

p. Select the Legend at the bottom of the pie chart and press **Delete**.

The chart resizes when the legend is removed. The legend is not necessary because you included data labels.

After reviewing the presentation, you decide that the chart on Slide 12 needs revising. You want the list of superfruits in the legend. You will swap the data from a single-series chart to a multi-series chart. Refer to Figure 5.28 as you complete Step 3.

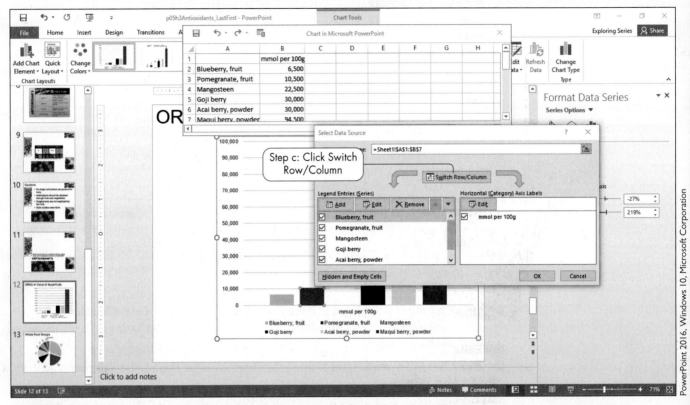

FIGURE 5.28 Switch Row/Column Dialog Box

a. Select the chart on Slide 12.

b. Click **Select Data** in the Data group on the Chart Tools Design tab.

   The Select Data Source dialog box opens, as does Excel. The Legend Entries (Series) pane shows the *mmol per 100g* series entry, and the Horizontal (Category) Axis Labels display the food category.

c. Click **Switch Row/Column**.

   The Legend Entries (Series) pane now displays the food categories, and the Horizontal (Category) Axis Labels pane now displays the *mmol per 100g* entry (see Figure 5.28).

d. Click **OK** and close the Excel worksheet.

   The data points (bars) show that *Maqui berry, powder* exceeds the other superfruit ORAC-H values. Two of the bars display the same color, and one marker is white which makes it difficult to see. Modifications are necessary. You will correct this problem in Hands-On Exercise 4.

e. Save the presentation. Keep the presentation open if you plan to continue with the next Hands-On Exercise. If not, close the presentation and exit PowerPoint.

Chart Refinement

Charts should be refined to ensure that the message is conveyed quickly and accurately. Adding a chart title or subtitle, axis titles, data labels, or a legend can help clarify the message, but you must balance the need for clarity with the need for simplicity. This can be a challenge, so ask a classmate or coworker to review your chart and explain their understanding of what your message is.

In this section, you will learn how to refine a chart by changing the chart type to better showcase the information, change a chart layout, and format chart elements.

Changing a Chart Type

STEP 1 ⟫ After creating the chart, you can experiment with other chart types to see which chart type conveys the message most effectively. For example, you may find that due to the number of bars created by the data, your column chart is cluttered and difficult to read. Changing the chart type to a line chart may show the same information in a clean, easy-to-understand format. If you wanted to convey the increase in the cost of fuel by monthly average for the past two years, you would have 24 bars in a bar chart. However, if you changed the bar chart to a line chart, your data points would be markers connected by line segments which would clearly show the peaks when the fuel price increased and valleys when it decreased.

Change a Chart Type

Each of the chart types available includes subtypes or variations. The variations include changing from 2-D formatting to 3-D formatting, stacking the data, changing the marker shape, and exploding slices, to name a few. Changing the subtype can give the chart a totally different look or can change the purpose of the chart dramatically and may be enough to emphasize the desired point.

> **To change the chart type or subtype, complete the following steps:**
>
> 1. Select the chart.
> 2. Click the Chart Tools Design tab.
> 3. Click Change Chart Type in the Type group.
> 4. Click the chart type you want from the left pane or the chart subtype from the top of the right pane.
> 5. Click OK.

Change a Chart Layout

STEP 2 ⟫ Each chart type has predefined layouts that you can quickly apply to your chart. These layouts reposition various chart elements. For example, the legend may be displayed at the top of the chart in one layout, at the bottom of the chart in another layout, or not at all in a third layout. Although you can change each element of the layout individually by manually selecting a style for the individual elements, using a predefined layout keeps your charts consistent and maintains a professional feel to your presentation.

To change a chart layout, complete the following steps:

1. Select the chart.
2. Click the Chart Tools Design tab.
3. Select one of the following:

   - Click Quick Layout in the Chart Layouts group and select the desired chart layout
   - Click Add Chart Element in the Chart Layouts group and select the desired chart element

PowerPoint determines the measurement or increments on the chart's Y-axis automatically based on the data entered in the worksheet. However, you can change the measurement used—but be careful when changing the measurements of the axes. Changing the Y-axis measurement to a smaller increment can exaggerate the data peaks and valleys displayed in the chart. Changing the measurements to larger increments can flatten or smooth out the data peaks and valleys. Figure 5.29 shows the ORAC-H Value of Superfruits as a line chart using the default Y-axis measurements. Figure 5.30 shows the same chart with the measurements changed to a minimum of 500 and a maximum of 500,000, which flattens the data peaks and distorts the information unless the chart is examined carefully.

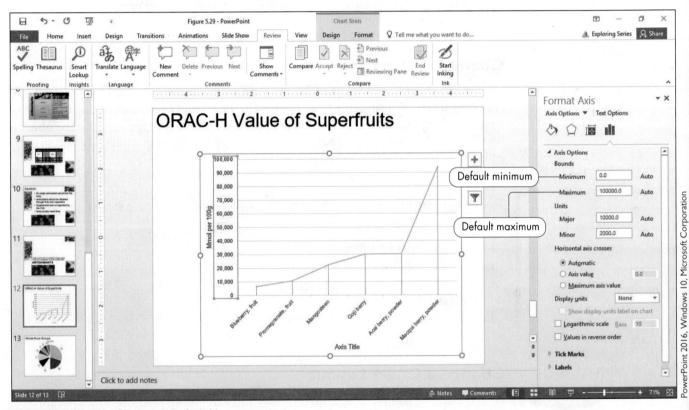

FIGURE 5.29 Line Chart with Default Measurements

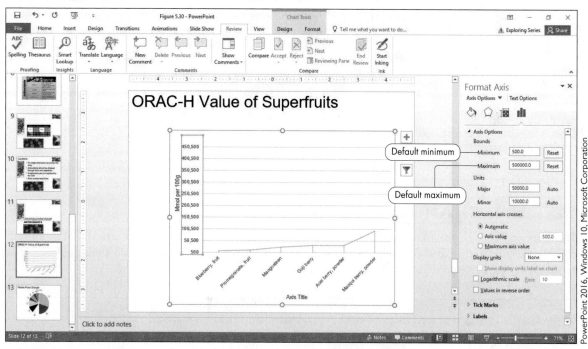

FIGURE 5.30 Line Chart with Manually Changed Measurements

Additionally, when the measurements use Excel's Auto feature, they automatically adjust if you make changes to the data to which the maximum and minimum values need to adapt. By contrast, manual measurements do not adapt unless manual readjustments are applied; thus, changes to the Excel data may also require additional changes to the axis measurements for the chart.

To change the chart axis, complete the following steps:

1. Select the chart, and click the Chart Tools Design tab.
2. Click Add Chart Element in the Chart Layouts group.
3. Click Axes.
4. Click Primary Horizontal, Primary Vertical, or More Axis Options.
5. Select the desired axis options.

Modify Chart Elements

STEP 3 ▶▶ You can change chart elements by changing shape fills, outline styles, and shape effects on the chart objects just as you changed shapes in SmartArt. This can add strong visual appeal to a chart. For example, if you created a bar chart showing the selling price of paintings you could replace the bars with a paintbrush shape.

To make formatting changes to an element, complete the following steps:

1. Click the element you want to change to select it, or click the element from the list available when you click the Chart Elements arrow in the Current Selection group on the Format tab.
2. Click Format Selection in the Current Selection group.
3. Make the changes desired in the Format pane.

Quick Concepts

10. How can you ensure that a chart conveys your message quickly and accurately? *p. 367*

11. Why would you want to use a predefined layout for your chart? *p. 367*

12. Name three components of a chart's layout. *p. 367*

Hands-On Exercises

Skills covered: Change a Chart Type • Change a Chart Layout • Modify Chart Elements

4 Chart Refinement

In your final review of the county health fair presentation, you modify the charts you have created by changing a chart type for ease of reading and correcting problems with chart layouts and elements.

STEP 1 ›› CHANGE A CHART TYPE

The chart on Slide 12 contains data about the amount of antioxidants per 100 grams of each type of superfruit. You decide to convert the chart into a bar chart so that the viewer can read down a list to quickly identify the superfruit providing the most antioxidants. Refer to Figure 5.31 as you complete Step 1.

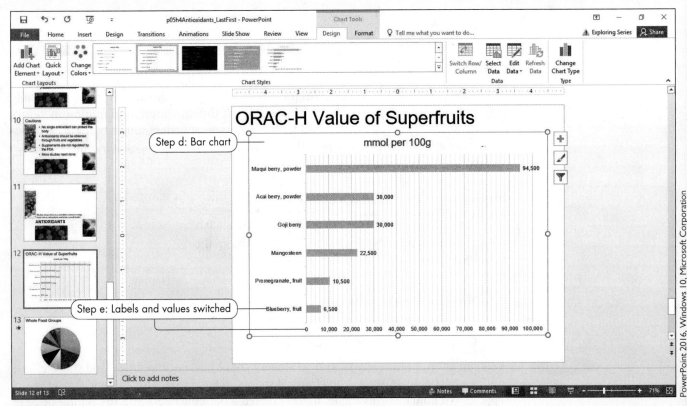

FIGURE 5.31 Column Chart Changed to Bar Chart

a. Open *p05h3Antioxidants_LastFirst* if you closed it at the end of the Hands-On Exercise 3, and save it as **p05h4Antioxidants_LastFirst**, changing h3 to h4.

b. Select the chart on Slide 12.

c. Click the **Chart Tools Design tab** and click **Change Chart Type** in the Type group.

d. Select **Bar** as the chart type and accept the default subtype, Clustered Bar. Click **OK**.

The column chart type changes to the bar chart type.

e. Click **Select Data** in the Data group, click **Switch Row/Column**, click **OK**, and then close Excel.

The superfruits are listed down the vertical axis, and the values are displayed along the horizontal axis.

TROUBLESHOOTING: If you do not see the superfruits listed down the vertical axis, click Add Chart Element in the Chart Layouts group on the Chart Tools Design tab. Click Axes and click Primary Vertical.

f. Save the presentation.

STEP 2 ›› CHANGE A CHART LAYOUT

You decide that including data labels would help the county health fair viewers understand the data. You change the layout of the bar chart so that the labels are easily added and also decide to change the fill of the bars by applying a style to make them more visible when projected. Refer to Figure 5.32 as you complete Step 2.

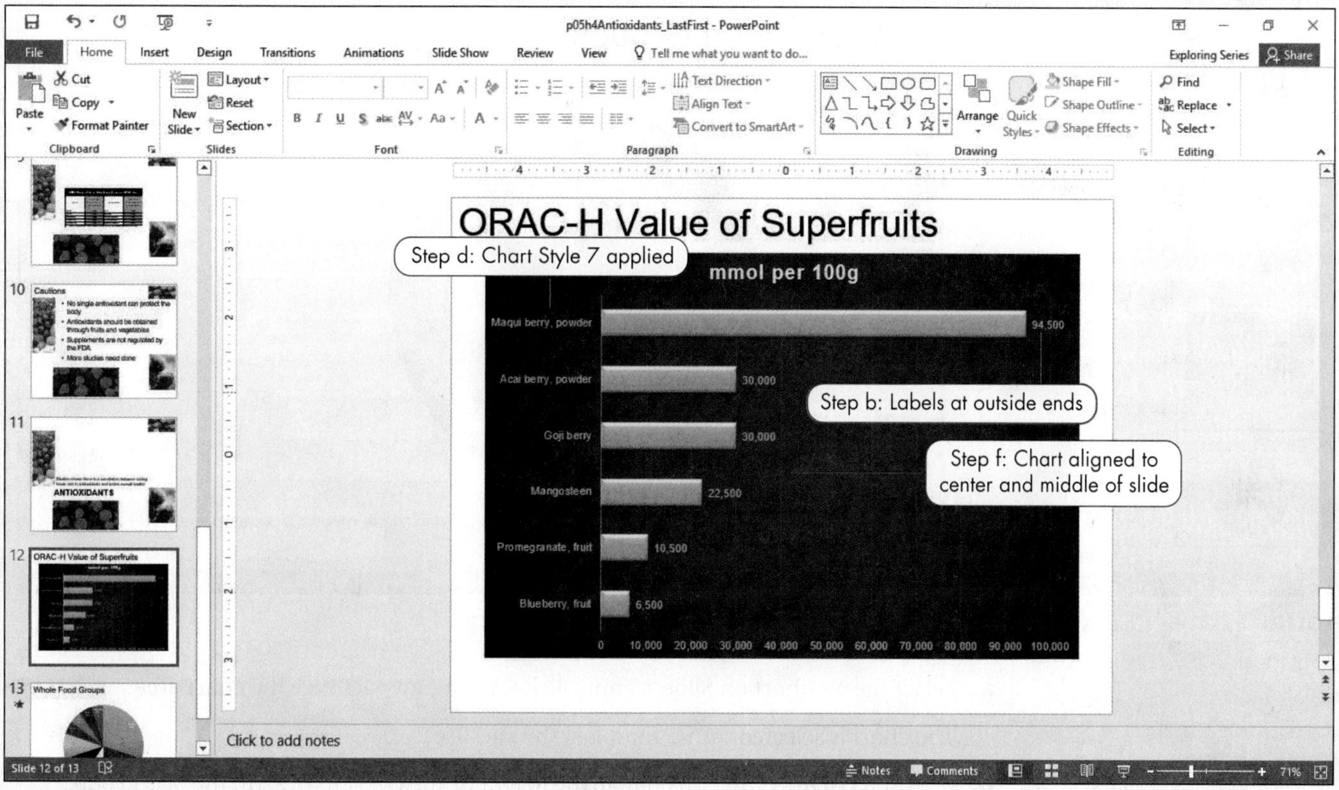

FIGURE 5.32 Modified Bar Chart

a. Ensure that the chart on Slide 12 is selected.

b. Click the **Chart Tools Design tab**, click **Quick Layout** in the Chart Layouts group, and then click **Layout 2**.

Layout 2 puts data labels at the outside ends of the bars and removes the horizontal axis. Layout 2 also moves the legend underneath the chart title. The legend is unnecessary and will be addressed in the next instruction.

c. Click **Add Chart Element** in the Chart Layouts group, point to **Legend**, and then select **None**.

The legend is deleted.

d. Ensure that **Style 7** is selected and click **More** in the Chart Styles group on the Chart Tools Design tab.

A dark background is applied to make the chart more readable and to add contrast.

e. Click the border of the chart to select it, click the **Format tab**, and then change the width of the chart to **9"** in the Size group.

f. Align the chart to the center and the middle of the slide.

g. Save the presentation.

After reviewing the pie chart on Slide 13, you decide several elements of the chart need to be formatted. The white slice blends with the background, so the color style of the chart needs to be changed. You also want the category name and percentage on the inside end of each pie slice. Finally, because you want to discuss each food group with the county health fair attendees, you apply an animation to bring the slices in one at a time. Refer to Figure 5.33 as you complete Step 3.

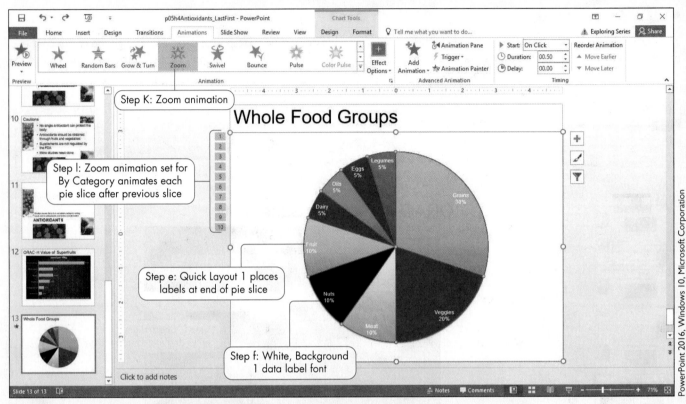

FIGURE 5.33 Pie Chart with Formatted Data Labels

a. Select the pie chart on Slide 13 and click the border to activate the chart area.

The chart is selected rather than just the pie slices.

b. Click the **Format tab** and change the height of the chart to **6.7"** in the Size group.

The change in the chart height moves part of the chart off the slide.

c. Click **Align** in the Arrange group and click **Align Bottom**. Click **Align** again and click **Align Center**.

The bottom chart border aligns with the bottom of the slide.

d. Click any slice of the pie and click **Quick Layout** in the Chart Layouts group on the Chart Tools Design tab.

Clicking a slice of the pie once selects all slices of the pie.

> **TROUBLESHOOTING:** If you double-click a pie slice, the Format Data Point pane opens. Click Close and the pie slice is selected.

e. Click **Layout 1** (first row, first column) in the Quick Layout group.

The category name and the percentage now appear at the end of each pie slice. Because of the color scheme, some labels are not visible.

f. Click the **Design tab**, and click **Style 5** (first row, fifth column) in the Chart Styles group. Click any pie slice label once to select all the data labels. Click the **Format tab**, click the **Text Fill arrow** in the WordArt Styles group, and then click **White, Background 1** under Theme Colors.

The text is changed to a theme style that coordinates with the presentation. The previous black text color was difficult to see on some of the slices, but the white color makes it easier to read the text on all the slices.

g. Select the legend on the bottom of the pie chart and press **Delete**.

The legend is unnecessary when data labels are used.

h. Select the title *Percentage* at the top of the chart and press **Delete**.

The title is unnecessary because the percent symbol appears next to the percentage displayed on each pie slice.

i. Click the **Animations tab**, click **More** in the Animation group, and then click **Zoom** (Entrance category).

j. Click **Effect Options** in the Animation group.

The Effect Options gallery opens.

k. Click **Slide Center** in the Vanishing Point category.

l. Click **Effect Options** again and click **By Category** in the Sequence category.

m. Click **Preview** in the Preview group.

Each pie slice now individually zooms out from the center of the pie when the slide show plays.

n. Save and close the file. Based on your instructor's directions, submit:

p05h1Poster_LastFirst

p05h4Antioxidants_LastFirst

Chapter Objectives Review

After reading this chapter, you have accomplished the following objectives:

1. Create a poster or a banner

- Charts convey relationships among words, numbers, or graphics. Posters and banners are specialized charts.
- Customize slide size: Use the Custom Slide dialog box to create a custom size slide such as a 17" x 22" slide used for a poster.

2. Draw a table

- Tables organize information, making it possible to more easily see relationships among words, numbers, or graphics.
- Tables can be inserted by specifying the number of columns and rows needed or by drawing the table.
- When you have multiple cell heights and widths in a complex table, use the flexible and efficient Draw Table feature to create the table.

3. Create a table structure

- Simplify table data: Make the table data as simple as possible to convey your message.
- Change row height, column width, and table size: Change the size of a cell or the table to accommodate your information or call attention to it.
- Align text within cells, rows, and columns: Aligning text enhances the readability of the data.

4. Format table components

- Set a background fill: Use the background fill options to add interest to a table.
- Change table borders: Change border style, weight, and color to separate and organize table information.
- Apply a table special effect: Add special effects to a cell, selected cells, or a table for interest.

5. Change table layout

- Insert columns and rows: You can insert rows above or below an existing row, or insert columns to the left or right of an existing column to accommodate additional information.
- Delete columns and rows: You can delete rows or columns to change the overall layout of a table.

6. Share information between applications

- Link and embed objects: Tables created in Word or Excel can be embedded in or linked to a PowerPoint presentation.

- Embedding creates a larger file than linking because linking simply places a copy of the table into the presentation and all editing takes place in the source application.
- Other objects, such as charts, can also be linked to or embedded in a presentation.

7. Create and insert charts

- Understand basic chart types: Choose the type of chart that best portrays your message.

8. Identify and modify chart elements

- The chart area is made up of the chart and all its elements. The plot area contains the data. The data series contains the data points representing a set of related numbers.

9. Modify a chart within Excel

- PowerPoint charts are based on Excel worksheets. Information is entered into a worksheet and plotted to create the PowerPoint presentation.
- Switch row and column data: Switch row and column data to change emphasis.

10. Change a chart type

- Change a chart type: Each chart type organizes and emphasizes data differently. Select the chart type that conveys the intended message of the chart.
- Change a chart layout: Use a predefined layout to keep your charts consistent and maintain a professional feel for your presentation. You can also edit the layout manually by choosing from chart title and axis title options, legend options, data label options, data table options, and axes and gridline options and by changing backgrounds in chart elements.
- Modify chart elements: The shape style (fill, outline, and effects) can be changed for individual chart elements. You can also use the Format Selection option to affect a current selection, which enables you to choose from fill, border color, border styles, shadow, and 3-D format options.

Key Terms Matching

Match the key terms with their definitions. Write the key term letter by the appropriate numbered definition.

a. Bar chart
b. Chart area
c. Column chart
d. Data series
e. Destination file
f. Embedded object
g. Gridline
h. Label
i. Legend
j. Line chart

k. Linked object
l. Multi-series data chart
m. Object linking and embedding (OLE)
n. Pie chart
o. Single-series chart
p. Source file
q. X-axis
r. Y-axis

1. _____ The file that contains an inserted object, such as a PowerPoint presentation with an Excel worksheet embedded in it. **p. 348**

2. _____ A part of the destination file that is updated when the source file is updated because the information is stored in the source file but displayed as the object in the destination file. **p. 349**

3. _____ A chart displaying two or more sets of data. **p. 357**

4. _____ A part of the destination file that, once inserted, no longer maintains a connection to the source file or source application in which the object was created. **p. 349**

5. _____ The horizontal axis, which usually contains the category information, such as products, companies, or intervals of time. **p. 358**

6. _____ A type of chart used to show comparisons among items, where the information is displayed horizontally. **p. 357**

7. _____ A line that extends from the horizontal or vertical axes and that can be displayed to make the chart data easier to read and understand. **p. 358**

8. _____ A type of chart used to show proportions of a whole. **p. 358**

9. _____ A feature that enables you to insert an object created in one application into a document created in another application. **p. 348**

10. _____ A type of chart used to show changes over time or comparisons among items where the information is displayed vertically. **p. 356**

11. _____ A chart displaying only one set of data. **p. 357**

12. _____ A chart element found in multi-series charts that helps identify the data series, assigns a format or color to each data series, and then displays that information with the data series name. **p. 359**

13. _____ The vertical axis, which usually contains the values or amounts. **p. 358**

14. _____ The file that contains the original table or data that is used or copied to create a linked or embedded object, such as a Word document or an Excel worksheet. **p. 348**

15. _____ A chart element that identifies data in the chart. **p. 358**

16. _____ The chart and all of its elements, bounded by the placeholder borders. **p. 358**

17. _____ A type of chart used to display a large number of data points over time. **p. 356**

18. _____ A chart element that contains the data points representing a set of related numbers. **p. 357**

Multiple Choice

1. Which of the following is used to arrange and organize information with text to illustrate relationships among words, numbers, and/or graphics?

   (a) Animation
   (b) Chart
   (c) SmartArt diagram
   (d) Image

2. Which of the following is *not* a part of table structure designed to maximize the understanding of data in the table?

   (a) Title
   (b) Subtitle
   (c) Column header
   (d) Background fill

3. What is the chart element that identifies data in the chart?

   (a) Label
   (b) Data series
   (c) Tick marks
   (d) Legend

4. A PowerPoint slide displaying a table object that is a copy or representation of a file stored in Excel that does *not* get updated displays what type of object?

   (a) Embedded object
   (b) Linked object
   (c) Included object
   (d) Outsourced object

5. Which of the following is a *true* statement regarding creating charts for display in a PowerPoint presentation?

   (a) Once you have entered data in a worksheet, you cannot reenter the worksheet to edit data.
   (b) You can paste a copy of an Excel chart into a PowerPoint slide by using the Paste Special command.
   (c) You can create a chart by clicking the SmartArt icon in the palette in a content placeholder.
   (d) When you create a chart in PowerPoint, you use an Access database to enter the data you wish to plot.

6. The purpose of a legend is to identify:

   (a) The type of information defined by the X-axis.
   (b) The type of information defined by the Y-axis.
   (c) What marker colors and patterns represent.
   (d) The type of chart.

7. To show the proportions of each pet type to total pet sales for a pet store, which type of chart should you use?

   (a) Column
   (b) Bar
   (c) Line
   (d) Pie

8. To show the growth of population in your city over the past 30 years, the best choice for your chart type would be:

   (a) Pie.
   (b) Bar.
   (c) Line.
   (d) Column.

9. To compare the sales of three brands of washing machines for the past two years, the best choice for your chart type would be:

   (a) Pie.
   (b) Column.
   (c) Radar.
   (d) Doughnut.

10. When using object linking and embedding, the file that contains an inserted object is the:

   (a) Table file.
   (b) Chart file.
   (c) Source file.
   (d) Destination file.

Practice Exercises

1 Coffee Club Poster

FROM SCRATCH

You are designing a poster to advertise the Saturday Morning Coffee Club at the 1st and Main Coffee House. The poster will be stapled to bulletin boards and placed in the store to remind customers of the event. The owner wants the poster to be simple but eye-catching, so you decide to create a poster that announces the ongoing event with general information. Once the poster is designed, you plan to take the file to a local print shop for reproduction, but before doing so you need a copy for the owner to review. You print a copy scaled to fit a standard 8.5" × 11" page. Refer to Figure 5.34 as you complete this exercise.

FIGURE 5.34 Scaled Advertising Poster

a. Begin a new presentation using the Retrospect theme and save it as **p05p1CoffeeClub_LastFirst**.

b. Create a handout header with your name and a handout footer with the file name, your instructor's name, and your class. Include the current date.

c. Click **Layout** in the Slides group on the Home tab and click **Picture with Caption**.

d. Click the **Design tab**, click **Slide Size** in the Customize group, and then select **Custom Slide Size** to open the Slide Size dialog box.

e. Select the existing number for Width and type **17**.

f. Select the existing number for Height and type **22**. Note that the *Slides sized for* option now displays Custom as its paper size and the Orientation is now set to Portrait for Slides and for Notes, Handouts & Outlines. Click **OK** and click **Maximize**.

g. Click the icon in the content placeholder to add a picture. Locate *p05p1CoffeeCup.jpg* and click **Insert**.

h. Click the **title placeholder** and type the following information. Press **Enter** after each line.
Saturday Morning Coffee Club at
1st and Main Coffee House

i. Click the **text placeholder** and type the following information. Press **Enter** after each line.
Join us each Saturday for Coffee and Tea specials.
Local artists, authors, or musicians will present their current works!
9 a.m. – 12 noon

j. Click the **File tab**, click **Print**, click the **Full Page Slides arrow**, and then click **Handouts, 1 Slide**.

k. Click the 1 Slide arrow and ensure that Scale to Fit Paper is selected. Click **Print**.

The poster prints on the size of paper loaded in the printer. Because desktop printers generally have a nonprintable region, the poster may have a white border surrounding it. Because you printed a handout instead of the full-page slide, the header and footer further reduce the size of the poster.

l. Save and close the file. Based on your instructor's directions, submit p05p1CoffeeClub_LastFirst.

2 Garden Club Presentation

Gardening is a seasonal activity. Each season demands specific tasks to be completed, depending on the climate zone. Some gardens require bulbs to be planted a few seasons prior to the bloom period, and some plants can be added to the garden once spring has arrived. You have been asked to create a presentation explaining this planning process. Refer to Figure 5.35 as you complete this skill.

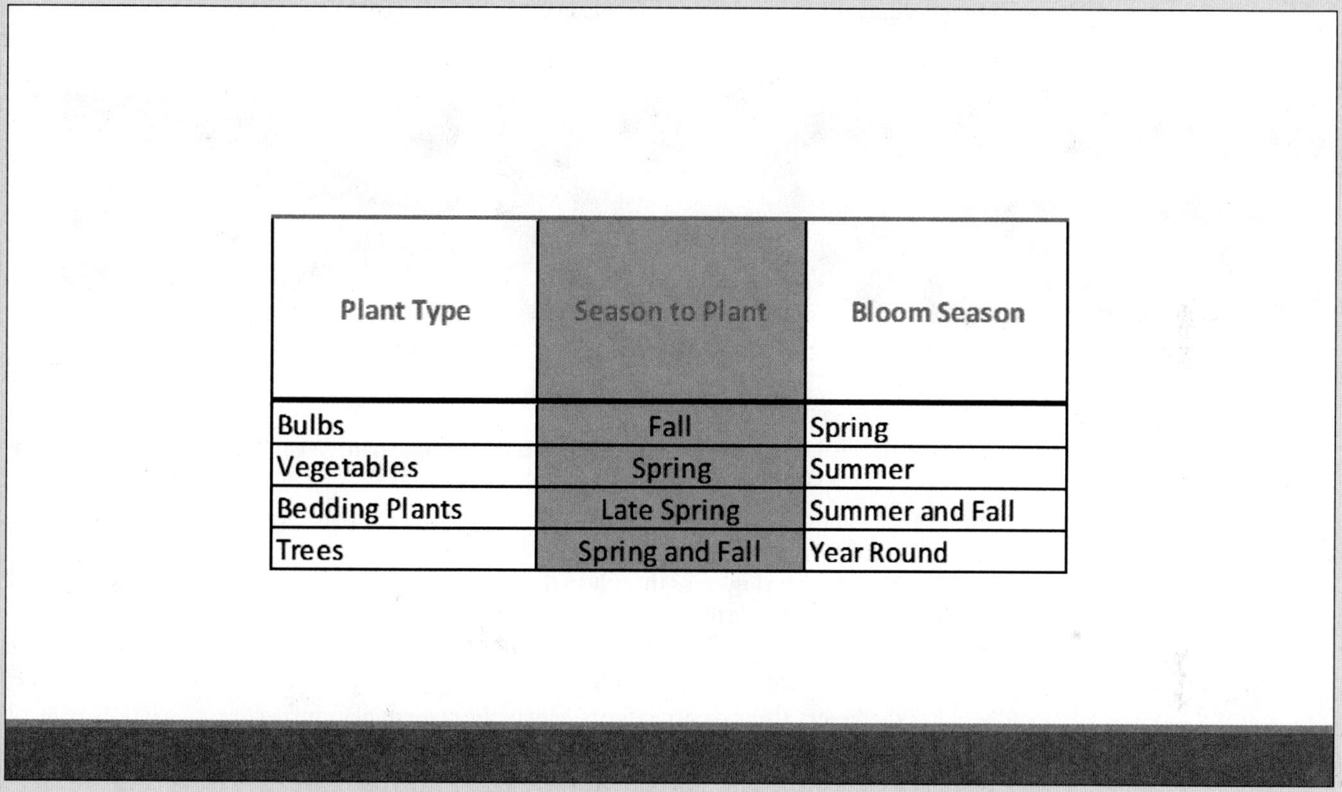

Plant Type	Season to Plant	Bloom Season
Bulbs	Fall	Spring
Vegetables	Spring	Summer
Bedding Plants	Late Spring	Summer and Fall
Trees	Spring and Fall	Year Round

FIGURE 5.35 Planning Your Garden Activities Presentation

a. Open *p05p2Garden* and save the presentation as **p05p2Garden_LastFirst**.

b. Create a handout header with your name and a handout footer with your instructor's name and your class. Include the current date.

c. Open *p05p2Activities.xlsx* and save the file as **p05p2Activities_LastFirst.xlsx**.

d. Select the **range A2:C6** to select the table data in the Excel file. Click **Copy** in the Clipboard group on the Home tab.

e. Click the **PowerPoint file** on the Windows taskbar to make the presentation the active file. Click **Slide 2**. Click **Paste arrow** in the Clipboard group on the Home tab and click **Paste Special**.

f. Click the **Paste link option** in the Paste Special dialog box. Ensure **Microsoft Excel Worksheet Object** is selected in the As box, and click **OK**.

g. Close the Excel file. Double-click the **table object** in the presentation.

h. Select **row 2** in Excel, click the **Font Color arrow**, and then select **blue** under Standard Colors.

i. Observe the color change to the column headings in the presentation. Save the changes in the Excel file and close Excel.

j. Click the **Format tab** and change the width of the table to **8"** in the Size group.

k. Click the **Format tab** and click **Align** in the Arrange group. Click **Align Center** and click **Align Middle**. Save and close the file, and submit based on your instructor's directions.

l. Save and close the file. Based on your instructor's directions, submit p05p2Garden_LastFirst.

3 Electricity

FROM SCRATCH You want to create a presentation about the generation of electricity. You are concerned about the burning of fossil fuels (coal, oil, and gas) because of the environmental implications. You will concentrate your presentation on new technologies that are being tested, but before you can do so you need to get basic facts concerning electricity into the presentation. You start the presentation by embedding two Excel charts. Refer to Figure 5.36 as you complete this exercise.

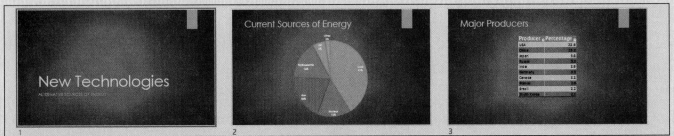

PowerPoint 2016, Windows 10, Microsoft Corporation

FIGURE 5.36 Energy presentation

a. Create a new presentation based on the **Ion template, Orange variation**. Save the presentation as **p05p3Energy_LastFirst**.

b. Create a handout header with your name and a handout footer with your instructor's name and your class. Include the current date.

c. Type **New Technologies** as the title in the title placeholder and type **Alternative Sources of Energy** in the subltitle placeholder.

d. Add a new slide using the **Title and Content** layout. Type **Current Sources of Energy** in the title placeholder.

e. Click the **Insert Chart icon** in the palette in the content placeholder.

f. Click **Pie** as the chart type and click **OK**.

g. Type the following data into the worksheet to create the pie chart. Close Excel.

	Source
Coal	41
Nuclear	14.8
Gas	20.1
Hydroelectric	16
Oil	5.8
Other	2.3

h. Click **Quick Layout** in the Chart Layouts group on the Chart Tools Design tab.

i. Click **Layout 1**.

j. Click the **Format tab** and click **Chart Title** from the Chart Elements list in the Current Selection group. Click **Delete**.

k. Change the chart Height to **6"** in the Size group on the Format tab.

l. Align the chart to the center and the bottom of the slide.

m. Add a new slide using the **Title Only** layout. Type **Major Producers** in the title placeholder.

n. Click the **Insert tab** and click **Object** in the Text group.

o. Click **Create from file**, click **Browse**, and locate *p05p3Energy*. Click **OK**.

p. Click **Link** and click **OK**.

q. Save and close the file. Based on your instructor's directions, submit p05p3Energy_LastFirst.

Mid-Level Exercises

1 School Spirit Banner

CREATIVE CASE

FROM SCRATCH

You belong to a student organization that prepares posters and banners for school activities. Next Friday your team, the Coalville Eagles, faces the Kamas Tigers at 7 p.m. at Coalville High School. You prepare a banner for this event. Refer to Figure 5.37 as you complete this exercise.

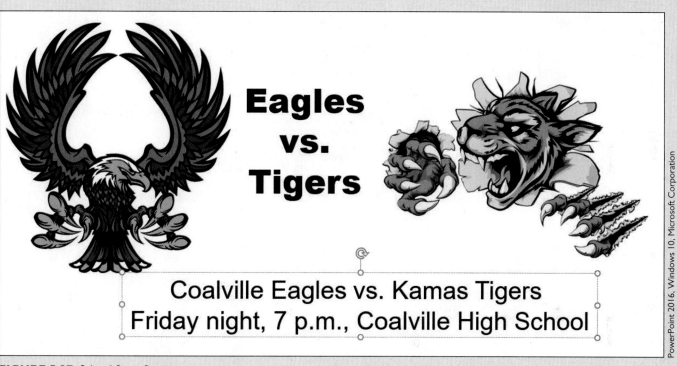

FIGURE 5.37 School Spirit Banner

a. Save a blank presentation as **p05m1Spirit_LastFirst**.

b. Create a handout header with your name and a handout footer with your instructor's name and your class. Include the current date.

c. Create a custom page size of **36" × 18"**, a standard size for small banners.

d. Type **Eagles vs. Tigers** as the slide title using the font of your choice.

e. Create a two-line subtitle. Type **Coalville Eagles vs. Kamas Tigers** as the first line of the subtitle. Type **Friday night, 7 p.m., Coalville High School** as the second line of the subtitle.

f. Insert the online images of your choice to represent the Eagles and the Tigers. If you want, you may replace the eagle and tiger mascots with the mascots of your choice, making sure you also change the team names in the title and subtitle placeholders.

g. Arrange the images and placeholders on the page as you see fit. Make any other changes such as additional text and a background change as desired.

h. Save and close the file. Based on your instructor's directions, submit p05m1Spirit_LastFirst.

You put together a presentation for a successful retail store. The store owners wish to expand their operation by requesting venture capital. Instead of creating PowerPoint tables, you decide to link to a worksheet that already contains sales data. Refer to Figure 5.38 as you complete this exercise.

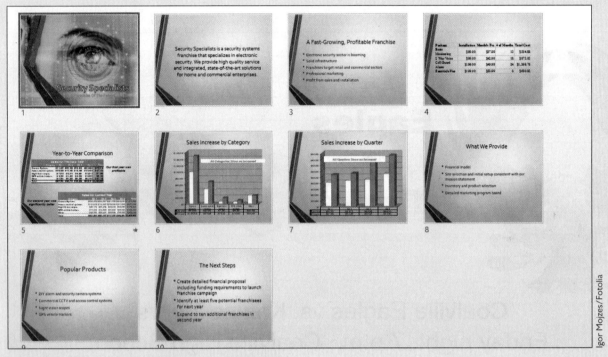

Igor Mojzes/Fotolia

FIGURE 5.38 Microsoft Excel Objects in a Presentation

a. Open *p05m2Capital* and save it as **p05m2Capital_LastFirst**.

b. Create a handout header with your name and a handout footer with your instructor's name and your class. Include the current date.

c. Open the *p05m2Sales* Excel workbook and save it as **p05m2Sales_LastFirst**.

d. Copy the data in the **Previous Year** tab for the **range A1:F8** in Excel, switch to PowerPoint, and then paste the data as a picture on Slide 5. Keep the source formatting. Change the table size by **locking the aspect ratio** and change the table height to **2"**. Drag the worksheet object to the left of the text *Our first year was profitable* and under the slide title.

e. Copy the data in the **Current Year** tab for the **range A1:F8** in Excel, switch to PowerPoint, and then paste the data to the same slide (Slide 5), keeping the source formatting. Change the table size by **locking the aspect ratio** and change the table height to **2"**. Drag the worksheet object to the right of the text *Our second year was significantly better*.

f. Copy the *Increase by Category* Excel chart and paste (with Use Destination Theme & Embed Workbook selected) to Slide 6 in the presentation. Resize the chart area height to **5.5"**. Reposition the chart below the slide title. Change the font size for the vertical axis and the horizontal data table axis to **12 pt**.

g. Copy the *Increase by Quarter* Excel chart and paste (with Use Destination Theme & Embed Workbook selected) to Slide 7 in the presentation. Size the chart area height to **5.5"**. Reposition the chart below the slide title. Change the vertical and horizontal data table axis font size to **12 pt**.

h. Use PowerPoint's Insert Object feature to create a new object on Slide 4: a new Microsoft Excel Worksheet. Create the following table in Excel **cells A1:E8** and use a formula in **cell E2** to calculate the Total Cost for Alarm Systems based on the installation cost and the cost per month for the required number of months. Auto fill the formula down to **cell D8** to copy the formula for the **range E2:E8** (to enable Excel to figure the total cost of the system). Format columns B, C, and E as **Currency**.

Package	Installation	Monthly Fee	# of Months	Total Cost
Basic Monitoring	99	37.99	12	=B2+(C2*D2)
2 Way Voice	99	42.99	18	
Cell Guard Alarm	199	49.99	24	
Essentials Plus	199	53.99	8	

i. Change the font size to **20 pt**. Resize the Excel window to fit the data cell range. Resize the columns to fit data by **double-clicking the right column border**.

j. Exit Excel and size the new Excel object to a width of **8.25"** in PowerPoint. Resize columns widths as necessary.

k. Apply **Align Center** and **Align Middle** to the new Excel object.

l. Save and close the file. Based on your instructor's directions, submit p05m2Capital_LastFirst.

3 Learning from an Expert

You and a classmate have been asked to create a presentation about a subject that interests you personally. Together, you have decided to create a presentation about the use of social networking in business. Create a new presentation using the Ion theme available in the Themes palette and save it as **p05m3Social_LastFirst**. Each of you must research two different types of social networking that are often used. Find as much information as you can about how companies use social networking to communicate with their customers and the number of customers or users that each social network has in at least four major countries.

Create the following slides: (1) a Title slide, (2) two Content with Caption slides, and (3) a Picture with Caption slide. Create a title and subtitle as appropriate on the Title slide. Briefly describe each of the social-network advertising options and add a descriptive chart or table for the two types of social networking on the Content with Caption slides. Finally, summarize your social networking research and add an image that enhances your presentation on the final slide in the presentation. Save and close the file. Based on your instructor's directions, submit p05m3Social_LastFirst.

Beyond the Classroom

Profession Presentation

Research the profession you are most interested in pursuing after graduation and create a presentation about the profession. Save the presentation as **p05b1Profession_LastFirst**. Create a handout header with your name and a footer with your instructor's name and class. Include the date. In addition to an introduction and summary slide, create three key topic slides. On the first topic slide, outline two key job-search strategies for your chosen profession. The second slide should be a chart illustrating data for expected job growth in the profession. Enter the data for the chart in a worksheet, and format the chart in an attractive, easy-to-read format. Apply appropriate titles and labels as needed to ensure that the chart is easily and accurately understood. The third slide should provide a typical job description or want ad for your profession. After the three key topic slides, create the summary slide that lists the resources you used to obtain the data in your presentation. Save and close the file. Based on your instructor's directions, submit p05b1Profession_LastFirst.

Chart Improvements

The presentation *p05b2Tips* includes four charts that confuse the message they are supposed to deliver. In some cases, the wrong chart type has been applied, and in others the formatting of the chart is distracting. In the Notes pane of each slide, design tips are given that you can read to help you identify the errors in each chart. Open the file and immediately save it as **p05b2Tips_LastFirst**. Read the notes associated with each slide, and edit the chart on the slide so it incorporates the tips. Make all modifications necessary to create a professional, easy-to-understand chart. Read the design tips in this slide show. Save and close the file. Based on your instructor's directions, submit p05b2Tips_LastFirst.

Capstone Exercise

Bryce Adventure Camp is a successful outdoor retreat dedicated to the appreciation of the splendor and inspiration of nature for good health. The operation has been so successful in its two years of operation that the owners opened retreats in two additional locations. They now want to open another retreat to allow even more people to enjoy the exhilaration of nature in magnificent settings. They are meeting with officers of a venture capital corporation, which offers funding for unique opportunities. The representatives have asked for an overview of Bryce Adventure Camp's philosophy, services and activities, sales for this year and last year, a year-to-year comparison, and charts showing the increase. The owners of Bryce Adventure Camp asked you for help in preparing the presentation for the meeting.

Create a Poster

The owners of Bryce Adventure Camp have reserved a meeting room at a local conference center. They want a large, foam-backed poster on an easel next to the conference room door. They have asked you to prepare the poster that a local company will print.

a. Open *p05c1Campposter* and save it as **p05c1Campposter_LastFirst**.

b. Create a handout header with your name and a handout footer with your instructor's name, and your class. Include the current date.

c. Change the width of the page to **17"** and the height of the page to **22"** in the Slide Size dialog box. Click **OK**. Click **Maximize**.

d. Type **Gardenia Room, 9 a.m.** in a new text box.

e. Apply the **Fill – White, Outline – Accent 1, Shadow** WordArt style and change the font size to **96 pt**.

f. Position the left top edge of the new text box at **1.88"** horizontal and **20.28"** vertical positions from the top left corner.

g. Print a copy of the poster as a handout, one per page, using the Scale to Fit Paper option.

h. Save and close the file, and submit based on your instructor's directions.

Create an Activity Costs Table

Some slides of the Bryce Adventure Camp slide show have been created, including an agenda, an introduction to the resort, and a list of adventures for the body and activities for the spirit. Now you insert a table showing the packages available in the Day Spa.

a. Open *p05c1Campshow* and save it as **p05c1Campshow_LastFirst**.

b. Create a new slide following Slide 4 using the Title and Content layout.

c. Type the title **Adventure Prices: $10 per voucher**.

d. Create a four-column, seven-row table. Do not worry about width or height of rows or columns.

e. Type the following table:

Adventure	Duration	Vouchers Required Private	Vouchers Required Group (min 3 people)
Guided hike	1 hour	3	1
Rappelling	2 hours	8	4
ATV tours	2 hours	10	4
Fitness classes	1 hour	3	1
Horseback riding	2 hours	6	2
Zip line	1 ride	1	

Modify Table Structure and Format Table

The table structure needs to be modified by adding an additional row. You also format the table to obtain the desired appearance. Size the table and apply a table style.

a. Change the table structure by adding an additional row at the bottom of the table. Merge the cells in the new row. Type **Camp Package: 10 Adventure Vouchers/$90 (All vouchers are non-refundable)** in the new row.

b. Set the table size to a height of **5.5"** and a width of **9"**.

c. Apply the **Medium Style 3 - Accent 1 table style** (third row, second column, Medium category) to the table.

d. Select the column headings and center them horizontally and vertically in the row.

e. Select columns **2**, **3**, and **4** and center the text horizontally.

f. Arrange the table so that it is centered horizontally on the slide and does not block the slide title.

Link Excel Tables and Charts

Bryce Adventure Camp's owners have tables and charts showing sales figures for this year and the previous year. These figures show that all three branches of their Adventure Camp have increased revenue and profit each year, and the charts emphasize the data.

a. Create a Title Only slide after Slide 5 and type **Sales Have Increased at Each Camp** as the title.

b. Open the *p05c1Campprofits* workbook in Excel, save it as **p05c1Campprofits_LastFirst.xlsx**, and then move to the worksheet containing the sales data for the previous year. Copy the data and paste it into Slide 6 of the presentation. Change the Paste options to **Keep Source Formatting**.

c. Repeat Step b to paste the worksheet data for the current year into Slide 6.

d. Size the two worksheets on Slide 6 to a height of **2.5"** and a width of **8"**.

e. Arrange the two tables attractively on the slide.

f. Create a Title Only slide after Slide 6 and type **All Camps Show an Increase** as the title of the new Slide 7. Use the destination theme and link the *Increase by Camp* Excel chart to the new slide. You do not need to copy the WordArt arrow that overlays the chart.

g. Size the chart to a height of **4.5"** and a width of **7.5"**.

h. Change the font size for the X-axis labels, Y-axis labels, and legend to **16 pt**.

i. Align the chart in the center of the slide.

j. Create a Title Only slide after Slide 7 and type **All Quarters Show an Increase** as the title of the new Slide 8. Use the destination theme and link the *Increase by Quarter* Excel chart to the new slide.

k. Size the chart to a height of **4.5"** and a width of **7.5"**.

l. Align the chart in the center of the slide.

Create a Bar Chart

To identify their guests' reasons for visiting the adventure camps, the owners included this question in a guest satisfaction survey. They provide the answers as a bar chart to make the venture capitalists aware that demand for the camp is unlikely to go down.

a. Create a *Title and Content* slide after Slide 8 and type **Top Five Reasons for Visiting Camp** as the title of the new Slide 9.

b. Create a column chart using the default Clustered Column type with the following data:

Location/Sight-seeing	52%
Adventure Opportunities	22%
Relaxation	13%
Children's Activities	8%
Spa and Fitness Facilities	5%

c. Size the chart to a height of **5"** and a width of **8.5"**.

d. Align the chart in the center of the slide.

Modify and Format a Bar Chart

You modify and format the bar chart to improve the appearance.

a. Apply **Quick Layout 2** to the chart.

b. Remove the title and the legend.

c. Click **Add Chart Element** in the Chart Layouts group, select **Gridlines**, and choose **Primary Major Horizontal**.

d. Change the colors of the chart to **Colorful 3**.

e. Select the **Plot Area** and add a picture fill using *p05c1Bryce.jpg*.

f. Change the data labels position to **Center**.

g. Save and close the file. Based on your instructor's directions, submit:

p05c1Campposter_LastFirst

p05c1Campshow_LastFirst

PowerPoint

Interactivity and Advanced Animation

LEARNING OUTCOME | You will develop presentations featuring interactivity and animation to build and retain audience attention.

OBJECTIVES & SKILLS: After you read this chapter, you will be able to:

CASE STUDY | Teaching Aids

As the teaching assistant for a computer literacy instructor, you prepare numerous teaching aids to help students. You begin by modifying a presentation in a quiz format to help students review charts and graphs. The existing presentation includes slides that display a question and a list of choices. Next, you insert sound action buttons so that if a student answers correctly, the student hears applause; if the student answers incorrectly, the student hears feedback indicating it is an incorrect choice. You add action buttons for students to use to navigate through the presentation and hyperlinks to open a reference table and an assignment. You also include your email address in the slide show in case the students want to contact you.

After modifying the Charts and Graphs Review presentation, you modify a presentation designed to help the computer literacy students understand PowerPoint's advanced animation features. Finally, you create animation examples for students to view.

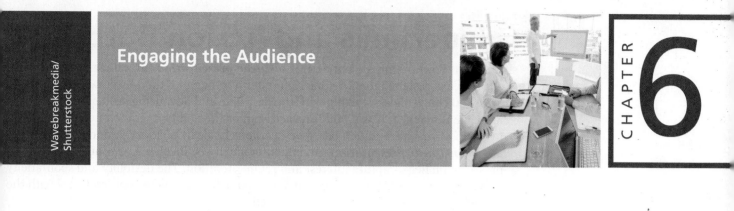

Wavebreakmedia/
Shutterstock

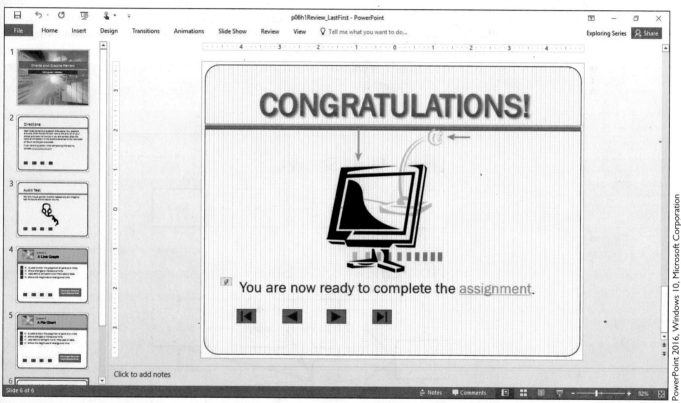

FIGURE 6.1 Teaching Aids Animated Presentation

PowerPoint 2016, Windows 10, Microsoft Corporation

CASE STUDY | Teaching Aids

Starting Files	Files to be Submitted
p06h1Review	p06h1Review_LastFirst
p06h1Quiz_Media folder	p06h2Animation_LastFirst
p06h2Animation	

Hyperlinks and Action Buttons

A typical PowerPoint presentation is a ***linear presentation***. In a linear presentation, each slide is designed to move one right after another, and the viewer or audience progresses through slides, starting with the first slide and advancing sequentially until the last slide is reached. If you add ***interactivity***, or the ability to branch non-sequentially to a part of the presentation based on decisions made by a viewer or audience, you create a ***non-linear presentation***. Adding interactivity by involving your audience in your presentation helps capture interest and retain attention. The flexibility and spontaneity of a non-linear presentation typically frees you to become more conversational with the audience, which leads to even more interaction.

You can add interactivity by creating ***hyperlinks*** that branch to slides or other locations containing additional information or by adding ***action buttons***. An action button is a ready-made button designed to serve as an icon that can initiate an action when clicked, pointed to, or run over with the mouse. Figure 6.2 demonstrates the linear versus non-linear navigation options in a presentation. In the non-linear slide show, Slide 1 could include a menu option enabling the viewer to choose any of the remaining five slides, and the remaining slides could be designed to enable the viewer to navigate back to the first slide or to other related slides.

In this section, you will add interactivity to a slide show by adding hyperlinks, action buttons, and a trigger.

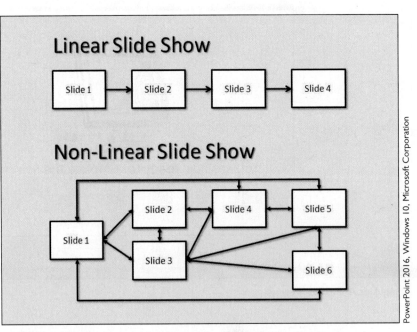

FIGURE 6.2 Linear Versus Non-Linear Navigation Options in a Presentation

Inserting and Using Hyperlinks

You can insert a hyperlink to enable a presenter to tailor the flow and content of a presentation based on audience questions or to enable single viewers to navigate through a slide show at their own pace, visiting the slides desired to gain more information in areas of interest or to review as needed. To activate a hyperlink, display the presentation in Slide Show view or Reading view and position the pointer over a hyperlink; the pointer becomes a hand. Click the hyperlink and you jump to a new location. The first time you click a hyperlink, the color of the hyperlink may change so that you know the link has been accessed previously. The colors assigned to the unused link and the used link are set by the theme.

PowerPoint enables you to attach a hyperlink to any selected object, such as text, shapes, images, charts, and even SmartArt or WordArt. The hyperlink can link to a(n):

- Existing file
- Webpage
- Slide in the open presentation
- New document
- Email address

To insert a hyperlink, complete the following steps:

1. Select the object or text you want the link attached to.
2. Click the Insert tab.
3. Click Hyperlink in the Links group.
4. Click the type of link you want in the *Link to* pane on the left side of the Insert Hyperlink dialog box.
5. Select and add any additional desired options and information related to the link location you selected.
6. Click OK.

TIP: USING OTHER METHODS TO INSERT HYPERLINKS
You can also use the keyboard shortcut Ctrl+K or you can right-click the selected object or text and select Hyperlink from the shortcut menu to open the Insert Hyperlink dialog box.

Link to an Existing File or Webpage

When the Insert Hyperlink dialog box opens, the *Link to* pane displays *Existing File or Web Page* as the default selection. If you are attaching the link to text and you selected the text before opening the dialog box, the text appears in the *Text to display* box at the top of the dialog box. If you did not pre-select text, the word to the right of the insertion point displays. You can delete any text that appears and enter the text you want to display on your slide in this box.

Often, hyperlinks link to webpages. At the bottom of the dialog box is an Address box where you enter the **uniform resource locator (URL)**, or web address, of the webpage you wish to link to. If you know the URL, you can type it in the Address box, but it is better to copy and paste a link to avoid errors caused by misspelling or incorrect punctuation.

If you do not know the URL, you can find it in one of several ways. If you visited the page recently, click Browsed Pages to show a list of the websites you have recently visited. Click the address from the list of URLs shown. You can also click *Browse the Web* (located below the *Text to display* box) to open your browser and navigate to the desired webpage. When you locate the page, click the PowerPoint icon on the Windows taskbar to return to PowerPoint. The URL displays in the Address box in the Insert Hyperlink dialog box. Lastly, you can copy the URL from the webpage address box by selecting the address and pressing Ctrl+C, minimizing the browser, and then pasting the URL in the Address box by pressing Ctrl+V.

Figure 6.3 shows how you would create a link to the National Park Service website. The text is selected so that a link to the website giving information about the park can be attached. The Insert Hyperlink dialog box is open and recently browsed pages are displayed. The hyperlink to the National Park Service website is shown in the Address box.

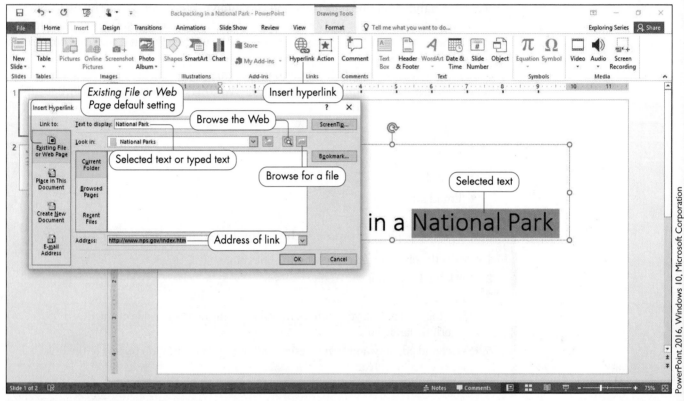

FIGURE 6.3 Insert Hyperlink Dialog Box

To link to an existing file stored on your computer or other storage device, from the Insert Hyperlink dialog box, click *Current Folder*, *Recent Files*, or *Browse for File* to navigate to the location of the desired file. If you know the exact file name and location, you can type it in the dialog box instead of browsing to locate the file. When you click the link during your presentation, the application in which the file was created opens and your file displays.

TIP: LINKING PICTURE FILES

What if you have a company logo that you want to use in all presentations you create? Every time you insert the logo, the picture file is embedded multiple times in a presentation, wasting storage space on your drive. Rather than embed the picture, you can create a picture link to keep your PowerPoint file sizes much smaller. To create a picture link, click the Insert tab and click Pictures in the Images group. Browse for the picture you want, click the Insert arrow, and select *Link to File*. PowerPoint inserts a link to the picture instead of embedding the picture file in your slide show. The link stores the entire path to the file, the location of the picture, and the picture size. Always save your objects to the same folder and storage device where you store your presentation. Then, link to that location so that the link will not be broken when you present. If you ever change the logo, replace the old logo file with the new logo file in the same location and with the same file name. When a presentation is opened that is linked to the picture, the new logo appears, so you do not have to replace the logo in every presentation.

To add an email link to a slide, select the Email Address option in the Insert Hyperlink dialog box and type the address in the *Email address* box. As you type, the protocol designator *mailto:* is automatically added before the email address. Creating an email link enables your viewer to contact you for more information and is especially helpful if you post your presentation on the Web. You can add any text on the slide, such as *Contact me for further information*, by typing it on the slide and selecting it or by typing the text in the *Text to display* box. Add a subject for the email to help you identify incoming mail. PowerPoint automatically formats it as a link for you. Figure 6.4 displays the *Email address* options in the Insert Hyperlink dialog box.

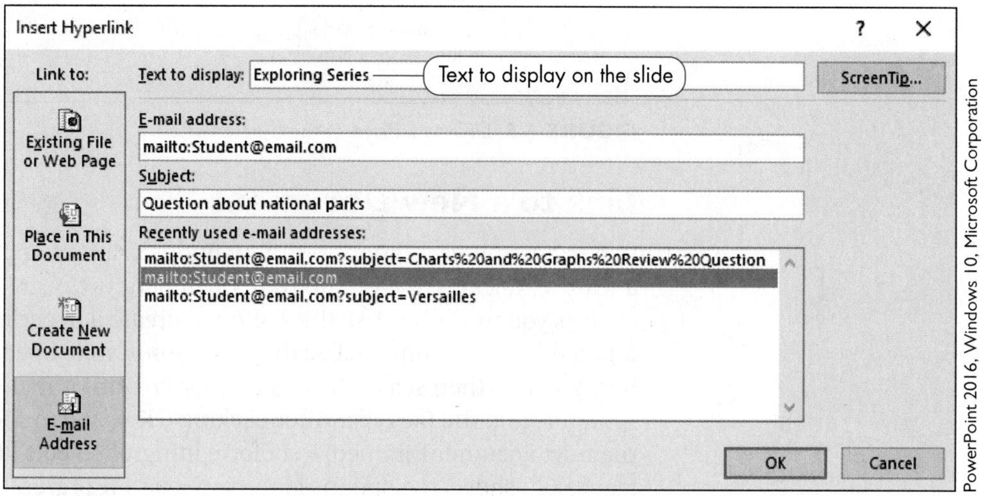

FIGURE 6.4 Creating an Email Link

Link to a Slide in the Active Presentation

You may want to create a link to another slide in a presentation. For example, you may create a menu of topics that are covered in the presentation. When you click a menu option, the presentation jumps to the slide containing the related content. Each topic slide should also include a link back to the menu. You can use links to branch to the slides that focus on your audience's anticipated questions or comments.

To create a link to another slide in the presentation, complete the following steps:

1. Select *Place in This Document* from the Insert Hyperlink dialog box.
2. Locate the desired slide in the list of slides that displays.
3. Select the slide to which you wish to link.
4. Click OK to close the dialog box (see Figure 6.5).

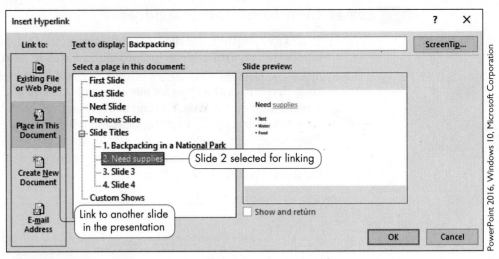

FIGURE 6.5 Link to a Place in the Document

Link to a New Document

In a training presentation, you may find it helpful to open a program and demonstrate a feature. Clicking the Create New Document option in the Insert Hyperlink dialog box enables you to do this. Use this option to create a hyperlink to a new PowerPoint presentation or other document. Use the Change button to open the *Create New Document* dialog box. You can then select the location for creating the new document and designate the file name and the file type. After clicking OK, you can specify whether you want to open the new document immediately for editing or to edit later in the *Insert Hyperlink* box. Figure 6.6 shows the options for creating a new presentation with the file name *Supplies* and opening it for immediate editing.

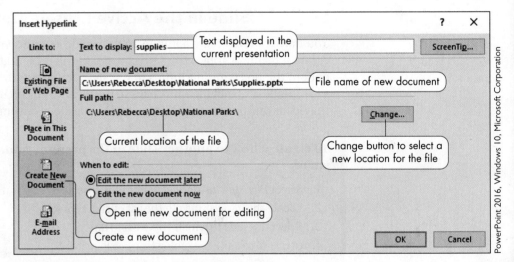

FIGURE 6.6 Linking to a New Document

Adding Action Buttons

STEP 2 ⟩⟩ Another way to add interactivity is by using an action button that, when you click, point to, or drag the mouse over it, initiates an action. Action buttons are excellent tools for navigating a slide show and are especially useful if you want to create a presentation for a *kiosk*, an interactive computer terminal available for public use, such as on campus, at a mall, or at a trade show. An interactive slide show is perfect for a kiosk display.

Actions can be associated with any object, not just an action button. Select an object, click the Insert tab, and then click Action in the Links group. The Action Settings dialog box opens so that you can select the type of action and how you want the action to be initiated.

Add Sound to an Object

STEP 3 ⟩⟩ Sound can be added to a hyperlink attached to an object to capture your audience's attention or to add emphasis to the subject of the link. To attach a sound to a hyperlink, click to select the *Play sound* check box in the Action Settings dialog box. Click the *Play sound* arrow and select the sound you want to play when the object is clicked or moused over during the show. To assign a sound file you have saved to your computer, scroll to the bottom of the list, click Other Sound, browse for the sound, and then select it.

TIP: USING GAMES AS QUIZZES

PowerPoint has a Quiz Show template that includes sample quiz question layouts such as True or False, Multiple Choice, and more. You can locate it by searching in the *Search for online templates and themes search box*, which is visible as you begin a New presentation.

Be sure to create a storyboard to plan for the slides for the quiz and for the interactive elements required by your plan. A standard quiz presentation would probably contain slides to introduce the quiz, directions, questions, feedback slides, and an ending slide.

Sound can be added to the answers to the questions to indicate a correct or incorrect answer. The answers could also link to the feedback slides, and the *correct* feedback slide would link to the next question. The *incorrect* feedback slide would link to the same question slide so the viewer could try again.

Using Action Buttons for Navigation

STEP 4 ⟩⟩ Slide Show view includes default navigation buttons on the bottom-left of a slide that return the presentation to the previous slide, advance to the next slide, activate a pen tool, open Slide Sorter view, zoom, or display a shortcut menu. If your presentation will be used by multiple people with varied skill levels, you may want to keep these default buttons. If, however, you wish to provide your users with additional choices, you may want to create custom buttons.

Table 6.1 lists the 12 different ready-made action buttons that PowerPoint includes in the Shapes gallery.

Table 6.1 PowerPoint Ready-Made Action Buttons

Action Button Icon	Name	Default Button Behavior
◁	Back or Previous button	Moves to previous slide
▷	Forward or Next button	Moves to next slide
◁|	Beginning button	Moves to the first slide in the slide show
|▷	End button	Moves to the last slide in the slide show
🏠	Home button	Moves to the first slide in the slide show by default but can be set to go to any slide
ⓘ	Information button	Can be set to move to any slide in the slide show, a custom show, a URL, another presentation, or another file in order to reveal information
↩	Return button	Returns to previous slide view regardless of the location in the slide show
▣	Movie button	Can be set to play a movie file
🗋	Document button	Can be set to load a document in the application that was used to create it
🔊	Sound button	Can be set to play a sound when clicked
?	Help button	Can be set to open the Help feature or a Help document
☐	Custom button	Can be set to move to a slide in the slide show, a custom show, a URL, another PowerPoint presentation, a file, or a program; also can be set to run a macro, add an action to an object, or play a sound

Creating Custom Buttons

 STEP 5 »» Action buttons can contain shapes such as arrows and symbols. *Custom buttons* can be created and set to trigger unique actions in a presentation. In addition to being a hyperlink to another location, custom buttons can display information or link to videos, documents, sound, and the Help feature.

To insert an action or custom button, complete the following steps:

1. Click the Insert tab.
2. Click Shapes in the Illustrations group. The Shapes gallery can also be accessed from the Home tab by clicking Shapes in the Drawing group.
3. Click the action button you want in the *Action Buttons* section of the Shapes gallery.
4. Click the desired location to create the button on the slide (or hold and drag to control the button size).
5. Select the Mouse Click or Mouse Over tab in the Action Settings dialog box.
6. Select desired options in the Action Settings dialog box.
7. Click OK.

Figure 6.7 shows the Action Buttons section displayed in the Shapes gallery with the action button designed to indicate sound selected.

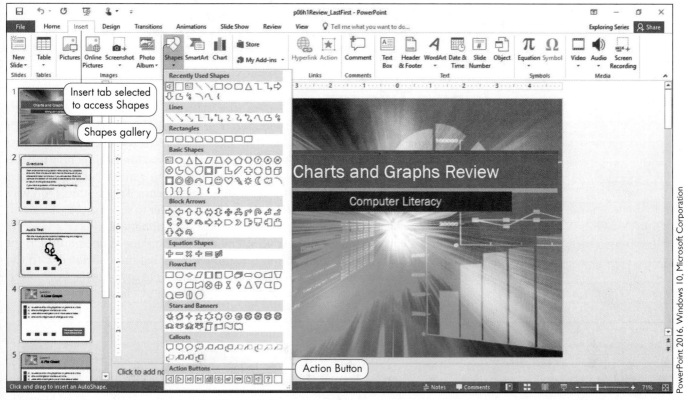

FIGURE 6.7 Action Buttons Displayed in Shapes Gallery

When you release the mouse after creating an action button, the Action Settings dialog box opens. Click the *Mouse Click or Mouse Over* tab to select how to initiate the action. Regardless of which method you select, the action options are the same. You can choose to have the action button hyperlink to another location in the slide show, a Custom Show, a URL, another PowerPoint presentation, or another file. An action button can even initiate a new program. To link to a specific slide in the slide show, click the *Hyperlink to* arrow and select a slide from the list. To have the action button run a specific program, click *Run program* and browse to locate the program you wish to open. You can also program the action button to run a macro or to add an action to an object. Figure 6.8 shows the settings for an action button that returns to the first slide.

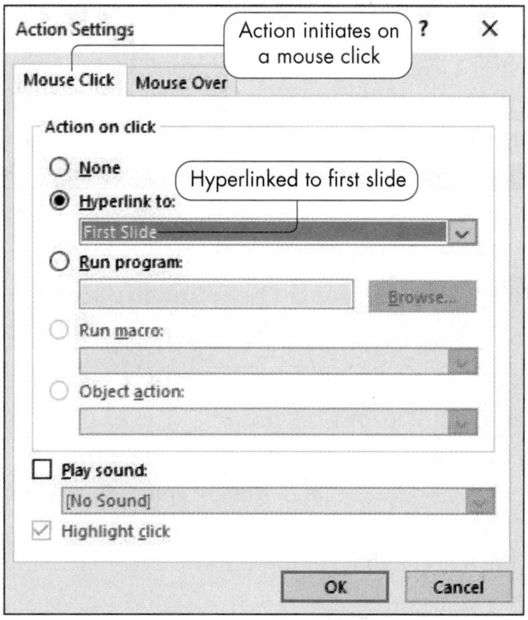

FIGURE 6.8 Action Settings Dialog Box

Using a Trigger

Another way to introduce interactivity into your presentation is through the use of a trigger. A *trigger* launches an animation that takes place when you click an associated object or a bookmarked location in a media object. An *animation* is an action used to draw interest to an object in a presentation. For example, you can use text as a trigger. The trigger is set up so when you click the text, an image appears. Triggers are a fun way to add interactivity to presentations—the viewer clicks a trigger to see a surprise element. Remember this key point about triggers: a trigger must use animation.

Figure 6.9 displays a slide with a trigger. The Animation Pane is open on the right side of the slide and shows the object and the animation or action associated with the trigger. The trigger is attached to the words *You are now ready to complete the assignment*. The slide is interactive because the viewer initiates the process by clicking the trigger.

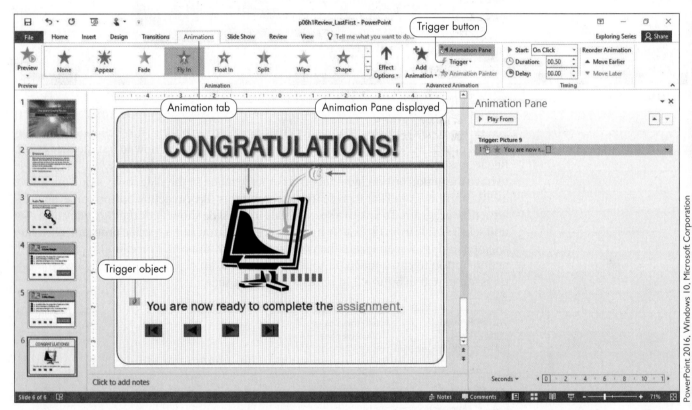

FIGURE 6.9 Create a Trigger

To set up a trigger, complete the following steps:

1. Select the object that will serve as the trigger.
2. Click the Animations tab.
3. Add the animation effect of your choice from the Animation group.
4. Click Trigger in the Advanced Animation group.
5. Select the *On Click of* or *On Bookmark* option to determine how the animation is triggered.
6. Select the object or bookmark that will launch the animation from the displayed list.

Add a ScreenTip

STEP 6 >> Sometimes, the viewer needs more information to determine the purpose of the hyperlink object or text. To help a viewer determine whether or not to click a hyperlink, use a ScreenTip. When the viewer points to the hyperlink, the ***ScreenTip*** displays with the additional information.

To add a ScreenTip to a hyperlink, click ScreenTip in the Insert Hyperlink dialog box. Type the text you want to display in the Set Hyperlink ScreenTip dialog box.

TIP: ADDING DEFINITIONS TO TECHNICAL TERMS

ScreenTips are an excellent way to define technical or new terms in a presentation. To use a ScreenTip in this manner, select the term in the text on your slide, click the Insert tab, and then click Hyperlink in the Links group. Link to *Place in This Document* and select the slide you are currently in. Finally, click ScreenTip and type the definition for the word you selected.

Check and Modify Hyperlinks and Action Buttons

STEP 7 >> Before delivering or publishing a presentation, check all action buttons to see if they perform as you intended. Test each of the hyperlinks in Slide Show view to see if it takes you to the proper location. (You can also check hyperlinks by right-clicking each link and selecting Open Hyperlink.) Check to see if the ScreenTips you entered display and are correct. Close each linked location, and make sure you return to the presentation. If you find a hyperlink that does not link properly, leave Slide Show view and immediately fix the link so you do not forget to do it later. Once you have edited the link, repeat the testing process until you are assured that every link works.

To edit hyperlinks in the Edit Hyperlink dialog box, complete the following steps:

1. Select the hyperlinked object.
2. Click Hyperlink in the Links group on the Insert tab. You can also press Ctrl+K or right-click the selected object and click Edit Hyperlink.
3. Modify the existing hyperlink after the Edit Hyperlink dialog box opens.
4. Click OK.

To remove a hyperlink, click Remove Link in the Edit Hyperlink dialog box or right-click the selected object and click Remove Hyperlink from the shortcut menu. If you delete the object to which a hyperlink is attached, the hyperlink is also deleted.

Quick Concepts

1. What is a presentation that enables the user to progress through the slides using action buttons and hyperlinks? *p. 390*

2. What are the main advantages of adding an email link to a presentation? *p. 393*

3. Which type of event is a trigger used to launch animation in a presentation? *p. 398*

Hands-On Exercises

Watch the Video
for this Hands-On
Exercise!

HOE1 Training

Skills covered: Insert an Email Hyperlink • Edit an Email Hyperlink • Add an Action to an Object • Create Sound Action Buttons • Edit Sound Action Buttons • Create Action Buttons for Navigation • Create a Custom Action Button • Insert Hyperlinks • Modify Hyperlinks • Test Hyperlinks

1 Hyperlinks and Action Buttons

One of your responsibilities as a teaching assistant is to provide materials for a computer literacy class. You create a presentation to help students review charts and graphs in a quiz format. Students answer questions and receive feedback on whether they selected a "correct" or "incorrect" answer. Students can also open a reference guide and an assignment from the presentation.

STEP 1 ➤➤ INSERT AND EDIT AN EMAIL HYPERLINK

The following table displays the storyboard used in creating the Charts and Graphs presentation. The storyboard notes all interactive elements you want to include in the presentation. You will modify this slide show to add the interactive elements. You will begin by inserting your email address so that, if necessary, a student could contact you with questions. Refer to the table below to add the following interactive elements to the slides in the presentation.

Slide	Content	Interactive Element
1	Title Slide	None
2	Directions	• Email hyperlink • Four navigation buttons: Beginning, Back or Previous, Forward or Next, End
3	Speaker Test	• Object with sound action attached
4	Question One	• Four sound action buttons (one for each answer) • Chart with animation trigger • Four navigation buttons: Beginning, Back or Previous, Forward or Next, End
5	Question Two	• Four sound action buttons (one for each answer) • Chart with animation trigger • Four navigation buttons: Beginning, Back or Previous, Forward or Next, End
6	Ending Slide	• Existing file hyperlink • Four navigation buttons: Beginning, Back or Previous, Forward or Next, End

a. Open *p06h1Review* and save it as **p06h1Review_LastFirst**.

> **TROUBLESHOOTING:** If you make any major mistakes in this exercise, you can close the file, open *p06h1Review* again, and then start this exercise over.

b. Create a handout header with your name and a handout footer with your instructor's name and your class. Include the current date.

c. Click **Slide 2** and position the insertion point after the colon following *contact*. Press **Spacebar**, type your email address, and then press **Spacebar**.

Because PowerPoint recognizes the format of an email address, it creates an automatic hyperlink to your email.

d. Right-click your email address and click **Edit Hyperlink**.

e. Click in the **Subject box**, type **Charts and Graphs Review Question**, and then click **OK**.

f. Save the presentation.

Because the quiz review slide show uses audio cues to indicate whether a student answers the question correctly, it is important for the student to have a working headset. You will create an action attached to an image of a headset so the student can test to see if his or her headset is working. Refer to Figure 6.10 as you complete Step 2.

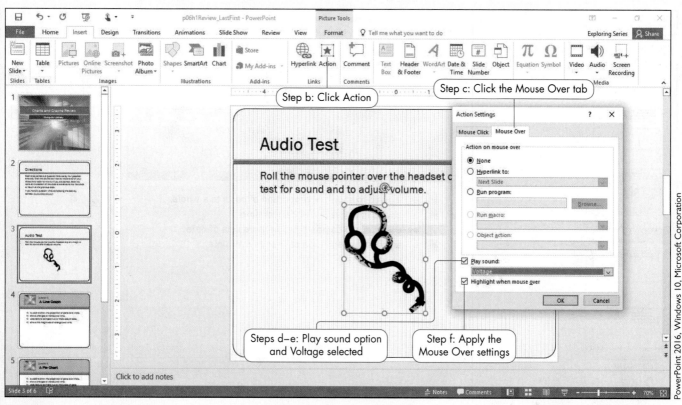

FIGURE 6.10 Action Settings

a. Click **Slide 3**, select the **headset picture**, and click the **Insert tab**.

b. Click **Action** in the Links group.

The Action Settings dialog box opens so that you can assign an action to the selected image.

c. Click the **Mouse Over tab**.

By selecting the Mouse Over tab, you assign any applied actions to occur when the mouse moves over the selected object.

d. Click to select the **Play sound check box** and click the **list arrow**.

PowerPoint includes a variety of sounds you can attach to objects, or you can select the Other Sound option and browse to locate a sound you have saved.

e. Click **Voltage**.

f. Ensure that the **Highlight when mouse over check box** is selected, and click **OK**.

With this option selected, the image will be surrounded by a border when the mouse rolls over the top of it, which makes it easy to note the mouse-over area.

> **TROUBLESHOOTING:** You will not be able to hear the Voltage sound or see the highlight border unless you are in Slide Show view.

g. Save the presentation.

You will create action buttons next to the answers on each of the question slides so that when clicked, the action button will play an audio response letting the student know whether he or she selected the correct answer. Refer to Figure 6.11 as you complete Step 3.

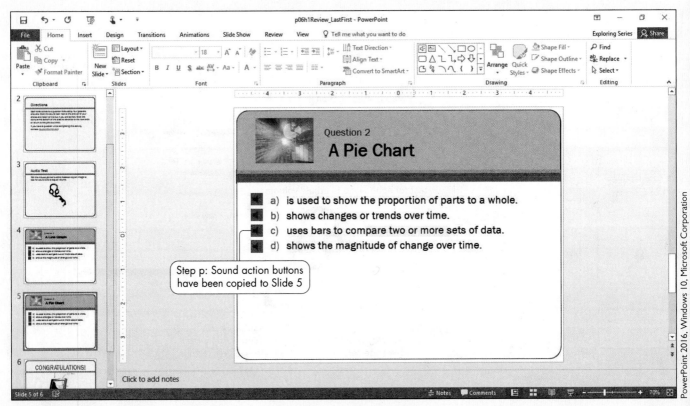

FIGURE 6.11 Action Assigned to an Object

a. Click **Slide 4** and click the **Insert tab**. Click **Shapes** in the Illustrations group.

The Shapes gallery opens, and the action buttons display at the bottom of the gallery.

b. Click **Action Button: Sound**.

The Shapes gallery closes, and the pointer becomes a crosshair pointer.

c. Click in an empty portion of the slide to create the button.

Do not worry about the size or position of the button at this time. You will adjust both in a later step. The Action Settings dialog box opens to the Mouse Click tab.

d. Click the **Play sound arrow** and select **Other Sound**.

e. Locate the *p06h1Incorrect* file in the p06h1Quiz_Media folder and click **OK**.

The sound file is assigned to the action button. Because this is not the correct answer, the viewer hears *Incorrect* when the button is clicked.

f. Click **OK** to close the Action Settings dialog box.

The action button now has sound attached to it, and the sound plays when the presentation is viewed in Slide Show view and Reading view.

g. Click the **Format tab** with the action button still selected and click the **Size dialog box launcher** in the Size group. Set **Height** to **0.35"** and **Width** to **0.35"**.

h. Click **Position** in the Format Shape pane and set **Horizontal position** to **0.5"** and **Vertical position** to **2.5"**. Press **Enter**.

i. Keep the sound action button selected and press **Ctrl+D** three times.

Three duplicates of the original sound action button are created. It is easier to edit duplicates than to re-create the button because the duplicates are already sized. The last duplicate created is now selected, so you will edit it first.

j. Click **Size & Properties** in the Format Shape pane. Set **Horizontal position** to **0.5"** and **Vertical position** to **3.9"** in the Format Shape pane. Press **Enter**.

The last duplicate you made moves into position to the left of answer *d*.

k. Right-click the selected button and click **Hyperlink**. Click the **Play sound arrow** and select **Other Sound**. Locate and select the *p06h1TryAgain* file and click **OK** to close the Add Audio dialog box. Click **OK** to close the Action Settings dialog box.

The sound action button has been edited to play a different sound file. Because this is not the correct answer, the viewer hears *Try Again* when the button is clicked.

l. Click the third sound action button from the top. In the Format Shape pane, in the Position options, set **Horizontal position** to **0.5"** and **Vertical position** to **3.43"**. Press **Enter**.

m. Right-click the selected button and click **Hyperlink**. Click the **Play sound arrow** and select **Other Sound**. Locate and select the *p06h1Sorry* file and click **OK** to close the Add Audio dialog box. Click **OK** to close the Action Settings dialog box.

Once again, the sound action button has been edited to play a different sound file. Because this is not the correct answer, the viewer hears *Sorry* when the button is clicked.

n. Click the second sound action button from the top, click in the **Format Shape pane**, click in the **Position options**, and then set **Horizontal position** to **0.5"** and **Vertical position** to **2.97"**. Press **Enter**. Click **Close** to close the Format Shape pane.

o. Right-click the selected button and click **Hyperlink**. Click the **Play sound arrow**, click **Applause**, and then click **OK** to close the Action Settings dialog box.

This is the correct answer, so the viewer hears applause when the button is clicked.

p. Hold down **Shift** and click to select the four sound action buttons. Press **Ctrl+C** to copy them to the Clipboard. Click **Slide 5** and press **Ctrl+V** to paste the buttons on Slide 5. Click away from the selected buttons to deselect them.

It is fastest to copy, paste, and edit the buttons to additional slides, although the sound action buttons will need to be repositioned.

q. Ensure that you are on Slide 5, select the top sound action button (the sound action button for answer *a*), right-click, and then click **Hyperlink**. Click the **Play sound arrow**, select **Applause**, and then click **OK** to close the Action Settings dialog box.

This is the correct answer, so the viewer hears applause when the button is clicked.

r. Select the second sound action button (the sound action button for answer *b*), right-click, and then select **Hyperlink**. Click the **Play sound arrow** and select **Other Sound**. Select the *p06h1Incorrect* file and click **OK** to close the Add Audio dialog box. Click **OK** to close the Action Settings dialog box.

s. Save the presentation.

You want navigation buttons with consistent placement on the slides in your slide show. You will create the buttons on one slide, and copy and paste them to other slides. Refer to Figure 6.12 and the table below as you complete Step 4.

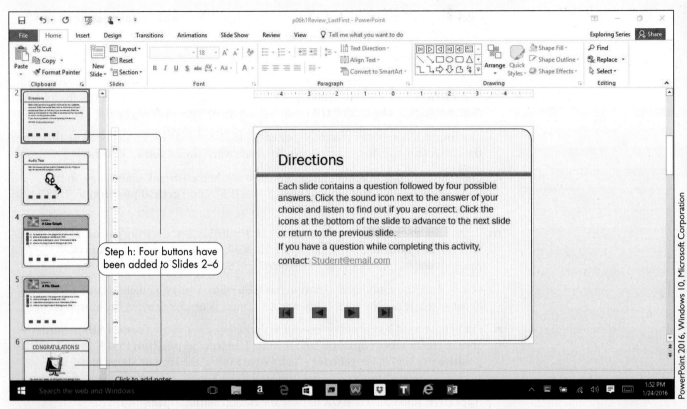

FIGURE 6.12 Action Buttons for Navigation

a. Click **Slide 2**, click the **Insert tab**, click **Shapes** in the Illustrations group, and then click **Action Button: Beginning** from the Action Buttons category of the Shapes gallery.

b. Click anywhere on the slide to create the action button.

The Action Settings dialog box opens, and the Beginning action button is preset to hyperlink to the first slide.

c. Click **OK**. Keep the button selected, and click the **Size dialog box launcher** in the Size group. Ensure that the Size section is expanded.

d. Set **Height** to **0.35"** and **Width** to **0.5"**. Press **Enter**.

e. Ensure the Position section is expanded and set **Horizontal position** to **0.92"** and **Vertical position** to **6.25"**. Press **Enter**.

f. Create three additional buttons using the default settings in the Action Settings dialog box and the information included in the following table:

Action Button	Height	Width	Horizontal Position	Vertical Position
Back or Previous	0.35"	0.5"	2.11"	6.25"
Forward or Next	0.35"	0.5"	3.27"	6.25"
End	0.35"	0.5"	4.46 "	6.25"

g. Close the Format pane. Select and copy the four action buttons.

h. Paste the action buttons on Slides 3 through 6.

i. Save the presentation.

You want to provide students with the option of opening a Charts and Graphs Reference Guide before answering quiz questions. You will create a customizable action button for students to click to open the guide. Refer to Figure 6.13 as you complete Step 5.

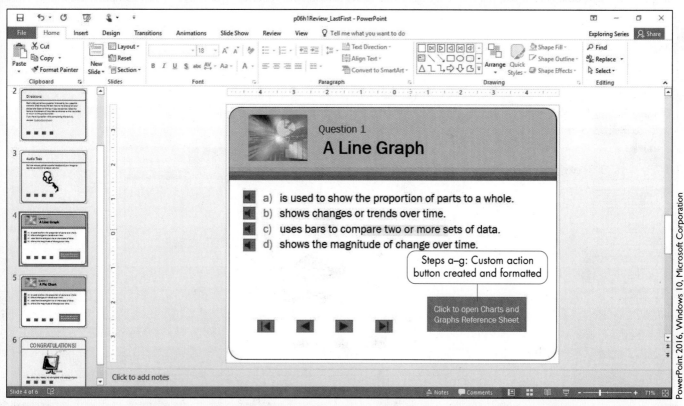

FIGURE 6.13 Custom Action Button

a. Click **Slide 4** and click the **Insert tab**. Click **Shapes** in the Illustrations group, and click **Action Button: Custom**.

b. Click the bottom right of the slide to create an action button.

c. Click **Hyperlink to** on the Mouse Click tab in the Action Settings dialog box, click the arrow, scroll down, and then select **Other File**.

d. Locate and select the *p06h1Guide* file and click **OK** to close the *Hyperlink to Other File* dialog box. Click **OK** to close the Action Settings dialog box.

e. Type **Click to open Charts and Graphs Reference Sheet** inside the selected custom action button.

f. Click the **Size dialog box launcher** in the Size group, and set **Height** to **1"** and **Width** to **3"**. Press **Enter**.

g. Ensure the **Position** section is expanded and set **Horizontal position** to **6"** and **Vertical position** to **5.58"**. **Close** the Format Shape pane.

h. Click the **border of the button object** to select the entire object and text, press **Ctrl+C** to copy the custom action button, and then paste it to Slide 5.

i. Save the presentation.

After completing the review quiz, you want the students to complete an assignment on charts and graphs. To include interactivity, you will add a ScreenTip to a picture that instructs the student to click the picture. You will create a hyperlink to an existing file using text in a text box. Finally, you will create a trigger that launches the text. Refer to Figure 6.14 as you complete Step 6.

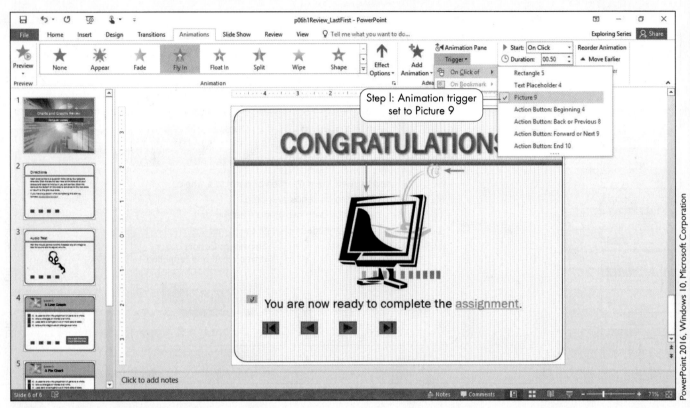

FIGURE 6.14 Slide 6 Trigger and Hyperlink

    a. Click **Slide 6** and select the **monitor picture**.

    b. Click the **Insert tab** and click **Hyperlink** in the Links group.

    c. Click **Place in This Document** and click **Slide 6**.

    You are linking the monitor picture to the same location in the document so that you have access to the ScreenTip option.

    d. Click **ScreenTip**, type **Click Me!** in the Set Hyperlink ScreenTip dialog box, and then click **OK**.

    The ScreenTip displays when the presentation is viewed in Slide Show or Reading view.

    e. Click **OK** to close the Insert Hyperlink dialog box.

    f. Select the word *assignment* in the text box.

    g. Click **Hyperlink**.

    h. Click **Existing File or Web Page**, then navigate to and insert *p06h1Assignment*. Click **OK**.

    i. Verify that the address for the *p06h1Assignment* file appears in the Address box and click **OK**.

    The word *assignment* is underlined, indicating it is a hyperlink.

    j. Ensure that the text box border is selected, and click the **Animations tab**.

    k. Click **Fly In** in the Animation group.

    With an animation assigned, the Trigger option is available.

l. Click **Trigger** in the Advanced Animation group, point to *On Click of*, and then click **Picture 9**.

Picture 9 (the monitor image) triggers the text animation when clicked in Slide Show or Reading view.

m. Save the presentation.

STEP 7 » TEST HYPERLINKS

In addition to viewing a slide show while you are developing it to ensure that it plays correctly, it is critical to test all interactive components of a slide show containing hyperlinks, action buttons, and triggers. You test the *Charts and Graphs Review* slide show before getting approval from your supervisor to create additional questions. Refer to Figure 6.15 as you complete Step 7.

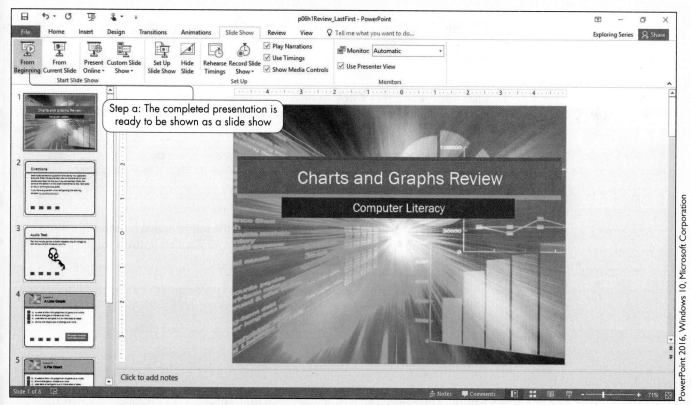

FIGURE 6.15 Completed Interactive Slide Show

PowerPoint 2016, Windows 10, Microsoft Corporation

a. Click the **Slide Show tab** and click **From Beginning** in the Start Slide Show group.

b. Advance to **Slide 2** and click the **email hyperlink**. Close the email screen without saving.

> **TROUBLESHOOTING:** When testing sounds, you may need to adjust your volume to hear the sounds playing. You may want to use a headset if you are in a public computer lab.

c. Click the **Forward or Next action button** to move to Slide 3. Point to the headset image.

> **TROUBLESHOOTING:** You will not be able to hear the Voltage sound or see the highlight border unless you are in Slide Show view. If the Voltage sound does not play when you mouse over it, exit the slide show and right-click the image of the headset. Click Hyperlink, click the Mouse Over tab, and then check *Play sound*. Select Voltage from the list of sounds and click OK. Return to Slide Show mode.

d. Continue advancing through the slides in the presentation using the action buttons for navigation. Be sure to test each button.

> **TROUBLESHOOTING:** If any of the action buttons do not work, exit the slide show. In any slide, right-click the action button. Click Edit Hyperlink and check the slide showing in the *Hyperlink to:* box. If no slide is showing or if the wrong slide is showing, click the arrow and select the right slide from the list. Click OK. Copy the button and paste it on all other slides containing the button. Return to Slide Show mode.

e. Click **Slide 4** and click each of the sound action buttons. Answer *b* should play the applause sound. The remaining sound action buttons should play a sound that indicates the choice of answer was incorrect.

> **TROUBLESHOOTING:** If any of the sound action buttons play the wrong sound, exit the slide show. Select the sound action button that plays the wrong sound, right-click, and then click Hyperlink. Change the linked sound to the correct choice. Return to Slide Show mode.

f. Click **Slide 4** and click **Click to open Charts and Graphs Reference Sheet** to open the Word document. Close the document after opening. Repeat for Slide 5.

> **TROUBLESHOOTING:** If the Word document did not open, exit the slide show. Right-click the custom action button and click Hyperlink. Click the *Browse for File* button and locate and insert *p06h1Guide*. Click OK twice. Return to Slide Show mode.

g. Ensure that you are on Slide 5 and click each of the sound action buttons. Answer *a* should play the applause sound. The remaining sound action buttons should play a sound that indicates the choice of answer was incorrect.

> **TROUBLESHOOTING:** If any of the sound action buttons play the wrong sound, follow the Troubleshooting instructions in Step e.

h. Advance to **Slide 6** and point to the image to view the ScreenTip.

> **TROUBLESHOOTING:** If the ScreenTip does not display, exit the slide show, right-click the image, and then click Edit Hyperlink. Click *Place in This Document*, click Slide 6, and then click ScreenTip. Type Click Me!. Click OK twice. Return to Slide Show mode.

i. Click the image to trigger the text box animation.

> **TROUBLESHOOTING:** If the text box does not fly onto the slide, exit the slide show. Select the text box, click the Animations tab, and then check to see if the Fly In animation is assigned. Then, click Trigger in the Advanced Animation group, click *On Click of*, and then check to see if *Picture 9* is selected. Return to Slide Show mode.

j. Click **assignment** to ensure that the *Charts and Graphs* assignment opens. Close the document after opening. End the slide show.

> **TROUBLESHOOTING:** If Word does not open and display the *p06h1 Assignment* file, exit the slide show. Right-click the assignment hyperlink and click Edit Hyperlink. Click the *Browse for File* button and locate and select *p06h1 Assignment*. Click OK twice.

k. Save and close the presentation. You will submit this file to your instructor at the end of the last Hands-on Exercise.

Advanced Animation

In the previous section, you used an animation trigger to control the flow of information on a slide. By fully utilizing the different types of animations and animation options, you can engage the audience's interest and direct their focus to important points in your presentation. Carefully plan animations, however, to ensure that they enhance the message of the slide. Used indiscriminately, animations can be distracting to the audience.

Table 6.2 shows PowerPoint's four animation types. Each of these animation types has properties, effects, and timing that can be modified.

TABLE 6.2 PowerPoint Animation Types	
Type	**Content**
Entrance	Controls how an object moves onto or appears on a slide
Emphasis	Draws attention to an object already on a slide
Exit	Controls how an object leaves or disappears from a slide
Motion Paths	Controls the movement of an object from one position to another along a predetermined path

Pearson Education, Inc.

In this section, you will apply multiple animations to an object, modify a motion path, specify animation effects, set animation timing, control the flow of text, and fine-tune your animations using the Animation Pane.

Applying Multiple Animations to an Object

STEP 1 ▶▶ Multiple animations can be applied to an object. For example, you could apply an entrance animation that causes your company logo to fly onto a title slide, an emphasis animation that causes the logo to grow and shrink, a motion animation that causes the logo to move in a circle, and an exit animation that causes the logo to fly off the slide. You can control the timing of the animations as well as the trigger that starts the animation sequence. This complex set of animations may not be necessary, but it shows the power of the animation effects. Keep in mind, though, when you use too many animations on one object or slide, the result can be distracting and take away from the message of the object or slide.

Figure 6.16 shows multiple animations applied to a slide. Numbered animation tags indicate the order in which the animations will play.

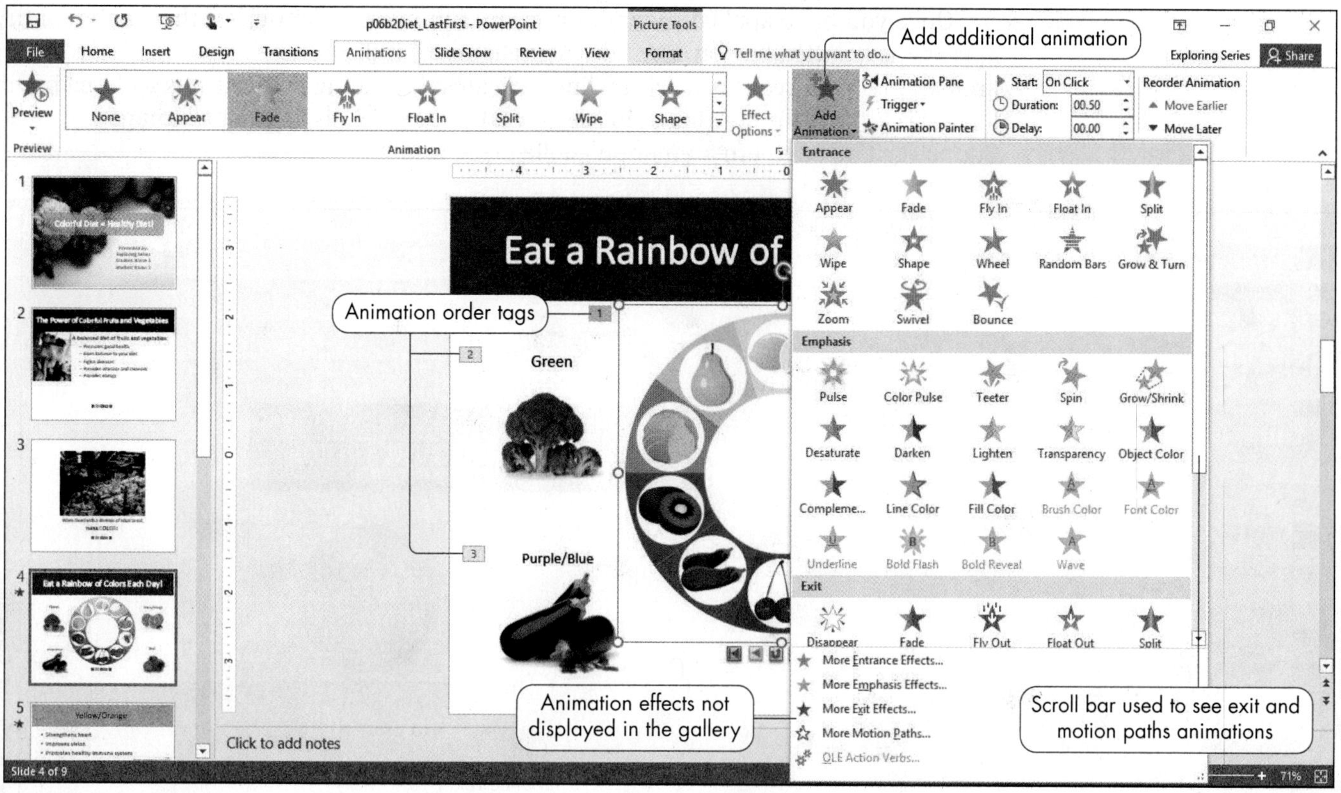

PowerPoint 2016, Windows 10, Microsoft Corporation

FIGURE 6.16 Slide with Multiple Animations Applied

To add multiple animations to an object, complete the following steps:

1. Select the object and click the Animations tab.
2. Apply an animation from the Animation gallery.
3. Click Add Animation in the Advanced Animation group.
4. Click an animation to apply it to the object.
5. Continue adding animations.

Animation sequences should be checked as you create them to make sure they respond in the way you expect. At any time, click Preview in the Preview group to see the animation sequence in Normal view. You can also check the sequence in Slide Show or Reading view.

Applying a Motion Path Animation

Because the eye is naturally drawn to motion, using a motion path (a predetermined path that an object follows as part of an animation) to animate an object can capture and focus a viewer's attention on key objects or text. Motion paths are linear, curved, or follow a predetermined shape. PowerPoint includes a variety of interesting motion paths such as arcs, turns, shapes, and loops. You can also draw a custom path for the object to follow. More motion path choices are available after you click More in the Animation group.

To apply a motion path animation, complete the following steps:

1. Select the object and click the Animations tab.
2. Click More in the Animation group.
3. Scroll down to the Motion Paths category.
4. Click a motion path animation to apply it to the selected object.

Once you have applied the motion path animation to an object, the motion path appears as a dotted line on the slide. A small arrow indicates the starting point for the animation, and a red arrow with a line indicates the ending point. If it is a closed path like a circle, only the starting point displays. Figure 6.17 displays a ball image with the Bounce Left motion path animation applied.

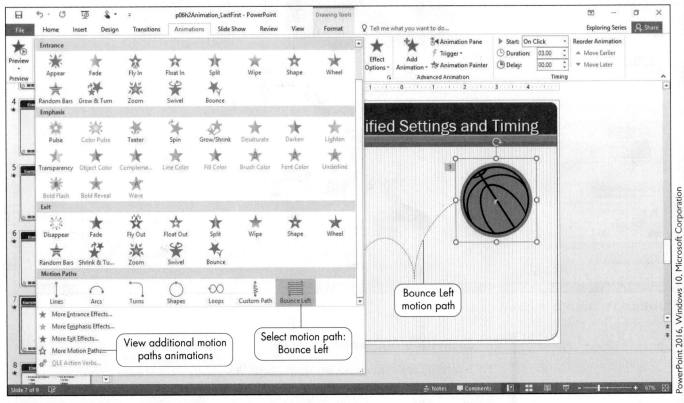

FIGURE 6.17 Bounce Left Motion Path

Create a Custom Path

STEP 2 》》 A *custom path* is an animation path that can be created freehand instead of following a preset path. You can draw a path in the direction and the length you determine rather than in a standard path available in the Animation gallery.

> **To create a custom path, complete the following steps:**
>
> 1. Select the object and click the Animations tab.
> 2. Click More in the Animation group.
> 3. Select the Custom Path animation from the Motion Path gallery.
> 4. Position the crosshair pointer in the approximate center of the object you wish to animate.
> 5. Drag in the direction you want the object to follow. The crosshair pointer becomes a Pencil tool that you drag until you have the desired path.
> 6. Double-click to end the path.

By default, a custom path animation uses the Scribble option, which enables you to draw the path by using the pointer like a pencil. You can draw a Curve or Line path by clicking Effect Options in the Animation group before you draw the path. Figure 6.18 shows a custom path animation drawn using the Scribble option.

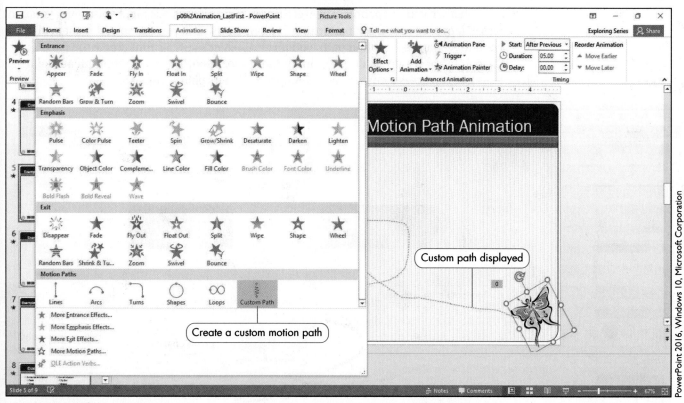

FIGURE 6.18 Custom Path

Several additional motion paths are available to apply when you choose More Motion Paths in the Animation gallery. The Change Motion Path dialog box provides several choices within the categories of Basic, Lines_Curves, and Special Paths. Figure 6.19 shows an image with the Stairs Down motion path applied.

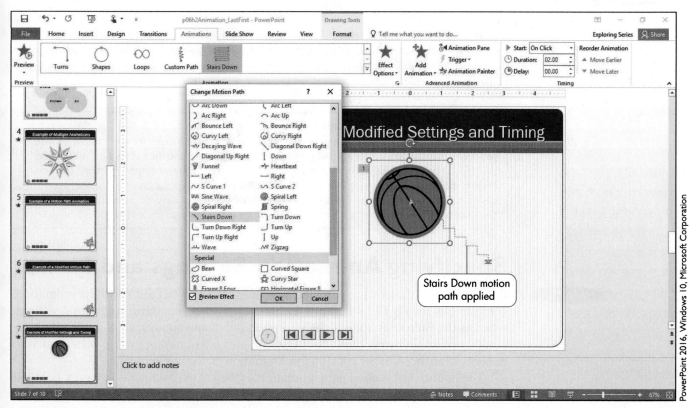

FIGURE 6.19 Path Example From the Lines_Curves Category

Whether you apply one of PowerPoint's motion paths or create your own, you can resize, move, or rotate the path using the same methods you use to edit a shape. If you want to reshape the motion path, you must display the points that create the path. Once the points are displayed, drag a point to its new location. The path automatically adjusts. Figure 6.20 shows a custom path animation with its points displayed.

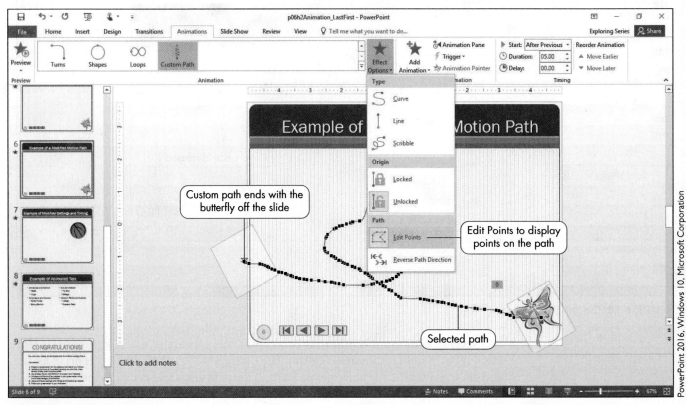

FIGURE 6.20 Reshaping a Path

To display the points, select the path, click Effect Options in the Animation group, and then click Edit Points. Drag points on the path as needed. You can add or delete points by right-clicking the path to display the editing menu and clicking Add Point or Delete Point.

> **TIP: REVERSING A CUSTOM PATH**
> If you want an object to end at an exact location on a slide, it may be easier for you to draw a motion path from its ending point than from its beginning point. Once you have the path drawn, reverse the path by clicking Effect Options in the Animation group and clicking Reverse Path Direction. Then, to prevent the object from jumping from its original location to the new location when the animation begins, lock the path by clicking Effect Options and clicking Locked. Finally, drag the object to the new beginning point.

Specifying Animation Settings and Timing

 Each of the animations has associated settings that vary according to the animation. For example, the Fly Out animation includes direction, smoothing, and sound settings, whereas the Fade animation includes only sound. Some options, such as direction, are readily accessible by clicking Effect Options in the Animation group. Others such as *Bounce end* are accessed by clicking the Animation dialog box launcher.

The Bounce Left motion path animation applied to the ball image in Figure 6.21 has the *Smooth start* and *Smooth end* settings set to 0 seconds. The *Smooth start* and *Smooth end* settings enable an object to accelerate and decelerate along its motion path. In this figure, the image begins to slow after 1.5 seconds because the Bounce end has been set for that. The ball disappears after animating because the *After animation* setting is set to Hide After Animation.

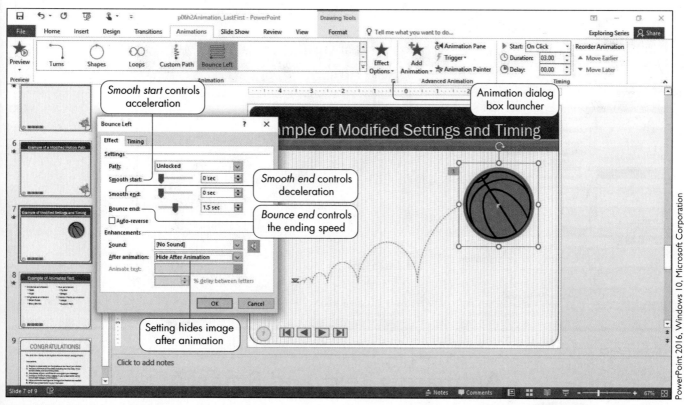

FIGURE 6.21 Animation Settings

Attaching timing settings to animations frees you from constantly advancing to the next object and lets you concentrate on delivering your message. Previously, you have set timing options in the Timing group on the Animations tab, and that is the quickest way to set the method for starting an animation, to set the duration of an animation, and to set the delay. The Animation dialog box launcher also provides access to these settings, but the dialog box it opens gives you several additional settings. You can set the number of times an animation is repeated, set the animation to rewind when it is done playing, and determine how the animation is triggered on the Timing tab of the dialog box. Figure 6.22 shows an animated SmartArt object. In addition to animating a SmartArt object as one object, you can select the individual shapes that make up the SmartArt object and animate them individually. The Circle dialog box is open, showing the Timing tab options available for the selected SmartArt object.

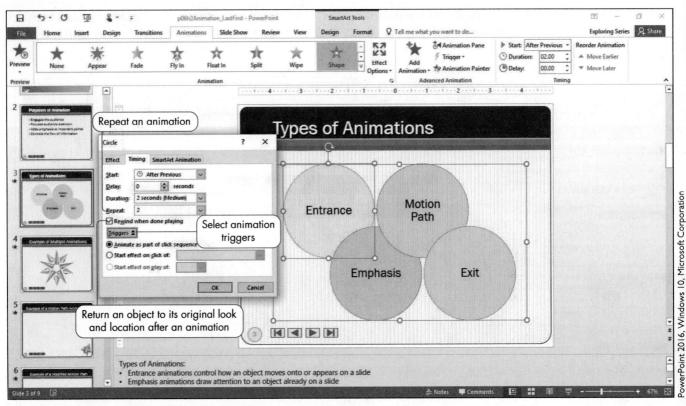

FIGURE 6.22 Timing Options for Circle Animation

Animating Text and SmartArt

STEP 4 ▶▶ Although animating non-bulleted text in placeholders and text boxes uses the same method as other objects, bullet text has additional animation options available. These options help you keep audience attention and can keep the audience from reading ahead. You can bring text onto the slide by animating the text as one object, animating all paragraphs to come in together, or by sequencing the text animation by text outline level. A paragraph in PowerPoint can be a line of text, several lines of text, or even a blank line. Whenever you press Enter to move the insertion point to a new line, you create a new paragraph.

> **To determine the animation sequence of bullet text, complete the following steps:**
>
> 1. Select the text and click the Animations tab.
> 2. Apply an animation effect.
> 3. Click Effect Options in the Animation group.
> 4. Select the desired text grouping option from the Sequence list.

To assign animations beyond the first level, click the Animation dialog box launcher and click the Text Animation tab. Click the *Group text* arrow and animate text for up to five outline levels. Figure 6.23 shows text animated by second-level paragraphs.

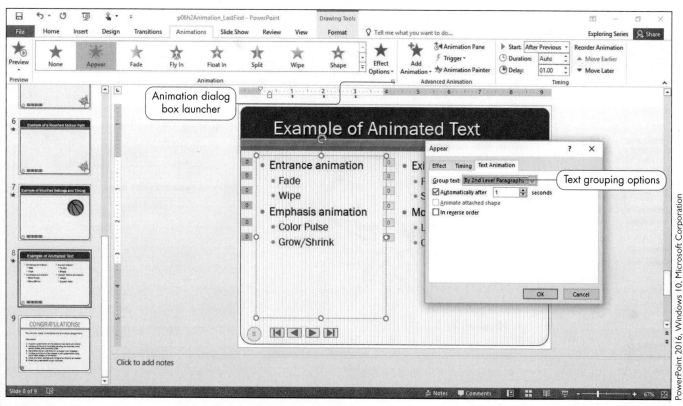

FIGURE 6.23 Text Animations by Second-Level Paragraphs

TIP: LAYERING TEXT ON TEXT

When following the 7×7 per slide text guideline, which suggests using no more than seven lines with seven words on a slide, you may find that you have more text to display on a slide than there is room available. If this happens, create two text boxes. Animate the first text box, and click the Animation dialog box icon launcher. Click the *After animation* arrow and click Hide After Animation. Select the second text box and animate using the Appear animation. Set the animation to play *After previous*.

Using the Animation Pane

STEP 5 ⟫ As you work with complex animations, it is helpful to view the Animation Pane. The Animation Pane provides a summary of animation effects used. The display begins with a tag indicating how the animation starts. A *0* tag indicates the animation starts with the previous animation. A numbered tag indicates the animation begins with a mouse click, and the number indicates the animation order. No tag indicates that the animation automatically starts after the previous animation. The Office software color-codes animation effects by type of animation: green indicates an entrance animation; red indicates an exit animation; yellow indicates an emphasis animation; and blue indicates motion paths.

An icon displays to the right of the tag that represents the type of animation effect applied. Next, a portion of the name of the animated object displays. Finally, a timeline displays the duration of an animation as a bar that can be used to adjust timing. To adjust animation timing, drag the edge of the timeline bar. To open the Animation Pane, click the Animations tab and click Animation Pane in the Advanced Animation group. The size of the Animation Pane can be adjusted by positioning the pointer along the left edge of the pane. When it changes to a double-headed arrow, hold and drag it to the left. This may make it easier to adjust the timing. Figure 6.24 shows a slide containing animated objects, with the Animation Pane open.

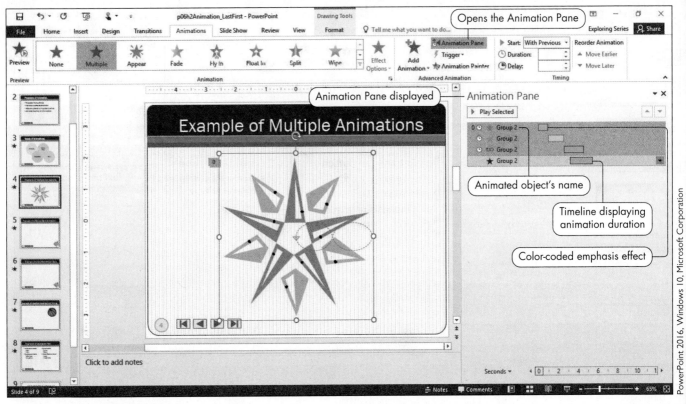

FIGURE 6.24 Animation Pane

Quick Concepts ✓

4. Which animation effect does an Entrance animation type apply to an object? **p. 410**

5. How will applying a motion path to an object or text enhance your presentation? **p. 411**

6. What animation effects are edited and controlled in the Animation Pane? **p. 417**

Hands-On Exercises

Watch the Video for this Hands-On Exercise!

MyITLab®
HOE2 Training

Skills covered: Apply Multiple Animations to an Object • Create a Custom Motion Path • Modify a Custom Motion Path • Specify Animation Settings and Timing • Animate Text and SmartArt • Use the Animation Pane to Modify Animations

2 Advanced Animation

In your role as the teaching assistant for the computer literacy class, you begin modifying a presentation designed to help the students understand PowerPoint's animation features. You create examples of animation for students to view.

STEP 1 ❯❯ APPLY MULTIPLE ANIMATIONS TO AN OBJECT

To illustrate an example of multiple animations applied to one object, you apply an entrance, emphasis, motion, and exit animation to an image. After testing the animations, you use the Animation Pane to select and modify the animations. Refer to Figure 6.25 as you complete Step 1.

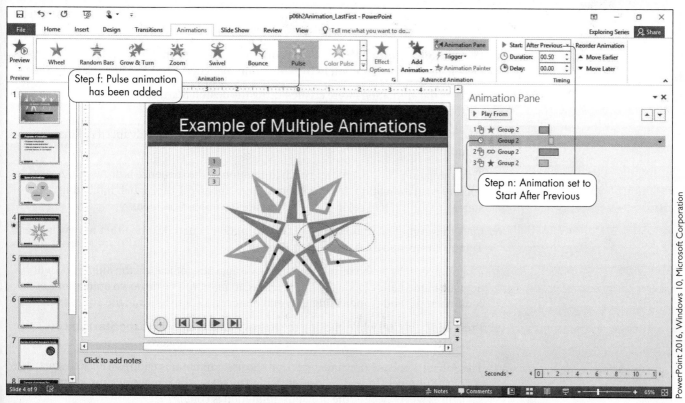

FIGURE 6.25 Multiple Animations Applied to an Object

a. Open *p06h2Animation* and save it as **p06h2Animation_LastFirst**.

> **TROUBLESHOOTING:** If you make any major mistakes in this exercise, you can close the file, open *p06h2Animation* again, and then start this exercise over.

b. Create a handout header with your name and a handout footer with your instructor's name and your class. Include the current date.

c. Click **Slide 4**, then select the **star image** and click the **Animations tab**.

d. Click **More** in the Animation group and click **Grow & Turn** in the Entrance category.

The Grow & Turn animation previews, and an animation tag numbered 1 is assigned to the image.

e. Click **Add Animation** in the Advanced Animation group.

f. Click **Pulse** in the Emphasis category.

The Pulse animation previews and an animation tag numbered 2 is assigned to the image.

g. Click **Add Animation** in the Advanced Animation group.

h. Scroll down the Animation gallery and click **Loops** in the Motion Paths category.

The Loops animation previews, the Loops motion path displays, and an animation tag numbered 3 is assigned to the image.

i. Click **Add Animation** in the Advanced Animation group.

j. Scroll down the Animation gallery and click **Shrink & Turn** in the Exit category.

The Shrink & Turn animation previews, and an animation tag numbered 4 is assigned to the image.

k. Click **Preview** in the Preview group.

Preview displays the animation sequence without regard to how each animation is set to start.

l. Click the **Slide Show tab** and click **From Current Slide** in the Start Slide Show group. Click to play each animation in the animation sequence. Press **Esc** after viewing Slide 4.

Because the animations were created using the default *Start: On Click* timing option, you must click to start each animation in the sequence.

m. Click the **Animations tab** and click **Animation Pane** in the Advanced Animation group.

The Animation Pane opens, and each animation in the sequence is displayed. As you point to each animation, the animations are numbered 1 through 4, indicating they start with a click, and color-coded to indicate the animation type.

n. Click the animation numbered **2** in the Animation Pane, click the **Start arrow** in the Timing group, and then click **After Previous**.

The number next to the second animation disappears, indicating the animation will activate immediately following the previous animation. The next two animations are renumbered 2 and 3, indicating they still require a click to activate the animation.

o. Press and hold **Ctrl** while clicking the last two animations. Click the **Start Arrow** and click **After Previous** to change their timings to After Previous.

The Animation Pane now indicates that the first animation requires a click to start. All of the numbers have disappeared, which indicates the remaining animations in the sequences will play after the previous animation is completed.

TROUBLESHOOTING: If it is difficult to see all four timeline bars, adjust the size of the Animation Pane by positioning the pointer along the left edge of the pane. When it changes to a double-headed arrow, hold and drag it to the left.

---

p. Test the animation sequence in Slide Show view to ensure that the animations play correctly.

q. Close the Animation Pane.

r. Save the presentation.

The next example of an animation in the presentation is a custom motion path animation. You will create a motion path to move an image around the slide, and you will copy the image and path to another slide and modify the path to smooth it. Refer to Figure 6.26 as you complete Step 2.

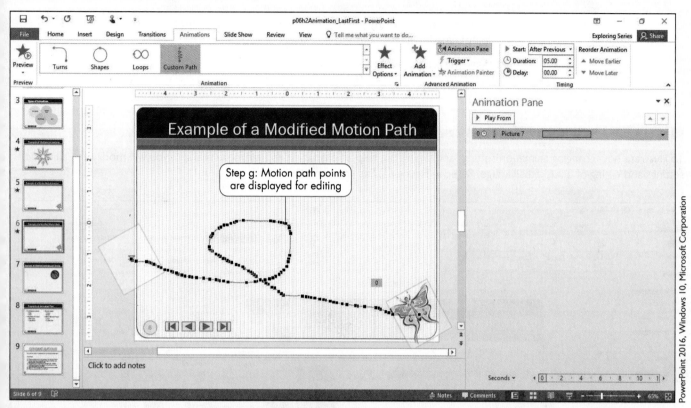

FIGURE 6.26 Original Custom Path Animation Ready to Be Modified

a. Click **Slide 5** and select the **butterfly image**.

b. Click **More** in the Animation group.

c. Click **Custom Path** in the Motion Paths category.

d. Click in the approximate center of the butterfly and drag the **Pencil tool** in a loop and off the left side of the slide. Refer to Figure 6.26. Double-click to end the path.

The animation previews, and when the preview finishes, you see the path with its green starting point and red ending point.

e. Select **02.00** in the Duration box in the Timing Group and type **05.00**.

Increasing the duration increases the amount of time it takes to complete the animation.

f. Select and copy the image. Click **Slide 6** and click the **Home** tab. Click the **Paste arrow** and select the **Use Destination Theme paste option** (first choice).

The image and its associated animation are pasted on Slide 6.

g. Ensure that you are on Slide 6 and click the **Animations tab**, then click the animation's path. Click **Effect Options** in the Animation group, and click **Edit Points**.

The points that create the motion path appear.

h. Click a point on the path and drag the point to a new position.

The path reshapes based on the new point position.

i. Click a point on the path, right-click, and then click **Delete Point**.

> **TROUBLESHOOTING:** If you press Delete on the keyboard, the entire path disappears. Click Undo on the Quick Access Toolbar and repeat Step i.

j. Continue to delete any points that cause a jerky animation motion, or right-click any point causing a jerky motion and select **Smooth Point**.

k. Save the presentation.

STEP 3 ›› **SPECIFY ANIMATION SETTINGS AND TIMING**

To illustrate how changing animation settings and timing can help an animation appear more realistic, you will modify the animation settings and timing of a basketball image. Refer to Figure 6.27 as you complete Step 3.

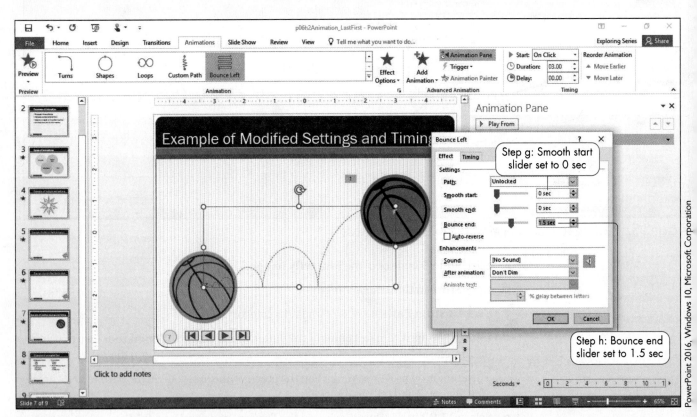

FIGURE 6.27 Bounce Left Animation Settings

a. Click **Slide 7** and click the **basketball image** to select it.

b. Click **More** in the Animation group, and click **More Motion Paths**.

c. Click **Bounce Left** in the *Lines_Curves* section and click **OK**.

d. Point to the red ending point of the animation. When the double-headed arrow displays, drag it to the left to extend the distance the animation will cover.

> **TROUBLESHOOTING:** Be sure the pointer displays as the double-headed arrow before dragging the red ending point of the animation. Otherwise, you will move the entire animation instead of extending the distance the animation will cover.

e. Click the **Duration up arrow** in the Timing group until the duration time is set at **03.00**.

The animation will now take three seconds to complete.

f. Click the **Animation dialog box launcher** in the Animation group to show additional animation effect options.

The Bounce Left dialog box opens.

g. Drag the **Smooth start slider** to **0 sec**.

The animation now starts at a higher speed rather than starting slowly and speeding up.

h. Drag the **Bounce end slider** to **1.5 sec** and click **OK**. (The *Smooth end* setting automatically becomes 0 sec.)

The animation previews automatically. The animation begins to slow after 1.5 seconds.

i. Save the presentation.

STEP 4 ▶▶ ANIMATE TEXT AND SMARTART

You want to demonstrate how to control the flow of information to the computer literacy students. To do so, you will animate text and a SmartArt diagram. You will apply the Appear animation effect on text content placeholders so that students will not be distracted by movement and can concentrate on reading the text. You will apply a Shape entrance animation so that the animation shape matches the circle shapes used in the SmartArt. Refer to Figure 6.28 as you complete Step 4.

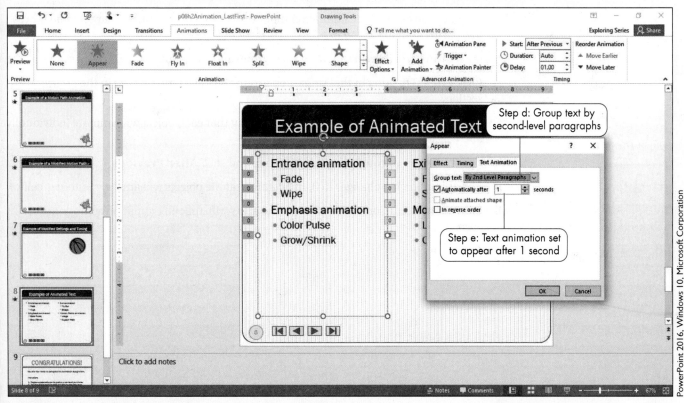

FIGURE 6.28 Animated Text Settings

a. Click **Slide 8** and click the **left content placeholder** to select it.

Selecting text enables you to apply an animation; selecting the content placeholder is faster.

b. Click **Appear** in the *Entrance* section of the Animation group.

Animation 1 and 2 tags appear next to the first and second first-level bullets and their associated second-level bullets.

c. Click the **Animation dialog box launcher** to display the Appear dialog box. Click the **After animation arrow** on the Effects tab, and click the last color option.

Text that has been viewed dims to the new color after viewing.

d. Click the **Text Animation tab** in the Appear dialog box, click the **Group text arrow**, and then select **By 2nd Level Paragraphs**.

First-level text and second-level text will animate one at a time.

e. Click **Automatically after**, click the **up spin arrow** to reach **1**, and then click **OK**.

The animation tags change to 0, indicating that they will start automatically. Preview displays the text entering, pausing for 1 second, and then dimming when the next animated text appears.

f. Click the **left content placeholder**, click **Animation Painter**, and then click the **right content placeholder**.

The animation timing and settings are copied to the placeholder.

g. Click **Slide 3**, and select the **SmartArt diagram**.

h. Click **More** in the Animation group and click **Shape** in the *Entrance* section.

Preview displays a Circle animation that begins at the edges of the SmartArt and moves inward to complete the shape.

i. Click **Effect Options** in the Animation group and click **Out** in the *Direction* section.

j. Click **Effect Options** in the Animation group and click **One by One** in the *Sequence* section.

Animation tags 1 through 4 appear, indicating that each object will animate individually and will start on a mouse click.

k. Click the **Start arrow** in the Timing group and click **After Previous**.

The animation tag changes to 0, indicating that the objects will animate automatically.

l. View the presentation in Slide Show view and verify that all animation settings are set correctly.

m. Save the presentation.

After viewing the presentation, you realize that you would like each animation to start automatically when the slide appears. You also want to modify the timing of some animations. You will open the Animation Pane to efficiently locate and change animation settings. Refer to Figure 6.29 as you complete Step 5.

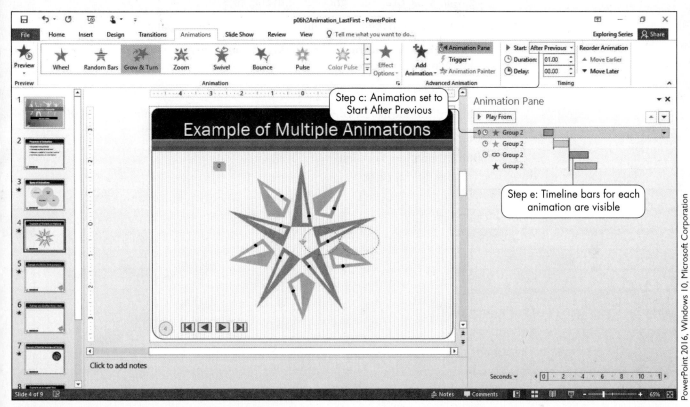

FIGURE 6.29 Timeline Bars for Modified Animation

a. Ensure that you are on the Animations tab. Click **Animation Pane** in the Advanced Animation group.

b. Click **Slide 4** and click the **star image**. Notice the Animation Pane.

All animations in the Animation Pane are selected. The animation 1 tag next to the first bullet indicates that this animation plays first and requires a mouse click to launch.

c. Click the **first animation** in the Animation Pane to select it and click the **Start arrow** in the Timing group. Click **After Previous**.

The animation 1 tag changes to a 0.

d. Repeat Step c for Slides 5 through 7.

e. Click **Slide 4** and drag the left border of the Animation Pane to the left until the timeline bar next to each animation is visible.

The timeline bars show that each animation starts immediately after the preceding animation. The loop animation takes longer to complete than the other three animations.

f. Drag the right edge of the timeline bar for the second animation to the right until the ScreenTip displays *End: 2.6s*.

The Pulse animation duration is increased.

TROUBLESHOOTING: Be sure the pointer displays as the double-headed arrow with vertical lines in the middle. A plain double-headed arrow will not work for this task.

---

g. Click the **last animation** to select it, click the **Start arrow**, and then click **With Previous**.

The beginning points for the third and fourth animations align so they begin at the same time.

h. Position the pointer over the fourth animation timeline bar and drag the bar so that it begins at **3.2s**. Drag the right edge of the bar to **5.5s**.

The time the animation starts and the duration of the animation is changed.

i. Click the **first animation** and click **Play From** in the Animation Pane to test the animation. Close the Animation Pane.

j. View the presentation in Slide Show view.

k. Save and close the file. Based on your instructor's directions, submit:

p06h1Review_LastFirst

p06h2Animation_LastFirst

Chapter Objectives Review

After reading this chapter, you have accomplished the following objectives:

1. Insert and use hyperlinks.

- Hyperlinks connect two locations and can be used to add interactivity to a slide show.
- Hyperlinks can be activated by a mouse click or a mouse over.
- Hyperlinks can be attached to any object and can take the viewer to another slide in a slide show, to an existing file, to a webpage on the Internet, to another program, or to the screen to begin an email.
- Link to an existing file or webpage: Use the Insert Hyperlink dialog box to specify the URL of the webpage to link to or browse for a desired file on your computer.
- Link to an email address: Creating an email link enables the viewer to contact you for more information or for additional questions or follow-up after a presentation.
- Link to a slide in the active presentation: This can be used to create a menu of topics, or to focus your audience's attention on anticipated questions or comments.
- Link to a new document: This option can be used to link to a new PowerPoint presentation or other document to demonstrate features or provide additional examples for the original presentation topic.

2. Add action buttons.

- Actions are instructions to PowerPoint to perform a task such as jumping to another slide, playing a sound, or opening another program.
- You can attach actions to any object or use an action button—a pre-made icon with actions attached.
- Activate an action button with a mouse click or a mouse over.
- Add sound to an object: Sound can be added to a hyperlink attached to an object to capture your audience's attention or to add emphasis to the subject of the link.
- Use action buttons for navigation: Action buttons are typically used to navigate a slide show (Back or Previous button, Forward or Next button, Beginning button, End button, Home button, and Return button) or to display some type of information (Information button, Movie button, Document button, Sound button, and Help button).
- Create custom buttons: Custom buttons are created and set to trigger unique actions in presentations. These buttons can be used as hyperlinks to another location, videos, documents, sound, or the Help feature.

3. Use a trigger.

- A trigger is an animation option that controls when an event takes place.
- In order for the event to take place, a viewer must click an object that has an animation trigger attached.

- Add a ScreenTip: ScreenTips can be added to hyperlinks to offer the viewer additional information.
- Check and modify hyperlinks and action buttons: Before delivering or publishing a presentation, test each hyperlink in Slide Show view or by right-clicking each link and selecting Open Hyperlink. Check all actions buttons to see if they perform as you intended.

4. Apply multiple animations to an object.

- You can apply more than one animation effect to an object.
- Multiple animations direct the flow of information or enhance the message of a slide.

5. Apply a motion path animation.

- In a motion path animation, an object follows a predetermined path to capture and focus a viewer's attention.
- Motion paths can be linear, curved, or follow a predetermined shape.
- Add, delete, and move points on a motion path to edit it.
- Create a custom path: Creating a custom motion path enables you to draw a path in any direction and of any length.

6. Specify animation settings and timing.

- Animation settings vary according to the animation type and are modified using the Animations tab or the Animation dialog box associated with the selected animation effect.
- Attaching timings to animations frees you from constantly advancing to the next object and lets you concentrate on delivering your message.

7. Animate text.

- Animating text controls the flow of information to the audience.
- You can bring text onto the slide by animating the text as one object, animating all paragraphs to come in together, or sequencing the text animation by text outline level.

8. Use the Animation Pane.

- The Animation Pane provides a summary of animation effects used.
- Tags indicate how an animation starts; the type of animation effect applied; a portion of the name of the animated object; and a timeline with bars that displays the start, end, and duration of animations.

Key Terms Matching

Match the key terms with their definitions. Write the key term letter by the appropriate numbered definition.

a. Action button

b. Animation

c. Custom button

d. Custom path

e. Emphasis

f. Entrance

g. Exit

h. Hyperlink

i. Interactivity

j. Kiosk

k. Linear presentation

l. Motion path

m. Non-linear presentation

n. ScreenTip

o. Trigger

p. Uniform resource locator (URL)

1. _____ The ability to branch or interact based on decisions made by a viewer or audience. **p. 390**

2. _____ An object that displays when the viewer mouses over a hyperlink or other object and provides additional information about the hyperlink or object. **p. 399**

3. _____ An action button that can be set to trigger unique actions in the presentation. **p. 396**

4. _____ A ready-made button designed to serve as an icon that can initiate an action when clicked, pointed to, or moused over. **p. 390**

5. _____ A presentation that progresses according to choices made by the viewer or audience that determine which slide comes next. **p. 390**

6. _____ An interactive computer terminal available for public use. **p. 395**

7. _____ A PowerPoint animation type that controls the movement of an object from one position to another along a predetermined path. **p. 410**

8. _____ An action used to draw interest to an object in a presentation; a movement that controls the entrance, emphasis, exit, and/or path of objects in a slide show. **p. 398**

9. _____ The address used to locate a resource or webpage on the Web. **p. 391**

10. _____ A presentation where each slide is designed to move one right after another, and the viewer or audience progresses through slides, starting with the first slide and advancing sequentially until the last slide is reached. **p. 390**

11. _____ A PowerPoint animation type that draws attention to an object already on a slide. **p. 410**

12. _____ A connection that branches to another slide or another location that contains additional information. **p. 390**

13. _____ A PowerPoint animation type that controls how an object moves onto or appears on a slide. **p. 410**

14. _____ An animation path that can be created freehand instead of following a preset path. **p. 412**

15. _____ A PowerPoint animation type that controls how an object leaves or disappears from a slide. **p. 410**

16. _____ An object that launches an animation that takes place when you click an associated object or a bookmarked location in a media object. **p. 398**

Multiple Choice

1. The term used for a connection from one location to another is:
   - (a) Hyperlink.
   - (b) Trigger.
   - (c) Motion path.
   - (d) Object.

2. When you click an object on the slide or when you launch an animation with a bookmark in a video and an animation effect occurs, which of the following is used?
   - (a) Hyperlink
   - (b) Mouse over
   - (c) Action button
   - (d) Trigger

3. Which of the following refers to an interactive slide show?
   - (a) Sequential presentation
   - (b) Linear presentation
   - (c) Non-linear presentation
   - (d) Abstract presentation

4. To define a new or technical term in a presentation, you can use a(n):
   - (a) ScreenTip.
   - (b) URL.
   - (c) Trigger.
   - (d) Motion path.

5. Which of the following is *not* a default navigation button included in Slide Show view?
   - (a) Previous
   - (b) Forward
   - (c) Display shortcut menu
   - (d) Help

6. Which of the following is a *true* statement regarding multiple animations?
   - (a) To add a second animation, click the Insert tab and click Add Animation.
   - (b) Multiple animations can be added to shape objects but not text objects.
   - (c) Individual animations that are part of an animation sequence display in the Animation Pane.
   - (d) All of the above.

7. An animation path that can be created freehand is called a(n):
   - (a) Emphasis.
   - (b) ScreenTip.
   - (c) Custom path.
   - (d) Action button.

8. Attaching a timing setting to animations enables the presenter to more effectively:
   - (a) Concentrate on delivering the message.
   - (b) Close the presentation at the end.
   - (c) Change timing during the presentation on the fly.
   - (d) All of the above.

9. When animating bulleted text, you can:
   - (a) Animate all of the text to come in together.
   - (b) Animate the text to come in as one paragraph.
   - (c) Animate the text to come in by text outline level.
   - (d) All of the above.

10. When working with complex animations, it is helpful to use the:
    - (a) Trigger.
    - (b) Custom path.
    - (c) Animation Pane.
    - (d) Information button.

Practice Exercises

1 Copyright and the Law

The IT manager of your company has observed some violations of software copyright in the organization. He immediately removed the offending software but feels that perhaps it is a lack of understanding about copyright rather than deliberate theft. He has asked you, as a company trainer, to prepare and deliver a presentation about basic copyright principles for company employees. You will create a custom action button, attach sound actions, and create navigation buttons. You will link to an existing Word document with a Microsoft End User License Agreement as a sample. You will also include a link to the Microsoft volume licensing site. You will edit a hyperlink that links to a website with further information about copyright and copyright protection. Finally, you will add an Appear entrance animation that groups text by second-level paragraphs so the presenter can discuss each level. Refer to Figure 6.30 as you complete this exercise.

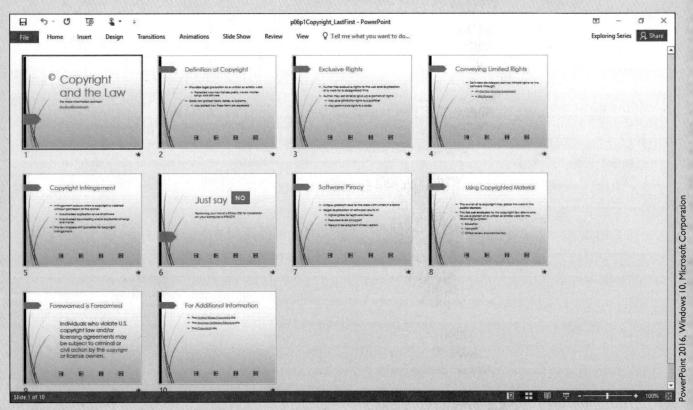

FIGURE 6.30 Slides 1 Through 10 of Completed Copyright and the Law Slide Show

a. Open *p06p1Copyright* and save it as **p06p1Copyright_LastFirst**.

b. Create a handout header with your name and a handout footer with your instructor's name and your class. Include the current date.

c. Click **Slide 1** and position the insertion point after the colon following *contact* on the Title slide. Press **Enter**, type your email address, and then press **Spacebar**.

d. Click **Slide 6** and click the **Insert tab**. Click **Shapes** in the Illustrations group, and click **Action Button: Custom**. Click to create a button in the top right of the slide. You will size and position the button in a later step.

e. Click the **Play sound check box** on the Mouse Click tab in the Actions Settings dialog box, click the **Play sound arrow**, and then click **Other Sound**.

f. Locate and select *p06p1No* and click **OK** twice.

g. Click the **Size dialog box launcher** in the Size group and set **Height** to **1"** and **Width** to **1.5"**. Click **Position** in the Format Shape pane and set **Horizontal position** to **6.25"** and **Vertical position** to **1.42"**.

h. Type **NO** in the action button. Select the text, apply bold, and then change the font size to **40 pt**.

i. Click **Slide 2** and click the **Insert tab**. Click **Shapes** in the Illustrations group, and click **Action Button: Beginning**. Click to create a button near the bottom of the slide. Click **OK** to accept the default action settings.

j. Click the **Size dialog box launcher** in the Size group to return to the Size options in the Format Shape pane. Size the button to **0.35"** by **0.35"** and position the button at a horizontal position of **6.4"** and a vertical position of **6.5"** (if necessary, refer to Step g instructions). Close the dialog box.

k. Click **Shape Fill** in the Shape Styles group, and click **Aqua, Accent 2, Lighter 60%** (third row, sixth column).

l. Ensure that you are on Slide 2 and click **Shapes More** in the Insert Shapes group on the Format tab to create action buttons for *Back or Previous*, *Forward or Next*, and *End* (three more buttons). Repeat Steps j through k to accept the default action settings for each button. Size the buttons and change the Shape Fill (Step k), but do not worry about the button positions. You will position the buttons in the next step.

m. Select the left-facing arrow **Action Button: Back or Previous** and position it at **3"** horizontally and **6.5"** vertically from the top-left corner. Select the right-facing arrow **Action Button: Forward or Next** and position it at **4.7"** horizontally and **6.5"** vertically from the top-left corner. Select **Action Button: End** and position it at **8.1"** horizontally and **6.5"** vertically from the top-left corner. Close the Format Shape pane.

n. Copy all four buttons and paste them on Slides 3 through 10.

o. Click **Slide 4** and select the text *End User License Agreement*. Click the **Insert tab** and click **Hyperlink** in the Links group. Click **Existing File or Web Page**, click **Browse for File**, locate and select *p06p1Eula*, and then click **OK** twice.

p. Select the text *Site License*. Click **Hyperlink** in the Links group, click **Existing File or Web Page**, and then type www.microsoftvolumelicensing.com in the **Address box**. Click **OK**.

q. Click **Slide 10** and right-click the **United States Copyright hyperlink**. Click **Edit Hyperlink**. Edit the web address to http://copyright.gov and click **OK**.

r. Click **Slide 2**, and select the **content placeholder**. Click the **Animations tab**, and click **Appear**.

s. Click the **Animation dialog box launcher** in the Animation group and click the **Text Animation tab**. Click the **Group text arrow**, click **By 2nd Level Paragraphs**, and then click **OK**.

t. Select the content placeholder on Slide 2, double-click **Animation Painter** in the Advanced Animation group, and then click each content placeholder in the remaining slides to copy the animation settings to each. Click the **Animation Painter button** to toggle it off when done.

u. Click **Slide 1** and select the **copyright symbol**. Click **More** in the Animation group and click the **Split** Exit effect. Open the Animation Pane. Drag the right end of the timeline bar until the ScreenTip reads **Start 0s**, **End 2.5s**. Close the Animation Pane.

v. View the presentation, observe the animations, and test each hyperlink.

w. Save and close the file. Based on your instructor's directions, submit p06p1Copyright_LastFirst.

2 GeGo Power!

You work in the lab of a food products company and have created several formulations of a nutritious new hot drink. You conducted a series of focus groups to study and determine consumer preferences. The focus group study also sought to determine whether consumers would be inclined to give up their morning coffee in favor of the new drink, code name "GeGo." You now want to present the results of the study to the food products company officials in the hopes they will agree to test it in the local college market in the fall. You will create a presentation that will include a study summary revealing the focus group preferences. You want to include the option to see detailed results for those who want to see them. You realize that creating a button as a trigger for the results is an excellent option. In this exercise, you will use an image as the trigger button to animate the table. Finally, you will add animation. Refer to Figure 6.31 as you complete this exercise.

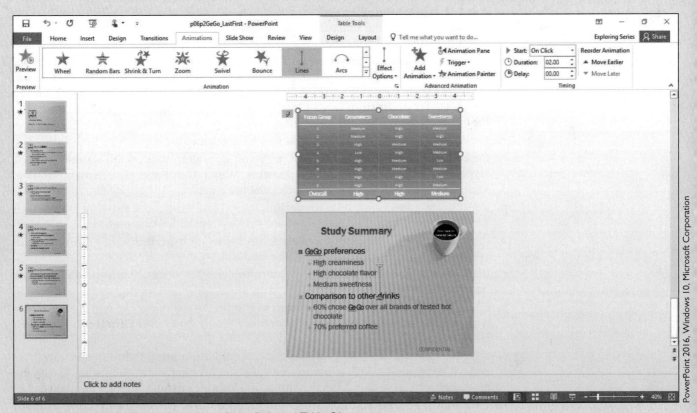

FIGURE 6.31 Slide 6 Zoomed to 40% to Show Slide and Table Object

a. Open *p06p2GeGo* and save it as **p06p2GeGo_LastFirst**.

b. Create a handout header with your name and a handout footer with your instructor's name and your class. Include the current date.

c. Click **Slide 1**, and click the outside border of the **GeGo logo**. Click the **Animations tab**, click **More** in the Animation group, and then click **Zoom** under Entrance.

d. Click **More** in the Animation group, click **More Motion Paths**, click **Vertical Figure 8** in the *Special* section, and then click **OK**.

e. Click the **GeGo logo**. Open the Animation Pane. Click the **arrow** on the right end of Group 2 and click **Start With Previous**. Close the Animation Pane.

f. Click **Slide 2**, click the **content placeholder**, and then click **Fade**.

g. Select the **content placeholder** again, double-click **Animation Painter** in the Advanced Animation group, and then click each of the **content placeholders** on Slides 3 through 5. Click the **Animation Painter** in the Advanced Animation group to turn off the feature when done.

h. Click **Slide 6**, and click the **View tab**. Click **Zoom** in the Zoom group, type **40%** in the Percent text box, and then click **OK**.

With the view reduced, a portion of a table containing the focus group results is visible at the top of the design window.

i. Click the table to select it, click the **Animations tab**, and then click **More** in the Animation group.

j. Click **Lines** in the Motion Paths category to apply the animation to the table.

k. Position the pointer over the red end. When it changes to the double-headed arrow, press and hold **Shift** to constrain movement to a straight line as you drag the red end arrow to the top of the letter *d* in the word *drinks* on the slide.

The table descends and covers the text when triggered.

l. Click the **table**. Click **Trigger** in the Advanced Animation group, point to *On Click of*, and then click **Group 7**.

Group 7 is the grouping of the hot chocolate image and the text box reading *Click here for detailed results*.

m. Click **Slide 4**. Select the words **nutrient recommendations (DRI)**. Insert a hyperlink to http://fnic.nal.usda.gov/dietary-guidance/dietary-reference-intakes.

n. View the presentation. When Slide 4 appears, test the hyperlink. When Slide 6 appears, click the **hot chocolate** image to trigger the table animation.

o. Save and close the file. Based on your instructor's directions, submit p06p2GeGo_LastFirst.

Mid-Level Exercises

1 Creative Presentation

CREATIVE CASE

FROM SCRATCH

You will use a Microsoft Office Online template, *Presentation on brainstorming*. Because it is a presentation template, it includes suggested text to jump-start the creative process. In this exercise, you will download the template and modify it. You will add a navigation bar using custom action buttons that link to the related slides. As an alternative method for navigating, you will change the agenda items to hyperlinks that link to the associated slide. Finally, you will animate text using the animation effects and settings you select.

a. Access the New Presentation pane. Search for the *Presentation on brainstorming* template. Choose the template with that name in the results or a similar template. Save the presentation as **p06m1Creativity_LastFirst**.

b. Create a handout header with your name and a handout footer with your instructor's name and your class. Include the current date.

c. Click **Slide 1** and replace the subtitle *Your Name* with your own name.

d. Click **Slide 2**, create a Custom Action button, and click **Cancel** to bypass the Action Setting dialog box at this time. Resize the button height to **0.59"** and width to **1.5"**. Change the Shape Fill to **Blue** (under *Standard Colors*).

e. Change the Shape Outline color to Theme Color **Indigo, Accent 5** (first row, ninth column).

f. Type **Overview** in the action button, select the text, and then change the font size to **16 pt**.

g. Duplicate the button five times. Change the label of the duplicate buttons to **Objectives**, **Rules**, **Activity**, **Summarize**, and **Next Steps**. Position the buttons just above the slide bottom accents with Agenda as the first button and the remaining buttons listed in the order above. With all six buttons selected, align the bottoms and distribute the buttons horizontally.

h. Select the text on each action button and add a hyperlink to **Place in This Document** to the slide title to correspond to each of the action button titles you just created.

i. Copy the buttons and paste them on Slides 3 through 8.

j. Click **Slide 2**, select **Overview**, and add a hyperlink to Slide 3.

k. Click **Slide 2** and continue adding hyperlinks for each agenda item to its associated slide.

l. Add the animation effects and settings you choose to the text in the presentation, using at least one each of the following animations: entrance, emphasis, exit, and motion path.

m. View the presentation and make any changes using the Animation Pane. Adjust or add additional animations, if desired.

n. Save and close the file. Based on your instructor's directions, submit p06m1Creativity_LastFirst.

2 Patient Assessment Flow Chart

In this exercise, you will create hyperlinks for a patient assessment flow chart for the Fire and Rescue Academy. Your task is to turn each shape in the flow chart into a clickable button with an action assigned. When clicked, the button will link to its associated slide. You will create a button to return the viewer to the flow chart after viewing a slide. You will assign a mouse-over action to an image that plays the sound of an ambulance. Finally, you will add triggers to launch a sequence of animated images.

a. Open *p06m2Assmnt* and save it as **p06m2Assmnt_LastFirst**.

b. Create a handout header with your name and a handout footer with your instructor's name and your class. Include the current date.

c. Click **Slide 2**, select **Scene Size-Up**, and add a hyperlink for the label to Slide 3.

d. Continue converting each shape label text in the Patient Assessment Flow Chart into a hyperlink to the associated slide. Note that the Focused Assessment and the Rapid Trauma Assessment labels share a common slide, Slide 5. Each of these two button labels, therefore, must link to Slide 5.

e. Enable the viewer to move quickly back to the flow chart slide by doing the following: on Slide 3, create an Action Button: Return that links to Slide 2. Resize the button to **0.5"** high by **0.5"** wide. Position it horizontally at **7.5"** from the top-left corner and vertically at **7"** from the top-left corner. Copy the button to Slides 4 through 9.

f. Click **Slide 7** and insert a mouse-over action that plays the *p06m2Ambulance* audio clip for the ambulance picture.

g. Create an animation sequence for the images in Slide 3. All animations should fly in. The top picture should start on click. Clicking the slide again should trigger the appearance of the middle image. Clicking the slide a third time should trigger the appearance of the bottom image.

h. Click **Slide 5** and use the Animation Pane to reorder the animations. The *Focused Assessment* subtitle currently appears last but should appear first, followed by its associated bullet points. The *Rapid Trauma Assessment* subtitle should appear next, followed by its associated bullet points.

i. Test each of the buttons and triggers you created in Slide Show view.

j. Edit any buttons that do not link correctly.

k. Save and close the file. Based on your instructor's directions, submit p06m2Assmnt_LastFirst.

3 Internet History Game

COLLABORATION CASE

FROM SCRATCH

You have been assigned to work with one or more other classmates to develop an interactive PowerPoint game on some aspect of Internet history. You should begin by searching for a Microsoft PowerPoint quiz template. The quiz needs to have a variety of question types such as multiple choice and true/false. Because everyone's schedule is varied, you should use either your Outlook account, another email account, or OneDrive to pass the presentation file. Do a final proofreading of all text, and test all interactivity and animations and adjust them as needed. Save the quiz as **p06m3Quiz_LastFirst**.

a. It will be helpful to create a storyboard to plan the slides for the game and the interactive elements required by your plan.

b. The first slide should contain the name of the game, your first and last names, and your partners' first and last names. Make the names into hyperlinks for each student's email address.

c. Be sure to include a slide that gives directions for the game.

d. The question slides should use animation to reveal the answers. One of the slides needs to use a trigger. Each slide, except the last one, requires action buttons to navigate to the next question slide.

e. Pass the presentation to the next student so that he or she can perform the same tasks, and so on.

f. After all students have contributed to the presentation, save and close the file. Based on your instructor's directions, submit p06m3Quiz_LastFirst.

Beyond the Classroom

Professionalism

GENERAL CASE ✓

FROM SCRATCH

Many professions have support organizations that are created to serve the membership and to enhance the professional growth of the members. Research the professional organizations available to you in your field of interest. Create a slide that shows a minimum of two routes you could choose to pursue for your field of interest, illustrating the professional path(s) available to you. Include hyperlinks to the organizations. Include additional information or additional slides in the presentation if desired. Animate the path to enhance the presentation and use the Animation Pane to adjust the duration of the animations as necessary. Create a handout header with your name and a handout footer with your instructor's name and your class. Include the current date. Save the file as **p06b1Professional_LastFirst** and close the file. Based on your instructor's directions, submit p06b1Professional_LastFirst.

Colorful Diet = Healthy Diet Presentation

DISASTER RECOVERY ✚

You are part of a group assigned to create a presentation on healthy eating. Your group was given one hour in a computer lab to prepare, so first you sketched out a storyboard, and then you divided responsibilities. One member of the group researched the benefits of eating fruits and vegetables, and two members created the design of the presentation, including locating pictures. As information was located, it was typed into the presentation.

Open *p06b2Diet* and save it as **p06b2Diet_LastFirst**. Create a handout header with your name and a handout footer with your instructor's name and your class. Include the current date. Check the presentation design to ensure that all aspects display properly and that the introduction slide, body slides, and conclusion slide appear in the correct order. Test hyperlinks, action buttons, and triggers to ensure that they link properly. Edit any hyperlinks that do not link correctly. Resize the action buttons and distribute them horizontally. Apply entrance, emphasis, motion path, and exit animations to the slides or make other changes to the slide show as desired. Use the Animation Pane to set timings as desired. Finally, carefully proofread the text and check the images. Save the file as **p06b2Diet_LastFirst** and close the file. Based on your instructor's directions, submit p06b2Diet_LastFirst.

Capstone Exercise

As a volunteer in the Humanities and Languages department at your college, you are often asked to prepare presentations to run at various kiosks, locations, and meetings around campus. The presentation topics vary, but all have the goal of educating students about humanities, languages, and other cultures. This week, you were asked to prepare a presentation based on information about Versailles to inspire students to think about having a study abroad experience during their college years.

Adding ScreenTips and Hyperlinks to an Email Address, a Webpage, and a Slide

In this exercise, you will include your email address on the first slide so that you can be contacted. You will include a hyperlink to the website of Versailles on the Welcome slide of the presentation.

a. Open *p06c1Versailles* and immediately save it as **p06c1Versailles_LastFirst**.

b. Create a handout header with your name and a handout footer with your instructor's name and your class. Include the current date.

c. Click **Slide 1**, and type your name replacing the *Exploring Series* subtitle text. Create a hyperlink that links your name to your email address. Type **Versailles** as the email Subject. Include the ScreenTip **Email Me for More Information**.

d. Click **Slide 3** and select the words **Welcome to Versailles**. Link to the website at http://en.chateauversailles.fr/homepage. Type **Official website of Versailles** as the ScreenTip.

e. Ensure that you are on Slide 3 and select the text **gardens**. Create a link to **Slide 6**.

f. Save the presentation.

Creating a Navigation Bar with Action Buttons and Adding Sound to an Object

You want to add interactivity to the slide show by enabling the viewer to easily navigate between slides, so you create a navigation bar.

a. Click **Slide 2** and insert an **Action Button: Beginning**. Click to create a button near the bottom of the slide. Click **OK** to accept the default action settings.

b. Size the button to **0.35"** by **0.35"** and position the button at a horizontal position of **6.5"** and a vertical position of **6.5"**.

c. Create an **Action Button: Back or Previous** with the default settings and size it to **0.35"** high and

0.35" wide. Set the horizontal position at **7.00"** and the vertical position at **6.5"**.

d. Create the following action buttons with default settings and size them to **0.35"** high and **0.35"** wide:
- **Action Button: Forward or Next** to a horizontal position of **7.50"** and vertical position of **6.5"**.
- **Action Button: End** to a horizontal position of **8.00"** and vertical position of **6.5"**.

e. Copy the action buttons and paste them to **Slides 3 through 9**.

f. Click **Slide 7** and select the first instance of the word **Crowns**. Add the **Chime** sound..

g. Save the presentation.

Creating Animations and Using a Trigger

To emphasize the message of the presentation, you will animate the information on a couple of slides. You will also apply a trigger to one of the animations.

a. Click **Slide 2** and apply a **Bold Reveal Emphasis animation** to the first set of bullets. Set the animation to start **With Previous**.

b. Apply a **Fade Entrance animation** to the second set of bullets. Set the animation to start **After Previous**.

c. Apply a **Zoom Entrance animation** to the last set of bullets. Set the animation to start **After Previous**.

d. Click **Slide 7**. Apply a **Grow & Turn Entrance animation** to the **Crown** image. Set the animation to start **With Previous**.

e. Click **Slide 8**. Apply a **Bean Special motion path** to the **Crown** image. Set the animation to start **With Previous**.

f. Click **Slide 9**. Apply a **Spin Emphasis animation** to the **Sun King** image. Set the animation to start **With Previous**. Apply a second animation for **Grow & Turn** using the Add Animation button. Set it to start **After Previous**.

g. Open the Animation Pane and adjust the End time for the second animation to **5s**.

h. Save the presentation.

Testing Hyperlinks, Action Buttons, and Animations

Before using the presentation at various campus functions, you know it is critical to check all hyperlinks, action buttons, animations, and triggers to ensure that they are working correctly. If any feature does not work, exit the slide show and edit the presentation immediately so you are not relying on your memory when editing.

a. View the slide show from the beginning.

b. Click **Slide 2**, and click **Action Button: Forward or Next** to see if it takes you to Slide 3.

c. Click **Action Button: Back or Previous** to see if it returns you to Slide 2.

d. Click **Action Button: End** to see if it successfully jumps to the *Life is good* slide.

e. Click **Action Button: Beginning** to see if it successfully jumps to the *Chateau de Versailles* slide.

f. Ensure that you are on Slide 1 and click the **email hyperlink** to test it. Close the email program and return to the presentation.

g. Click **Slide 3** and test the **Welcome to Versailles** hyperlink. Close the browser and return to the presentation.

h. Ensure that you are on Slide 3 and click the **gardens** hyperlink to see if it jumps to Slide 6.

i. Click **Slide 7** and test the **Crowns** hyperlink to hear the sound. Observe the animation on the crown image. Adjust as desired.

j. Click **Slide 8** and observe the animation on the crown image. Adjust as desired.

k. Click **Slide 9** and observe the animation on the Sun King image. Adjust as desired.

l. Save and close the file. Based on your instructor's directions, submit p06c1Versailles_LastFirst.

PowerPoint

Customization

LEARNING OUTCOME

You will customize PowerPoint options, features, and presentations to increase productivity and the effectiveness of slide shows.

OBJECTIVES & SKILLS: After you read this chapter, you will be able to:

CASE STUDY | Survival Solutions

You are the owner of Survival Solutions, a store that provides family emergency preparation supplies. You believe that preparation provides peace of mind before, during, and after an emergency. Because of your knowledge about family emergency planning and communication, you are often invited to be a guest speaker. The two topics on which you are invited to present most often are "Emergency Preparedness" and "What to Do Before, During, and After a Disaster."

To make it easier and more time efficient when you create presentations, you modify PowerPoint's settings and personalize the Ribbon to create a tab with the tools you use frequently. You then use the tools to create a logo for Survival Solutions. To help create recognition for your business, you modify the slide masters that control the layout and appearance of handouts, notes, and slides. You add the new logo, and change the theme colors to match your logo colors. Finally, you create a custom show from a presentation you have used in the community so that you can have flexibility on topics based on audience request. You also control the detail displayed to the audience by hiding and unhiding slides.

Customizing PowerPoint and the Slide Show

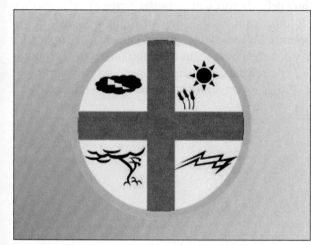

CHAPTER 7

FIGURE 7.1a Survival Solutions Logo

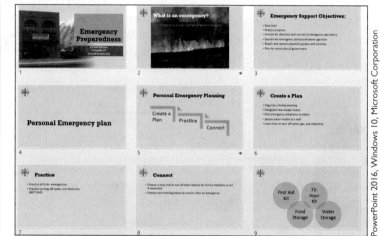

FIGURE 7.1b Survival Solutions Presentation

PowerPoint 2016, Windows 10, Microsoft Corporation

CASE STUDY | Survival Solutions

Starting Files	Files to be Submitted
p07h1Preparedness	p07h1SSLogo_LastFirst
P07h2Store	p07h1Preparedness_LastFirst
P07h2Plan	p07h2SurvivalTemplate_LastFirst.potx
	p07h3Survival_LastFirst

PowerPoint Customization

You can become a PowerPoint power user by setting PowerPoint's options to meet your individual needs and by modifying PowerPoint's working environment to include customized tabs. Changing the default PowerPoint options can help you work more productively and smoothly, while adding a personalized tab that contains the features you use most to the Ribbon enables you to work with less effort.

In this section, you will learn how to set General options for working with PowerPoint, change how PowerPoint corrects and formats your text, customize how you save your documents, and use other more advanced options. You will also learn how to customize the Ribbon by adding a new tab to make some features more easily accessible. Finally, you will use the new tab to create a logo.

Setting PowerPoint Options

To work powerfully and efficiently in PowerPoint, you should choose options that match your work needs. ***PowerPoint Options*** provide you with a broad range of settings that enable you to customize the ribbon to meet your needs. You can configure many of the features in PowerPoint using these options. To access the options, click File to display the Backstage view and select Options to open the PowerPoint Options dialog box. Although this discussion will highlight many of the settings, you should spend time exploring all the options. Figure 7.2 shows the Backstage view with the Options feature indicated.

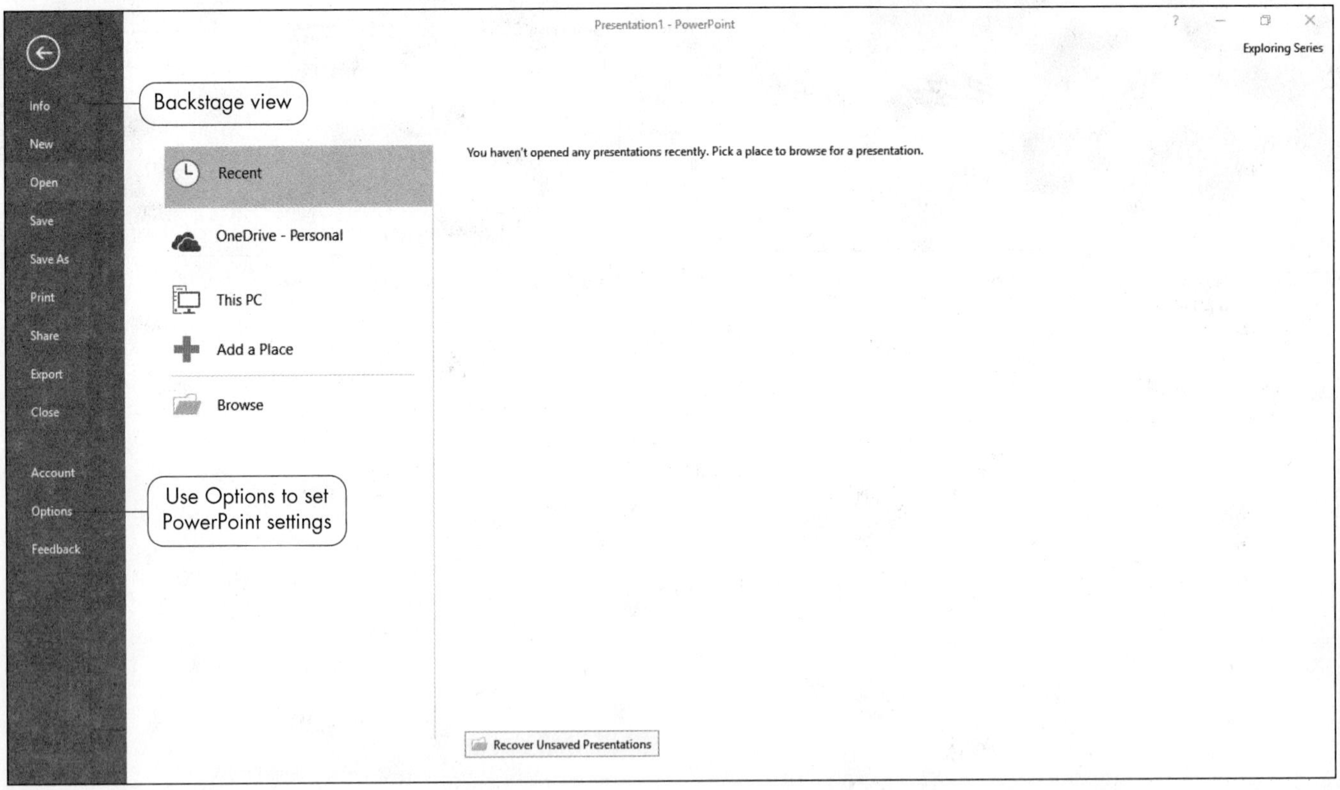

PowerPoint 2016, Windows 10, Microsoft Corporation

FIGURE 7.2 Accessing PowerPoint Options

Determine General Options

STEP 1 Figure 7.3 shows the PowerPoint Options dialog box with General options displayed. The options are displayed as categories along the left side of the dialog box. Click a category to view the options available in that category. The General options category includes the options that impact PowerPoint when you open it, such as setting interface options, personalization, and start-up options.

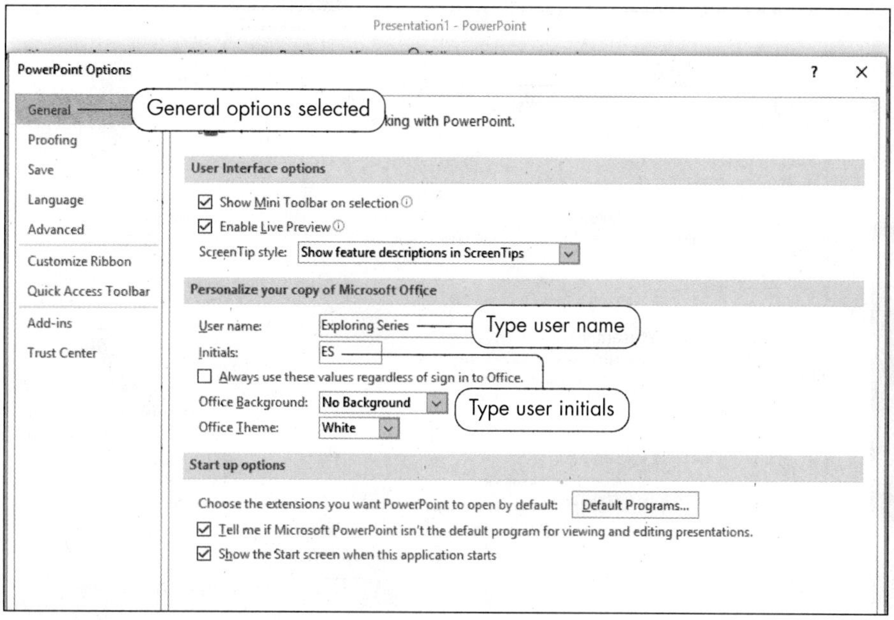

PowerPoint 2016, Windows 10, Microsoft Corporation

FIGURE 7.3 PowerPoint General Options

Each of the sections can help you customize your presentations.

- *User Interface options* enable you to customize the screen display through which you communicate with the software. You can determine whether to show the Mini toolbar when text is selected, whether to use Live Preview, and how ScreenTips display.
- *Personalize your copy of Microsoft Office* enables you to specify your name in User name and Initials. You should add your user name and initials the first time you work with PowerPoint, because when you work with others on presentations your information is used to identify your comments and is included in the presentation information if you created the presentation or were the last person to modify it. Figure 7.4 shows Exploring Series as the author name because *User name* was set in General options.
- *Start up options* enable you to choose whether you are notified if PowerPoint is not your default program for viewing and editing presentations, and whether the ***Start screen*** displays when PowerPoint starts. The Start screen is the screen you first view when you open PowerPoint and is divided into four main areas: a list of files you have recently opened, the Open Other Presentations option, the Search for Online Templates option, and the thumbnails of the various themes built-in to PowerPoint. If you deselect the *Show the Start screen when this application starts* option, you will open a new presentation when you start PowerPoint.

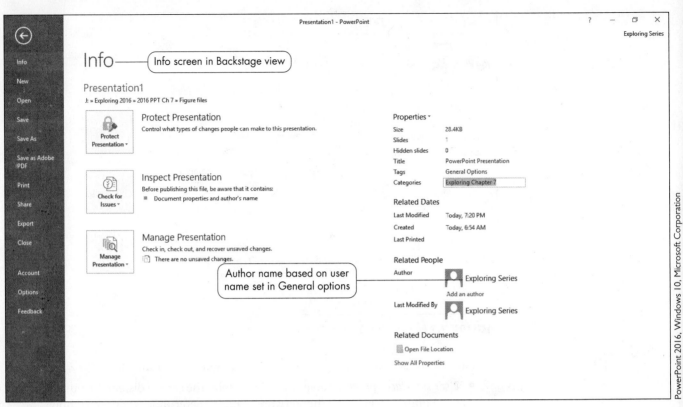

FIGURE 7.4 Author Name in the Backstage View

Set Proofing Options

STEP 2)) Proofing options enable you to change how PowerPoint corrects and formats your text. Click AutoCorrect Options on the Proofing tab to open the AutoCorrect dialog box. Review each of the tab options in the dialog box to understand what PowerPoint automatically changes as you type. Then select or deselect check boxes to apply the settings of your choice. For example, AutoCorrect automatically resizes the font of text you type as a title to fit the size of the title text placeholder. If you want the title text to be uniform on every slide, click the AutoFormat As You Type tab in the AutoCorrect dialog box and deselect the *AutoFit title text to placeholder* check box. Figure 7.5 shows the Proofing options and the AutoCorrect dialog box with the AutoFormat As You Type tab open.

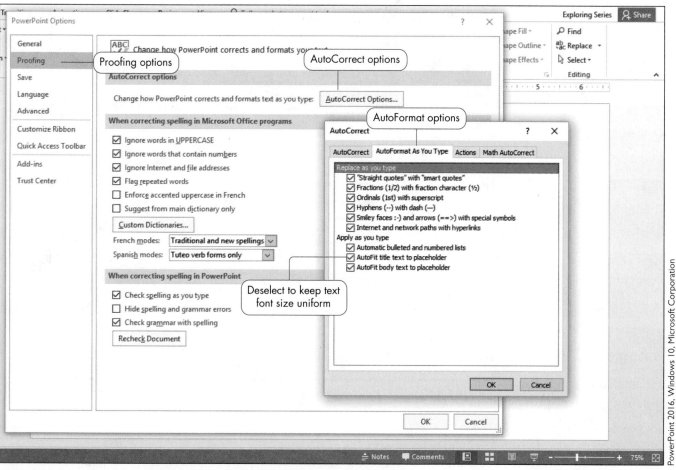

FIGURE 7.5 PowerPoint Proofing Options and AutoCorrect Options Box

Customize Save Options

PowerPoint Save options enable you to customize when and where your documents are saved and can be an invaluable resource. By default, PowerPoint saves your presentation every 10 minutes so that if PowerPoint closes unexpectedly and you did not have a chance to save, you can recover the presentation. All but the changes you made since the last time the AutoRecover saved will be available to you the next time you open PowerPoint. The recovered presentation will display in a pane on the left side of the screen so that you can restore it. You can change the setting for how often you want PowerPoint to save your presentation using the Save options. You can also change where the program saves the AutoRecover version. To save time navigating to folders, change the location to where your presentations are saved. For example, if you always save your presentations to a folder you created for assignments, enter that location as your default file location. Figure 7.6 shows Save options.

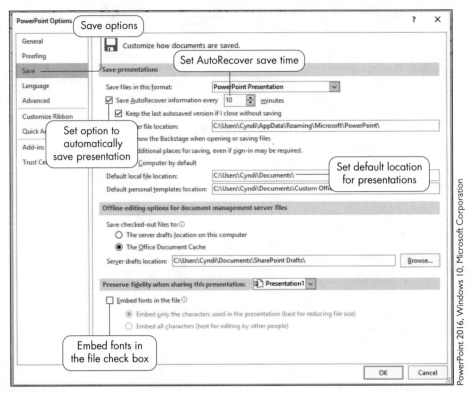

FIGURE 7.6 PowerPoint Save Options

TIP: EMBED FONTS

Although PowerPoint includes many font choices, you might want to use another TrueType font you find on the Web. TrueType fonts are scalable fonts supported by Windows that display and print smoothly at any point size. After downloading the font, you can embed it in your presentation to ensure that it is available when you work on or display your presentation on another computer. Embedding a font also ensures that others reviewing and editing a presentation have access to that font. To embed a font, click Save in the PowerPoint Options dialog box, and click the *Embed fonts in the file* check box. Select the *Embed only the characters used in the presentation* option or the *Embed all characters* option. While selecting *Embed all characters* ensures that every character will be available in the future if needed while editing, it creates a larger file size.

Determine Language Preferences

Language options enable you to change the Office language used for editing, display, Help, and ScreenTips. The languages available to you depend on the version of Microsoft Office you use and any additional language packs installed on your computer. When you set the default editing language in PowerPoint, the language changes for all of your Microsoft Office programs.

Choose Advanced Options

Advanced options enable you to set your preferences for editing, cutting, copying, pasting, sizing and quality of images, setting chart data point properties, setting display options, working in Slide Show view, and printing, as well as several General options. For example, in the Editing options section, you can change the number of undos (which reverses your last action) from the default of 20 to any number from 3 to 150. The more you increase the number of undo levels, however, the more of your computer's RAM (random access memory) is used to store the undo history. If you set your undo levels to a high number, you may experience a computer slowdown. Figure 7.7 shows some of the Advanced options available.

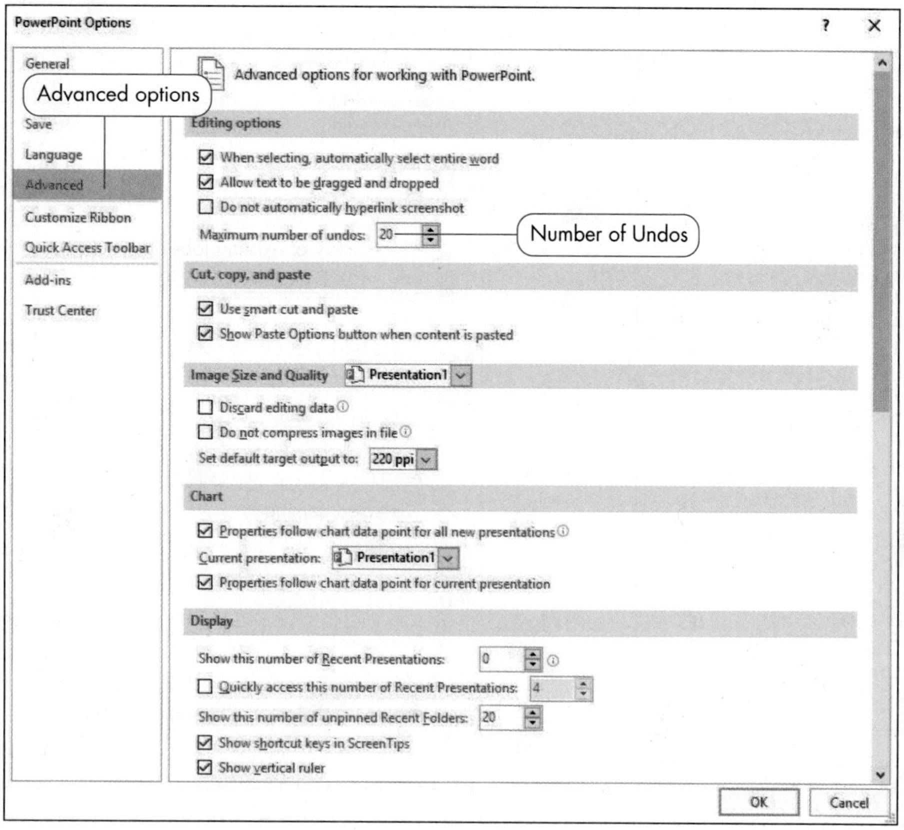

PowerPoint 2016, Windows 10, Microsoft Corporation

FIGURE 7.7 PowerPoint Advanced Options

Customizing the Ribbon

STEP 3 The ***Customize Ribbon*** tab in the PowerPoint Options dialog box enables you to create a personalized tab on the Ribbon as well as modify the settings of any tab. Ribbon customization enables you to rearrange features on the standard Ribbon to enable you to easily access the features you use most often or to add a tab to include features that are not available on the standard Ribbon. You can change the order of the tabs, change the order of the groups that appear within the tabs, and create new groups within a tab as well as creating a new tab.

Figure 7.8 shows all of the possible Customize Ribbon options on the left, with the current arrangement of the Ribbon in the right pane. To expand the view to display the groups within a tab, click Expand group (+) next to the group name, and to collapse the view to hide the groups, click Collapse group (-). To change the order of the existing tabs or groups, drag and drop a selected tab or group to a new position or use Move Up and Move Down.

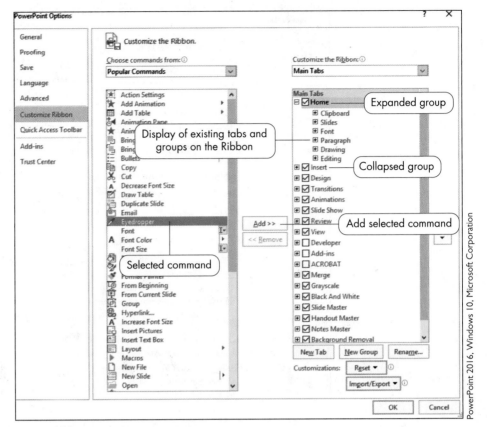

FIGURE 7.8 Customize Ribbon Options

TIP: RESTORE THE RIBBON

You can restore the Ribbon to its original arrangement by clicking Reset and clicking Reset all customizations. Reset also enables you to reset individual Ribbon tabs.

Add a New Tab

To have access to the commands you use most, add a new tab to the Ribbon and add frequently used commands to the new tab. When you personalize your Ribbon by adding a new tab, the new tab only appears in the Office application in which you created it.

To create a new tab, complete the following steps:

1. Click File, Options, and then Customize Ribbon, or right-click the Ribbon and select Customize Ribbon.
2. Select the existing tab you want the new tab to appear after.
3. Click New Tab.

The new tab is created and named *New Tab (Custom)*. The new tab also contains a new group named *New Group (Custom)*. To add additional groups, click New Group. You can rename tabs or groups by clicking Rename or by right-clicking the tab and selecting Rename. When you rename a group, you can select a colorful symbol to represent the contents of the group. Figure 7.9 shows that a new tab containing a new group has been created on the Ribbon.

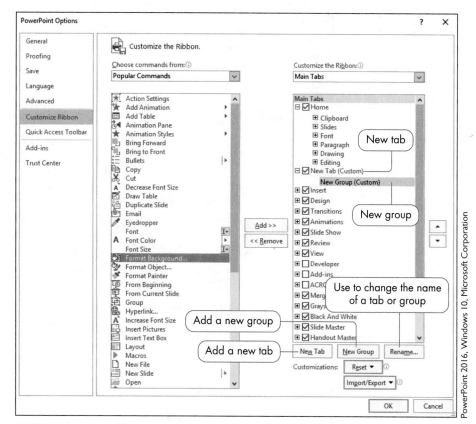

FIGURE 7.9 New Tab and New Group Options

Add Commands to a Group

To add commands to an existing tab or group or to a newly created tab, click a command name on the left and click Add. Popular commands that you can add are displayed in the default view, but you can click the *Choose commands from* arrow to choose additional commands and macros. For example, instead of using the arrow keys on the keyboard to **nudge** an object (move in small, precise increments), you can add the nudge commands to a group in a personalized tab. Figure 7.10 displays a customized tab and group with added nudge commands.

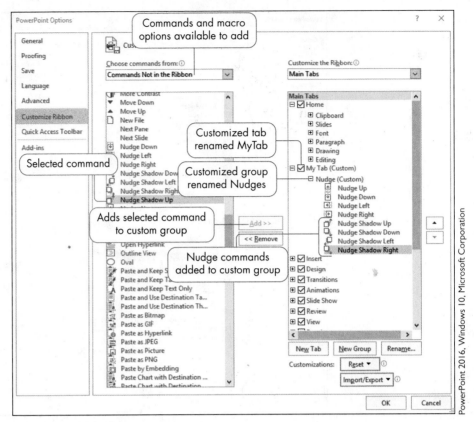

FIGURE 7.10 Customized Tab and Group

After customizing the Ribbon to maximize your productivity, you may want to use it on other computers you use or share it with others who could benefit. You can do so by exporting it as an exported Office User Interface (UI) customization file, which uses the extension *.exportedUI*.

To import or export a customized Ribbon, complete the following steps:

1. Click the File tab to display the Backstage view and click Options.
2. Click in the left pane.
3. Click Import/Export.
4. Click *Import customization file* or *Export all customizations*.
5. Locate the desired file with the *.exportedUI* extension and click Import, or navigate to the desired file location, type a file name, and then click Save.

Quick Concepts ✓

1. List two options that can be set in General PowerPoint Options and explain the benefit of being able to change each of the options. **p. 442**
2. Why would you choose to enable Embed fonts in the file option in Save options? **p. 446**
3. How can you restore the Ribbon to its default setting? **p. 448**

Hands-On Exercises

Watch the Video for This Hands-On Exercise!

MyITLab® HOE1 Training

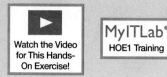

Skills covered: • Determine General Options • Choose Advanced Options • Set Proofing Options • Add a New Tab • Add Commands to a Group

1 PowerPoint Customization

You decide to modify several of PowerPoint's settings to meet your needs. Because you often use PowerPoint's illustration tools, you create a custom Ribbon tab to make these tools easy to access. You then use the new Ribbon tab and group to create a new logo for your store, Survival Solutions.

STEP 1 » DETERMINE GENERAL OPTIONS

Because you plan on working with others on several presentations, you decide to personalize your copy of Microsoft Office by adding your name and your initials. Refer to Figure 7.11 as you complete Step 1.

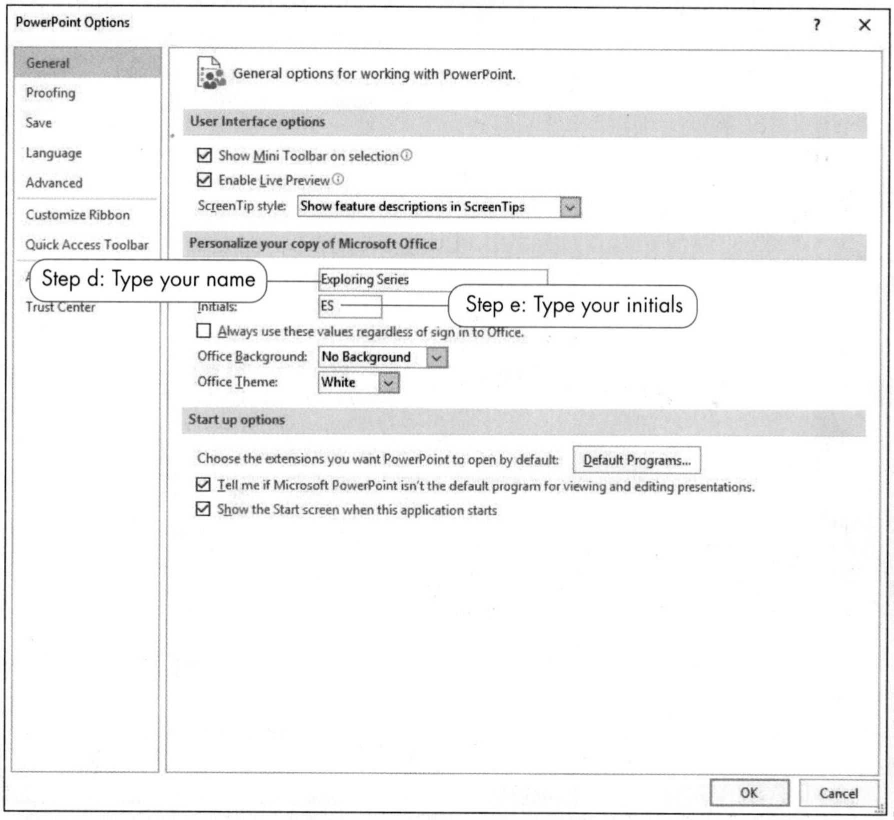

FIGURE 7.11 Personalizing Microsoft Office

a. Open the *p07h1Preparedness* presentation and save it as **p07h1Preparedness_LastFirst**.

> **TROUBLESHOOTING:** If you make any major mistakes in this exercise, you can close the file, open *p07h1Preparedness* again, and then start this exercise over.

b. Create a handout header with your name and a handout footer with your instructor's name and your class. Include the current date.

c. Click the **File tab** and click **Options**.

The PowerPoint Options dialog box opens.

d. Type your name in the **User name box**.

e. Type your initials in the **Initials box**.

f. Keep the PowerPoint Options dialog box open for the next step.

> **TROUBLESHOOTING:** If you are working in a public lab, you should restore the Ribbon to its original arrangement after making changes to the Ribbon as part of these exercises.

STEP 2 ⟩⟩ CHOOSE ADVANCED OPTIONS AND SET PROOFING OPTIONS

You decide to turn off background printing. Background printing enables you to continue working as you print but increases the print response time. You use your company name, Survival Solutions, in most of the presentations you create. To minimize the chances for a typographical error, you set AutoCorrect to replace the initials "ss" with Survival Solutions. To improve the spelling checker results, you also activate the *Check grammar with spelling* feature so the correct usage of words can be identified. Refer to Figure 7.12 as you complete Step 2.

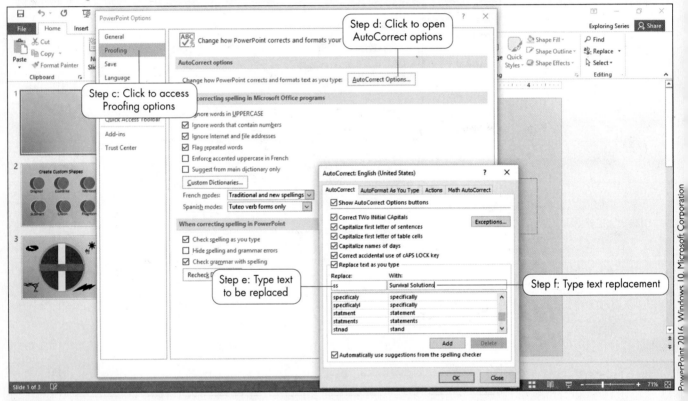

FIGURE 7.12 Proofing Options

a. Click **Advanced** in the left pane of the PowerPoint Options dialog box.

b. Scroll until you see the Print section and click the **Print in background check box** to deselect it.

The *Print in background* option is deselected.

c. Click **Proofing** in the left pane of the PowerPoint Options dialog box.

d. Click **AutoCorrect Options** and ensure that the AutoCorrect tab is selected.

The AutoCorrect tab in the AutoCorrect dialog box opens.

e. Type **ss** in the Replace box.

f. Type **Survival Solutions** in the With box and click **OK**.

Because you are only adding one text replacement, you click OK. If you wanted to add additional text replacements, you would click Add and click OK when all replacements are made.

g. Ensure that proofing is still selected and that the Check grammar with spelling check box is selected and click **OK**.

The PowerPoint Options dialog box closes, and you return to Slide 1 of the presentation.

h. Click the **title placeholder**. Type **ss** and press **Spacebar**.

Survival Solutions replaces the original placeholder text.

> **TROUBLESHOOTING:** If the text is not replaced, do the following: click the File tab, click Options, click Proofing, and then click AutoCorrect Options. Make sure the *Replace text as you type* check box is selected. Repeat Steps d through f.

i. Type **is the write place for getting prepared** after *Survival Solutions* in the title placeholder.

A wavy line displays underneath the word *write*, indicating it is the wrong word choice in this context.

j. Right-click **write** and select **right**.

The incorrect word is replaced, and the sentence is now grammatically correct.

k. Save the presentation.

Because you work with shapes often, you decide to create a tab on the Ribbon that includes the commands for shapes and the commands for manipulating shapes in one location. You will create a new customized tab, practice using the commands in the tab, and then use the commands to create a logo for Survival Solutions. Refer to Figure 7.13 as you complete Step 3. You may also refer to Figure 7.1 to view the completed logo.

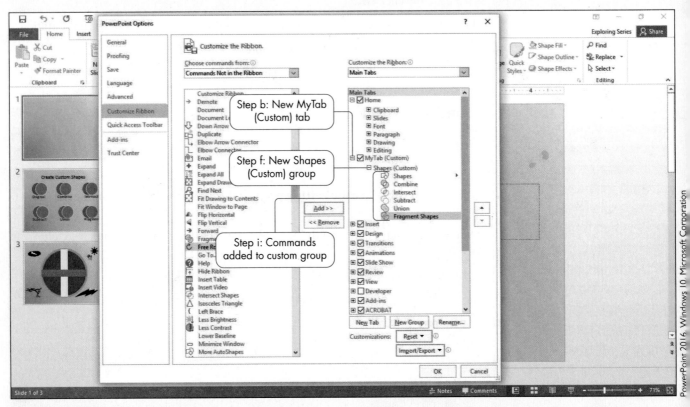

FIGURE 7.13 New Tab and Group

a. Select **Slide 2**. Click the **File tab**, click **Options**, click **Customize Ribbon** in the PowerPoint Options dialog box, and then click **New Tab** near the bottom of the right side of the Customize the Ribbon dialog box.

A new tab is created in the Main Tabs list and positioned between the Home tab and the Insert tab. The tab is named *New Tab (Custom)* and contains a new group named *New Group (Custom)*.

> **TROUBLESHOOTING:** If the new tab is positioned elsewhere, click Reset, select *Reset all customizations*, and then click Yes. Repeat Step a. As an alternative, you can select the new tab and click the Move Up and Move Down arrows to reposition the new tab.

b. Select **New Tab (Custom)**, click **Rename**, type **MyTab** in the Display name box, and then click **OK**.

The new tab displays as *MyTab (Custom)*.

c. Select **New Group (Custom)** and click **Rename**.

The Rename dialog box opens.

d. Click the **Key icon** (third row, seventh column) in the Symbol section; do not close the Rename dialog box.

You can display icons on the Ribbon to make it smaller if you want. Also, icons will display if your monitor has a low screen resolution setting. In either of these cases, a key icon will represent the new custom group.

e. Type **Shapes** in the **Display name box** and click **OK**.

The group displays as *Shapes (Custom)*.

f. Select **Shapes** in the *Choose commands from* column on the left side and click **Add**.

The shape commands are now added to the Shapes (Custom) group.

g. Click the **Choose commands from arrow** and click **Commands Not in the Ribbon**.

h. Scroll down the list of commands, click **Combine Shapes**, and then click **Add**.

Combine Shapes is added to MyTab (Custom) in the Shapes (Custom) group below the Shapes commands.

i. Add the following commands to MyTab (Custom) in the Shapes (Custom) group:

- Combine
- Intersect
- Subtract
- Union
- Fragment

j. Click **OK** to close the PowerPoint Options dialog box.

k. Click the **MyTab tab** and note that the Shapes group contains six buttons.

> **TROUBLESHOOTING:** All but the Shapes feature are dimmed because they require two shapes to be selected before they can be used.

l. Select the **red circle** above the Combine label, press and hold Shift, and then click the **blue circle** above the Combine label. Click **Combine** in the Shapes group.

The overlapping area of the two circles is cut out, making the background visible.

> **TROUBLESHOOTING:** If the new shape is blue, the blue circle was selected first. Click Undo on the Quick Access Toolbar, click outside the circles, and then repeat Step l.

m. Select the **red circle** above the Intersect label, press and hold Shift, and then click the **blue circle**. Click **Intersect** in the Shapes group.

The overlapping area is retained and other areas are cut from the shape.

n. Select the **red circle** above the Subtract label, press and hold Shift, and then click the **blue circle** above the Subtract label. Click **Subtract** in the Shapes group.

The overlapping area of the blue circle is cut from the red circle, creating a crescent shape.

o. Select the **red circle** above the Union label, press and hold Shift, and then click the **blue circle** above the Union label. Click **Union** in the Shapes group.

The circles join and become a single shape with a red fill.

p. Select the **red circle** above the Fragment label, press and hold Shift, and then click the **blue circle** above the Fragment label. Click **Fragment** in the Shapes group.

The circles break into individual pieces.

q. Select the **red rectangle** on Slide 3, press and hold Shift, and then click the vertical **yellow rectangle** to add it to the selection. Click **Union** in the Shapes group to form a red cross.

r. Select the **green circle**, press and hold Shift, and then click the **blue circle** to add it to the selection.Click **Combine** in the Shapes group. Select the **green circle**, click the **Format tab**, and then click **Bring Forward**.

The overlapping area of the two circles is cut out, which reveals a yellow circle that had been hidden by the shapes. The green circle moves to the front and becomes a border for the logo.

s. Select the **black jagged line shape** in the bottom-right corner, press and hold **Shift**, and then click the adjacent **yellow jagged line shape** to add it to the selection. Click **Intersect** in the Shapes group on the MyTab tab.

The intersection of the shapes is a thin jagged black line.

t. Copy the jagged line and paste and position it under the first line to represent the shaking that might occur during an earthquake. Click a jagged line, press and hold **Shift**, and then click the other jagged line to add it to the selection. Click the **Format tab** and click **Group** in the Arrange group two times. Size the group to **1.3"** high by **1.85"** wide.

u. Select the **black cloud shape**, press and hold **Shift**, and then click the **yellow lightning shape** to add it to the selection. Click **Subtract** in the Shapes group on the MyTab tab.

The lightning shape is subtracted from the cloud shape.

v. Drag each of the four black disaster symbols onto the yellow circle, one in each quadrant, and then press **Ctrl+A** to select all objects in the logo. Group the objects.

The group includes the large green circle and its boundary box and sizing handles, the red cross and its boundary box and sizing handles, and each of the four disaster symbols with their boundary boxes and sizing handles.

w. Right-click the selected group and select **Save as Picture**. Navigate to where you are saving your homework files and type **p07h1SSLogo_LastFirst** in the File name box.

x. Click the **Save as type arrow**, ensure that the file type is set as PNG Portable Network Graphics Format, and then click **Save**.

TROUBLESHOOTING: If you are working in a public lab, you should restore the Ribbon to its original arrangement after making changes to the Ribbon as part of these exercises.

---

y. Save and close the presentation. You will submit these files to your instructor at the end of the last Hands-On Exercise.

Master Basics

By customizing a PowerPoint presentation, you put your unique creative ideas to work. However, you will still want to maintain a consistent, professional look throughout the presentation. *Masters* control the layouts, background designs, and color combinations for handouts, notes pages, and slides, giving the presentation a consistent appearance. The slide master controls the formatting and layout of the slides and the notes and handout masters control the printed output of slides. By modifying the masters, you make changes that affect the entire slide show and supporting materials. This is more efficient than individually changing each slide in the presentation. The design elements you already know about, such as themes and layouts, can be applied to each type of master. Slide masters can also be reused in other presentations.

In this section, you learn how to modify masters. Specifically, you will learn how to customize the layout and formatting of handouts, notes, the slide master, and slide layouts controlled by the slide master.

TIP: FRESH START

Modifications to masters can be made at any time as you create the presentation, but it is best to begin with a blank presentation. This gives you a clean workspace, enabling you to concentrate on the design of your slide show, handouts, and notes.

Modifying Handout and Notes Masters

You can print handouts and notes pages of your presentation. Printed handouts display thumbnails of the slides for audience use. Printed notes pages display individual slides with notes and are typically used by the presenter. You might want to customize these types of printouts to display exactly the information you want in the position that is most advantageous.

Customize the Handout Master

STEP 1 ›› The *handout master* contains the design information about the layout and formatting of audience handout pages. The handout master controls the orientation of the page; the number of slides per page; and the layout of fields such as the header, footer, date, and page number.

To modify the handout master, complete the following steps:

1. Click the View tab.
2. Click Handout Master in the Master Views group.
3. Make the changes you want to the handout master using the features on the Handout Master tab.
4. Click Close Master View to return to Normal view.

When the handout master is selected, a placeholder for handout page elements as well as modified Ribbon options displays. The Ribbon is modified to include the Handout Master tab as well as the Home, Insert, Review, and View tabs. All other tabs do not display.

The Handout Master tab includes the Page Setup group, which enables you to change the orientation of the handouts from the default portrait setting to landscape and to determine the slide size by selecting Standard, Widescreen, or a custom screen size. You can select the number of slides you want to appear on the handouts in this group by clicking Slides Per Page and selecting the number of slide thumbnails you want to print per handout page. You can also print the slide outline from this option. Figure 7.14 shows an open handout master with the Slides Per Page options displaying.

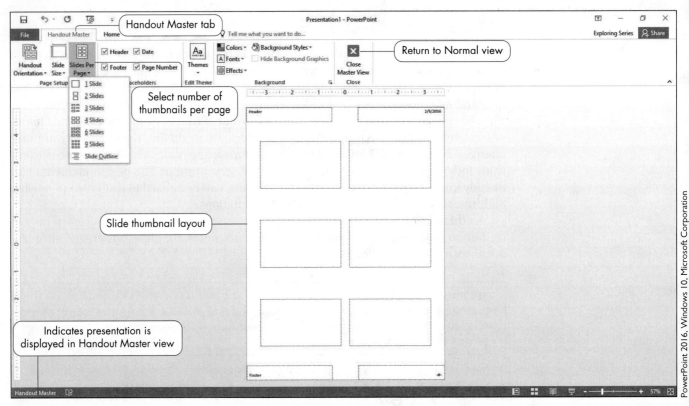

FIGURE 7.14 Handout Master

On the handout master, you modify the header, date, footer, or page number fields using the Placeholders group. You can omit any of these fields from the handout by deselecting the field's check box in the Placeholders group. Initially, the placeholders for the header and date fields are at the top of the page. The footer and the page number field placeholders are at the bottom of the page. You can move each placeholder by dragging it to a new location. In Figure 7.15, the date placeholder is moved to the bottom of the page. The footer is moved to the top of the page, and the page number is removed. Although the term *footer* implies that the location is always at the bottom of a page or slide, sometimes PowerPoint slide templates reposition footers at the top or on the sides.

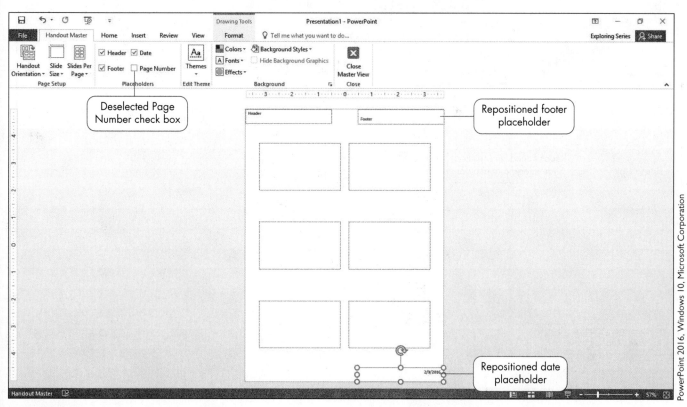

FIGURE 7.15 Customized Handout Master

You can modify the handout master even further using the options from the other tabs displayed on the Ribbon. For example, if you want to have a company logo on each handout page, use Pictures in the Images group on the Insert tab. As you revise the handout master, keep in mind that the handouts are to supplement your presentation. Audience members appreciate handouts that are uncluttered and easy to read, as they often take notes on the handouts that you give them. After modifying the master, click Close Master View in the Close group on the Handout Master tab to return to Normal view.

Customize the Notes Master

 The *notes master* contains design information for notes pages. Often, the speaker uses notes pages to prepare for and deliver the presentation and may occasionally distribute detailed notes pages to an audience. You can specify the fields, the format, and the layout of the notes master similar to the handout master. Figure 7.16 shows a customized notes master that includes resized content placeholders, a company logo, and repositioned placeholders.

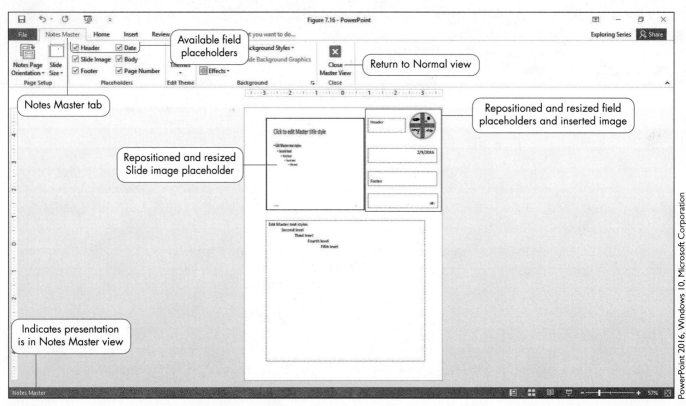

FIGURE 7.16 Customized Notes Master

To modify the notes master, complete the following steps:

1. Click the View tab.
2. Click Notes Master in the Master Views group.
3. Make the changes you want to the notes master using the features on the Notes Master tab.
4. Click Close Master View to return to Normal view.

Modifying a Slide Master

 Each of the layouts available to you when you choose a design theme has consistent elements that are set by a *slide master* containing design information. The slide master also includes associated slide layouts such as a title slide layout, various content slide layouts, and a blank slide layout. You may access the tabs and add objects such as images, SmartArt, shapes, and sounds when modifying the slide master. Transitions can be added to the slide master and animations can be applied to the objects on the slide master.

Customize a Slide Master

The slide master is the top slide in a hierarchy of associated layouts based on the slide master. As you modify the slide master, elements in the slide layouts related to it are also modified to maintain consistency. The associated slide layouts designate the location of placeholders and other objects on slides as well as formatting information. The slide master can be saved as a template and can be applied to other slide presentations.

In Slide Master view, the slide master is the larger, top slide thumbnail shown in the left pane. The title slide layout is the second slide in the pane. The number of slide layouts following it varies depending upon the template. Figure 7.17 shows the default Office Theme slide master and its related slide layouts. The ScreenTip for the slide master indicates it is used by one slide because the slide show is a new slide show comprised of a single title slide.

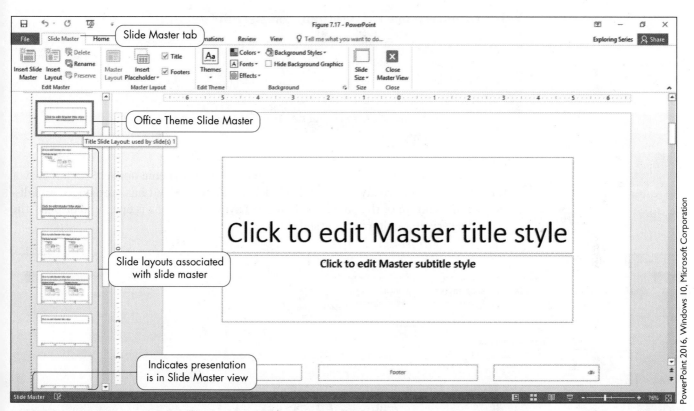

FIGURE 7.17 Slide Master View

The slide master is the most efficient way of setting the fonts, color theme, and effects for the entire presentation. To set these choices, click the slide master thumbnail in the left pane to display the slide master. The main pane shows the placeholders for title style, text styles, a date field, a footer field, and a page number field. Select the text in the master title style placeholder or any level of text in the placeholder and modify the font appearance. You can also make adjustments to the footer, date, and page number fields.

You can move and size the placeholders on the slide master. The modifications in position and size are reflected on the associated slide layouts. This may conflict with some of the slide layout placeholders, however, as repositioning a placeholder may place it on top of a placeholder in the other layout. You can solve this by moving the placeholders on the individual slide layouts as needed.

Delete, Add, and Rename Slide Layouts

STEP 4 ›› If you only need a limited number of layouts, delete the extras to save file size. The title slide layout cannot be deleted, but all other layouts can be removed. Click the slide layout thumbnail you wish to delete and click Delete in the Edit Master group on the Slide Master tab. You can preserve a slide layout within the master even if it is not used in the presentation by clicking Insert Slide Master and clicking Preserve. This will ensure that slide masters in a presentation cannot be deleted.

To add and rename a slide layout, complete the following steps:

1. Click the View tab, and click Slide Master in the Master Views group.
2. Click Insert Layout in the Edit Master group.
3. Click the added slide layout thumbnail to select it.
4. Click Rename in the Edit Master group.
5. Select the default *Custom Layout* name and type a new name.
6. Click Rename.

Figure 7.18 shows the slide master with the Parallax theme applied. All but two of the original associated layouts have been deleted. A new layout has been added and displays at the bottom of the pane. The Rename Layout dialog box is open and displays the name PowerPoint assigns to new slide layouts.

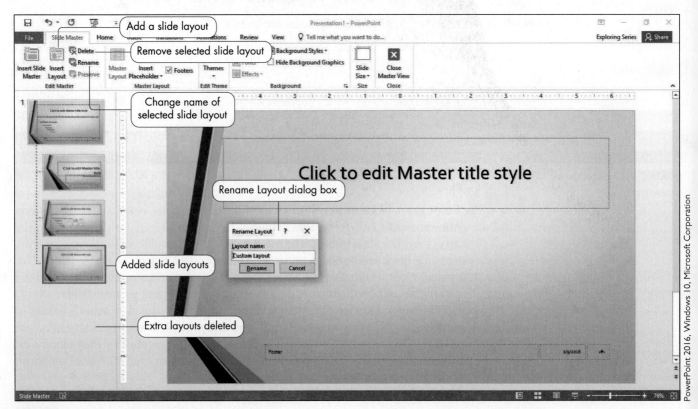

FIGURE 7.18 Adding and Renaming a Custom Layout

Work with Slide Layout Placeholders

You can add, remove, and size placeholders anywhere on a slide to customize a slide layout. You can add specific types of placeholders (see Figure 7.19), including the standard Content placeholder. The Content placeholder contains content buttons in a palette within the placeholder. These buttons enable you to add a table, chart, SmartArt, and other media. If you are creating a template for others to use, you can add prompts with instructions for users by inserting a text placeholder.

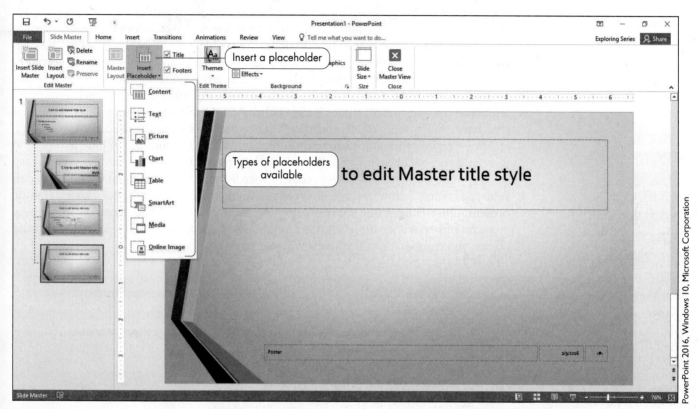

FIGURE 7.19 Placeholder Types

To add a placeholder to a selected layout, complete the following steps:

1. Click the View tab, click Slide Master in the Master Views group, and select the layout to which you want to add a placeholder.
2. Click Insert Placeholder or click the Insert Placeholder arrow in the Master Layout group on the Slide Master tab.
3. Click the desired placeholder type to select it.
4. Drag to create the placeholder in the size that you want.

Once you select a type of placeholder, you can continue adding similar placeholders by clicking Insert Placeholder. To change the type of placeholder, click the Insert Placeholder arrow and make a selection from the list.

> **TIP: REMOVE SLIDE LAYOUTS AND PLACEHOLDERS**
> Select the slide thumbnail first. Click Delete in the Edit Master group on the Slide Master tab to delete the entire slide layout. If you want to remove placeholders from a slide layout, click the placeholder border and press Delete.

Customize the Slide Master Color Theme

Creating custom colors as part of a theme adds a creative touch to a presentation. Using the custom colors on the slide master ensures that the slide layouts maintain continuity.

For example, after adding a logo to the slide master, you can use the logo colors on elements of the slide master. The associated slide layouts use the same colors.

Consider your audience and the message of your presentation as you select colors on your slide master. Look at things around you to come up with color combinations. Other PowerPoint presentations that you may see—in addition to magazines, websites, and other graphically designed materials—will give you a good idea of what colors work well together.

Choose combinations that provide high contrast. Think of your favorite team colors, and you are probably thinking about high-contrast color combinations. If black-and-white printouts are made for the audience, then the choice of colors for the text should provide even more contrast so the handouts are legible. Generally, the slides will be easiest to read when a dark text is placed on a lighter background. You may have seen presentations where the background is dark and the text is light. In making color choices, you need to consider your audience. Some members of your audience may have problems reading light text on a dark background. Additionally, if cost is an issue, printing a dark background increases the print cost due to the amount of ink needed.

Colors convey meanings to your audience. Write the word *hot* in blue letters, and your audience will be confused. Write *hot* in red or orange, and the audience will grasp what you are trying to say. Certain colors evoke feelings. Blue, green, and violet are cool, relaxing colors. Yellow, orange, and red are invigorating, warm, action colors. If your presentation is long, using a warm color will quickly wear your audience out. The Color Associations reference table shows common colors, associations people make with the colors, and emotions that are linked with the colors.

TABLE 7.1   Color Associations

Color	Associations	Emotions	Uses
Red	Danger, blood, strength, courage, fire, energy	Love, power, passion, rage, excitement, aggression, determination, decision making, romance, longing	Make a point or gain attention. Stimulate people into making quick decisions.
Orange	Fall, warmth, fun, joy, energy, creativity, tropics, heat, citrus fruit	Pleasure, excitement, strength, ambition, endurance, domination, happiness, enthusiasm, playfulness, determination, success, stimulation	Emphasize happiness and enjoyment. Stimulate thought. Ensure high visibility. Highlight important elements.
Yellow	Sunshine, bright, warnings	Cheerful, joy, happiness, warmth, optimism, intellect, energy, honor, loyalty, cowardice, lightheartedness, jealousy	Gain a positive response. Gain attention.
Green	Nature, calm, refreshing, money, growth, fertility	Tranquility, growth, safety, harmony, freshness, healing, restive, stability, hope, endurance, envy, jealousy	Present a new idea. Suggest safety. Promote "green" products.
Blue	Sea, sky, peace, calm, cold, impersonal, intellect, masculine, expertise, integrity	Truth, dignity, trust, wisdom, loyalty, harmony, stability, confidence, calming, tranquility, sincerity, healing, understanding, melancholy, belonging	Build trust and strength. Promote cleanliness. Suggest precision. Suppress diet.
Violet	Wealth, royalty, sophistication, intelligence, spirituality, wisdom, dignity, magic, feminine	Power, stability, luxury, extravagance, creativity, frustration, gloom, sadness	Promote children's products. Gain respect and attention.
Black	Formal, mystery, death, evil, power, elegant, prestigious, conservative, the unknown	Authority, boldness, seriousness, negativity, strength, seductiveness, evil	Provide emphasis. Contrast with bright colors and make reading easy.
White	Snow, cleanliness, safety, simplicity, youth, light, purity, virginity	Perfection, distinction, enlightenment, positivity, successful, faith	Provide emphasis. Suggest simplicity. Promote medical products.
Gray	Neutral, science, architecture, commerce, cold	Easy-going, original, practical, solid	Complement other colors. Unify colors. Bring focus to other colors.
Brown	Earth, richness, masculine, harvest, fall	Conservative, steady, dependable, serious, stability	Build trust.

Pearson Education, Inc.

Color themes are combinations of 12 colors used for the text, lines, background, and graphics in a presentation. Color themes contain four text and background colors, six accent colors, and two hyperlink colors. Because standard Office color themes may not include the color combinations that are used by your school, business, or other organization, you can customize your own color theme.

As you focus your attention on creating your own color theme for the slide master, you have 16 million colors from which to choose. You may change any of the 12 colors used in a color theme to any of the 16 million colors available to customize it to your needs. When selecting colors for your color theme, avoid making each of the 12 colors completely different—choose one color family, use different shades of the colors in the family, and add two or three accent colors. Select colors that work well together. Use light and dark shades of the same color within your color theme for a unified, professional appearance.

STEP 5 ❯❯
To customize the color theme for a slide master, complete the following steps:

1. Click the View tab and click Slide Master in the Master Views group.
2. Click the slide master thumbnail in the Slides pane.
3. Click Colors in the Background group.
4. Select a Built-In color theme or select Customize Colors.

If you select Customize Colors, the Create New Theme Colors dialog box opens showing the current theme colors. A preview of how the colors are applied on a slide is shown in a Sample pane. Click the color box next to the name of the color element that you want to change and choose a Theme color, a Standard color, or More Colors. Figure 7.20 displays the Create New Theme Colors dialog box.

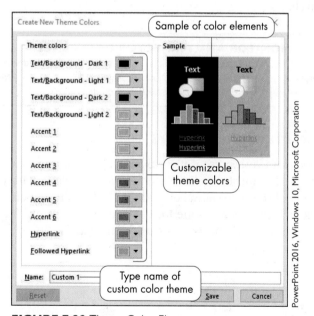

FIGURE 7.20 Theme Color Elements

When you select More Colors, the Colors dialog box that displays offers two tabs for selecting colors. The Standard tab contains 127 colors and 14 shades of white to black. The Custom tab enables you to make selections based on the ***RGB*** color model, where numbers are assigned to red, green, or blue, and the mixture of red, green, or blue light creates a color representation. A zero for each represents black. The number 255 for each of the colors in the model represents white. The RGB model uses 16 million colors. Using this system, you can match any color where you know the three RGB numbers. A similar color model, ***HSL***, balances hue, saturation, and luminosity to produce a color. The numbers for black and white are represented the same way as in the RGB model.

Figure 7.21 shows the Custom tab in the Colors dialog box with the RGB color model selected. Drag the crosshairs in the color box to the color family you wish to use, for instance green. The slider to the right of the color box is used to select the shade of that color. If you know the RGB number, you can use the spin boxes to increase or decrease the numbers, or you can type the numbers into the boxes for each of the colors. After selecting the color, click OK to place that color into the theme. The Sample box in the Create New Theme Colors dialog box displays the current color and the new color. As you make changes to the theme element colors, look at the sample to get an idea of how your color theme will look on the slide.

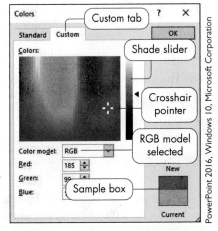

FIGURE 7.21 Custom Tab in the Colors Dialog Box

After making your selections, type a name for the new color theme in the Name box and click Save.

TIP: MONITOR AND PROJECTOR DIFFERENCES
Monitors and projectors show colors in different ways. To avoid surprises, always test your presentation color themes on the projector you will use for your presentation. If you are unable to do this, keep your color theme simple and use standard colors.

Use Multiple Masters

If you want your presentation to contain two or more themes, use **multiple masters** and insert a slide master for each theme. For example, you may use a different theme for each section of the slide show. For example, a slide show about yard tips for each season could include four themes—one for each season. Figure 7.22 shows multiple masters, one using the Facet theme and one using the Parallax theme.

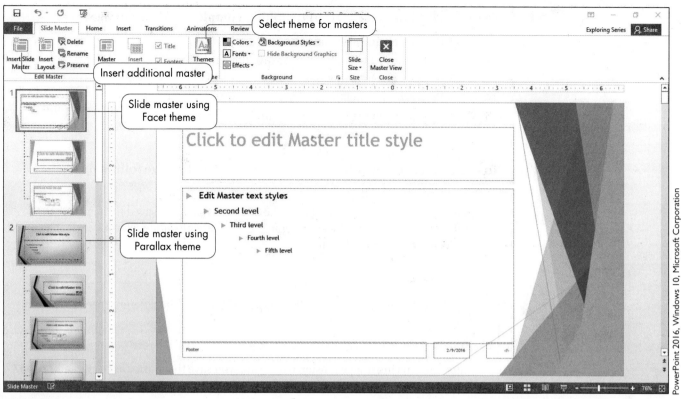

FIGURE 7.22 Multiple Masters

To create multiple masters, complete the following steps:

1. Click the View tab and click Slide Master in the Master Views group.
2. Click Themes in the Edit Theme group.
3. Select a built-in theme or browse for a custom theme you have saved to apply the theme to the existing slide master and its associated layouts.
4. Click below the last slide layout in the Slide Master pane.
5. Click Themes in the Edit Theme group.
6. Select a built-in theme or browse for a saved theme to apply the theme to the new slide master and its associated layouts.

Saving a Slide Master as a Template

To reuse the modified slide master with any presentation, save the file as a ***template***, a file that incorporates formatting elements such as theme and layouts. PowerPoint saves the master as a template with an extension of ***.potx*** and retains the changes in the file. A best practice for you to follow, making it more efficient to locate template files, is to save them to the Templates folder at *C:\Program Files\Microsoft Office\Templates*. By using this practice your templates will appear in the Start screen in the personal templates section when you launch PowerPoint.

> **TIP: BEST PRACTICE WHEN WORKING WITH A TEMPLATE**
> Although you can save any presentation as a template, it is best to start a template with a blank presentation and then design the slide master. This way you save the design you create without saving slides with content. When you save a presentation as a template, you are saving the slides too, and any unwanted slides have to be deleted when the template is used. Also, if you are creating a template for others to use, add instructional prompts to the master using a text placeholder before saving as a template.

STEP 6 »

To save a file as a presentation template, complete the following steps:

1. Click the File tab and click Save As.
2. Navigate to the location you want to save the template in.
3. Click the *Save as type* arrow.
4. Click PowerPoint Template.
5. Type a file name in the File name box and click Save.

To use your custom presentation template, complete the following steps:

1. Click the File tab and click New.
2. Select Personal, next to Featured in the Start screen, if you saved the template to the default location. If you saved the template to another location, click Open, navigate to the location, select your template, and then click Open.

Quick Concepts

4. What are the benefits of using slide masters? What are the different types of masters and the benefits of each? *p. 457*

5. Explain the importance of color use in your presentation. *p. 464*

6. After customizing a slide master, why would you save the master as a template? *p. 467*

Skills covered: Customize the Handout Master • Customize the Notes Master • Customize a Slide Master • Delete, Add, and Rename Slide Layouts • Customize the Slide Master Color Theme • Save a Slide Master as a Template

2 Master Basics

Because you deliver many presentations to local groups on emergency preparedness, you decide to customize a master for handouts and notes that includes your logo and contact information. Then you create a slide master and several slide layouts that you can use for presentations so people identify your business when they see your presentations and advertising.

STEP 1 ⟫ **CUSTOMIZE THE HANDOUT MASTER**

At the beginning of your presentations, you will give your audience a handout of your presentation that displays four slides per page. You choose this layout because you want the audience to have room to write notes below the slide thumbnails. For identification purposes and to save time in the future, you decide to modify the master so it includes your logo and business name. You will also reposition the date field placeholder so it appears below the header. Refer to Figure 7.23 as you complete Step 1.

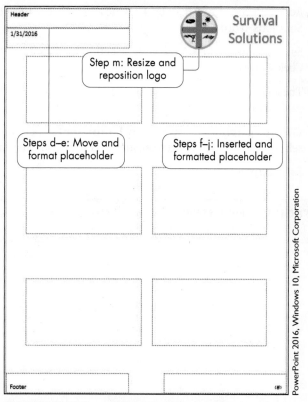

FIGURE 7.23 Survival Solutions Handout Master

a. Create a new blank presentation and save it as **p07h2Survival_LastFirst**.

b. Click the **View tab** and click **Handout Master** in the Master Views group.

The Handout Master tab opens and the master displays.

c. Click **Slides Per Page** in the Page Setup group and select **4 Slides**.

Four slide placeholders display on the handout for positioning purposes. You will still need to pick the number of placeholders you want to print when you are ready to print the handouts.

d. Drag the **date placeholder** immediately below the header placeholder using the Smart Guides to align the two placeholders.

e. Click the **Home tab**, ensure that the date placeholder is selected, and then click **Align Left** in the Paragraph group. Deselect the date placeholder.

The Header field and the content of the date placeholder align on the left.

f. Click the **Insert tab** and click **WordArt** in the Text group.

g. Click **Fill – Blue, Accent 1, Shadow** (first row, second column).

h. Type **Survival**, press **Enter**, and then type **Solutions**.

i. Select the text, click **Text Fill** in the WordArt Styles group, and then click **Red** in the Standard Colors category.

The text is now red.

j. Change the font size to **28 pt**.

k. Drag the **WordArt** to the top-right corner of the handout and use the Smart Guides to ensure that the top and right borders of the WordArt align with the top and right edges of the page.

l. Click **Insert**, click **Pictures** in the Images group, and then navigate to the location where you saved the logo you created in Hands-On Exercise 1, *p07h1SSLogo_LastFirst*. Click the **logo** and click **Insert**.

m. Resize the logo to **1"** high by **1"** wide and drag the **logo** to the left of the Survival Solutions WordArt.

n. Select the **logo**, press **Ctrl** while selecting the WordArt, and then click the **Home tab**. Click **Copy** in the Clipboard group.

The logo and WordArt are saved together as an item to the Clipboard so that you can paste it in other locations.

o. Click the **Clipboard Dialog Box Launcher** to open the Clipboard. View the copied selection in the Clipboard to ensure that it was saved. Close the Clipboard.

p. Save the presentation.

> **TROUBLESHOOTING:** If the logo and WordArt do not appear in the Clipboard, select both objects, and press Ctrl+C. When the copy appears in the Clipboard, close the Clipboard.

Sometimes the notes you add to your slides are very detailed and take a great deal of space. PowerPoint automatically resizes the font to fit the text to the page, which can make the text difficult to read. You will change the notes master to provide more space for notes and add your logo and business name. Refer to Figure 7.24 as you complete Step 2.

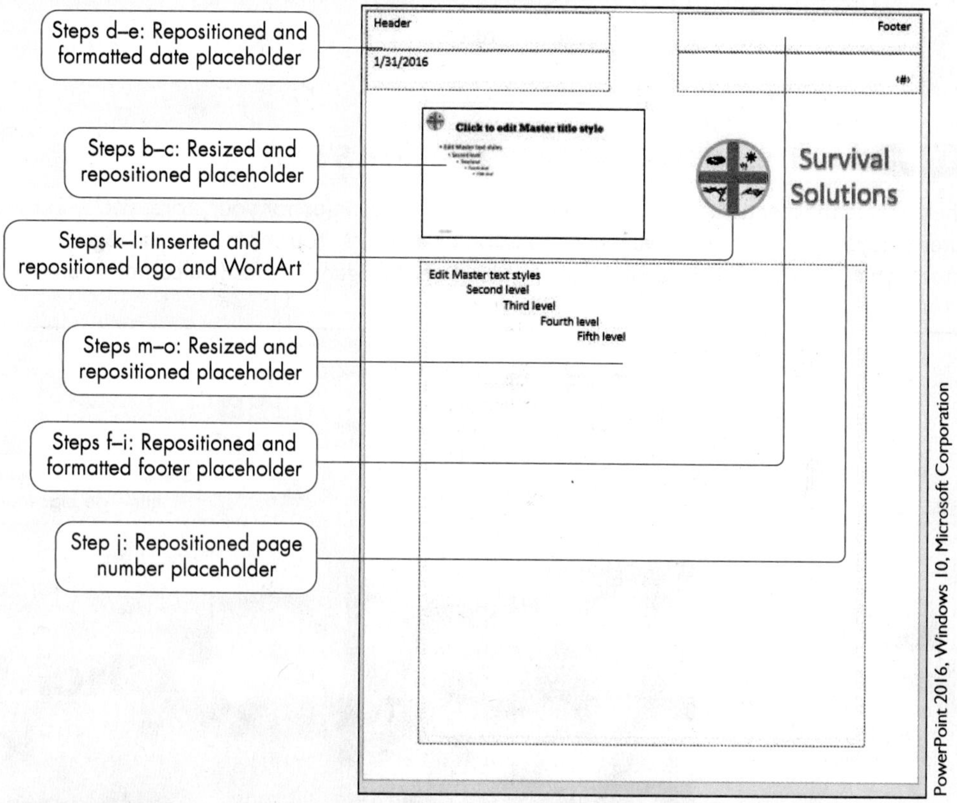

FIGURE 7.24 Survival Solutions Notes Master

a. Click the **View tab** and click **Notes Master** in the Master Views group.

The Notes Master tab opens and the notes master displays.

b. Click the **first text placeholder**, click the **Format tab**, and then click the **Size Dialog Box Launcher**. Scale the placeholder to **50%** of its current size.

The placeholder reduces in size to 1.69" high by 3" wide.

c. Click **Position**. Ensure that the position is set to a Horizontal position of **0.75"**, and a Vertical position of **1.25"** from the Top Left Corner. Close the task pane.

d. Drag the **date placeholder** beneath the header placeholder.

e. Click the **Home tab** and click **Align Left** in the Paragraph group.

The header information and the date are left aligned.

f. Drag the **footer placeholder** to the top right of the page.

g. Right-click the **footer placeholder** and select **Format Shape**.

The Format Shape pane opens.

h. Click **Text Options**, click the **Textbox icon**, change the **Vertical alignment** to **Top**, and then close the task pane.

i. Click **Align Right** in the Paragraph group.

j. Drag the **page number placeholder** beneath the footer placeholder.

k. Click the **Clipboard Dialog Box Launcher** to open the Clipboard. Point to the **logo** and **WordArt** in the list, click the **arrow**, and then click **Paste** to paste the logo. Close the Clipboard.

The objects are pasted on the Notes page.

l. Drag the **logo** and **WordArt** so they are approximately centered in the white space to the right of the Slide Image placeholder.

m. Select the **body placeholder** (the placeholder containing the text levels), click the **Format tab**, and then resize the placeholder to **6.25"** high and **6"** wide.

n. Drag the **body placeholder** up until it fits on the page.

o. Save the presentation.

STEP 3 ›› **CUSTOMIZE A SLIDE MASTER**

To help create the identity of your business and to build recognition for your store, you will create a Survival Solutions slide master that you can use to create presentations for local events. You will include the logo you created on the slide master and a photograph of your store on the Title slide master. Refer to Figure 7.25 as you complete Step 3.

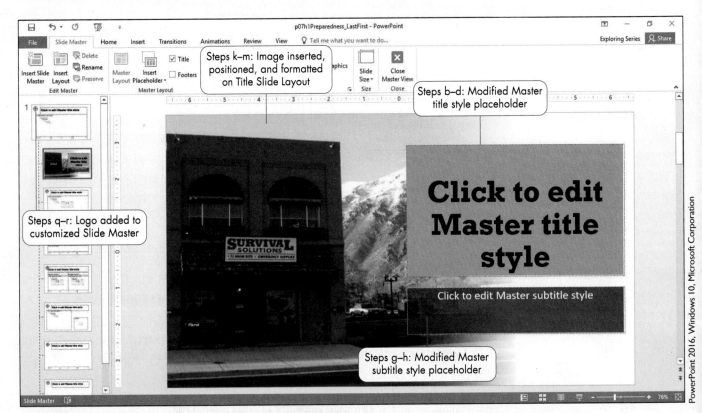

FIGURE 7.25 Survival Solutions Slide Master and Title Slide Layout

a. Click the **View tab** and click **Slide Master** in the Master Views group.

The Slide Master tab opens with the Office Theme slide master selected.

b. Select the **Title Slide Layout**, select the **Master title style placeholder**, click the **Format tab**, and then click the **Size Dialog Box Launcher** in the Size group.

The Format Shape pane opens.

c. Resize the placeholder so it is **3.6"** high by **6.15"** wide.

d. Click **Position**. Set the **Horizontal position** to **6.88"** from the Top Left Corner and the **Vertical position** to **0.87"** from the Top Left Corner, and click **Close** to close the Format Shape pane.

The placeholder moves to the right side of the slide.

e. Click the **Shape Fill arrow**, click **More Fill Colors**, and then click the **Custom tab**. Type **206** in the Red box, type **172** in the Green box, and then type **152** in the Blue box. Type **40** in the **Transparency box** and click **OK**.

The placeholder fill changes to a semitransparent fill.

f. Click the **Home tab**, change the font to **Rockwell**, and then ensure the font size is **60**. Change the font style to **Bold**.

> **TROUBLESHOOTING:** If Rockwell is not available, select any serif font available, such as Times New Roman.

g. Select the **Master subtitle style placeholder** and click the **Format tab**. Click the **Size and Position Dialog Box Launcher** in the Size group, and resize the placeholder to **1.25"** high by **6.15"** wide. Position it horizontally at **6.88"** from the Top Left Corner and **4.8"** vertically from the Top Left Corner.

The subtitle style placeholder is positioned below the title style placeholder.

h. Click the **Format tab**, click **Shape Fill**, click **More Fill Colors**, and then click the **Custom tab**. Type **128** in the Red box, type **47** in the Green box, and then type **53** in the Blue box. Type **20** in the Transparency box and click **OK**.

The placeholder fill changes to a slightly transparent brick-red fill.

i. Click the **Home tab**, select the text, and then change the font color to **White, Background 1**.

j. Click the **Slide Master tab** and click the **Footers check box** in the Master Layout group to deselect it.

The footers are only removed from the title slide layout because it is the selected layout.

k. Click the **Insert tab**, click **Pictures** in the Images group, locate and select *p07h2Store.png* from the data files, and then click **Insert**.

l. Click the **Size and Position Dialog Box Launcher** in the Size group. Position the picture at **0"** from the Top Left Corner and **0"** vertically from the Top Left Corner.

m. Click the **Send Backward arrow** in the Arrange group on the Format tab and click **Send to Back**.

The picture is positioned behind the two placeholders.

n. Click the **Office Theme Slide Master thumbnail**, which is located at the top of the list.

The slide master is selected, and changes made to it will be reflected in associated slide layouts.

o. Select the **Master Title style placeholder** and change the size to **1.38"** high by **10.55"** wide. Position it horizontally at **1.86"** and vertically at **0.42"** from the Top Left Corner.

p. Click the **Home tab** and ensure that the font is set to Rockwell and the font style to Bold.

q. Click the **Clipboard Dialog Box Launcher** to open the Clipboard. Point to the logo and WordArt in the list, click the **arrow**, and then click **Paste**. Delete the WordArt so only the logo remains on the slide. Close the Clipboard.

> **TROUBLESHOOTING:** If the logo and WordArt are no longer available, click the View tab, click Handout Master in the Master Views group, copy just the logo, and then return to Slide Master view. Paste the logo on the slide.

r. Position the logo horizontally at **0.25"** and vertically at **0.25"** from the Top Left Corner.

s. Save the presentation.

Several of the slide layouts associated with the Office Theme slide master you are modifying are not needed, so you will delete them. You will need a layout that includes a picture placeholder in the bottom-right corner of the slide that you will use to put pictures of supplies, however, so you create a custom layout. Refer to Figure 7.26 as you complete Step 4.

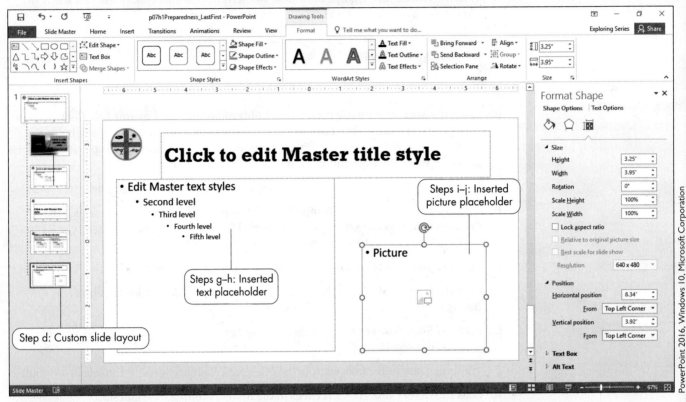

FIGURE 7.26 Custom Slide Layout Renamed Supplies

a. Click **Two Content Layout** in the thumbnail list of layouts associated with the slide master.

The Two Content layout displays.

b. Click the **Slide Master** tab and select **Delete** in the Edit Master group.

The Two Content layout is deleted and the Comparison layout, the next layout in the list, displays.

c. Delete the following layouts:

- Title Only
- Blank
- Content with Caption
- Picture with Caption
- Title and Vertical Text
- Vertical Title and Text

The Office Theme slide master and four associated layouts remain (Title Slide, Title and Content, Section Header, and Comparison).

d. Ensure that the last layout in the thumbnail list is selected and click **Insert Layout** in the Edit Master group.

A new layout, Custom Layout, appears at the bottom of the list of layout thumbnails, and the slide displays in the Slides pane. The layout includes title, date, footer, and page number placeholders.

e. Click **Rename** in the Edit Master group and type **Supplies** in the Layout name box in the Rename Layout dialog box. Click **Rename**.

The name of the new layout is changed to Supplies.

f. Click the **Footers check box** in the Master Layout group to deselect it.

The footers at the bottom of the slide layout are removed.

g. Click the **Insert Placeholder arrow** in the Master Layout group, click **Text**, and then drag to create a text placeholder on the left side of the slide.

h. Click the **Format tab** and click the **Size Dialog Box Launcher** in the Size group. Resize the placeholder to **5.33"** high and **7.02"** wide. Position it horizontally at **0.43"** and vertically at **1.83"** from the Top Left Corner.

The placeholder is resized and positioned on the slide.

i. Click the **Slide Master tab**, click the **Insert Placeholder arrow** in the Master Layout group, click **Picture**, and then drag to create a picture placeholder on the bottom-right of the slide.

j. Resize the placeholder to **3.25"** high and **3.95"** wide. Position it horizontally at **8.34"** and vertically at **3.92"** from the Top Left Corner (see Figure 7.26). Close the Format Shape pane.

k. Save the presentation.

STEP 5 ›› CUSTOMIZE THE SLIDE MASTER COLOR THEME

To further refine your custom master, you will create a custom color theme using the colors in your logo and your store picture. Refer to Figure 7.27 as you complete Step 5.

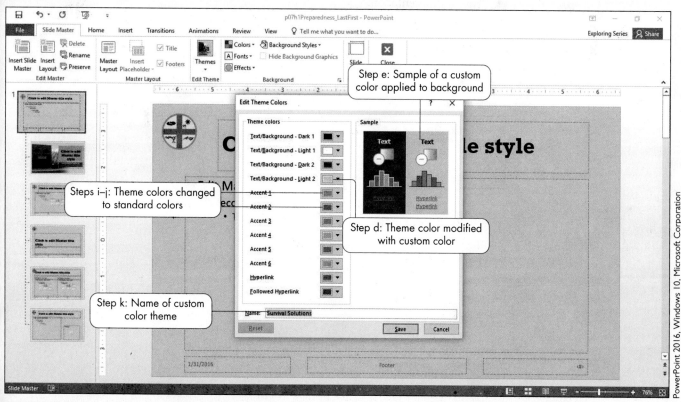

FIGURE 7.27 Create New Theme Colors Dialog Box

a. Click the **Office Theme Slide Master thumbnail** at the top of the thumbnail list.

b. Click **Colors** in the Background group.

c. Click **Customize Colors**.

The Create New Theme Colors dialog box displays the theme colors used in the Office theme that your slide master has been using.

d. Click the **Text/Background - Light 2 arrow** and click **More Colors**.

The Colors dialog box opens with the Custom tab active.

e. Type **193** in the Red box, type **231** in the Green box, type **250** in the Blue box, and then click **OK**.

The Create New Theme Colors dialog box opens the custom color in the color box and in the sample.

f. Click **Save** and click **Background Styles** in the Background group.

Note that the four text and background colors from the color theme display within the 12 thumbnails, and the thumbnails in the second column show the custom color you created.

g. Click **Style 2** (first row, second column) to apply the custom color to the slide master.

h. Click **Colors** in the Background group, right-click **Custom 1**, and then select **Edit**.

The custom color theme you created opens so you can make additional modifications.

i. Select the **Accent 1 color box** and select **Green** in the Standard Colors category.

j. Select the **Accent 2 color box** and select **Red** in the Standard Colors category.

k. Type **Survival Solutions** in the **Name box** and click **Save**.

l. Save the presentation.

STEP 6 » SAVE A SLIDE MASTER AS A TEMPLATE

To be able to use the slide master you just created, you save it as a template. Then, to test the masters you created, you will insert slides from a Survival Solutions slide show you previously presented to a community group. You will view the slide show, and you will preview the handout master and the notes master. Refer to Figure 7.28 as you complete Step 6.

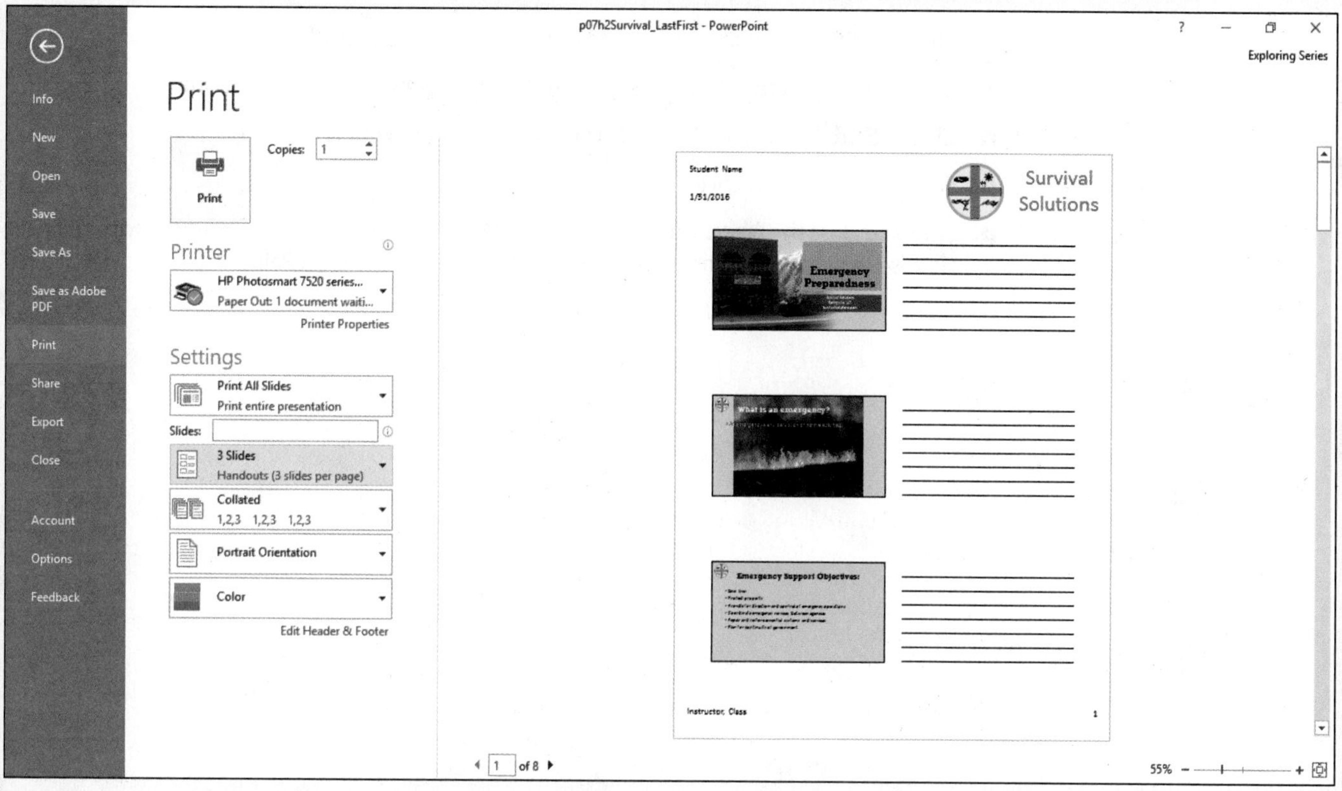

PowerPoint 2016, Windows 10, Microsoft Corporation

FIGURE 7.28 Handout Page Based on Custom Slide Master

a. Click the **File tab** and click **Save As**. Navigate to the location of your homework files.

b. Click the **Save as type arrow** and select **PowerPoint Template**. The file location will automatically change to the Custom Office Templates folder when you change the file type to PowerPoint Template.

c. Name the file **p07h2SurvivalTemplate_LastFirst** and click **Save**.

d. Click **Close Master View** in the Close group. Ensure that the Format Shapes task pane is closed.

e. Ensure that the Home tab is open, click the **New Slide arrow** in the Slides group, and then select **Reuse Slides**.

The Reuse Slides pane opens.

f. Click **Browse** in the Reuse Slides task pane and select **Browse File**.

g. Locate and select *p07h2Plan* and click **Open**.

The 24 added slides appear as thumbnails in the Reuse Slides pane.

h. Right-click any of the slides in the list and select **Insert All Slides**. Close the Reuse Slides pane.

The slides appear in the Slides pane with the slide master you created.

i. Click the **File tab**, click **Save As**, change the file type to PowerPoint Presentation, locate and then select *p07h2Survival_LastFirst*. Click **Save** and click **Yes**.

By saving the file as a PowerPoint Presentation (.pptx file) and not as a PowerPoint Template (.potx file), you do not overwrite the template you created. You will be able to use the template with other presentations.

j. Create a Notes and Handouts header with your name and a footer with your instructor's name and your class. Include the current date.

k. Delete Slide 1.

The empty title slide is deleted, and the title slide from the inserted presentation becomes the new Slide 1.

l. Click the **File tab**, click **Print**, and then click **Full Page Slides**.

m. Click **3 Slides** in the Handouts section. View the preview of the handout.

n. Click **3 Slides** and click **Notes Pages** in the Print Layout section.

o. Scroll to view the notes on some slides.

p. Save and close the presentation. Keep PowerPoint open if you plan to continue with the next Hands-On Exercise. If not, close the presentation and exit PowerPoint.

Custom Shows

Custom shows are composed of a subset of slides assembled for a presentation. Often, a main show (the original presentation) is developed and a number of different presentations based on the main show are created. For instance, you may plan for a 40-minute presentation only to find out at the last minute that your time has been cut to 25 minutes. Rather than show all of the slides in the presentation, moving quickly past less important slides, you can create a custom show using only the critical slides. You can also create multiple custom slide shows in a presentation that are linked so that the presentation pulls slides from each. Custom shows enable you to focus your presentation on the needs of your audience.

An alternative to creating a custom show is to designate hidden slides in a slide show. You might choose to create hidden slides if you wish to have a few slides to reserve in case they are needed later. As you give your presentation, you can reveal hidden slides within the sequence based on your audience needs and the time constraint. You can also use hidden slides to reveal increasingly detailed slides and complex concepts as needed, or you can skip the slides without the audience being aware that you are skipping material. You will experiment with hiding slides and revealing them as you display a slide show.

In this section, you will learn how to create multiple custom shows from a single presentation and how to run and navigate a custom slide show. Finally, you will designate and display hidden slides.

Creating a Custom Show

STEP 1 ⟫ In ***basic custom shows***, you select slides from one main presentation and group them to create other presentations, enabling you to adapt a single presentation to a variety of audiences. If your main presentation contains ten slides, you might designate the first, third, eighth, and tenth slides for one custom show and the first, fifth, and sixth slides for another. The main presentation contains all of the slides needed in the custom shows.

> **To create a custom show, complete the following steps:**
> 1. Click the Slide Show tab.
> 2. Click Custom Slide Show in the Start Slide Show group.
> 3. Select Custom Shows.
> 4. Click New.
> 5. Type a name in the *Slide show name* box.
> 6. Click the slide you want to include in the custom show and click Add. Continue adding slides and click OK.
> 7. Repeat Steps 4 through 7 to create additional custom shows.

Figure 7.29 shows the Custom Shows dialog box and the Define Custom Show dialog box that opens when you click New. The dialog boxes have been rearranged so they are both visible. The slides in the main presentation are listed in the left pane of the Define Custom Show dialog box and are identified by the slide number and the title of the slide. The slides in the custom show are listed in the right pane and are numbered based on their position in the new show.

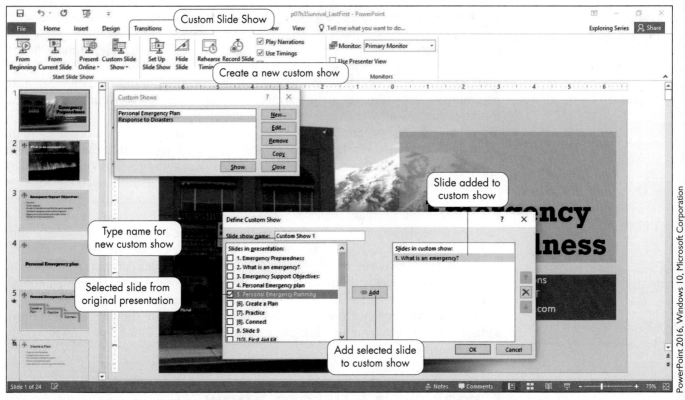

FIGURE 7.29 Creating a Custom Show

Hyperlinked custom shows connect a main custom show to other custom shows using hyperlinks. For example, you might be giving a presentation to a group of potential students who are exploring college majors. One slide in your presentation could have links to parts of your slide show that discuss individual majors. After you quickly poll your audience, you find that everyone is interested in hearing you talk about the nursing major, while half are interested in the business major, and only one or two people want to hear about the other programs. As you present the hyperlinked show, you can decide whether to branch to the supporting shows containing other program information or not. To create a hyperlinked custom show, all of the slides must be in the same presentation. This presentation is then divided into custom shows. A hyperlinked custom show might include ten slides from the main presentation, three slides from another part of the show, and five slides from yet another.

Create the main custom slide show, as previously described, by opening the original presentation and selecting the slides that will be in the main show. Name this custom show with a unique name, such as Proposal_Links, so that you will be able to identify it later as the show that contains the hyperlinks. Create the supporting custom slide shows, as described, by selecting slides from the presentation and naming each show with a different name.

TIP: MAIN CUSTOM SHOW

Name the basic custom slide show with the word *Main* or *Original* as part of the name to make it easy to identify. For instance, a cooking hyperlinked custom show might be called Main Vegetable Presentation. The supporting custom slide shows might be named Cooking Beans, Peeling Tomatoes, or Roasting Vegetables.

After you create all of the custom shows, click the Home tab to return to the original presentation, if necessary. Use the Slide Thumbnail pane to select the slide in the main custom slide show that contains the hyperlinks.

> **To create a custom slide show with hyperlinks, complete the following steps:**
>
> 1. Select the text or other object that you plan to click to view the supporting slides.
> 2. Click the Insert tab and click Hyperlink in the Links group.
> 3. Click Place in This Document in the Insert Hyperlink dialog box, as shown in Figure 7.30.
> 4. Scroll to the bottom of the slide list where the Custom Shows list begins and click the name of the supporting slide show. A preview of the first slide in that show will appear in the Slide preview box.
> 5. Click the *Show and return* check box so that the supporting slide show will return to the main show after all of the slides have been shown.
> 6. Repeat these steps to set up the remaining hyperlinks.

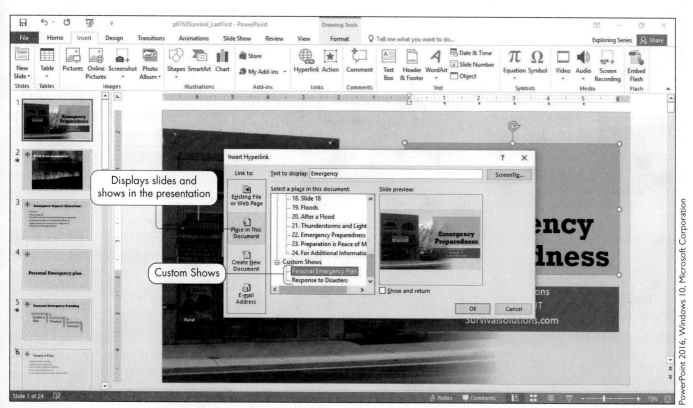

FIGURE 7.30 Insert Hyperlink Dialog Box

Designating and Displaying Hidden Slides

 Although custom shows fit many needs, in some cases you may prefer to skip detailed slides in the main presentation and only show them if the audience requests additional information. Hiding slides within the sequence of the presentation depends on your ability to anticipate what your audience might ask. For example, a presentation on budgeting might include slides that speak of the budgeting process as a concept. Your audience might ask to see some actual numbers plugged into a budget. If you anticipate this question, you can create a slide in advance with this information and hide it within the presentation. During the presentation, if no one asks to see numbers in a budget, you continue through the slide show. But if someone asks, you can show the hidden slide, and then continue through the presentation. The next time you make a presentation, the slide will again be hidden.

To hide a slide, complete the following steps:

1. Select the slide you want to hide in Slide Sorter view or in the Slides pane in Normal view.
2. Click the Slide Show tab.
3. Click Hide Slide in the Set Up group.

Slide Sorter view is active in Figure 7.31, displaying a slide number with a slash—the symbol indicating that a slide is hidden. The thumbnail also appears grayed out. To display a hidden slide, select it in the Slide Thumbnail pane and click Hide Slide again. During the presentation, when you arrive at the location of the hidden slide, you reveal the slide by pressing H.

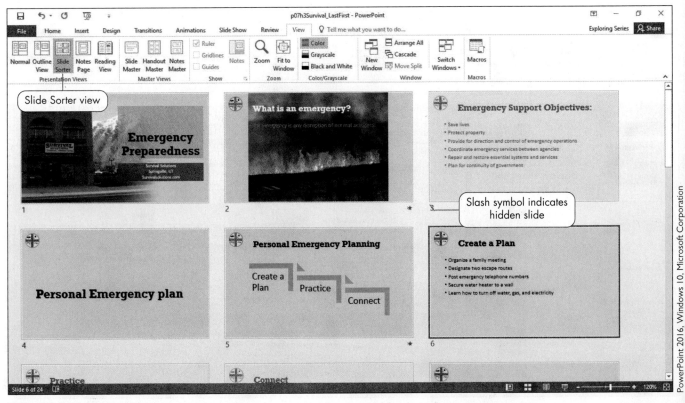

FIGURE 7.31 Hidden Slide

TIP: DISPLAY A SPECIFIC SLIDE IN SLIDE SHOW VIEW
While in Slide Show view, if you know the slide number of a hidden slide, type the number on the keyboard and press Enter to display it. Any slide in the slide show, not just hidden slides, can be quickly displayed using this method.

As you print your slide presentation, you may decide to print the hidden slides or not. Print Preview contains a check box to designate whether to print the hidden slides. It is a good idea to print the hidden slides on the notes pages for the presenter. This way, as the speech is being delivered, the presenter is reminded of the hidden slides and their content.

Running and Navigating a Custom Show

 STEP 3 ⟩⟩ Once a custom slide show has been created and/or hidden slides created, the presentation must be saved. You can then display the custom show from the beginning or at any time while showing the main show.

> **To show the basic custom slide show from the beginning, complete the following steps:**
>
> 1. Open the presentation and click the Slide Show tab.
> 2. Click Custom Slide Show.
> 3. Click the name of the custom show you wish to present.

The show will begin automatically. To show the custom show during the display of the main show, right-click and select Custom Show. Then, select the title of the custom show you wish to display.

> **To show a hyperlinked custom slide show, complete the following steps:**
>
> 1. Open the presentation.
> 2. Click the Slide Show tab.
> 3. Click Custom Slide Show.
> 4. Select the name of the main custom slide show.

The custom presentation will begin. When a slide is reached that contains a hyperlink, click the hyperlink and continue through the supporting slides. Advance through all of the supporting slides and return to the main custom slide. Select another hyperlink if one appears on this slide or continue displaying the slides in the main custom slide show.

Quick Concepts ✔

7. What is the main advantage of creating a custom show? *p. 479*

8. How can you print hidden slides? *p. 482*

9. Explain why you might want to create a hyperlinked custom show. *p. 483*

Watch the Video for This Hands-On Exercise!

MyITLab®
HOE3 Training

Skills covered: Create a Custom Show • Designate and Display Hidden Slides • Run and Navigate a Custom Show

3 Custom Shows

The main slide show, or original slide show, for Survival Solutions was designed so that you can create custom shows based on it to allow flexibility while presenting. You can present a custom show on how to prepare for emergencies or a custom show on responses to specific disasters depending upon audience questions and feedback. The slide show also contains several general slides that can be followed up with reserved slides containing greater detail. You will hide the detail slides, display hidden slides, and then practice navigating custom shows.

STEP 1 ▶▶ CREATE A CUSTOM SHOW

You create two custom slide shows based on the main Survival Solutions presentation so that you can select the show that best meets your audience's interests. Refer to Figure 7.32 as you complete Step 1.

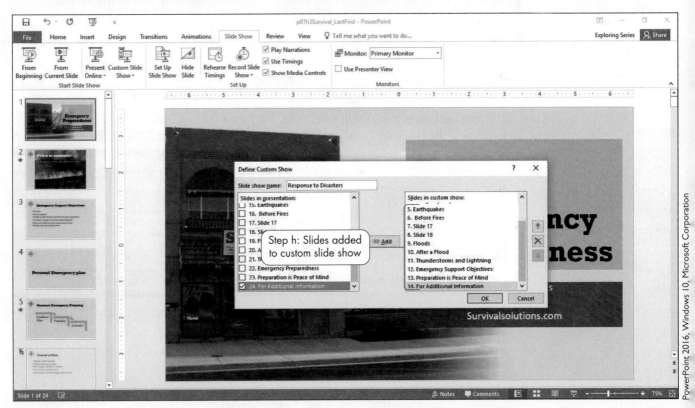

FIGURE 7.32 Response to Disasters Custom Show

a. Open *p07h2Survival_LastFirst* if you closed it at the end of the Hands-On Exercise 2, and save it as **p07h3Survival_LastFirst**, changing h2 to h3.

This presentation is the main (original) show from which you will select slides for custom shows.

> **TROUBLESHOOTING:** Be sure you start with the correct file. Start with the Survival presentation file, not the Survival template file.

b. Click the **Slide Show tab** and click **Custom Slide Show** in the Start Slide Show group.

c. Select **Custom Shows** and click **New**.

The Define Custom Show dialog box opens.

d. Type **Personal Emergency Plan** in the Slide show name box.

e. Select **Slides 1** through **14** and **Slides 23** and **24**. Click **Add**.

Slides 1 through 14, 23, and 24 are added to the custom show. The slides are renumbered in the custom show.

> **TROUBLESHOOTING:** If you select the wrong slide, click the name of the slide on the right side of the Define Custom Show dialog box and click Remove.

f. Click **OK**.

g. Click **New** and type **Response to Disasters** in the Slide show name box.

h. Add the following slides in this order: 1, 2, 14, 22, 15 through 21, 3, 23, and 24.

i. Click **OK** and click **Close**.

j. Save the presentation.

STEP 2 ▶▶ DESIGNATE AND DISPLAY HIDDEN SLIDES

To allow for differing presentation times and audience interest, you will hide slides showing detailed personal emergency planning (Slides 6–8) and storage recommendations (Slides 10–13). If time allows, you will display these slides. Refer to Figure 7.33 as you complete Step 2.

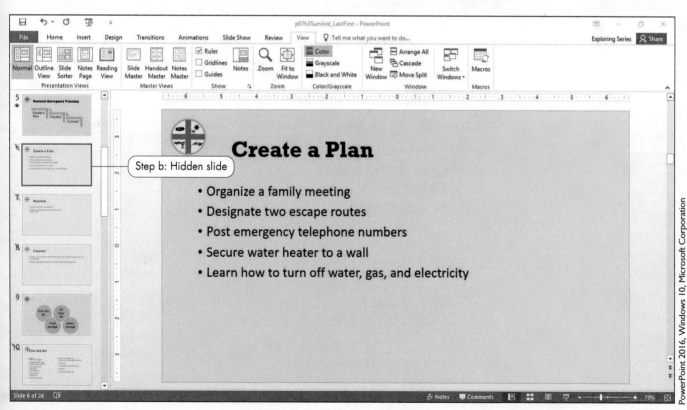

FIGURE 7.33 Hidden Slide

a. Select the **Slide 6 thumbnail**.

b. Ensure that the Slide Show tab is selected and click **Hide Slide** in the Set Up group.

   A slash appears through the slide designation 6 next to the thumbnail.

c. Hide **Slides 7**, **8**, and **10** through **13**.

> **TROUBLESHOOTING:** If you hide a slide by mistake, select the slide and click Hide Slide in the Set Up group on the Slide Show tab again.

d. Click the **View tab** and click **Slide Sorter** in the Presentation Views group.

   Slide Sorter view displays the Hide Slide symbol on Slides 6 through 8 and 10 through 13.

e. Click **Normal**.

f. Save the presentation.

STEP 3 ›› RUN AND NAVIGATE A CUSTOM SLIDE SHOW

To check slide order and practice displaying custom slide shows and hidden slides, you view the Personal Emergency Plan custom show.

a. Click the **Slide Show tab** and click **Custom Slide Show**.

b. Select **Personal Emergency Plan**.

c. Advance through the presentation until you reach the *Personal Emergency Planning* Smart Art diagram.

d. Click **H** on the keyboard.

   Slide 6 displays, followed by Slides 7 and 8, all of which are part of a hidden sequence of slides. Then the next non-hidden slide displays, and the slide show advances through all remaining non-hidden slides. If additional hidden slides follow after this sequence, they can be displayed by pressing H on the keyboard, as in Step d.

e. Advance to the end of the presentation and exit the slide show.

f. Save and close the file. Based on your instructor's directions, submit the following:

   p07h1SSLogo_LastFirst

   p07h1Preparedness_LastFirst

   p07h2SurvivalTemplate_LastFirst.potx

   p07h3Survival_LastFirst

Chapter Objectives Review

After reading this chapter, you have accomplished the following objectives:

1. Set PowerPoint options.

- Set PowerPoint's options to meet your individual needs and maximize your productivity.
- Determine General options: General options are options that impact PowerPoint when you open it such as setting interface options, personalization, and start up options.
- Set Proofing options: Proofing options enable you to change how PowerPoint corrects and formats text.
- Customize Save options: Save options enable you to customize when and where your documents are saved.
- Determine Language preferences: Use Language preferences to change the Office language used for editing, display, Help, and ScreenTips.
- Choose Advanced options: Advanced options enable you to set your preferences for editing, cutting, copying, pasting, sizing and quality of images, setting chart data point properties, setting display options, working in Slide Show view, and printing, as well as several other options.

2. Customize the Ribbon.

- Customize the Ribbon to efficiently access PowerPoint features that you use most often or are not available on the standard Ribbon.
- Add a new tab: Personalize the Ribbon by adding a new tab to which you can add frequently used commands. A new tab includes a new group that is used to contain the commands you add.
- Add commands to a group: In addition to adding any popular commands, you can add commands not on the Ribbon, macros, or any command already contained on other tabs that you want quick access to.

3. Modify handout and notes masters.

- Masters control the consistency of your presentations, notes, and handouts. You can customize these masters so that your printouts provide the information you want to display in the position that is most advantageous.
- Customize the handout master: A handout master controls the layout and formatting of audience handout pages.
- Customize the notes master: The notes master controls the design information for notes pages.

4. Modify a slide master.

- A slide master controls the design elements and slide layouts associated with the slides in a presentation.
- Customize a slide master: Customizing a slide master modifies the same elements in the associated slides to maintain consistency.
- Delete, add, and rename slide layouts: Slide layouts include a title slide layout, various content slide layouts,

and a blank slide layout. Unneeded layouts can be deleted. New slide layouts can be added and renamed.
- Work with slide layout placeholders: You can add, remove, and size placeholders anywhere on a slide to customize a slide layout. You can add specific types of placeholders.
- Customize the slide master color theme: Using custom colors adds a creative touch to a presentation, and creating the custom colors on the slide master theme maintains continuity.
- Use multiple masters: Adding multiple themes to a presentation enables you to use a different theme for different sections of a slide show.

5. Save a slide master as a template.

- After you modify a slide master, you can save the file as a template so that you can reuse the slide master with any presentation.
- PowerPoint saves the master as a template with an extension of .potx and retains the changes in the file.

6. Create a custom show.

- Once a slide show is developed, you can create a number of custom slide shows based on subsets of slides from the main (original) show.
- Creating custom shows enables you to keep all the shows you need for various audiences within one file.
- You can display the custom show that relates to your audience's interests.

7. Designate and display hidden slides.

- You can create and hold slides in reserve in anticipation of audience questions. You can then hide the slide with the reserved or detailed information until the appropriate time during the presentation.
- While presenting in Slide Show view, display a hidden slide by pressing H on the keyboard.

8. Run and navigate a custom show.

- Display a custom show from its beginning, at any time while showing the main show, or by clicking a hyperlink.
- To show the basic custom show from the beginning, open the presentation, click the Slide Show tab, click Custom Slide Show, and then click the name of the custom show you wish to present. The show begins automatically.
- To branch to a custom show while presenting the main (original) show, right-click and select Custom Show. Then select the title of the custom show you wish to display.
- To display a hyperlinked custom slide show, click a link on a slide displayed during the main slide show.

Key Terms Matching

Match the key terms with their definitions. Write the key term letter by the appropriate numbered definition.

a. .exportedUI
b. .potx
c. Basic custom show
d. Color theme
e. Custom Show
f. Customize Ribbon
g. Handout master
h. HSL
i. Hyperlinked custom show
j. Master

k. Multiple masters
l. Notes master
m. Nudge
n. PowerPoint Options
o. RGB
p. Slide master
q. Start screen
r. Template
s. TrueType fonts

1. _____ Scalable fonts supported by Windows that display and print smoothly at any point size. **p. 446**

2. _____ The top slide in a hierarchy of slides that contains design information for the slides. **p. 460**

3. _____ The file extension assigned to a PowerPoint template. **p. 467**

4. _____ A numeric system for identifying the color resulting from the combination of red, green, and blue light. **p. 465**

5. _____ Contains the design information for audience handout pages. **p. 457**

6. _____ Consists of the color combinations for the text, lines, background, and graphics in a presentation. **p. 465**

7. _____ The screen that displays by default when PowerPoint is opened that provides options for opening existing presentations or new presentations from online or from a built-in theme. **p. 443**

8. _____ Begins with a main custom show and uses hyperlinks to link between other shows. **p. 480**

9. _____ A broad range of settings that enable you to customize the environment to meet your needs. **p. 442**

10. _____ Move an object in small, precise increments. **p. 449**

11. _____ A predesigned file that incorporates formatting elements, such as theme and layouts, and may include content that can be modified. **p. 467**

12. _____ Contains the design information for notes pages. **p. 459**

13. _____ A single presentation file from which you can create separate presentations. **p. 479**

14. _____ Contains design information that provides a consistent look to your presentation, handouts, and notes pages. **p. 457**

15. _____ Located in the PowerPoint Options dialog box and enables you to create a personal tab on the Ribbon that includes features that are not available on the standard Ribbon. **p. 447**

16. _____ The file extension assigned to an exported User Interface customized file. **p. 450**

17. _____ A grouped subset of the slides in a presentation. **p. 479**

18. _____ A color model in which the numeric system refers to the hue, saturation, and luminosity of a color. **p. 465**

19. _____ A presentation containing two or more themes on the slide master. **p. 466**

Multiple Choice

1. Which of the following options can be changed in the General options within PowerPoint Options?

   (a) Image Size and Quality
   (b) User name
   (c) AutoCorrect
   (d) Customize Ribbon

2. Which of the following statements is *not* true regarding customizing the Ribbon?

   (a) All available PowerPoint commands are displayed on the default Ribbon.
   (b) Custom tabs and groups can be added to the Ribbon.
   (c) Tabs and groups can be renamed.
   (d) Commands can be removed from one tab and added to another.

3. Which AutoCorrect option enables you to automatically resize the font of text as you type a title to fit the size of the title text placeholder?

   (a) Math AutoCorrect
   (b) Actions
   (c) AutoFormat As You Type
   (d) AutoCorrect

4. By default, notes masters contain:

   (a) Three slide thumbnails per page.
   (b) Only a slide thumbnail and note text.
   (c) Note text, date, header, and footer.
   (d) A header, date, slide thumbnail, note text, footer, and page number.

5. Which of the following is *not* a true statement regarding a slide master?

   (a) A slide master controls the position of the slide thumbnail in handouts and notes pages.
   (b) A slide master saved as a template can be used with multiple presentations.
   (c) A slide master is the top slide in a hierarchy of slides that stores design information and slide layouts.
   (d) A presentation can contain more than one slide master.

6. Which of the following is *not* a true statement about slide layouts associated with a slide master?

   (a) Slide layouts can be renamed or deleted.
   (b) Slide layouts contain the same theme (color theme, fonts, and effects) as the slide master.

   (c) Slide layouts cannot be modified by adding additional placeholders.
   (d) Slide layouts can use either portrait or landscape orientation.

7. Custom slide shows are:

   (a) Multiple presentation files with slides copied from a main presentation file.
   (b) Shows created by selecting slides from a main presentation and saved with the presentation file.
   (c) Shows with a modified slide master.
   (d) Shells for building presentations.

8. Custom slide shows *cannot* contain:

   (a) Slides that are not a part of the original presentation.
   (b) Hyperlinks to other slide shows.
   (c) Hidden slides.
   (d) More than 10 slides.

9. Custom slide shows can be viewed using all of the following methods *except* by:

   (a) Clicking the Slide Show tab, clicking Custom Slide Show, and then clicking the name of the custom show.
   (b) Right-clicking in Slide Show view, selecting Custom Show, and then selecting the name of the custom show.
   (c) Pressing Ctrl+C while in Slide Show view and selecting the name of the custom show.
   (d) Clicking a hyperlink on a slide while in Slide Show view.

10. Which of the following statements is *true* about hidden slides?

    (a) A hidden slide does not show when you advance from one slide to another when displaying a slide show.
    (b) A hidden slide is created using Hide Slide in the Custom Slide Show group on the Slide Show tab.
    (c) A hidden slide cannot be used during a custom slide show.
    (d) A hidden slide can be revealed when displaying a slide show by pressing 1.

Practice Exercises

1 Mountain Biking Presentation

You are preparing a presentation to a local youth group about mountain bike safety and general mountain biking rules of the trail. You want the title slide to include a mountain scene with a mountain bike popping up on a trail. To begin, you will change PowerPoint options to include an AutoCorrect phrase for efficiency and to change the AutoRecover time to five minutes. You will modify the Ribbon structure you created in Hands-on Exercise 1 to add positioning features. You will use PowerPoint's Combine Shapes feature to complete the mountain scene, and you will add and position an image of a mountain bike. Finally, you will enter sample text in the title slide text and a content slide so you can view the finished handouts and notes masters. Refer to Figure 7.34 as you complete this exercise.

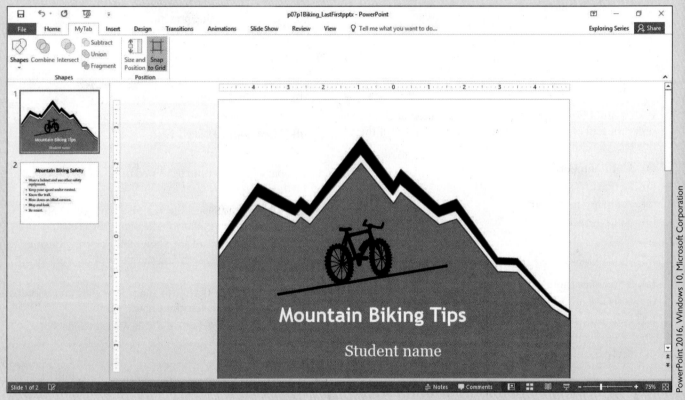

FIGURE 7.34 Mountain Biking Title Slide

a. Open *p07p1Biking* and save it as **p07p1Biking_LastFirst**.

b. Create a handout header with your name and a handout footer with the file name, your instructor's name, and your class. Include the current date.

c. Click the **File tab**, click **Options**, and then click **Proofing**.

d. Click **AutoCorrect Options** and click the **AutoCorrect tab**. Type **mb** in the **Replace box** and type **Mountain Biking** in the **With box**. Click **Add** and click **OK**.

e. Click **Save** in the left pane of the PowerPoint Options dialog box, select the number in the *Save AutoRecover information every* box, and then type **5**.

f. Click **Customize Ribbon** and click **MyTab (Custom)**.

> **TROUBLESHOOTING:** If you do not have a tab named MyTab (Custom), complete Hands-on Exercise 1, Step 3.

g. Click **New Group** and click **Rename**. Type **Position** in the Display name box and click **OK**.

h. Select **Size and Position** in the Popular Commands list and click **Add**.

i. Click the **Choose commands from arrow** and select **Commands Not in the Ribbon**.

j. Select **Snap to Grid** and click **Add**. Click **OK**.

k. Select the **black mountain shape** (click the top peak of the black mountain shape), press and hold **Shift**, and then click the **blue shape with the orange outline** (click the top peak of the blue mountain shape) to add it to the selection. Click the **MyTab tab** and click **Subtract** in the Shapes group. A jagged white line now exists where the blue shape was cut out of the black mountain shape.

l. Click the **Insert tab**, click **Pictures**, select *p07p1Bike.jpg*, and then click **Insert**.

m. Drag the back wheel of the mountain bike image as close to the straight black trail line as possible. If the grid setting does not enable you to align the back tire with the trail, click the **MyTab tab** and click **Snap to Grid** in the Position group to deactivate it. Drag the image until the back wheel aligns with the trail line. Resize the image as desired.

n. Click in the **title placeholder** and type **mb Tips**. AutoCorrect replaces *mb* with *Mountain Biking*.

o. Type your name in the **subtitle placeholder**.

p. Add a new slide using the Title and Content layout.

q. Click in the **title placeholder** and type **mb Safety**. Type the following bulleted points:
- **Wear a helmet and use other safety equipment**
- **Keep your speed under control**
- **Know the trail**
- **Slow down on blind corners**
- **Stop and look**
- **Be smart**

r. Click the **File tab**, click **Print**, click **Full Page Slides**, and then click **Notes Pages**. View the Notes Pages preview. Click **Notes Pages** and click **Handouts 4 Slides Horizontal**.

s. Save and close the file. Based on your instructor's directions, submit p07p1Biking_LastFirst.

2 Sunshine Log Homes

FROM SCRATCH

Your manager prepared a presentation discussing the positive features of building a home using the services of Sunshine Builders. You have been asked to modify the handouts so that the printouts have two slides per page and contain the date, company name and logo, and page number. The manager would also like the company name and logo on the slides. Because your manager will be using this same format in the future, you will save a file with the masters as a template. Refer to Figure 7.35 as you complete this exercise.

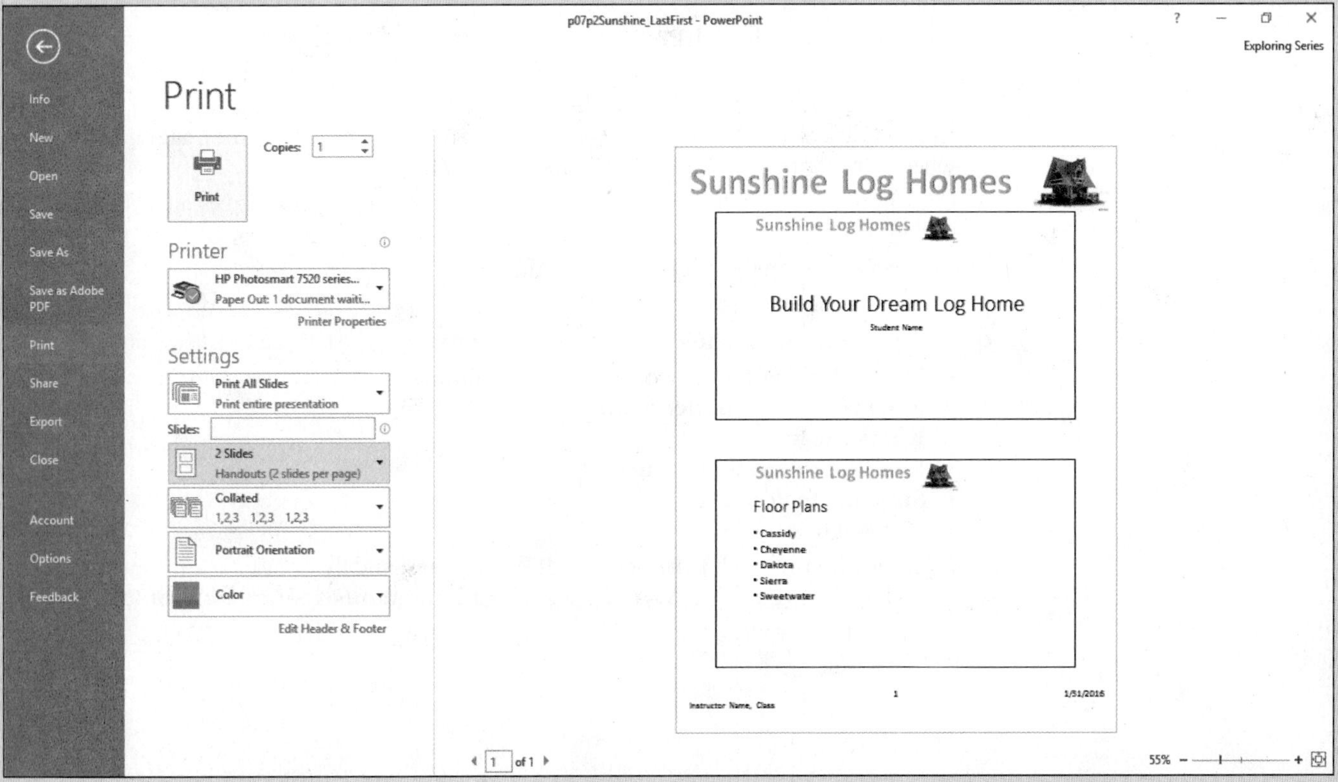

PowerPoint 2016, Windows 10, Microsoft Corporation

FIGURE 7.35 Sunshine Log Homes Handout

a. Open a new blank presentation and save it as **p07p2Sunshine_LastFirst**.

b. Click the **View tab** and click **Handout Master** in the Master Views group.

c. Click **Slides Per Page** in the Page Setup group and select **4 Slides**.

d. Deselect the **Header check box** in the Placeholders group.

e. Select the **Page Number placeholder**, click the **MyTab tab**, and then click **Size and Position** in the Position group.

f. Set the following in the Format Shape pane and close the pane:

- Size: Height **0.5"**, Width **1"**.
- Position: Horizontal **3.25"** from the Top Left Corner and Vertical **9.5"** from the Top Left Corner.
- Text Box: Vertical alignment **Top Centered**.

g. Drag the **date placeholder** to the bottom-right corner of the page, aligning its bottom border with the bottom edge of the page and the right border with the right edge of the page.

h. Click the **Insert tab**, click **WordArt** in the Text group, click **Fill – Gold, Accent 4, Soft Bevel** (first row, fifth column), set the font size to **48 pt**, and then type **Sunshine Log Homes**. Drag the WordArt to the top-left corner of the page, aligning its top border with the top edge of the page and the left border with the left edge of the page.

i. Click the **Insert tab**, click **Pictures** in the Images group, locate *p07p2Cabin.jpg*, and then click **Insert**.

j. Click the **MyTab tab** and click **Size and Position** in the Position group. Set the following in the Format Picture pane and close the pane:
- Size: Height **1"**, Width **1"**.
- Position: Horizontal **6.35"** from the Top Left Corner and Vertical **0"** from the Top Left Corner.

k. Select the **WordArt** and **log home image**, click the **Home tab**, and then click **Copy** in the Clipboard group.

l. Click the **View tab** and click **Notes Master** in the Master Views group. Deselect the **Header** and **Date check boxes** in the Placeholders group.

m. Click the **Home tab** and click the **Clipboard Dialog Box Launcher** to open the Clipboard pane. Point to the WordArt and image in the list, click the **arrow**, and then click **Paste**. Deselect the objects. Close the Clipboard.

n. Set the horizontal position of the WordArt to **0"** from the Top Left Corner and set the vertical position to **0"** from the Top Left Corner.

o. Set the horizontal position of the picture to **6.35"** from the Top Left Corner and set the vertical position to **0"** from the Top Left Corner.

p. Click the **View tab**, click **Slide Master** in the Master Views group, and then paste the WordArt and the image on the Office Theme slide master.

q. Set the horizontal position of the WordArt to **1.33"** from the Top Left Corner and set the vertical position to **0"** from the Top Left Corner. Set the horizontal position of the picture to **7.65"** from the Top Left Corner and set the vertical position to **0"** from the Top Left Corner.

r. Select the **Master title style placeholder**, set the following in the Format Shape pane, and then close the pane:
- Size: Height **1.25"**, Width **8"**.
- Position: Horizontal **1.33"** from the Top Left Corner, Vertical **1.08"** from the Top Left Corner.

s. Select the **Master text placeholder**, set the following in the Format Shape pane, and then close the pane:
- Size: Height **4.3"**, Width **8"**.
- Position: Horizontal **1.33"** from the Top Left Corner, Vertical **2.42"** from the Top Left Corner.

t. Close the slide master. Click the **File tab** and click **Save As**. Click the **Save as type arrow** and select **PowerPoint Template**. Name the file **p07p2SunshineTemplate_LastFirst**. Click **Save**. Close the file, and close PowerPoint.

u. Open PowerPoint, and click the **Personal** link next to the Featured link on the right side of the screen. Double-click **p07p2SunshineTemplate_LastFirst** to open the template. Create a handout header with your name and a handout footer with the file name, your instructor's name, and your class. Include the current date.

v. Type **Build Your Dream Log Home** in the title placeholder on Slide 1, and your name in the subtitle placeholder. Type the following text in the notes pane: **Sunshine Log Homes is well known as one of the premier custom log home builders in the Mountain area. If innovative design, distinctive quality, and impressive value are important to you, we are your builder!**

w. Create a new slide using the Title and Content layout. Type **Floor Plans** in the title placeholder and enter the following as bullets: **Cassidy, Cheyenne, Dakota, Sierra**, and **Sweetwater**.

x. Add the following text in the notes pane: **One of the most exciting parts of your log home-building experience is selecting your floor plan. Our floor plans reflect today's log home design trends.**

y. Click the **File tab**, click **Print**, and then click **Full Page Slides**. Click **Notes Pages** and note the preview of the printed notes pages. Click **Notes Pages** and click **2 Slides (Handouts)**. Note the preview of the handout.

z. Click **Save As**, locate and select *p07p2Sunshine_LastFirst*, and then click **Save**, being careful not to save the presentation over the template file. Close the file. Based on your instructor's directions, submit the following:

p07p2Sunshine_LastFirst

p07p2SunshineTemplate_LastFirst

3 Luxury Estates Presentation

You are a realtor selling luxury country estates. This week, you have appointments with two potential customers, so you will create a presentation using recent photographs and information about the estates you personally selected as being the most suitable. You will create custom shows for each customer including a slide personalizing the show and slides highlighting the estates. You will hide slides with cost information on each estate so they can be shown if the customer expresses an interest in the property. Refer to Figure 7.36 as you complete this exercise.

FIGURE 7.36 Luxury Estates Presentation

a. Open *p07p3Luxury* and save it as **p07p3Luxury_LastFirst**.

b. Create a handout header with your name and a handout footer with your instructor's name and your class. Include the current date.

c. Click the **Slide Show tab** and click **Custom Slide Show** in the Start Slide Show group. Select **Custom Shows** and click **New**.

d. Type **Roberts** in the Slide show name box.

e. Select **Slides 1, 2, 4, 5, 6, 10, 11, 12**, and **19**, click **Add**, and then click **OK**.

f. Click **New** and type **Lewis** in the Slide show name box.

g. Select **Slides 1, 3, 7, 8, 9, 13, 14, 15, 16, 17, 18**, and **19**, click **Add**, and then click **OK**. Click **Close**.

h. Select **Slides 6, 9, 12, 15**, and **18** in the Slides pane and click **Hide Slide** in the Set Up group.

i. Ensure that the Slide Show tab is still selected, click **Custom Slide Show** in the Start Slide Show tab, and then click **Roberts**.

j. Advance to Slide 5 and press **H** on the keyboard to reveal Slide 6, which is a hidden slide. Advance to the end of the presentation and exit. Repeat with the Lewis show. Advance to Slide 8 and press **H** on the keyboard to reveal Slide 9, which is a hidden slide.

k. Close the file. Based on your instructor's directions, submit p07p3Luxury_LastFirst.

Mid-Level Exercises

Family Reunion

CREATIVE CASE

FROM SCRATCH

You are creating a PowerPoint presentation for a family reunion and have asked family members to provide a picture labeled with names, recent family information, and the connection to your great-grandfather. You will modify PowerPoint options and the Ribbon to put the tools you need on one tab, and combine shapes to create a family logo. You will include the logo on the handout, notes, and slide masters to create a theme. You will also modify the slide master with your preferences for a font theme and color theme and create three new slide layouts. You will save your work as a template so others may use it.

a. Open a blank presentation and save it as **p07m1Reunion_LastFirst**.

b. Set PowerPoint options to save AutoRecover information every **15 minutes** (Save option) and to set the default target output to **150 ppi** (Advanced option), if necessary.

c. Customize the Ribbon to put the buttons you use most on one custom tab with groups. You can modify the MyTab tab you created in previous exercises or reset the Ribbon to its original state and create a new tab with groups.

d. Click the **Title box** and type your **great-grandfather's name**. Combine shapes to create a family logo and position it in the bottom-right corner of the slide. Copy it to the Clipboard.

e. Modify the handout and notes masters to include your logo in the position of your choice. Make at least one change to the placeholders (e.g., location, font, size) and make any other changes.

f. Display the slide master. Create a new Color theme by customizing at least two theme colors. Save the new theme with the name **Family Reunion**.

g. Select the **title slide layout** and insert and position a 6" by 4" picture placeholder on the slide for your great-grandfather's image. Rearrange or reformat the title and subtitle placeholders to fit on the empty area of the slide.

h. Replace the title text with **Enter Great-Grandfather's Name**. Replace the subtitle text with **Enter reunion date, time, and location**.

i. Remove the date and page number placeholders from the title slide layout. Make additional design changes as desired.

j. Replace the text in the footer placeholder with your family name and the word *Reunion*. Use the *Header and Footer* dialog box on the Insert tab to apply the footer to the title slide layout only.

k. Delete all other slide layouts. Insert a new slide layout named **Family Information**.

l. Remove the footer, date, and page number placeholders from the Family Information slide layout. Add a text placeholder that fills the blank space of the slide.

m. Copy the Family Information slide and paste it on the Slide Thumbnail pane. Rename the slide layout **Family Relationship**.

n. Remove the text placeholder on the Family Relationship slide layout. Insert a SmartArt placeholder that fills the blank space of the slide.

o. Click the **File tab** and click **Save As**. Click the **Save as type arrow** and select **PowerPoint Template**.

p. Open PowerPoint, and click the **Personal** link next to the Featured link on the right side of the screen. Double-click **p07m1Reunion_LastFirst.potx** to open the template.

q. Select the **Picture placeholder** on the **title slide layout** in the open slide master. Apply the animation of your choice. Save the template, replacing the previous template.

r. Click the **Slide Master tab** and click **Close Master View** in the Close group.

s. Create a title slide and a Family Information slide using your own family information and family photo.

t. Create a handout header with your name and a handout footer with your instructor's name and your class. Include the current date.

u. Save the file as **p07m1Reunion_LastFirst.pptx**, being careful to save over the presentation file and not the template file.

v. Close the file. Based on your instructor's directions, submit the following:
p07m1Reunion_LastFirst
p07m1ReunionTemplate_LastFirst.potx

PTA Fundraising Shows

The PTA at the elementary school has quarterly meetings where discussions focus on plans for fundraising throughout the year. At the beginning of the year, all of the plans are put into a presentation. Two presentations cover the plans for each fundraising project. The slides contain the project description, dates, and committee assignments. One slide details the budget and is hidden during the general member meeting and displayed to the PTA board meeting. You create two custom shows that contain the title slide, the slides pertaining to the most recent project and the next project, the budget slide, and a thank-you slide.

a. Open *p07m2PTA* and save it as **p07m2PTA_LastFirst**.

b. Create a handout header with your name and a handout footer with your instructor's name and your class. Include the current date.

c. Create a custom show named **Fall Projects** using Slides 1 through 6 and 9 through 11.

d. Create a custom show named **Winter Projects** using Slides 1, 2, and 5 through 11.

e. Hide Slide 10.

f. Display the Fall Projects custom show. Show the hidden slide.

g. Display the Winter Projects custom show. Show the hidden slide.

DISCOVER

h. Use the Set Up Slide Show dialog box to display the Winter Projects custom slide show. Also set the Laser pointer color to **green**.

i. Display the entire presentation. Use the Laser pointer to draw attention to details on slides.

j. Close the file. Based on your instructor's directions, submit p07m2PTA_LastFirst.

3 **IT Department Meeting**

COLLABORATION CASE

FROM SCRATCH

As the administrative clerk for the IT director of your company, you are responsible for preparing a PowerPoint agenda presentation for every IT department meeting. Because this is a task that encompasses several areas, you rely on IT department employees to provide pertinent information. The title slide includes meeting details, and each agenda item is listed on a single slide with the name of the person responsible for the discussion of this item. Another type of slide contains additional resources related to the agenda item, such as text, graphics, or SmartArt. You will create a slide master template so that the structure of the presentation is prepared. You will create the design of the slide master to match the company's colors and include the company logo. Each employee is responsible for providing information to you. This can be accomplished using Outlook or SkyDrive. Save the master as a template named **p07m3AgendaTemplate_LastFirst.potx** and close it. Open the template and put in agenda information for an organization of which you are a member. Save the file as **p07m3Agenda_LastFirst**. Close the file. Based on your instructor's directions, submit the following:

p07m3AgendaTemplate_LastFirst.potx

p07m3Agenda_LastFirst

Beyond the Classroom

Mix Presentation

As a trainer in your company's Human Resources department, you are responsible for researching new software that could be helpful for employee use. One group you present to is the IT department, which would implement the installation of the software. Another group would be administrators who would approve or disapprove the purchase and installation of the software. The third group you would present to would be the employees who would be using the software. Microsoft released a new software, Office Mix, that looks promising for your company. Office Mix is a free add-in for PowerPoint. Research Office Mix and develop a presentation that contains information that will be useful to all of these groups. Save the file as **p07b1Mix_LastFirst**. Use your knowledge of slide masters to create appropriate layouts. Create a custom color theme. Use hyperlinks, illustrations, images, sounds, video, animation, and transitions as appropriate. Create three custom slide shows—one for each group on Office Mix. Close the file. Based on your instructor's directions, submit p07b1Mix_LastFirst.

Templates Gone Haywire

DISASTER RECOVERY ✚

Your 14-year-old brother has been working on a presentation for his science class. Open the presentation he created, *p07b2Corrections*. Save the file as **p07b2Corrections_LastFirst**. Notice your brother tried revising a design template but has become confused. His handouts print with a blue background, he gets blank pages when he tries to view notes pages, and the animation and transitions he applied create a mixed-up jumble of words and graphics flying all over the screen. You sit down and help him with the templates. First, however, you set General options so that the User Name displays your name and Initial displays your initials. Set the Office theme to Colorful. Change the Save options so PowerPoint AutoRecover saves every 10 minutes. You correct the handout master so that the background is white. You revise the notes master so the placeholders necessary to display the header, slide image, and body appear, as well as the footer and page number. You make adjustments to the animations and transitions so they enhance the slide show rather than distract the audience. Close the file. Based on your instructor's directions, submit p07b2Corrections_LastFirst.

Capstone Exercise

You are an advisor for the School of Arts at your university and will be visiting local high schools to recruit new students. You want to create a presentation that will allow you to show custom slide shows based on the interests of the students with whom you are speaking. In this capstone exercise, you will create a custom presentation demonstrating the skills learned in this chapter.

Set PowerPoint Options and Customize the Ribbon

The computer you have been given is one that was in the department's front office. The person using it before you had set custom options and made Ribbon changes. You decide to change the PowerPoint options to fit your needs, reset the Ribbon to its original state, and then customize the Ribbon to meet your needs.

a. Create a new blank presentation and save it as **p07c1Arts_LastFirst**.

b. Apply the **Crop** theme and the **Teal** variant of the theme.

c. Create a slide footer that reads **www.artschool.edu**. Include a slide number on all slides. Do not include the slide footer and slide number on the Title slide.

d. Create a handout header with your name and a handout footer with the instructor's name and your class. Include the current date.

e. Set PowerPoint General options to include your user name and initials, if necessary.

f. Set PowerPoint Save options to AutoRecover information every 5 minutes, to keep the last autosaved version if you close without saving, and to embed all fonts.

g. Reset all customizations on the Ribbon.

h. Add a custom group following the Drawing group in the Home tab. Name the custom group **Combine Shapes**.

i. Include the following buttons from the *Commands Not in the Ribbon* list in the Combine Shapes group: Combine Shapes, Fragment Shapes, Intersect Shapes, Subtract Shapes, and Union Shapes.

Combine Shapes

To add interest to the title slide, create a custom shape to frame an image of the School of Arts building.

a. Create a Round Same Side Corner Rectangle shape with the following specifications:
  - Picture Fill: *p07c1University.jpg*.

  - Size: Height **3.51"**, Width **10.15"**.
  - Position: Horizontal **1.6"** from the Top Left Corner, Vertical **2.37"** from the Top Left Corner.

b. Create a Flowchart: Delay shape using the following specifications:
  - Size: Height **3.9"**, Width **5.5"**.
  - Rotation: **270°**.
  - Position: Horizontal **3.32"** from the Top Left Corner, Vertical **1.15"** from the Top Left Corner.

c. Join the rectangle shape and the flowchart shape using Union.

d. Copy the resulting shape to the Clipboard.

Modify Masters and Save the Template

You decide that the frame you created belongs on the Title slide master so that you can use it with other images in the presentation. You will cut the frame from the title slide and paste it on the Title slide master. Then you will change the Color theme, format the master title style as WordArt, and modify the master subtitle text. Next, you will modify the handout master and the notes master. You will save the presentation as a template for reuse with other presentations.

a. Cut the frame group from the title slide, switch to Slide Master view, and then paste the university image on the Title slide master.

b. Apply the **Candara font theme**.

c. Apply the **Paper color theme**. Then customize the theme by creating new theme colors using the following specifications:

Element	Red	Green	Blue
Text/Background – Dark 1	12	12	12
Text/Background – Dark 2	44	41	0
Text/Background – Light 2	227	234	207
Accent 4	181	84	117
Hyperlink	251	74	24
Followed Hyperlink	251	147	24

d. Apply the **Milk Glass** effect.

e. Select the shape with the image and send it to the back.

f. Delete the master subtitle style placeholder.

g. Position the master title style placeholder horizontally **.82"** from the Top Left Corner and vertically **4.75"** from the Top Left Corner.

h. Apply an **Appear animation** to the title placeholder.

i. Apply the **Split transition** to the Title slide master.

j. Delete all slide layouts except for title slide layout and insert three new slide layouts.

k. Select the first slide layout and rename it **Department**.

l. Replace the text in the title placeholder with **Place title here**.

m. Fill the blank portion of the slide layout with a picture placeholder.

n. Delete the bullet from the picture placeholder and replace the word *Picture* with **Place picture here**.

o. Select the second slide layout and rename it **Degrees**.

p. Fill the blank portion of the slide layout with a text placeholder.

q. Select the third slide layout and rename it **Pictures**.

r. Hide Background Graphics on the Pictures layout.

s. Delete the master title style placeholder.

t. Switch to Handout Master view and move the footer placeholder immediately below the header placeholder. Move the page number placeholder immediately below the date placeholder.

u. Insert *p07c1Arts.jpg* and modify it using the following specifications:
  - Size: Height **1"**, Width **2"**.
  - Position: Horizontal **2.75"** from the Top Left Corner, Vertical **9"** from the Top Left Corner.

v. Switch to Notes Master view and type **Slide** before the number field in the page number placeholder.

w. Close Notes Master view and save the presentation as a template named **p07c1ArtsTemplate_LastFirst**.

x. Add slides to the presentation by reusing **all** of the slides in *p07c1School*.

y. Remove the new **Slide 2**.

z. Save the presentation as **p07c1Arts_LastFirst**, saving over the presentation you began at the beginning of this exercise. Be careful not to save over the template you created.

Set Up and Display Custom Shows

You will create four custom slide shows using a single presentation. Both will contain a title slide, information slides related to a department in the School of Arts, and content slides.

a. Create a custom show named **Dance Department** and use **Slides 1** through **7**, **21**, and **22**.

b. Create a custom show named **Music Department** and use **Slides 1**, **2**, **8** through **12**, **21**, and **22**.

c. Create a custom show named **Theatrical Arts Department** and use **Slides 1**, **2**, **13** through **15**, **21**, and **22**.

d. Create a custom show named **Arts/Visual Communications Department** and use **Slides 1**, **2**, and **16** through **22**.

e. Display the custom shows. You do not need to click to advance as the transitions are set to advance automatically.

f. Save the presentation. Close the file. Based on your instructor's directions, submit p07c1Arts_LastFirst.

Collaboration and Distribution

LEARNING OUTCOME — You will demonstrate how to review, secure, and share a presentation.

OBJECTIVES & SKILLS: After you read this chapter, you will be able to:

CASE STUDY | The Harbor Business Center

ACSL Development is a large, internationally owned commercial real estate development company specializing in properties that serve as business hubs with access to cutting-edge technology. The centers are designed to meet the demands of leading global companies. You are an intern working for the vice president of marketing, Susil Akalushi. Susil has asked you to prepare a presentation under her supervision. The presentation must describe ACSL's latest project, the Harbor Business Center, a $58.5 million, mixed-use project offering luxurious new office space. Office suites are finished to a high standard of style and décor with state-of-the-art communication technology. The project is centrally located two blocks from the city harbor area and one block from the state and federal courthouses.

After completing the presentation, you send it to Susil for her review. She reviews your presentation and sends it back to you with comments regarding the changes you need to make. You make the requested changes and prepare the presentation for sharing with other company employees by protecting the presentation and checking it for issues. You package the presentation for distribution.

Collaborating, Preparing, Securing, and Sharing a Presentation

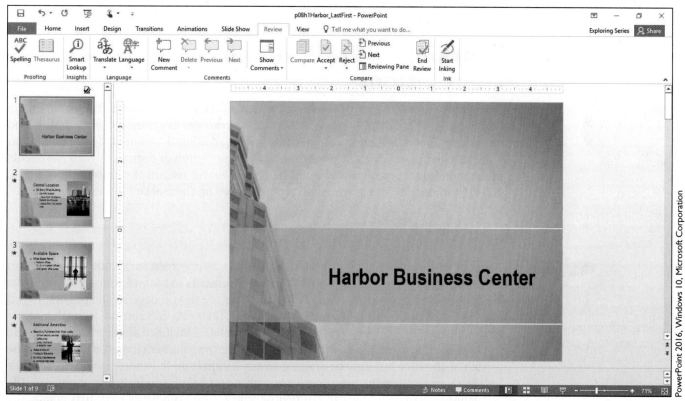

FIGURE 8.1 The Harbor Business Center Presentation

CASE STUDY | The Harbor Business Center

Starting Files	Files to be Submitted
p08h1Harbor	p08h3Harbor_LastFirst
p08h1HarborAkalushi	p08h3HarborPicture_LastFirst

Presentation Collaboration

Collaboration is a process by which two or more individuals work together to achieve an outcome or goal. Many times, a presentation results from the collaborative efforts of a team of people. Collaborating with others in a presentation sparks the creativity and problem-solving skills of all group members, which makes the final project a better project than one in which one individual has sole responsibility. Today's technology enables you to collaborate easily with others, and Office applications include features to facilitate this process.

In this section, you will learn how to add, edit, print, and delete comments. You will learn how to add annotations while displaying a presentation and how to save the annotations. You will merge and compare presentations and review and manage the changes made by others. You will also view presentation properties.

Working with Comments and Annotations

After you have created your PowerPoint presentation, you may want to route it to others for review. After receiving your presentation, the *reviewer* examines the presentation and can add text notes or draw markings on a slide for additional commentary or explanation while displaying a slide show presentation. A presentation or document with comments and annotations contains *markup*. When the reviewer returns the presentation to you, you determine the changes you wish to make based on the markup in the presentation.

Add Comments

STEP 1 ⟩⟩ Think of *comments*, text notes attached to a slide, as onscreen sticky notes that you can insert and remove as needed. You can insert comments to remind yourself of revisions you want to make or as reminders of where you are as you develop the project. If you distribute the presentation to others for review, they can add comments with suggestions. The name of the person inserting the comment is included along with the date and the reviewer's account icon. If nothing is selected, the comment icon is positioned at the top left of the slide but may be dragged to any location on the slide. If you select text or an object, or position the insertion point within text before you insert the comment, the comment icon appears next to the text or object. The Comments pane lists comments in the order they are added to the slide. To move from one comment to another, use the Previous and Next buttons in the Comments pane.

As you review comments, you can choose to incorporate any suggestions you agree with or to ignore any you do not wish to incorporate. Usually, you would delete a comment after your decision. This helps you determine where you are in the review process. If you are part of a work group, you may choose to leave the comments for others to see, and you may choose to reply to existing comments.

> **To insert a comment, complete the following steps:**
> 1. Click the Review tab.
> 2. Click New Comment in the Comments group. The Comments pane opens.
> 3. Type the comment in the comment box.
> 4. Click outside the box to close it.

When you open a presentation that has new comments, a pop-up displays to alert you to the comments. To view a comment, select the comment icon on the slide or Comments on the status bar at the bottom of the screen to show the Comments pane. Comments do not display during Slide Show view. If you want to edit an existing comment, select the comment, then click inside the comment text box to make your changes. If more than one comment is located on the slide, the fill of the selected comment icon changes color to indicate it is the active comment. Otherwise, the comment icon is simply outlined. Delete a comment by clicking Delete in the comment box or by selecting it and clicking Delete in the Comments group on the Review tab. Figure 8.2 shows the Comments pane and a slide with an open comment.

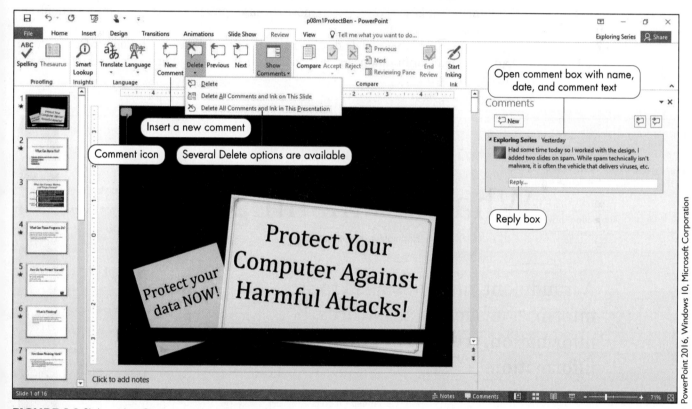

FIGURE 8.2 Slide with a Comment

> **TIP: DELETE ALL COMMENTS**
> To delete all of the comments on the current slide, click the Delete arrow in the Comments group and click *Delete All Comments and Ink on This Slide*. To delete all of the comments in the presentation, click the Delete arrow and then *Delete All Comments and Ink in This Presentation*.

Insert Annotations

Annotations are markings that are written or drawn on a slide for additional commentary or explanation while a slide show is displayed, similar to the way a sports commentator may draw a play during the broadcast of a football game. To add an annotation while playing a slide show, right-click a slide, select Pointer Options, and then select Pen or

Highlighter. Pen creates a thin line, and Highlighter creates a thick line. Drag the mouse (or your finger or stylus on a touch screen) to draw or write on the slide. To turn off the pen or highlighter, right-click, select Pointer Options, select Arrow Options, and then select Automatic. When you exit the slide show, you will be prompted to keep or discard the ink annotations.

Emphasize Content During a Presentation

You can call your audience's attention to the portion of the slide you want to emphasize without creating ink markup (annotations). You do this either by using the Zoom In option or by using your mouse as a laser pointer while displaying a presentation. To use Zoom In during a presentation, right-click and select Zoom In to display a transparent selection box. You can then drag the box over the content that you want to emphasize. To remove the emphasis, simply right-click once more to return to the presentation.

To use a laser pointer, start the presentation in either Slide Show view or Reading view, press and hold Ctrl, hold down the left mouse button, and then drag the mouse to make the laser pointer appear on the slide. When you release the left mouse button, the laser pointer disappears. You can also right-click the mouse, point to Pointer Options, and then click Laser Pointer. To remove the laser pointer, return to Pointer Options and click Laser Pointer again.

Figure 8.3 shows a slide displaying in Slide Show view with Pointer Options open and displaying annotations made with the pen and highlighter, as well as Arrow Options to turn them off.

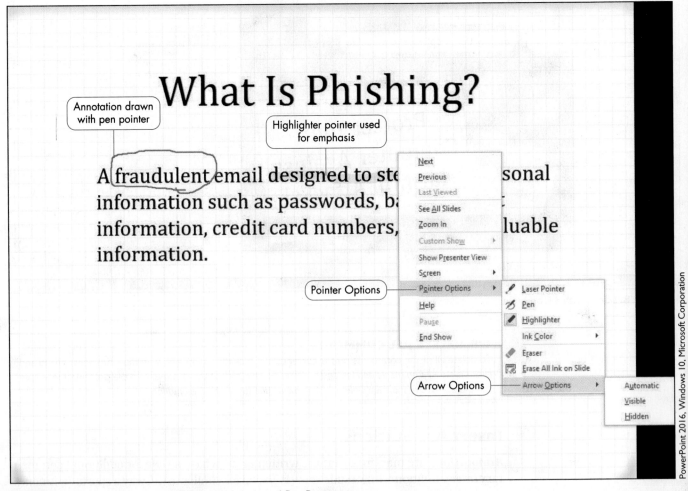

FIGURE 8.3 Annotations Created with Highlighter and Pen Pointers

Showing, Hiding, and Printing Markup

STEP 2 〉〉 A comment or saved annotation is only visible if you have Show Markup active. Show Markup is in the Show Comments arrow in the Comments group of the Review tab. Show Markup is a toggle that displays or hides inserted comments and saved annotations. Figure 8.4 displays a slide with both annotations and comments. The slide is displayed in Normal view. The annotations still display because they were kept when the slide show ended.

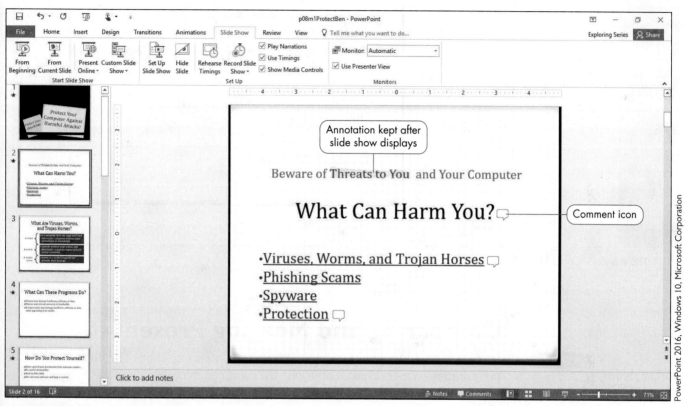

FIGURE 8.4 Annotations in Normal View

Because it is sometimes easier to review comments and annotations in print format, you may choose to print the comments and annotations that have been stored on your slides. When you choose to print comments and annotations (markup), the comments print on a separate page from the slides that display the annotations. To print comments and ink markup, click the File tab and click Print. Select Full Page Slides (or whatever layout is desired); if your slide show contains comments or annotations, the *Print Comments and Ink Markup* option is active. This option is grayed out if the presentation does not contain comments or annotations. Figure 8.5 displays the *Print Comments and Ink Markup* option.

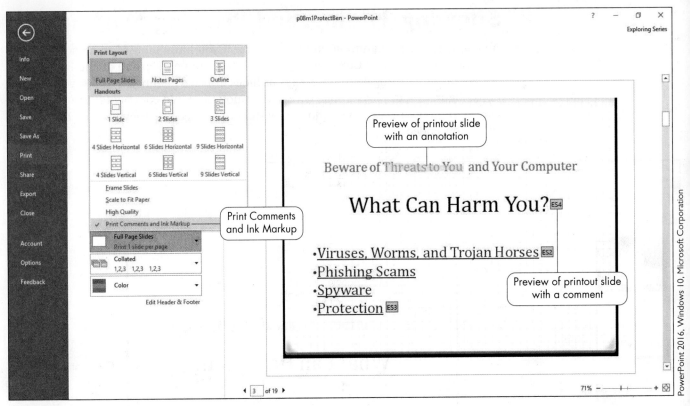

FIGURE 8.5 Print Comments and Ink Markup Option

Comparing and Merging Presentations

STEP 3 ▶▶ PowerPoint enables you to compare versions of a presentation. The differences in the presentations are marked as revisions that you can accept or reject. This is extremely beneficial in a collaborative project, because after all team members submit their version of the presentation someone can merge all the changes into one presentation. To compare and merge presentations, you need a minimum of two presentations: the original and the presentation with changes.

To compare and merge presentations, complete the following steps:

1. Open the original presentation.
2. Click the Review tab and click Compare in the Compare group.
3. Locate and select the changed version of the presentation in the *Choose File to Merge with Current Presentation* dialog box.
4. Click Merge.

Once you have clicked Merge, the Revisions pane opens. The pane opens, by default, to a Details tab with two sections. The top section, Slide Changes, lists the changes to the slide currently selected. The bottom section, Presentation Changes, lists any slides that have been added or removed from the original presentation. The Revisions pane also includes a Slides tab that indicates whether the current slide has been changed and which slide contains the next set of changes.

The Slide Changes section of the Details tab displays icons and abbreviated text representing changes to objects on the slide. To accept an individual change, click the change in the Revisions pane and click Accept in the Compare group. You can also click the icon representing the object on the slide and select a check box in the Revisions check list that opens. You can see the change that will result when you click a check box. To accept all changes on the current slide, click the Accept arrow in the Compare group on the Review tab and click Accept All Changes to This Slide or Accept All Changes to the Presentation.

If you accept a change and then decide you no longer want the change, click Reject in the Compare group. Any changes that you do not accept are discarded when you complete the review. To complete the review, click End Review in the Compare group. Figure 8.6 shows the Revisions pane with the Details tab selected. The Slide Changes section shows changes for slide properties on the current slide. The Presentation Changes section shows two changes in the presentation. All changes made in the slide are displayed in the Revisions check box on the slide. In this case, two slides were inserted.

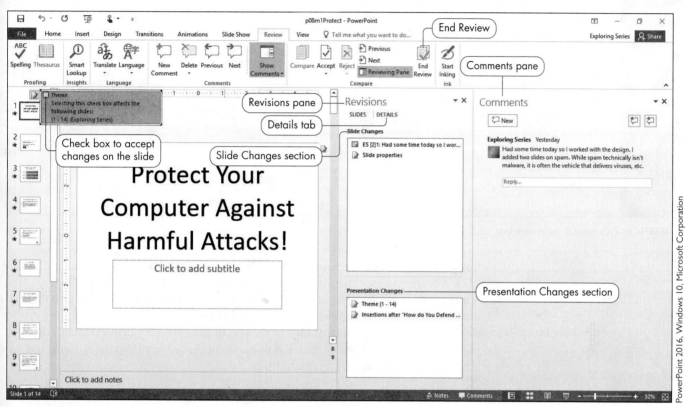

FIGURE 8.6 Revisions Pane

Viewing Presentation Properties

STEP 4 》》 To view the original author(s) of a presentation and its creation date, or to see who last modified the presentation and when the modification took place, view the presentation properties (*document properties* or *metadata*). Document properties are the attributes about a presentation that describe it or identify it. Metadata is data that describes other data. In addition to the author and modifier properties, you can view many details such as the title, file size, keywords, and statistics. Some of the properties are created and updated automatically, and some are created by the user. The presentation properties help you organize and search for your presentations.

To view presentation properties, click the File tab to display the Backstage view. The panel on the right side of the screen displays some properties. Click Show All Properties at the bottom of the panel to see all properties. You can change document properties not automatically set by PowerPoint by clicking the property box and typing the change. Figure 8.7 displays the properties for a presentation on protecting your computer.

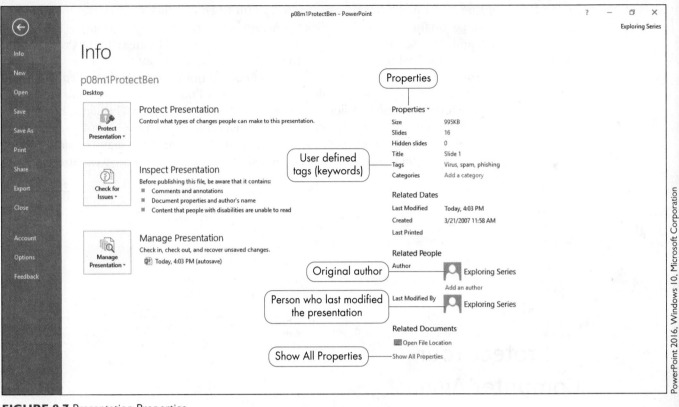

FIGURE 8.7 Presentation Properties

To set multiple document properties, click the Properties arrow in the right pane and click Advanced Properties. A dialog box displays in the Backstage view. The Title and Author properties are entered automatically but can be changed. You can also change the Subject, Manager, Company, Category, and Comments. The words you type in the Keywords property box display as tags when you display the Properties panel in the Info section in the Backstage view. Figure 8.8 displays the Advanced Properties dialog box for a presentation on protecting your computer.

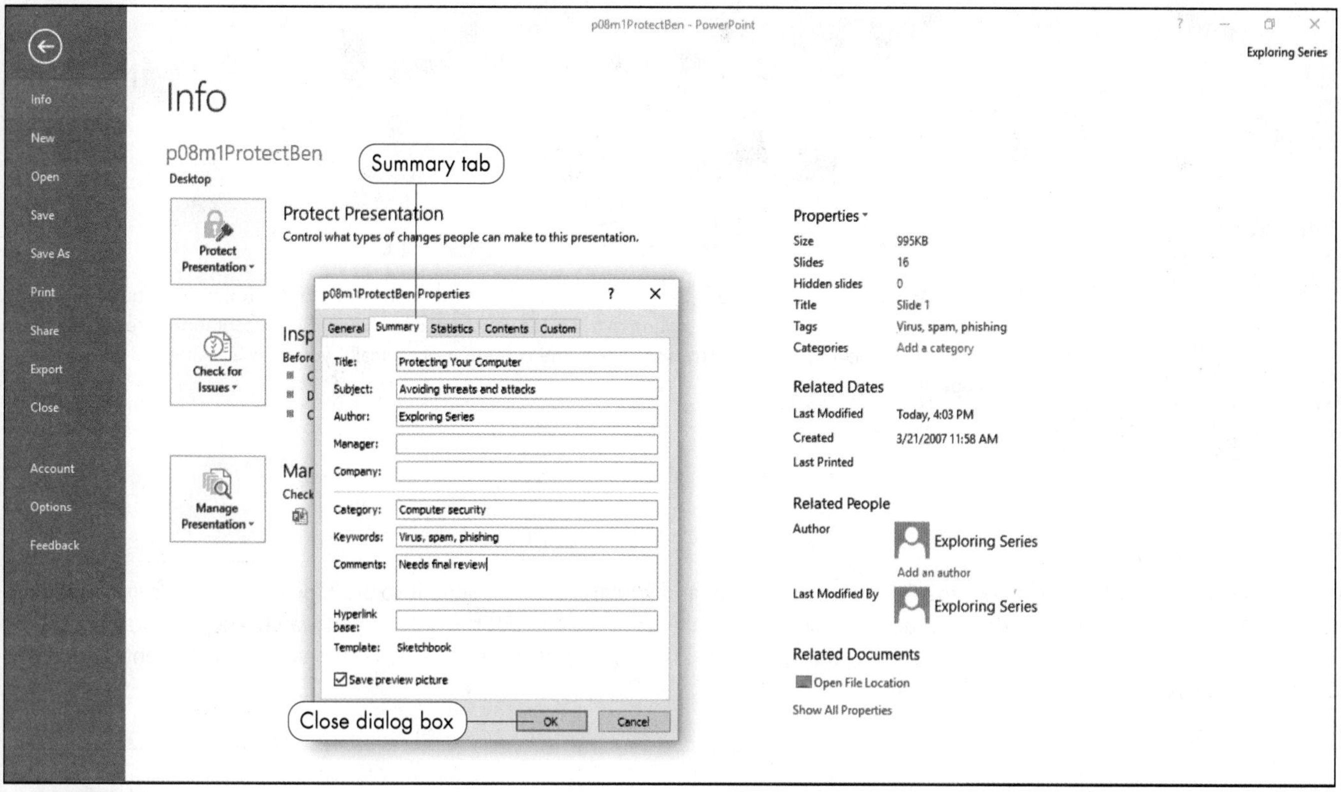

FIGURE 8.8 Advanced Properties Dialog Box

Quick Concepts

1. When working on a project, why is collaboration important? *p. 502*

2. Explain how comments can be edited or deleted. *p. 503*

3. Why is it beneficial to be able to compare two versions of a presentation? *p. 506*

PowerPoint 2016, Windows 10, Microsoft Corporation

Hands-On Exercises

Watch the Video
for this Hands-
On Exercise!

MyITLab®
HOE1 Training

Skills covered: Insert
Annotations • Insert a
Comment • Show Markup •
Hide Markup • Print Markup •
Compare Presentations • Merge
Presentations • View Presentation
Properties • Change Presentation
Properties

1 Presentation Collaboration

You review the Harbor Business Center presentation and add comments and annotations. You print a copy of the presentation, comments, and ink markup for your records. When the presentation is returned to you by the reviewer, you compare and merge the presentations. Finally, you view and edit the presentation properties.

STEP 1 ➤➤ INSERT ANNOTATIONS AND A COMMENT

You have completed the Harbor Business Center presentation, and you are ready to send it to Susil for her review. Before sending it to her, you review the presentation in Slide Show view. You have a question about the data as you watch the presentation, so you add annotations to mark the location that raised your question. Then you ask the questions as comments in the presentation. Refer to Figure 8.9 as you complete Step 1.

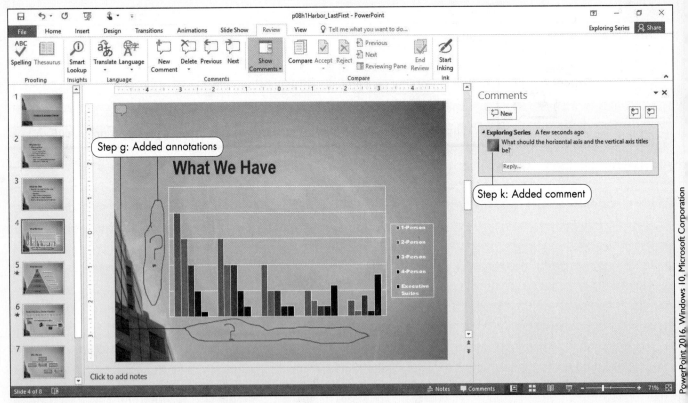

FIGURE 8.9 Harbor Annotations and Comment

a. Open the *p08h1Harbor* presentation and save it as **p08h1Harbor_LastFirst**.

   The Harbor Business Center presentation opens. It has formatting problems that will be addressed in a later step.

b. Create a handout header with your name and a handout footer with your instructor's name and your class. Include the current date.

c. Click the **File** tab and click **Options**. Ensure your initials appear in the Initials box, and click **OK**.

Figures in this chapter display the initials *ES* for "Exploring Series," and it is also used as the name.

d. Click the **Slide Show** tab and click **From Beginning** in the Start Slide Show group.

e. Click three times to advance to the fourth slide, titled *What We Have*. Note that no vertical or horizontal axis titles exist to describe what the columns in the chart represent.

f. Right-click the **slide**, point to *Pointer Options*, and then select **Pen**.

g. Draw a circle around the location where a horizontal axis title would typically appear and draw a question mark within the circle.

h. Draw a circle around the location where a vertical axis title would typically appear and draw a question mark within the circle.

i. Press **Esc** and click **Keep** to save the ink annotations.

j. Click the **Review tab** and click **New Comment** in the Comments group.

A comment icon appears in the top-left corner of Slide 4. The Comments pane opens a new comment box with your name displayed.

k. Type **What should the horizontal axis and vertical axis titles be?** in the comment box.

l. Save the presentation.

STEP 2 » SHOW, HIDE, AND PRINT MARKUP

You view the slide with the markup showing, and you hide the markup. You also preview the comment and the annotations printouts in Print Preview. Refer to Figure 8.10 as you complete Step 2.

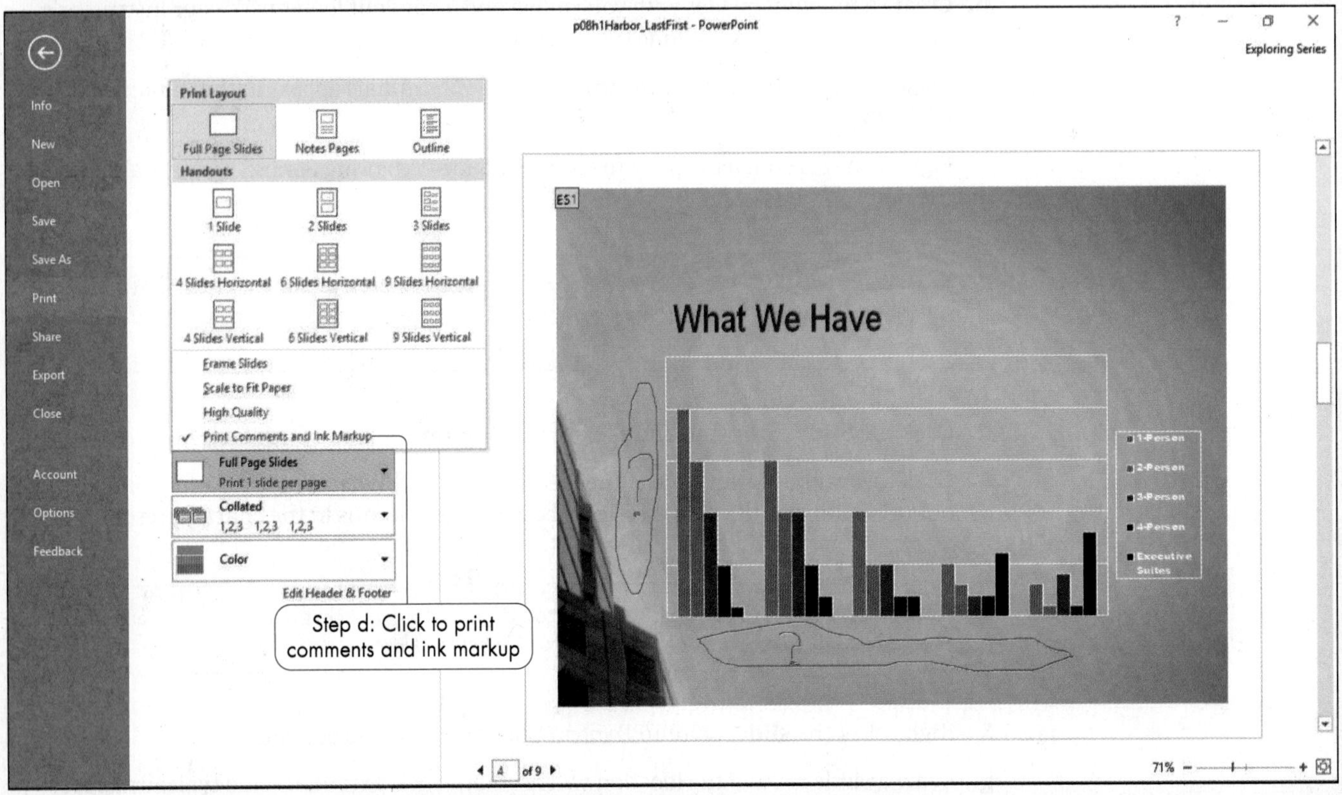

FIGURE 8.10 Preview of Annotations Printout

a. Click the **Show Comments arrow** in the Comments group on the Review tab. Click **Show Markup** to deselect it.

Clicking Show Markup toggles the feature off so the Comment pane and the annotations no longer display.

b. Click **Show Comments** in the Comments group and click to select **Show Markup**.

The comment and the annotations display on the slide.

c. Click the **File tab** and click **Print**.

d. Click the **Full Page Slides arrow** and note that *Print Comments and Ink Markup* is checked. Click the **Full Page Slides arrow** again to close it.

The annotations on Slide 4 display and will print if Slide 4 is printed. In the top-left corner of the slide, the initials of the person who made the comment are displayed.

TROUBLESHOOTING: If *Print Comments and Ink Markup* is not selected, click the check box.

e. Click **Next Page** in the navigation control at the bottom center of the Backstage Print view to advance to page 5.

Page 5 displays the comment on Slide 4.

f. Save the presentation.

Susil has returned her version of the Harbor Business Center presentation. You merge her presentation with your original, and accept and reject changes. You remove all remaining comments, and save the merged version of the presentation. Refer to Figure 8.11 as you complete Step 3. Although you will not access this particular view, it is used here to illustrate the final presentation.

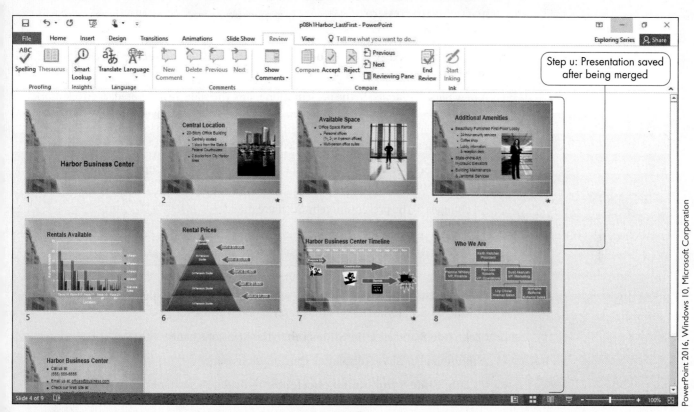

FIGURE 8.11 Merged Harbor Business Center Presentation

a. Click the **Review tab** and click **Compare** in the Compare group.

The *Choose File to Merge with Current Presentation* dialog box opens.

b. Navigate to your student data files, select *p08h1HarborAkalushi*, and then click **Merge**.

The first slide of the presentation displays in Normal view. The Revisions pane opens with the Details tab active. The Slide Changes section displays one item, a comment from Susil. The Presentation Changes section shows two changes to the presentation: a theme change on Slides 1 through 8 and insertions after "Harbor Business Center." The Comments pane also opens. One comment from Susil exists.

c. Ensure that the icon in the Slide Changes section is selected and read the comment on the slide.

The comment box with Susil's comment takes the focus.

d. Click **Theme (1–8)** in the Presentation Changes section.

The Revisions box attached to the thumbnail of Slide 1 in the Slides pane opens and indicates that the theme change made by Susil impacts Slides 1 through 8.

e. Click **Accept** in the Compare group.

A checked icon appears next to the Theme (1–8) item in the Presentation Changes section, indicating that the change was accepted. A check mark also appears above the Slide 1 thumbnail in the Slides pane.

f. Select **Insertions after "Harbor Business Center"** in the Presentation Changes section.

A Revisions box displays between Slide 1 and Slide 2 that reads *Inserted "Central Location" (Susil Akalushi).*

TROUBLESHOOTING: Exploring Series might display instead of Susil Akalushi because the author used it in the data file. Continue the exercise regardless of the name that displays.

---

g. Click the **Inserted "Central Location" (Susil Akalushi) check box** above Slide 2 in the Slides pane to select it.

A new Slide 2 is added to the presentation using the slide Susil created. A check mark also appears on the slide thumbnail in the Slides tab indicating a change was made. A check appears next to the Slide 2: Central Location item in the Presentation Changes section indicating the change was accepted.

h. Click the **Accept arrow** in the Compare group and select **Accept All Changes to the Presentation**.

All changes to the presentation by Susil are made.

TROUBLESHOOTING: Be sure to use the Accept arrow. Accept is gray and unavailable.

---

i. Click the **Slide Show tab** and click **From Beginning** in the Start Slide Show group. Advance through the slides in the presentation. Press **Esc**.

j. Click **Slide 8** and click the **Slides tab** in the Revisions pane.

A thumbnail of Slide 8 displays in the Revisions pane.

k. Click the **Slide 8 thumbnail check box** in the Revisions pane to deselect it. Note that the organization chart is a SmartArt style that displays in 3D format when checked and not in 3D format when deselected.

l. Click the **Slide 8 thumbnail check box** again. Click the **Review tab** and click the **Reject arrow** in the Compare group. Click **Reject All Changes to This Slide** to select it.

All changes to Slide 8 are rejected. The organization chart is no longer displayed in 3D format.

m. Click the **Details tab** in the Revisions pane and select **Rectangle 2: Who We Are**. Click **All changes to Rectangle 2**. Click the *Reject arrow* in the Compare group. Click **Reject All Changes to This Slide**.

The title changes from *Harbor Business Center Team* to *Who We Are* because you rejected Susil's changes.

n. Click **Slide 1**, and select the comment in the Slide Changes section of the Details tab in the Revisions pane. Click **Delete** in the Comments group.

o. Click **Next** in the Comments group.

The Slide Changes section of the Details tab displays the two comments and three changes on Slide 5.

p. Read a comment and click **Next** in the Comments group. Read the next comment and click **Next** again in the Comments group.

The presentation advances to Slide 9.

q. Read the comment on Slide 9 regarding animating the content placeholders on Slides 2 through 4.

r. Click Slide 2, select the **content placeholder**, click the **Animations tab**, and then click **More** in the Animation group. Click **Wipe** in the Entrance category. Click **Effect Options** in the Animation group and click **From Left**. Click the **Start arrow** in the Timing group and select **After Previous**.

s. Deselect the **content placeholder** and select it again to enable the Animation Painter feature. Double-click **Animation Painter** in the Advanced Animation group and copy the content placeholder animation to the content placeholders on Slides 3 and 4. Deselect the **Animation Painter**.

t. Click the **Review tab**, click the **Delete arrow** in the Comments group, and then click **Delete All Comments and Ink in This Presentation**. Click **Yes** and close the Revisions and Comments panes.

u. Save the presentation. If you get a message about ending the review, click **Save** again.

STEP 4 » VIEW AND CHANGE PRESENTATION PROPERTIES

To help you organize your presentation files and to help you and Susil locate the file through the Windows Search feature, you create document properties. Refer to Figure 8.12 as you complete Step 4.

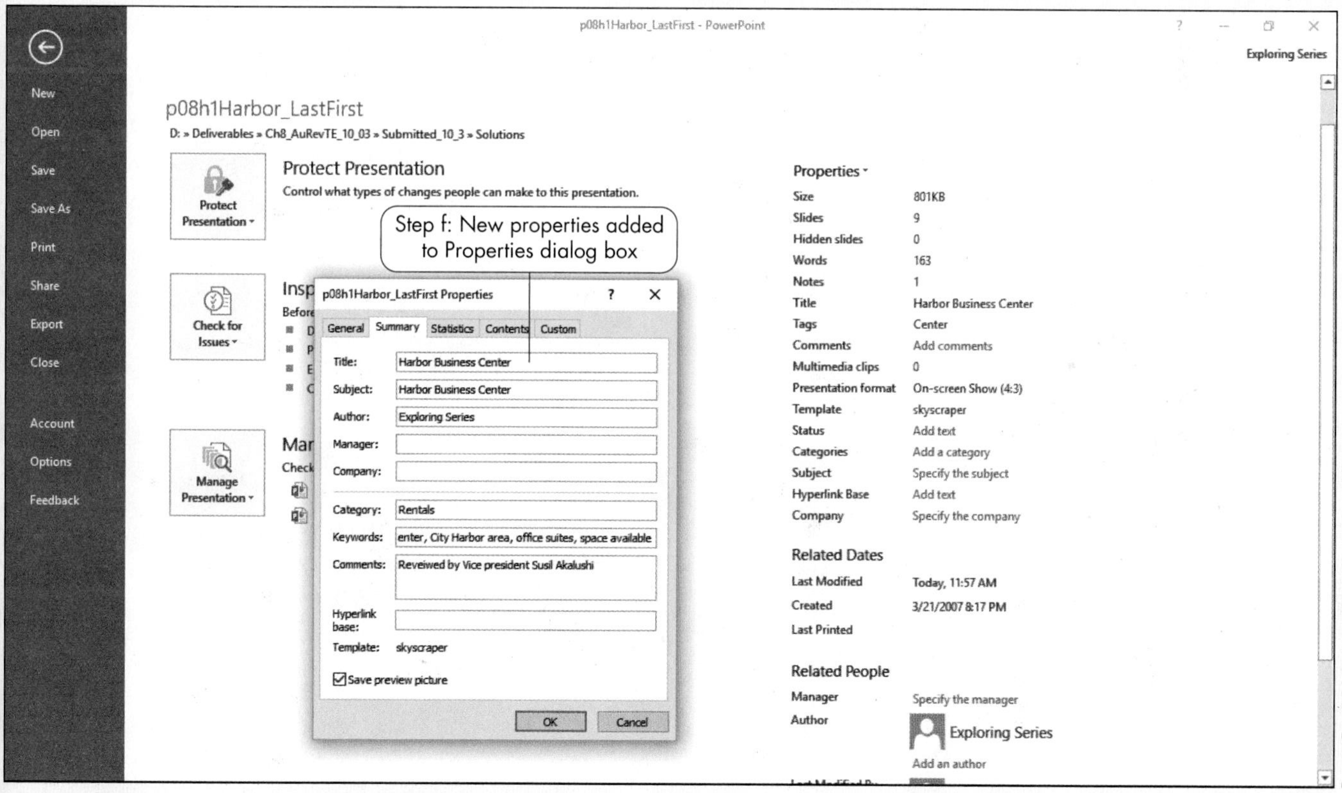

PowerPoint 2016, Windows 10, Microsoft Corporation

FIGURE 8.12 Document Properties

a. Click the **File tab** and note the properties that are displayed on the right side of the Backstage view.

b. Click **Add a tag** next to the Tags property and type **Center**.

Center becomes a keyword that you can use to search for the presentation.

c. Click **Show All Properties** at the bottom of the Properties pane and note the additional properties that display.

d. Click **Properties** at the top of the Properties pane and click **Advanced Properties**.

The Properties dialog box displays and includes the following properties: Title, Author, and Keywords (Center) on the Summary tab.

e. Click in the **Subject box** on the Summary tab and type **Harbor Business Center**.

f. Add the properties shown in the following table:

Type of Property	Property Information
Keywords	City Harbor area, office suites, space available
Category	Rentals
Comments	Reviewed by Vice president Susil Akalushi

TROUBLESHOOTING: Be sure to keep the keyword *Center* from the merged presentation.

g. Click **OK** in the Properties dialog box.

h. Save the presentation. Keep the presentation open if you plan to continue with Hands-On Exercise 2. If not, close the presentation and exit PowerPoint.

Preparation for Sharing and Presentation Security

Once you complete a slide show, you can present it or distribute it to others to view. If you want to distribute the presentation to others, take advantage of PowerPoint's tools for preparing and securing a presentation for distribution. In addition to the ability to add and remove document properties that was covered in the previous section, these two collections of tools enable you to do the following:

- Check the content of the presentation for accessibility issues.
- Run a compatibility check to identify features that viewers using previous versions are not able to see.
- Mark the presentation as final and make it read only.
- Add a password.
- Allow people viewing rights but restrict their rights to edit, copy, and print.
- Attach a digital signature.

To access these features, click the File tab to display the Backstage view as shown in Figure 8.13.

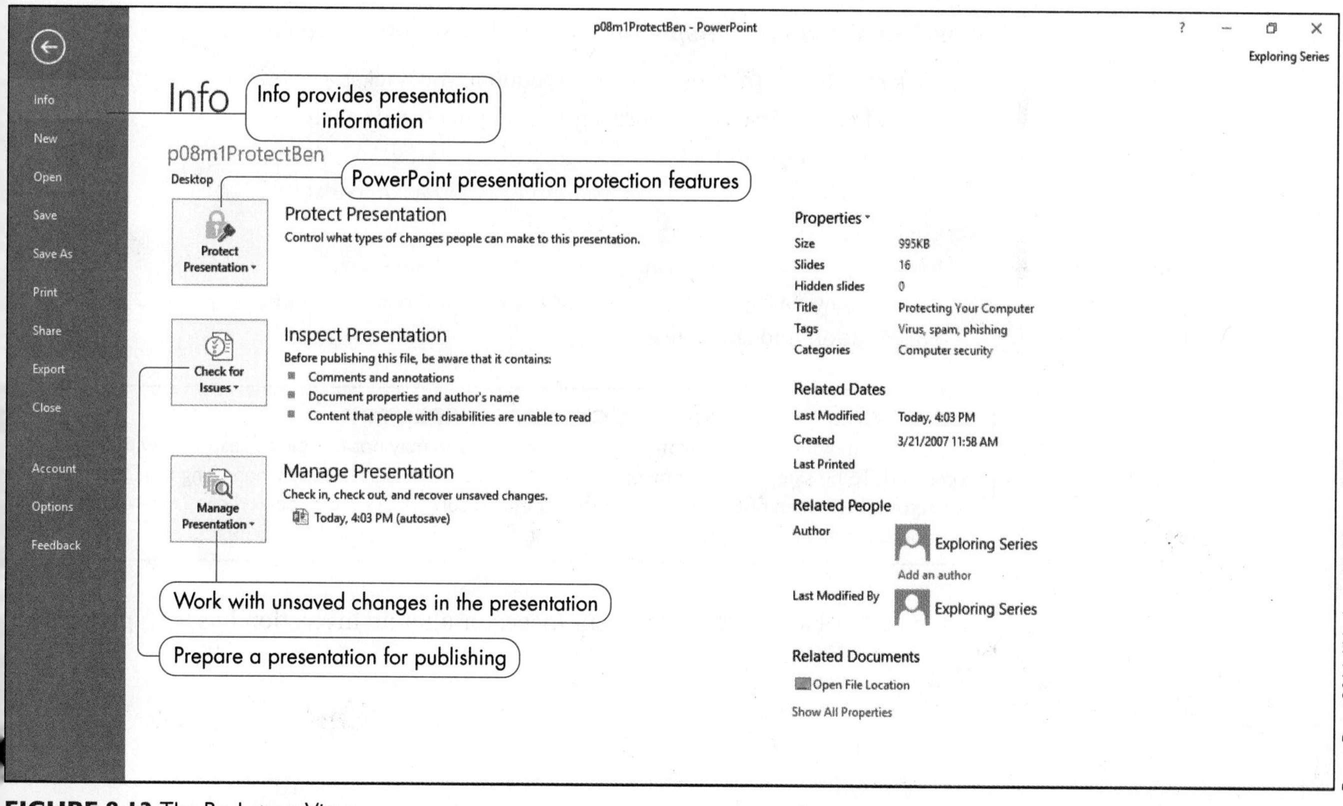

FIGURE 8.13 The Backstage View

In this section, you will learn how to inspect a presentation for issues before sharing and to secure a presentation for distribution.

Checking a Presentation for Issues

While adding details to the presentation properties helps you organize and locate your presentations, you may not wish other people to have access to that data. Your presentation may also contain content that someone with disabilities cannot view or someone using an earlier version of PowerPoint cannot view. The ***Check for Issues commands*** enable you to uncover issues that may cause difficulties for viewers.

Access Document Inspector

 To check for hidden and personal data in the presentation or in its properties, use the ***Document Inspector***. You can search the following content areas:

- Comments and Annotations
- Document Properties and Personal Information
- Content Add-ins
- Task Pane Add-ins
- Embedded Documents
- Macros, Forms, and ActiveX Controls
- Custom XML Data
- Invisible On-Slide Content
- Off-Slide Content
- Presentation Notes

To use the Document Inspector, complete the following steps:

1. Click the File tab to display the Info section in the Backstage view.
2. Click Check for Issues and click Yes if prompted to save your file.
3. Select Inspect Document.
4. Click the check box next to the content that you wish to inspect.
5. Click Inspect.
6. Review the results in the Document Inspector dialog box.
7. Click Remove All next to the types of content you want to remove from your presentation and click Close.

> **TIP: BE CAUTIOUS USING DOCUMENT INSPECTOR**
> If you remove hidden content from your presentation, you may not be able to restore it with the Undo command. To be safe, make a copy of your presentation and use the copy when using the Document Inspector. Then when distributing the presentation, be sure to use the inspected copy to avoid sharing personal information or other still intact content.

Figure 8.14 shows the Document Inspector after an inspection has been performed.

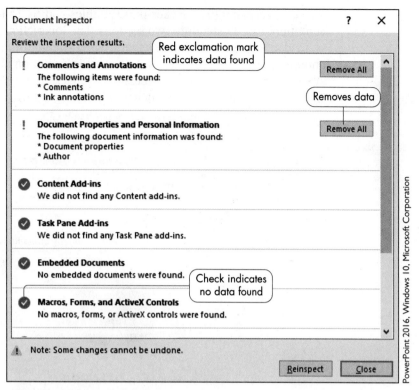

FIGURE 8.14 Document Inspection Results

Check Accessibility

Because you want your presentation to be accessible for users with varying challenges when you distribute it, you should use the Accessibility Checker before sharing it. The **Accessibility Checker** helps you identify and resolve problems with accessibility issues in your presentation. **Accessibility** in PowerPoint refers to the ease with which a person with physical challenges is able to access and understand a presentation. To fix some of the issues the Accessibility Checker identifies, you may have to change, reformat, or update your content.

The Accessibility Checker locates accessibility issues and assigns them to one of three categories:

- **Error**: Issues where content is unreadable. For example, no **alternative text (alt text)** means a text-based description of an image is not available.

- **Warning**: Issues where content is difficult to read. For example, a table is difficult to read because of complex formatting.

- **Tip**: Issues that may or may not make content difficult to read. For example, the order in which text should be read is unclear due to the order of objects on a slide.

To use the Accessibility Checker, complete the following steps:

1. Click the File tab to display the Info section in the Backstage view.
2. Click Check for Issues.
3. Select Check Accessibility.
4. Review and fix the issues in the Accessibility Checker pane that opens on the right side of Normal view.
5. Close the Accessibility Checker pane after fixing the issues.

The Accessibility Checker pane enables you to find and fix the issues in the presentation. It is divided into two sections. The top section lists the inspection results and is divided into Errors, Warnings, and Tips. The bottom section describes why an issue should be fixed and provides a link to more information about making documents accessible. Figure 8.15 shows the Accessibility Checker pane with two errors displayed in the Inspection Results section along with a warning and a tip.

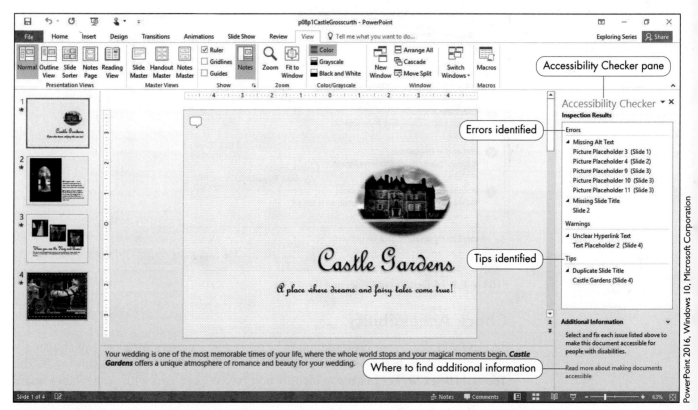

FIGURE 8.15 Accessibility Checker

Check Compatibility

STEP 2 ▶▶ Whenever you share your presentation with others, you need to consider what software they are using. If they are using an earlier version of PowerPoint, they may not be able to see or use some of the features available in the latest version of PowerPoint. You can check your presentation for features not supported by earlier versions of PowerPoint by activating the *Compatibility Checker*. The Microsoft PowerPoint Compatibility Checker dialog box appears and warns you about features you used in your presentation that may be lost or degraded when you save the presentation to an earlier format for distribution.

> **To use the Compatibility Checker, complete the following steps:**
> 1. Click the File tab to display the Info section in the Backstage view.
> 2. Click Check for Issues.
> 3. Select Check Compatibility.
> 4. Read any messages that are generated and see what action to take.
> 5. Click OK to close the pane when finished.

Figure 8.16 displays the Microsoft PowerPoint Compatibility Checker dialog box with two warnings about the compatibility with PowerPoint 97–2003 applications.

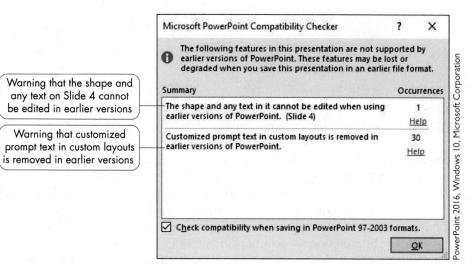

Warning that the shape and any text on Slide 4 cannot be edited in earlier versions

Warning that customized prompt text in custom layouts is removed in earlier versions

FIGURE 8.16 Compatibility Checker

Protecting a Presentation

Anyone can open, copy, or change any part of a presentation unless you protect its integrity by using PowerPoint's Protect Presentation features. You can make a presentation read only, require a password, or add a digital signature. Figure 8.17 displays the Protect Presentation features available in PowerPoint.

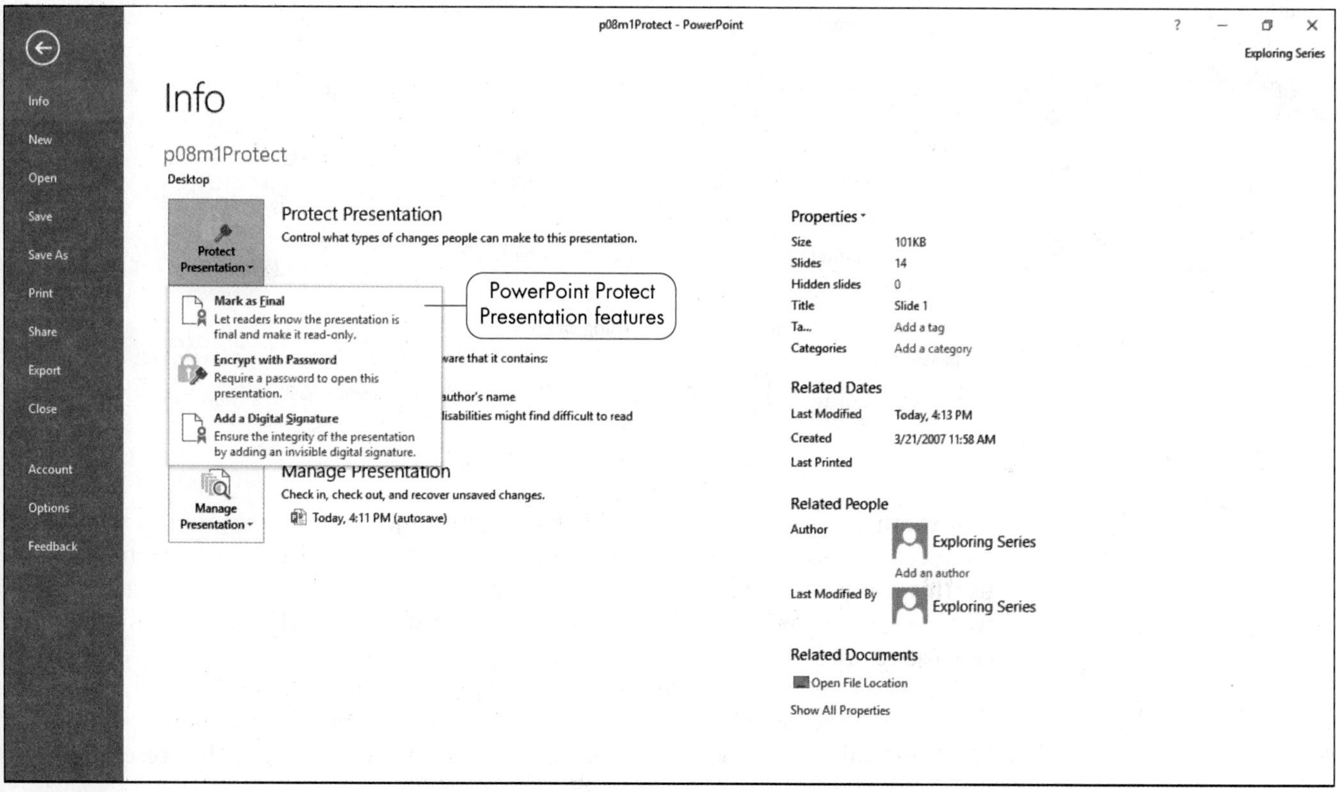

FIGURE 8.17 PowerPoint's Protect Presentation Features

Protect with a Password

 >> Use *encryption* to protect the privacy of your presentation by converting the presentation into unreadable scrambled text that needs a password to be opened. Set a password on your presentation to prevent other people from opening or changing your presentation. Once you set a password, you can change it or remove it only if you know the original password.

To encrypt a presentation with a password, complete the following steps:

1. Click the File tab to display the Info section in the Backstage view.
2. Click Protect Presentation.
3. Select Encrypt with Password.
4. Type a password in the Encrypt Document dialog box.
5. Reenter the password in the Confirm Password dialog box and click OK.

You are prompted to reenter the password as a security measure to ensure that you enter the password with no typographical errors. This is critical because if you type the password incorrectly or forget the password, you will not be able to open your presentation or change the password. Also be careful about what you type in capital letters and what you type lowercase. Passwords are intentionally case sensitive. Avoid creating passwords using dictionary words, words spelled backwards, common misspellings, and abbreviations. Do not use sequences or repeated characters such as 123456, 33333, or abcdef. Never use personal information such as your name, birthday, or driver's license number. See the Table 8.1 for Microsoft's recommendations for creating a strong password for online safety. These guidelines can help you set a pattern for all passwords you use.

TABLE 8.1 Password Tips

Tip	Background	Example
Think of a sentence or two about something meaningful to you. Use about 10 words.	Creating a sentence about something meaningful will help you remember the password.	King is an English Bulldog. He is my best friend. *10 words*
Turn your sentence into a row of letters.	Using the first letter of each word will help you remember the password.	kiaebhimbf *10 characters*
Add complexity.	Make some of the letters uppercase. For example, make only the letters in the first half or last half of the alphabet uppercase.	kiaebhiMbf *10 characters*
Add length with numbers.	Put two numbers that are meaningful to you between sentences.	kiaeb18hiMbf *12 characters*
Add length with punctuation.	Put a punctuation mark at the beginning of the password	!kiaeb18hiMbf *13 characters*
Add length with symbols.	Put a symbol at the end of the password.	!kiaeb18hiMbf& *14 characters*

Source: https://www.microsoft.com/security/pc-security/password-checker.aspx

Pearson Education, Inc.

Another method you can use to set a password for your presentation is to click the File tab, select Save As, select Browse, select Tools, and then select General Options. If you use this method to encrypt your document, you have more options. You can set one password to open the presentation and a different password to modify the presentation. You can also remove automatically generated personal information when you save. This does not, however, remove properties you have added. After setting it, a password takes effect the next time you open the presentation. When you attempt to open the presentation, the Password dialog box opens. Enter the password and click OK to open the presentation.

Mark as Final

 After you prepare your presentation for distribution, you can mark it as a final version. This feature deactivates most PowerPoint tools and converts the presentation to read-only format. Doing this allows viewers to watch your presentation but not to edit it unless they turn off the Mark as Final feature—which is easy to remove if changes are needed. A Mark as Final designation lets your viewers know they are viewing a finished presentation.

To mark a presentation as final, complete the following steps:

1. Click the File tab to display the Info section in the Backstage view.
2. Click Protect Presentation.
3. Select Mark as Final.
4. Click OK in the warning message box that appears stating *This presentation will be marked as final and then saved.*
5. Click OK in the PowerPoint information message box (see Figure 8.18).

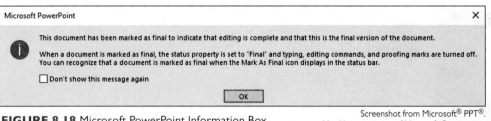

FIGURE 8.18 Microsoft PowerPoint Information Box

Screenshot from Microsoft® PPT®.
Used by permission of Microsoft Corporation

A Marked as Final message bar appears below the Ribbon and a Mark as Final icon displays on the status bar. If you wish to make changes, however, you can click Edit Anyway on the warning bar. You can also turn off final status by clicking the File tab, clicking Protect Presentation, and then clicking Mark as Final. Figure 8.19 shows a presentation marked as final.

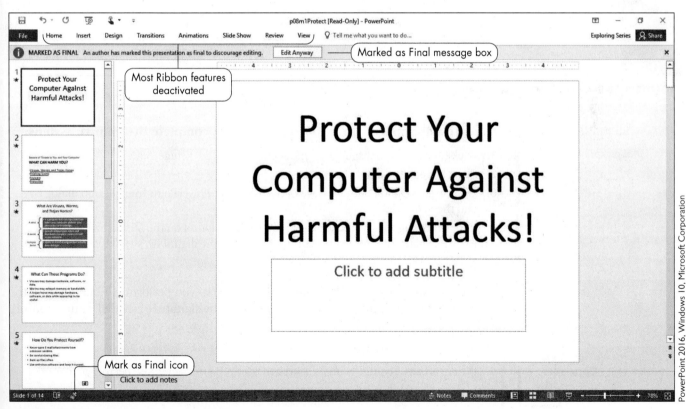

FIGURE 8.19 Presentation Marked as Final

Add a Digital Signature

A ***digital signature*** is an invisible, electronic signature stamp that is encrypted and attached to a certificate. The certificate is attached to the presentation. This is similar to signing a paper document. If you want those with whom you share your presentation to be able to verify the authenticity of your digital signature, you can obtain a digital ID from a Microsoft partner. You can also create your own digital ID; however, it will only enable you to verify that a presentation has not been changed on the computer on which you have saved the presentation. Figure 8.20 shows the beginning of the process to get a digital signature.

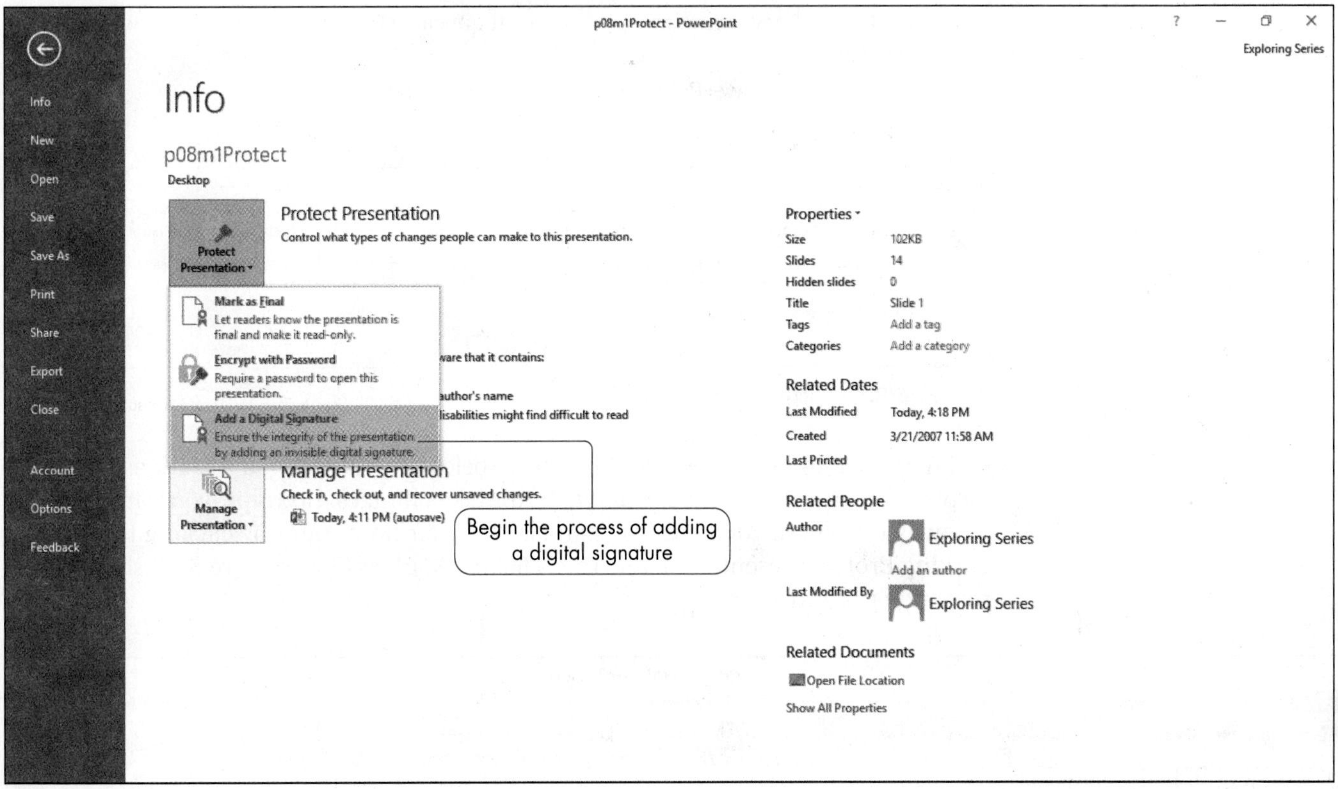

FIGURE 8.20 Beginning the Process of Getting a Digital Signature

To create a digital ID with a Microsoft partner, complete the following steps:

1. Click the File tab to display the Info section in the Backstage view.
2. Click Protect Presentation.
3. Select Add a Digital Signature, read the Microsoft PowerPoint Information dialog box, and then click Yes.
4. Choose among the Available Digital ID providers found on the Microsoft Office website. Each will have a different method to get the digital ID, so follow the onscreen steps to complete the process.

Adding a digital signature should be the last step you perform when preparing the document because, if you make any changes after the signature is added, your signature is invalidated.

Quick Concepts

4. Which areas of content can be searched using the Document Inspector? *p. 518*
5. Explain why you should use the Accessibility Checker. *p. 519*
6. What does the Compatibility Checker do? *p. 520*
7. Describe two methods that can be used to set a password for your presentation. *p. 522*

Hands-On Exercises

Watch the Video for this Hands-On Exercise!

MyITLab® HOE2 Training

Skills covered: Inspect the Presentation • Check for Compatibility • Set a Password • Remove a Password • Mark as Final

2 Preparation for Sharing and Presentation Security

Now that you have incorporated Susil Akalushi's changes in the Harbor Business Center presentation, you prepare the presentation for sharing with other company employees. You check the presentation for issues and protect the presentation.

STEP I ›› **INSPECT THE PRESENTATION**

Before you send the presentation out to other ACSL Development employees, you use the Document Inspector to check the document for information that you may not want others to view. Refer to Figure 8.21 as you complete Step 1.

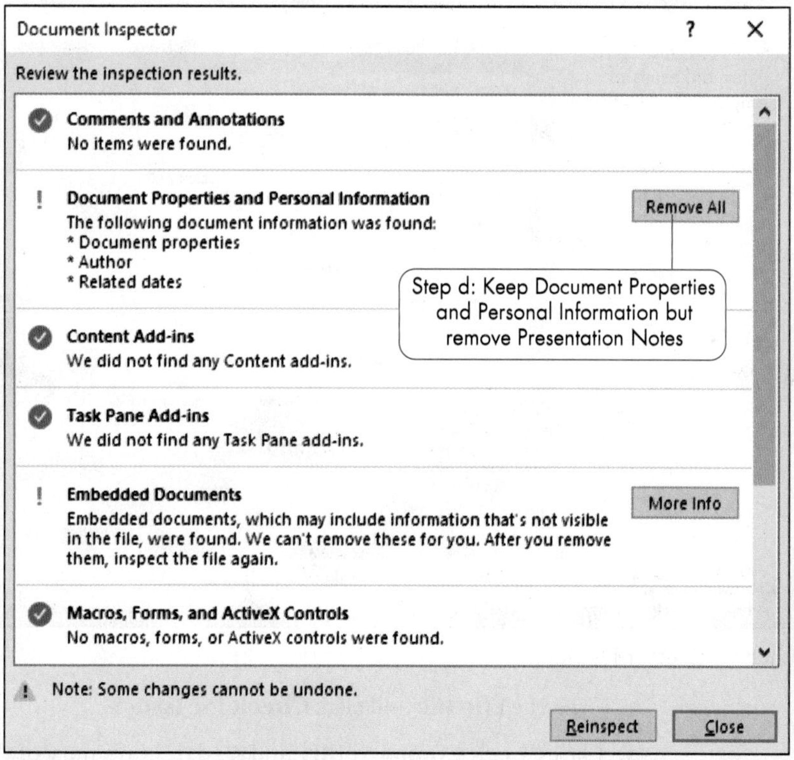

<figure>

Document Inspector   ?   ✕

Review the inspection results.

✓ **Comments and Annotations**
No items were found.

! **Document Properties and Personal Information**   [Remove All]
The following document information was found:
* Document properties
* Author
* Related dates

> Step d: Keep Document Properties and Personal Information but remove Presentation Notes

✓ **Content Add-ins**
We did not find any Content add-ins.

✓ **Task Pane Add-ins**
We did not find any Task Pane add-ins.

! **Embedded Documents**   [More Info]
Embedded documents, which may include information that's not visible in the file, were found. We can't remove these for you. After you remove them, inspect the file again.

✓ **Macros, Forms, and ActiveX Controls**
No macros, forms, or ActiveX controls were found.

⚠ Note: Some changes cannot be undone.

[Reinspect]   [Close]

PowerPoint 2016, Windows 10, Microsoft Corporation

</figure>

FIGURE 8.21 Document Inspector

a. Open *p08h1Harbor_LastFirst*, if you closed it at the end of the Hands-On Exercise 1, and save the presentation as **p08h2Harbor_LastFirst**, changing *h1* to *h2*.

b. Click the **File tab**, click **Check for Issues**, and then select **Inspect Document**.

The Document Inspector dialog box opens and displays a list of items the inspector will search for.

c. Click **Inspect**.

No comments or annotations were found because you removed them in Hands-On Exercise 1. Document properties and personal information were found, as well as embedded documents and presentation notes.

d. Keep the Document Properties and Personal Information and click **Remove All** in the Presentation Notes section.

Because *p08h2Harbor_LastFirst* is a duplicate of *p08h1Harbor_LastFirst*, this is a convenient method to create a copy for distribution that has changes from the original document.

e. Click **Close**.

f. Save the presentation.

STEP 2 ›› CHECK FOR COMPATIBILITY

Some of the ACSL Development employees still use older versions of Office because the company has not updated software in all departments to the latest version of Office. You check the Harbor Business Center presentation's compatibility with the earlier versions of Office. Refer to Figure 8.22 as you complete Step 2.

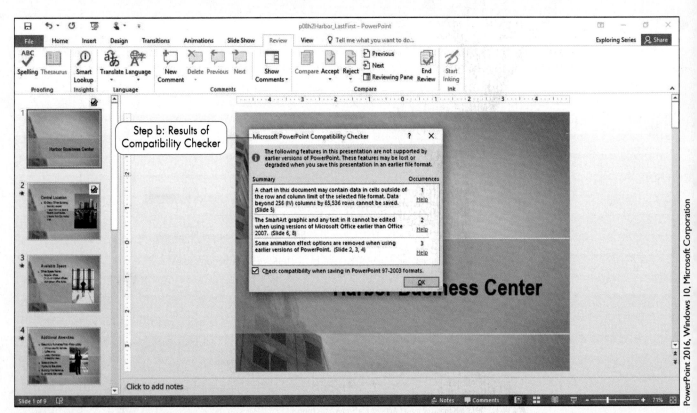

FIGURE 8.22 Compatibility Checker Results

a. Click the **File tab** and click **Check for Issues**.

b. Click **Check Compatibility** and read the summary of the features that cannot be supported in earlier versions of Microsoft Office.

Three issues are identified. The chart on Slide 5 contains data in cells outside of the row and column limit, and Slides 6 and 8 contain SmartArt graphics that cannot be edited when using versions of Microsoft Office earlier than Office 2007. Slides 2, 3, and 4 may not have some of the animation effects when used in earlier versions of PowerPoint.

> **TROUBLESHOOTING:** A compatibility pack may download as part of this step. If installed, presentations created in versions newer than 2003 will be automatically converted but some effects and features may be lost.

c. Click **OK**.

Compatibility issues have been identified, but nothing has been changed.

d. Save the presentation.

To secure the Harbor Business Center presentation, you add a password to the file. Then, to make it easier for Susil to access the file, you use the Save As General Options to remove the password and set a new one. Refer to Figure 8.23 as you complete Step 3.

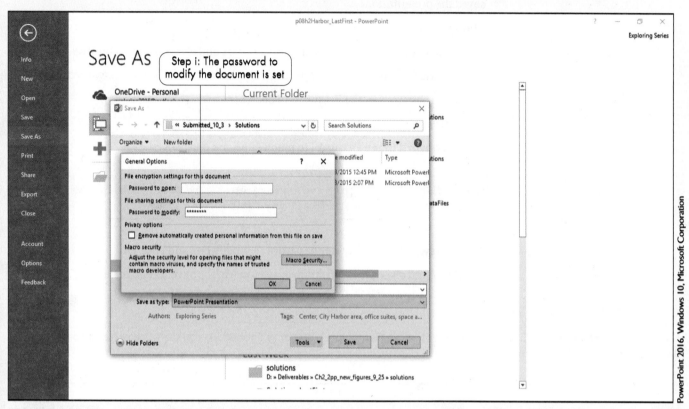

FIGURE 8.23 General Options for Setting a Password

a. Click the **File tab**, click **Protect Presentation**, and then click **Encrypt with Password**.

The Encrypt Document dialog box opens.

b. Type **h@Rb0R!c3nT3R?** and click **OK**.

> **TROUBLESHOOTING:** This is a secure password created from the name of the project, Harbor Center, and created using uppercase and lowercase letters and numbers and symbols from the top and bottom keyboards. It is 14 characters long.

c. Type **h@Rb0R!c3nT3R?** when you are prompted to reenter the password and click **OK**.

The Protect Presentation section changes to a yellow color and reads *A password is required to open this presentation.*

> **TROUBLESHOOTING:** If you typed the two passwords differently, you receive a warning that the passwords did not match and that the password was not created. Repeat the process until the passwords match. Never copy a password and paste it into the duplicate password box because if you copy and paste a typographical error, you will not be able to open the file or remove the password.

d. Save and close *p08h2Harbor_LastFirst* and reopen the presentation.

The Password dialog box opens.

e. Type **h@RbOR!c3nT3R?** in the Password dialog box and click **OK**.

The Harbor Business Center presentation opens.

f. Click the **File tab** and click **Save As**. Click **Browse** to navigate to the location where you saved the presentation.

The Save As dialog box opens.

g. Click **Tools** just to the left of Save in the dialog box and click **General Options**.

The General Options dialog box opens and displays asterisks in the Password to open box.

h. Delete the password in the Password to open box.

The password to open is removed.

i. Type **password** in the Password to modify box and click **OK**.

> **TROUBLESHOOTING:** This is a very insecure password and would not be safe. It will, however, enable your instructor to open your file and verify that you have set a password.

j. Type **password** in the Reenter password to modify box and click **OK**.

k. Click **Save** and click **Yes** when prompted to confirm the Save As and replace the existing file.

STEP 4 >> MARK AS FINAL

You want the employees of ACSL Development to know that the presentation is finished, so you mark the presentation as final. Refer to Figure 8.24 as you complete Step 4.

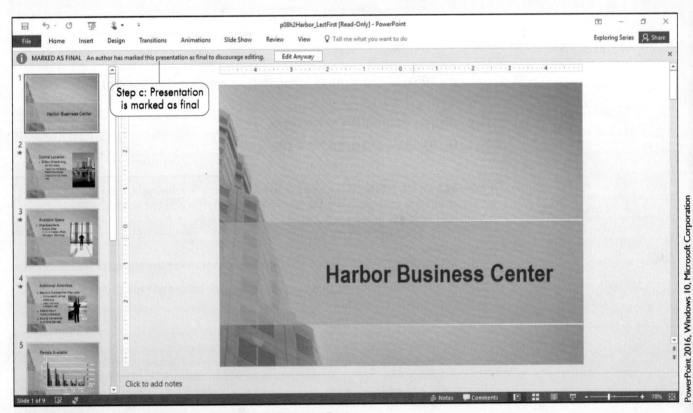

FIGURE 8.24 Harbor Business Center Presentation Marked as Final

a. Click the **File tab** and click **Protect Presentation**.

> **TROUBLESHOOTING:** If you closed the presentation after Step 3, the Password dialog box appears prompting you to enter the password to modify the presentation. If you do not enter the password, the presentation opens as a read-only version.

b. Select **Mark as Final** and click **OK** in the Microsoft PowerPoint Information dialog box that appears indicating that the presentation will be marked as final and then saved.

c. Click **OK** in the additional Microsoft PowerPoint Information dialog box indicating that the document has been marked final.

A Marked as Final message bar appears below the Ribbon and reads *An author has marked this presentation as final to discourage editing.*

d. Click the **Home tab**.

The Ribbon appears over the message bar (Marked as Final). Most features have been greyed out, preventing the user from making changes.

e. Close the file. You will submit this file to your instructor at the end of the last Hands-On Exercise.

Presentation Sharing

You spent a great deal of time creating a professional presentation that delivers your message—now how will you deliver that message to your audience? Will you present it, or will you distribute it to your audience? If you are going to distribute it, what file format will you use? What distribution methods are available?

PowerPoint includes multiple distribution options using a variety of file formats. Among the variety of methods you can use to distribute your presentation are burning it to a CD or DVD, presenting it on the Web, delivering it on a network location, or printing the presentation in an image format. These methods may require different file formats. In this section, you will save your presentation using several file types and examine PowerPoint's distribution options.

Selecting a Presentation File Type

By default, PowerPoint saves a presentation in the .pptx file format, an open format that uses *Extensible Markup Language (XML)*. XML is a set of encoding rules that creates a file format that is designed to provide maximum flexibility when storing and exchanging structured information. Microsoft Office moved to the use of XML file formats with Office 2007 and continues its use with Office 2016. Among the many benefits of XML are more compact files, improved damaged-file recovery, better privacy and control over personal information, better integration, and easier detection of documents that contain macros.

Change File Type

While you can change the file type of a PowerPoint presentation using the Save As feature, you may find it helpful to use Export to determine the file type you wish to use. Export includes a Change File Type option that provides a list of commonly used file types and a description of the file type to help you determine if it is appropriate for your needs.

To change a file type using this method, complete the following steps:

1. Click the File tab and click Export.
2. Click Change File Type (see Figure 8.25).
3. Select a file format from the Presentation File Types, Image File Types, or Other File Types sections.
4. Click Save As at the bottom of the list.
5. Navigate to the location where you want to store the file, type a file name in the File name box, and then click Save.

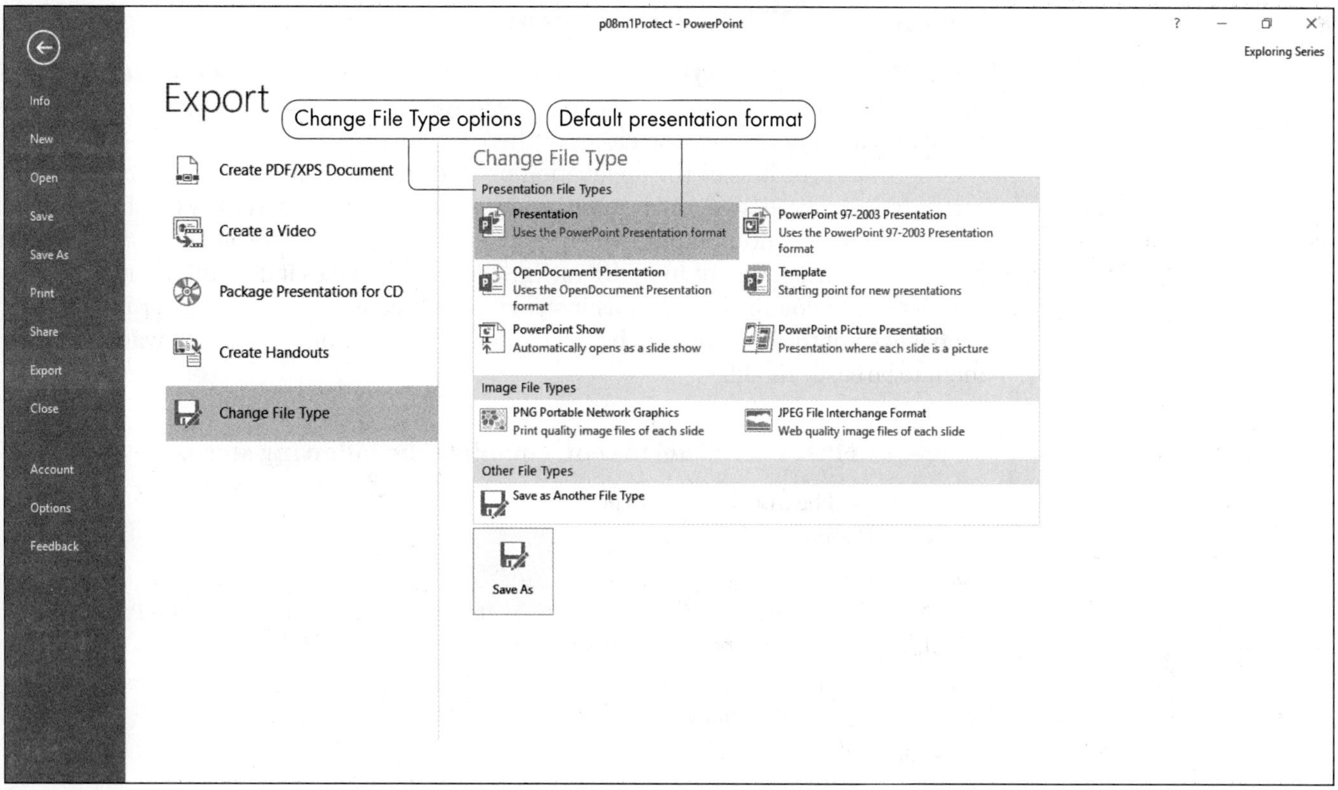

FIGURE 8.25 Export Pane with Change File Type Option Selected

One option in the Change File Type list enables you to save a presentation as an *OpenDocument presentation (.odp)*, a presentation that conforms to the OpenDocument standard for exchanging data between applications. This standard is an open XML-based format used in both free software and proprietary software, such as Microsoft Office, that seeks to make records and documents accessible across platforms and applications. Some PowerPoint features are fully supported when saved as an OpenDocument presentation, but others are only partially supported or not supported at all. Be sure to save your presentation in a PowerPoint format before saving as an OpenDocument presentation to ensure that you have a backup of the original format if needed.

After creating a presentation, you may want to save the individual slide or slides as graphic images. You can save each slide or all slides in the presentation as PNG Portable Network Graphics (.png) image(s) that use lossless compression and provide print-quality image files of each slide. You can also save each slide or all slides in the presentation as JPEG File Interchange Format (.jpg) image(s) that use a lossy format, which makes the file size smaller and makes the files suitable for Web-quality images.

Create a PowerPoint Picture Presentation

STEP 1 ▶▶ PowerPoint has the PowerPoint Picture Presentation option. This option *flattens* (converts all objects on a slide to a single layer) the content of each slide and then saves the slides in the .pptx presentation format. By converting each slide into an image, the slides become harder for others to modify. In addition, the presentation file size is much smaller and it is easier to email or download. To save a presentation in the PowerPoint Picture Presentation file format, click the File tab, click Export, click Change File Type, and then click PowerPoint Picture Presentation. Click Save As at the bottom of the list. Type the name of the presentation in the File name box and click Save. If you use the same file name as the original presentation, PowerPoint saves the PowerPoint Picture Presentation as a copy of the original.

Create a PDF/XPS Document

The **PDF file format (.pdf)** (created by Adobe Systems) and **XPS file format (.xps)** (created by Microsoft) are excellent file formats to use when distributing files to others. This is because documents saved in either of these formats are fixed file formats—they retain their format regardless of the application used to create them. These formats enable the presentation to be viewed and printed by any platform. This is extremely helpful if you are sending your presentation out to viewers who do not have Microsoft Office. Saving your presentation or document in a PDF or XPS file format makes it difficult to modify. When you distribute documents such as instructions, directions, legal forms, or reports, you probably want the document to be easy to read and print, but you do not want the document to be easily modified.

To create a PDF or XPS document, complete the following steps:

1. Click the File tab and click Export.
2. Click Create PDF/XPS Document.
3. Click Create PDF/XPS.
4. Navigate to the location where you want to store the document when the *Publish as PDF or XPS* dialog box appears and type a file name in the File name box.
5. Select the *Optimize for Standard (publishing online and printing)* or *Minimize size (publishing online)* option.
6. Click Publish.

Create a Video

Take advantage of the excitement of video by converting your presentation into an engaging video. PowerPoint includes an option for converting your presentation content into video that you can share with anyone. PowerPoint outputs your presentation as a Windows Media Video (WMV) video clip and includes all recorded timings and narrations, if used in the presentation; all slides that are not hidden; and all animations, transitions, and media.

Before creating a video, create your presentation and record any narration and timings you want as part of the video. You can use your mouse as a laser pointer to draw a viewer's attention to objects on your slides. Save the presentation.

To convert your presentation to a video, complete the following steps:

1. Click the File tab and click Export.
2. Click Create a Video.
3. Click Presentation Quality to display video quality and size options and select the desired option.
4. Click Don't Use Recorded Timings and Narrations, or click Use Recorded Timings and Narration if you wish to use any recorded timings and narration or laser pointer movements.
5. Click the Seconds to spend on each slide spin arrows to change the default time of 5 seconds if you are not using recorded timings and narrations.
6. Click Create Video.
7. Navigate to the location where you want to store the video when the Save As dialog box appears and type a file name in the File name box.
8. Click Save.

Before you determine the video quality and size for the presentation, you need to determine the output for the video. If you plan on the presentation video being displayed on a computer or high definition (HD) display, you need to create a high-quality video (1440 × 1080 pixels). This creates a large file size. If you plan to upload the video to the Internet or burn it to a DVD, you need to create a medium-quality video (960 × 720 pixels). This creates a moderate file size. If you plan on the video being played on a portable device, you need to create a low-quality video (640 × 480 pixels). This creates the smallest file size, but text would be difficult to read. Figure 8.26 displays the *Create a Video* options with the default setting for computer and HD displays.

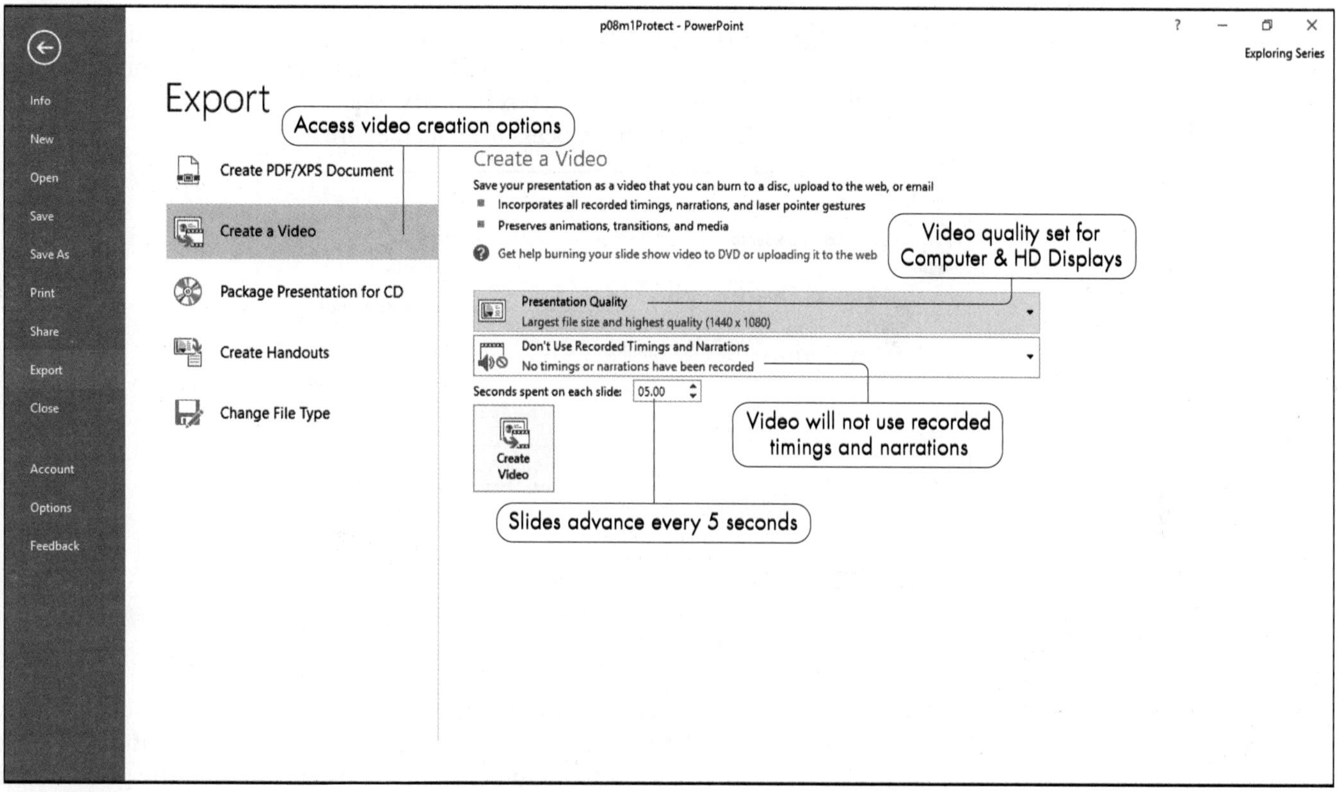

PowerPoint 2016, Windows 10, Microsoft Corporation

FIGURE 8.26 Export Pane with Create a Video Option Selected

The length of time it takes to create a video depends on the content in the presentation and the length and quality of the video. The presentation will be recorded in real time, so it may take several hours to record. You can monitor the progress of the recording on the status bar. To play the video, locate and double-click the file.

Package Presentation for CD

STEP 2 »» ***Package Presentation for CD*** is a PowerPoint feature that enables you to copy your presentation to a CD, DVD, or a storage location such as a hard drive, a network location, or a USB device. You can save the fonts you used, as well as linked or embedded items. After you have packaged your presentation for CD, you can then distribute it to others. You may package your presentation on a CD for your personal use, too. If you are presenting at another location, you can package your presentation and carry the CD with you. At the new location, you can play the presentation from the CD if the computer you are using to present has PowerPoint installed.

To package your presentation, complete the following steps:

1. Save the presentation you want to package.
2. Insert a CD into the CD drive if you want to copy the presentation to a CD. Omit this step if you are copying the presentation to a folder on a USB device, a hard drive, or to a network location.
3. Click the File tab and click Export.
4. Click Package Presentation for CD.
5. Click Package for CD in the right pane.

TIP: BE AWARE OF YOUR DEVICE'S DRIVES
Keep in mind that not every device has an optical drive to play a CD or DVD. You can use the Package Presentation for CD feature to copy your presentation to a network location or a USB device as another method of distribution for your presentation.

The Package for CD dialog box opens (see Figure 8.27). Click in the Name the CD box and type a name for your CD. If you wish to include additional presentations or files on the CD, click Add. The Add Files dialog box appears. Select the presentation you want to include and click Add. Repeat this process until all files are added.

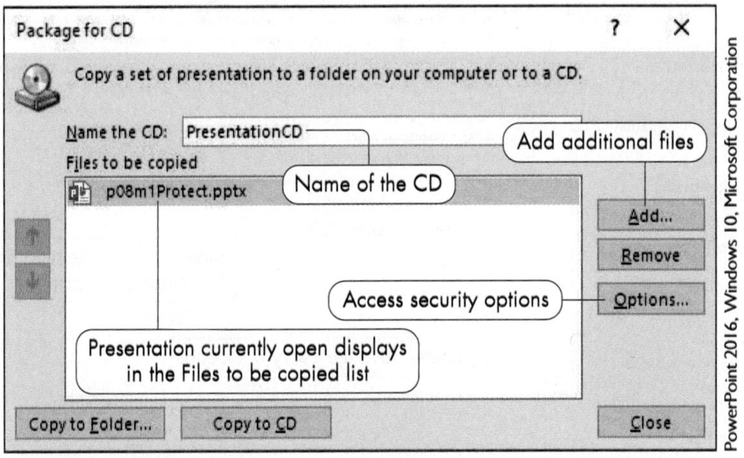

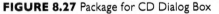

FIGURE 8.27 Package for CD Dialog Box

Click Options in the Package for CD dialog box to specify what files will be included and to set the privacy and security options that you want for the presentation. You can choose whether or not you want to include files you have linked to in the presentation and whether you want to embed TrueType fonts. ***TrueType fonts*** are digital fonts that contain alphabetic characters and information about the characters, such as the shape of the character, how it is horizontally and vertically spaced, and the character mapping that governs the keystrokes you use to access them. This is important if you want the font to display as the font designer created it and as you used it in the presentation. If you have used a nonstandard font in your presentation, you cannot be sure the computer on which you are going to display your presentation has the same font. If it does not have the same font, the computer substitutes another font, which can create havoc in your presentation design. If you embed the TrueType fonts you used in your presentation, you will have a larger file, but you can be sure that your presentation displays fonts accurately.

To ensure the security and privacy of your presentation, the Package for CD options also enable you to set a password for opening the presentation and a second password for modifying the presentation. You can also check the option to inspect the presentation for inappropriate or private information and remove it, a feature you explored earlier in this chapter. After setting the options you want, click OK. Figure 8.28 displays the Options dialog box.

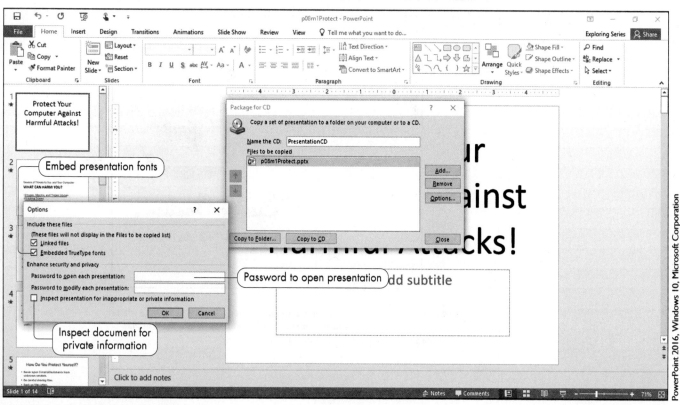

FIGURE 8.28 Package for CD Options

Once you have selected the options you want, click either Copy to Folder or Copy to CD. If you click Copy to Folder, you can copy the files to a new folder on your hard drive or a storage location such as a USB drive. You can create a name for the folder, browse to the location you wish to store the folder, and then copy the presentation to that location. If you click Copy to CD, for security purposes, you are asked if you want to include linked files. If you trust the linked files, click Yes. At that point, you see instructions for writing to your CD writer. These instructions vary depending on the device you use to burn CDs.

After you have packaged your presentation for CD and distributed it, the individual receiving the CD simply places the CD in his or her CD drive, and the CD loads and displays your presentation. If you included more than one presentation on the CD, the presentations load and display in the order in which you added them to the CD. This is the default setting for Package for CD. If the presentation was packaged to a folder, locate and open the folder and double-click the presentation name. This starts PowerPoint, and opens the presentation.

Create Handouts in Microsoft Word

In addition to the excellent handouts you can create in PowerPoint, you can prepare handouts in Word. When you create your audience handouts through Word, you can take advantage of all of Word's word-processing tools. In addition, you are given several helpful layouts not available in PowerPoint. For example, when you create notes page handouts in PowerPoint, the handouts consist of a thumbnail of the slide at the top of the page with its related notes beneath it—one slide per sheet of paper. If you have many slides, this can be an inefficient use of paper. By sending your presentation to Word, you can select a layout that puts thumbnails of the slides on the left side of the page and the related notes on the right side. Depending on the length of your notes, you may fit several slides per sheet of paper. This saves paper but can be time-consuming, as Word has to create a table and insert the slides and notes in the table cells. Figure 8.29 shows a notes page in PowerPoint, and Figure 8.30 shows its counterpart in Word.

Your wedding is one of the most memorable times of your life, where the whole world stops and your magical moments begin. ***Castle Gardens*** offers a unique atmosphere of romance and beauty for your wedding.

1

FIGURE 8.29 PowerPoint Notes Page

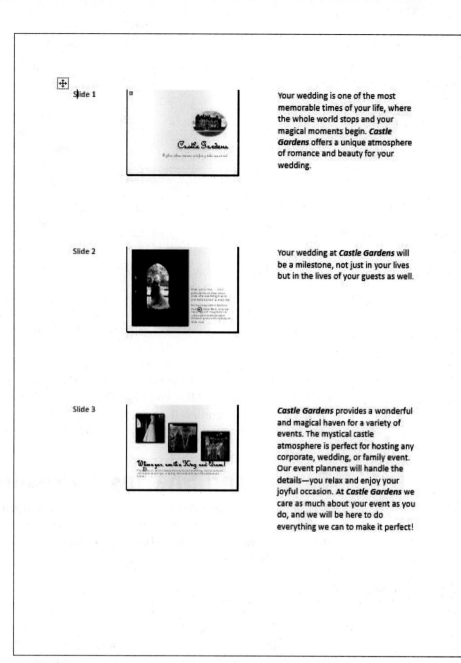

FIGURE 8.30 Word Notes Page

PowerPoint 2016, Windows 10, Microsoft Corporation

To create handouts in Word, complete the following steps:

1. Click the File tab and click Export.
2. Select Create Handouts.
3. Click Create Handouts in the right pane.
4. Click the layout you want for your handouts in the Send to Microsoft Word dialog box (see Figure 8.31).
5. Click OK.

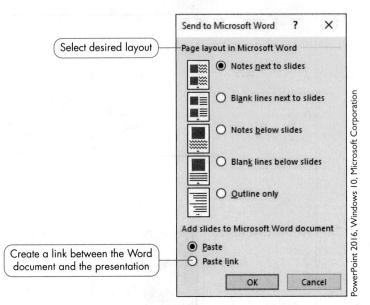

Select desired layout

Create a link between the Word document and the presentation

FIGURE 8.31 Word Layouts for PowerPoint Notes and Slides

The Send to Microsoft Word dialog box includes an option to paste a link between the Word document and the presentation so that changes you make in either one are reflected in the other. After you click OK in the dialog box, Microsoft Word opens and displays your presentation in the page layout you selected. When you are done making changes in Word and done printing the handout, click Close to quit Word.

Saving and Sharing a Presentation

A variety of methods exist for sharing a presentation with others, depending on your audience and how you want to connect with them. You can share the presentation by using email, inviting people to OneDrive to view or collaborate on it, using the Present Online feature, or publishing the slides.

Send Using Email

One easy-to-use method for distributing a presentation is to send it by email. If your default email client is Outlook, you can send the presentation file directly from PowerPoint. Recipients receive the presentation as an attachment to the email.

To email a presentation from PowerPoint, complete the following steps:

1. Click the File tab and click Share.
2. Click Email.
3. Click Send as Attachment or another send option (see Figure 8.32).
4. Type or select the email addresses of the recipient(s) in the To box that opens in your default email application.
5. Change the subject line from the name of the presentation if you want and add a message informing the recipient(s) of your purpose for sending the presentation.
6. Click Send.

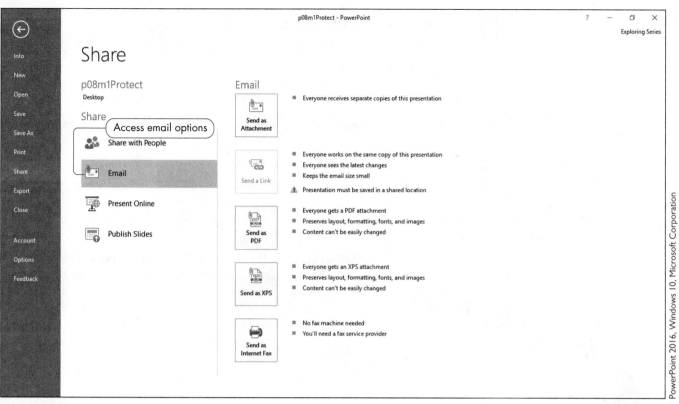

FIGURE 8.32 Share Pane with Email Option Selected

If you do not use Outlook as your default email client, you can still send your presentation via email.

To send you presentation in other email clients, complete the following steps:

1. Save the presentation in the file type that meets your needs and close the presentation.
2. Open your email client.
3. Click Attach, locate the file, and then attach the file to the email.
4. Type or select the email addresses of the recipient(s) in the To box.
5. Change the subject line to the subject you want and add a message informing the recipient(s) of your purpose for sending the presentation.
6. Click Send.

Share with People on OneDrive

STEP 3 ⟩⟩ You can use PowerPoint to send your presentation to *OneDrive*, an app used to store, share, and access files and folders via the Internet. OneDrive is part of Microsoft's online services designed to help users communicate and collaborate, and it currently provides free cloud storage for photos, videos, and documents. OneDrive enables you to store, access, and share your files from any device with Internet access—no need to carry a USB or external drive with you. When you share a presentation stored in OneDrive, you can share a link to OneDrive with others rather than sending an attachment. This enables you to maintain a single version of the presentation and enables others to edit the presentation in their browsers. To log in to OneDrive, you will need a Microsoft account and password. If you use Outlook.com or Xbox Live, you already have a Microsoft account. It was formerly referred to as a Windows Live ID.

TIP: TO OBTAIN A MICROSOFT ACCOUNT

A Microsoft account uses an email address and a password. Create your credentials for a Microsoft account, and you will have access to many services. It enables you to log in to such sites and services as Office 365, OneDrive, Outlook.com, Office Online, Xbox Live, and Skype. To sign up for a Microsoft account, visit https://onedrive.live.com/about/en-us/.

To save and share a presentation using OneDrive, complete the following steps:

1. Click the File tab and click Share.
2. Click Share with People. Click Save to Cloud.
3. Click OneDrive – Personal on the Save As pane. Then click Browse.
4. Click the OneDrive folder (see Figure 8.33). Click Save.
5. Return to Share and click Share with People.
6. Type the names or email addresses of those you want to share the presentation with or use the Address Book. You can include a personal message, and you can determine whether the users can view or edit the presentation (see Figure 8.34).
7. Click Share.

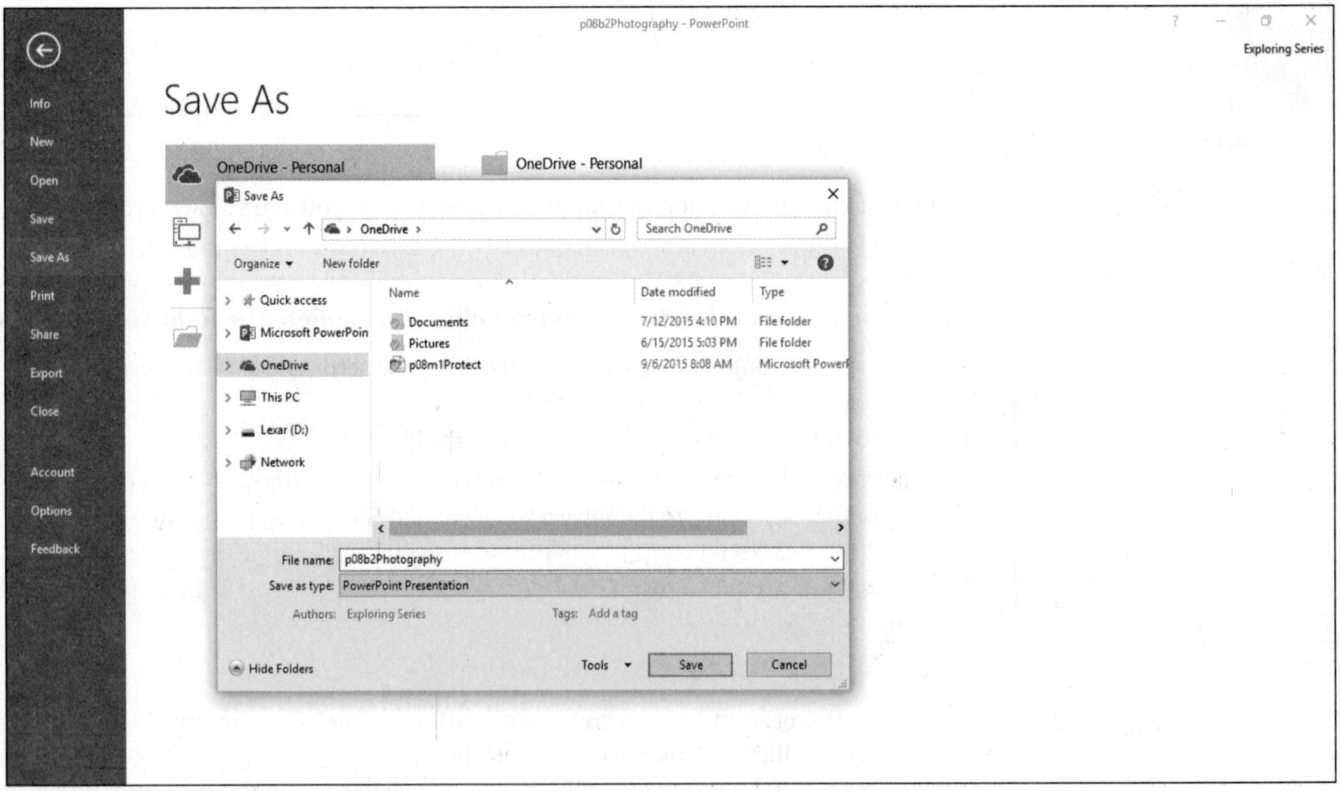

PowerPoint 2016, Windows 10, Microsoft Corporation

FIGURE 8.33 Saving to OneDrive

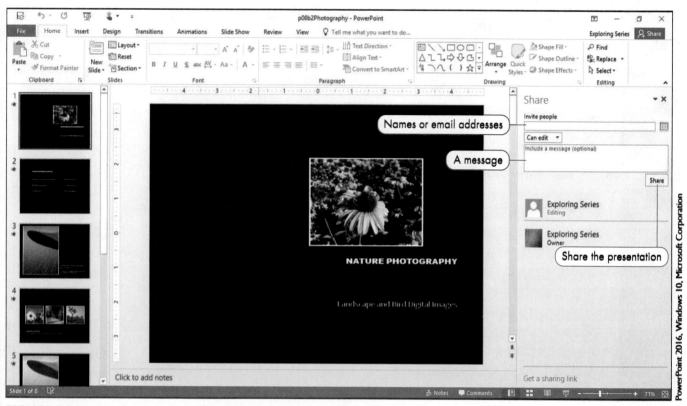

FIGURE 8.34 Inviting People to View Your Presentation

The Share pane also provides a feature for a Sharing Link. You can select whether to create a link that allows others to edit the documents or to create a link allowing others only to view the documents. The link can be copied and then pasted into an email.

Present Online

You may also use *Present Online* to transmit a presentation over the Internet in real time to invited participants who are in different locations. To do this, you use a Microsoft account to log in to the Office Presentation Service, a free service provided by Microsoft for PowerPoint users. To share the presentation, you send the URL for the presentation to your invited participants, and they watch your presentation on their Internet browser at the same time you deliver it. There is an option to enable remote viewers to download the presentation.

To present a presentation online, complete the following steps:

1. Click the File tab and click Share.
2. Click Present Online.
3. Click Present Online in the right pane (see Figure 8.35).
4. Sign in using your Microsoft account if prompted to do so.
5. Click Copy Link and share the link with participants via text messaging, instant messenger program, or email. Click Send in Email to send the link through Outlook.
6. Click Start Presentation.
7. Advance through the slide show and exit the slide show when you have displayed all slides.
8. Click End Online Presentation in the Present Online group to end the online presentation. When warned that everyone viewing the presentation will be disconnected if you continue, click End Online Presentation (see Figure 8.36).

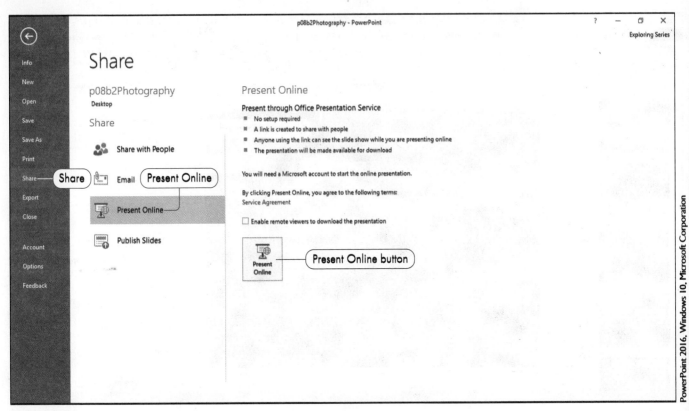

FIGURE 8.35 Share Pane with Present Online Option Selected

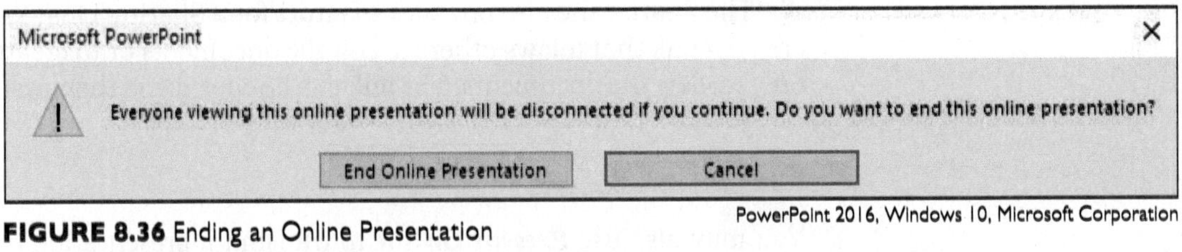

FIGURE 8.36 Ending an Online Presentation

PowerPoint 2016, Windows 10, Microsoft Corporation

TIP: TO PUBLISH SLIDES

An additional option, Publish Slides, lets you share and reuse individual PowerPoint slides by storing them in a slide library on a server or at a SharePoint site. This option requires Microsoft PowerPoint Professional Plus 2010 software. A SharePoint site is generally found in a corporate environment, but check with your instructor or lab manager to see whether a SharePoint site is available for your use.

Collaborate in a Business Environment

OneDrive for Business provides cloud storage so that files can be stored, shared, and synced from any location or device with Internet connection. In an office environment, you may have access to OneDrive for Business. Access to OneDrive for Business enables collaboration between team members on a presentation or project and provides additional services unavailable in PowerPoint. All team members are able to save to and obtain files from a centralized browser-based location, depending on their permissions.

Using OneDrive for Business for collaborating enables you to do the following:

- Store your presentations in a cloud-based workspace for convenient access from anywhere.

- Share presentations in a folder or workspace so team members have access to each other's work.

- Work on presentations at the same time and see the changes as they are being made.

- Use any device to view and sync your files.

OneDrive enables work teams to share files and work together on a presentation. OneDrive provides tools to make sharing and updating documents easy. Slides can be saved directly to a folder that has been created, and saved slides are available to team members for reuse in other presentations.

You and your coworkers can access the slide folder and do the following:

- Add slides to the folder.
- Reuse slides in the folder in a presentation.
- Track changes made to slides.
- View the latest version of a slide or presentation.
- Search for specific presentations being stored on OneDrive.

Quick Concepts

8. Explain when you might want to change file types for a presentation. Discuss two different file types you would use. **pp. 530–531**

9. What are the benefits of saving a presentation using PowerPoint Picture Presentation? **p. 531**

10. What is the difference between sharing a presentation in OneDrive and sending the presentation as an attachment? **pp. 538–539**

Hands-On Exercises

Skills covered: Create a PowerPoint Picture Presentation • Package a Presentation • Share With People

3 Presentation Sharing

You want to share the Harbor Business Center presentation with an associate. You decide to save the presentation as a PowerPoint Picture Presentation to flatten the content to a single image per slide, and to invite your associate to view the presentation on OneDrive. You also package the presentation to a folder so that others can watch the presentation on most computers.

STEP 1 ›› CREATE A POWERPOINT PICTURE PRESENTATION

You want to save the Harbor Business Center presentation as a PowerPoint Picture Presentation so each slide is flattened as an image, making it more difficult to modify. Refer to Figure 8.37 as you complete Step 1.

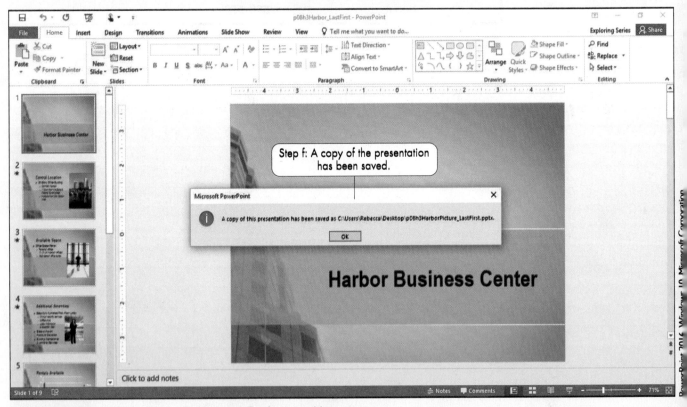

FIGURE 8.37 PowerPoint Picture Presentation Confirmation Message

a. Use File Explorer to make a copy of *p08h2Harbor_LastFirst*. Rename the copied presentation **p08h3Harbor_LastFirst**.

> **TROUBLESHOOTING:** If you open *p08h2Harbor_LastFirst* and try to save it using another file name, PowerPoint removes the *Marked as Final* designation. You need to preserve those settings so that your instructor can verify that you completed Hands-On Exercise 2.

b. Open *p08h3Harbor_LastFirst* and type **password** when prompted to enter the password, then click **OK**.

You protected the presentation with a password in Hands-On Exercise 2.

c. Click **Edit Anyway** on the Marked as Final message bar.

The Marked as Final message bar is removed, and the status bar no longer contains the Marked as Final icon.

d. Click the **File tab**, click **Export**, and then click **Change File Type**.

A list of file types display in the right pane, the Change File Type pane.

e. Click **PowerPoint Picture Presentation** and click **Save As** at the bottom of the pane.

A Save As dialog box displays.

f. Change the file name to **p08h3HarborPicture_LastFirst**, adding *Picture* to the file name. Click Save.

A Microsoft PowerPoint dialog box displays indicating a copy of the presentation has been saved and giving the full path and file name of the copy.

g. Click **OK**.

The dialog box disappears and the *p08h3Harbor_LastFirst* presentation is onscreen.

h. Save *p08h3Harbor_LastFirst* and leave it open.

STEP 2)) **PACKAGE A PRESENTATION**

You use the Package a Presentation for CD feature to package the Harbor Business Center presentation.

a. Ensure that *p08h3Harbor_LastFirst* is open.

> **TROUBLESHOOTING:** If you closed *p08h3Harbor_LastFirst* while completing the previous step, you will need to type the password when prompted and click OK.

b. Click the **File tab** and click **Export**.

The Export options display in the Backstage view.

c. Click **Package Presentation for CD** and click **Package for CD** in the right pane.

The Package for CD dialog box appears. The default name assigned by PowerPoint, PresentationCD, displays and the presentation file name is shown in the Files to be copied list.

d. Type **Harbor Business** in the **Name the CD box**.

e. Click **Copy to Folder**.

The Copy to Folder dialog box displays the name of the folder and the location in which it will be saved.

f. Click **Browse**, navigate to the location where you save your solution files, and then click **Select**.

g. Click **OK** and click **Yes** to include linked files.

File Explorer opens and displays the PresentationPackage folder, an AUTORUN file (the instruction file that starts the presentation when a CD is inserted), and the presentation file.

h. Close File Explorer and close the Package for CD dialog box.

i. Leave *p08h3Harbor_LastFirst* open for the next step.

STEP 3 » SHARE WITH PEOPLE

You want to share the presentation by inviting your associate (your instructor) to see it on OneDrive. Refer to Figure 8.38 as you complete Step 2.

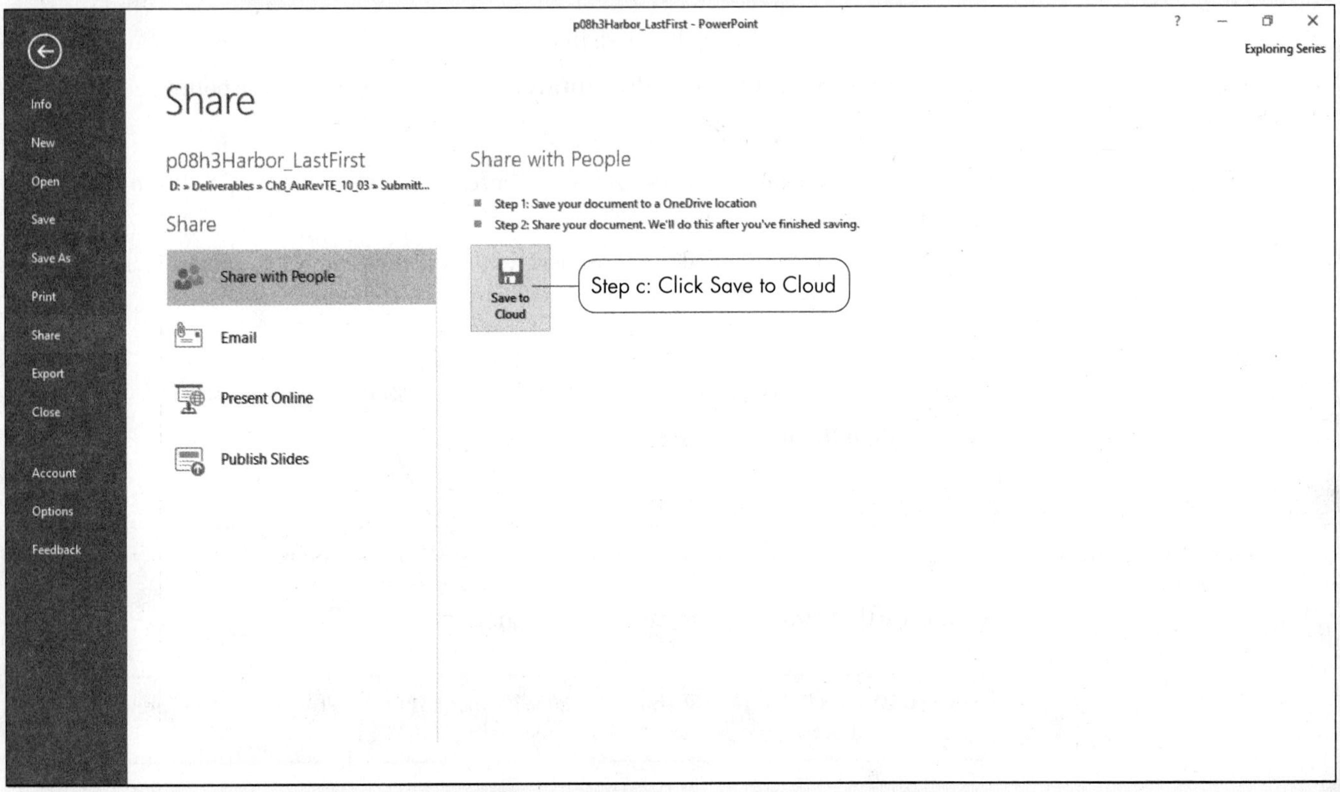

FIGURE 8.38 Share Pane with Share with People Option Selected

> **TROUBLESHOOTING:** You will not be able to do this step if you do not have a Microsoft account. To obtain a Microsoft account, refer to the Tip that appears near Figure 8.33.

a. Ensure *p08h3HarborPicture_LastFirst* is open.

b. Click the **File** tab and click **Share**.

c. Click **Share with People** and click **Save to Cloud** in the right pane.

d. Click **OneDrive** in the Save As pane. Click **Browse**.

The Save As dialog box opens where you can select the location for saving the file before sharing it.

e. Click the **OneDrive folder** in the left pane. Click **Save**.

The presentation is now saved on OneDrive. Next, you return to the presentation.

f. Click the **File tab** and click **Share**. Click **Share with People** and then click **Share with People** in the right pane.

You return to the presentation and the Share pane opens.

g. Type the names or email addresses of those you want to share the presentation with. Click the **Can Edit arrow** and select **Can View**.

h. Click **Share**.

i. Save and close the file. Based on your instructor's directions, submit:

p08h3Harbor_LastFirst
p08h3HarborPicture_LastFirst

Chapter Objectives Review

After reading this chapter, you have accomplished the following objectives:

1. Work with comments and annotations.

- To facilitate the collaboration process, PowerPoint provides tools that team members can use to review a presentation.
- Add comments: The Review tab contains the Comments group, which has tools for adding a new comment on a slide, for editing or deleting existing comments, and for moving between comments.
- Insert annotations: Ink annotations, such as highlighting or drawings, can be added during a slide show and saved as the slide show is closed.
- Emphasize content during a presentation: You can call your audience's attention to the portion of the slide you want to emphasize without creating ink markup (annotations) by either using the Zoom In option or using your mouse as a laser pointer.

2. Show, hide, and print markup.

- When the annotations are saved, they display on the slides in Normal view. When comments have been added to a slide, the slide shows the markup.
- Show Markup is located in the Comments group on the Review tab and can be toggled on or off to be hidden or displayed.
- You can keep a record of markups made to a presentation by printing the comments and ink annotations. Comments will print on a separate page for each slide, whereas annotations print on the slide for which they were created.

3. Compare and merge presentations.

- PowerPoint enables you to compare two versions of a presentation.
- The differences in the presentations are marked as revisions that you can accept or reject.

4. View presentation properties.

- PowerPoint automatically stores data about your documents as document properties, including the name of the author creating the presentation, as well as data such as the number of slides in the show and the number of words.
- You can add additional properties such as a subject, keywords, manager, company, category, and comments that can be used to search for and locate documents.

5. Check a presentation for issues.

- Access Document Inspector: Before distributing the slideshow, you can use the Inspect Document feature to find the document properties and strip out the properties you do not want others to see.
- Check accessibility: The Accessibility Checker checks a presentation for issues that people with disabilities may find hard to read.

- Check compatibility: The Compatibility Checker inspects the presentation for features not supported by earlier versions of PowerPoint.

6. Protect a presentation.

- Protect with a password: For security and privacy reasons, you may want to encrypt a presentation and set a password to open a document or modify a document.
- Mark as Final: To indicate that the presentation is completed, use the Mark as Final feature.
- Add a digital signature: To authenticate your presentation to others with a digital signature, you must sign up with a third-party signature service. You can create your own digital signature for your use to authenticate that a presentation has not been modified since you last worked on it.

7. Select a presentation file type.

- PowerPoint includes many options for saving a document based on your needs and the needs of your audience.
- Change file type: The file types are available in the Save As feature, but accessing the Change File Type option provides you with a list of commonly used file types and a description of the file type to help you determine if it is appropriate for your needs.
- Create a PowerPoint Picture Presentation: This option flattens the content of each slide and converts the slide into an image. This makes it harder for others to modify them.
- Create a PDF/XPS document: You can use these file formats when you want to distribute the file to others for viewing and printing regardless of the platform they have.
- Create a video: This file type can be shared with anyone. It includes all recorder timings, narrations, animations, transitions, and media in the original presentation.
- Package presentation for CD: This allows you to copy your presentation to a CD, DVD, or other storage locations such as a hard drive, network location, or USB device.
- Create handouts in Microsoft Word: Handouts created in Word provide more options for use of word-processing tools and additional layouts not available for handouts created in PowerPoint.

8. Save and share a presentation.

- You have a variety of methods for sending a presentation to others. The method of distribution you select depends on your audience and how you want to connect with them.
- You can send the presentation to your audience using email, save the presentation to OneDrive, or transmit the presentation using the Present Online service.

- Send using email: If your default email client is Outlook, you can send the presentation directly from PowerPoint. Otherwise, you can save the presentation and attach it to an email using your preferred email client.
- Share with people on OneDrive: You can use OneDrive to store, access, and share your presentation anywhere there is an Internet connection. You can maintain a single version of the presentation while you and others view and edit it.

- Present online: Sharing a presentation this way allows you to transmit it over the Internet to invited participants at different locations using the Office Presentation Service.
- Collaborate in a business environment: OneDrive for Business can be used by work teams to collaborate on projects, share files, and develop presentations simultaneously.

Key Terms Matching

Match the key terms with their definitions. Write the key term letter by the appropriate numbered definition.

a. Accessibility

b. Accessibility Checker

c. Alternative text (alt text)

d. Comment

e. Compatibility Checker

f. Digital signature

g. Document Inspector

h. Document property

i. Encryption

j. Extensible Markup Language (XML)

k. Markup

l. Metadata

m. OneDrive

n. OneDrive for Business

o. OpenDocument presentation (.odp)

p. PDF file format (.pdf)

q. Present Online

r. Reviewer

s. TrueType font

t. XPS file format (.xps)

1. _____ A Microsoft service that enables the transmission of a presentation in real time over the Internet to a remote audience. **p. 541**

2. _____ An app used to store, share, and access files and folders via the Internet. **p. 539**

3. _____ A digital font that contains alphabetic characters and information about the characters, such as the shape, spacing, and character mapping of the font. **p. 534**

4. _____ A presentation that conforms to the OpenDocument standard for exchanging data between applications. **p. 531**

5. _____ Comments and ink annotations that appear in a presentation. **p. 502**

6. _____ A tool that aids in identifying and resolving accessibility issues in a presentation. **p. 519**

7. _____ A tool that checks for features in a presentation that are not supported by earlier versions of PowerPoint. **p. 520**

8. _____ A method used to protect the contents of your presentation by converting it into unreadable scrambled text that requires a password to be opened. **p. 521**

9. _____ A set of encoding rules that create a file format that is designed to provide maximum flexibility when storing and exchanging structured information. **p. 530**

10. _____ A tool that detects hidden and personal data in the presentation. **p. 518**

11. _____ The ease with which a person with physical challenges is able to access and understand a presentation. **p. 519**

12. _____ An invisible, electronic signature stamp that is encrypted and attached to a certificate that can be added to a presentation. **p. 523**

13. _____ Data that describes other data. **p. 507**

14. _____ A more secure electronic file format created by Adobe Systems that preserves document formatting and is viewable and printable on any platform. **p. 532**

15. _____ A text-based description of an image. **p. 519**

16. _____ A text note attached to a slide that can be inserted or removed as needed. **p. 502**

17. _____ Someone who examines the presentation and provides feedback. **p. 502**

18. _____ An electronic file format created by Microsoft that preserves document formatting and is viewable and printable on any platform. **p. 532**

19. _____ A Microsoft service that provides cloud storage so that files can be stored, shared, and synced from any location or device with Internet connection for workplace collaboration. **p. 542**

20. _____ An attribute, such as an author's name or keyword, that describes a file. **p. 507**

Multiple Choice

1. The process whereby a team works together to accomplish a goal is referred to as which of the following?

(a) Unification

(b) Collusion

(c) Collaboration

(d) Deliberation

2. Which of the following is an Adobe electronic file format that preserves document formatting?

(a) PDF

(b) XPS

(c) PNG

(d) XML

3. Markup may consist of all of the following *except*:

(a) Comments inserted by the presentation creator.

(b) Annotations.

(c) Comments inserted by a reviewer.

(d) Passwords created for opening and modifying a presentation.

4. Which of the following statements regarding annotations in a presentation is *not* true?

(a) Annotations are markings on a slide.

(b) Annotations can be preserved as you close a presentation.

(c) Saved annotations are visible even when Show Markup is inactive.

(d) Annotations can look like they are drawn with a pen or a highlighter.

5. Which of the following document properties is *not* created automatically by PowerPoint but can be added?

(a) Number of slides in the presentation

(b) Last date of modification

(c) Keywords

(d) Date the presentation was created

6. Which of the following is *not* checked by the Document Inspector?

(a) Comments and annotations

(b) Version compatibility

(c) Document properties and personal information

(d) Presentation notes

7. Which of the following is a *true* statement regarding passwords?

(a) One password may be set to open a document, and a second password may be set to modify a document.

(b) Mary_Sept18_1990 is a more secure password than M@ryO9LB_L990.

(c) A password can only be set through the *Prepare for Sharing* feature.

(d) A digital signature is the same thing as setting a password.

8. Which of the following may be packaged with your presentation when you use the *Package for CD* feature?

(a) All TrueType fonts used in the presentation

(b) Any files linked to the presentation

(c) Any embedded items

(d) All of the above

9. All of the following statements about creating handouts in Microsoft Office Word are true *except*:

(a) Create Handouts is available from the Review tab.

(b) Creating handouts in Microsoft Word enables you to use word-processing features to format the handouts.

(c) Word provides layouts not available in PowerPoint.

(d) A link can be pasted between PowerPoint and Word so changes can update in either document when made.

10. When merging presentations, the Revision pane contains which of the following?

(a) A list of all comments and annotations created in the presentation

(b) A list of features in the presentation that are not supported by earlier versions of PowerPoint

(c) A list of changes to the slide currently selected and any slides that have been added or removed in the presentation

(d) A digital signature ensuring the integrity of the presentation

Practice Exercises

1 Castle Gardens

Castle Gardens provides wedding packages that include the use of fabulous gardens or a castle great hall, a wedding planner, pewter tableware, old English décor, photography, and videography. You create a PowerPoint presentation advertising Castle Gardens and submit it to the owner, Ms. Grosscurth, for review. She reviewed the slides, added comments, and made changes. You merge the presentations and accept and reject changes. You view the presentation and highlight words and phrases you think create the emotional appeal of Castle Gardens and you keep the ink annotations when you exit Slide Show view. You print a copy of the comments and annotations to create a record of the changes you made and hide the markup. Refer to Figure 8.39 as you complete this exercise.

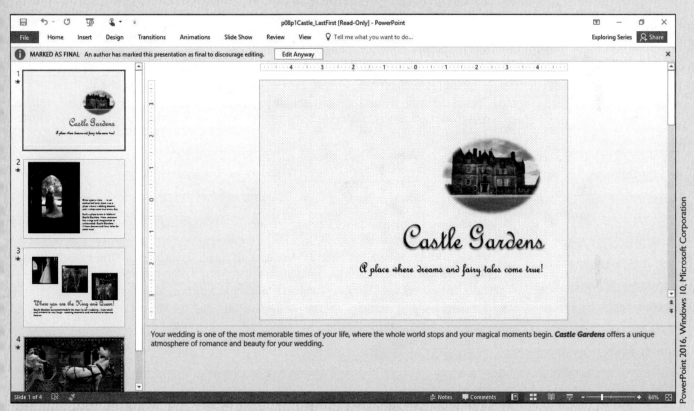

FIGURE 8.39 Castle Gardens Presentation

a. Open *p08p1Castle* and save it as **p08p1Castle_LastFirst**. Click the **File tab**, click **Options**, and then change the user name to your name and the initials to your initials (if necessary). Click **OK**.

b. Create a handout header with your name and a handout footer with your instructor's name and your class. Include the current date.

c. Click **Slide 1**, click the **Review tab** and click **New Comment** in the Comments group. Type **Ms. Grosscurth, this is the beginning of the presentation we discussed. Please review it and make suggestions for changes. Thanks!**

d. Save the presentation and click **Compare** in the Compare group on the Review tab.

e. Navigate to your student data files, select *p08p1CastleGrosscurth*, and then click **Merge**.

f. Click **Slide 1**, select and read the first comment in the Slide Changes section displayed in the Details tab of the Revisions pane, the comment requesting that Ms. Grosscurth review the presentation.

g. Click **Delete** in the Comments group.

h. Click **Insertions at beginning of presentation** in the Presentation Changes section. Click **All slides inserted at this position** in the Slides pane. Select and read the next comment in the Slide Changes section, the comment requesting that you change the color tone of the castle picture.

i. Select the image of the castle and click the **Format tab**. Click **Color** in the Adjust group. Click **Temperature: 4700 K** in the Color Tone section.

j. Click the **Review tab**, click **Next** two times in the Comments group, and then read the comment on Slide 2. Click **Next** in the Comments group.

k. Click **Slide 3**, read the comment, select the text *The castle*, and then type **Castle Gardens**.

l. Click **Next** two times in the Comments group and read the comment for Slide 4 at the top of the Slide Changes section.

m. Click the **Accept arrow** in the Compare group and click **Accept All Changes to the Presentation**. All of the changes are accepted, but the comments remain.

n. Close the Revisions pane. Close the Comments pane.

o. Click the **Slide Show tab** and click **From Beginning** in the Slide Show group.

p. Ensure that you are on Slide 1. Right-click anywhere on the slide, point to Pointer Options, and then select **Highlighter**. Highlight the following words in the presentation, selecting the highlighter on each slide:

Slide #	Words to Highlight
1	dreams, fairy tales
2	wishes came true
3	most lavish wedding

q. Exit the presentation and click **Keep** in the Microsoft PowerPoint dialog box asking if you want to keep your ink annotations.

r. Click the **File tab**, click **Print**, and then click **Full Page Slides**. Click **4 Slides Horizontal** in the Handouts section. Note the annotations display on the print preview.

s. Drag the vertical scroll bar down and note that comments from all four slides display.

t. Return to the presentation and click the **Review tab**, click the **Show Comments arrow**, and then click **Show Markup** to toggle the display of the markup off.

u. Save the presentation. Click the **File tab**, click **Protect Presentation**, and then select **Mark as Final**. Click **OK** two times.

v. Close the file. Based on your instructor's directions, submit p08p1Castle_LastFirst.

2 Martin Luther King, Jr. Commemoration Flyer

You are part of a student council committee working on the annual Martin Luther King, Jr. Commemoration. You have created a one-page flyer that can be emailed to students and also printed and handed out in the Student Center. In this exercise, you change the presentation properties, check the presentation for issues, save the presentation as a PDF file to preserve the formatting and image when printing, and then create handouts in Microsoft Word. Refer to Figure 8.40 as you complete this exercise.

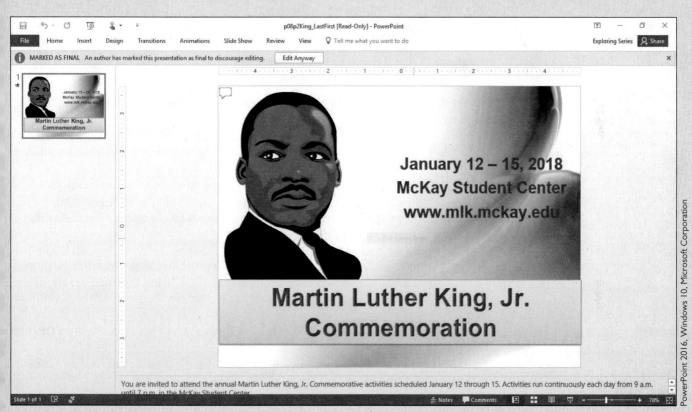

FIGURE 8.40 Martin Luther King, Jr. Commemoration Flyer

a. Open *p08p2King* and save it as **p08p2King_LastFirst**.

b. Create a handout header with your name and a handout footer with your instructor's name and your class. Include the current date.

c. Click **Slide 1**, click the **Review tab**, and click **New Comment** in the Comment group. Type **Remind all students of this event**.

d. Click the **Show Comments** arrow in the Comments group on the Review tab. Click **Show Markup** to deselect it and hide the comment.

e. Click the **File tab**, click **Properties** in the right pane, and then click **Advanced Properties**. Make the following changes to the properties:

Property	Change
Title	Martin Luther King, Jr. Commemoration
Subject	Annual MLK Commemoration Flyer
Category	Civil rights
Keywords	Martin Luther King Jr., Commemoration, Flyer, MLK, Ad, civil rights
Comments	Flyer to be mailed, and printed and distributed in the Student Center

f. Click **OK**.

g. Ensure that you are in the Backstage view, click **Check for Issues**, and then click **Check Accessibility**.

h. Note the Accessibility Checker shows two errors and one tip for making the document more accessible. Click **Picture 4 (Slide 1)** in the Inspection Results section of the Accessibility Checker and read why this error needs to be fixed and how to fix the error in the Additional Information section.

i. Click the picture of **Martin Luther King, Jr.**, and click the **Format tab**. Click the **Size dialog box launcher**.

j. Click **Alt Text** in the Format Picture pane and type the following:

Alt Text	Text-Based Representation
Title	Martin Luther King, Jr.
Description	This is an image of Martin Luther King, Jr., an African American leader in the civil rights movement, an activist, and an American clergyman.

k. Proofread what you typed and fix errors as needed. Click **Close** in the Format Picture pane. Leave the Accessibility Checker open.

l. Click **Slide 1** in the Errors section of the Inspection Results section of the Accessibility Checker and read why this error needs to be fixed and how to fix the error in the Additional Information section.

m. Click in the **title placeholder** and type **Martin Luther King, Jr. Commemoration**.

n. Click **Slide 1** displayed under Tips in the Inspection Results section of the Accessibility Checker and read the tip on why reordering the objects on the slide can benefit the comprehension of someone who cannot view the slide.

o. Click the **Home tab**, click **Arrange** in the Drawing group, and then select **Selection Pane**. Ensure that Title 1 is selected and click the **Bring Forward arrow** twice so that the title will be read first by a text reader. Select **Subtitle 2** and click the **Bring Forward arrow** once so that the subtitle will be read next by a text reader. Close the Selection pane and the Accessibility Checker pane.

p. Save the presentation. Click the **File tab**, click **Export**, and then click **Create PDF/XPS Document**.

q. Ensure **Create PDF/XPS** in the right pane is selected and navigate to the folder containing your files. Click **Publish**.

r. Close Adobe Acrobat Reader, Adobe Acrobat, or the window in which the flyer opened.

s. Click the **File tab**, click **Export**, and then click **Create Handouts**.

t. Click **Create Handouts** in the right pane.

u. Click **Notes below slides**. Click **OK**.

v. Delete **Slide 1** in the top-left corner when Word opens. Navigate to where you are saving your files and save the document as **p08p2KingHandout_LastFirst**. Close Word.

w. Click the **File tab**, click **Protect Presentation**, and select **Mark as Final**. Click **OK** twice.

x. Click the **File tab**, click **Share**, and click **Email**. Click **Send as Attachment**. Type the email address of your instructor in the To box of your default email application. Click **Send**.

y. Close the file. Based on your instructor's directions, submit:
p08p2King_LastFirst
p08p2KingHandout_LastFirst

Mid-Level Exercises

1 Protecting Your Computer Training Presentation

As an employee of your company's IT department, you sometimes prepare technology training materials. You are currently preparing a presentation on threats to computer security and computer safety tips. You ask Ben, a colleague in human resources, to review the presentation and insert comments with suggestions. Because the presentation is password protected, you share the password with him. When he returns the presentation, you merge and compare the presentations and decide which suggestions to incorporate. Then you prepare the presentation for distribution and select a presentation file type.

a. Open *p08m1Protect* and save it as **p08m1Protect_LastFirst**.

b. Create a handout header with your name and a handout footer with your instructor's name and your class. Include the current date.

c. Use Protect Presentation to encrypt the presentation with a password for opening. Use **Th>3@t$** as the password.

d. Click **Slide 1**, then create a comment that reads **Ben, please review the presentation and make suggestions. Do I need to add anything? Thank you.**

e. Compare and merge *p08m1ProtectBen* with the open *p08m1Protect_LastFirst*.

f. Note that the Revisions pane lists two changes in the *Presentation Changes* section. Accept both of the presentation changes: *Theme (1-14)* and *Insertions after "How do You Defend Against Spyware."*

g. Start on Slide 1 and advance one by one through the comments on each slide using Next in the Comments group. Read each of the comments and make the following changes based on the comments. Delete the comments after making the changes.

Slide	Comment	Change
2	bb2	Link the *Viruses, Worms, and Trojan Horses* bullet to Slide 3.
2	bb3	Remove the *Protection* bullet.
2	bb4	Change all slide titles to sentence case (the first letter of the sentence is capitalized, with the rest being lowercase unless requiring capitalization for a specific reason) on all slides except Slide 1. (Tip: Use Change Case in the Font group of the Home tab.)
5	bb5	Find and replace all occurrences of *E-mail* with *email*. (Tip: Use Match Case)

h. Check the spelling in the presentation. Change all occurrences of *trojan* to **Trojan**. Ignore the suggestion for *OnGuard*.

i. Accept all changes in the presentation. Close the Revisions and Comments panes if necessary.

j. View the presentation as a Slide Show. Annotate Slide 13, the *What is spam?* slide, by highlighting *spam* in the title to remind you to add a Spam hyperlink to the menu slide. Keep the ink annotations when you exit the slide show. On Slide 2, add **Spam** to the bulleted list and hyperlink it to Slide 13.

k. View the Print Preview for Handouts (4 slides Horizontal per page). Scroll through Print Preview and note the comments. Print as directed by your instructor.

l. Run the Compatibility Checker to check for features not supported by earlier versions of PowerPoint. Note that the SmartArt graphic on Slide 3 and any text in it cannot be edited when using versions of Microsoft Office earlier than Office 2007.

m. Change the file encryption settings for the presentation in General Options. Delete the password in the Password to open box.

n. Make the following changes to the properties:

Property	Change
Title	Protect Your Computer Against Harmful Attacks
Subject	Computer Safety
Category	Training
Keywords	Computer safety, viruses, worms, Trojan horses, spam
Comments	Presentation for Employee Education Program. Reviewed by Ben B.

o. Save the presentation and use the Export option Change File Type to save a version of the file to a PowerPoint Show so that it automatically opens as a slide show. Use the name **p08m1ProtectShow_LastFirst**.

p. Save and close the files. Based on your instructor's directions, submit:

p08m1Protect_LastFirst

p08m1ProtectShow_LastFirst

2 Impressionist Artists

MyITLab®
Grader

You have been refining a presentation on impressionist artists for your Nineteenth Century Art class. In this exercise, you prepare the presentation for distribution, create a handout in Microsoft Word, and then package the presentation. Finally, you present the presentation online to class-mates who will be unable to be in class the day you present.

a. Open *p08m2Impressionism* and save it as **p08m2Impressionism_LastFirst**.

b. Create a handout header with your name and a handout footer with your instructor's name and your class in the presentation. Include the current date.

c. Inspect the presentation for hidden metadata or personal information. Check every type of information, including off-slide content.

d. Remove Document Properties and Personal Information. Do not remove presentation notes.

e. Run the Compatibility Checker to check for features not supported by earlier versions of PowerPoint. Note that earlier versions cannot change the shape and text on Slides 1 and 3.

f. Create handouts in Microsoft Word with notes next to the slides. Insert your name, instructor's name, and class in a header and print as directed by your instructor. Save the Word handout as **p08m2Handout_LastFirst**. Close Word.

g. Use the Package Presentation for CD feature to copy the presentation and media links to the folder where you saved your solution files. Name the CD **Impres_LastFirst**.

h. Use your Microsoft account (or create one) so that you can access the Office Presentation Service.

DISCOVER **i.** Send an email sharing the link for the online presentation with your instructor and start the slide show. After viewing the presentation, end the online presentation.

j. Save and close the file. Based on your instructor's directions, submit:

p08m2Impressionism_LastFirst

p08m2Handout_LastFirst

Impres_LastFirst

3 Rescue Pets

COLLABORATION
CASE
CREATIVE
CASE

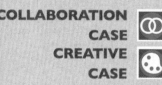

You and your friends volunteer at the local animal shelter each week. You have been asked to put together a short presentation about some of the success stories for matching animals with loving families. The presentation will be used to solicit donations, to recruit more volunteers, and to attract more adoptive families. You and your friends can use OneDrive or pass the presentation among group members as an attachment using your Microsoft accounts.

a. Open *p08m3Pets* and save it as **p08m3Pets_LastFirst**.

b. Add your name on the title slide. Create a handout header with your name and a handout footer with your instructor's name and your class in the presentation. Include the current date.

c. Add one slide with a description and a photo of a pet.

d. Save the presentation and pass it to the next student so that he or she can add their name and add a slide with a pet photo and description. Continue until all group members have created a slide in the presentation.

e. Use Comments to share ideas about the presentations.

f. Ensure that you are on the Review tab, and click the **Show Comments arrow**. Click **Show Markup** to deselect it and hide the comments.

g. Inspect the document and run the Accessibility Checker and the Compatibility Checker. Correct all errors.

h. Create and publish a PDF of the presentation. Name the PDF **p08m3PetsHandout_LastFirst**. Close Adobe Acrobat Reader, Adobe Acrobat, or the window in which the PDF opened.

i. Use the Package Presentation for CD feature to copy the presentation and media links to the folder where you saved your solution files. Name the CD **PetsCD_LastFirst**.

j. Save and close the file. Based on your instructor's directions, submit:

p08m3Pets_LastFirst

p08m3PetsHandout_LastFirst

PetsCD_LastFirst

Beyond the Classroom

Flat Stanley Team Project

GENERAL CASE ✓

Jeff Brown created Flat Stanley, a completely flat boy, in a children's book in 1964. In 1995, Dale Hubert started the Flat Stanley Project to encourage international literacy and community building—a project that has had a phenomenal worldwide impact on collaboration in education. Research the project at www.flatstanley.com. Your goal is to participate in a collaborative project using Flat Stanley by joining with a team of two to three other students in your class.

Each team member must create a Flat Stanley, or download the Flat Stanley template from the website. Team members should journal Flat Stanley's activities for several days by recording them with a digital camera. Each student should create a presentation using their images. Name each presentation **p08b1FS_LastFirst**. Send the presentations to each other via email so everyone can add comments and annotations. When they return the presentations to you, compare and merge the documents. Accept and reject changes as needed to create a cohesive presentation of Flat Stanley's activities. Delete any comments and annotations after reading them. Insert a handout header with your name and a handout footer with your instructor's name and your class. Include the current date. Create presentation properties that could help you locate the presentation. Inspect the document and remove anything that appears except the properties. Check the compatibility of the presentation with earlier versions of PowerPoint. Save the presentation as a PowerPoint Show named **p08b1FlatStanley_LastFirst**. Present the slide show online to your teammates, or package the presentation to a folder including all links. Save and close the file. Based on your instructor's directions, submit:

> p08b1FS_LastFirst
> p08b1FlatStanley_LastFirst

Photography Class Project

DISASTER RECOVERY ✚

As a project for your Art Appreciation class, you contacted a local photographer, Katherine Hulce, and asked her to share several of her digital images with you. The photographer gave you permission to use her images but retained the copyright. You created a presentation to introduce her work and emailed the presentation to her. She returned the presentation with some added images, annotations, comments, and changes.

Open *p08b2Photography* and save it as **p08b2Photography_LastFirst**. Compare and merge the presentation with *p08b2PhotographyHulce*. Accept all changes to the presentation and end the review. As you view each slide, you notice two other photographers are mentioned on Slide 2. Change the slide title to singular and delete their names, leaving only Katherine Hulce's information. Run the Document Inspector to ensure no other photographers' information is included. Remove all comments, annotations, document properties, and personal information. Change the background to Aqua, Background 2. Create a handout header with your name and a handout footer with your instructor's name and your class. Include the current date. Add the photographer's name as key words in the presentation properties. Save the presentation and resave it as a PowerPoint Picture Presentation with the name **p08b2PhotographyShow_LastFirst**. Mark the presentation as final. Save and close the file. Based on your instructor's directions, submit:

> p08b2Photography_LastFirst
> p08b2PhotographyShow_LastFirst

Capstone Exercise

Your sister is starting a bakery business that specializes in wedding cakes. She has put together a presentation that she will use to introduce her services to prospective brides but wants you to give her some ideas for improving it. She emailed the presentation to you so that you can make suggestions and return it to her so that she can incorporate the suggestions in her slides. Then she returns the presentation for you to compare and merge. After accepting the changes, you prepare the presentation for distribution to the brides.

Create Annotations and Comments, Hide Markup

You open the presentation your sister sent to you, then add comments on some slides and make an annotation.

a. Open the *p08c1Cakes* presentation and save it as **p08c1Cakes_LastFirst**.

b. Create a handout header with your name and a handout footer with your instructor's name and your class. Include the current date.

c. Play the slide show from the beginning. On Slide 1, change your pointer options to **Highlighter** and highlight the subtitle text. On Slide 3, highlight the word *desert*.

d. Keep the ink annotations as a reminder of changes you want to suggest when you reach the end of the presentation.

e. Create a comment that reads **Hey Sis, why don't you use this spot to give your business phone number?** on Slide 1. Drag the comment balloon so it is next to the highlighted text.

f. Add a comment that reads **This would be cute as your last slide in the presentation.** On Slide 2.

g. Add a comment that reads **I think you mean dessert.** on Slide 3.

h. Save the presentation.

Merge Presentations

Your sister made the changes you suggested and removed all comments and annotations from her copy. She has returned the presentation to you. You compare and merge your sister's presentation with the presentation you created.

a. Replace **subtitle text** with **(555) 555-5555** on Slide 1. Move Slide 2 to the end of the presentation. Change **desert** to **dessert** on the new Slide 2. Then delete all comments and annotations in the presentation.

b. Compare and merge the onscreen *p08c1Cakes_LastFirst* presentation with *p08c1CakesKathryn*.

c. Accept all changes.

d. Close the Revisions and the Comments panes.

e. Save the presentation.

Inspect the Presentation and Check Compatibility

You inspect the presentation to ensure that only the metadata you want is retained. You run the Compatibility Checker to see if any of the features you used are not supported by earlier versions of PowerPoint.

a. Inspect the presentation for any hidden or personal information. The Document Inspector locates document properties and custom XML data. Do not remove these items. Close the Document Inspector.

b. Run the Compatibility Checker to see if any of the features you used are not supported by earlier versions of PowerPoint. The slide master and layout levels will be lost if you save the presentation in an earlier file format. You do not need to make changes for the earlier version as part of this exercise. Click **OK**.

c. Save the presentation.

Share the Presentation

You are ready to share the presentation as a PowerPoint Picture Presentation that can be emailed to prospective brides or uploaded to the business website.

a. Click Export and select Change File Type.

b. Save the presentation as a PowerPoint Picture Presentation named **p08c1CakesPPPP_LastFirst**.

c. Save the presentation.

Mark as Final

After making a shareable version of the presentation, you plan to indicate that the original presentation is complete. You mark the presentation as final.

a. Mark the presentation as **Final**.

b. Verify that the presentation has been marked as final by checking the status bar for the Mark as Final icon.

c. Close the file. Based on your instructor's directions, submit:

p08c1Cakes_LastFirst
p08c1CakesPPPP_LastFirst

You have worked hard to meet your goal of becoming a school teacher. You are excited to start teaching in the fall and want to be prepared. You began a slide show to introduce science to your students and now want to modify the original slide show to add additional information and visual impact. You will insert slides, change layouts, insert a picture and a video, add WordArt, insert a SmartArt diagram, reuse a slide, and create a table. You will also add a transition and animations.

Set Up Presentation

You open the original slide show, rename the file, and save it.

a. Open *pApp_Cap1_Science* and save the file as **pApp_Cap1_Science_LastFirst**.

b. Create a Notes and Handouts header and footer with the date, the page number, your name in the header, and your instructor's name and your class in the footer.

c. Replace *Student Name* with your name on **Slide 1**.

Use WordArt, Format a Background, Add a Video

You decide to enhance the presentation introduction by changing text to WordArt. In addition, you change the background to enhance the slide show. You add a video clip to a slide.

a. Click **Slide 2**. Select the text in the title placeholder and apply the WordArt style **Fill - White, Text 1, Outline - Background 1, Hard Shadow - Background 1**.

b. Select the title placeholder and change the shape fill to **Red, Accent 6, Darker 25%**.

c. Click the **View tab**, select **Outline view**, select the **subtitle placeholder** on Slide 2, and then type **The word "Science" means "knowledge" in Latin**. Switch to Normal view.

d. Insert a new slide after **Slide 2** using the **Two Content layout**. Type **Science is:** in the title placeholder. Type **A collection of knowledge that is used to explain the world around us.** in the left content placeholder and **A way of uncovering new pieces of knowledge.** in the right content placeholder.

e. Click the **Design tab** and click **Format Background**. Insert a picture fill using *pApp_Cap1_DNA*.

f. Select both content placeholders, then change the font size to **36 pt** and the font color to **Gray-80%, Background 2**.

g. Change the transparency of the background to **50%**.

h. Use the content placeholder on **Slide 4** to insert the video *pApp_Cap1_Questions*.

i. Add a speaker note that reads **Science explains what is happening in the world around us. Science uses the scientific method to do this.**

Add SmartArt and Shapes

You create a SmartArt graphic and shapes to explain The Scientific Method. After completing the diagram, you animate it.

a. Create **Slide 5** using the **Blank layout**. Insert a **Vertical Bending Process** SmartArt diagram.

b. Open the Text pane and type the following:
  - **Ask a question**
  - **Do research**
  - **Construct hypothesis**
  - **Test hypothesis**
  - **Draw a conclusion**

c. Remove the four empty [Text] bullet points.

d. Close the Text Pane. Deselect the Draw shape, select the SmartArt, and then **Align Left**.

e. Select the *Draw a conclusion* shape and make two copies.

f. Position one copy of the *Draw a conclusion* shape at **8.9"** horizontally from the **Top Left Corner** and **0.84"** vertically from the **Top Left Corner**. Replace the *Draw a conclusion* text with **Try again**.

g. Select the remaining copy of the *Draw a conclusion* shape and replace the *Draw a conclusion* text with **Hypothesis is proven**. Drag the shape containing the *Hypothesis is proven* text to the right using the SmartGuides to align it with the center of the *Draw a conclusion* shape and with the left side of the *Try again* shape.

h. Create an arrow connecting the *Draw a conclusion* shape to the *Try again* shape. Change the weight of the arrow to **6 pt** and change the shape outline to **Red, Accent 6**.

i. Group the arrow and the *Try again* shape. Deselect the grouped shapes.

j. Create an arrow connecting the *Draw a conclusion* shape to the *Hypothesis is proven* shape. Change the weight of the arrow to **6 pt** and change the shape outline to **Red, Accent 6**.

k. Group the new arrow and the *Hypothesis is proven* shape.

l. Select the SmartArt and apply the **Float In** animation. Set the animation to start **With Previous**.

m. Select the *Try again* group and apply the **Wipe** animation with the **From Left** effect.

n. Select the *Hypothesis is proven* group and apply the **Wipe** animation with the **From Left** effect.

o. Add a speaker note that says **Trying again is not a failure. When results disprove a hypothesis the scientist has gained new knowledge.**

Add Content and Animation

You reuse a previously created slide to add content, and you modify the layout on the reused slide to make it easier to read and understand.

a. Select **Slide 3** and use the Reuse Slides feature to add the slide *pApp_Cap1_Fields* so that it becomes Slide 4. Close the Reuse Slides pane.

b. Change the slide layout to **Blank**.

c. Select the SmartArt and change the layout to **Organization Chart**.

d. Change the height of the SmartArt to **7.5"** and the width to **11.78"**.

e. Reposition the SmartArt so that it is in the **center** of the slide.

f. Select the **Biology shape**, click **Layout** in the Create Graphic group on the Design tab, and change the layout to **Both**.

g. Repeat Step f for the Chemistry and Physics shapes.

h. Change the SmartArt style to **Powder**.

i. Change the SmartArt colors to **Colorful Range – Accent Colors 5 to 6**.

j. Apply the **Wipe animation** (Entrance category) to the SmartArt. Change the sequence of the animation to the **One by One effect**.

Add a Table

You add a table to the slide show showing science disciplines that combine knowledge of all three fields of science to uncover facts.

a. Insert a **Title and Content** slide at the end of the slide show.

b. Add the title **Disciplines Requiring Combined Knowledge**.

c. Create a table with **4 columns** and **6 rows** in the content placeholder.

d. Type the following table:

Discipline	Biology knowledge	Chemistry knowledge	Physics knowledge
Biochemistry	X	X	
Genetics	X	X	
Forensic science	X	X	X
Geology	X	X	X
Nuclear chemistry		X	X

e. Select the cells with Xs as their content and change the paragraph alignment to **Center**.

Insert and Modify a Picture

You want to introduce the Applied Science section with a picture. You insert a picture and add a picture frame to the image.

a. Create a new slide, **Slide 8**, with the **Panoramic Picture with Caption** layout. Insert *pApp_Cap1_Structure*.

b. Apply the **Metal Oval** picture style.

c. Type **Applied Science** in the title placeholder. Delete the subtitle placeholder.

d. Select the title placeholder and change the shape fill to **Red, Accent 6, Darker 25%**.

e. Change the height of the title placeholder to **1.75"**.

f. Change the size of the font in the title placeholder to **96 pt**.

Finalize the Presentation

To ensure the professionalism of the presentation, you review the presentation and make changes.

a. Check the spelling of the presentation and correct any misspelled words.

b. View the presentation in **Slide Show view** and note that Slide 4 does not appear in the correct order in the slide show. Close the slide show.

c. View the presentation in **Slide Sorter view**. Drag Slide 4 so it becomes Slide 6.

d. Apply the **Orbit transition** to all slides.

e. Change the transition timing so that all slides advance automatically after 8 seconds.

f. View the presentation in **Reading View**.

g. Save and close the file. Based on your instructor's directions, submit pApp_Cap1_Science_LastFirst.

As a member of the local school district's STEM committee, you have been asked to help create the opening presentation for the upcoming exhibition at the Regional Expo Center. The exhibition is intended to build interest in expanding the STEM curriculum within the local school district and to seek funding from local business owners and taxpayers. Some of the slides will be printed as posters and handouts for distribution at the conference. Charts will be used to highlight facts about the planets and a table will display pertinent facts about the exhibition schedule. You will also apply some animations, insert hyperlinks, and work with the slide master.

Create the Presentation

    a. Start PowerPoint. Open *p00ac2Planets* and save the file as **p00ac2Planets_LastFirst**.

    b. Set the Slide Size to **Widescreen (16:9)**. Ensure that the Orientation for Slides is **Landscape** and Handouts is set to **Portrait**.

Design a Table and Change the Table Layout

    a. Click **Slide 2** and insert a table with 3 columns and 4 rows. Change the design to **Medium Style 2 – Accent 2**. Add the following information to the table:

Left Column	Middle Column	Right Column
Welcome to Our World	9:00 AM	10:00 AM
Sizing Up the Planets	10:00 AM	11:00 AM
Reaching for the Stars	11:00 AM	12:00 PM
Let's Get Involved (Luncheon)	12:00 PM	1:30 PM

    b. Insert a new top row to the table. Add the following information to the new row:

Left Column	Middle Column	Right Column
EVENT	START	END

    c. Add a new first column to the table. Merge all the cells in the first column and format the cell in the first column with a picture fill using the *p00ac2World* file.

    d. Size table to **3.2" high by 11.08" wide**. Center all of the text in the table vertically and horizontally. Apply the **Riblet Cell Bevel effect** to all cells of the table.

Create and Insert a Chart, Change a Chart Type, and Change the Chart Layout

    a. Click **Slide 3**, copy the chart found in the downloaded Excel file *p00ac2Size,* and paste it on the slide. Use the destination theme. Change the height of the object to **4.4"** and center it on the slide.

    b. Click **Slide 4** and insert a **Clustered Column** chart. When Excel opens, resize the chart data range to **A1:B10**. Delete the contents of the cells in columns C and D. Replace the remaining content in the Excel worksheet with the following data:

    Cell A2: Mercury

    Cell A3: Venus

    Cell A4: Earth

    Cell A5: Mars

    Cell A6: Jupiter

    Cell A7: Saturn

    Cell A8: Uranus

    Cell A9: Neptune

    Cell A10: Pluto (dwarf planet)

    Cell B1: Average Distance in Astronomical Units

Cell **B2**: **0.381**

Cell **B3**: **0.7219**

Cell **B4**: **1.002**

Cell **B5**: **1.52**

Cell **B6**: **5.2**

Cell **B7**: **9.55**

Cell **B8**: **19.25**

Cell **B9**: **30**

Cell **B10**: **39.5**

Close Excel.

c. Change the chart to a **Line with Markers** chart. Apply **Style 8** in the Chart Style group to the chart. Set the Fill to **Teal, Accent 2, Lighter 60%.** Close the Format pane.

Insert and Use a Hyperlink and Add an Action Button

a. Click **Slide 5** and insert a hyperlink from the text *MARS STUDENT IMAGING PROJECT* to the webpage **http://mars.nasa.gov/msip**. Add the ScreenTip **Click for additional information** to the hyperlink.

b. Click **Slide 6**, select the phrase *Contact us today!*, and insert an email hyperlink to **Student@email.com**

c. Insert a hyperlink from the text *HOW CAN I HELP?* to the downloaded Word document *p00ac2Feedback*.

d. Insert an **Action Button: Beginning** shape by clicking in the bottom-left corner of the slide. Set the action button to link to **Slide 2** (Exhibition schedule) when clicked. Size the action button to **0.57" by 0.99"**. Move the action button to the **lower-right corner** of the slide. Copy the button to **Slides 3-5**.

Apply a Motion Path Animation and Specify Animation Settings and Timings

a. Click **Slide 5** and apply a **Fly In Entrance animation** to the text placeholder on the left. Set the Effect Options so that the text flies in from the top left. Set the Delay to **00.75**. Use the Animation Pane to set the animation for each bullet to **Start After Previous**.

b. Apply the **Fly In Entrance animation** to the text placeholder on the right. Set the Effect Options so that the text flies in from the top right. Set the Duration to **01.00** and the Delay to **01.25**. Set the Start to **After Previous**. Close the Animation Pane.

c. Click **Slide 7** and add an action to the words *TO INSPIRE OUR CHILDREN* so that when they are clicked, the **Applause** sound is played.

Customize the Ribbon

a. Create a custom tab to the right of the Home tab. Name the tab **Shapes**. Name the group in the tab **Combine Shapes**. Include the following buttons from the *Commands Not in the Ribbon* list in the Combine Shapes group: Combine Shapes, Intersect Shapes, Subtract Shapes, and Union Shapes.

Use Combine Shapes Commands

a. Switch to **Slide Master view**. There are three shapes in the top-right corner of the top-level Slide Master. Combine the three shapes. Remove the slide number placeholder from the slide.

Modify a Slide Master, Handout, and Notes Master

a. Apply the **Calibri Font theme** to the Slide Master. Beginning with the Section Header Layout, delete the remaining slide layouts that are not associated with a numbered slide.

b. Switch to **Handout Master view**. Change the page setup to **2 Slides** per page. Delete the Header placeholder.

c. Switch to **Notes Master view**. Type **Page** followed by a space before the number field in the Page Number placeholder. Close Notes Master view.

Hide Slides and Create a Custom Slide Show

a. Hide **Slide 5** in the presentation.

b. Create a new custom slide show named **Planets Show** using Slides 1, 2, 3, 4, and 6 (in that order). Start the custom show from the beginning.

Work with Comments and Annotations

a. Click **Slide 2**. Use the Highlight tool with the default color to highlight the words *Start* and *End* in the table. Disable the highlight tool and proceed through the presentation to the Planetary Size Range slide.

b. Ensure that the Planetary Size Range slide is selected and use the Pen tool to draw a **circle** around the left axis. Stop making annotations and exit the slide show. Save the annotations that you have made.

c. Insert the comment **Should we allow 15 minutes between each event as a break time?** on Slide 2.

d. Insert the comment **Let's get rid of these labels.** on Slide 3.

Check a Presentation for Issues and Protect a Presentation

a. Run the Compatibility Checker to see which features are used that are not supported by earlier versions of PowerPoint, but do not make any changes as a result.

b. Save the presentation. Mark the presentation as final.

c. Close the presentation and exit PowerPoint. Based on your instructor's directions, submit p00ac2Planets_LastFirst.

Microsoft Office 2016 Specialist PowerPoint

Online Appendix materials can be found in the Student Resources located at www.pearsonhighered.com/exploring.

MOS Obj Number	Objective Text	Exploring Chapter	Exploring Section
1.0 Create and Manage Presentations			
1.1 Create a Presentation			
1.1.1	create a new presentation	**Chapter 1**, Introduction to PowerPoint	Planning and Preparing a Presentation
1.1.2	create a presentation based on a template	**Chapter 1**, Introduction to PowerPoint	Planning and Preparing a Presentation
1.1.3	import Word document outlines	**Chapter 2**, Presentation Development	Importing an Outline
1.2 Insert and Format Slides			
1.2.1	insert specific slide layouts	**Chapter 1**, Introduction to PowerPoint	Adding Presentation Content
1.2.2	duplicate existing slides	**Chapter 3**, Presentation Design	Capstone Exercise
1.2.3	hide and unhide slides	**Chapter 7**, Customization	Designating and Displaying Hidden Slides
1.2.4	delete slides	**Chapter 2**, Presentation Development	Hands -On Exercise 1
1.2.5	apply a different slide layout	**Chapter 2**, Presentation Development, Online Appendix	Modifying a Presentation Based on a Template, Online Appendix
1.2.6	modify individual slide backgrounds	**Chapter 2**, Presentation Development	Modifying a Presentation Based on a Template
1.2.7	insert slide headers, footers, and page numbers	**Chapter 1**, Introduction to PowerPoint	Inserting a Header or Footer
1.3 Modify Slides, Handouts, and Notes			
1.3.1	change the slide master theme or background	**Chapter 2**, Presentation Development	Modifying a Theme
1.3.2	modify slide master content	**Chapter 2**, Presentation Development	Modifying the Slide Master
1.3.3	create a slide layout	**Chapter 2**, Presentation Development, Online Appendix	Modifying the Slide Master, Online Appendix
1.3.4	modify a slide layout	**Chapter 1**, Introduction to PowerPoint	Adding Presentation Content
1.3.5	modify the handout master	**Chapter 7**, Customization	Modifying Handout and Notes Masters
1.3.6	modify the notes master	**Chapter 7**, Customization	Modifying Handout and Notes Masters
1.4 Order and Group Slides			
1.4.1	create sections	**Chapter 2**, Presentation Development	Using Sections
1.4.2	modify slide order	**Chapter 1**, Introduction to PowerPoint	Reviewing the Presentation

MOS Obj Number	Objective Text	Exploring Chapter	Exploring Section
1.4.3	rename sections	**Chapter 2**, Presentation Development	Using Sections
1.5 **Change Presentation Options and Views**			
1.5.1	change slide size	**Chapter 1**, Introduction to PowerPoint	Printing in PowerPoint
1.5.2	change views of a presentation	**Chapter 1**, Introduction to PowerPoint	Opening and Viewing a PowerPoint Presentation
1.5.3	set file properties	**Chapter 8**, Collaboration and Distribution, Online Appendix	Viewing Presentation Properties, Online Appendix
1.6 **Configure a Presentation for Print**			
1.6.1	print all or part of a presentation	**Chapter 1**, Introduction to PowerPoint	Printing in PowerPoint
1.6.2	print notes pages	**Chapter 1**, Introduction to PowerPoint	Printing in PowerPoint
1.6.3	print handouts	**Chapter 1**, Introduction to PowerPoint	Printing in PowerPoint
1.6.4	print in color, grayscale, or black and white	**Chapter 1**, Introduction to PowerPoint	Printing in PowerPoint
1.7 **Configure and Present a Slide Show**			
1.7.1	create custom slide shows	**Chapter 7**, Customization	Creating a Custom Slide Show
1.7.2	configure slide show options	Online Appendix	Online Appendix
1.7.3	rehearse slide show timing	**Chapter 1**, Introduction to PowerPoint	Opening and Viewing a PowerPoint Presentation
1.7.4	present a slide show by using Presenter View	**Chapter 1**, Introduction to PowerPoint	Opening and Viewing a PowerPoint Presentation
2.0 **Insert and Format Text, Shapes, and Images**			
2.1 **Insert and Format Text**			
2.1.1	insert text on a slide	**Chapter 1**, Introduction to PowerPoint	Opening and Viewing a PowerPoint Presentation
2.1.2	apply formatting and styles to text	**Chapter 2**, Presentation Development	Reusing Slides from an Existing Presentation
2.1.3	apply WordArt styles to text	**Chapter 3**, Presentation Design	Creating WordArt and Modifying WordArt
2.1.4	format text in multiple columns	**Chapter 1**, Introduction to PowerPoint, Online Appendix	Adding Presentation Content, Online Appendix
2.1.5	create bulleted and numbered lists	**Chapter 1**, Introduction to PowerPoint	Adding Presentation Content
2.1.6	insert hyperlinks	**Chapter 4**, Enhancing with Multimedia	Using the Internet as a Resource
2.2 **Insert and Format Shapes and Text Boxes**			
2.2.1	insert or replace shapes	**Chapter 3**, Presentation Design	Creating Shapes
2.2.2	insert text boxes	**Chapter 3**, Presentation Design	Creating Shapes
2.2.3	resize shapes and text boxes	**Chapter 3**, Presentation Design	Creating Shapes

MOS Obj Number	Objective Text	Exploring Chapter	Exploring Section
2.2.4	format shapes and text boxes	**Chapter 3**, Presentation Design	Applying Quick Styles and Customizing Shapes
2.2.5	apply styles to shapes and text boxes	**Chapter 3**, Presentation Design	Applying Quick Styles and Customizing Shapes
2.3	**Insert and Format Images**		
2.3.1	insert images	**Chapter 4**, Enhancing with Multimedia	Inserting a Picture
2.3.2	resize and crop images	**Chapter 4**, Enhancing with Multimedia	Transforming a Picture
2.3.3	apply styles and effects	**Chapter 4**, Enhancing with Multimedia	Transforming a Picture
2.4	**Order and Group Objects**		
2.4.1	order objects	**Chapter 3**, Presentation Design	Arranging Objects
2.4.2	align objects	**Chapter 3**, Presentation Design	Arranging Objects
2.4.3	group objects	**Chapter 3**, Presentation Design	Modifying Objects
2.4.4	display alignment tools	**Chapter 3**, Presentation Design	Modifying Objects

3.0　Insert Tables, Charts, SmartArt, and Media

3.1	**Insert and Format Tables**		
3.1.1	create a table	**Chapter 1**, Introduction to PowerPoint	Adding a Table
3.1.2	insert and delete table rows and columns	**Chapter 1**, Introduction to PowerPoint	Adding a Table
3.1.3	apply table styles	**Chapter 5**, Posters, Tables, and Statistical Charts	Formatting Table Components
3.1.4	import a table	**Chapter 5**, Posters, Tables, and Statistical Charts	Sharing Information Between Applications
3.2	**Insert and Format Charts**		
3.2.1	create a chart	**Chapter 5**, Posters, Tables, and Statistical Charts	Creating and Inserting Charts
3.2.2	import a chart	Online Appendix	Online Appendix
3.2.3	change the Chart Type	**Chapter 5**, Posters, Tables, and Statistical Charts	Changing a Chart Type
3.2.4	add a legend to a chart	Online Appendix	Online Appendix
3.2.5	change the chart style of a chart	Online Appendix	Online Appendix
3.3	**Insert and Format SmartArt graphics**		
3.3.1	create SmartArt graphics	**Chapter 3**, Presentation Design	Creating SmartArt
3.3.2	convert lists to SmartArt graphics	**Chapter 3**, Presentation Design	Creating SmartArt
3.3.3	add shapes to SmartArt graphics	**Chapter 3**, Presentation Design	Modifying SmartArt
3.3.4	reorder shapes in SmartArt graphics	**Chapter 3**, Presentation Design	Modifying SmartArt
3.3.5	change the color of SmartArt graphics	**Chapter 3**, Presentation Design	Modifying SmartArt
3.4	**Insert and Manage Media**		
3.4.1	insert audio and video clips	**Chapter 4**, Enhancing with Multimedia	Adding Video

MOS Obj Number	Objective Text	Exploring Chapter	Exploring Section
3.4.2	configure media playback options	**Chapter 4**, Enhancing with Multimedia	Using Video Tools
3.4.3	adjust media window size	**Chapter 4**, Enhancing with Multimedia	Using Video Tools
3.4.4	set the video start and stop time	**Chapter 4**, Enhancing with Multimedia	Using Video Tools
3.4.5	set media timing options	**Chapter 4**, Enhancing with Multimedia	Using Video Tools

4.0 Apply Transitions and Animations

4.1 Apply Slide Transitions

MOS Obj Number	Objective Text	Exploring Chapter	Exploring Section
4.1.1	insert slide transitions	**Chapter 1**, Introduction to PowerPoint	Applying Transitions and Animations
4.1.2	set transition effect options	**Chapter 1**, Introduction to PowerPoint	Applying Transitions and Animations

4.2 Animate Slide Content

MOS Obj Number	Objective Text	Exploring Chapter	Exploring Section
4.2.1	apply animations to objects	**Chapter 1**, Introduction to PowerPoint	Applying Transitions and Animations
4.2.2	apply animations to text	**Chapter 1**, Introduction to PowerPoint	Applying Transitions and Animations
4.2.3	set animation effect options	**Chapter 1**, Introduction to PowerPoint	Applying Transitions and Animations
4.2.4	set animation paths	**Chapter 6**, Engaging an Audience, Online Appendix	Applying a Motion Path Animation, Online Appendix

4.3 Set Timing for Transitions and Animations

MOS Obj Number	Objective Text	Exploring Chapter	Exploring Section
4.3.1	set transition effect duration	**Chapter 1**, Introduction to PowerPoint	Applying Transitions and Animations
4.3.2	configure transition start and finish options	**Chapter 6**, Engaging an Audience, Online Appendix	Using the Animation Pane, Online Appendix
4.3.3	reorder animations on a slide	**Chapter 6**, Engaging an Audience, Online Appendix	Applying Multiple Animations to An Object, Online Appendix

5.0 Manage Multiple Presentations

5.1 Merge Content from Multiple Presentations

MOS Obj Number	Objective Text	Exploring Chapter	Exploring Section
5.1.1	insert slides from another presentation	**Chapter 2**, Presentation Development	Reusing Slides from an Existing Presentation
5.1.2	compare two presentations	**Chapter 8**, Collaboration and Distribution, Online Appendix	Comparing and Merging Presentations, Online Appendix
5.1.3	insert comments	**Chapter 8**, Collaboration and Distribution, Online Appendix	Comparing and Merging Presentations, Online Appendix
5.1.4	review comments	**Chapter 8**, Collaboration and Distribution, Online Appendix	Working with Comments and Annotations, Online Appendix

5.2 Finalize Presentations

MOS Obj Number	Objective Text	Exploring Chapter	Exploring Section
5.2.1	protect a presentation	**Chapter 8**, Collaboration and Distribution, Online Appendix	Protecting a Presentation, Online Appendix

MOS Obj Number	Objective Text	Exploring Chapter	Exploring Section
5.2.2	inspect a presentation	**Chapter 8**, Collaboration and Distribution, Online Appendix	Checking a Presentation for Issues, Online Appendix
5.2.3	proof a presentation	**Chapter 1**, Introduction to PowerPoint	Reviewing the Presentation
5.2.4	preserve presentation content	**Chapter 8**, Collaboration and Distribution, Online Appendix	Selecting a Presentation File Type, Online Appendix
5.2.5	export presentations to other formats	**Chapter 8**, Collaboration and Distribution, Online Appendix	Selecting a Presentation File Type, Online Appendix

Glossary

.exportedUI The file extension assigned to an exported User Interface (UI) customized file.

.potx The file extension assigned to a PowerPoint template.

Accessibility Checker A tool that aids in identifying and resolving accessibility issues in a presentation.

Accessibility The ease with which a person with physical challenges is able to access and understand a presentation.

Access A relational database management system in which you can record and link data, query databases, and create forms and reports.

Action button A ready-made button designed to serve as an icon that can initiate an action when clicked, pointed to, or moused over.

Adjustment handle A yellow circle on a shape that is used to change the shape.

Alternative text (alt text) A text-based description of an image.

Animation An action used to draw interest to an object in a presentation; a movement that controls the entrance, emphasis, exit, and/or path of objects in a slide show.

Annotation A marking that is either written or drawn on a slide for additional commentary or explanation while the slide is displayed.

Area chart Used to emphasize the magnitude of change over time.

Background Styles gallery A gallery providing both solid color and background styles for application to a theme.

Background The portion of a picture that can be deleted when removing the background of a picture.

Backstage view A component of Office that provides a concise collection of commands related to an open file.

Bar chart Used to show comparisons between items.

Basic custom show A single presentation file that is separate from a main (original) presentation that includes some of the slides of the main presentation.

Bitmap image An image created by bits or pixels placed on a grid to form a picture.

Bookmark A method used to mark specific locations in a video.

Brightness A picture correction that controls the lightness or darkness of a picture.

Bubble chart Used to show fluctuations or the range of change between the high and low values of a subject over time.

Callout A shape that be can used to add notes, often used in cartooning.

Chart area The chart and all of its elements bounded by the placeholder borders.

Chart elements icon An icon used to show, hide, or format the chart title, data labels, or legend.

Chart filters icon Shows or hides data in a chart.

Clipboard An area of memory reserved to temporarily hold selections that have been cut or copied and allows you to paste the selections.

Cloud storage A technology used to store files and to work with programs that are stored in a central location on the Internet.

Codec (coder/decoder) A digital video compression scheme used to compress a video and decompress for playback.

Collaboration A process by which two or more individuals work together to achieve an outcome or goal.

Collapsed outline An Outline view that displays only the slide number, icon, and title of each slide in Outline view.

Colors gallery A set of colors available for every theme.

Color theme Consists of the color combinations for the text, lines, background, and graphics in a presentation.

Column chart Used to show data changes over a period of time or comparisons among items.

Column headers The text in the top row of the table that identifies the contents of the columns.

Command A button or area within a group that you click to perform tasks.

Comment A text note attached to a slide that can be inserted or removed as needed.

Compatibility Checker A tool that checks for features in a presentation that are not supported by earlier versions of PowerPoint.

Compression A method applied to data to reduce the amount of space required for file storage.

Contextual tab A tab that contains a group of commands related to the selected object.

Contrast The difference between the darkest and lightest areas of a picture.

Copyright The legal protection afforded to a written or artistic work.

Copy A command used to duplicate a selection from the original location and place a copy in the Office Clipboard.

Crop The process of reducing an image size by eliminating unwanted portions of an image or other graphical object.

Custom button An action button that can be set to trigger unique actions in a presentation.

Customize Ribbon tab A tab in the PowerPoint Options dialog box that enables you to create a personal tab on the Ribbon that includes features that are not available on the standard Ribbon.

Custom path An animation path that can be created freehand instead of following a preset path.

Custom Slide Show A grouped subset of the slides in a presentation.

Cut A command used to remove a selection from the original location and place it in the Office Clipboard.

Data series A chart element that contains the data points representing a set of related numbers.

Deck A collection of slides.

Destination application The application into which an object is being inserted, such as PowerPoint.

Destination file The file that contains an inserted object, such as a PowerPoint presentation with an Excel worksheet embedded in it.

Dialog Box Launcher A button that when clicked opens a corresponding dialog box.

Dialog box A box that provides access to more precise, but less frequently used, commands.

Digital signature An invisible, electronic signature stamp that is encrypted and attached to a certificate that can be added to a presentation.

Distribute To divide or evenly spread selected shapes over a given area.

Document Inspector A tool that detects hidden and personal data in the presentation.

Document property An attribute, such as an author's name or keyword, that describes a file.

Doughnut chart Used to show the relationship of parts to a whole; like a pie chart, but can contain more than one data series.

Effects gallery A range of special effects for shapes used in the presentation.

Embedded object An inserted part of the destination file that, once inserted, no longer maintains a connection to the source file or source application in which the object was created.

Embed A method of storing an object from an external source within a presentation.

Emphasis A PowerPoint animation type that draws attention to an object already on a slide.

Encryption A method used to protect the contents of your presentation by converting it into unreadable scrambled text that requires a password to be opened.

Enhanced ScreenTip A small message box that displays when you place the pointer over a command button. The purpose of the command, short descriptive text, or a keyboard shortcut if applicable will display in the box.

Entrance A PowerPoint animation type that controls how an object moves onto or appears on a slide.

Excel An application that makes it easy to organize records, financial transactions, and business information in the form of worksheets.

Exit A PowerPoint animation type that controls how an object leaves or disappears from a slide.

Expanded outline An Outline view that displays the slide number, icon, title, and content of each slide in the Outline view.

Exploded pie chart A pie chart emphasizing data by separating, or exploding, slices from the pie.

eXtensible Markup Language (XML) A set of encoding rules that creates a file format that is designed to provide maximum flexibility when storing and exchanging structured information.

Eyedropper tool A tool used to recreate an exact color.

Flatten A method used to convert all objects on a slide to a single layer.

Flip To reverse the direction an object faces.

Flow chart An illustration showing the sequence of a project or plan containing steps.

Fonts gallery A gallery that pairs a title font with a body font.

Footer Information that displays at the bottom of a document page.

Foreground The portion of the picture that is kept when removing the background of a picture.

Format Painter A feature that enables you to quickly and easily copy all formatting from one area to another in Word, PowerPoint, and Excel.

Freeform shape A shape that combines both curved and straight-line segments.

Gallery An area in Word which provides additional text styles. In Excel, the gallery provides a choice of chart styles, and in Power Point, the gallery provides transitions.

Gradient fill A fill that contains a blend of two or more colors or shades.

Gridline A line that extends from the horizontal or vertical axis, and that can be displayed to make chart data easier to read and understand.

Group (PowerPoint) Multiple objects connected so they are able to move as though they are a single object.

Group A subset of a tab that organizes similar tasks together.

Handout master Contains the design information for audience handout pages.

Header An area with one or more lines of information at the top of each page.

Hierarchy A method used to organize text into levels of importance in a structure.

HSL A color model in which the number system refers to the hue, saturation, and luminosity of a color.

Hyperlinked custom shows A main custom show that uses hyperlinks to link to one or more other presentations enabling the user to quickly move between presentations.

Hyperlink A connection that branches to another slide or another location that contains additional information.

Infographic Informational graphic that is a visual representation of data or knowledge.

Infringement of copyright A situation that occurs when a right of the copyright owner is violated.

Interactivity The ability to branch or interact with a presentation based on decisions made by a viewer or audience.

Kelvin The unit of measurement for absolute temperature used to measure the tone of an image.

Kiosk An interactive computer terminal available for public use.

Label A chart element that identifies data in the chart.

Landscape orientation A document layout when a page is wider than it is tall.

Layout Determines the position of the objects or content on a slide.

Leaders The lines used to connect a label to a slice of pie in a pie chart.

Legend A chart element found in multi-series charts used to help identify the data series; assigns a format or color to each data series and then displays that information with the data series name.

Linear presentation A presentation where each slide is designed to move one right after another, and the viewer or audience progresses through slides, starting with the first slide and advancing sequentially until the last slide is reached.

Line chart Used to display a large number of data points over time.

Line weight The width or thickness of a shape's outline.

Linked object An inserted part of the destination file that is updated when the source file is updated because the information is actually stored in the source file, not the destination file.

Link A connection from the presentation to another location such as a storage device or website.

Live Preview An Office feature that provides a preview of the results of a selection when you point to an option in a list or gallery. Using Live Preview, you can experiment with settings before making a final choice.

Lock Drawing Mode Enables the creation of multiple shapes of the same type.

Margin The area of blank space that displays to the left, right, top, and bottom of a document or worksheet.

Markup Comments and ink annotations that appear in a presentation.

Master Contains design information to control the layouts, background designs, and color combinations for handouts, notes pages, and slides, giving the presentation a consistent appearance.

Metadata Data that describes other data.

Microsoft Office A productivity software suite including a set of software applications, each one specializing in a particular type of output.

Mini toolbar A toolbar that provides access to the most common formatting selections, such as adding bold or italic, or changing font type or color. Unlike the Quick Access Toolbar, the Mini toolbar is not customizable.

Motion path A PowerPoint animation type that controls the movement of an object from one position to another along a predetermined path.

Multimedia Various forms of media used to entertain or inform an audience.

Multiple Masters A presentation containing two or more themes in the slide master.

Multi-Series chart A chart showing two or more sets of data.

Narration Spoken commentary that is added to a presentation.

Non-linear presentation A presentation that progresses according to choices made by the viewer or audience that determine which slide comes next.

Normal view (PowerPoint) The default PowerPoint workspace.

Notes master Contains the design information for notes pages.

Notes Page view Used for entering and editing large amounts of text to which the speaker can refer when presenting.

Nudge Move an object in small, precise increments.

Object linking and embedding (OLE) A feature that enables the insertion of an object created in one application into a document created in another application.

OneDrive for Business A Microsoft service that provides cloud storage so that files can be stored, shared, and synced from any location or device with Internet connection for workplace collaboration.

OneDrive Microsoft's cloud storage system. Saving files to OneDrive enables them to sync across all Windows devices and to be accessible from any Internet-connected device.

Opaque A solid fill, one with no transparency.

OpenDocument presentation (*.odp) A presentation that conforms to the OpenDocument standard for exchanging data between applications.

Outline view (PowerPoint) A view showing the presentation in an outline format displayed in levels according to the points and any subpoints on each slide.

Outline view A structural view of a document that can be collapsed or expanded as necessary.

Outline A method of organizing text in a hierarchy to depict relationships.

Package Presentation for CD A PowerPoint feature that enables you to copy a presentation, its fonts, linked items, and embedded items to a CD or folder for distribution.

Paste A command used to place a cut or copied selection into another location.

PDF file format (.pdf) A more secure electronic file format created by Adobe Systems that preserves document formatting and is viewable and printable on any platform.

Photo Album A presentation containing multiple pictures organized into album pages.

Picture fill Inserts an image from a file into a shape.

Picture A graphic file that is retrieved from storage media or the Internet and placed in an Office project.

Pie chart Used to show proportions of a whole.

Plain text format (.txt) A file format that retains only text but no formatting when you transfer documents between applications or platforms.

Plot area The region containing the graphical representation of the values in the data series.

Point The smallest unit of measurement used in typography, 1/72 of an inch.

Portrait orientation A document layout when a page is taller than it is wide.

Poster Frame The image that displays on a slide when a video is not playing.

PowerPoint Options A broad range of settings that enable you to customize the environment to meet your needs.

PowerPoint presentation An electronic slide show that can be edited or delivered in a variety of ways.

PowerPoint show An unchangeable electronic slide show format used for distribution.

PowerPoint An application that enables you to create dynamic presentations to inform groups and persuade audiences.

Presenter view Specialty view that delivers a presentation on two monitors simultaneously.

Present Online A Microsoft service that enables the transmission of a presentation in real time over the Internet to a remote audience.

Public domain The rights to a literary work or property owned by the public at large.

Quick Access Toolbar A toolbar located at the top-left corner of any Office application window, that provides fast access to commonly executed tasks such as saving a file and undoing recent actions.

Quick Style A combination of formatting options that can be applied to a shape or graphic.

Reading View Displays the slide show full screen, one slide at a time, complete with animations and transitions.

Recolor The process of changing a picture by adjusting the image's colors.

Reviewer Someone who examines the presentation and provides feedback.

RGB A numeric system for identifying the color resulting from the combination of red, green, and blue light.

Ribbon The command center of Office applications. It is the long bar located just beneath the title bar, containing tabs, groups, and commands.

Rich Text Format (.rtf) A file format that retains structure and most text formatting when transferring documents between applications or platforms.

Rotate To move an object around its axis.

Saturation A characteristic of color that controls its intensity.

ScreenTip An object that displays when the viewer mouses over a hyperlink or other object and provides additional information about the hyperlink or object.

Section A division to presentation content that groups slides meaningfully.

Selection net A selection of multiple objects created by dragging a rectangle around all of the objects you wish to select.

Selection pane A pane designed to help select objects.

Shape A geometric or non-geometric object, such as a rectangle or an arrow, used to create an illustration or highlight information.

Sharpening A technique that enhances the edges of the content in a picture to make the boundaries more prominent.

Shortcut menu A menu that provides choices related to the selection or area on which you right-click.

Single-series chart A chart showing only one set of data.

Slide The most basic element of PowerPoint, similar to a page in Word.

Slide master The top slide in a hierarchy of slides based on the master that contains design information for the slides.

Slide show A series of slides displayed onscreen for an audience.

Slide Show view Displays the completed presentation full screen to an audience as an electronic presentation.

Slide Sorter view Displays thumbnails of presentation slides enabling a view of multiple slides.

Slides pane Pane on the left side of Normal view that shows the slide deck with thumbnails.

SmartArt A diagram that presents information visually to effectively communicate a message.

SmartGuide A guide that displays when an object is moved that helps align objects in relation to other objects.

Softening A technique that blurs the edges of the content in a picture to make the boundaries less prominent.

Source application The application you use to create an original object, such as Word or Excel.

Source file The file that contains the original table or data that is used or copied to create a linked or embedded object, such as a Word document or an Excel worksheet.

Stacking order The order of objects placed on top of one another.

Start screen The screen that displays by default when PowerPoint is opened that provides options for opening existing presentations or new presentations from online or from a built-in theme.

Status bar A bar located at the bottom of the program window that contains information relative to the open file. It also includes tools for changing the view of the file and for changing the zoom size of onscreen file contents.

Stock chart Use to show fluctuations or the range of change between the high and low values of a subject over time.

Storyboard A visual plan of a presentation that displays the content of each slide in the slide show.

Surface chart Used to plot a surface using two sets of data.

Table style A combination of formatting choices for table components available to you that are based on a theme.

Tab Located on the Ribbon, each tab is designed to appear much like a tab on a file folder, with the active tab highlighted.

Tell me what you want to do box Located to the right of the last tab, this box enables you to search for help and information about a command or task you want to perform and also presents you with a shortcut directly to that command.

Template A predesigned file that incorporates formatting elements, such as a theme and layouts, and may include content that can be modified.

Text box (PowerPoint) An object that provides space for text anywhere on a slide; it can be formatted with a border, shading, and other characteristics.

Text pane A pane for text entry used for a SmartArt diagram.

Texture fill Inserts a texture such as canvas, denim, marble, or cork into a shape.

Theme A collection of design choices that includes colors, fonts, and special effects used to give a consistent look to a document, workbook, presentation, or database form or report.

Title bar The long bar at the top of each window that displays the name of the folder, file, or program displayed in the open window and the application in which you are working.

Toggle commands A button that acts somewhat like light switches that you can turn on and off. You select the command to turn it on, then select it again to turn it off.

Tone A characteristic of lighting that controls the temperature of a color. See also *Kelvin*.

Transparency The visibility of fill.

Trigger An object that launches an animation that takes place when you click an associated object or a bookmarked location in a media object.

TrueType fonts Scalable fonts, supported by Windows, that contain alphabetic characters and information about the characters, such as the shape, spacing, and character mapping of the font, that enable them to display and print smoothly at any point size.

Ungroup To break a combined grouped object into individual objects.

Uniform resource locator (URL) The address used to locate a resource, or webpage, on the Web.

Variant A variation on a chosen design theme.

Vector graphic An image created by a mathematical statement.

Vertex The point where a curve ends or the point where two line segments meet in a shape.

View The various ways a file can appear on the screen.

WordArt A feature that modifies text to include special effects, such as color, shadow, gradient, and 3-D appearance.

Word An application that can produce all sorts of documents, including memos, newsletters, forms, tables, and brochures.

X-axis The horizontal axis that usually contains the category information such as products, companies, or intervals of time.

XPS file format (.xps) An electronic file format created by Microsoft that preserves document formatting and is viewable and printable on any platform.

XY (scatter) chart Used to show the relationships among the numeric values in several data series, or plot two groups of numbers as one series of XY coordinates.

Y-axis The vertical axis that usually contains the values or amounts.

Z-axis The axis in three-dimensional charts that is used to plot the depth of a chart.

Zoom slider A feature that displays at the far right side of the status bar. It is used to increase or decrease the magnification of the file.

Index

trigger
   defined, 398
   using, 398–399
TrueType fonts, 534
.txt (plain text format), 155